# THE 12 KEY OUTCOMES OF YOUR MAGIC YEAR

**1. PURPOSE**
An Inspiring Written Purpose That You L...

**2.**
Written & Framed Goals

**3. HABITS**
Defined Habits You're 100% Committed To

**6. HEALTH**
A Personalized Magic Morning Routine

**5. HAPPINESS**
The Growth Mindset Installed

**4. PEOPLE**
An Uplifting Inner Circle

**7. MONEY**
A Personal Financial Plan Created

**8. COMMUNITY**
Living Where You Love With People You Love

**9. LOVE**
Creating Your Relationship Vision

**12. AWAKENING**
Experiencing Ayahuasca or a Vipassana

**11. FAMILY**
Written Family Vision & Values Statement

**10. SEXUALITY**
Creating a Weekly Sensuality Ritual

## A BIG THANK YOU TO OUR FIRST EDITION READERS

Welcome friends. Hello from Nosara, Costa Rica. You're receiving one of the first 2500 copies of this book ever printed. This is a special early edition copy. Pretty cool, right? *Magic Year* is a guide to transforming your life in just 12 months. I hope it makes a BIG difference for you.

As you're reading, what you can especially help me with is…

1. Add a quick review to Amazon.com at bit.ly/magicyearbook. That would be a HUGE help! Also please follow @magicyearteam on Instagram.

2. Review the table of contents then choose the sections of the book to read that you either have the most expertise in or the most interest in. Any and all feedback is welcomed to my WhatsApp if you know me or to ryan@magicyear.com.

3. My target audience is people who are getting ready for a big change in their lives -- people interested in personal growth who sense there is something more to life than what they are currently experiencing. People who want both success and happiness. These people may be at the beginning or in the middle of their personal growth and transformation journey and want a good guide to transformation.

Be sure to also check out our online course at www.magicyear.com. The course provides videos, worksheets, accountability, community, and coaching as you go about living your magic year. Thanks for being a first edition reader!

With love and purpose,
Ryan

# MAGIC YEAR

## A 12 Month Online Course & Group Coaching Program Designed to Transform Your Life

www.magicyear.com

# TABLE OF CONTENTS

| | |
|---|---|
| **TABLE OF CONTENTS** | **2** |
| **DEDICATION** | **12** |
| **ABOUT OUR FAMILY** | **13** |
| **INTRODUCTION** | **14** |
| | |
| **CH 1: THIS IS NOT A NORMAL BOOK** | **21** |
| A Magic Life | 21 |
| Your Magic Year | 22 |
| The 12 Key Outcomes of this Book | 24 |
| Achievers and Seekers | 25 |
| Who Are We? | 30 |
| How We Created Our Magic Life | 31 |
| The Magic Life We're Building | 32 |
| One Year to Transform Your Life | 33 |
| The Magic Year Challenge | 34 |
| Two Life Changing Experiences | 35 |
| Your Life Upgrade Manual | 37 |
| How this Book is Structured | 39 |
| A World of Magic Awaits | 40 |
| | |
| **CH 2: ESCAPING THE MATRIX** | **43** |
| What is The Matrix? | 43 |
| Breaking Free | 48 |
| What is Muggledom? | 49 |
| Following Your Bliss | 50 |
| How This Book Came to Life | 52 |
| The Inspiration for This Book | 53 |
| Building on the Shoulders of Giants | 54 |
| My Goals For Writing | 56 |
| | |
| **CH 3: MY BIG UPGRADE** | **60** |
| How My Mom Made Me An Achiever | 60 |
| Becoming a Tech Entrepreneur - 2002-2012 | 61 |
| The Downside of Overwork | 63 |
| How I Learned To Heal Anxiety and Stress | 65 |
| Losing My Mom To Brain Cancer | 67 |
| Doing an MBA at Harvard Business School | 68 |
| Learning Yoga & Meditation In India | 69 |
| Moving to San Francisco | 70 |

| | |
|---|---|
| How Breathing Healed My Nervous System | 71 |
| The Festival That Changed Everything: Burning Man | 72 |
| Wake Up Call: Losing My Dad to Leukemia | 74 |
| The Fourth Sign I Needed to Slow Down | 74 |
| How To Calm Your Nervous System | 76 |
| American Fuckface | 77 |
| My Journey So Far | 80 |

## STEP 1: PURPOSE MAGIC — 86

| | |
|---|---|
| My Journey With Purpose | 86 |
| The Two Phases: Exploration and Execution | 90 |
| How to Escape From a Boring & Passionless Life | 92 |
| Scheduling Exploration Journeys | 96 |
| Who Gives You Your Purpose? You do. | 97 |
| Why Are You Alive? | 99 |
| The Formula for Inner Peace and Happiness | 100 |
| Creating Your Purpose Statement | 105 |
| Draw Your Purpose | 109 |
| How You Know You've Found Your Purpose | 111 |
| The How - Making Your Purpose Real | 112 |
| The Value of Writing Your Own Obituary Early | 113 |
| Becoming a Purpose-Driven Leader | 114 |
| Burn the Boats & Make Money Doing What You Love | 117 |
| What Authentic Leaders Are Great At | 120 |
| Recommended Books on Purpose | 120 |
| Key Outcome from This Chapter | 120 |

## STEP 2: GOALS MAGIC — 124

| | |
|---|---|
| My Journey With Goals | 124 |
| Creating Your Big Goal | 125 |
| Developing Radical Self-Belief | 126 |
| My Big Goal | 128 |
| Write Down Your Goals | 129 |
| Create an Annual Goal Writing Process | 130 |
| Print Out This Goals Sheet & Frame It | 131 |
| Create Your One Page Life Plan | 132 |
| Life KPIs - How to Measure Your Goals | 134 |
| The Formula of Success | 135 |
| How to Be Fearless With Your Goals | 136 |
| Be Crystal Clear On What You Want From Life | 138 |
| Thoughts Become Things | 139 |
| Create Your Vision | 140 |
| Create Your Bucket List | 143 |
| Go on Epic Adventures | 144 |

| | |
|---|---:|
| Recommended Books on Goals | 147 |
| Key Outcome from This Chapter | 147 |

## STEP 3: HABITS MAGIC — 151

| | |
|---|---:|
| What's Your Habit Stack? | 151 |
| How to Add a New Habit to Your Life | 157 |
| How to Track Your Daily Habits | 160 |
| Living Life As An Experiment | 161 |
| A Template for Creating Your Life Experiments | 162 |
| The Experiment We Designed to Get Over Fear | 164 |
| A Few Experiments From My Own Life | 165 |
| Self-Discipline - The Key Habit of Winners | 170 |
| The Secret to Self-Confidence | 172 |
| Honor Your Word To Others | 175 |
| Preparation - Winning Before the Game Begins | 176 |
| Do This Before You Go To Sleep | 178 |
| Writing Down Your Values | 178 |
| Recommended Books on Habits | 183 |
| Key Outcome from This Chapter | 183 |

## STEP 4: PEOPLE MAGIC — 187

| | |
|---|---:|
| My Journey With People | 187 |
| Surround Yourself With Extraordinary People | 188 |
| Relationships Lead to Happiness | 192 |
| Find Extraordinary Mentors | 192 |
| Finding Great Mentors Using FedEx | 196 |
| Finding Mentors Via Your Podcast | 196 |
| Use Your Educational Network | 197 |
| Use Professional Networks | 198 |
| Show Up Early to Events | 199 |
| Networks Filled With Great People | 199 |
| Meeting Epic People at Festivals | 200 |
| The Value of Mastermind Groups | 202 |
| WhatsApp Groups Really Matter | 203 |
| Public Speak Every Chance You Get | 204 |
| Developing Deep & Authentic Relationships | 206 |
| Avoid Conspiracy Theorists | 209 |
| Keep Relationships Even in Failures | 211 |
| Recommended Books on People | 211 |
| Key Outcome from This Chapter | 212 |

## STEP 5: HAPPINESS MAGIC — 217

| | |
|---|---:|
| My Personal Metric of Life Success | 217 |
| My Journey With Happiness | 219 |

| | |
|---|---|
| Conscious Drugs Messed Up My Consistency | 219 |
| How Do You Know When Too Much is Too Much? | 220 |
| The Vow Of Unconditional Happiness | 224 |
| Life is Happening For You, Not To You | 226 |
| Accept Continual Change As the Way of Life | 228 |
| Reframe Suffering as Learning | 229 |
| Make a Comeback & Create a Magic Decade | 231 |
| Thrive on Criticism | 232 |
| Fuck Fitting In | 235 |
| How to Heal PTSD | 237 |
| Become A Mental Black Belt | 238 |
| Choose a Growth Mindset | 240 |
| Never Complain | 242 |
| Choosing a Positive Outlook | 243 |
| Quit Your Job? | 245 |
| Forgiveness Is a Key to Happiness | 246 |
| Be Like a Kid | 248 |
| Your Best Work Comes From Flow States | 250 |
| The Eight Sources of Joy | 251 |
| Live in the Moment | 252 |
| Give Your Master Gift Before You Die | 254 |
| Study Happiness Philosophy | 255 |
| Buddha, Epicurus, & 3 Existentialists Walk Into a Bar | 257 |
| Express Your Emotions, Bro | 260 |
| Start a Gratitude Journal | 261 |
| Realize That Happiness Leads to Success | 263 |
| Realize That Everything is Impermanent | 264 |
| Understand Happiness Chemicals | 265 |
| Celebrate Your Wins | 267 |
| Know The Five Biggest Regrets of the Dying | 267 |
| What Robin Sharma Wishes He'd Known By 40 | 269 |
| Don't Fear Death | 271 |
| Only Do The Fuck Yeses | 272 |
| Live the Four Agreements | 274 |
| Create a Daily Affirmation | 275 |
| Focus on What You Can Control | 278 |
| Programs That Changed My Happiness & Health | 279 |
| Get on a 'High-Flying Disc' Before Key Decisions | 280 |
| Morgan's Ten Principles for Living | 281 |
| Recommended Books on Happiness | 282 |
| Key Outcome from This Chapter | 282 |

## STEP 6: HEALTH MAGIC — **287**

| | |
|---|---|
| My Journey With Health | 289 |

Don't Be An Average American — 291
Never Eat Processed or Packaged Foods — 293
Eat a Paleo Diet — 294
Get Into Ketosis Monthly — 295
Appetite Suppressants That Actually Work — 296
Use Your Mornings for Self Care (Not Work) — 297
Prime Your State Before You Do Anything — 299
Don't Overwork — 300
Lift & Sweat Every Fucking Day — 302
Sauna Your Way to the Top — 303
Fast Often — 304
Sleep... A Lot — 306
Go See a Functional Medicine Doctor — 308
Run From Alcohol & Vaping — 310
Reduce Your Stress Chemicals — 311
How to Reduce Amygdala Attacks — 313
Do a Daily Cold Plunge — 316
Do AcroYoga — 317
Book a Craniosacral & Reiki Session — 318
Try Shirodhara (Ayurvedic Oil Dripping) — 319
Do Some Holotropic Breathing — 319
Get Daily Sun Exposure for 15 Minutes — 320
Do A Monthly Float Session — 321
Do A Cupping & Gua Sha Session — 322
Take a Digital Detox Every Quarter — 323
Do a Darkness Retreat Like Aaron Rogers — 324
Male Testosterone Supplements — 325
Daily Meditation — 326
The Science of Meditation — 327
Creating Your Miracle Morning Routine — 328
Recommended Books on Health — 330
Key Outcome from This Chapter — 331

## STEP 7: MONEY MAGIC — 335

My Journey With Money — 337
The Eight Forms of Wealth — 338
Understand What Money Actually Is — 340
My Four Rules for Money — 342
Tracking Your Spending — 343
Creating Your Personal Financial Statement — 344
The 7 Steps for Building Wealth — 346
The Four Types of Freedoms — 348
Time Freedom — 350
Be Like Jack — 351

| | |
|---|---|
| The Two Types of People: Workers & Investors | 352 |
| What Do the Rich Do Differently | 353 |
| The Automatic Millionaire | 355 |
| The Automatic DecaMillionaire | 356 |
| Avoid These Money Traps If You Can | 358 |
| Become the Authority in Your Field | 360 |
| Learn The Basics of Investing | 361 |
| Acquire Cash Flowing Assets | 364 |
| Make Money While You Sleep | 365 |
| How to Make $10M+ By Building Companies | 366 |
| Sell a Product, Not a Service | 368 |
| How to Value a Company | 368 |
| How to Angel Invest The Right Way | 370 |
| The Traits of Billionaires | 372 |
| Recommended Books on Money | 373 |
| Key Outcome from This Chapter | 373 |

## STEP 8: COMMUNITY MAGIC — **376**

| | |
|---|---|
| You Can Go Live Anywhere, Right Now | 377 |
| Slow Travel Around the World | 379 |
| Move Globally With a Digital Nomad Visa | 380 |
| Use Geoarbitrage To Keep Costs Low | 383 |
| Using Remote Work To Achieve Location Freedom | 384 |
| Finding My Home as a Dual-Culture Kid | 385 |
| Learn From the Blue Zones | 386 |
| Move to Nosara? | 387 |
| Why I Love Intentional Communities | 388 |
| Coliving and New Urbanism | 390 |
| Try Living in a Peaceful Place Like Bali | 392 |
| Living in Walkable Cities | 394 |
| Smart Cities | 395 |
| Recommended Books on Community | 396 |
| Key Outcome from This Chapter | 396 |

## STEP 9: LOVE MAGIC — **399**

| | |
|---|---|
| My Journey Finding Magical Love | 400 |
| Meeting My Wife At Burning Man | 402 |
| Our First Meeting | 403 |
| Camp Mystic MidBurn | 404 |
| The First Conversation | 405 |
| The Vision For Our Relationship | 407 |
| Creating an Relationship Adventure Book | 410 |
| Steal These Marital Vows (And Customize Them) | 413 |
| Reimagining Marriage, Family, & Divorce | 415 |

| | |
|---|---|
| Divorce the Conscious Way | 417 |
| What Love Means to Me | 417 |
| Develop Yourself First | 418 |
| Develop Your Masculine & Feminine Skills | 419 |
| Creating Polarity in Your Romantic Relationship | 420 |
| How to Find Your Romantic Partner | 421 |
| 25 Tips to Win A Heart | 423 |
| Create a Relationship North Star | 424 |
| Tips on Creating With Your Spouse (Holy Hell) | 425 |
| Relationship MDMA Ceremonies | 428 |
| Our Guide to Open Relating | 429 |
| The Most Common Types of Open Relating | 430 |
| Our Form of Marital Relationship | 430 |
| Full Devotion & Full Freedom | 432 |
| Make the Primary Relationship Solid First | 432 |
| Some Potential Benefits of Open Relating | 435 |
| How Monogamy Led Me to Lose My Sex Drive | 436 |
| The Key Lessons We've Learned About Open Relating | 436 |
| Recommended Books on Love | 440 |
| Key Outcome from This Chapter | 440 |

## STEP 10: SEX MAGIC — 443

| | |
|---|---|
| My Journey with Sex | 445 |
| Getting Outside of the Box | 446 |
| Fast Sex vs. Slow Sex | 447 |
| Create Your Weekly Sensuality Temple | 449 |
| Learn Tantra | 450 |
| Become a Tantric Sex God | 451 |
| Bring a Tantrika Into Your Bedroom | 453 |
| Destigmatizing Dakinis & Sex Workers | 455 |
| Sexuality: Resurrect Your Fucking King | 456 |
| Orgasms Can Cure Hysteria | 457 |
| Deep Dick Medicine (DDM) | 458 |
| The Secrets to the Pussy | 459 |
| Get A Couples Erotic Massage | 460 |
| Go To a Play Party | 461 |
| Set the Scene for Your Sex | 465 |
| Find a Dom | 466 |
| Try Some Shibari | 468 |
| Name Your Masculine & Feminine | 469 |
| Wait for Sex on the First Date | 469 |
| Listen to Napoleon Hill About Sex Transmutation | 470 |
| Recommended Books on Sexuality | 471 |
| Key Outcome from This Chapter | 471 |

## STEP 11: FAMILY MAGIC — 474

- Our Family Purpose Statement — 475
- Having Our First Baby — 476
- Creating a LuvBubble Around Our Friends & Family — 477
- Our Dream for a New Way of Living — 479
- Create a Ten Year Family Vision — 481
- Our Family Values — 483
- How to Give Your Kids a Big Leg Up in Life — 484
- Repairing Conflict In Front of the Children — 485
- Raising Curious & Adventurous Kids — 486
- Parenting Is Really Hard — 487
- Recommended Books on Family — 488
- Key Outcome from This Chapter — 489

## STEP 12: AWAKENING MAGIC — 491

- What I Mean by "Awakening" — 494
- My Personal Awakening Process — 498
- How Ten Days in Silence Helped Me — 502
- What I Learned from Vipassana — 504
- How Plant Medicines Helped Me End Overwork — 505
- My Experience With Plant Medicines — 506
- My Time With Iboga — 507
- The Softer San Pedro & Peyote — 509
- My First Heart Opening Ceremony — 509
- How Ayahuasca Changed Everything — 510
- Starting the Healing Process — 513
- My Experience With 5MeO-DMT — 514
- A Guide to Entheogens — 516
- Recommended Books on Awakening — 522
- Key Outcome from This Chapter — 522

## A BONUS STEP: OPTIMISM MAGIC — 525

- My Journey With Optimism — 526
- Optimism As Your Secret Advantage — 526
- Why I'm Optimistic For the World — 527
- Grandma Would Be Proud of Humanity — 532
- Why Do Some Think the World is Getting Worse? — 534
- The Progress With Renewable Energy — 535
- The Human Development Report — 536
- The New Renaissance — 538
- We Are Consciousness First, Human Second — 539
- Recommended Books on Optimism — 540

**THE LIFE THAT IS NOW POSSIBLE**     **542**
  The New You     544

## THE MAGIC YEAR CHALLENGE

If you're reading this, you could be the first to complete *The Magic Year Challenge*

**The Magic Year Challenge** - *The challenge to complete all 111 action items in this book within 12 months. The first two people to complete the Magic Year Challenge will win an all-expense paid trip to Costa Rica to hang out with the author.*

The first two people who complete all 111 action items inside this book and let me know via Instagram DM (@magicyearteam) or email at ryan@magicyear.com will win an all-expense paid week-long trip to Nosara, Costa Rica for a week of vacation and 1:1 life coaching sessions. This prize is open to readers of this book as well as anyone taking the *Magic Year Course* available on our website at www.magicyear.com. Please include action item reflection answers and photos of the habit changes (pictures of you at the gym, in the cold plunge, meditating, etc.).

# DEDICATION

My inspiration for writing this book is my son, Apollo. My **Magic Year** -- the year I got everything aligned in my life -- was his first year of life. When he's ready, I plan to give him a copy of this book and use it as part of his life curriculum. Son, I hope you will use this book as a guide for creating a life filled with magic, joy, adventure, friendship, love, vitality, healing, contribution, flow, and prosperity. In other words, a magic life. If you remember nothing else from this book, remember these 12 tips...

1) Do what you love to do. Obsess over your passions to find the gifts that you're meant to share with the world.

2) Miracle mornings create miracle lives. Exercise every single day.

3) Keep living life as a continual set of experiments. Keep what works.

4) Remember the formula for success: Vision + Belief + Action + Consistency = Results

5) As Joseph Campbell said, follow your bliss. And as Franz Kafka said, follow your obsession. I like to combine them and say, follow your joy.

6) The purpose of life is to enjoy it fully, be kind, learn, grow, and give your gifts to the world while lovingly training the next generation.

7) Along the journey of life, everything that happens "to you" is really happening "for you." Turn your challenges into gifts.

8) Create a cash flow engine. Spend 20% less than you earn every month after taxes and invest the difference in long-term cash flow generating assets like stocks, bonds, and real estate.

9) The secret to creating massive wealth is to build a business that makes money while you sleep. Figure this out and the world becomes your oyster.

10) Always remember who you are: an Infinite God temporarily inside a human body. We believe you are an immortal being and that your soul will continue long after your current body ceases to exist.

11) Find yourself an incredible life partner that you can create new realms and universes with and continue the family legacy of love, flow, joy, and magic. There is no more magical experience than having a baby with someone you love!

12) Your parents love you beyond words. While we may not always be in these bodies, our energy is always here to surround you in a LuvBubble.

**Bonus Tip:** Doing the hokey pokey might just be what it's all about.

# ABOUT OUR FAMILY

*Ryan, Morgan, and Baby Apollo in Costa Rica*

Hi there. We're Ryan & Morgan Allis. We are an American husband and wife who are joyous parents to our son Apollo. We are based in Nosara, Costa Rica, but often spend a couple months at a time on extended nomadic trips to the USA, Bali, Australia, and Spain -- places we absolutely love. We are completely obsessed with living a **magic life** and encouraging people to follow their bliss and live fully expressed lives in touch with their authentic desires.

Our shared purpose, or **dharma**, is to reimagine how human beings live, love, learn, and play -- and to share the lessons we learn as we continue to adopt an "alternative lifestyle" of semi-nomadic and deeply passionate living. We are working on pioneering an example for a new way of living a magical family life along with hundreds of our friends in Nosara, Costa Rica. Come visit! We are big conscious art and music festival fans – and have attended Burning Man and Envision 12 times between us. We are also the creators of the Magic Friends Festival in Costa Rica, which for now is just for our inner circle but may expand someday.

In a former life, Ryan was CEO and co-founder of a software company called iContact, which he led to a $169 million sale to a public company and is the founder of Hive (www.hive.org), a global community of purpose-driven leaders and Magic Year (www.magicyear.com) a personal transformation course inspired by this book. He went to UNC-Chapel Hill for college and has an MBA from Harvard Business School. Morgan has been a fashion line entrepreneur, a business strategist, and a biohacker, creator, sensuality coach, and prolific painter. While Ryan is the primary author of this book, Morgan contributed many of the ideas, title, and inspiration.

# PART 1

## INTRODUCTION

# INTRODUCTION

"In a civilization of human beings sleepwalking through the finest years of their lives, fuel the majesty of your audacity by regularly reaching for what the herd claims to be impossible."
- Robin Sharma, author

This book is designed to help you create a **magic life** within one year. How do I define a magic life? Well, it's a life you absolutely love…

- You're making money doing what you love
- You're living where you want
- You have a clear life purpose and written goals that light you up
- You have inspiring and uplifting friends
- You're having great sex with a partner you care about
- You have positive and supportive daily habits
- You're truly healthy and happy

Yep, it's possible. This is the version of you that is happy, healthy, wealthy, and fully alive. The version of you with your inner spark intact and your soul truly happy. That is where we're going.

Regardless of your age or place in life, a magic life is possible. Yes, it will take intentionality, effort, and consistency, but it's within your reach. Some changes and a lot of joyous and consistent effort will be necessary. But you have a really good guide in your hands for designing the next version of yourself.

Are you in?

After spending the last 20 years learning, achieving, messing up, exploring the edges of personal growth and transformation, and building communities of purpose-driven leaders, I'm deeply committed to helping people actually create magic lives for themselves.

When I was 27 two things happened to me that changed my life forever.

1. I sold the marketing software company, iContact, that I'd spent 10 years building for $169M.

2. My mom passed away from Stage 4 Glioblastoma brain cancer.

Suddenly, I had all the money I needed. But no amount of money could keep my mom alive. I resisted her death, creating lots of needless suffering in me and kicking off lots of inner questioning of the meaning of life. For once, I didn't feel in control of what happened.

This dark night of the soul made me realize that life is short and catalyzed me into a twelve year journey to find true inner happiness and optimal health. I followed my mom's dying advice. She told me, "Ryan, always follow your bliss."

After she passed, I went to Harvard Business School for an MBA and then used my part of the proceeds from the sale of iContact to fund a 12 year adventure across 40 countries, leading to life changing experiences and magical encounters in California, India, Bali, Thailand, and Costa Rica.

Along the way, I discovered Burning Man, ayahuasca, vipassana, tantra, open relating, biohacking, purpose-driven leadership, the formula of success, and a new philosophy of joyous and simple living -- and created a magical family of my own.

I also created Hive.org, a global community of purpose-driven leaders with 3,600 alumni in 135 countries. So far we've put on purpose workshops in 15 countries -- and are planning to expand further in 2024. I love teaching people how to discover their purpose, write down their goals, create the right habit stacks, build cash flowing engines doing what they love, and create the life of their dreams.

Today, I live in Nosara, Costa Rica, a small beachside surf and yoga town, with my wife Morgan, young son Apollo, and close friends. We're living the life of our dreams. We are truly happy. We figured out some of the secrets to lasting health, wealth, happiness, and presence -- and we want to share them with you.

So yes, *Magic Year* is everything I learned during the last 20 years of my life on this journey of achievement and exploration -- packaged into a twelve step structure designed to help anyone create the life of their dreams.

If you apply what's in this book and do the action items inside -- you can design the life you've always been dreaming of and be well on the path toward making it real one year from today.

To get there, we will cover these topics in a lot of depth: Purpose, Goals, Habits, People, Happiness, Health, Money, Community, Love, Sex, Family, and Awakening. If you choose to follow the premise of the book -- of actually doing all the action items and implementing the habit stacks within, you can shift a lot in the next year.

There are some edgy topics in this book that aren't in most books on personal growth -- topics like tantra, open relating, community living, and medicine work. Enjoy these sections. I hope they will give you a guide to some of the more hidden parts of transformation work.

There are exactly **111 action items** in this book. If you actually do all 111 of them, you will undoubtedly change your life and be on the path to creating the life of your dreams. Yes, you do have to do the action items inside to create the change you seek. You can't just passively read and expect transformation. I challenge you to do every single one and see what happens. And I challenge you to join our online course at www.magicyear.com for added community, coaching, workbooks, accountability, and support (and invites to our events!).

So think of *Magic Year* as your personal guide to creating the life of your dreams in every single aspect of living. At the beginning of each chapter you'll find the key concepts and definitions for that chapter. At the end of each chapter (starting with the Purpose Chapter), you'll find an implementation guide that recaps the action items.

Now, let's take a moment to anchor into your own mind the future vision of you. This is called **advance visualization**.

Imagine for a moment the upgraded version of yourself a year from today, the version that becomes possible after applying the knowledge from this book.

Envision a fully integrated, healthy, healed, fit, confident, abundant, and relaxed version of yourself. Imagine a happier, more content you, adept at flowing with the ups and downs of life and embracing the lessons stemming from challenges. Imagine yourself with a complete life reboot. Yes, imagine the version of yourself who:

1. Spent 10 days at a Vipassana silent meditation retreat (visit dhamma.org to schedule yours), emerging with a clearer and happier mind.

2. Finally decided to shed those extra 25 pounds that's been hanging around -- either through diet and daily exercise or a combination of diet, daily exercise, and new

clinically proven appetite suppressants like Tirzepatide or Semaglutide.

3. Committed to healing your central nervous system, prioritizing frequent digital detoxes by taking time away from your phone and immersing yourself in nature for at least three days every quarter, and scheduling weekly full-body massages and cranial sacral sessions.

4. Limited television and social media use to two hours per week, redirecting the extra time towards exercising, reading, and socializing with family and friends and building a cash flowing creative project.

5. Took a couple weeks out of your life to sit with the Ayahuasca plant medicine in Costa Rica or Peru and was able to heal childhood trauma and overcome the fear of death.

6. Chose to explore beautiful, lower-cost places such as Thailand, Bali, and Costa Rica, and then actually moved to a community of inspiring individuals (read the Community chapter for more on this!).

7. Overcame PTSD and anxiety through daily breathing practices and by working with a practitioner who utilized cutting edge entheogenic therapeutics like ketamine, psilocybin, or MDMA during guided sessions -- the same therapeutics that have been shown to heal PTSD in military veterans.

8. Realized life is short and proactively planned incredible adventures with your family and friends every six months.

9. Left the job you dreaded and decided to actually make money doing something you truly enjoyed. I'll show you how to do that while actually earning more every month -- either via a remote job or by building a business that turns into a passive cash flow engine that makes you money while you sleep.

10. Took the time to write down your goals, create a written purpose, get an accountability coach, and then take consistent action toward generating massive results in your life every week for a year.

11. Decided to hire a sex coach (gasp!) and invite them into the bedroom to help you uplevel your sex life with your partner(s) and bring you to new heights of pleasure, presence, confidence, and awakening.

12. Realized that being happy is a relatively simple by-product of daily exercise, not eating processed foods, minimizing sugar and alcohol, installing your miracle morning routine, learning to not worry by letting go of obsessing about control, spending lots of time with people you care about, and choosing to be unconditionally happy.

These are merely a few examples of the changes you can make and actions you can undertake inspired by this book. This version of yourself is attainable, it truly is.

No matter your geography, income, or education -- this book works when applied. Through my writing (or through the online video course version of this book at www.magicyear.com), let us be your personal coach for the next year of your life through this book and course. We promise to be kind and friendly AND also take a stand for your potential and hold you to your highest vision of yourself.

Yes, we're looking to create a version of you that is:

1. Happy
2. Healthy
3. Wealthy
4. Fully Alive

So yes, if you implement the action items in this book, you're going to go through a massive life upgrade in the next year. The path won't always be linear, but once you commit and initiate action, you'll find the universe moving with you.

This book is designed to help you create an inspiring vision for the next phase of your life, escape from the cultural conditioning **matrix** of wherever you live, subscribe instead to a positive and uplifting **information diet**, surround yourself with interesting, smart, motivated, healthy, and kind people, create what really matters to you – and live a life true to yourself and your dreams.

So whether you want to upgrade every area of your life -- or simply improve a few elements -- this is a comprehensive and in-depth guide. Together, let's create an upgraded life for yourself—a life you deeply love and in which you're thriving in all areas.

As you implement this book, send me the stories of what happens, and share with the world what you learn. Post about it, share about it, and tell your friends about the journey that you're going through. Send stories to ryan@magicyear.com.

Drumroll please… magic friends… here's (nearly) everything I've learned over the last 20 years about building a life of meaning, purpose, joy, pleasure, contribution, and magic. I hope you enjoy it!

Welcome to the start of your upgrade process and your magic life. Welcome to a catalyst in your awakening process, and welcome to a book that might just change your life. Enjoy the adventure. Let's jump in.

Yours in Purpose,
Ryan P. Allis
Nosara, Costa Rica
July 15, 2023


P.S. - *Magic Year* is designed as both a book and a course. If you want to actually DO the course as you read the book, go to www.magicyear.com. The online course provides videos, content, assignments, templates, community calls, accountability, coaching, and more. It's for the people who are committed to personal growth and actually transforming your life in the next 12 months!

# CHAPTER 1

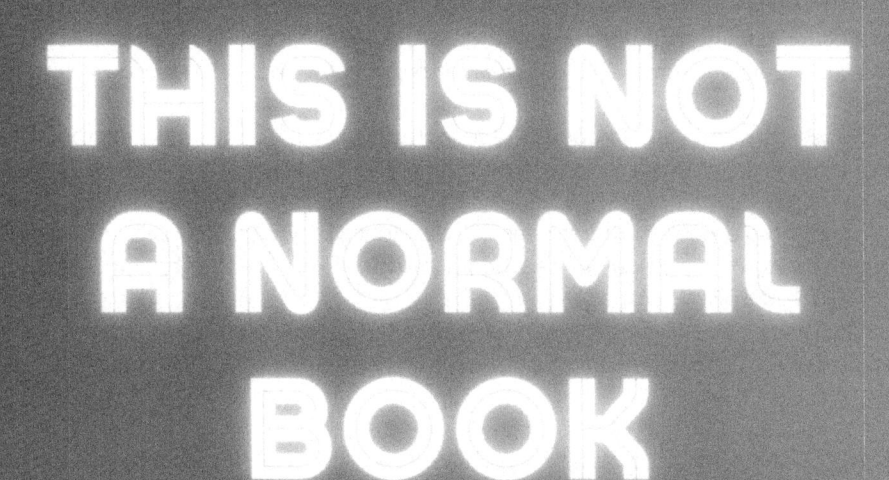

# THIS IS NOT A NORMAL BOOK

**MAGIC YEAR**

MAGIC YEAR - 20

# KEY CONCEPTS FROM CHAPTER ONE

**1. MAGIC LIFE**

The life of someone who works on what they love, lives where they want, has created a clear purpose and written goals, has inspiring friends around them, has positive habits, is having great sex, and is truly healthy and happy.

**2. MAGIC YEAR**

A 12 month period of focus on upgrading all the major areas of your life. This will be the next 12 months of your life if you choose to accept the challenge of this book.

**3. ACHIEVERS**

People committed to becoming the best version of themselves and going after their dreams and goals consistently.

**4. SEEKERS**

People obsessed with living life to its fullest, continual experimentation and transformation, and learning the deeper secrets of the universe.

**5. TRIAD OF TRANSFORMATION**

The three most life changing and transformative experiences of my life: Ayahuasca, VIpassana, and Burning Man.

**6. GEOARBITRAGE**

Earning your income from one place and then working remotely in another country where costs are much lower. (Example: earning American pay rates but rotating between Bali, Thailand, & Costa Rica).

**7. HABIT STACK**

The collection of all your current habits. If you can upgrade your habit stacks in each of the 12 areas of this book, you can completely transform your life.

**8. ESCAPE PLAN**

Your plan to get out of your mediocre environment and your mediocre life by upgrading where you live to an inspiring place with nature, friends, community, and healthy organic food.

**9. INTUITION**

The little voice inside of your head from your Higher Self that guides you toward the right path. When you don't listen to it, bad things start to happen.

**10. TIME FREEDOM**

When you can do whatever you want with your time, either because you have very low expenses or you have lots of money.

**11. LOCATION FREEDOM**

When you have the freedom to live and work from wherever you choose. You can work from anywhere with a strong internet connection.

**12. BURNING MAN**

The world's best arts and music festival (tied in my mind with Envision). Around 75,000 people attend every August in Black Rock City, Nevada.

# CH 1: THIS IS NOT A NORMAL BOOK

*"How do you build a good life? Relentlessly follow your intuition. Build with people who also love to grow. Take responsibility for your healing. Love yourself so deeply that you feel at home in your own body and mind. Teach yourself to forgive. Never stop being a kind person." - Yung Pueblo*

## A Magic Life

This book is written to help you create a **Magic Life**. So, how do I define a Magic Life? It's a life you absolutely love. As I shared in the introduction, here are the seven parts of a magic life:

- You're making money doing what you love
- You're living where you want
- You have a clear life purpose and written goals that light you up
- You have inspiring and uplifting friends
- You have positive and supportive daily habits
- You're having great sex with a partner you care about
- You're truly healthy and happy

Yep, this is possible for you to create for yourself -- and that's where we are going with this book. If you implement the habits and lessons in this book -- my goal is that within one year of today you'll be able to authentically and honestly check off each of the above seven components when looking at your own life. Read the above list again.

*Magic Life - The life of someone who works on what they love, lives where they want, has created a clear purpose and written goals, has inspiring friends around them, has positive habits, is having great sex with a partner they care about, and is truly healthy and happy.*

This is the version of you that is happy, healthy, wealthy, and fully alive. The version of you with your inner spark intact and your soul truly happy. This is the life we are going to design together. But it's not just about life design -- it's about life creation too.

Yes, this book is designed to actually change your life -- in a big way. If you play all out with this book, you have the opportunity to design and then actually create the life of your dreams. So let's do it. Let's play all out. Let's go all in on this adventure together.

Let's design and then create lives of meaning, flow, adventure, and passive income. In our new life we're designing, let's leave all the mediocrity, BS, and blah behind. Let's say no to perceived obligations that don't light us up inside. Let's say no to people that don't light us up inside.

Let's protect our souls from resignation and cynicism and actually follow our bliss. Let's create lives of inspiration rather than lives of obligation. Let's create cash flow engines from businesses doing what we love. Let's prepare ourselves for -- and then create the relationships of our dreams. Let's create lives of ecstatic pleasure rather than lives of rote boredom that feel like Groundhog Day on repeat. Yes, it is possible. Yes, you can be free.

Can you get behind this? Is it something you want? Do you really want it? You have to want it. Give me any motivated person and within one year I can transform their lives. Are you our next success story at Magic Year?

Step-by-step we'll transform each major area of your life -- until you have designed AND are actually living the life you've always dreamed of.

Why did I write this book? Simple: to help people not have to take as long as I did to learn the lessons inside. I wrote this book to be a guide to upgrading yourself, transforming yourself in all aspects, and going through the process of creating a happier, healthier, and wealthier life in which you're fully connected to yourself and others, are living an inspiring purpose, and are making your money doing what you love.

This book is written and designed as a comprehensive system for living. It is a guidebook to the process of life upgrading and life optimization.

It's a book for people who want to capture the spark inside of them, re-ignite it, follow their bliss, and design a non-traditional life outside of the Matrix and definitely outside of the 9-5 rat race of working in a field that dulls your soul.

This book is for people who are curious, into experimentation, and want something more in their life. People who are on the verge of (or in the middle of) their personal transformation process. If you want a guide to the process of personal transformation -- well, you've found it.

I promise you this: if you go all in with this book -- not just reading it -- but doing all 111 of the action items, your life will change forever. So go all in. Commit now, and your life will never be the same.

So let's go. Let's go all in and see what happens.

## Your Magic Year

I am absolutely obsessed with how this book actually helps you. Here's some guidance to make the best use of it.

1. **Read it.** Read the book. One step per day is a good pace--so over 12-14 days. The second time you go through it, actually do all 111 of the action items as you go either on your own or via our online course at magicyear.com (for added support and videos).

2. **Implement it.** Spend one month focusing on implementing and mastering the action items and habit stack within each of the 12 major steps. This will be your **Magic Year.**

3. **Live it.** Magic Days Turn into Magic Weeks, Magic Years, Magic Decades, and Magic Lives.

### How to Read This Book

Read this book all the way through once, then go back and do all 111 action items in a notebook or Google Doc, or via our online course at www.magicyear.com.

If you read about an hour a day for 14 days and you'll be done with the first step, which is reading the book itself.

Then, on your second time around, devote a month to implementing and living the habits suggested in each chapter, and actually doing all 111 action items in the book. This will become your **Magic Year.**

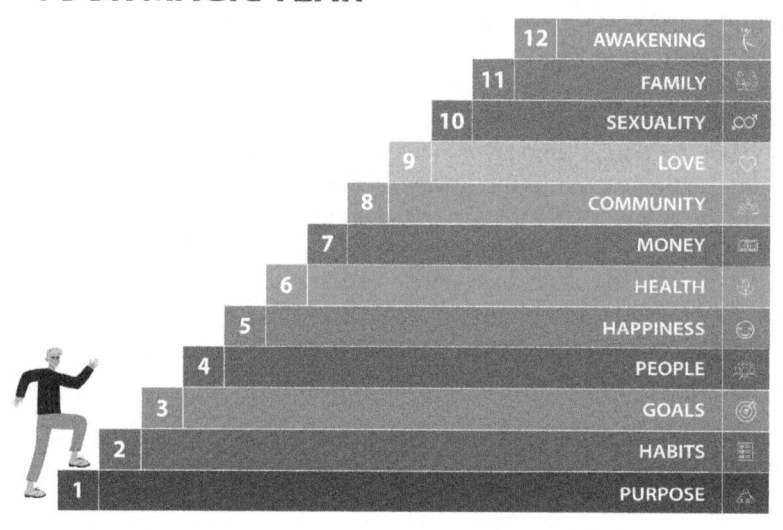

*Magic Year - A 12 month period of focus on upgrading all the major areas of your life. This will be the next 12 months of your life if you choose to accept the challenge of this book.*

## YOUR MAGIC YEAR

|  |  |
|---|---|
| 12 | AWAKENING |
| 11 | FAMILY |
| 10 | SEXUALITY |
| 9 | LOVE |
| 8 | COMMUNITY |
| 7 | MONEY |
| 6 | HEALTH |
| 5 | HAPPINESS |
| 4 | PEOPLE |
| 3 | GOALS |
| 2 | HABITS |
| 1 | PURPOSE |

If you want to actually DO the course as you read the book (or after), go to www.magicyear.com. We are building an online course there with videos, weekly content, assignments, templates, community calls, accountability, and more. You'll get about 20% of the value from this book from reading it and 80% of the value from this book from doing it. Read it, do it, become it.

If you live this book -- each month will build on the prior month -- so you'll be stacking a set of new habits as you go -- and re-creating yourself from the inside out. If you fully commit to the changes, your life will change. You don't have to keep everything -- just keep what works and what you find makes a difference for you.

Each month, I encourage you to do the action items in that month's section. Some are written reflections and some are daily or weekly habits to integrate into your life. The positive habits that you build in the earlier section should continue throughout the year and you build one layer on top of the prior. Be rigorous with yourself and actually do all the recommended habits for at least 30 straight days -- every single day of that month. That's how you will create massive change and lasting transformation!

So let's say you're reading this book in December. You would take the following year and focus one month on doing all the exercises and implementing the habit stack from each section, so that January was about goals, February was about habits, March was about Purpose, and so on.

Each month, you focus on doing the action items in that section. The habits that you build in the earlier section continue throughout the year, and you build one layer on top of the prior. That's why I call it "**habit stacking**."

I added in an extra bonus step (step 13: optimism) as well as the end. You can either do that as month 13 or replace the family step with that (if you don't have or don't want to have kids).

While this book may take only a couple weeks to read in full, it will certainly take much longer than a couple weeks to fully become the person that this book guides you toward becoming.

Embodiment takes time. So keep returning to this guide as you continue in life-- referencing sections as needed.

Let's be real. Transformation usually takes a decade or so. So stay on the path and keep following what brings you alive while creating habits that create the life you dream of.

To get started, all that's needed is a willingness to read, reflect, experiment, and implement what works for you -- and a burning desire inside of you to live a better life going forward.

Your destiny is in your hands, my friend. So don't let yourself live a mediocre and unreflected-upon life like many people. Life's too short for that. You've got a guide right in front of you now that somehow you manifested to help you. Put it to work. Take the actions. Get the upgrade.

Follow us on Instagram and TikTok at @magicyearteam. We'll be sharing all your success stories there, so send them in as you start seeing changes in your life!

## The 12 Key Outcomes of this Book

Each step in this book and the course has a key outcome. Here are the key outcomes for each of the twelve sections. If you actually, "do" this book or its accompanying course -- here's what you have accomplished by the end of it.

- Step 1: Purpose - A written down and inspiring purpose statement
- Step 2: Goals - Written down and framed goals and one-page life plan
- Step 3: Habits - An optimized list of defined habits that you're 100% committed to
- Step 4: People - An uplifting inner circle of family, friends, and mentors
- Step 5: Happiness - The Growth Mindset installed (life happening "for you" not "to you")
- Step 6: Health - A personalized Magic Morning Routine
- Month 7: Money - Personal financial plan created
- Month 8: Community - Living where you love with people you love
- Month 9: Love - Creating your relationship vision
- Month 10: Sexuality - Creating a weekly sensuality ritual
- Month 11: Family - Creating a family vision and values statement
- Month 12: Awakening - Experiencing an ayahuasca journey or Vipassana

## THE 12 KEY OUTCOMES OF YOUR MAGIC YEAR

1. **PURPOSE** — An Inspiring Written Purpose That You Love
2. **GOALS** — Written & Framed Goals
3. **HABITS** — Defined Habits You're 100% Committed To
4. **PEOPLE** — An Uplifting Inner Circle
5. **HAPPINESS** — The Growth Mindset Installed
6. **HEALTH** — A Personalized Magic Morning Routine
7. **MONEY** — A Personal Financial Plan Created
8. **COMMUNITY** — Living Where You Love With People You Love
9. **LOVE** — Creating Your Relationship Vision
10. **SEXUALITY** — Creating a Weekly Sensuality Ritual
11. **FAMILY** — Written Family Vision & Values Statement
12. **AWAKENING** — Experiencing Ayahuasca or a Vipassana

Enjoy the process as you go, and send in your questions and success stories to me at ryan@magicyear.com!

## Achievers and Seekers

To understand me, you should know this. I spent my entire 20s being an **achiever**—going after big, hairy, audacious goals—and my entire 30s being a **seeker**—going as deep as I could with personal transformation and cathartic and often spiritual peak experiences. Lots of yoga, meditation, plant medicine, and Burning Man festivals later, now in my 40s, I've integrated both parts of me and am now both an achiever and a seeker.

It's been quite the journey. In my first two decades as an adult, here's what I focused on:

| Age | What I Did The Last Two Decades | What I Was Obsessed With |
| --- | --- | --- |
| **20s** | Mastered the external world of business and entrepreneurship. Sold a company for $169 million. Got an MBA from Harvard. | External Success |
| **30s** | Mastered the internal world of wellness, meditation, sexuality, energy, love, and fatherhood. | Internal Happiness |

In my 20s, I worked to master the external worlds of business, marketing, and entrepreneurship. I built a software company called iContact to 300 employees, 70,000 customers, and $50M per year in sales and sold it for $169 million in 2012, finished an MBA from Harvard Business School in 2016, founded a global community of purpose-driven leaders called Hive, traveled to 40+ countries, and became a personal growth junkie. I wasn't exactly a hippie back then (like I am now). I was focused on being in the top 1% of goal oriented people. I was an **achiever**.

*Achievers - People committed to becoming the best version of themselves and going after their dreams and goals consistently.*

In my 30s, I went on a big, decade-long adventure. I worked to master the internal world of wellness, meditation, sexuality, happiness, and love. I got into festival culture and attended Burning Man eight times, met my wife Morgan there, got married to her, had our baby boy Apollo, became a health nut. and lived between Bali, Austin, SF, LA, Boulder, and Costa Rica in a very fun and joyous decade full of growth, experiments, and play. I was focused on being in the top 1% of consistently happy people. I was a **seeker**.

*Seekers - People obsessed with living life to its fullest, continual experimentation and transformation, and learning the deeper secrets of the universe.*

I was definitely obsessed with living my life to its fullest and learning the deeper secrets of the universe. I've found a few of them -- and I'm going to share them with you in this book.

So, if you're both an achiever AND a seeker – and curious about how to live an extraordinary life of meaning and joy, this book is for you.

### Achievers
People committed to becoming the best version of themselves and going after their dreams and goals consistently

### This Book

### Seekers
People obsessed with experiencing life to its fullest, continual experimentation, and learning the deeper truths of the universe

The book is designed for people who are on a path of personal growth and transformation and want a modern guide to life upgrading. My primary audience I'm writing for is achievers and seekers who want to make something of themselves and are willing to put in the effort to actually create the life of their dreams (not just talk about it or dream about it, but fucking do it). You see, the key to becoming a successful achiever <u>and</u> a knowledgeable seeker is to balance these two parts of you, like the ying and the yang.

> **!** Never seek so deeply and quickly that you can't continue to consistently achieve your dreams. And never become so single-minded and boring that all you become is a one-dimensional person whose investment portfolio looks incredible but is as deep as a papercut.

Make your goal to be deeply happy first and deeply successful second. For it is lasting happiness that leads to true success, and not the other way around.

As I wrote about earlier, today I'm almost 40 and am living the life of my dreams with my family in a health, surf, and yoga town in Costa Rica. I live an incredibly magical life in paradise focused on health, happiness, tantra, and community. But it wasn't always that way. I used to be super serious, obsessive about building companies, and pretty intense.

These days I spend my time helping build a community of inspiring families and friends near Nosara, Costa Rica, writing books that help people live more joyful lives, and coaching high-growth CEOs (what I used to be).

In this book, I'm focused on taking the lessons from my two decades as an adult and creating an optimal plan for joyful and meaningful living that anyone can apply to creating a magic life. This book is designed to be a road map for you to create the life of your dreams, live an upgraded life, and then find a community that will support you in sustaining your big life upgrade.

You can think of this book as the completely unofficial sequel to the 2007 book, *The Four Hour Workweek*. Similar to that Tim Ferriss classic, this book shares an entirely new way of unconventional living that is now possible -- and gives a detailed, step-by-step roadmap to living it. So don't just read this book. Do this book. Set a goal to do all 111 of the action items inside this book. If you actually do all of them, your life will be forever transformed. Create a special notebook or Google Doc for the reflection exercises inside.

> **!** Set a goal to do all 111 of the action items inside this book. If you actually do all of them your life will be forever transformed. Create a special notebook or Google Doc for the reflection exercises inside -- or do them at the magicyear.com course.

I give lots of appreciation to the original human guinea pig and **lifestyle designer**, Tim Ferriss. He's been a role model for me since 2007, and we have been in similar friend circles since 2018, when we met at our Burning Man Camp -- the extraordinary Camp Mystic, and when we lived in Austin, TX at the same time.

Yes, this book is written to be exceptionally transparent and truthful. We go deep -- get real -- and share the hardships, the successes, the fuck ups, and the lessons. I talk about overcoming "conscious" drug addiction (to psilocybin, MDMA, and LSD mainly), about sex and tantra, and about the difference between healthy obsessions (what makes you happier over time) and unhealthy obsessions (what makes you less happy over time).

I find it's better to provide a loving and thoughtful guide to navigating these edgy topics than to pretend that mistakes and challenges don't exist and sell you some puff piece of fake reality.

You see, sometimes, when you're a **seeker,** you go too far exploring and have to return home. You sometimes only know you went too far over the edge when you find yourself over the edge. You say to yourself, "let me try this one more thing." And then a few days later you realize, "Shit, I might have gone a little too far."

Hopefully, by providing this guide, you can go further into the depths of growth, transformation, and awakening than I ever could venture myself, while being even safer.

There are parts of these edgy realms that are worth careful and experienced guidance and looking at the lessons of many years of human experimentation and learning rather than a "fuck around and find out" laissez faire attitude that can lead to disaster or a fear-based puritan avoidance that can lead to soul-repressed boredom.

So yes, you're probably going to read about some topics that you might not find in a traditional "personal growth" book. I wanted to write about the full human experience and not just provide a "you can do it and everything will be great" sheltered guide.

So yes, we'll be talking about purpose, habits, goals, and money -- the traditional topics of personal growth -- but we'll also be going deep on sex, love, and spiritual awakening.

In writing this book, I asked myself "What book would Tony Robbins write if he'd done ayahuasca, Burning Man, and a few Vipassanas"? Boring this shall not be.

In the Awakening section of the book, I will cover what I call the Triad of Transformation: **Burning Man**, **Vipassana**, and **Ayahuasca**—three experiences that completely changed my life. If you get a chance to do just one of these three -- it will for sure be a life altering adventure. And if you do all three -- get ready for some major life transformation. Just make sure you have good guides along the way.

*Burning Man -* The world's best arts and music festival (tied in my mind with Envision in Costa Rica). Around 75,000 people attend every August in Black Rock City, Nevada.

*Vipassana -* A ten day silent meditation retreat designed to help you let go of the past and become the new version of yourself. Sign up for one at www.dhamma.org.

*Ayahuasca - A plant brew* often grown and made in Central and South America. Drinking ayahuasca often leads to an 8-14 hour intense spiritual experience that leads people into greater connection to their heart and nature and compassion for all beings. Do with care and a good guide.

For those of you who have already been to every festival, tried every "medicine," experienced the grand **Triad of Transformation** (Vipassana, Burning Man, and Ayahuasca), and have your miracle morning routine on lock -- some of this guide may be old hat -- so skip around to what fascinates you most.

*Triad of Transformation - The three most life changing and transformative experiences of my life: Ayahuasca, Vipassana, and Burning Man.*

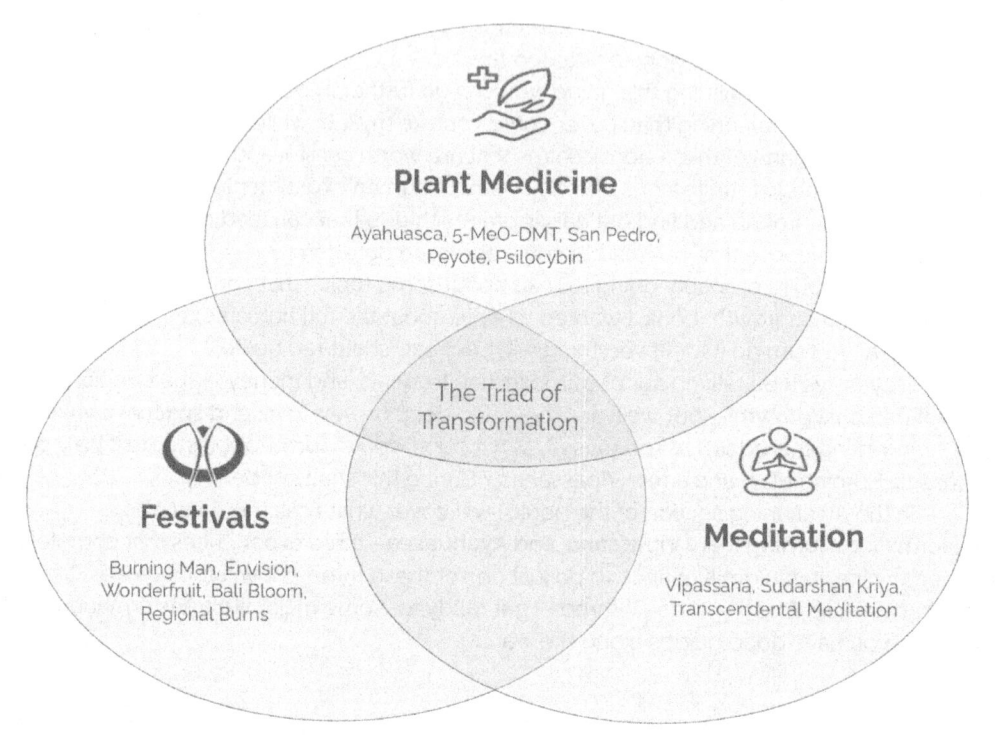

**Plant Medicine**
Ayahuasca, 5-MeO-DMT, San Pedro, Peyote, Psilocybin

**Festivals**
Burning Man, Envision, Wonderfruit, Bali Bloom, Regional Burns

**Meditation**
Vipassana, Sudarshan Kriya, Transcendental Meditation

The Triad of Transformation

*The Triad of Transformation*

If you're already far down the road of biohacking, life optimization, community connection, and purpose-driven living – then this guide may help prepare you for the next stage of life and give you a few new experiments to try.

You'll find some great nuggets for upgrading your life, whether you're just hearing the phrase "personal transformation" for the first time and are curious or if you've personally meditated with Ram Dass, drank the mushroom shakes at the Full Moon Party in Koh Phangan, sat with Ayahuasca ten times, and already spent a few weeks with that Indian Tantra cult.

For those of you who perhaps are just entering or are in the midst of your own personal transformation process (or wondering what the fuck personal transformation actually is), the 12 sections within may turn out to be life changing.

Just go slow. Don't do everything in the same month (or year, for that matter). Remember that transformation is a ten year (and multi-life) process. Slow and smooth is better than fast and unpredictable.

As I like to say, your soul has been here for many lifetimes and will be here for many more. There's no need to learn all the lessons at once. Give yourself a few years to really lock in your **magic life**.

# Who Are We?

Ryan, Morgan, and Baby Apollo in Costa Rica in June 2023

Hi, I'm Ryan. My wife is Morgan, and our baby is Apollo. We are Americans living the remote work digital nomad dream. We live most of the year in Nosara, Costa Rica, and work on what inspires us.

You'll find us writing, making art, creating courses, and creating communities and festivals for our friends.

I work from my laptop these days, mostly writing books, creating the *Magic Year* course, and training coaches who coach high achievers. Morgan is working on building Nosara into a **magic town** of art, connection, nature, and play -- and convincing all our friends to move here too!

On the side, we're also occasional sex coaches. Not really professionally. But for our friends (and friends of friends) who are in relationships where they've lost a little spark. We come into the bedroom and help guide couples to regain polarity and the magic spark and inspiration that come from passionate, frequent sex. We enjoy doing that occasionally -- as well as attending "temple parties" which are adult sensual play parties.

Our shared purpose/dharma as a couple is to help **reimagine how human beings live, love, learn, and play** -- and to share the lessons we learn as we live an "alternative lifestyle" of semi-nomadic and sensual living. We're literally on this planet on a shared mission to pioneer a new way of living and help people realize that *magic can be real*.

We feel very lucky to live this type of life -- and we know it is possible for you too. We met at the Burning Man festival in 2018.

We used to live in Los Angeles, Boulder, and Austin. Today, we use **geoarbitrage** to keep our costs low -- living globally for much less than we would spend to live in America year round.

*Geoarbitrage* - Earning your income from one place and then working remotely in another country where costs are much lower. (Example: earning American pay rates but rotating between Bali, Thailand, & Costa Rica.)

We like to cap the amount of time we spend in the USA at 25% of our time. The energy in America is usually a little dense for us. By keeping our time in the USA capped at 90 days per year -- it keeps us continually learning, growing, and experimenting -- and giving our son an extraordinary education based on the pillars of curiosity, play, nature, and adventure. Apollo's already lived in four countries (Indonesia, Costa Rica, Australia, and the USA) and he's just two. He goes to an outdoor daycare with domes and yurts, and he's about to start soon at a bilingual outdoor play-focused Waldorf school near Nosara.

We love to be where there are very interesting, globally-minded and health conscious people -- and full of fantastic flexible-schedule adventures and curiosity-based Montessori or Waldorf based schools.

We plan to raise our children in many different countries — exposing them to a variety of cultures and ways of living. We're adventurous, inspired, and are here to live a beautiful life. We created and now host an annual Family Festival in Costa Rica called LuvBubble as well as our in-person retreats that focus on teaching the lessons of this book. You're invited to join us for one of these someday.

While I wrote 95% of the words in the book, Morgan inspired at least half of the ideas in this book, especially those around the topic of joy, pleasure, and play.

We're writing this book for people who have a different way of living calling out to them. This book is for people who have an inner voice in their soul that says, "There's more out there."

## How We Created Our Magic Life

These days we live in a small beach house in Costa Rica -- 15 minutes south of Guiones Beach in Nosara -- in the Blue Zone of the Nicoya Peninsula. We live about 50 feet from the ocean--just a few steps from the waves. We have Banyan trees, hammocks, and a garden. Two of our closest friends live with us in a tiny home on our land.

We are living a pretty simple life these days -- and we've never been happier. We're creating a daycare for the area near the Waldorf School called Casa De Las Estrellas. I'm creating the *Magic Year* course and online coaching program (I hope you join it!).

Our son Apollo will soon be two years old -- and we're thinking about having our second baby soon. We've gotten our family's monthly living expenses down to about $15,000 per month, including housing, childcare, food, travel, car, and all other expenses.

While that might sound like a lot of money to some, just a year ago we were spending $40,000 per month living a much more complicated life in Austin, Texas. We've simplified and downsized--and found what really matters to us (friends, family, and a paradise location). We find that a **simple life**, spent with close family and friends doing something meaningful in a beautiful place, is the best type of life for us.

*Simple Life* - An uncomplicated life without lots of possessions or things to hold you back, where you focus on optimizing for time spent creating meaningful things with people you love.

Everything we don't spend, we put into long term savings and investments. We're now slowly becoming real estate investors here in the Nosara area -- and are loving the process.

Every Thursday night, we co-host a music night for our community in the area and get to see many of our friends. Soon, we'll be starting up the weekly Garza Ecstatic Dance on Friday nights. We've created the life of our dreams -- through a lot of intentionality and planning. Now, it's time for you to create the life of your dreams.

My intention with this book is to give you a guide that you can use to upgrade your life within 12 months -- toward a life of meaning, purpose, connection, and wellness. No matter how old you are today, you too can shift into a life where you are thriving in every dimension.

Will the process be over in 12 months? No, personal transformation is a continual process. But if you do the action items in this book you'll be well on your way!

## The Magic Life We're Building

Yes, it's safe to say... My wife, Morgan, and I have chosen to live an unconventional life. There are many differences between a **Standard Life** versus the **Magic Life** we choose to live.

*Standard Life - A life stuck in a cycle of overwork and depression, characterized by a lack of meaning and purpose, depression, ill-health, and disconnection from self and community.*

*Magic Life - The life of someone who is working on what they love, lives where they want, has created a clear purpose, has inspiring friends around them, has uplifting habits, is having great sex, and is healthy and happy.*

Here's a comparison of the standard life versus the life we choose to live.

| The Standard Life | Our Magic Life |
|---|---|
| Get stuck in a 9-5 job | Work remotely 4-5 hours per day |
| No location freedom | Can live and work anywhere |
| Take 2-3 weeks off per year for vacation | Our life is essentially a continuous vacation, at the same cost of being in one place |
| Rarely travel outside home country | Live between USA & Costa Rica |
| Take lots of prescription drugs | Take supplements |
| Eat lots of processed foods | Eat a keto/paleo diet |
| Numb themselves via alcohol | Alcohol-free |
| Have sex less than 1x per week | Have sex 3+ times per week |
| Friends are very homogeneous and uninspiring | Our friends are interesting and from all over the world |

| | |
|---|---|
| Watch 20+ hours per week of TV/movies | Watch max 2-3 hours per week TV/movies, usually uplifting documentaries and Disney movies |
| Expose your consciousness to violent media | Watch only uplifting and encouraging content |
| Cheat on partner / spouse and hide and lie about it | Have an open relationship with deep devotion, honest communication, and mutual encouragement |
| Have a few hobbies outside of work | Always trying new activities like Tae Kwon Do, Shibari rope tying, Padel, Volcano hiking, horseback riding, surfing, and more |
| Goal is to be money rich, no matter how much you have to work | Goal is to be time rich first and money rich second |

What type of life do you want to create for yourself? I'm here to help you follow the "magic life way" and ultimately create a life that inspires you.

## One Year to Transform Your Life

What if someone challenged you to actually create the life of your dreams in a year? How would you do it? What would you need to change about your life? What would you need to change about yourself?

Well, this is the exact premise of this book. So, yes, what if you gave yourself 12 months to completely transform your life in every area?

You see, when I became a new dad in June 2022, everything changed for me.

Suddenly, I was the co-leader of a 7 pound 3 oz. human baby boy named Apollo. Within days, a massive urge came over me to get anything and everything that wasn't working in my life fixed quickly. It wasn't about me anymore. It was about the family. I was the co-leader of my family. It was time to get myself together in every dimension of life.

I spent the next year following Apollo's birth writing this book and taking a close and hard look at my purpose, goals, habits, people, happiness, health, money, community, love, sensuality, and family. Every area of life. How could I get myself ready, lead my family, and have an extraordinary next decade of life?

This year was my **Magic Year**.

At the time of Apollo's birth, I was 192 pounds, which is pretty big for a 5'10" guy. I was clinically obese with over 24% body fat and a 32 BMI.

The week our little baby boy came out, I decided to make a big change. Unlike my dad, I wasn't going to let my health kill me early. Over the following 12 months, I changed a lot of things about my life. Mediocrity wasn't going to cut it any more.

By Apollo's first birthday in June 2023, I was 147 pounds (down 45 pounds) and had a very healthy 14.4% body fat. During the year, I also completely changed my company to focus on doing what I actually love (writing books and coaching CEOs), and we decided to move into the community of our dreams in Nosara, Costa Rica. I wrote this book during that magical year -- and the time period inspired the title of this book.

That year was my **Magic Year**. Now, it's time for yours.

So what do you think would happen if you decided to spend one year of your life actually doing what is in this book. Actually doing what brings you alive? Actually following your joy? Actually following your healthy obsessions? Actually building passive cash flow engines step-by-step that compound over time? Actually bringing into your life inspiring and uplifting friends and mentors?

What fears come up when you think about actually taking action to create the life you dream of?

*How would you not run out of money?*
*What if something bad happened?*
*Would you lose your friends?*
*Would your family still love you?*
*Would you be ridiculed for being different?*

Fear is a big blocker toward needed change. I'm here to get you through it and over it. Let's give you some better questions. Instead of all those fear-based questions above, ask yourself repeatedly...

*What magic might happen?*
*What might I learn?*
*Who might I meet?*
*Who might I become?*
*How might I change for the better?*

Yes, decide to spend one year working on actually creating the life of your dreams. Get yourself out of the endless, stress-filled **rat race** driven by OPE (other people's expectations) and actually create a life you love.

*Rat Race - The mindless race to do work you don't enjoy that barely keeps you afloat financially. Being stuck in a cycle of consumption, debt, and overwork and never choosing to do what you actually want to do with your life.*

## The Magic Year Challenge

As you read this book, I encourage you to consider taking on this **Magic Year Challenge** with me. Spend one year of your life to actually create the life of your dreams and see what is possible. We have a big prize available for the first two people to actually complete the challenge.

*Magic Year Challenge - The challenge to complete all 111 action items in this book within 12 months. The first two people to complete the Magic Year Challenge will win an all-expense paid trip to Costa Rica to be coached by the author 1:1.*

This will be fun! The first two people who send in evidence that they have completed all 111 action items to me on Instagram DM (@magicyearteam) or via email at ryan@magicyear.com will win an all-expenses paid week long trip to Nosara, Costa Rica to have a week long vacation and 1:1 life coaching sessions with me and my colleague Joe McVeen.

Evidence can include your action item reflection answers in Google Doc and photo documentation of all habit changes (you in a cold plunge, meditating, at the gym, etc.). This prize is open to readers of this book as well as anyone taking the *Magic Year Course* on our website. We'll post to our newsletter list and IG once two people have successfully claimed this challenge. Let's go!

## Two Life Changing Experiences

What got me on this journey of personal transformation? Well, in 2012, something incredible happened to me, followed by something devastating.

The incredible thing first: After 10 years of focused and consistent effort to build an entrepreneurial venture to $50 million per year in revenues, we sold the software company I'd co-founded in 2002 as a freshman in college in North Carolina for $169 million. I was 27 at the time. This was the peak experience of my achiever phase -- and the result of ten years of really hard work.

This was a life changing experience for me that kicked off the next leg of my upgrade journey.

After paying the venture capitalists their return and sharing the proceeds with my co-founder and all our employees (we made every employee a partial owner), I ended up earning $15 million after-taxes.

It was life changing money. But something was missing inside. I had financial wealth. But I didn't quite have happiness yet. And I hadn't discovered the deeper meaning and purpose for my life yet.

I was 50 pounds overweight, had chronic neck pain, and terrible anxiety from a decade of exhaustive overwork. I wasn't healthy, nor particularly happy, even though it seemed like I had everything on the surface.

Then something devastating happened. My beloved 59 year old mom, Pauline, who had invested so much time and love into raising me, was diagnosed with terminal brain cancer. My mom was dying of brain cancer, and there wasn't anything I could do about it, no matter how much I tried to save her life with the latest medical treatments and studies.

Her death that Spring woke me up to the brevity of life -- and her dying wish for me was to "always follow my bliss."

Since then, I've been on a grand journey around the world to find what was missing inside of me. To find true happiness. To find true health. To discover an untroubled inner life, or inner peace and deep fulfillment. And to find my deeper purpose in life. My magic gift.

Between California, Bali, Thailand, India, Costa Rica, and the deserts of Burning Man, I not only found what I was missing, but I also found a repeatable process that can help anyone become truly happy and actually create a purpose-driven life of their dreams. In this book, I will share this process with you. Just commit. Do the steps. Realize that it's a multi-year process. And your life will start transforming.

It took me 12 years and about $5 million of my own (rather hard-earned) money to learn the lessons in this book. As part of living the life that taught me the lessons inside, I've traveled to 45 countries and attended over 30 personal growth workshops, courses, and experiences ranging from meditation in India, to Tony Robbins in Florida, to Landmark Forum in California, to Burning Man in Black Rock City, to Envision in Costa Rica.

I was an **achiever, seeker, explorer, adventurer,** and **experimenter**. I was searching for inner happiness, true health, and the love of my life.

In 2018, I finally found my wife Morgan, and we've been on an extraordinary journey of mutual growth-inducing marital bliss since then.

In my 30s, as a seeker, I experimented with 25 different plant medicines (probably too many → see the Awakening Chapter), spent many weeks in silence at Vipassana, attended eight Burning Man festivals, visited Esalen more than I can count, and I even dated a few brilliant women in California who taught me their secrets to healthy living (thank you, Nadia, Rebecca, and Danielle!).

Then, in June 2022, my wife Morgan gave birth to our son Apollo. That event catalyzed me into wanting to take everything I'd learned and actually create the life of our dreams before Apollo got too old. I'd gotten a little fat and boring again. It was time to mix things up -- and become the example of a man that I wanted to be for my son.

In 2023, we moved to Nosara, Costa Rica, got our little family beach house on a 1/3rd of an acre, and decided to live a beautiful, simple, and thriving life next to friends and family.

It was a winding path for me. But it doesn't have to be as much of a winding path for you. With the right guide to creating the life of your dreams -- you can go further than I ever imagined. You can both accomplish more of what matters to you and be happier.

You can now stand on my shoulders and learn what I've learned, in a couple weeks of reading or less -- and then apply the action items and the recommended **habit stack** to your own life.

*Habit stack - The collection of all your current habits. If you can upgrade your habit stacks in each of the 12 areas of this book, you can completely transform your life.*

This book has many definition callouts like the one above that will help you keep track of the sometimes unusual language I'll be using. There are about 200 words or phrases in this book that I define because I've either made them up or because they are a bit esoteric and warrant definition. I like to culture hack. By creating some new concepts, I hope to make a positive difference to the lexicon of personal growth, just like Tim Ferriss did when he invented the term "lifestyle design" in 2007.

Each chapter has a visual guide at the beginning of it that lays out the major concepts for that chapter. Study these visual guides in-depth.

Regardless of your age, study this book like you'd study for an important exam or work project. Except now, this isn't about getting an A+ or getting promoted. This is about upgrading your life and your very understanding of what is possible for the rest of your life.

Regardless of how old you are today, anything you dream of, that you believe in fully, that you also take consistent action toward is possible. It only takes a couple years to create the life of your dreams from scratch if you have the right guide.

Regardless of how old you are today, anything you dream of, that you believe in fully, that you also take consistent action toward is possible. It only takes a couple years to create the life of your dreams from scratch if you have the right guide.

This book will guide you through upgrading every major area of your life, including your purpose, goals, habits, people, happiness, health, money, community, love, sex, family, and spiritual awakening process. If you're committed, what took me 12 years might only take you 12 months to learn and perhaps another 12 months to perfect.

So, if you're serious about upgrading your life, re-discovering your magic spark and gift inside, and actually creating the life of your dreams, make this book your consistent companion.

Sleep next to it. Underline it. Highlight it. Make lots of notes. Put it under your pillow at night. And create a single Google Doc or notebook to capture all your action items and reflections from it.

## Your Life Upgrade Manual

Every decade or so, I like to write a book and leave little breadcrumbs for those who come after me. I'm fully aware that I won't be around forever in this body. My hope is that it will be easier for you to be able to go further than I could – by using this guide to get further on the path of awakening and growth.

So, if you're stuck in the land of suburban dread, overwork, paycheck-to-paycheck living, unhealthy eating, mundane mediocrity, obesity, and strip malls – think of this book as your ticket to freedom and full spectrum wellness that will teach you what you need to know to craft your **escape plan** -- and then execute on it.

*Escape Plan - Your plan to get out of your mediocre environment and your mediocre life by upgrading where you live to an inspiring place with nature, friends, community, and healthy organic food.*

Think of this book as a **Life Upgrade Manual** or as a guide to a new way of living.

| The Old Way | The Magic Way |
|---|---|
| Suburban Dread | Community Living |
| Office Work | Remote Work |
| Morning Commutes | Miracle Mornings |
| Obesity | Fitness |
| Lots of Sugar & Alcohol | Keto & Paleo Diets |
| Bad & Infrequent Sex | Frequent Great Sex |
| Cold Winters | Paradise Living |
| High Living Costs | Low Cost Living |
| Obsession with TV & Social Media | Obsession with Living Passionately |
| Boring Lives | Festivals & Community Gatherings |
| News-Obsessed Worry | Living a Joyous & Present Life |

MAGIC YEAR - 38

| | |
|---|---|
| Kids Raised By Parents | Kids Raised By Parents & Community |
| Stuck in Your Home Country | Travel & Living in Many Countries |
| Lack of Touch | Group Cuddles |
| Busyness and Stress | Lower Cost, Low Stress Living |
| Little Time With Friends | Meaningful Presence With Friends |
| Disconnection & Marital Separation | Weekly Temples With Your Partner |
| Living With Fear & Worry | Living in Delight and Joy |
| Uninspired Friends | A Passionate Global Tribe |

Welcome to a new way of living. Welcome to your handbook to get you started on this journey of living a happy, healthy, vibrant, alive, wealthy, sensually alive, and passionate life.

Like I said -- it's not a normal book. It took me 12 years and quite a few million dollars of adventuring, seeking, and exploration to learn how to distill the lessons in this book.

Building on the shoulders of giants before, I pushed the boundaries of growth-oriented human potential exploration just a little bit further to help you do the same and someday pass on your learnings to the next generation to continue the long march of progress in human consciousness evolution.

Implement it section by section, and you are going to have a truly extraordinary (if a little bumpy and growth-filled) next twelve months. Go slow, take it month-by-month. Don't change everything in 30 days. But definitely start listening to your **intuition** inside and acting in alignment with your authentic desires. Take some chances. Jump off a figurative cliff or two -- and learn to build your airplane in mid-air.

*Intuition - The little voice inside of your head from your Higher Self that guides you toward the right path. When you don't listen to it, bad things start to happen.*

In this book, I'll be making sure that you have clear written goals, good habits, uplifting people around you, and an optimal mindset. I'll check in to ensure you've got your physical and mental **habit stack** on lock with healthy fuel, a strong body, and a calm mind.

In the money section, I'll introduce you to the concepts of **time freedom**, **income freedom**, and **net worth freedom**.

*Time Freedom - When you earn more than your monthly living expenses in passive income from your businesses and investments, giving you freedom to invest your time as you choose.*

*Location Freedom - When you have the freedom to live and work from wherever you choose. You can work from anywhere with a strong internet connection.*

*Net Worth Freedom - When your passive cash flow from your businesses and investments is high enough to more than cover your total annual expenses, so that your net worth continues to grow over time.*

I'll help you ensure that you're fully alive with your spirit unleashed -- living with an inspiring purpose, a loving family, with work you enjoy, and expressed sensuality that connects you to your healthy primal nature.

I'll end the book with a section focused on the process of **awakening**. I'll cover the process of awakening to your true nature as an infinite being and how to appropriately use **meditation** and **entheogens** that have been used for millennia to help homo sapiens transcend the illusion of ego-based separation.

*Entheogens* - Psychoactive substances which are used for religious, shamanic, or spiritual purposes. Entheogens can alter perception, mood, and cognitive processes, often leading to profound insights or experiences of unity and transcendence.

The awakening I'm referring to in that final section is the transformation from:

1. Overly serious to continual bliss (also known as ananda)
2. Overly heady to integrated between body, mind, and spirit
3. An inability to feel to an ability to reconnect to your heart
4. Self-centered to we-centered
5. Following your obligation to following your obsession
6. Following others expectations to following your joy
7. Mediocre to extraordinary
8. Lonely and individualistic to community-driven

While you could learn many of these concepts yourself in a single magic mushroom or ayahuasca journey or by doing a Vipassana, having a guide to these esoteric realms might just be helpful and save you some time and brain cells.

It's going to be a fun book. One word of warning, though. Don't just read it once. While that may help a little – it won't do the trick of actually transforming every area of your life. Instead, refer back to the book time and again as you implement the lessons. Like the 1937 classic *Think and Grow Rich*, this isn't meant to be read once and forgotten. If you really want to create the life of your dreams, keep referring back to it time and again -- and yes, actually do the action items.

## How this Book is Structured

"No amount of security is worth the suffering of a mediocre life chained to a routine that has killed your dreams." - Maya Mendoza, author

The first part of this book is my personal transformation story—sharing exactly how I ended up where I am today as happy and healthy and the co-leader of a loving family -- a family that makes a very intentional and conscious choice to live life differently.

I share the real inner vulnerable story -- not just the standard polished veneer of some privileged Harvard grad former tech entrepreneur (me). I share the real stuff, the juicy stuff, and the inner story of my personal upgrade journey. I went from being an obese, anxiety-ridden workaholic American entrepreneur to a healthy and happy writer/course builder/CEO coach living in the Blue Zone of Costa Rica with my family. There's a damn good story there.

The second part of the book is a guidebook to upgrading your life, with 12 steps, each with its own chapter. Each chapter focuses on an area of your life -- and how to optimize it for living a happy and meaningful life. Consider this book a journey you will go on. It's nearly time to begin the deep work. Get ready.

## A World of Magic Awaits

Yes, I know that life can sometimes feel lonely and overwhelming. I've been there. Life can especially feel lonely in the land of headiness, mental debate, hypercompetition, social media overwhelm, and disconnection from our bodies and each other that has permeated much of our global culture.

But, friends, know that there is a whole other world out there. A world of connection, wellness, art, music, authentic people, adventure, purpose, and play. A world of wellness, festivals, magic, desert pyramids, art, music, and full expression. This is the world I live in. And you can enter this world too. You just have to know where to go to find it. I plan to guide you there.

Yes, there is a world where you too can live in a beachside home for less than living in America, just like my friends here in Costa Rica. I'll point you to the best places for community connection and perfect weather that have exceptional schools and lots of activities for kids.

This book will be your guide. I'll tell you where to go -- and how to get there. I don't have all the answers. No one does. But I have some. And I hope to share as much as we can with you in the pages ahead.

A world of achievement, growth, adventure, joy, play, and flow is out there. But you have to commit to getting out of the world of mediocrity and escape first from the matrix surrounding your old way of being and living.

As Robin Sharma writes, "The majority of people on the planet today are allowing large amounts of mediocrity to overwhelm their lives. Watch how they work, what they think, the words they deploy, the food they eat, the habits they apply, and the way they behave, and it's clear they have given away their sovereign power to false beliefs, past hurts, current challenges, daily disturbances, and inexcusable excuses."

Fuck mediocrity. Let's create a **magic life**. It's time to start your Magic Year!

# CHAPTER 2

# ESCAPING THE MATRIX

**MAGIC YEAR**

MAGIC YEAR - 42

# KEY CONCEPTS FROM CHAPTER TWO

**1. THE MATRIX** 
Mind conditioning from news media, advertising, and social networks that holds us back from becoming the best version of ourselves. The Matrix around you often prevents free thinking, creates limiting beliefs, and leads to mediocrity.

**2. INFORMATION DIET** 
The information that reaches your brain on a daily basis. Controlling and limiting what you intake from social media and the news media is especially important to maintaining a happy, healthy, wealthy, and fully alive life.

**3. THE DRAG** 
A depression that can sink in from overexposure to the Matrix if you don't surround yourself with positive and uplifting people, create meaning in your life, install positive habits, and carefully curate your information diet.

**4. AMERICAN MATRIX** 
The particular type of mind conditioning that comes from living in America -- a wonderful country with a few faults: an obsessive focus on work and money and destructive patterns of obesity, violent media, and prescription drug addiction.

**5. THE THREE EPIDEMICS** 
The three major American epidemics of obesity, prescription pills, and loneliness.

**6. FLOW STATE** 
When you're so engaged in what you're doing that time melts away, you can achieve superhuman performance, and your inhibitions of revealing your true self are extinct.

**7. MUGGLES** 
People who have forgotten or haven't yet discovered their magical abilities.

**8. MUGGLEDOM** 
Where Muggles live. The standard society, filled up with people who have forgotten that they are infinite beings and powerful creators.

**9. MAGIC YEAR** 
A 12 month period of focus on upgrading all the major areas of your life. This will be the next 12 months of your life if you choose to accept the core challenge of this book.

**10. ANANDA** 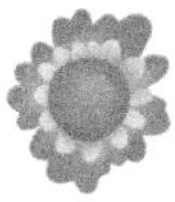
A Sanskrit word meaning a feeling of intense pleasure or eternal bliss. The concept of Ananda inspired Joseph Campbell's famous encouragement to "Follow your bliss."

**11. MIRACLE MORNINGS** 
The daily routine you do in the first 2 hours of being awake that is designed to bring you into optimal performance and happiness for the rest of the day. Ideally includes exercise, cold plunge, supplements, sun exposure, saunas, etc.

**12. RAT RACE** 
The mindless race to do work you don't enjoy that barely keeps you afloat financially. Being stuck in a cycle of consumption, debt, and overwork and never choosing to do what you actually want to do with your life.

# CH 2: ESCAPING THE MATRIX

*"The Matrix many of us are trapped in is the 'reality' offered to us by society. We are expected since we are born, to behave in a certain way, to work for certain things, to get good grades, to get a good job, to have insurance of all kinds, to worry about retirement, to raise kids and put them through the same motions as we went through, and thus being a part of one never-ending cycle which is paved with good intentions, but littered with crushed souls." - Dolly Garland*

## What is The Matrix?

Here's a very important definition for this book. I consider "**The Matrix**" to be the web of cultural conditioning that occurs through media, advertising, and general thought within a country, often preventing free thinking. It's the water we swim in, often unknowingly.

Eventually, the Matrix often erodes our self-belief and turns us into shells of our former joyous selves, where anything and everything was possible.

Here's how author Tom Bilyeu describes the Matrix: "What I mean when I say escape the matrix is to get out from under the limiting beliefs that we all have that hold us back."

Here's my definition:

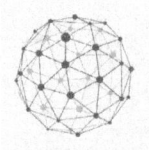

*The Matrix - Mind conditioning from news media, advertising, and social networks that holds us back from becoming the best version of ourselves. The Matrix around you often prevents free thinking, creates limiting beliefs, and leads to mediocrity.*

So the way I use the term, The Matrix in this book – I am referring to the general thinking of a society that holds us back from becoming the best and fullest expression of ourselves.

My friend and author Vishen Lakhiani calls this concept "The Culturescape" in his great book *The Code of the Extraordinary Mind*.

The great 20th century German existentialist philosopher Martin Heidegger called this concept "The Chatter" and argued that we have to escape the chatter of society to become authentic and realize our full potential.

Escaping the chatter couldn't be more important in a time of endless scrolling and social and news apps that intentionally prey on our dopamine and fear cycles in order to addict us and bring us back over and over, increasing their advertising revenues. We must say no to The Matrix -- and to the many insidious ways it infiltrates our minds through the algofeeds.

While some of the data sources in your personal information matrix may be uplifting and positive – it's a good bet that many contain messages of violence, fear, criticism, and exclusion. And it's a good bet that many encourage habits or products that simply aren't good for people (eat lots of sugar, take this pill to make yourself better, and spend all your money on things you don't really need).

It takes intentionality and willpower, to tune out bad influences and to be intentional with your **information diet**. Curating your information diet is one of the most important acts you can do as a conscious creator.

*Information Diet* - *The information that reaches your brain on a daily basis. Controlling and limiting what you intake from social media and the news media is especially important to maintaining a happy, healthy, wealthy, and fully alive life.*

Getting rid of violent movies and television shows from your consciousness is critical to actually seeing how wonderful and incredible life is and avoiding **The Drag**.

*The Drag* - *A depression that can sink in from overexposure to the Matrix if you don't surround yourself with positive and uplifting people, create meaning in your life, install positive habits, and carefully curate your information diet.*

The Drag is what can happen to you emotionally and energetically when you feel demotivated, disconnected, and lonely after being continually exposed to a violent, unhealthy, and disconnected media culture that is energetically toxic.

The media matrix (which makes money by selling ads and subscriptions) often leads us to think that life is difficult and terrible by showing fear-based content that is addicting yet nearly completely irrelevant to our lives.

Each country has its own slightly different media-driven matrix—the collection of norms, attitudes, judgments, cultures, and expectations of political correctness for what you can say and how you must act to "fit in."

One of the reasons that my family likes living abroad most of the year is that it gets us outside of the **American Matrix** so that we can see what is universal truth beyond our local bubble.

*The American Matrix* - *The particular type of mind conditioning that comes from living in America -- a wonderful country with a few faults: an obsessive focus on work and money and destructive patterns of obesity, violent media, and prescription drug addiction.*

The American Matrix makes it "normal" to eat a Big Mac with fries and a Coca Cola, weigh over 220 pounds, work 50+ hours per week, watch three hours of television and social media videos per day, pile on credit card debt, take antidepressant pills, go see a violent movie, read about conflict all day long, watch our military drones kill people in foreign countries, numb ourselves with alcohol, and then wonder why we're not happy. It's time to opt-out, get out, and create something new.

While it should be obvious that these actions aren't going to lead to a fulfilling life, sadly, it's the water us American fish are swimming in that has made us mostly blind to the fact that we live in a deeply depressed and disconnected society that has lost its way. It's the unhealthy inputs that create the unhealthy outputs.

I choose to live in Costa Rica because here there is intentionally no military, beautiful protected nature, and there's an opportunity to raise our kids in a peaceful and healthy society that believes in "Pura Vida." Not to mention, it consistently ranks as one of the happiest countries in the world and costs about half as much to live here as any American suburb.

Paradise at half the cost with all my happy, health-obsessed, growth obsessed friends? Sign me up!

The **American Matrix** makes it normal for the average American to be at least three of these six:

- Obese
- Anxious
- Depressed
- TV-Obsessed
- Pill-popping
- Workaholics

If you're being honest with yourself, **which are you?**

In America, we see that media, advertising, and culture often encourage overeating, overwork, anxiety, and pill-based solutions that treat symptoms rather than the actual problem. This has led to a country where...

- 20% of adults are on mental health medications[1]
- 46% of adults are classified as obese (BMI >30)[2]
- 52% of adults have diabetes or pre-diabetes[3]
- 66% of Americans are on some form of prescription drug[4]
- 73% of Americans are classified as overweight or obese (BMI >25)[5]
- 70 million ADHD prescriptions are given annually[6]
- 337 million antidepressant prescriptions are given annually[7]
- 6.3 billion prescriptions are dispensed annually (19 per person)[8]
- Over 1 billion pounds of toxic pesticides are used annually[9]

**Seriously. What. The. Actual. Fuck.**

Why do we allow ourselves to suffer from a simultaneous **obesity epidemic**, **pill epidemic**, and **loneliness epidemic**. What happened to us? What happened to the confident and healthy nation that put a man on the moon in 1969?

*The Three Epidemics* - The three major American epidemics of obesity, prescription pills, and loneliness.

---

[1] Mental Health - https://www.insurancejournal.com/news/national/2021/04/22/610924.htm
[2] Obesity - https://www.cdc.gov/obesity/data/adult.html
[3] Diabetes - https://www.aicr.org/news/half-of-us-adults-have-diabetes-or-prediabetes/
[4] Prescription Drugs - https://hpi.georgetown.edu/rxdrugs/
[5] Obesity - https://data.oecd.org/healthrisk/overweight-or-obese-population.htm
[6] ADHD Prescriptions - https://www.nytimes.com/2022/07/09/style/medication-depression-anxiety-adhd.html
[7] Anti-depressants - https://www.drugdiscoverytrends.com/the-pandemic-is-fueling-the-demand-for-natural-alternatives-to-antidepressants
[8] Prescriptions - https://www.iqvia.com/insights/the-iqvia-institute/reports/the-use-of-medicines-in-the-us
[9] Pesticides - https://www.ncbi.nlm.nih.gov/pmc/articles/PMC2946087/

Is it the food we're eating? The breakdown of local communities? The pursuit of profit above purpose? The endless doom loop of social media scrolling? The divisive and fear-driven news media? A history of multiple unnecessary wars that had little to do with us? Are pharmaceutical companies prioritizing Wall Street over wellness? Violent movies that destroy our souls and turn us into zombies? Or all of the above.

We've sadly gone from a nation of shooting stars to a nation of school shooters.

What killed the soul of America -- and how do we revitalize our bold nation that is a melting pot full of innovators, pioneers, creators, hard workers, and community-driven leaders.

How do we create a generation of kids that isn't traumatized-- a generation of kids taught to be kind to others, think empathically about their broader community, to spend time in nature, and to always follow what brings them alive?

It's time to change the pattern, unsubscribe from the soul-numbing violence shown to us in Hollywood and from our past war-mongering political leaders, and invest in the mental health of our children and adults and in a new story of peace, trust, and wellness.

If I could dose everyone in America with a serving of ayahuasca, I could -- this would single-handedly change everything in a couple weeks and raise the consciousness of the whole country. Perhaps we should put aya in the water instead of fluoride? (Real thought).

As Morpheus said in the Matrix, "You take the blue pill... the story ends, you wake up in your bed and believe whatever you want to believe. You take the red pill... you stay in Wonderland, and I show you how deep the rabbit hole goes." Choose the red pill and wake the fuck up – and get out of the system that makes you a fat cog in a hypercompetitive machine.

And as Carnivore Aurelius says on Instagram, "Maybe your life doesn't suck and the world isn't unfair. Maybe you're just meant to spend your time in the sun, eat real foods, care for those you love, raise a family, fight for a purpose, and dance around the fire… but instead you sit in an office bombarded with toxic fluorescent light, get blackout drunk on the weekends, suck on cherry vapes, eat junk drenched in seed oils, and live in an apartment the size of a shoebox in a city infested with rats."

Powerful truth bombs there.

Yes, the truth is that life can be easy, wonderful, and fun, and that a very large majority of people are kind. If you unsubscribe from the madness of "the news" and experience the goodness of people through day-to-day first-person experiences, this becomes obvious very quickly. You just have to focus on the goodness of everyday people in your hometown and as you travel around the world.

As Jason Nemer, the founder of Acroyoga, says, "You can trust people. You can trust a lot of people. You don't have to live in fear of strangers. It seems crazy to me that, in many cultures, we teach our children to fear and not talk to strangers. I've been all over the world. I've traveled the world, and I've never had anything bad happen to me. I assume the best in people. I assume that I can trust them.

So yes, I encourage you to DELETE the news apps from your phone and block the news websites from your browsers. They aren't helpful and just make us sad and fearful. Instead of informing us -- they are de-forming us and dividing us. They are making us needlessly scared. You must break free.

While I love my homeland of America and see the positives of its systems of technology and innovation, its arrogant attitude toward fighting wars it didn't actually need to fight (Vietnam, Iraq, and Syria) and allowing corporations to have the same legal rights as people has caused us to lose our way since 1950. We need to stop fighting wars over territories that are not ours when there are no present threats to our people. We also need to put the culture wars behind us and find common ground.

Watching NBC News and reading the New York Times in the 1990s was essential to staying informed. Today, it's a surefire way to gain needless information and depression. Unsubscribe and turn it off.

Will I ever be based again in the United States? Well, maybe someday. Wake me up when semi-automatic assault rifles are banned, corporations can't fund political campaigns, we're not the biggest carbon emitter per capita in the world, and we aren't fighting a proxy war with Russia. Until then, I'm going to build my family's life in a peaceful Blue Zone.

> To break free from the illusions of the Matrix, you must realize that you've been a willing participant in an education system designed for the industrial age, designed for compliance, and designed to make you an employee within a competitive and goal-oriented military industrial complex rather than a free-thinking creator.

Is there some evil plot by the global elites to lock us into a matrix and become cogs in their profit-making machine? No, there isn't.

The truth is that in post-World War II America, we had no choice but to become a society that became experts at production and efficiency. GDP was societal survival in the 1940s-1980s. And so we created the military-industrial complex (a term coined by President Eisenhower in 1961) that led to massive advances in technology and production that ultimately led us to winning the arms race and the Cold War.

The propaganda of the Matrix was in some ways essential to nation-state survival in a time before human beings could communicate across borders, religions, and cultures.

The downside, of course, was that free-thinking creators didn't really fit into the cog-in-an-industrial machine and compliance focused, work-obsessed culture that came from scaling up assembly lines, supply chains, and global trade ad infinitum.

While we gained national highway systems, GPS systems, the information technology revolution, and rising economic output, we created a crisis of meaning, loneliness, and human connection -- that ultimately led to the counter-cultural protests of the 1960s and later the major protests against the overprotective restrictions during COVID.

Free thinkers be damned. Get back into your box. Memorize this. Get back in line. Play your role in society, take your pills, and pretend to be happy. There was little room for the "crazy ones, the misfits, the rebels, the troublemakers, the round pegs in the square holes, the ones who see things differently."

Kids were labeled ADHD and problem-children when they were just fucking being kids. As author Chris Finlay so eloquently says:

> "From when we're age five, we're put into these classrooms. We're told to sit down, be quiet, concentrate and pay attention. Very little of it was about honoring the individual and their own unique talents. The next thing is you work for someone. There is the slavery of thinking that you should be an employee. There are so many things you could do. there are so many things you could be. You could be a transformation speaker, you could be a healer, an artist, you could be a dancer, you could be all these things. You see yourself in a certain way. I'd say that you are actually much more. The possibilities that exist for you in your life are actually beyond your wildest dreams." - Chris Finlay

# Breaking Free

Hey there, fellow Earthling! I hope I now have your attention. Did you know that you're wired to be a hunter-gatherer, a social creature with 150 close friends, and a passionate lover under the stars?

You're not actually meant to be a corporate cog sitting in a cubicle and stressed out all the time.

That's right - your evolution has primed you for a life of adventure, exploration, and connection with nature and other humans. So, why are you now stuck doing spreadsheets and endless Zoom calls all day, feeling unfulfilled, lonely, and restless? Don't worry; you're not alone!

Many of us have lost touch with our primal instincts, leading to feelings of disconnection, boredom, and burnout. The truth is, something is wrong - but it's not with you. It's with our society, which has conditioned us to prioritize productivity, efficiency, and material success over our innate human needs. This problem is just as big in China, Korea, and Japan as it is in the USA. The Europeans, Central Americans, and South Americans seem to have things more in balance.

But don't despair; it's not too late to reconnect with your true nature, connect with your friends, and find your passion again. So, go ahead and take a break from those spreadsheets, and go skinny-dipping in a nearby lake or river, join a hunting or fishing trip, or take a walk under the stars with someone you love. Your mind and body will thank you, and you'll find that you can focus better and be more productive when you honor your natural needs.

Do you remember that last moment in your life when you felt an intense passion burning within you? The last time you were truly passionate (or even obsessed) about something. Maybe you had a fast beating of your chest or just a fiery feeling. Go back to that moment in your life. How old were you? Where were you? Who was around you?

If you can remember that feeling and anchor it inside of you -- so much is possible.

> The goal is to live in such a way that you feel flow, excitement, and passion for what you're creating every day. If you're not -- you're not doing the right thing with your time. Only through flow can we have the persistence to create our most important works.

Starting today, I encourage you to live in such a way that this feeling of **flow, passion,** and **obsession**, can return. Choose to live a life of experimentation, exploration, and growth-- where no external critic or even your scared inner child can hold you back.

> *Flow State - When you're so engaged in what you're doing that time melts away, you can achieve superhuman performance, and your inhibitions of revealing your true self are extinct.*

This is exactly what you realize during a good night of tripping at Burning Man -- when you recognize this is all a game preparing you for something bigger in the future. You realize that there are a lot of bullshit confines in the world that aren't in alignment with love -- and that you can choose to leave these behind. My friend and author Vishen Lakhiani calls these "brules" (an abbreviation of bullshit rules) in *The Code of The Extraordinary Mind*.

> To break free from the illusions of The Matrix, you have to realize that you don't have to meet the expectations of society, your parents, or anyone for that matter. Instead, you should focus on defining and chasing your own dreams. Yes, actually do what you love. That's the whole fucking thing. Just do what you love that makes a difference for others – and figure out how to monetize it.

You see, the key to breaking free from the Matrix is to **never compromise your own dreams**. If you need to take a pay cut or reduce your living standards for a few years to work on what you truly love and give to the world what you are meant to give -- fine. But **don't you dare die with your gifts left inside of you**.

If you do that, I'll kick your ass in the next life. Hopefully, this book will help ensure that doesn't happen.

## What is Muggledom?

In Harry Potter, **muggles** are those who have forgotten or haven't yet discovered their magical ability. Muggles, of course, live in **Muggledom**. And part of my goal with this book is to help you **escape the matrix,** get yourself out of Muggledom, and into living the life of your dreams **with a community of inspiring and encouraging friends**.

> Muggles - People who have forgotten or haven't yet discovered their magical abilities.

> Muggledom - Where Muggles live. The standard society, filled up with people who have forgotten that they are infinite beings and powerful creators.

**You, my friend, are not a muggle.** By the very fact that you picked up this book, it is evidence that you are on the right path. Welcome to a new path. I'm here to be your guide. And I believe in you. No matter what you've been through or where you are -- I believe in you.

The truth is, none of us are Muggles. We are all part of God. We are all magical, infinite creators born of miracles. Yes, you are part of an extraordinary species of Homo sapiens, but you are so much more than just a human. Your true nature is a soul that is temporarily residing inside a human body. Welcome to The Human Experience.

So, my friend, remember who you truly are. Reclaim your fierceness. Reclaim your inner joy. Reclaim your childlike wonder. A path forward within awaits. An extraordinary life awaits you. You just have to realize who you are and what you are capable of.

This book will help you realize that you...

- Are a powerful creator
- Are infinite in nature

- Are consciousness
- Are part of God
- Will thrive if you surround yourself with uplifting and inspiring people
- Can achieve anything you set your mind to
- Can live anywhere you want
- Can actually make a great living by following your obsessions and joys and doing what brings you alive
- Can actually create the life of your dreams
- Can accomplish anything through a combination vision, action, and consistency
- Can have the partner and marriage of your dreams
- Can have the family of your dreams
- Can be an inspiring purpose-driven leader up to extraordinary things
- Give up your ego and decide to follow the path of joy and service and surrender and see where it leads you
- Are happiest when you are living near your friends
- Are in fact extremely magical and that's a true miracle that you are here today.

*"You forget who you are. Born of stardust. Nuclear fusion. The blood of mammoths spilled on frozen seas by your ancestors. You are made of miracles. A survivor of every plague, pestilence, and war. You are 30 trillion cells, serving one true master (spirit). Don't forget who you are." - Aubrey Marcus*

This book is designed to wake you from your soul's slumber and give you a guidebook to leading yourself through a massive personal upgrade. This book provides a path forward for those who want to create what is next for themselves.

So yeah, not a normal book. Thank God. Normal books are boring.

# Following Your Bliss

*"If you follow your bliss you put yourself on a kind of track that has been there all the while, waiting for you." - Joseph Campbell*

In the biography *Joseph Campbell: A Fire In the Mind,* authors Stephen and Robin Larsen explain how Campbell followed his "inner guidance" and his "own intuitions and premonitions."

This was their way of describing how one of the great minds and writers of the 20th century followed his internal compass above all else. As a young man, Campbell studied at Dartmouth and Columbia University and traveled the world extensively, absorbing himself in mythology, anthropology, art, and religion. During a short time working in his family business, Campbell found that the world of money deadened his soul.

Watching the workers, he wrote in his journal, "They sacrifice their joy and adventures to money -- and the money merely enables them more dull plodding -- to bring more people into the world so that the same futile work and sorrow may be carried on for another span of years."

Campbell decided to let go of money and instead, do what he wanted with his life. This decision later brought him much fame and allowed him to influence the entire field of storytelling so much that George Lucas once credited Campbell for the narrative arc of the *Star Wars Trilogy*.

Campbell deeply studied Hinduism, and after reading the sacred Sanskrit Hindu scripture, *The Upanishads*, he decided to devote his life to seeking "**ananda**" (a feeling of intense pleasure or joy signifying eternal bliss).

> *Ananda - A Sanskrit word meaning a feeling of intense pleasure or eternal bliss. The concept of Ananda inspired Joseph Campbell's famous encouragement to "Follow your bliss."*

Campbell would later say, "If you follow your bliss, you put yourself on a track that has been there all the while, waiting for you, where the life that you ought to be living becomes the one you are living. Wherever you are – if you are following your bliss, you are enjoying that refreshment, that life within you, all the time."

In the 1970s and 1980s, my mom, Pauline, became deeply inspired by Joseph Campbell's philosophy around **seeking ananda** and **following your bliss**. She taught me to, above all, follow my dreams, follow my obsessions, and to follow my joys.

In fact, as the very last thing she did before her glioblastoma brain tumor took over, she wrote in black marker on top a picture of her riding her bike as a little 3 year girl, "**Ryan, always follow your bliss**."

These five words -- her last written words -- changed the path of my life since she passed in May 2012 and led me on a 12 year journey that culminated in meeting the love of my life, having our son Apollo, and moving to Nosara, Costa Rica to live a beautiful, simple, and happy family life.

I've lived an unconventional life true to her guidance -- and it has brought me everything I've ever dreamed -- a beautiful family, financial freedom, deep purpose, and a life of adventure.

This book is designed to provide you with both a deep commitment to following your own joy as well as a **system for living** that you can use to create the life of your dreams, no matter your age today.

The entire philosophy of this book can be summed up by this:

> Actually follow what brings you alive with intentionality and consistency and your life will become magical beyond measure.

As Robin Sharma says, "The secret to happiness is simple, find out what you truly love to do and then direct all of your energy towards doing it."

We'll keep coming back to this principle over-and-over, especially in the purpose and happiness chapters ahead!

## How This Book Came to Life

What I'm good at and love to do in the world is gather information from many sources, add in my own life experiences, and then synthesize it into the essence of what is needed to create positive change in life.

I love to synthesize complexity into simplicity -- with the goal of service, contribution, and hopefully to tangibly making your life better. I'm a conscious collection of around 86 billion brain neurons tuned to become an information synthesizer for you.

My goal is to sift through the good stuff out there, have my own experiences and lessons in life, and find the absolute gems to create a book that can be transformative and truly life changing for my readers.

I've been slowly "working" on this book since 2012 and collecting the lessons for it since 2002. After ten years of collecting notes, I wrote the core of this book during a workcation in Ubud, Bali, during November 2022-February 2023.

In perhaps the most productive 3 months of my life -- I went from 0 words to 100,000+ words in 90 days.

During the time I was writing this book in Bali, almost every day I would go to the local community wellness space, Titi Batu in Ubud, Bali – do my **miracle morning** routine (see below), and then write for 2-3 hours each day. I then finished this book while living in Nosara, Costa Rica. Ubud and Nosara are two of my favorite places in the world.

*Miracle Morning - The daily routine you do in the first 2 hours of being awake that is designed to bring you into optimal performance and happiness for the rest of the day. Ideally includes exercise, cold plunge, supplements, sun exposure, saunas, etc.*

What's my miracle morning routine? It has thirteen steps...

### My Miracle Morning Routine

1. Get 8+ hours of sleep (lights out and devices off by 10pm)
2. A cup of Green Tea
3. 10 Minutes of morning sun exposure
4. Take Supplements: Fish Oil, Tongkat Ali, Beef Liver, 5-HTP, & Magnesium
5. Bench 130 lbs x 30 (strength training) and do 30 pull ups and 100 situps
6. 3 minutes in the hot tub
7. Swim 100 meters in the pool
8. 3 min in the Cold Plunge at 45-50° F
9. 5 mins in the Steam Sauna then 5 mins in the Dry Sauna (at around 176° F)
10. Alternate nostril breathing and breath of fire (Bhastrika Pranayama)
11. Visualization: imagining my day ahead and feeling grateful
12. Shower
13. Eat breakfast (usually scrambled eggs with avocado and sausage or chicken salad)

Only then do I begin my writing or other work. If I do these steps (they take me about 60 minutes plus a short drive to the gym/wellness center), I feel fantastic and am set up for a mentally healthy and productive day ahead of clear and calm thinking and extraordinary creativity. I'll write more about these later in the book in the health pillar.

## The Inspiration for This Book

I was inspired to write this book as a guide to living a happy and magical life for our young son, Apollo. We plan to read it to him as he grows up -- and give him his own special copy when he turns 14 in 2036 -- and guide him through its contents.

The original inspiration to begin this project was my mother, Pauline. She passed away in May 2012 from a brain tumor when I was 27 years old. She inspired me to follow my bliss and dream big. She taught me to be an entrepreneur and a world traveler -- and to **follow my obsessions for as long as they stay obsessions**. I've had three major obsessions throughout my adult life so far:

- Obsession 1: building a successful business
- Obsession 2: building a community of purpose-driven leaders
- Obsession 3: building a family that travels the world and *actually* lives in joyous flow

In this book, I'll share what I've learned from all three of these obsessions. I published my first book, *Zero to One Million*, in 2008 with McGraw Hill on the topic of entrepreneurship. At the time, I was the CEO of a quickly growing software company and had become obsessed with the simple question of "how to build a company from zero to one million dollars in sales."

Eventually that company (iContact) reached $50 million in annual sales, and we sold it for $169 million, a really significant success -- especially considering we built it in North Carolina, which wasn't known for as many high-growth tech startups. I was incredibly goal oriented at the time.

Now, in this book, I am writing a guide to creating the life of your dreams in 12 months -- using everything I've learned from my 20s and 30s. While it took me 20 years and a few million dollars to learn what I know today – I can help you figure most of it out in 1 year and for $20. The magic of human progress.

I began this project by writing down everything I had learned a few months after she passed – which now, many years later, has become this book. I thank my mom for always encouraging me and for the inspiration to capture and share the lessons of my life.

You see, I believe that the purpose of life is to enjoy it, be kind, learn, grow, and give your gifts to the world fully while lovingly training the next generation. Let's repeat that...

### The Purpose of Life

The purpose of life is to enjoy it, be kind, learn, grow, and give your gifts to the world fully while lovingly training the next generation.

Ultimately, I see each of us as nodes of consciousness, where part of our purpose in living is to share what we learn with others. Thus, as I go through life, I do my best to publish what I learn. This is how consciousness evolves, learns, and expands. This process of the evolution of collective consciousness on Earth is accelerating faster than ever now that we have self-learning AI. It will be incredible to see where we are in a couple decades from now when our son Apollo is an adult.

As part of contributing what I've learned, back in 2014, for my 30th birthday, I published a very long 1,284 page slide deck, calling it *Lessons from My 20s*. The original slides can be found at www.hive.org/20s. The slides went viral, getting picked up in many news outlets, and have been seen over 6 million times.

Eight years later, in 2022, my son Apollo was born in Austin, Texas. My little 7 pound baby boy coming out of my wife Morgan was a moment I'll never forget. His birth inspired me to take those 1,200 slides, add in all the lessons from my 30s, and create a book that I could someday give to him when he's a bit older.

This is what motivated me to take all the notes I've ever collected on living, re-read all my favorite books, document my own life experiences -- and create this book as a special guidebook to extraordinary living for my son and hopefully for you as well. I will publish the first full release version of this book on my 40th birthday – August 14, 2024 (and some early preview editions before then).

So, in summary, the inspiration for this book was…

1. My mom who died of cancer and taught me life is short

2. My son who I want this to be a guide for someday

3. Me turning 40 and wanting to create a masterwork and share what I've learned before I, too, someday pass on.

### What is Worth Obsessing Over?

Obsess over growth, not comfort.
Obsess over learning, not predictability.
Obsess over contribution, not safety.
Obsess over happiness, not money.
Obsess over kindness, not yourself.
Obsess over your obsessions. And always follow your bliss.

## Building on the Shoulders of Giants

In addition to my own life lessons, this book builds on and integrates the ideas found in many great books. These below books especially influenced this book. Thank you to their authors!

### The Books That Most Influenced This Book

1. *The Four Hour Work Week* by Tim Ferriss
2. *Tools of Titans* by Tim Ferriss
3. *The Monk Who Sold His Ferrari* by Robin Sharma
4. *The Everyday Hero Manifesto* by Robin Sharma
5. *The 5AM Club* by Robin Sharma
6. *Think and Grow Rich* by Napoleon Hill
7. The Law of Success by Napoleon Hill

8. *Rich Dad Poor Dad* by Robert Kiyosaki
9. *The Untethered Soul* by Michael Singer
10. *The Surrender Experiment* by Michael Singer
11. *The Great Work of Your Life* by Stephen Cope
12. *Abundance* by Peter Diamandis
13. *Factfulness* by Hans Rosling
14. *The Rational Optimist* by Matt Ridley

## MY FOUR BIGGEST LITERARY INFLUENCES

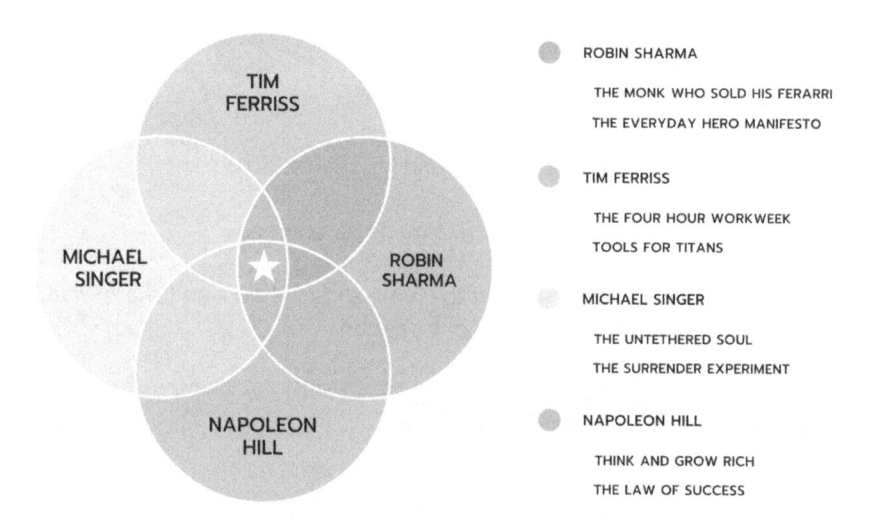

**ROBIN SHARMA**
THE MONK WHO SOLD HIS FERARRI
THE EVERYDAY HERO MANIFESTO

**TIM FERRISS**
THE FOUR HOUR WORKWEEK
TOOLS FOR TITANS

**MICHAEL SINGER**
THE UNTETHERED SOUL
THE SURRENDER EXPERIMENT

**NAPOLEON HILL**
THINK AND GROW RICH
THE LAW OF SUCCESS

I have to give a LOT of credit for this book to one of my favorite authors, Robin Sharma. I have quoted him dozens of times in this book. His books, *The Monk Who Sold His Ferrari, The 5AM Club,* and *The Everyday Hero Manifesto* hugely influenced my life.

I also have to give a lot of credit to my friend Tim Ferriss, who created an absolute tour de force with *The Four Hour Workweek* and *Tools of Titans* -- books that have changed countless lives for the better. Robin and Tim are by far the most quoted and referenced writers in this book.

I give a lot of credit as well to Napoleon Hill, perhaps the original success author, who conducted a twenty year study of over 500 people between 1908 and 1928 to determine the common traits that led to successful lives.

Without their decades of work laying the foundation for me -- I could not have written this book.

Lastly, I give extraordinary thanks to former billion dollar tech company CEO turned meditation and yoga center owner and writer Michael Singer. I read his instant classic, *The Untethered Soul*, during my first ten-day silent meditation Vipassana in 2015 (I wasn't supposed to read books in a Vipassana, but did anyway) -- and that book ended up forming the foundation of my spiritual belief system.

I also give major props to authors Robert Kiyosaki, Simon Sinek, Tony Robbins, Peter Diamandis, Dale Carnegie, Jen Sincero, Ryan Holiday, Brene Brown, Janet Hardy, Dossie Eaton, and Hans Rosling, who have all helped me form the way I think as a human being, global citizen, CEO coach, purpose-driven leader, and entrepreneur.

You see, I love **idea sex** -- bringing together the best ideas from hundreds of books and many life experiences into one synthesized place. I'm like an AI bot -- building a corpus of information that I like to refine, update, and share.

The difference is that I actually get to live life -- and learn from that as well. An AI bot can't actually take ayahuasca, do a Vipassana, make love, or go to Burning Man -- well at least not yet.

## My Goals For Writing

So what are my goals for writing this book? Simple. To change your life, massively, for the better -- and to show you that a new way of living is possible -- no matter how old you are today or where you live or how much money you make.

> **My Goal for Writing This Book**
>
> To change your life, massively, for the better -- and to show you that a new way of living is possible -- no matter how old you are today or where you live or how much money you make.

My goal is to change your life using nothing but the beautiful technology of paper and ink, or electrons and pixels if you're reading this digitally.

My goal for this book is to enable you, as the reader, to **escape the matrix**, live anywhere, heal your body, become truly free, reach your financial goals, start an epic family (if you wish), become a sensual master, and absolutely love your life. You're in for a treat.

I want you to be able to answer the following questions while reading this book. I'll be asking you some deep questions like...

Why are you alive?<br>
What are you here to create next?<br>
Where do you want to live next?<br>
What are the habits you're committed to?<br>
What is your wealth plan?<br>
What experiments are you committed to trying?<br>
What do you want to leave behind?

My goal is to help you live an intentional and thoughtful life of contribution, joy, love, and magic – and if you choose, escape the lower energy matrix of mediocrity that so many people get stuck in.

My intention and hope is to bring together the wisdom from living a bold and adventurous life and from reading many great books to create one synthesized book that can be used as a guidebook to upgrading your body, mind, spirit, and bank account, becoming the next version of yourself, escaping the Matrix, and leaving Muggledom for good.

I hope you're enjoying this book so far!

The next chapter "My Big Upgrade" is my personal story of how I went through a massive upgrade and personal transformation process over the last 12 years, and what I learned going from a workaholic overachiever to a rudderless overseeker -- and how I got my life back into a healthy balance between achieving and seeking, while achieving long-term happiness.

If you want to skip my story and jump straight into the 12 step program, you can skip ahead to the purpose chapter. Either way, let's keep going!

# CHAPTER 3

# MY BIG UPGRADE

# KEY CONCEPTS FROM CHAPTER THREE

### 1. EXTERNAL WORLD
Everything that can be seen. The world of business, finance, government, science, etc.

### 2. INTERNAL WORLD
Everything that cannot be seen. Your thoughts, your habits, your memories, your desires, and your emotions.

### 3. BURNOUT CULTURE
The standard American (and now Japanese/Chinese) culture of working so much that you lose your health, often becoming reliant on stimulants to wake you and depressants to numb you.

### 4. PANIC ATTACKS
An intense episode of fear or anxiety that can last a few hours. Panic attacks can be lessened by calming the nervous system through breath, time in nature, time away from digital devices, and removing all stimulants.

### 5. STANDARD LIFE
A life stuck in a cycle of overwork and depression, characterized by a lack of meaning, depression, ill-health, and disconnection from self and community.

### 6. MAGIC LIFE
A life you absolutely love. The life of someone who is working on what they love, lives where they want, has created a clear purpose, has inspiring friends around them, and is healthy and happy.

### 7. BREATH OF FIRE
Inhaling through the nostrils while lifting the arms in a shoulder press motion, then exhaling forcefully through the nostrils while bringing the arms back to the body. Do this 20 times for three rounds, holding your breath in between each round. Also known as Bhastrika.

### 8. NERVOUS SYSTEM
Your body's command center. Originating from your brain, it controls your movements, thoughts and automatic responses to the world around you. It also controls other body systems such as digestion and breathing.

### 9. STIMULANTS
Stimulants speed up messages traveling between the brain and body. They can make a person feel more awake, alert, confident or energetic. Stimulants include caffeine, nicotine, amphetamines and cocaine. Large doses can result in anxiety, panic, seizures, headaches, aggression and paranoia.

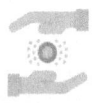

### 10. REIKI
A Japanese healing technique that involves the transfer of energy from the practitioner's hands to the patient's body to promote physical, emotional, and spiritual healing. The word Reiki is composed of two Japanese words: "rei," meaning universal, and "ki," meaning life force energy.

### 11. HOLOTROPIC BREATHING
Rapid, deep, breathing in and out for 30+ minutes designed to oxygenate your brain and naturally get into a psychedelic-like state. Do under guidance and with supervision until you're experienced.

### 12. AMERICAN FUCKFACE
An overweight and stressed-out American workaholic. Who I was for much of my 20s before I spent my 30s learning to master my health, energy, and inner world.

# CH 3: MY BIG UPGRADE

This book is all about how to transform and upgrade your life. In this chapter, I'll share my personal transformation journey – so you can read about how I did it and what I learned. Then, I'll begin the "12 steps to creating the life of your dreams" in the next chapter. I plan to answer these two questions in this chapter:

1) How did I go from being the son of a preacher and a social worker to becoming a self-made tech entrepreneur millionaire by the age of 27? (Hint: it has a lot to do with writing down ambitious goals and consistently taking massive action towards achieving them. Goals are the first step in the 12-step process of this book.)

And, more importantly...

2) How did I transform from an overweight, stressed, anxious, and overworked entrepreneur with panic attacks, heartburn, and chronic neck pain in my late 20s into a purpose-driven, healthy, happy, and joyous family man by my late 30s?

## How My Mom Made Me An Achiever

I was born in August 1984 in Pittsburgh, Pennsylvania, the only child of an Episcopalian minister from Pennsylvania and a Buddhist social worker from England.

So, I'm half-American and half-British. My mom was into Joseph Campbell, yoga, and living on the beach, while my dad was a sociable person, always taking care of everyone in his church.

Growing up, I lived in Rhode Island (1986-1994) and Florida (1994-2002). I was a relatively average suburban kid growing up in the 1990s who loved playing soccer, baseball, Nintendo, and computers. I was a normal American kid growing up in the 1990s.

When I was four, my mom stopped working to spend more time with me. Therefore, we relied on a single income from my dad, which amounted to about $32,000 per year, an average middle-class income at the time.

My mom encouraged and nurtured my intelligence, and I was mostly an all-A student. This achievement later helped me get into Harvard for grad school. As a kid, I loved sports, playing baseball and soccer when I was young and participating in track and cross country in high school.

*I loved playing baseball and soccer as a kid growing up in Florida*

I was exceptionally lucky to have a supportive and loving family. For me, the value of having two parents who loved each other and were kind to each other was immense. This gave me a big leg up in life. My mom got me interested in business, entrepreneurship, and travel from a young age.

After getting my first computer from my uncle in 1995, I started my first business at the age of 11 — offering computer help to senior citizens near my home in Florida. I remember earning $463 in the summer of 1995 from computer help. I was thrilled!

I then started my second business at the age of 14 — doing website design for e-commerce websites. This got me interested in internet marketing, which was a really good thing to be learning about in 1998 when e-commerce was so new.

On my 16th birthday, my mom, Pauline, gave me three books:

- *Think and Grow Rich* (about goals and belief)

- *Rich Dad Poor Dad* (about saving and investing)

- *The Lexus and The Olive Tree* (about globalization).

These three books changed the course of my life and turned me into the entrepreneur and writer that I'm today—and someone who is absolutely obsessed with helping people live purpose-driven lives of meaning and joy.

## Becoming a Tech Entrepreneur - 2002-2012

At 18, I went to UNC-Chapel Hill for university and studied economics. In my first semester of college, I caught the entrepreneurial bug and started an internet software company called iContact that, after a few years of very hard work, became quite successful.

I lived in the office that first summer, dropped out of college, and did whatever it took to keep costs low while we grew revenues. In our first year, we did $12k in sales. In year two, we did $250k in sales. And in year three, when I was 21 years old, we had surpassed $1M in sales.

Importantly, we built a system that **made money while we slept** (the key to making lots of money, which I'll write about in the Money Chapter).

By 2011, every day we were earning around $136,000 in sales—meaning that every time I went to sleep for the night, we would wake up with about $45,000 more in sales by morning. It was quite a system. And, of course, investors like to invest in systems that work 24/7.

When I was 25, we reached #81 on the INC 500, meaning we were the 81st fastest-growing company in the entire United States.

And by the time I was 26, we had grown to 300 employees, 70,000 paying customers, and $50 million per year in sales. We were doing over $4M in sales per month when we sold the company (over $130,000 per day).

It was quite the ride. I learned a lot as a young CEO.

*The company I co-founded, iContact in 2011, outside of our offices in Raleigh, NC*

After a decade of intense work, we sold the company for $169 million to a public company called Vocus. This was in February 2012.

Just growing up in the middle class, the son of a preacher and a social worker, and selling your company for over $100 million dollars at 27? It happened to me. This decade of **consistent focus** kicked off a lot of positive events in my life (and also caused many challenges to my health that I'll write about later on).

Because of iContact's success, I had many incredible opportunities—like helping with the email marketing campaigns for former U.S. President Barack Obama in 2008 and 2012. And in 2012, I got invited to be a National Co-Chair of Tech for Obama, alongside Marc Benioff from Salesforce.com.

I share these photos not to brag but to reinforce that anything is possible for your life if you believe that anything is possible.

*Me, Marc Benioff, and President Obama in April 2012 when I was a Co-Chair of Tech For Obama*

The opportunities continued to come during this decade of focusing on hard work and external success as a tech entrepreneur. I was invited by Elizabeth Gore to join the United Nations Foundation Global Entrepreneur Council, and through our meetings, I got to meet global luminaries like UN Secretary-General Kofi Annan, Infosys Founder Narayana Murthy, CNN Founder Ted Turner, Archbishop Desmond Tutu, and Queen Rania. I even once went on a date with Barbara Bush, President George W. Bush's daughter, in New York City, whom I met through some global charity work. I was living in a very different world back then.

*A proud moment with Kofi Annan, Ted Turner, Muhammad Yunus, Queen Rania, and many other exceptional leaders in 2011 in Washington D.C. with the United Nations Entrepreneur Council (I am 2nd from the right, top row)*

## The Downside of Overwork

But what was the downside of this success? There's a ying to every yang.

While I had mastered the **external world** of business entrepreneurship, I had a lot to learn about the **internal world** of the body, mind, and spirit.

*External world - Everything that can be seen. The world of business, finance, government, science, etc.*

*Internal world - Everything that cannot be seen. Your thoughts, your habits, your memories, your desires, and your emotions.*

With so much overwork, I had become somewhat spiritually lost, anxious, and rather one-dimensional as a human being.

Throughout my 20s, I was a severe workaholic. I worked 12 hours per day, 6 days per week, for 10 years to build iContact. Yes, that's roughly 37,000 hours of work.

My LinkedIn resume, Facebook feed, and bank account may have looked great — but my soul felt confused. And I certainly wasn't yet a master in the art of living. I often wondered, "Why was I here?"

I thought that anxiety, heartburn, neck pain, and burnout were normal for entrepreneurs — and simply came with the territory of building a successful business. I didn't yet know that an entirely different form of in-flow living was possible.

**Burnout culture** was a real force I had to battle with in my 20s.

*Burnout Culture - The standard American (and now Japanese/Chinese) culture of working so much that you lose your health, often becoming reliant on stimulants to wake you and depressants to numb you.*

Here's a powerful piece of writing by my friend Lindsay Briner, who coaches entrepreneurs and leaders on how to achieve stable flow (instead of hypomanic flow, which can lead to burnout).

## Burnout Culture Must End by Lindsay Briner

The culture of "killing it" is killing us. I see it firsthand everyday. The Y-Combinator "hustle" culture, the boss babe memes, all of it.... is a dying paradigm because it simply does not actually work. All these memes are outgrowths of a variety of deeply embedded societal belief systems that we have inherited and blindly repurposed. To self-sacrifice to be worthy of success, that we have to work harder to achieve more, that we have to prove ourselves to be safe, that we have to ultimately kill ourselves to reach our goals.

At the core of the high achiever gestalt I believe is an abandonment of self; stemming from unmet needs as a child to be held, nurtured and cherished. All this results in coping-mechanisms and beliefs that we have to be perfect to be worthy of anything. When we are not perfect, it's a fundamental humiliation of failure that feels like death itself.

I've had many clients vulnerably and painfully admit they believe if the company does not succeed, it equates to complete identity loss, suicide, the ultimate shame. They are in TERROR of dropping the ball.

The reality is they are already dropping the ball by neglecting themselves.

BURNOUT is when the external circumstances of a capitalistic system reinforces our own conditioning, LOCKS our mind and body into a survival pattern and downward loop of self-deprecation, distraction and unsustainable everything.

BURNOUT is leading from fear, anxiety, cortisol and adrenaline, and projections of the hero, the martyr, the saint, the perfectionist.

When we can identify the pattern, label it as a hoax, the false self narrative, the cosmic joke... then we can sidestep the pattern. We can learn to pick up the remote control to change the channel of our pattern-matching algorithms...

A cultural shift is occurring. It's becoming the new norm. We don't have a choice any more. Our leaders are burnt out. Collectively we are realizing inner peace and performance are compatible.

Here's how I figured out that a big change was needed in my life in order to stop working all the time and getting past the point of burnout often.

# How I Learned To Heal Anxiety and Stress

"When your brain is in a stress state, almost everything is perceived as a potential threat." - Emily Nagoski, Ph.D., author, *Come as You Are*

Everything started coming to a screeching halt for me in April 2011. I was on a cruise ship with 1200 other entrepreneurs about to leave the Miami port. It was the first ever Summit Series cruise for entrepreneurs — an incredible opportunity and experience.

I had just tried to escape the ship — but they had just disembarked from the port a few minutes earlier.

I was having a **panic attack**. A bad one. My second one ever. I felt trapped. I needed to get off that ship.

*Panic attack - An intense episode of fear or anxiety that can last a few hours. Panic attacks can be lessened by calming the nervous system through breath, time in nature, time away from digital devices, and removing all stimulants.*

But there was nothing that was going to get me off that ship—barring jumping and swimming, which thankfully I wasn't crazy enough to attempt. Although I thought about it.

My good friend Elizabeth Davis took me back to my cabin—and kept me away from the balcony. For the next six hours, I was exceptionally paranoid, hyper-talkative, and unnaturally brilliant—solving calculus equations in my mind.

That day, I had eaten nothing but a brownie and grapes—and had two coffees and a Red Bull energy drink. I was running off excitement and adrenaline.

I should have eaten more, but I was moving quickly and hyped. I had just met three of my heroes for the first time—the author Tim Ferris, the entrepreneur Gary Vaynerchuk, and the social entrepreneur Jacqueline Novogratz from Acumen Fund. During the main stage talk from Tim Ferriss that afternoon, something had snapped in my head. I was stressed out beyond belief.

At the time, I was 26 and still the CEO of iContact. We were up to 300 employees and things were getting super stressful.

- One of our employees had recently committed suicide without any explanation.
- Salesforce.com had just walked away from buying our company for $95 million at the last possible moment.
- Our fastest-growing competitor, MailChimp, was literally giving away their product, cannibalizing our revenue.

I should have hired a COO two years earlier to be the experienced operator of the business—but none of that was relevant now.

Now, I was freaking out on a cruise ship—having the worst panic attack of my life. And I wasn't sure if I'd make it through the night. I felt utterly trapped on a massive boat as it left the shore.

Thank God for Elizabeth being there. I talked with her all night from 9 pm to 3 am, paranoid, scared, with thoughts racing…

Something had to change. I could no longer work 80-hour weeks and fly all over the world building my fast-growing software company. I needed to learn a more sustainable way to create, work, and build value.

By 3 am that night (about 10 hours from the first symptoms and five hours after the peak), I was finally calming down. Whatever chemicals had been triggered in my brain were finally dissipating.

## ✋ The First Sign I Needed to Slow Down: The Panic Attack on the Cruise

Thank God for this wake-up call... as it led to some major changes in my life in the next few years. And thank God I stayed on that cruise, because the next night I'd meet someone who would change the direction of my life entirely.

His name was Bear Kittay. Bear ended up making a big difference in my life.

Bear Kittay and I in 2012 at Summit Series in Eden, Utah

I first saw Bear's trademark big blue furry bear hat in the front row of a Roots concert, the well known band with Questlove that had been flown in for the cruise by the organizers.

Bear told me he was a 26-year old from New York who lived in San Francisco and was an entrepreneur — helping build a political software company at the time.

I told him I lived in North Carolina and was a software entrepreneur. We were the same age and clicked as two entrepreneurs on a path of growth and learning. He insisted I come visit him sometime in California. I said I would, got his number, and left it at that.

Bear would later come to play a big role in my life a year later when he invited me to my first Burning Man, a festival that changed my life and led me to meeting my wife Morgan there in 2018. More on that story soon enough.

So what actually happened to me on that boat? I later learned (after talking to a psychologist) that what I'd experienced on the Summit Series Cruise was a classic hypomanic attack—characterized by paranoia and talkativeness—and that this was rather common in entrepreneurs who overworked and overstressed themselves and didn't eat properly while overstimulating their nervous system.

I had become so stressed out as a workaholic entrepreneur, working 80-hour weeks for a decade—that I lost my health. I had ballooned to 212 pounds (heavy for 5'10") and had terrible heartburn and 10-hour-long panic attacks every few years. I knew I needed a major change in my life and work schedule.

It was 2011, and this was before I knew about yoga, meditation, vipassana, ayahuasca, and ACTUALLY listening to the signs the universe was trying to tell me—first softly, then loudly.

I didn't listen to the anxiety attack on that boat. I went right back to work the following Monday after the short cruise—back into the pressure-packed world of running a venture capital-backed fast-growing startup. I thought I was 26 and invincible. I was wrong.

It would take an even bigger sign from the Universe to teach me to slow down and actually prioritize my health and happiness.

## Losing My Mom To Brain Cancer

It was six months later (now November 2011), and I got a phone call from my dad saying that I needed to come home to Florida as soon as possible. Something was wrong.

I flew down, and my Dad told me that my 59-year-old mom, Pauline, had been diagnosed with a stage four glioblastoma brain tumor in the back left of her brain.

The doctors weren't too hopeful. Over the next six weeks, the tumor grew (even with radiation treatment) from the size of a dime to the size of a fist.

Within three months, my beloved mom could no longer walk, and within four months, she could no longer talk.

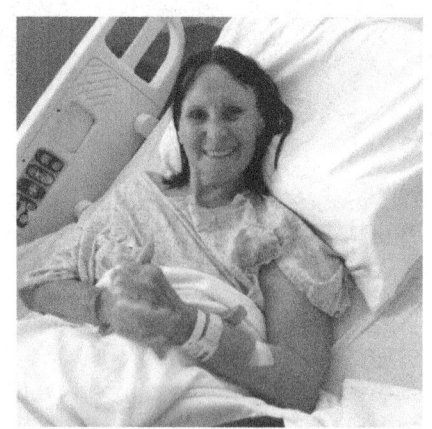

*My mom Pauline just after being diagnosed with a Glioblastoma brain tumor*

She passed away on May 25, 2012 – just six months after her diagnosis. Her early passing absolutely rocked my world.

The Second Sign I Needed to Slow Down: Losing My Mom to Brain Cancer

I like to think that every challenge in life has a gift that comes with it. The silver living gift was that her passing woke me up from the automatic and unquestioned life I was living as an overworked and obese American CEO.

I realized that life was short -- and that quality of life really mattered. Accomplishments matter. But happiness matters just as much as accomplishments – if not more.

I went from idolizing overworked, hard-charging tech billionaires to idolizing people who were physically and spiritually healthy and who were living the lives of their dreams. This sentence is worth repeating...

> I went from idolizing overworked, tech billionaires to idolizing people who were *physically and spiritually healthy and who were living the lives of their dreams.*

Just before my mom left for hospice care, while she could still write, she wrote her final written words to me on a postcard from Venice, Italy. On it, she wrote "Ryan, Live life fully and know how to pack for the trip."

I knew it was now my turn for a major change in life. A BIG CHANGE was needed. I needed to follow her advice and go live my life fully.

Two months after my mom's brain cancer diagnosis, we received an offer from a public company called Vocus (now Cision) to buy my company, iContact, for $169 million.

It was a time of major shifts.

After some consideration, we said yes, partly influenced by what I was going through, and we closed on the deal on February 27, 2012.

Ten years of hard work had paid off. A decade of consistency, dedication, and yes, unhealthy overwork had paid off. When all was said and done, I had earned about $15M after taxes – by the time I was 27. It was a big win.

The moment we sold the company, I flew down to Florida to spend some time with my mom and do our best to enjoy the last couple months of her life. I will always remember those last few months with her -- and her continual encouragement to follow my bliss until the very end.

After she passed away in May 2012, we gathered the core family for her life celebration in Florida -- and I began wondering what would be next.

It was time for something new.

Now it was time to go back to school, fulfilling both a personal wish and a dream of my mom, and to learn how to actually heal my overextended body and central nervous system. I write a LOT more about this in the Health and Awakening sections coming up later in this book.

# Doing an MBA at Harvard Business School

My mom's sudden passing from brain cancer led me to decide to sell my company and go back to school - to get a Masters in Business Administration (MBA) from Harvard Business School. They have a great program for people who want to study:

1. Purpose-driven leadership

2. How business, government, and politics interact and how the world truly works

3. How trillions of dollars of wealth and resources move around the world to create what humans desire

I was very excited to attend HBS. You see, back in 1979, my mom had gotten into a Ph.D. program at Oxford University and forewent the incredible opportunity to move to Pennsylvania to marry my dad.

Yet, she always held out hope that her son, in whom she invested so much love and time, would someday get a graduate degree from a top school.

Fortunately, back in 2011, the HBS Entrepreneurship Chair, Bill Sahlman, did a case study on my company, iContact, and invited me to fly up to Boston to speak to the class about the case.

Professor Sahlman helped me get in. I ended up being the fifth person ever to get accepted into Harvard Business School without getting a college degree first. I had dropped out of UNC-Chapel Hill after two years in order to build iContact. The admissions office thankfully decided that my entrepreneurial experience was sufficient evidence of my ability to critically reason, think strategically, and contribute to the class discussions.

I loved my two years there, learning everything I could about global business, macroeconomics, impact investing, world politics—and the way the world of 2012 actually worked—studying the interplay between business, government, and politics and creating a better world.

I loved my time at HBS and ended up as the Co-President of the Social Enterprise Club, a member of the HBS Africa Club, and a member of the Harvard Graduate School Leadership Institute.

*Section F at Harvard Business School, Class of 2014*

## Learning Yoga & Meditation In India

Just two weeks before I started HBS, in August of 2012, I met a woman named Nadia at my 28th birthday party in San Francisco who would change my life. She was from Berkeley, California, and was half-Iraqi and half-American. She had attended Stanford and had become a fan of meditation. We would soon start dating each other -- and had a three year relationship that taught me so much about slowing down and not being so intense.

After my first year at HBS, I moved to San Francisco, took two years off from school (before eventually finishing), and Nadia and I lived together. Nadia was the first to introduce me to yoga and meditation—a process that began a ten-year journey to heal my central nervous system.

In 2014, Nadia took me to India for a yoga program at the Isha Yoga Ashram in Coimbatore. It was the classical "Silicon Valley Tech CEO" heads to India type of experience.

After learning to do **sun salutations** (a basic yoga flow), some terrible neck pain that I had for 13 years from a car crash went away. Most of the pain went away within 10 minutes—and the rest went away over the course of a few months of continued practice.

Yes, the chronic neck pain that I had lived with for 13 years went away after doing something as simple as a daily yoga stretch.

I suddenly became curious about this yoga and meditation thing. I added sun salutation stretches to my morning magic routine.

*The 12 Step Process of a Sun Salutation. Try it. Like now. Right now.*

## Moving to San Francisco

After my first year at HBS, I took two years off and moved to San Francisco to live with my girlfriend, Nadia, build a tech startup called Connect, start a global community of leaders called Hive.org, and continue my personal transformation journey.

Living in San Francisco from 2014 to 2018 was like living in the epicenter of the technology revolution. It felt like we were all part of a new Renaissance in human creativity and innovation as companies like Airbnb, Uber, Twitter, Salesforce, Facebook, and Google scaled up nearby. I loved the unique and expressive people I met in San Francisco and the beauty of the nature of Marin County and the wonders of Northern California, including Yosemite and the Redwood forests. I highly recommend hiking through Muir Woods in Marin County, California, and visiting Yosemite if you get the chance, whether with your family or on a personal retreat.

I loved the retreat centers of Northern California, including Esalen, Harbin Hot Springs, 1440 Multiversity, Spirit Rock, and Earthrise at Ions, where some of the best thinking and writing work of my life has been done.

In San Francisco, I was also exposed to the Landmark Forum, Art of Living Meditation, and a community of Burning Man and biohacking aficionados who changed the direction of my life and eventually led me to my wife in 2018.

## How Breathing Healed My Nervous System

Back in San Francisco, Nadia introduced me to The Art of Living, a global non-profit organization that teaches people to meditate. I took their main three-day course (available online and in-person) called The Happiness Program. It was in this program I first learned a meditation technique that I wasn't bored by!

The meditation technique involved doing alternate nostril breathing, **breath of fire** (see diagram below), and holding my breath for various lengths of time.

*Breath of fire - A meditation and breathing technique involving Inhaling through the nostrils while lifting the arms in a shoulder press motion, then exhaling forcefully through the nostrils while bringing the arms back to the body. Do this 20 times for three rounds, holding your breath in between each round. Also known as Bhastrika.*

Position: Sitting

- Make a fist of your hands, place it in front of your shoulders
- Inhale forcefully while throwing your hands up and opening your fists.
- Exhale forcefully while drawing your hands down and closing your fists
- Practice this 20 rounds/cycle for 3 cycles
- After the practice, close your eyes and observe your breath

The Art of Living's full process is called the Sudarshan Kriya, or simply, "the kriya." You can learn this process by doing the Art of Living Happiness program, which I highly recommend.

After doing this 30-minute breathing process, I actually felt calm for the first time in 15 years. It turned out that doing this breathing exercise for 30 minutes per day ended years of anxiety and frequent panic attacks.

> My nervous system was simply overstimulated

It seems obvious to me now that my **central nervous system** was completely fried after ten years of misuse and over-stress.

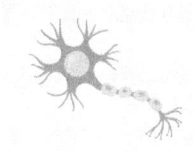

*Nervous System - Your body's command center. Originating from your brain, it controls your movements, thoughts and automatic responses to the world around you. It also controls other body systems such as digestion and breathing.*

At the time, to be honest, I didn't even really know what a nervous system was. I thought it was just the nerves in my body that passed signals of touch or pain. I had never really learned about the central nervous system. Somehow, I had gotten through the American public education system without ever being taught that:

1) I was a living organism that had a complex central nervous system

2) The central nervous system (CNS) could **retain traumatic experiences in the body**

3) Traumatic experiences can have long-lasting effects on the CNS, including changes in brain structure and function. Trauma can lead to alterations in the size and activity of certain brain regions, such as the amygdala, hippocampus, and prefrontal cortex.

4) If you let too many of these traumatizing experiences stay in your body, your mind can get extremely anxious and your body can get sick

5) By breathing in and out quickly and deeply over and over you can oxygenate your brain and activate your parasympathetic nervous system, which can help you heal your body from the inside.

This process of trauma release and CNS healing is obvious to me now -- but I had to learn this for myself. If you want to explore this area of healing yourself:

1) Take a holotropic breathing course in your area
2) Look up *Wim Hof Breathing* on YouTube
3) Take The Art of Living Happiness Course online or in-person from www.artofliving.com; and
4) Read the book, *The Body Keeps the Score* by Dr. Bessel van der Kolk.

I share a few more suggestions below from my own experience.

Around this time (2015/2016), I started reading great books like *The Untethered Soul* by Michael Singer, *The Monk and the Ferrari* by Robin Sharma, and *The Surrender Experiment* by Michael Singer.

These books further opened my eyes to a new way of living -- a way of living I am now writing about and actually living every day. My personal transformation process had begun.

## The Festival That Changed Everything: Burning Man

Earlier, I wrote about Bear Kittay, who I met on that Summit Series entrepreneur cruise. The next year, Bear invited me to go to my first Burning Man festival. That single action changed the course of my life in a big way!

Burning Man is an eight-day-long festival that happens right before Labor Day in America each year (so late August/early September).

There was only one problem—it happened during my first week of Harvard Business School's MBA program. At HBS, you actually can't miss the first week of school or they kick you out. I couldn't get kicked out in my first week!

So, what did I do? After my last class of the week ended at 3 pm on Friday, I took a taxi to Boston's Logan Airport, boarded the 5 pm flight to Reno, Nevada. I then rented a car in Reno and made the 4-hour drive to Black Rock City, Nevada—the home of the Burning Man Festival.

I picked up a sleeping bag, a CamelBak backpack, some protein bars, some water, and some LED lighting on the way at the Reno Walmart, and then arrived at the Burning Man gate at 2 am.

I made it inside (there was a very short wait as most people had been there for five days already) by 3 am.

I couldn't find my camp as I had no idea yet how the street system at Burning Man worked, so I simply walked around from 3am to sunrise, marveling at the magic that I saw.

Girls kissing girls (gasp!) inside of orgy domes, ravers dancing to Skrillex on MDMA, interactive art installations in the middle of the desert, and thousands of laser lights electrifying the night sky. What a scene to witness after my first week in the conservative hallowed halls of Harvard.

That year, there was even an Occupy Wall Street art exhibit in which a Bank of America and Wells Fargo wooden office structure was burned in effigy—letting anger out over how the 2008/2009 financial crisis had given bailouts to the bankers but not to regular folks.

In twelve hours, I had gone from one of the bastions of American capitalism (Harvard Business School) to the center of cultural experimentation (Burning Man). I was captivated by what I saw—but I could only stay this time around for 36 hours.

The "wooden man" burned that night (which always happens the Saturday before Labor Day in America). Then on Sunday afternoon, I drove back to Reno, just making it onto my red-eye flight back to Boston.

I landed at Boston's Logan Airport at 7:30 am, took a taxi back to campus, and made it into my 8:50 am first class of the day, still with playa dust on my shoes. Wow, what a weekend! I promised myself I'd go back. I had a feeling someday I'd meet my wife there.

Of all the things I've ever done, going to Burning Man (now 8 times) has changed my life more than almost anything else—other than sitting with the plant medicine Ayahuasca.

I sold my house to someone I met at Burning Man. I met my wife at Burning Man. And many of my best friends are from my Burning Man Camp—Camp Mystic. Through my Burning Man camp, I started meeting very interesting, creative, and healthy people who had broken away from the standard American practice of "**work an office job, live in a box in a city, and live a meaningless existence.**" There was a new way of living that was possible.

Post-Burning Man, I was meeting people who were passionate about living, who were healthy and fit, committed to personal growth, excited about community, and most importantly, deeply happy. I would return to Burning Man nearly every year after that and still go every year now.

I started learning as much as I could from people like this—including my longtime hero and writer role model, Tim Ferriss, who a few years later would end up staying at Camp Mystic and being a groomsman in the same wedding as me.

## Wake Up Call: Losing My Dad to Leukemia

As you go through life, there are certain catalysts that give you no choice but to grow up. Losing my mom in 2012 was one of them when I was just 27 years old. Thankfully, then, I had 6 months' notice to say my goodbyes.

Two years later, in September 2014, my dad passed away suddenly and unexpectedly at the age of 76. I didn't even have a chance to say goodbye. The autopsy report later showed that he had died from sepsis, an infection to which he was susceptible due to an undiagnosed form of leukemia, a cancer in his blood-forming tissues.

There I was, having just turned 30 years old the month before, with both of my parents gone. I felt lost in the world with both my parents gone. I had no choice but to either collapse or create the strength within myself to fully develop the masculine and feminine sides of myself.

The Third Sign I Needed to Slow Down: Losing My Dad to Leukemia

For a while, I clung on to my girlfriend Nadia and my friends for a sense of home—but without a sense of family in the world, I was unsure where home even was. I would have to find the resolve inside myself to stabilize myself in a sea of change—while preparing to create my own family.

*My dad visiting me at Harvard Business School in 2013, the year before he passed from Leukemia.*

## The Fourth Sign I Needed to Slow Down

The following weekend, I was at Bear Kittay and Katiyana Kittay's wedding in California and had a full-on ten-hour panic attack—brought on by how overstimulated my brain had become from learning as much as I did on Ayahuasca about compassion and the nature of reality.

Bear had been my good friend since 2012 and was the very reason I moved to California and discovered Burning Man—so I wasn't going to miss his wedding for the world. But just after arriving, I started getting super paranoid.

I remember my friends having to kindly request the artist Android Jones to leave the master bedroom so I could lay down during the panic attack. He was finalizing the framing of his artwork—an incredible drawing of the bride and groom, a piece of artwork he called "Presence."

My friends Bear and Katiyana Kittay as drawn by Android Jones, overlaid on a map of the Burning Man festival, where they met in 2012

Following this third panic attack in 8 years – I knew things needed to change. Fortunately, the effects of the ayahuasca gave me no choice but to slow down for a bit.

As Anais Nin once wrote, "The day came when the risk to remain tight in a bud was more painful than the risk it took to blossom."

This was that day for me. I just couldn't live in my world of overwork anymore. I could no longer be An American Poster Child for Hustle-At-All-Costs Culture (an **American Fuckface**, as my wife calls it).

The Fourth Sign I Needed to Slow Down: Ayahuasca Induced Panic Attack

This was the fourth and final sign from the universe that I needed to slow down and really get my health right before I could build something meaningful again.

The universe could not possibly be screaming, "SLOW DOWN, RYAN," any louder.

- Sign #1 - April 2011 - Panic Attack on the Summit Series Cruise
- Sign #2 - May 2012 - Losing My Mom to Brain Cancer
- Sign #3 - September 2014 - Losing My Dad to Leukemia
- Sign #4 - May 2016 - Panic Attack After Ayahuasca

These four events were the initial wake up calls that my personal transformation process was in motion!

It was now May 2016. Both my parents had died of cancer. My girlfriend had left me. I'd finally graduated from Harvard Business School. I had no choice but to actually slow down, do the work, and fix myself from the inside out. No amount of overwork or hyperactivity could numb or suppress myself enough. I had to do the work. I didn't know what exactly to do so it took me a few extra winding years to make it to the other side. Thankfully, this guide now exists.

I'm hopeful it saves you a couple years of your life (or more!) as you go through your own personal transformation journey and become the person that you are meant to become. This is the sacred process of *becoming you*.

## How To Calm Your Nervous System

If you are experiencing an overstimulated nervous system, there are a few key things you can do to help regulate your body.

1. **Get Out of Your Current Environment** - I recommend getting out of your current physical environment that has overstimulated you and, for at least two months, removing yourself from anyone who has encouraged the behavior that has led to the overstimulation and decline in health.

2. **Move to a Calm Place** - Move for 60-90 days (or longer) to a warm and peaceful place like the West coast of Florida, Costa Rica, Nicaragua, Thailand, or Bali. Thailand and Bali are particularly good options as they are quite inexpensive, and you can live like a King or Queen on $3000 per month there. Check out Koh Phangan or Chiang Mai Thailand or Ubud or Canggu, Bali for some of our favorite retreat and healing locations. You can also check yourself into the Yoga Barn in Ubud, Bali or the ISHA Ashram in Coimbatore, India if you want a really out of the way place to calm your system for a few weeks.

3. **Get Off Any Stimulants -** If you're taking more than 60mg per day of caffeine (about one cup of tea), reduce your caffeine intake or eliminate it altogether. Also, get off any stimulants you might be on like adderall, modafinil, nicotine, cocaine, amphetamines, or kratom. Let your body completely reset itself by removing all stimulants for 2-3 weeks.

*Stimulants - Stimulants speed up messages traveling between the brain and body. They can make a person feel more awake, alert, confident or energetic. Stimulants include caffeine, nicotine, amphetamines and cocaine. Large doses can result in anxiety, panic, seizures, headaches, aggression and paranoia.*

4. **Book Cranial Sacral Sessions** - Find yourself a good cranial sacral practitioner and book 2-3 sessions with them. This type of bodywork will begin to relax your Central Nervous System (CNS), and help you heal. Cranial sacral therapy (CST) is a holistic healing technique that is based on the idea that the skull, spine, and pelvis should be in proper alignment in order to allow the cerebrospinal fluid to flow freely. This therapy helps release tension in the bones and soft tissues of the skull and spine.

5. **Book Reiki Sessions** - Find yourself a good reiki practitioner and book 2-3 sessions with them. Reiki is a form of energy healing that originated in Japan. It is based on the idea that energy, or "ki," flows through the body and that disruptions in this flow can lead to physical, emotional, and spiritual imbalances. Reiki practitioners use their hands to channel healing energy into the client's body in order to restore balance and promote healing.

*Reiki - A Japanese healing technique that involves the transfer of energy from the practitioner's hands to the patient's body to promote physical, emotional, and spiritual healing. The word Reiki is composed of two Japanese words: "rei," meaning universal, and "ki," meaning life force energy.*

6. **Start Meditating / Breathing Every Morning** - Take the 2.5 day Art of Living Happiness Course and every day do the breathing exercises they teach you (called the Sudarshan Kriya).

7. **Try Rapid Holotropic Breathing** - Watch YouTube videos on how to do Wim Hof or holotropic breathing (or find a local workshop) and start doing this type of breathing at least weekly to oxygenate your brain. Holotropic breathing is a technique that involves using rapid, deep breathing combined with music and other forms of stimulation to induce an altered state of consciousness. It is based on the idea that accessing non-ordinary states of consciousness can facilitate healing and personal growth. It's best to do your first few sessions under the guidance of a trained facilitator.

*Holotropic Breathing - Rapid, deep, breathing in and out for 30+ minutes designed to oxygenate your brain and naturally get into a psychedelic-like state. Do under guidance and with supervision until you're experienced.*

8. **Starting Sleeping 8 Hours Per Day** - If you're not already, make sure you're allowing yourself to sleep 8-9 hours per day. This is non-negotiable for anyone committed to health and optimal performance and productivity.

I'll write much more about healing the central nervous system in the health chapter of this book.

## American Fuckface

Even after meeting my wife, Morgan, and even after seven years of plant medicine, yoga, and meditation, I still would revert back into the "Default American Path" of stress and overwork a bit too much and not be consistent with my morning routines.

I had one more hurdle to overcome in 2021 and 2022 to put behind the realm of anxiety, stress, and obesity for good, create the life of our dreams that we live today in Costa Rica, and really lock into my magic mornings and weeks.

When we found out we were pregnant in October 2021, I was consulting with a hedge fund to help them with their marketing and fundraising.

When we came home to the USA to try to conceive in the summer of 2021, I had reconnected with a friend of mine from Burning Man who ran a hedge fund that was designed to eventually give half its profits to charity.

We decided to work together, and over the course of nine months, I helped raise $27 million for the fund, believing in its mission and the new investment technologies it was building.

The major downside was the stress and overwork. I went from the freedom-filled world of a consultant who had many clients to most of my time being focused on one client.

Add in the stress of pregnancy, and I suddenly became overly serious and let go of some of my better morning habits. From 10am to 5pm each day, I was raising money from serious investors. The environment you're in creates the environment inside, I quickly learned.

While we built a successful fundraising machine using a combination of webinars and email marketing, the impact on my physical and mental health was substantial.

I kept going because I wanted to keep a stable income and save money for the upcoming birth of my son.

By May 2022, when I stopped working with the firm, I had gained 30 pounds in 9 months and many of the physiological signs of overwork and stress that I had worked so hard to move away from had returned (anxiety, heartburn, weight gain).

I stopped working with the firm at the same time the time my son was born—and after a six-week paternity leave, I ended up going back to consult with (perhaps foolishly) in the same field—a fund of funds.

By October 2022, my wife had had enough with me putting so much of my creative energy and heart energy into such an up-and-down field.

In a particularly memorable verbal disagreement (we very rarely fight), she spontaneously called me an "**American Fuckface**."

To her, an American Fuckface was **an overweight, stressed-out workaholic**.

*American Fuckface - An overweight and stressed-out American workaholic. Who I was for much of my 20s before I spent my 30s learning to master my health, energy, and inner world.*

*In your own judgment, have you ever been that? Are you that now?*

An American Fuckface I had suddenly become, over the course of just 16 months back in America -- just by being in the American Cultural Matrix and being beaten down from the stress of pregnancy, childbirth, and a heavily regulated financial industry, and getting away from my tested habits and routine.

I knew in that moment I needed to get out of the patterns I was in. Even if our income was going to go down for a bit -- I needed out as soon as possible from this external environment that was impacting my internal environment so much.

Our sex life had been seriously impacted by my stress -- and at one point, due to stress and late-stage pregnancy, we went five months without sex. This was a big deal for a deeply in love couple who was used to connecting intimately multiple times per week.

Morgan said to me in the same conversation that she wanted to get out of America for a bit as she saw what the cultural conditioning of the general acceptance of a workaholic and overweight and disconnected environment had done to me.

Even though we had a two year lease on our house in Austin, we decided to go back to Bali -- and quickly.

We left a week later, negotiating out of our lease for three months of payments (a rather painful penalty, but it was necessary).

We arrived back in Ubud, Bali on October 25, 2022 for six months and I'll never forget the feeling once I arrived.

Complete nervous system relaxation

There was something about the calm rice fields of Bali, the orange and purple sunsets nightly, and the extraordinarily kind people who believe in karma that calmed my soul.

We had no idea how long we were going to stay in Bali (it ended up being 3 months). But we did learn this:

While we love to live in America for about 2-3 months each year, we benefit immensely from time away from being immersed in American culture and prefer to spend most of our time in places like Costa Rica and Bali.

Don't get me wrong... I love America. I love the drive to improve and compete. I love markets and business. I love that things like roads and supply chains "just work" here. I love that America is a global leader in innovation and technology. I love the sports culture. I love America as a global melting pot and as a relatively new upstart of freedom and democracy. It's where I was born and where I've lived 90% of my life, and it's where I played T-Ball, Little League, went to college, went to grad school, and started many businesses.

But I don't love the workaholicism, the alcoholism, the militarism, the obesity, the fear-based news cycle, the cancel culture, and the gun violence.

It's a country that has the potential to continue to be a beacon of light on the hill for so many, but the cultural fabric of America has seemed to temporarily break in the last five years.

Can America be repaired to the heights of its glory in the 1990s before an unnecessary war (Iraq), the election of an undemocratic bully (Trump), and a global pandemic (Covid) temporarily broke the foundations of culture and turned us into a divided nation?

I sure hope so. I am deeply hopeful America can heal over the next decade through principled leadership and community-level strengthening that works to create a stronger fabric of trust.

In the meantime, in order to help heal the world, I must first heal myself.

"Yesterday I was clever, so I wanted to change the world. Today, I am wise so I am changing myself." -Rumi

It took until moving back to Bali in the Fall of 2022 when I finally once and for all commit internally to give up the **Standard Life** and the thought of being a standard run-of-the-mill American overweight workaholic -- that the ingrained culture of "never enoughness" the country so often produces in its men (myself included).

|  | Me in My 20s | Me in My 30s |
|---|---|---|
| **Goal** | Build a financially successful tech company | Be happy, find my wife, have a family, heal |

|  |  |  |
|---|---|---|
| **Where I Lived** | North Carolina, Massachusetts, and California in the USA | Half the year living in relaxed tropical paradises like Bali and Costa Rica |
| **Key Events** | Selling my software company for $169 million. Attending Harvard Business School for an MBA. Attending my first Burning Man. | Going to India to learn meditation and yoga. Ceremonially using entheogenic medicines. |
| **Work** | Venture-backed software company CEO | Building a global community of heart-centered leaders called Hive.org, writing books, and consulting with SaaS CEOs |
| **Daily Work** | 10-12 hours per day | 4-5 hours per day |
| **Family Changes** | Losing both my parents to cancer | Meeting my wife at Burning Man, getting married, and having a baby |
| **My Personality** | Driven, intense, heady | Joyous, happy, calm, relaxed, heart centered |
| **Key Driver** | Achievement | Happiness |
| **Medical Issues** | Overweight, anxiety, heartburn, neck pain, panic attacks | None |
| **Happiness Level** | 5/10 | 9/10 |

I am so grateful to no longer be a workaholic and to have an integrated life that invests in family, creativity, adventure, and contribution.

## My Journey So Far

As we end this opening section about this book and my personal journey, here's a summary of my path along the way so you can see the big picture. There have been four distinct phases to my life so far.

### Phase 1: Childhood

- 1984 - Born in Pennsylvania to an American minister and a Buddhist social worker from England
- 1986 - Moved to Rhode Island as my dad became the pastor of a new church
- 1994 - Moved to Anna Maria Island, Florida with my family
- 1995 - Got my first computer from my Uncle Steve, started my first business teaching senior citizens how to use computers
- 1998 - Started a website design agency at age 14
- 2000 - Received a copy of *Think and Grow Rich* and *Rich Dad Poor Dad* from my mom

### Phase 2: Achieving

- 2002 - Went to UNC for college, founded iContact—an email marketing software company
- 2005 - iContact passed $1M in annual sales, raised our seed round of venture capital
- 2006 - Became a self-made millionaire for the first time by building a company
- 2007 - Raised $7M in Venture Capital for iContact from Updata Partners
- 2008 - Wrote a book on entrepreneurship called *Zero to One Million*
- 2010 - Raised $40M in Venture Capital for iContact from JMI Equity
- 2011 - iContact did $50M in annual sales and reached 300 employees and 70,000 customers
- 2012 - My mom passed away from brain cancer. Sold iContact for $169M to a public company called Vocus (now Cision), moved to Boston to get an MBA from Harvard Business School, went to Burning Man for the first time
- 2013 - Took Landmark Forum for the first time, got inspired to start Hive.org, a global community for purpose-driven leaders

## Phase 3: Seeking

- 2014 - My dad passed away from Leukemia. Moved to San Francisco to start Hive.org, a global community for purpose-driven leaders, visited India to learn meditation and yoga. I took two years off from HBS to build Hive.
- 2015 - Experienced Sassafras and Iboga for the first time -- two entheogenic plant medicines that began to open my heart and make me much more present and in touch with my softer side
- 2016 - Finally graduated from Harvard Business School's MBA program, sat with Ayahuasca plant medicine for the first time which completely changed my life. It made me more compassionate and opened my eyes to the true nature of the soul.
- 2017 - Moved to Encinitas, CA to heal and recover from 15 years as a workaholic
- 2018 - Met my future wife Morgan, an artist, at Burning Man
- 2019 - Morgan and I started dating, traveled the world for a year with her
- 2020 - We got married and moved to Bali, Indonesia. We were in Bali for nearly 2 years and loved it. There, I began to study tantra and really get in optimal health.

## Phase 4: Transforming

- 2021 - Moved to Boulder, Colorado -- a beautiful town at the edge of the Rockies
- 2022 - Had our son Apollo in Austin, TX -- and lived the life of a suburban American family for a year before moving to Costa Rica
- 2023 - Moved to Nosara, Costa Rica and now building our **magic life** in a beautiful tropical paradise
- 2024 - Published the final version of this book and created it's accompanying course at magicyear.com

Okay, that's enough about me. The rest of the book is going to be all about you. Starting with the very next chapter, the book is going to truly begin.

So now, let's get ready for the 12 Steps to Create a Magic Life. Your **magic life upgrade** begins now...

~~~~~~~

*It's time for Part 2--where the book really begins. Magic Friends--this is the adventure we're about to go on together... get ready! Do the work, see the transformation in yourself, live your **magic year**, and create your **magic life**. A new way of living is possible if you follow this roadmap ahead. If you'd like, join us in the online course edition at www.magicyear.com.*

## THE 12 KEY OUTCOMES OF YOUR MAGIC YEAR

**1. PURPOSE** — An Inspiring Written Purpose That You Love

**2. GOALS** — Written & Framed Goals

**3. HABITS** — Defined Habits You're 100% Committed To

**6. HEALTH** — A Personalized Magic Morning Routine

**5. HAPPINESS** — The Growth Mindset Installed

**4. PEOPLE** — An Uplifting Inner Circle

**7. MONEY** — A Personal Financial Plan Created

**8. COMMUNITY** — Living Where You Love With People You Love

**9. LOVE** — Creating Your Relationship Vision

**12. AWAKENING** — Experiencing Ayahuasca or a Vipassana

**11. FAMILY** — Written Family Vision & Values Statement

**10. SEXUALITY** — Creating a Weekly Sensuality Ritual

# PART 2

# THE 12 STEPS TO CREATING THE LIFE OF YOUR DREAMS

**MAGIC YEAR**

# STEP 1

## PURPOSE MAGIC

MAGIC YEAR - 85

# KEY CONCEPTS FROM THE PURPOSE CHAPTER

### 1. GIFT
What you're especially good at <u>and</u> enjoy doing. It can be one thing or many things.

### 2. DHARMA
One's higher purpose to serve others, which when fulfilled leads to a magical life. Another term for purpose, calling, mission, or raison d'être.

### 3. PURPOSE STATEMENT
A 15 word or less statement that describes what you want to do for the next few years of your life. Keep it understandable, memorable, and concise.

### 4. EXPLORATION PHASE
Adventuring, learning, and growing without a primary creative project in order to find what makes the latest version of you come alive

### 5. EXECUTION PHASE
An intense work period designed to create something new in the world and/or contribute to a mission that matters to you.

### 6. ESCAPE PLAN
Your plan to get out of your mediocre environment and your mediocre life by upgrading where you live to an inspiring place with nature, friends, community, and healthy organic food.

### 7. SOUL DEATH
Occurs when you no longer believe it's possible to do what you love and pursue your dreams. Can be revitalized by actually doing what you love and are most passionate about.

### 8. RAT RACE
The mindless race to do work you don't enjoy that barely keeps you afloat financially. Being stuck in a cycle of consumption, debt, and overwork and never choosing to do what you actually want to do with your life.

### 9. EXPLORATION JOURNEYS
A 2-3 month adventure designed to get you out of your comfort zone and culture matrix that you schedule after accomplishing a major life milestone.

### 10. PURPOSE-DRIVEN LIFE
The life of someone who intentionally reflects on the purpose for the next phase of their life -- and then goes and actually lives it.

### 11. FLOW STATE
When you're so engaged in what you're doing that time melts away, you can achieve superhuman performance, and your inhibitions of revealing your true self are extinct.

### 12. PURPOSE-DRIVEN LEADER
A leader who has aligned their personal purpose with their professional work, who becomes lit up with aligning all their energy and life force toward that bigger mission.

# STEP 1: PURPOSE MAGIC

"Don't ask what the world needs. Ask what makes you come alive and go do that. Because what the world needs is people who have come alive."
- Howard Thurman, Pastor

**YOUR MAGIC YEAR**

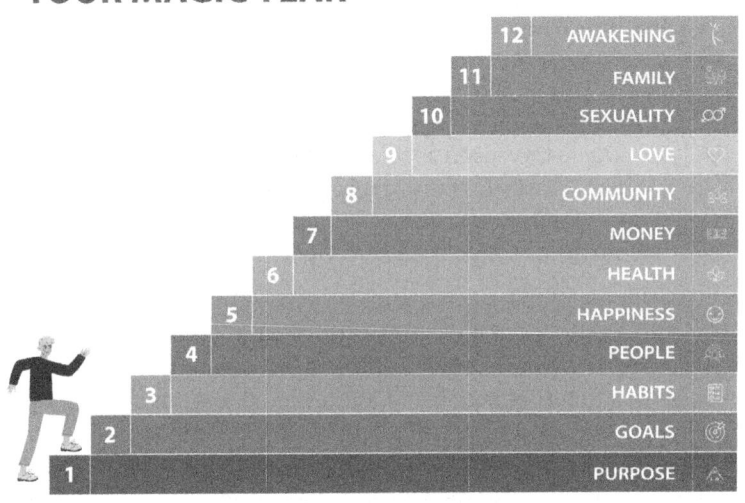

| 12 | AWAKENING |
| 11 | FAMILY |
| 10 | SEXUALITY |
| 9 | LOVE |
| 8 | COMMUNITY |
| 7 | MONEY |
| 6 | HEALTH |
| 5 | HAPPINESS |
| 4 | PEOPLE |
| 3 | HABITS |
| 2 | GOALS |
| 1 | PURPOSE |

We are now in the 12 Steps to Creating the Life of Your Dreams -- the second part of the book. Your *Magic Year* has officially begun. Let's keep going.. And let's start with the very important topic of purpose.

Without a clear written purpose it's hard to have clarity in the direction of your life. So let's make the primary focus of this chapter to get down on paper a written purpose statement that lights you up!

## My Journey With Purpose

Everybody has a **gift**. For some, it's music; for others, it's business, sports, writing, or science. Many people have more than one gift.

*Gift - What you're especially good at <u>and</u> enjoy doing. It can be one thing or many things.*

My gifts are in content creation, idea synthesis, making the complex simple, marketing, system building, community building, CEO coaching, life coaching, and helping people discover why they are alive. What are your gifts?

### Action Item #1: What Are Your Gifts?
Write down your gifts -- things that you are especially good at and that you really enjoy doing.

Above is the very first action item in this book. Remember, this isn't a book that you just read and reflect on—it's a book you act on. So be sure to do each action item!

**Pro tip:** When you start doing the action items, get a dedicated notebook or single Google Doc that you will use for all the written reflections. There are two types of action items: reflections and habit changes. Use the notebook/Google Doc to record all your reflections and the habit tracker founder in the habits section of this book to track your new habits each month. Actually do these 111 action items and watch your life transform. Sign up for the course at www.magicyear.com if you want videos, coaching, community, custom worksheets, and accountability as you go.

Your purpose usually sits at the intersection of **what you love to do**, **what you're good at** (your gifts), **what the world needs**, and **what you can be paid to do.**

We'll come back to the intersection of these four questions in a few pages when we take a stab at writing down our purpose statements. But first, a story.

I started thinking about "my purpose" in life back in 2012, when on the very first day of the MBA program at Harvard Business School, they had us write an essay with the prompt of:

"What is it you plan to do with your one wild and precious life?" - Mary Oliver, poet

That night, I wrote as eloquently as I could about how I wanted to live globally, get married, have a family, and be happy. I had no idea then that I wanted to become a full-time writer and CEO coach and live across Bali, America, and Costa Rica.

I hadn't yet even experienced the three things that changed my life the most -- the **triad of transformation** -- Burning Man, Vipassana, and Ayahuasca. I was a young 28 year old seedling still having panic attacks in my hyper-focused entrepreneurial shell, about to break through to discover a new world of balance and energy.

The following year in San Francisco, at the urging of a friend, I took a life changing personal growth course called the Landmark Forum and its follow-up courses, the Landmark Advanced Course and the Landmark Self-Expression and Leadership Program. These programs changed my life. I've taken these programs twice now, and I've recommended them to thousands of people.

The Landmark Forum and Landmark Advanced Course taught me two things:

1. Do what you say you're going to do, every single time.

2. Life is empty and meaningless -- UNLESS you create the meaning for yourself. This meaning that you create for your life is your **purpose**.

Even since then, I've been absolutely obsessed with the concept of purpose. Some people call purpose a **calling**, a **raison d'etre**, a **dharma**, a **mission**, or even a **big goal**.

Whatever you call it -- purpose is the key driving force that pulls you toward your future. Without purpose -- you squander your time. With it -- you can achieve anything.

> Whatever you call it -- purpose is the key driving force that pulls you toward your future. Without purpose -- you squander your time. With it -- you can achieve anything.

By 2013, the concept of dharma and purpose became an obsession for me, and I decided to devote much of my life to create communities of purpose-driven people.

Then, I read the book *The Great Work of Your Life* by Stephen Cope in 2017 in Bali -- and I became hooked on the concept of dharma.

I like to think of dharma as your higher purpose. When I was living in Ubud, Bali, I came across the following two definitions of dharma on the wall of the Dharma Coffee Cafe in Penestanan. Here's a photo from the actual cafe wall in Bali in January 2023.

> **Dharma**
> noun [dhər-ma]
>
> (1) The principles to do what is right, in-line with one's conscience.
>
> (2) One's higher purpose to serve others & when fulfilled leads to a magical life

So, when I use the term **dharma** in this book, I mean the second definition -- "one's higher purpose to serve others, which when fulfilled leads to a magical life."

> *Dharma - One's higher purpose to serve others, which, when fulfilled, leads to a magical life. Another term for purpose is calling, mission, or raison d'être.*

You can think of your purpose as your unique gift to the world. Your purpose will evolve over time as you change and grow, so focus on coming up with your purpose for the next phase of your life instead of trying to come up with just one life purpose that stays fixed and with you forever.

In 2013, I became so obsessed with the concept of purpose that I started a workshop called the *Hive Designing Your Life Workshop*. We hosted the very first Hive for 34 people from 12 countries at the Change.org headquarters in San Francisco in January 2014.

So far, we've hosted 36 Hive workshops in nine countries on the topic of finding your purpose and creating your life goals. We now have over 3,600 graduates of our Hive workshop in over 150 countries around the world. It's been an incredible journey building this workshop. We now host it about twice per year.

I've also become deeply passionate about the topic of **life design**.

*live your dream.* *Life Design - The practice of intentionally and thoughtfully living your life. Start designing your life by writing down your current purpose, goals, habits, and values.*

The graduates of one of the first Hive Global Leaders Programs in San Francisco, an organization I started in 2013. Learn more at www.hive.org.

So as you design your life -- it's a good idea to start with your **purpose statement**. This is usually a short statement that describes your purpose for the next few years of your life. Usually, these cover <u>what</u> you want to create, <u>who</u> you want to serve, and <u>where</u> you want to do it.

*Purpose Statement - A 15 word or less statement that you memorize that describes what you want to create or do for the next few years of your life.*

You want your purpose statements to be concise, memorable, and understandable. I've had many purposes throughout my life, -- as **your purpose is something that evolves with you**. It's not static in most cases. Here are a few of my past purpose statements:

| My Past Purpose Statements |  |
|---|---|
| 2006 | Help small businesses grow with email marketing |
| 2010 | Help create a world without poverty (I became very passionate about angel investing in East Africa during this phase). |
| 2013 | Start a workshop (Hive) that teaches leaders how to define and claim their purpose for the next phase of their life |
| 2018 | Find my long-term wife and partner who I can create a family with |
| 2020 | Reimagine community living |
| 2022 | Create a family that becomes an example for a new way of living, working, playing, loving, and learning |
| 2023 | Move to Costa Rica and live in a modern ecovillage with dozens of my friends |

and family from around the world

2024 Publish the Magic Year book and course and help transform 1M lives

Later in this chapter, I'll help you come up with refined wording for your **purpose statement** for this next phase of your life. For now, let's just come up with a first draft.

> **Action Item #2: Write Down A Draft Purpose Statement**
> Write down a 15 word or shorter purpose statement that answers the question, "What is the purpose for the next 3-5 years of your life." What are you here to do next? Brainstorm 3 possible drafts. Make your statement inspiring, memorable, and understandable.

## The Two Phases: Exploration and Execution

Personally, I like to work for 5-10 years on a really important and meaningful project to me -- and then take 1-2 years to explore widely without any "clear direction" other than to newly find what brings me alive. I call these phases exploration and execution.

*Exploration Phase - Adventuring, learning, and growing without a primary creative project in order to find what makes the latest version of you come alive*

*Execution Phase - An intense work period designed to create something new in the world and/or contribute to a mission that matters to you.*

So in essence, life is a continual alternation between phases of exploration and execution.

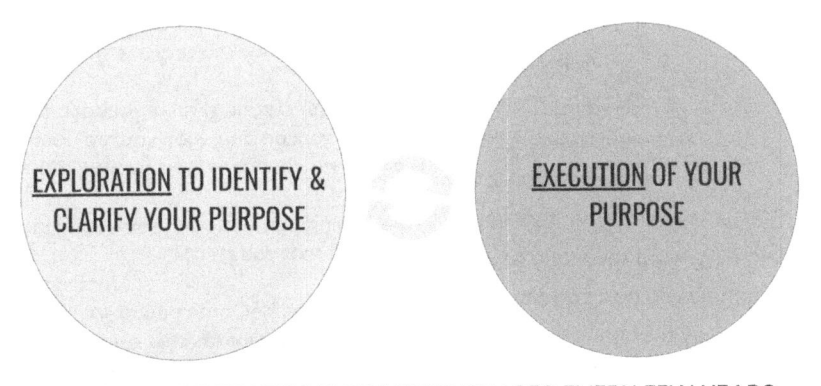

**EXPLORATION TO IDENTIFY & CLARIFY YOUR PURPOSE**

**EXECUTION OF YOUR PURPOSE**

ALTERNATE BETWEEN THESE TWO PHASES EVERY FEW YEARS

Until you find a clear purpose that motivates you deeply, your goal should be to explore, learn, & try many things so that you can see what the world needs and what makes you come alive.

> ❗ Until you find a clear purpose that motivates you deeply, your goal should be to explore, learn, & try many things so that you can see what the world needs and what makes you come alive.

Many people never figure out what they truly love to do and what their inner gift is -- because they don't do nearly enough exploring.

Looking back at my years since 2002, when I became an adult, around 67% of my years have been primarily execution focused and around 33% of my years have been primarily exploration focused.

- 2002-2011 - Execution - Building iContact a software company
- 2012-2015 - Exploration - Building Hive Purpose Workshop, Completing my MBA
- 2016 - 2018 - Execution - Scaling the Purpose Workshop to 3,500+ graduates
- 2019-2022 - Exploration - Finding my wife and starting my family
- 2023-2024 - Execution - Writing and publishing this book and course

That's a total of 15 years of execution focus and 7 years of exploration focus. This doesn't mean I wasn't working during the seven years of exploration. It just means that I was working a bit less, usually just as a CEO Coach and writer -- which allows me complete **time freedom** to live what I want and conduct many life experiments to find what I want to create and contribute to next.

After taking 2 years to live in Bali in 2020-2022 and focusing on getting married and having kids, now I'm ready for another 5-10 year execution cycle of building Nosara into a magical international town and bringing this course to the world!

Most people never take time to focus on exploration. I find that my exploration years are the years I grow the most and set myself up for finding my next joy and contribution to the world.

| THE EXPLORATION PHASE | THE EXECUTION PHASE |
|---|---|
| Going to school | Finding a mission or problem you are deeply passionate about solving or contributing to |
| Gaining skills | |
| Finding mentors | Joining (or creating) an organization that allows you to work on a mission you are passionate about, make money, and do work that you love |
| Traveling/adventuring | |
| Learning what you love | |
| Learning about yourself | Becoming committed to something bigger than yourself that you enjoy |
| Learning what the world needs | |
| Learning how you can contribute in a way that brings you alive | Usually a defined time period like 5-10 years before it's time for another exploration adventure |

Here's what these phases might look like as a visual graphic for someone who took an exploration year after college and then a multi-year adventure across Southeast Asia in her late 20s.

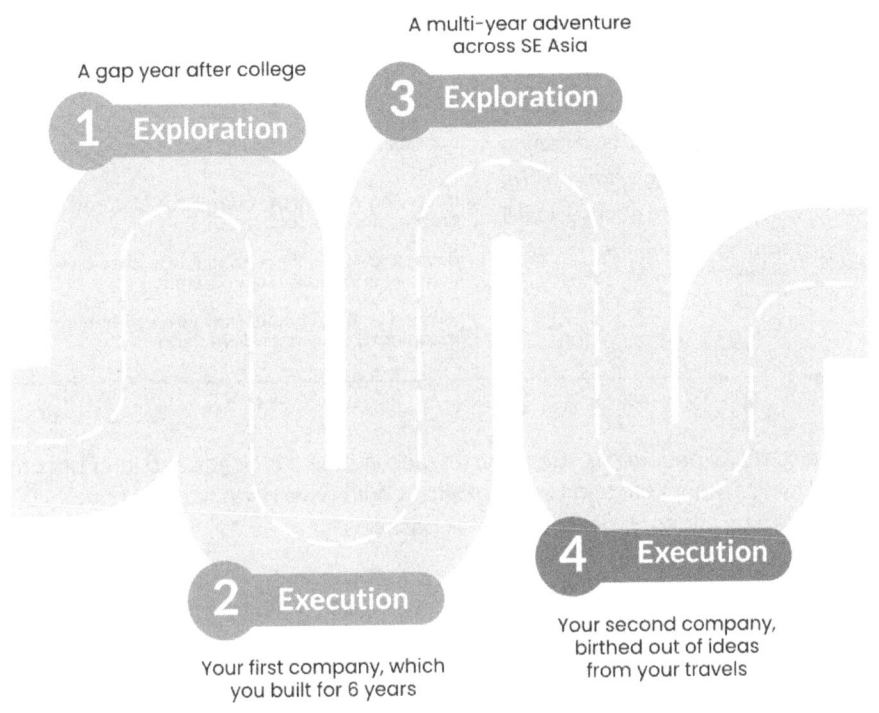

**1 Exploration** — A gap year after college

**3 Exploration** — A multi-year adventure across SE Asia

**2 Execution** — Your first company, which you built for 6 years

**4 Execution** — Your second company, birthed out of ideas from your travels

What will be the roadmap of your next few years? Are you overdue for an exploration phase soon? Are you on one now? Or is it time to put your head down and execute on something you're deeply passionate about?

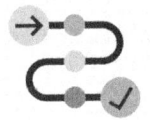

**Action Item #3: Execution or Exploration**
Write down whether you are in Execution or Exploration Phase primarily right now, as well as whether you plan to be in Execution or Exploration phase over the next year of your life.

# How to Escape From a Boring & Passionless Life

You can create any life you dream of if you stay focused on what you want and continue to take exploration adventures. Many people never realize that they are supposed to have exploration phases every so often to get to know themselves, learn what they love, and see what's possible.

Instead, they end up resigned and cynical, and from age 35 onwards they get stuck in a trap, unable to ever have the courage to explore and discover each new version of themselves that emerges every decade or so.

| THE EXPLORATION PHASE | THE 'RESIGNED & CYNICAL' PHASE |
|---|---|
| Going to school<br>Gaining skills<br>Finding mentors<br>Traveling/adventuring<br>Learning what you love<br>Learning about yourself<br>Learning what the world needs | Not taking the time to explore and learn what you really love to do and what lights you up inside<br>Taking the safe and meaningless route because it "pays the bills"<br>Not listening to your inner voice telling you to "get out"<br>Not giving yourself the permission to pursue your dreams and live boldly<br>Never finding the inner confidence to go after what you love and make a big difference<br>"Someday in the future" I'll work on something more meaningful that I really love to do |

**AGE** 0  5  10  15  20  25  30  35  40  45  50  55  60  65  70  75  80

I see so many people get stuck in a rat race in their 20s or 30s and later become resigned and cynical about life and the magic that could have been had they simply taken the road less traveled by and truly developed their passions.

> Don't let this happen to you. Don't get stuck in the rat race. Do what you love and never take or stay at a job you don't love.

So how do you avoid entering into a boring, soul sucking "resigned and cynical" phase from age 30-90?

1. By always following your passion, obsessions, and bliss, no matter how much courage it takes to do so.

2. By defining your purpose clearly and creating goals and habits in alignment with that purpose.

3. By going on epic exploration adventures with your family, actually doing your bucket list items, and experimenting with living in other countries. There's nothing like living in other countries to get you out of a lifestyle rut.

No matter how old you are -- if you are stuck doing something you don't enjoy and feel stuck inside -- get the fuck out of there. Take your family with you if you need to. Just save up a little bit of money, make your **escape plan**, and go.

> *Escape plan - Your plan to get out of a mediocre environment and your current life by upgrading how you live to a purpose-driven life with the right goals and habit stack and, if desired, upgrading where you live to an inspiring place with nature, friends, community, sensuality, and healthy food.*

**Get out of the Matrix. Run, Neo. Run.** Assuming you can earn at least $25k per year or have some money in savings, you can always go live for a couple months in Bali, Spain,

Colombia, Costa Rica, or Nicaragua in a $800 per month house while you figure out what you really want to do. It's better to be a passionate pauper (for a time while you recreate yourself), than it is to be a middle-class person who is "responsible" but dead inside.

> Don't ever let the life you ended up in be your jail.
> No matter your age, you can always reinvent yourself.

Fresh starts are possible for everyone. Including you. Go to that ashram in India, that monastery in Bhutan, that course in Costa Rica, that medicine ceremony in Peru, and that festival in the desert. Learn who the fuck you are, while you still have time.

Go do the things you want to do. Don't wait until your 65 to start living your life.

Because **if there's one thing that's true about life -- it's that we don't have as much time as we think we do**. Life goes by fast.

It doesn't matter how old you are. Yes, even 40-somethings and 50-somethings and 60-somethings can go on exploration adventures in between execution phases to experience somewhere new and learn about themselves.

In fact, you better -- otherwise you'll just die a really slow, boring death as you get fat and irrelevant and cling on to comfort and safety. And nobody wants that. Reinvent yourself continually -- if you aren't growing, you're dying. Constant renewal is the way.

Many people enter the **death spiral** of their lives 20-30 years before they need to because they become cynical and resigned to a life not in alignment with their flow, purpose, creativity, expression, and true desire.

The lesson here? Do what you love now -- or get ready to start declining soon after 50 on the slow march to the grave. Once your passion for living and soul goes, your body is not usually far behind.

> *Death Spiral - Getting ready to die before it's actually your time because you've lost your connection to your own passions and soul.*

The premature death spiral happens to people who become resigned and cynical and no longer believe it is possible to live the life of their dreams.

Their bodies begin breaking down early because they have nothing that is motivating them to keep going. Once the inner passion leaves and the soul dies, the body tends to decline quickly and dis-ease sets in.

This is what many people's lives look like -- losing their zeal, luster, and passion for living by their mid-50s and then, frankly, just giving up and getting ready to die long before their time. Fuck. That.

Once **soul death** sets in, it's not that long until the grave.

> *Soul Death - When you no longer believe it's possible to do what you love and pursue your dreams.*

| THE EXPLORATION PHASE | THE CYNICAL 'I HATE MY LIFE' PHASE | THE DEATH PHASE |
|---|---|---|
| Growing up<br>Going to school<br>Gaining skills<br>Finding mentors<br>Traveling/adventuring<br>Learning what you love<br>Learning what the world needs<br>Learning how you can contribute to society | Not taking the time to explore and learn what you really love to do<br><br>Taking the safe meaningless route because it "pays the bills"<br><br>Not listening to your inner voice and signals from your body and nervous system telling you to "get out"<br><br>Not giving yourself the permission to pursue your dreams and live boldly<br><br>Never finding the inner confidence to go after what you love and make a big difference<br><br>"Someday in the future" I'll work on something more meaningful that I really love to do | Your body breaking down and you dying earlier than you hoped because you lived a stressful unhealthy life<br><br>The regret at the end of your life of not actually pursuing your dreams<br><br>The regret at the end of your life of not actually living a life of meaning, flow, and contribution to others |

AGE  5  10  15  20  25  30  35  40  45  50  55  60  65  70  75  80

Avoiding premature soul death takes some real effort. I've seen way too many friends take the first job they get offered, increase their living expenses so they are dependent on their job, get stuck in a trap thinking they can't leave, get into debt for things they don't need, spend decades paying it off while living a boring life, then 40 years later retire to do what they wish they had actually done in their 20s and 30s while they were young.

Let's say now you're 55 years old and a little overweight, your drive is waning, your mental clarity is lacking, and you never really gave living your dreams a shot. You start getting achy, your testosterone is way down, and your immune system is a bit weaker. Suddenly, your cynicism and resignation turn into actual dis-ease within your body. You no longer trust the universe to keep you safe. And bam. You're in a **death spiral**, two or three decades before you should be.

Death spirals lead to early disease and early death. The way out of them is simple. **Figure out what you enjoy doing and go fucking do it now**. Your life is literally on the line.

People that enter the death spiral early often experience regret for not pursuing their dreams when they had time -- and regret for spending the best years of their lives stuck in a rat race rather than doing what they actually wanted to do.

While you can always turn it around and create a new story for your life, the key is to not wait until it's too late to live the life of your dreams. Avoid this by intentionally choosing to do what you love and following your bliss.

Get yourself out of the hamster wheel of constant work, high living costs, and no time to truly connect to yourself or the people you love. Get yourself out of the consumption-driven debt-fueled **rat race**.

*Rat race - Being stuck in a cycle of consumption, debt, and overwork and never choosing to do what you actually want to do with your life. The mindless race to do work you don't enjoy that barely keeps you afloat financially.*

Instead of the **rat race**, learn to live simply and near people who inspire you. Keep your costs low. Then, as you build your income and investments, you can slowly increase your monthly living expenses over time. More to come on this in the money chapter.

I like to say fuck the hamster wheel and fuck the rat race. Live now, my friends. Actually do what you love. Life's too short to not.

> Fuck the hamster wheel. And fuck the rat race. Live now, my friends. Actually, do what you love. Life's too short to not.

Do whatever you gotta do. Declare bankruptcy and move to another place if you have to. Just get the fuck out, and instead of the urban chaos where people don't have time to connect to themselves and others -- move into a **conscious community** (like Ubud, Nosara, Uvita, Koh Phangan, Encinitas, Topanga, Boulder, or Ibiza) where people know each other, support each other, and frequently gather to celebrate the magic of life.

Move to a place connected to nature where artists and healers can thrive. Slow down and actually enjoy the magic of the gift of life you've been given.

As Hunter S. Thompson said, "Life should not be a journey to the grave with the intention of arriving safely in a pretty and well preserved body, but rather to skid in broadside in a cloud of smoke, thoroughly used up, totally worn out, and loudly proclaiming "Wow! What a Ride!"

### Action Item #4: Are You Doing What You Love?
Write down the answer to this question: Are you doing what you love right now? If yes, stop there. If not, write down the answer to this question? Why not (answer honestly), and when will you start doing what you actually love with your work and career?

## Scheduling Exploration Journeys

So how do you stay fresh in each stage of your life? You ensure you stay fully alive at every stage of your life by continually going on exploration journeys after every major execution phase.

While going to another country in 1900 might have involved multiple weeks on a boat -- today it's as easy as a few hours watching a movie on a plane. We are so very lucky, in ways we don't even appreciate.

During my childhood, I was lucky to visit about 15 countries with my parents. As an adult, I've been to another 30 countries so far. Some of these have been short visits on a 2-3 week vacation, cruise, or work trip. But many of these countries have been longer visits -- including living in Bali, Indonesia, for two out of the last five years.

It's on these longer **exploration journeys** that I've become the person I am today. Don't skip them. Particularly if you are in a phase where you are seeking the next evolution of yourself--plan your next exploration journey now.

*Exploration Journey - An adventure of at least 2-3 months designed to get you out of your comfort zone and culture matrix that you schedule after accomplishing a major life milestone (like finishing college, selling a company, publishing a book, finishing a big project, getting married. etc.).*

Immersing yourself in a new culture for 2-3 months (while keeping your core **miracle morning** habits) is usually one of the absolute best ways you can uplevel everything about yourself.

These exploration journeys will also help you refresh the people around you, get out of the local Matrix (thought patterns and beliefs) of your culture, and allow you a chance to create new habits while calming down your nervous system -- which can get very overactivated in Western competitive cultures.

As you work toward living a purpose driven life and creating a new version of yourself every so often, you have to be willing to try new places.

Escape and get the fuck out of wherever you are. If you want.

**Action Item #5: Schedule Your Next Mini-Exploration Journey**
Schedule your next mini-exploration journey right now. Block off 2-3 weeks on your calendar and take an adventure of a lifetime to a country you don't live in (or just work remotely). Also, apply for a passport if you don't have one yet.

## Who Gives You Your Purpose? You do.

"Your future must be created by yourself clearly, crystal clearly, otherwise you'll be at the whim of society, the whim of others, the whim of the winds. When you have a clear and specific future created for yourself then you can actually make things happen."
- Werner Erhard, Founder of Landmark

Now that we've shared how important exploration journeys are to self-discovery and finding what makes us come alive as we evolve decade over decade -- now let's talk about purpose.

Who or what gives us our purpose? Who gives you your purpose for living? Well, you do. Not some meditating monk on a hill, some workshop leader, or God. (Well, technically speaking, you are part of God, but that's a long aside best discovered in a plant medicine ceremony or Vipassana.)

That's right, *you* create your own purpose for each phase of your life. It is you who programs yourself.

You see, life is inherently empty and meaningless UNLESS you create and discover that meaning for yourself.

So it's your role to create your own purpose for each phase of your life. Some people might LOVE playing the piano. Others might love building businesses. Others might absolutely love teaching children. Whatever your purpose on this planet is, I celebrate you. I celebrate you in your uniqueness.

So who gives you your purpose for living? Who decides what you love to do and how you can contribute to society? You do.

As Werner Erhard, the founder of the transformational workshop company Landmark, says, "Your future must be created by yourself clearly, crystal clearly, otherwise you'll be at the whim of society, the whim of others, the whim of the winds. When you have a clear and specific future created for yourself, then you can actually make things happen."

So yes, it's important to know the purpose of why you're alive right now. It's important to have a clear **purpose statement** for the next phase of your life that you share pretty much the same way every time you tell other people (which should be many times each week -- every time you meet someone new and you want them to know what you're all about). It's important to know your purpose statement by heart....

- So that you can tell others what you're all about.
- So you can share it powerfully in a group setting.
- So people know what you're all about and can send others with a similar mission your way.
- So that you can use your time on this planet the way you want to.

This statement will, of course, evolve over time as you learn, grow, and find different passions and interests. The key is to have a purpose statement for each phase of your life, and to continually update it.

As a reminder, a purpose statement is *a 15 word or less statement that you memorize* that describes what you want to do for the next few years of your life. Usually, these cover what you want to create, who you want to serve, and where you want to do it.

You see, when you have a purpose you really enjoy AND you can clearly articulate it, life becomes so much easier. People start automatically matching you up with people who can help you -- and things start happening much more in flow.

You see, there is a key universal principle we all live by. Do you want to know what this universal principle is?

Okay, here's the universal principle. Highlight this, underline this, circle this, and remember this:

You can have and be anything in life that you want. But you can't have everything and be everything. You have to focus and choose. Let's repeat that...

> You can have anything in life that you want. But you can't have everything. You have to focus and choose.

So here's the truth. Once you know what you want in life and who you want to really be — life gets way easier.

Because remember, you can have anything you want, but you can't have everything. You have to choose.

So as we prepare to create our own purpose statements for the *next phase of your life*, let's begin by laying out what the broader purpose of life is.

**What's the purpose of life?** The purpose of life is the evolution of consciousness.

**What's the purpose of your life?** To enjoy it, be kind, grow, and give your gifts to the world and the next generation.

**Why did your soul come here?** To learn, grow, and contribute to others and the continual evolution of consciousness and knowledge in the universe.

## Why Are You Alive?

> "You forget who you are. Born of stardust. Nuclear fusion. The blood of mammoths spilled on frozen seas by your ancestors. You are made of miracles. A survivor of every plague, pestilence, and war. You are 30 trillion cells, serving one true master (spirit). Don't forget who you are." - Aubrey Marcus

My friends. Never forget who you are. Yes, you are born of survivors of every asteroid, ice age, plague, famine, and war. You are the 1 in 30 trillion product of an extraordinary evolution. You are literal stardust evolved into multicellular consciousness. You have 86 billion neurons and are made up of 7 octillion atoms.

And now you're here. On Earth. Maybe for the first time. Maybe again. Who knows? The question is, of course, what will you use your time on Earth to create?

- What missions will you devote your life energy to?
- What types of companies/organizations do you want to create or work with? How will these companies serve others?
- What will you exchange your life force this time around to be part of?
- What is worthy of this next phase of your life?

And my favorite question of all time:

Why are you alive?

This is the question to ask yourself, repeatedly. I use it as a mantra in my meditations -- repeating it over and over to myself. I also ask everyone I know this question as a way of getting to know who they are and what they are all about.

I like to rephrase it as "why am I alive right now?" knowing that the answer will change.

Let's take a look at what some well known philosophers, authors, and creators have said about purpose and meaning.

- As the Algerian-French Existentialist Philosopher Albert Camus told us, "Life has no meaning unless you create the meaning for yourself."
- As Werner Erhard, the Landmark and EST Founder, says, "Everything is empty and meaningless."
- And as holocaust survivor Victor Frankl told us: "The meaning of life is to give your life meaning."
- The singer/songwriter Jason Mraz believes, "Life is empty and meaningless. It's you who give meaning to something. The world you see before you is entirely defined by your interpretation of it. Otherwise, life just is."

Even with all the wisdom abounding about how critical it is to **give your own life a deeper meaning**, most people never actively look for their deeper purpose on this planet. Instead, they get sucked into the dreaded vortex of passionless mediocrity--and their life gets designed by others instead of intentionally and thoughtfully by themselves. Don't let this happen to you. Design your own life -- in very specific detail.

So what is there to do here on Earth? Enjoy life, be kind, and follow your higher intuition. That's it. **That's the whole fucking thing.** Enjoy life, be kind, and follow your higher intuition toward doing something of meaning and contribution that brings you into flow and makes you feel alive.

Of course, knowing how to actually listen to your higher intuition and not your human addictions and human needs — that's the magic. That takes practice. But it becomes quite easy with deep meditation or an every few months self spiritual journey while on a microdose of MDMA and ketamine.

> "Don't just be yourself. Create yourself. How will you act? How will you look? What will you achieve? Design every detail of your future self. And then go to work making it real. Be relentless for who you're becoming."
> - Zach Pogrob, @BehaviorHack

## The Formula for Inner Peace and Happiness

My friend Chris Vasquez, the CEO of Quantum Talent Group, recently posted the following formula for inner peace and happiness on his Instagram. It's one of the most eloquent descriptions of how to find inner peace through living in alignment with your deeper callings. It's worth reading 2x.

### The Formula for Inner Peace and Happiness by Chris Vasquez

I built a successful company, became a multimillionaire, created a non-profit, got my dream penthouse, and traveled all around the world. I thought all this would bring me the happiness and peace I was searching for, but I was wrong. This is what I discovered.

1. Everything is temporary. There's no single person, event or accomplishment that will bring you permanent peace and happiness.

2. No matter where you are in your journey, if you lack inner peace, it's because you are being called to become something greater.

3. The gap between who you currently are and who you're meant to be is what creates your experience of suffering. And that's not a bad thing. Those painful emotions are simply signals from the universe that exist to motivate you to evolve.

4. The inner peace that you seek can only be achieved in one way: by living in alignment with who your conscience is calling you to be on a day to day basis. Your conscience is your divine GPS, installed to guide you on your path of self evolution.

5. Once you get clear on who you're called to become, your only job is to practice being that person and never breaking character

6. The act of honoring your highest self and your daily thoughts and actions is the only path to lasting fulfillment. It doesn't matter how successful you are, or how much you've accomplished in the past.

7. The health of your spirit demands that you continue to grow into greater versions of yourself, so don't avoid those uncomfortable feelings, don't label them as negative. Those calls from the universe are gifts that are begging to be opened.

8. You might be called to start a new business, become a mother, build your dream body, whatever it is, you must honor these calls.

9. Inner peace therefore is not a final destination, but a moment to moment reward that you earn by living in alignment with your higher self.

10. Your conscience already knows what you're meant to become. The question is, "Will you answer the call?"

So, what's calling you right now? What is your intuition telling you is next for your life? Are you fighting this calling? Or making plans to follow it? If there's one piece of advice I have -- it's to follow your inner calling. Not always immediately, but always within a couple months of feeling them consistently!

This is how you create the life of your dreams -- by following your bliss and your obsessions toward creating or building something (a business, a product, a course, a workshop, a family, a town, a community, an artwork) only you could build.

Do what only you could possibly do. This is how you give your gift and create your masterwork.

> Do what only you could possibly do. This is how you give your gift and create your masterwork.

## People Who Live With Purpose, And Those Who Don't

"We're on assignment. Bodies on consignment... And what is the purpose? What is the purpose and would you believe it? Would you believe it if you knew what you were for? And how you became so informed? Bodies of info performing such miracles. I am a miracle made up of particles. And in this existence I'll stay persistent. And I'll make a difference. And I will have lived it." - Nahko Bear, from the song Aloha Ke Akua

My friends, there are two types of people in the world.

1. People who live with a clear purpose
2. People who don't.

*Those Who Live With a Clear Purpose* | *Those Who Don't*

There are those who take the time to create and live their purpose -- and those who don't. There are those who listen to their inner calling to give their gifts to the world -- and those who don't. Those who do are often able to live with extraordinary energy and motivation and overcome challenges most could not dream of.

Too many people are waiting to "find" their purpose, when in fact purpose is something you continually create for yourself throughout life. I like to refine my purpose statement at the end of each year, the same week I create my goals and my vision board between December 26 and December 31 -- while everyone else is watching college football bowl games and taking time off.

Today, my current personal purpose statement is to "Create the world's most impactful online personal growth course (see MagicYear.com) and help transform the lives of over 1 million people."

This will be a fun journey ahead!

### My Current Purpose Statement

Create the world's most impactful online personal growth course and help transform the lives of over 1 million people

Once you have a clear purpose and goals for your life, you can direct your life rather than letting outside factors determine your direction.

As podcaster Aubrey Marcus says, "The more you wake up to who you are, the more unbearable it becomes to be who you are not."

And as Kant said, "You must be free so that you may become what you are capable of becoming."

And wow, when you have that purpose on lock, you will be able to much more easily withstand criticism and challenges when you are internally clear on your specific purpose on this planet.

The absolute #1 common denominator among every single highly driven and successful person I have ever met, regardless of field, is that they have committed their purpose and goals to writing and created for themselves a **purpose-driven life**.

*Purpose-driven life - The life of someone who intentionally reflects on the purpose for the next phase of their life -- and then goes and actually lives it.*

So, choose to be a purpose-driven person. Your energy and clarity will be magnified. If you can go through the process in this chapter to create your purpose, then you can add great meaning and motivation to your life.

**Action Item #6: Purpose-Driven Person?**
Write down the answer to this question: As of today, do you consider yourself to be a purpose-driven person? If so, what bigger purpose are you on -- and why does this purpose motivate you?

Let's take a look at one of my favorite poems about finding your spark and going after your dreams from our friend Prince EA. I encourage you to read it out loud to yourself and then reflect on what you take away from it.

### Everybody Lives But Not Everybody Dies
### A Poem By Prince EA

It is not death most people are afraid of. It is getting to the end of life, only to realize that you never truly lived.

There was a study done, a hospital study on 100 elderly people facing death close to their last breath. They were asked to reflect about their life's biggest regret.

Nearly all of them said they regretted not the things they did but the things they didn't do. The risks they never took the dreams they didn't pursue.

I ask you would your last words be; if only I had – hey, you wake up!

Why do you exist? Life is not meant to simply work, wait for the weekend and pay rent. No, no I don't know much. But I know this. Every person on this earth has a gift.

And I apologized to the black community but I can no longer pretend.

Martin Luther King? That man never had a dream, that dream had him.

See people don't choose dreams, dreams choose them. So the question I'm getting to is, do you have the courage to grab the dream that picked you? That befit you and grips you; or will you let it get away and slip through?

You know I learned a fact about airplanes the other day. This was – this was so surprising, see. I was talking to a pilot and he told me that many of his passengers think planes are dangerous to fly in. But he said actually, it is a lot more dangerous for a plane to stay on the ground.

I say what? Like how does that sound. What he said, he said, because on the ground the plane starts to rust, malfunction and wear, much faster than it ever would if it was in the air.

As I walked away I thought, yeah, makes total sense because planes were built to live in the skies. And every person was built to live out the dream they have inside. So it is perhaps the saddest loss to live a life on the ground without ever taking off.

See, most of us are afraid of the thief who comes in the night to steal all of our things. But there is a thief in your mind who is after your dreams. His name is doubt.

If you see him, call the cops and keep him away from the kids, because he is wanted for murder. For he has killed more dreams than failure ever did. He wears many disguises and like a virus will leave you blinded, divided and turn you into a kinda.

See kinda is lethal. You know what kinda is? There are a lot of kinda people, you kinda want a career change, you kinda want to get straight A's, you kinda want to get in shape. Simple math, no numbers to crunch. If you kinda want something, then you will kinda get the results you want.

What is your dream? What ignites that spark. You can't kinda want that, you got to want it with every part of your whole heart. Will you struggle? Yeah, yeah… you will struggle, no way around it. You will fall many times, but who's counting? Just remember, there's no such thing as a smooth mountain.

If you want to make it to the top then, there are sharp ridges that have to be stepped over. There will be times you get stressed and things you get depressed over.

But let me tell you something. Steven Spielberg was rejected from film school three times. Three times, but he kept going. The television execs fired Oprah, said she was unfit for TV but she kept going. Critics told Beyoncé that she couldn't sing. She went through depression. But she kept going.

Struggle and criticisms are prerequisites for greatness. That is the law of this universe and no one escapes it. Because pain is life but you can choose what type? Either the pain on the road to success or the pain of being haunted with regret.

You want my advice. Don't think twice. We have been given a gift that we call life.

So don't blow it. You're not defined by your past instead you were born anew in each moment. So own it now.

Sometimes you've got to leap and grow your wings on the way down. You better get the shot off before the clock runs out because there is ain't no overtime in life, no do over. And I know it sounds like I'm preaching or speaking with force but if you don't use your gift then you sell not only yourself, but the whole world, short.

So what invention that you have buried in your mind? What idea? What cure? What skill did you have inside to bring out to this universe? Uni meaning one, verse meaning song, you have a part to play in this song.

So grab that microphone and be brave. Sing your heart out on life's stage. You cannot go back and make a brand new beginning. But you can start now and make a brand new ending.

Okay, so you're ready to find your spark and go after your bliss. But how do you get clear on what the heck your purpose actually is for the next phase of your life?

You don't have to go on a vision quest in the desert without water, hike Kilimanjaro, or sit with shamans in the Amazon to do ayahuasca and 5-MEO-DMT (although that could potentially help--more on that later!).

You just have to go through a simple process about once per year to write down your purpose statement for the next phase of your life. I'll walk you through it.

## Creating Your Purpose Statement

*"When you are inspired by some great purpose, some extraordinary project, all your thoughts break their bonds. Your mind transcends limitations, your consciousness expands in every direction and you find yourself in a new, great and wonderful world. Dormant forces, faculties and talents become alive. And you discover yourself to be a greater person, by far, than you ever dreamed yourself to be."* - Patanjali, Indian Sage

A **purpose statement** is a 15 word or less sentence that makes it clear to others your primary purpose for living at the moment.

Here is the process I've used to help over 3,500 global leaders create their purpose statement over the last 10 years through the Hive workshops.

I believe that your purpose statement resides in the interaction of four key questions, which come from the Japanese concept of **Ikigai**.

1. What do I really love to do?
2. What does the world need?
3. What am I good at?
4. What can I be paid for?

Answer these four questions. Find what is at the intersection of all four questions -- and you'll have found your purpose, your calling, your mission, your area of contribution to the Grand Human Project, and your reason for being that pulls you forward into the next stage of your existence.

```
                    ♥
              What You
              Love Doing

         passion    mission

  What You    ★    What the
  Are Good At      World Needs

         profession  vocation

              What You Can
              Be Paid For

  ★ Your Purpose
```

    These four questions come from the Japanese Ikigai model. So ask yourself these questions, see what answers you come up with -- and then find the intersection of them all. Magic will ensue if you actually do what's at the center -- even if it means you need to reduce your living costs for some time as you build up in your new specialty.

    In my *Designing Your Life Workbook*[10] I've come up with some more in-depth questions for helping people find their purpose. If after answering the above four questions, you're still searching -- ask yourself these questions and write down the answers in a notebook. I created this workbook in 2014 with my girlfriend at the time, Nadia, who was one of the first to assist with the "Designing Your Life" course at Stanford. Since then, the workbook has undergone many interactions. This is the longer -- but more effective, path to coming up with your purpose statement.

1. What do I really love doing? When am I most in flow/in the zone? What excites me? What makes me come alive and be joyous?

2. What does the world need? What does humanity and the world need to thrive? List as many things as you can think of. 4 min

3. How can I create what the world needs while doing what I love?

4. What are all the things I could do in life that would serve humanity in a big way and allow me to do what you love?

5. What would I do with my life if I were actually doing exactly what I wanted to do, were completely unreasonable about it, and stopped coming up with reasons and excuses

---

[10] Available for free at https://bit.ly/designingyourlifeworkbook

for why I can't truly live up to my full potential now?

6. What's holding you back? What would it take for you to start doing what you really want to do? What steps can you take to get started now?

7. What are my personal financial goals? What do I want my annual income to be in 5 years? In 10? In 20? How much do I want to save and invest in the next 5 years? What do I want to have saved up in investments and savings by age 65?

8. How can I get paid to do what I love? What could I do in the next phase of my life that would serve humanity in a big way, allow you to do what I love, and create economic value that allows me to reach and surpass my personal financial goals?

9. What is the change I am committed to in the world? What is so compelling to you that you might be willing to dedicate the next phase of my life to making it happen? In other words, what might be my purpose for the next phase of my life.

**Action Item #7: Purpose Reflection Questions**
Open up a Google Doc and write down the answers to the above nine questions. Use the writing process to reflect on what you want to create next in your life.

I encourage you to take some time now or soon to answer the above nine questions in a Google Doc or in a notebook. Actually, do the above exercise. Don't just keep reading. Calendar some time in the next few days if you can't do it now. Having a clear purpose is an essential part of creating a happy, fulfilling, and deeply meaningful life -- so don't brush past this step unless you're already super clear on why you're alive and what you're here to do for the next few years!

**Action Item #8: Create Your Purpose Statement**
Now, go back to the draft purpose statement you wrote earlier in this chapter. Now that you've read more about how to find your authentic purpose, write 3 more draft purpose statements and then select the one you like best. Make sure the final is less than 15 words, easy to understand, and inspiring to yourself and others.

Pause your reading right now and write down at least 3 possibilities for your purpose statement. This will be important to have clear before you go forward -- even if it's a statement that you're simply exploring different options and places until you find it. Once you have some possibilities written down for your purpose statement:

- Count the number of words. Make sure it's fewer than 15 words so that you can remember it.
- Make sure it's simple enough that a 10 year old would understand it. Remove any jargon or industry-specific words.
- Lastly, share with a few people and see if they are inspired by it.

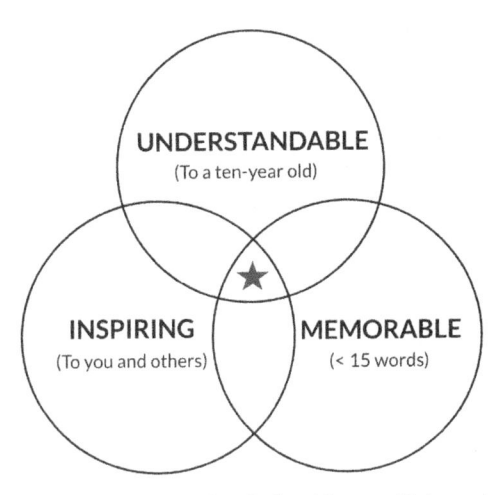

```
        UNDERSTANDABLE
         (To a ten-year old)


  INSPIRING        MEMORABLE
(To you and others)  (< 15 words)
```

The Three Characteristics of a Great Purpose Statement

Here are some purpose statements after this simplification process.

## Example Purpose Statements

Create the world's best university in North India for 18-29 year olds

Expand clean energy usage in Mexico to 50% of total power generation

Build the world's best workshop on life design and purpose

Travel the world for a year to discover what I truly love

Create a family filled with love that many other families look up to

And here are the eight elements of a great purpose statement:

1. Understandable to yourself and others when you say it
2. Inspiring to yourself and others when you say it
3. Easy to remember
4. Focused on serving others
5. Integrates service to others with financial sustainability
6. Bigger than your ego
7. When you say it aloud it feels as if it is coming through you
8. It resonates in your gut

Make sure your statement fits all of the above criteria. If you're still stuck at this point, brainstorm a few possibilities and then sleep on them. And remember that life is a series of alternations between exploration and execution.

Perhaps the purpose for the next year of your life should simply be to "Travel around the world and explore what I want to do next" or to "Save up $10,000 from my current job and then start a business that allows me to work remotely" or "Go back to school to prepare for my next career opportunity in a field I'm passionate about." Your purpose statement doesn't have to be something that lasts forever. It's just your purpose for the next phase of your life.

So if you don't know yet -- make your purpose simply to explore and learn and grow until you find what makes you truly come alive.

Once you've settled on your purpose statement, be sure to go through and check out your goals and habits from the earlier steps and make sure they still align with your new purpose statement. Your purpose, goals, and habits should all be in alignment.

## Draw Your Purpose

To make your purpose even clearer, I encourage you to draw the who, what, where of your purpose statement. Here are a few visual examples:

**WHAT**

Build the top university

**WHERE**

In Northern India

**WHO**

For 18-25 year olds

Create renewable energy

In Mexico

For businesses

MAGIC YEAR – 110

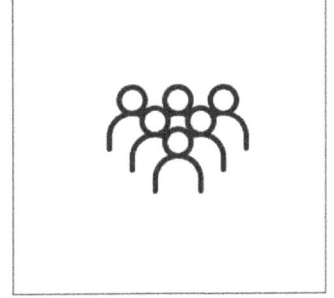

**Build a workshop**  |  **globally**  |  **for purpose-driven leaders**

You can draw each element of your purpose statement below.

# WHAT             # WHERE             # WHO

_____    _____    _____
_____    _____    _____
_____    _____    _____

What do you want to do?    Where do you want to do it?    Who will you serve?

**Action Item #9: Create Your Purpose Drawing**
Use the above template to draw the what, who, and where of your purpose. What will you do? Who will you serve? Where will you serve them? Draw it and write it out either in the book itself or on a notepad.

# How You Know You've Found Your Purpose

You know you've found your purpose when you find your **flow state**.

> *Flow state - When you're so engaged in what you're doing that time melts away, you can achieve superhuman performance, and your inhibitions of revealing your true self are extinct.*

Flow is the mental state in which a person performing an activity is fully immersed in a feeling of energized focus, full involvement, and enjoyment in the process of the activity.

Here's what basketball great Kobe Bryant said about getting into flow, "When you get in that zone, there's just supreme confidence that you know it's going in. Things just slow down, everything just slows down, and you just have supreme confidence ... everything becomes one noise, you don't hear this or that. Everything is just one thing."

One of the main popularizers of the concept of flow was Hungarian-American psychologist Mihaly Csikszentmihalyi. He stated, "In flow, the emotions are not just contained and channeled, but positive, energized, and aligned with the task at hand. The hallmark of flow is a feeling of spontaneous joy, even rapture, while performing a task."

Of course, you may ask, "How do you get into flow?" Simple. You work on what you love and what you're obsessed with. That's it.

And you give up on doing anything that doesn't bring you into the flow state (except for critical habits that are necessary for an optimal life).

When you do what you love, do what you're good at, and do it all for a greater reason than yourself -- flow emerges naturally.

Every single day of my life (7 days a week), I write for about 3 hours. These hours are always the most flow-filled moments of my day. I also play with my son every day -- which also gets me into deep flow.

I'm a prolific writer because I get into flow with it. I've done my 10,000+ hours of writing -- because I love it. I love the process of thinking, analyzing, synthesizing, and sharing.

Living a life without daily flow would be unthinkable for me. What is the thing you absolutely love to do so much that you could do it for 2-3 hours every day?

If you can find a way to earn money while being in flow, --holy shit you've found the secret to incredible professional performance and major contributions.

For most people, there comes a breaking point when they simply CANNOT STAND life as it is any longer -- and they make a choice that they are going to reconnect with their soul, give their gifts to the world, get into flow, and be themselves.

After a while, perhaps a few years of passionless mediocrity, it becomes so unbearable to be the shell of yourself any longer that you have a cathartic breakthrough and say, YOU'RE NEVER GOING BACK.

As my mom always told me, "Follow your bliss."

As HBS Professor Theresa Amabile writes, "The desire to do something because you find it deeply satisfying and personally challenging inspires the highest level of creativity, whether it is in the arts, sciences, or business."

So follow your bliss and follow your obsession to the ends of the Earth -- and your life will be one of magic, contribution, surprises, and very unique learning that you can share with others.

# The How - Making Your Purpose Real

Do you have a draft purpose statement written down? You should. If not, take a few minutes to write one down now. What is it you want to create during the next few years of your life that brings you alive?

Once you have a draft of your **purpose statement** written out, then the question becomes, -- how do you want to create this change in the world? What structure do you want to flow within?

- Do you want to be self-employed (a writer, an artist, a massage therapist, etc.)?
- Do you want to be an artist or athlete?
- Do you want to build or grow an existing business?
- Do you want to start a new business?
- Do you want to build or grow a non-profit?
- Do you want to work for the government?
- Do you want to work for yourself or someone else?
- Do you want to work in an office or remotely?

Here's the process I recommend using to go from a general idea of your purpose to deciding *how* you're going to make it real.

1. Explore widely to find what makes you come alive.
2. Create a written purpose statement, knowing it will evolve.
3. Determine the opportunity or problem you want to work on in world next
4. Decided on the sector you want to work in (big business, entrepreneurship, self-employment, non-profit, government, entertainment, arts, sports, etc.)

Once you've determined the change you seek, I encourage you to build or join an organization that is 100% in alignment with your personal mission.

You can use the below flowchart to decide which path is best for you. Which would be the most effective? Which would bring you the most joy?

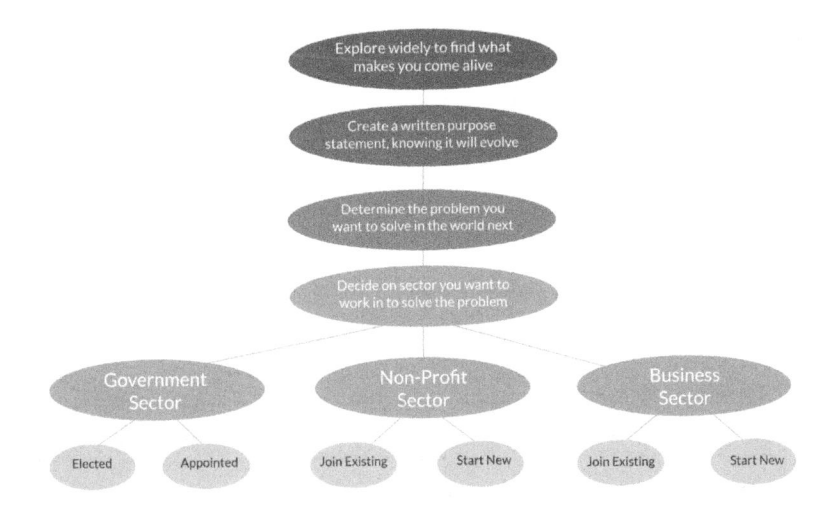

Personally, I've found that entrepreneurship (building a business you own) is a great path for those who want:

1. Time freedom

2. Money freedom

3. Location freedom

If you want to become financially wealthy while building something scalable that makes a difference for a lot of people -- the best way to do that is to build a business that earns money while you sleep. More on that later in the money chapter.

If you do choose to join someone else's organization -- ensure that you're working with someone you can really learn from -- and ensure that that organization's mission is very aligned with (if not exactly the same as) your purpose for the next phase of your life.

**Action Item #10: Your How**
How will you make your purpose real? Will you work for yourself or someone else? Will you build a business, a non-profit, or work in government, sports, arts, or entertainment? How will you achieve your personal financial goals while doing what you love and following your purpose? Write down the answers.

## The Value of Writing Your Own Obituary Early

Once you have your one page life plan created, I recommend opening up a Google Doc or notebook and taking a few minutes to complete what I call the Obituary exercise. Writing it now (hopefully many decades before your eventually passing) will help guide your decisions toward creating the life you truly want.

| Exercise: Write Your Own Obituary |
|---|

_____ _____ was born in _____ in the year _____ and was passionate about _____

_____

_____

_____ and served their community and world by _____

_____

_____

What brought them the most joy was _____

_____

_____.

They were married to _____ and had ____ kid(s) named

_____.

**Action Item #11: Write Your Obituary**
Use the above template to write down your own obituary. Writing it now (hopefully many decades before your eventually passing) will help guide your decisions toward creating the life you truly want.

At the end of the day, know that **your life is your message to the world**. So make sure it is inspiring. Write an inspiring epitaph now -- and then spend the next few decades making it real. Build yourself from the inside out -- one building block at a time.

# Becoming a Purpose-Driven Leader

"Each of us must make the personal choice to be a hero or not, to be committed to something bigger than ourselves or not, to go beyond the way we "wound up being" and have the purpose of our lives and our careers be about something that makes a difference or not, in other words, to be a leader or not." - Werner Erhard, Founder of EST and Landmark

Now that you have defined your **purpose statement** for the next phase of your life -- you know why you're alive. You're alive to be happy, help others, be kind, and make your purpose real in the world.

And once you have a clear purpose that you can express to others--now you can become a **purpose-driven leader** -- someone whose professional work is aligned with their personal purpose.

You see many people drift around rudderless. Leaders, on the other hand, move mountains toward making meaningful missions real.

Purpose-driven leaders work to become the best versions of themselves and inspire and coach teams to become the best versions of themselves and to give their best possible efforts toward achieving a mission that matters.

**Leader -** A person who is committed to something bigger than themselves and can lead others toward that vision.

**Purpose-Driven Leader -** A leader who has aligned their personal purpose with their professional work, who becomes lit up by aligning all their energy and life force toward that purpose.

For example, you could be a leader inside of a large corporation with a mission you're not that passionate about.

But to become a purpose-driven leader -- you'd have to either start or join a company or organization that has the same mission as you.

It's that simple.

There is a simple question to know if you're a purpose-driven leader or not. **Are you working professionally (what you do to earn money) on what you're most passionate about?** If your personal purpose is the same as your professional mission, you're a purpose-driven leader.

## The Purpose-Driven Leader
Personal Purpose = Professional Mission

## The Standard Run-of-the-Mill Leader
Personal Purpose ≠ Professional Purpose

While it's fine to work at an organization with a mission you're not that into in the short-term to gain skills or save up money -- in the long run -- the dream should be to be building an organization that you're deeply passionate about and committed to -- and doing what you love every day.

Your goal should make your purpose that way that you earn your income. Align your personal purpose with your professional mission. They should be one and the same. The flow that erupts when you're giving your efforts to what you love is extraordinary.

As Amazon founder Jeff Bezos has said, ""You can have a job, or you can have a career, or you can have a calling. If you can somehow figure out how to have a calling, you've hit the jackpot. Because that's the big deal."

Wow, it's an incredible feeling when you earn your income working on the mission that matters most to you. When your personal purpose is what you work on daily, work becomes greatly enjoyable—no matter the challenge.

As Robert Kiyosaki of *Rich Dad Poor Dad* fame writes, "There's great power when your personal mission and business mission are aligned. Many people start a business only to make money. Just to make money is not a strong enough mission. Money alone does not provide enough fire, drive, or desire."

Henry Ford was a man driven by a spiritual goal first and a business goal second. He wanted to make the automobile available to the masses, not just the rich. That is why his mission statement was: 'democratize the automobile'. When the spiritual mission and business mission are both strong and in line, the combined power builds huge businesses."

Sadly, way too few people have taken the time to create their personal purpose. And even those who do have a personal purpose rarely make it their full time professional pursuit. Don't be like that.

How can people expect to inspire a team to greatness if they aren't working on their purpose with their full passion and energy? Teams can tell whether you're a passionless corporate shrill or lit up on fire with energy.

The way great leaders get that "je ne sais quoi" quality about them is from their deep commitment to creating something that makes the world better

Imagine the insatiable energy and charisma you will have when you're actually working on what you're passionate about with your full time effort.

What are some characteristics of purpose-driven leaders? Purpose-driven leaders…

- Have aligned their personal purpose with their professional mission
- Know why and where they are leading.
- Paint a clear vision and communicate it succinctly, visually, and repeatedly.
- Are vulnerable and open with their team and share their struggles
- Inspire a team to move mountains to achieve the mission through their authentic enthusiasm.
- Have a calm and clear inner state. No anxiety or fear as they know they are using their time well on this planet.
- Realize that failure is definitionally impossible as long as learning occurs
- See themselves as not only human but as a force of energy making change happen in the world
- Have probably been through crucible moments of loss and suffering, experienced a Hero's Journey, and come out the other side
- Proactively invite feedback to get better
- Operate with the highest integrity of word and are careful about their commitments
- Seek to hire people who share the same mission and are experts in their specialty
- Understand how to make change within an existing system
- Think in terms of decades or longer

You see, **nearly superhuman feats are possible when you are deeply passionate about your mission**.

The proof is in this 530+ book (and year-long course). I could not have possibly created this book if I wasn't deeply passionate about transforming lives and the topics of growth, transformation, and awakening.

So, if you want to have the persistence to build a great business, work on solving a problem that you are passionate about and that aligns with your life purpose.

Are you working full time on your purpose in life? Have you aligned the way you make money with working on your purpose? Why or why not?

Growing an organization and building all the systems needed to make it scale can be hard. Only if you're deeply passionate about solving the problem will you get through the years of challenges. Don't take a job unless you care about the mission the business is working toward.

As HBS Professor Bill George says, "As a leader, you must choose your purpose carefully, because your passion for that purpose is what draws people to you as a leader. If you aren't clear about your purpose, why would others want to follow you?"

Whether as an entrepreneur, CEO, executive, or manager, make sure you're passionate about what you're leading your team toward accomplishing. If you're not passionate about achieving this goal, you are in the wrong organization. Don't begin the effort of building a company or joining a new team if you're not deeply passionate about the problem you are trying to solve. Building a successful team and company is so much easier when you are lit up by the deeper why. Always *start with why*.

## Burn the Boats & Make Money Doing What You Love

A hard skill to master is making the commitment to **only make money doing things you enjoy doing**. It took me until my 39th birthday in August 2023 to 110% commit to this.

Why is this important? Well, it's simple. If you love what you do, you'll enjoy life so much more and also have the persistence and dedication to truly become great at that thing. That mastery over time in the area you truly love will have compounding effects, allow you to serve others in a bigger and bigger way, enliven your soul, get you out of the drudgery of the 9-5 working for someone else doing something you don't love, and selling your life force energy for sustenance. Stop doing that -- and instead focus your time creating and serving missions that truly matter to you in ways that light you up inside and bring you into flow where time melts away.

Here's a letter I wrote to my wife Morgan the weekend before my 39th birthday sharing the internal struggle I was having committing to only making money helping people transform their lives and give up fully on the old ways I used to earn money -- from SaaS CEO coaching and crypto newsletter writing.

### My Inner World - A Dream for my 39th Year

*A Letter to My Beloved on My 39th Birthday*
*Burning The Boats to American Fuckface Island and Arriving Fully Into Magic Land*

My Queen Morgan,

I am truly so happy to be your partner and husband on this journey of life. Thank you for choosing me at the soul level.

I am writing this birthday letter to share some dreams and intentions for the next year of life.

My dream for my 39th year is to transition fully into earning money only doing what I love to do most (help others transform their lives through Magic Year).

This is the year I am transitioning into full artist and building the system for full prosperity for our family. By my 40th birthday I want to have $500k per month in sales (and $100k+ in net profits) from an automated course and scalable coaching system. I want to be the architect of the system and curriculum and vision holder, and the head coach trainer -- but be removed enough that I could depart for 30-60 days on an adventure an everything continue to grow and operate with excellence.

I have had to inside myself, be willing to live on less in the short-term in order to go fully into my art and service to others, which I know will actually end up making us more in the mid-term and long-run.

I know you're in and you get it. I just need to ask for your love and patience as we figure out the exact customer profile and value prop and sales model for the Magic Year course. We're close. I can feel it. Within weeks.

I don't want to get scared and run back to CEO Coaching or SaaS consulting just to make lots of "predictable money" again. I want to earn 100% of my monthly income from helping people create lives they love, something I love so much. If that means we only make $10k to $15k per month for a few months while we figure out the scalable sales model for the course, so be it.

I am feeling tender at this moment – as I sense we are right on the precipice of figuring out how to make the *Magic Year* course sales funnel work – but we haven't quite cracked that last nut yet. I sense Joe and I will figure that out together over the next 2-3 weeks.

I am feeling vulnerable – **what if I fail?** But then mentally, I burn the boats and commit. If I commit all the way to living in this new way, I know we will make it, figure it out, and thrive.

Joe has made a deep commitment with me to not taking any more fixed pay and working going forward for 1/3rd of profits. So we're both 110% in it now. We sell the course, or we don't make it. And 100% of the time when I commit to having to sell something I'm passionate about, it always works–even if I have to do some things that don't scale right away.

We are going to do a lot of prospect empathy work to understand the needs of our customers and see how we can get them over the hump and make a big difference in their lives. Seeing this in the chat log from yesterday's first webinar really motivated me:

- "I need motivation to take the first steps to start a new career!" - Vivian
- "I am in a major transformation of life meaning, career, and lifestyle." - Justin
- "I'm out of work and things are slow due to strikes so taking advantage of the time to make a change!" - Ryan
- "I'm just retired after a 34 year career.....feeling lost." - Constance
- "I'm rebuilding my life after my mom died. I was her caregiver for 5+ years." - Karla
- "I want to become my best self to help others do the same." - Constance

And seeing the purpose statements that the participants came up with motivated me even more!

- 'Infinite Love, Joy and Abundance for my family, community and global audience." - Joe
- "I will create a template to solve poverty, food security, housing, and income for all to thrive." - Lynda
- "Empowering minds through transformative education, fostering growth, and building compassionate communities, shaping positive change globally." - Olga
- "I'd like to mentor other people" - Cindy
- "To live a magical life full of ease, joy, and sacred wealth that inspires others." - Karla

This was so fulfilling to see. After ten months of writing the book and 3 weeks of laying the foundational structure for the course sales, we will be launching the book to the Hive list on

Monday/Tuesday and the webinars/course to the Hive list on Wednesday/Thursday. It's going to be a really exciting week. After 12 years of keeping meticulous track of the lessons I've been learning and a year of compiling the book, *Magic Year* is finally becoming real, my love!

For the next year of my life, I want to teach others how to apply the Magic Year to their life, in an online course format with group coaching and optional 1:1 coaching available. I want to teach others how to design lives of joy, play, presence, health, and magic.

I'm excited, and thank you for your support and trust as I become an **artist of service** instead of a **servant of money.**

From now on, I earn money only doing what I love and what brings me alive – and nothing else. I walk the way I teach, and nothing else.

I've had to get over the fear that you'd leave me if I wasn't super financially successful immediately and had to take a few months to figure it all out – and by getting over that, I've created a pathway for it actually to be so extraordinarily successful.

Whatever it takes, I'm done with SaaS and crypto (except for selling Coinstack when the time is right). The ships have been burned, and together we will thrive in this new land of soul-led purpose.

I sense this will help me further become the Man of Your Dreams and reach my full Embodied King potential.

I love you. I thank you. Forgive me as I have been learning to have the courage to walk in this way completely the last few years.

Thanks for helping me learn, refine, and now spread a message of magic, love, presence, wellness, joy, connection, play, sensuality, community, and so much more!

Your king,
-Ryan


So what's the lesson? Simple. Once you know what your purpose is, create a plan to transition to only making money from making your purpose real in the world and through serving others in a way that lights you up inside. This is the creators way. This is the magic way. Fuck drudgery and doing only what you can be safely paid well for. Do what you love and bring your gift and magic to the world, even if you have to take a short-term pay cut as you master the skills. That's what the world needs -- inspired people who will stop at nothing to hone their craft, get better, serve in ways that light them up inside, and give their gifts to others.
    This was the gift I gave myself for my 39th birthday. After 3 years of working on things I didn't always love to do in order to give my family a predictable income, I decided I was going to take a chance and bring the Magic Year course to the world. I'm all in. It's only when you get all in that God will start to truly move with you.

## What Authentic Leaders Are Great At

As I end this section on authentic purpose-driven leadership, I'll share with you what author Brene Brown says that authentic leaders are really good at:

1. **Cultivating Authenticity:** Letting Go of What People Think
2. **Cultivating Self-Compassion:** Letting Go of Perfectionism
3. **Cultivating a Resilient Spirit:** Letting Go of Numbing and Powerlessness
4. **Cultivating Gratitude and Joy:** Letting Go of Scarcity and Fear of the Dark
5. **Cultivating Intuition and Trusting Faith:** Letting Go of the Need for Certainty
6. **Cultivating Creativity:** Letting Go of Comparison
7. **Cultivating Play and Rest:** Letting Go of Exhaustion as a Status Symbol and Productivity as Self-Worth
8. **Cultivating Calm and Stillness:** Letting Go of Anxiety as a Lifestyle
9. **Cultivating Meaningful Work:** Letting Go of Self-Doubt and "Supposed To"
10. **Cultivating Laughter, Song and Dance:** Letting Go of Being Cool and "Always in Control"

"Being committed to something bigger than yourself is the source of power in leading and in exercising leadership effectively. Being committed to something bigger than yourself creates for a leader the kind of power that replaces the need for force. Being committed to something bigger than yourself is the source of the serene passion and charisma required to lead and to develop others as leaders, and the source of persistence when the path gets tough. ...In a certain sense, all leaders are heroes. Heroes are ordinary people who are given being and action by something bigger than themselves. Such commitments create something to which others can also be committed and have the sense that their lives are also about something bigger than themselves. This is leadership!"
- Werner Erhard and Michael Jensen

## Recommended Books on Purpose

- *The Great Work of Your Life* by Stephen Cope
- *True North* by Bill George
- *Start With Why* by Simon Sinek
- *Find Your Why* by Simon Sinek

## Key Outcome from This Chapter

**An Inspiring Written Purpose That You Love** - Be sure you've written down your purpose for the next 3-5 years of your life in 15 words or less. Make sure it's easy to remember, easy to understand, and inspiring to you and others,

MAGIC YEAR - 121

# PURPOSE CHAPTER ACTION ITEMS

1. **Your Gifts** - Write down your gifts -- things that you are especially good at and that you really enjoy doing.

2. **Purpose Draft** - Write down a 15 word or shorter purpose statement that answers the question "what is the purpose for the next 3-5 years of your life." What are you here to do next? Brainstorm 3 possible drafts. Make your statement inspiring, memorable, and understandable.

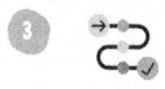

3. **Current Phase** - Write down whether you are in Execution or Exploration Phase primarily right now as well as whether you plan to be in Execution or Exploration phase over the next year of your life.

4. **Doing What You Love** - Write down the answer to this question: Are you doing what you love right now? If yes, stop there. If no, write down the answer to this question? Why not (answer honestly) and when will you start doing what you actually love with your work and career?

5. **Exploration Journey** - Schedule your next mini-exploration journey right now. Block off 2-3 weeks on your calendar when you will 100% definitely commit to going to another country that you don't live in and take an adventure of a lifetime (or just work remotely). Also apply for a passport if you don't have one yet.

6. **Purpose-Driven** - Write down the answer to this question: As of today, do you consider yourself to be a purpose-driven person? If so, what bigger purpose are you on -- and why does this purpose motivate you?

7. **Purpose Reflections** - Write down answers to the nine questions in the Creating Your Purpose Statement section. Use the writing process to reflect on what you want to create next in your life.

8. **Purpose Statement** - Go back to the draft purpose statement you wrote earlier. Now that you've read more about how to find your authentic purpose, write 3 more draft purpose statements and then select the one you like best. Make sure the final is less than 15 words, easy to understand, and inspiring to yourself and others.

9. **Purpose Drawing** - Use the template in this chapter to draw the what, who, and where of your purpose. What will you do? Who will you serve? Where will you serve them? Draw it and write it out either in the book itself or on a notepad.

10. **Your How** - How will you make your purpose real? Will you work for yourself or someone else? Will you build a business, a non-profit, or work in government, sports, entertainment? How will you achieve your personal financial goals while doing what you love and following your purpose? Write down the answers.

11. **Frame Your One Page Plan** - Fill out the above One Page Life Plan, then print it out and frame it and put it up in your home or office where you'll see it daily. Print out your free template at https://bit.ly/onepagelifeplan. Don't forget to frame it and actually hang it up! This one step will change everything!

12. **Your Obituary** - Write your own obituary using the template in this chapter. Writing it now (hopefully many decades before your eventually passing) will help guide your decisions toward creating the life you truly want.

# STEP 2

# GOALS MAGIC

**MAGIC YEAR**

# KEY CONCEPTS FROM THE GOALS CHAPTER

### 1. BIG GOAL

The main goal you are working toward during this phase of your life. Make sure you know what it is. Write it down. Print it out. Frame it. Tell other people about it.

### 2. MINDSET

Your attitude, focus, and motivation, which comes from your environment, information diet, and core people. By blocking out the noise, having an uplifting creator mindset, and taking consistent action toward your vision you can achieve extraordinary things.

### 3. GROWTH MINDSET

Someone who accepts responsibility for their life and believes that the challenges in their life are for them to grow. Has clear goals and purpose. Sees life as happening for them. The opposite of the victim's mindset.

### 4. RADICAL SELF-BELIEF

An extraordinary amount of self-confidence in yourself, coupled with an ability to tune out the noise and block out the critics. Commonly found in future billionaires or exceptional artists, musicians, and athletes.

### 5. LIFE KPIs

The measurable key performance indicators of your life that you track your week-to-week progress by.

### 6. REALITY DISTORTORS

People who are so confident and have such a locked in mindset that they can create reality from nothing but thought, belief, consistent action, and good energy.

### 7. THE SUCCESS FORMULA

Vision + Belief + Action + Consistency = Results

### 8. LIFE DESIGN

The practice of intentionally and thoughtfully living your life. Start with writing down your current purpose, goals, habits, and values.

### 9. INFORMATION DIET

The information that reaches your brain on a daily basis. Controlling and limiting what you intake from social media and the news media is especially important to maintaining a happy, healthy, wealthy, and fully alive life.

### 10. VISION BOARD

A Google Slide Deck or physical cardboard that contains images of what you want to bring into your life over the next 3-5 years

### 11. BUCKET LIST

A list of all the exciting and adventurous things you want to do for yourself and with your friends and family before you "kick the bucket."

### 12. EPIC ADVENTURES

Elements on your bucket list. Things that you'd absolutely love to do and would create lifelong memories.

# STEP 2: GOALS MAGIC

"Humans are not driven by the past. We're pulled forward by the future we're most committed to." - Dr. Benjamin Hardy

## YOUR MAGIC YEAR

| Step | Category |
|---|---|
| 12 | AWAKENING |
| 11 | FAMILY |
| 10 | SEXUALITY |
| 9 | LOVE |
| 8 | COMMUNITY |
| 7 | MONEY |
| 6 | HEALTH |
| 5 | HAPPINESS |
| 4 | PEOPLE |
| 3 | HABITS |
| 2 | GOALS |
| 1 | PURPOSE |

## My Journey With Goals

In order to be consistently happy, **you need something meaningful to strive for**. It can be big or small. It just needs to be meaningful to you.

It can be grand in scale, such as inventing a new scientific discovery, selling a company, launching a Netflix show, or designing a new city. Alternatively, it can be smaller in scale, like raising a great family, giving back to your local community, or becoming a preschool teacher who makes a difference in the lives of dozens of kids every year. The key is that it just needs to be meaningful to you.

I started writing down my goals in the year 2000 after my mom Pauline gave me the book *Think and Grow Rich*. The first ever goal I wrote down was an ambitious one. It was...

**My First Written Goal:** To build a company to $1M in sales by the time I turned 21

Yes, this was quite an ambitious goal for a teenager, yet I was determined to find a way to make it real. Below is the actual written goal from an old notebook I recently found.

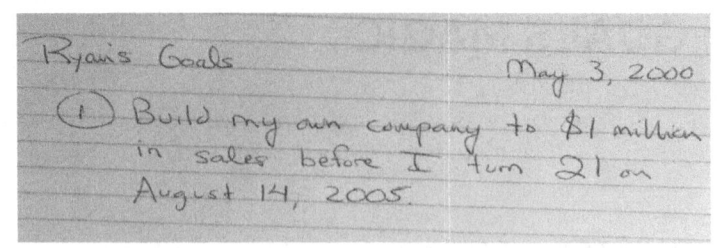

> Ryan's Goals                May 3, 2000
> ① Build my own company to $1 million in sales before I turn 21 on August 14, 2005.

At the age of 16, I was just a freelance website designer and high school student, earning around $4000 per year building websites. Who was I to proclaim I'd build a million-dollar company in 5 years?

I gave myself five years to go from $4k per year to $1 million per year. Pretty ambitious, right?

As John Maxwell says, "Successful and unsuccessful people do not vary greatly in their abilities. They vary in their desires to reach their potential."

What is going to be the goal that pulls you forward into your destined future? Remember, your future is created by your dreams and your goals, not your past. Pull yourself forward with a truly inspiring dream -- and you'll create for yourself a truly magical life and service, impact, and fun!

## Creating Your Big Goal

> "A dream is something you fantasize about that will probably never happen. A goal is something you set a plan for, work toward, and achieve."
> - Paul Levesque, WWE Wrestler

Once I wrote the goal down and made it my **Big Goal,** I started finding mentors who could help me make it happen.

> Big Goal - The main goal you are working toward during the next year or two of your life. Make sure you know what it is. Write it down. Print it out. Frame it. Tell other people about it.

Within a year of writing down my big goal of building a company to $1M in sales by 21, I was featured on the front page of the local newspaper, *The Bradenton Herald*, after I sent them a press release titled "16 Year Old Running a Bradenton Web Design Agency," and my web design business took off. From that article, I received a voicemail from a guy named J.R. Rogers who hired me during my senior year of high school to be the Vice President of Marketing for an arthritis nutraceutical company.

That year, we scaled his 3 person company from $2,000 per month in sales to $200,000 month in sales -- all through internet marketing (search engine optimization, pay per click advertising, and affiliate marketing -- all of which was new at the time).

I then applied to and got into UNC-Chapel Hill for college and moved there on my 18th birthday. During my first year in college I met my future co-founder of iContact, Aaron Houghton, at the Carolina Entrepreneurship Club.

We started the business together in 2002 -- and I knew that this would be the company that would reach $1M in annual sales.

So what happened? Did I achieve this very ambitious goal? No. I "failed."

I missed this goal by 18 days. I turned 21 on August 14, 2005. iContact, reached $1 million in annual sales on September 1, 2022. I missed it by 18 days.

Truth is, I would not have even come close to this goal had I not written it down five years earlier and then focused my mind, learning, and relationships toward making it real. **Mindset** was everything, here.

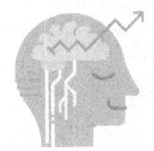

*Mindset - Your attitude, focus, and motivation, which comes from your environment, information diet, and core people. By blocking out the noise, having an uplifting creator mindset, and taking consistent action toward your vision you can achieve extraordinary things.*

I had realized early on in life that a clear vision, self-belief, consistent action, and having a **growth mindset** was essential to success.

*Growth Mindset - Someone who accepts responsibility for their life and believes that the challenges in their life are for them to grow. Has clear goals and purpose. Sees life as happening for them. The opposite of the victim's mindset.*

# Developing Radical Self-Belief

"Imagine the person you want to be, then BE that person now. When you do this, your imagined FUTURE directs your behavior, rather than your past.."
- Dr. Benjamin Hardy, *Be Your Future Self Now*

To achieve my **Big Goal** of building a company to $1M in annual sales by age 21, I had developed **radical self-belief**. I did this at age 17, within an environment (Matrix) where few people thought much of teenagers. This was a few years before Mark Zuckerberg showed the world what a teenager could create with "The Facebook" at Harvard.

*Radical self-belief - An extraordinary amount of self-confidence in yourself, coupled with an ability to tune out the noise and block out the critics. Commonly found in future billionaires or exceptional artists, musicians, and athletes.*

Through radical self-belief, I had succeeded beyond my wildest dreams. The company we founded, iContact, ended up growing bigger and bigger. When I was 26, it reached $50 million in annual sales and 300 employees. We later sold it for $169M -- and so, that reading of *Think and Grow Rich* eventually became worth many millions of dollars to me within just eleven years. From **thought to action to reality**.

*The iContact Executive Team in 2011, In Front of Our Office in Raleigh, North Carolina. I'm in the front right.*

**Thoughts. Become. Things.** As my friend Salman recently wrote...

"What if I told you that the secret to it all is simple? Our thoughts and our feelings create the blueprint for our reality. Every coherent thought and feeling is a lever to pull for generating change on a greater level, one that creates ripples far beyond that which our conscious minds are able to comprehend." - Salman Hatta

You see, anything that gets created in reality must first be blueprinted in the workshop of our minds. Our imaginations. And once you know what you actually want, it becomes one thousand times easier to actually get it.

Napoleon Hill wrote in his 1928 class *The Law of Success*, one of my favorite quotes: "Every great railroad and every outstanding financial institution and every mammoth business enterprise and every great invention began in the imagination of some one person."

Here are some examples of Big Goals that I've had over the last 20 years.

### Example Big Goals I've Had

- 2005 - Reach $1M in sales for my company
- 2007 - Raise a $7M Series A for my company
- 2008 - Publish my book on entrepreneurship, *Zero to One Million*
- 2010 - Raise a Series B for my company of at least $40M
- 2011 - Reach $50m in sales for my company
- 2012 - Sell my company for $100M+
- 2013 - Start Hive.org, offering a workshop on finding your purpose and designing your life

2016 - Graduate from Harvard Business School's MBA program
2018 - Move to San Diego and heal from too much plant medicine work
2019 - Meet my wife
2020 - Get married
2021 - Get Morgan pregnant
2022 - Have a healthy baby (Apollo)
2023 - Finish this book, lose 45 pounds
2024 - Publish this book and get 1 million people through *Magic Year*

It's extraordinary to see what life can bring to you when you write down your goals annually -- and you always know what your **big goal** is.

**Action Item #12: Your Big Goal**
What is the #1 goal in your life over the next year? Reflect on, decide on, and then write down your Big Goal.

Yes, It's fair to say that my mom had a big impact on me by giving me the book *Think and Grow Rich* at age 16. I learned that nearly anything was possible that I set my mind to and worked toward consistently for ten years.

This principle can be tracked back 2400 years to the time of Aristotle, who once wrote, "First, have a definite, clear practical ideal; a goal, an objective. Second, have the necessary means to achieve your ends; wisdom, money, materials, and methods. Third, adjust all your means to that end."

## My Big Goal

So, yes, create your own Big Hairy Audacious Goal (aka your big goal for the next phase of your life).... And then take massive action toward that big goal for 5-10 years. Your ten thousand mini-actions will eventually snowball as you find what works. You have to do what other people won't so you can create what other people can't.

While many people hope for extraordinary things to occur in their lives, exceptional achievers take matters into their own hands and make extraordinary things happen.

What's my Big Goal for this book? Simple... for it to sell 1 million copies over time. I even have a 1M tattoo on my back that I got while in Bali. It may take ten years -- but we'll get there.

*The tattoo I got that symbolizes selling 1 million copies of this book. Let's transform 1M lives!*

Now that's a visible commitment. I also have a new wristband on my wrist that keeps me focused on this big goal even when I can't see the tattoo on my back. It says "1M Books Sold."

*My wristband representing my Big Goal to sell 1 million copies of this book*

I love using wristbands to focus on my big goals. They have been a significant mental hack that I've employed since 2006 in my own journey towards clarity and consistency. I have found that what you focus on and commit to tends to get done. It also helps that people ask me about them a few times per month, bringing me back to my long term big goals!

**Action Item #13: Big Goal Wristband**
Once you decide on what your Big Goal is for the next year or two of your life, print out a wristband with the goal on it. You can make them at 24HourWristBands.com.

While many people hope for extraordinary things to happen in their lives, exceptional achievers take matters into their own hands and make extraordinary things happen. We don't simply rely on hope and prayer. **We take consistent massive action.**

As Christopher Sommer, the Former National Team Coach for USA Men's Gymnastics, once said, "Achieving the extraordinary is not a linear process. The secret is to show up, do the work, and go home. A blue-collar work ethic married to indomitable will. It is literally that simple."

Always remember the **Formula of Success**: Vision + Belief + Action + Consistency = Results.

## Write Down Your Goals

*"Dream up a good life. It's just about letting the universe know what you want and working toward it while letting go of how it comes to pass." - Jim Carey, actor*

Very few people actually write down their goals. Fewer still print them out, frame them, and hang them up in their office or bedroom.

In my experience, the rare person who does take those steps (to write down, print out, frame, and physically hang up their goals) are the rare ones who are the happiest, most likely to achieve the most, and make the biggest difference in the world.

The great "secrets" within the 1937 book *Think and Grow Rich* by Napoleon Hill were simply that:

1. You can have anything you want but not everything you want

2. If you get clear on what you DO want, your dreams are more likely to become real.

3. If you write down your goals and then come back to focusing on them, you will be many times more likely to make them real.

No, this "goal manifestation" process isn't black magic from the quantum realm. It's simply a demonstration of the truth that:

1) Thoughts become real, over time, through belief, focus, and taking consistent actions that align with that focus

2) When you write down your goals and make them visible, you think about them more, making you much more likely to take the actions needed to make the goals real.

3) When you tell others your goal, this naturally brings other minds together to assist you in making your inspired dreams come through -- forming a sort of mastermind group to help you make things real.

Yes, when you write down your goals, your subconscious mind begins to more actively think about bringing into your life the people, resources & knowledge you need to achieve them.

And when you know what you're up to in the world, your mind can naturally filter opportunities so you find those which match your goals.

So yes, those who set aside the time to write down & frame their goals are the most effective people at actually achieving their goals.

It's worth taking a moment now and writing down at least one goal you have for the next year of your life.

As Elizabeth Gilbert says, "You gotta create your life and write your story with your own hands."

## Create an Annual Goal Writing Process

"If you set your goals ridiculously high and it's a failure, you will fail above everyone else's success." - James Cameron, Producer of Avatar and Titanic

Now that we know about the importance of having a **Big Goal** that you're focused on, let's talk about the entire goal creation process.

Here are some questions worth asking yourself:

1. Have you ever written down your goals before?
2. When was the last time you wrote down your goals?
3. Are the goals you set usually too ambitious or too easy?

4. Have you ever printed out your goals and framed them on your wall?
5. What was the most ambitious goal you ever set? Did you achieve it?
6. Are you willing to try writing down your goals and posting them up in your bedroom or office for a year and seeing what happens?

Ever since the year 2000, I've taken three days between Christmas and New Year's (usually around December 28-30) to write down my goals for the following year and create a vision board. I've been amazed at what I've been able to see and experience, and just how much my life has been enriched since I began writing down goals and then pursuing them wholeheartedly. It's been 24 years now of writing down my goals at the end of each year.

Here's the exact process I use each year to create my annual goals between Christmas and New Year's Day...

1. Open up a Google Doc
2. Create headings for 1 yrs, 5 yrs, and lifetime
3. Write down 5-10 goals in each category
4. Print out one copy
5. Sign it and date it
6. Frame it
7. Hang it in your bedroom or office
8. Share it with your partner, parent, or best friend for accountability and encouragement

I also will go back to my goals sheet for the prior year and see how I did. I tend to make my goals ambitious enough so that I only achieve about half of them. Anything higher -- and I wasn't ambitious enough. I also put my big goal for that year at the top. Often I'll have the same Big Goal for 3-10 years at a time.

## Print Out This Goals Sheet & Frame It

You can use the below template to create your own goals sheet. Start by writing down your Big Goal for the next year. Your big goal is what you are organizing your life around over the next 12 months.

Once you have your **Big Goal** for the next year of life, then fill out the other boxes below -- the 90-day action plan, 1-year goals, 5-year goals, and Lifetime goals. Do this exercise again at the end of each year. Once you're done, frame it in a standard 8.5"x11" frame and hang it up on your wall.

Goals Sheet of _____

**Your Big Goal**

| 90 Day Action Plan | 1 Year Goals |
|---|---|
| 5 Year Goals | Lifetime Goals |

Signed on _____, _____ 20___    X_____

You can find the digital template for the goals sheet at https://bit.ly/annualgoalstemplate. Remember: **what you make visible becomes real.**

**Action Item #14: Write Down Your Goals**
Fill out the above goals sheet using the template at https://bit.ly/annualgoalstemplate. Then use it to create your one page life plan in the very next section.

# Create Your One Page Life Plan

"Everyone successful is purposeful, decisive, and a free thinker.
- Napoleon Hill, The Law of Success

Now that we have your purpose statement and goals written down, it's time to bring it all together and create your **one page life plan** -- which will tie together your purpose, goals, and habits into a single document that you can print out, frame, and hang in your office or bedroom.

You can either fill this out here in the book or find the digital version of the One Page Life Plan.[11]

| **Life Plan of** _____ |||
|---|---|---|
| Purpose Statement ||| 
| How I'll make It happen |||
| Metrics of Success by 2050 || Habits to Start |
| Habits to Stop || Habits to Continue |
| 90 Day Action Plan || 1 Year Goals |
| 5 Year Goals || Lifetime Goals |
| Signed on _____, ____ 20__ || X_____ |

### Action Item #15: Frame Your One-Page Life Plan
Fill out the above One Page Life Plan, then print it out and frame it and put it up in your home or office where you'll see it daily. Print out your free template at https://bit.ly/onepagelifeplan. Don't forget to frame it and actually hang it up! This one step will change everything!!

---

[11] Find the free One Page Life Plan template to print out at https://bit.ly/onepagelifeplan

# Life KPIs - How to Measure Your Goals

Goals are great. But how you measure and track your goals matters just as much. As management great Peter Drucker once wrote, "What gets measured gets managed." Key performance indicators (KPIs) are simply goals that can be measured and tracked quantitatively.

This is why I've created weekly "Life KPIs" for myself that I track every Friday.

*Life KPIs - The measurable key performance indicators of your life that you track your week-to-week progress by.*

Here's my personal KPI tracking sheet right now. As you can see, I currently have 17 KPIs that I'm tracking weekly for each area of my life.

| # | Life KPI | 4/14/23 Wk 5 | 4/21/23 Wk 6 | 4/28/23 Wk 7 | 5/5/23 Wk 8 | 5/12/23 Wk 9 | 5/19/23 Wk 10 | 5/26/23 Wk 11 | 6/2/23 Wk 12 | 6/9/23 Wk 13 |
|---|---|---|---|---|---|---|---|---|---|---|
| 1 | MRR from CEO Coaching | $40,000 | $42,500 | $47,500 | $47,500 | $47,500 | $47,500 | $47,500 | $47,500 | $47,500 |
| 2 | # of Paying CEO Coaching Clients | 2 | 2 | 2 | 2 | 2 | 2 | 2 | 2 | 2 |
| 3 | # of Paying SaaS Group Coaching Clients | 0 | 0 | 2 | 2 | 2 | 2 | 2 | 2 | 2 |
| 4 | Coinstack Subscribers | 92383 | 93523 | 95234 | 96233 | 97320 | 99,003 | 101,012 | 103,414 | 105,102 |
| 5 | Coinstack Unique Opens (Most Recent Post) | 33124 | 32421 | 34342 | 35622 | 36742 | 38344 | 39041 | 40122 | 42,264 |
| 6 | Coinstack Open Rate | 35.86% | 34.67% | 36.06% | 37.02% | 37.75% | 38.73% | 38.65% | 38.80% | 40.21% |
| 7 | Coinstack Unique Clicks | 568 | 520 | 532 | 489 | 332 | 450 | 562 | 467 | 438 |
| 8 | Magic Year All Time Posts | 0 | 0 | 0 | 0 | 0 | 0 | 0 | 0 | 0 |
| 9 | Magic Year BeeHiiv Subs | 0 | 0 | 0 | 0 | 0 | 0 | 0 | 0 | 0 |
| 10 | Magic Year BeeHiiv Opens | 0 | 0 | 0 | 0 | 0 | 0 | 0 | 0 | 0 |
| 11 | # of Friends Considering Moving to Costa Rica | 6 | 7 | 8 | 8 | 8 | 10 | 12 | 12 | 12 |
| 12 | LinkedIn Newsletter Subscribers | 2631 | 2644 | 2653 | 2685 | 2704 | 2724 | 2780 | 2820 | 2850 |
| 13 | Amount in Personal Checking + Savings | $24,682 | $23,432 | $22,241 | $20,423 | $16,234 | $12,422 | $6,030 | $25,324 | $32,639 |
| 14 | Weight at End of Week | 152.8 | 150.4 | 148.5 | 149.5 | 150.5 | 151.2 | 154.5 | 153.1 | 152.2 |
| 15 | Body Fat | 15.5% | 14.9% | 14.7% | 14.80% | 14.90% | 15% | 15.10% | 15.20% | 14.9% |
| 16 | Times I Made Love to Wife | 1 | 1 | 1 | 2 | 3 | 4 | 4 | 4 | 3 |
| 17 | Friends I Saw In Person This Week | 15 | 5 | 12 | 20 | 12 | 7 | 6 | 12 | 22 |

Source Image

Every Friday at 4 pm, I take half an hour to update the metrics on my sheet before I stop working for the weekend. Everything that really matters to me, which can be measured, is in this sheet, from Body Fat % to the amount of money in my bank account, to the number of times I made love to my wife that week. By definition, all KPIs are quantifiable.

Create your own Life KPI sheet. Write your **Big Goal** and any other overall life goals at the top, and then write down the specific measurements that contribute to achieving those goals below. These are your **Life KPIs**.

Every Friday, fill out where you are in each of your KPIs and track your progress over time. You can do it on a sheet of paper or on a spreadsheet. I use a spreadsheet because my KPIs and big goals tend to change every so often.

**Action Item #16: Create Your Life KPI Sheet**
Create your own Life KPI Sheet. Write down your Big Goal and then all the specific metrics that feed into achieving your big goal and any other major life goals you have. Every Friday, update it with the measurements from the prior week. You can use the template at https://bit.ly/lifekpis.

# The Formula of Success

*"There are those who make excuses and those who get it done. We only live once -- get it done." - Jalen Hurts, NFL Quarterback*

The formula for massive success in life is actually quite simple. It can be found within the 80,000 words of the book "*Think and Grow Rich*," repeated many times in slightly different words.

Are you ready? Okay—here's the foundation for massive success in life. It took me about 30 years to figure this one out.

1. **Vision:** Think about what you want, then decide on your Big Goal.
2. **Belief:** Actually believe you can achieve it.
3. **Action:** Take massive action toward your Big Goal.
4. **Consistency:** Stay consistent with these actions for 10 years.
5. **Results:** Achieve massive success.

Many people do step #1, but few people write down their big goal (Hill calls it the "Chief Definite Purpose") and fewer people actually take consistent action with their big goal for 5-10 years.

And thus, few people achieve massive success. It's the 1% of people who can create their own reality field (I call them **reality distorters**) and can stay consistent at something for 10 years who make it (whether in business, acting, the arts, or sports). I call these people reality distorters.

*Reality Distorters - People who are so confident and have such a locked in mindset that they can create reality from nothing but thought, belief, consistent action, and good energy, even against tall odds or general disbelief.*

Now, if you bring all these elements together, you get one of the most important formulas in this book.

**The Formula of Success**: Vision + Belief + Action + Consistency = Results

I will refer to this **Formula of Success** a few times in this book. I might even write a whole book on it someday. Keep coming back to this formula, and anytime something isn't working, see which part of the formula you're missing.

Very few people ever do step one (vision), and even fewer do step two (belief). And even fewer do step three (action). And even fewer do step four (consistency). But if you can be the rare duckling to do all four steps, anything is possible for your magic life.

**Action Item #17: Apply The Formula of Success**
Study The Formula of Success and write down how you can immediately apply it to your life. Vision + Belief + Action + Consistency = Results.

As Zach Porgrob from BehaviorHack writes, "People will tell you to be realistic to drag you down to their version of reality. Resist."

I've yet to meet a single entrepreneur, actor, artist, or athlete who actually followed the steps above and did not achieve major success in their field of choice within a decade.

So if Napoleon Hill were accurately titling his book, he would have called it "*Think, Take Action, Stay Consistent for Years, Grow Rich.*" Of course, that title probably wouldn't have sold 75 million copies. 🙂

Another way to think about this formula for achieving incredible things and making a big impact in the world is as follows.

1) **Clarity:** Get clear on what you want to achieve
2) **Obsession:** Get absolutely obsessed with the change you're wanting to make in the world
3) **Consistency:** Work toward this goal consistently for ten years

It's as simple as that. Get clear. Get obsessed. Stay consistent.

# How to Be Fearless With Your Goals

*"Everything you want is on the other side of fear."* - Jack Canfield

Back in 2014, when I turned 30, I set a really big goal. I wanted to build a non-profit workshop on designing your life that over 1 million people would eventually graduate from. I initially called it the Hive Global Leaders Program and now refer to it as the Hive Designing Your Life Workshop. You can learn more about it at www.hive.org. Our goal is to help over 1 million people intentionally and thoughtfully go through a process of **life design**.

*Life Design - The practice of intentionally and thoughtfully living your life. Start with writing down your current purpose, goals, habits, and values.*

This goal was so big, it scared me.
How would I manage to get 1 million people through a weekend workshop?
Wow, it has been quite a journey to create Hive. We've faced numerous challenges, including the impact of Covid when we had to shut down for two years. However, we believe we have finally figured out how to make our business model scale, giving us a real chance to reach our goal.
So, how are we doing so far? In my 30s, we hosted this in-person weekend workshop 40 times, and 4,000 people from 130 countries completed it. I have personally led nearly 30 of

these workshops, while others have led them about 10 times. Now, our focus is on systematizing and digitizing the program, enabling us to offer it online, train others to deliver the content, and reduce the price point.

My plan is to establish a "train the trainer" program, where I teach other graduates how to deliver the curriculum. While I'm not entirely certain yet how we will reach our goal (perhaps this book will help), I firmly believe that if we persevere, we will eventually get there.

Throughout this journey, I have had to overcome many personal challenges and doubts (who am I to create one of the world's largest courses on Designing Your Life?). However, I always come back to the inspiring quote by John Lewis, "If not us, who? If not now, when?"

Creating significant achievements requires fearlessness and taking one step at a time towards your dreams. Overcoming fears often involves experimenting and taking calculated risks.

Back in January 2023, I was apprehensive about leaving Bali and returning to the USA. With a 7-month-old baby, it was much easier to raise our little one in Bali, where full-time nanny care cost $1,000 per month compared to $5,000 per month in the USA. Because everything costs less in Bali, $1000 per month is actually a good wage there and is quite a bit more than what the nannies would usually earn there.

With a young baby, I was feeling worried that reducing the amount of childcare we had would hinder or slow down my progress in creating my Masterwork (this book) and sharing my gift with the world. Fear of course was simply False Evidence Appearing Real. It all worked out in the end just fine -- as it almost always does.

Here's an excerpt from my journal at that time.

### My January 22, 2023 Journal Entry

We're leaving Bali soon and not having the immense gift of full-time nanny care any longer and not really knowing how that is going to be for us. This is the cause of some of my concern about the unknown ahead. I just can't yet imagine what it's going to be like to either not have care available for Apollo. I'm worried I'll get stuck in the world of having to work a lot more to pay for the care and that I'll lose momentum on the book. I know that everything we want is on the other side of fear, so I'm leaning into it.

What ended up actually happening? Well, we went back to Austin a few weeks later, and we found a full-time nanny who charged us $5,000 per month. We also hired a part-time nanny to cover nights when Morgan needed help for a couple extra months until Apollo could sleep all the way through.

Yes, it ended up costing more – but we worked it out. It was nothing to be afraid of. I didn't die. And I was able to keep working on the book for about 15 hours per week while still maintaining my work coaching CEOs and doing marketing growth consulting, which paid our bills in the meantime.

As Mark Twain once said, "I've had a lot of worries in my life, most of which never happened." Most of your fears never become real – so why worry about them endlessly? Things tend to work out in the end if you stay focused on what you want. So if things aren't working out, it's not the end.

As Dr. Adam Gazzaley said, "Have no fear. You've got one chance here to do amazing things, and being afraid of being wrong or making a mistake or fumbling is just not how you do something of impact. You just have to be fearless."

Be fearless. Get clear on your goals. Go after them with all you've got. And love yourself along the way.

## Be Crystal Clear On What You Want From Life

*"You are behind the steering wheel of your life. There are no limitations to what you can do, have, or be—except the limitations you place on yourself by your own thinking." - Brian Tracy, author*

Many people go through life mostly on autopilot, not truly living an intentional life with defined dreams and goals -- and just letting the expectations of others (parents, friends, partners, and society) and chance guide their life -- rather than taking the steering wheel of their own lives.

The reality is that you can do anything in life, but you can't do everything at once.

Many people have limiting beliefs due to their upbringing or "what society tells them is possible" that cause them to not even dream… or if they do dream, to not believe in their own dreams.

What I encourage people to do it to:

1) Be clear on what you want from life (write it down and print it out);
2) Be clear on the positive impact you wish to make and how you wish to serve others;
3) Create a **reality field** around you in which you carefully curate your **information diet** and who you allow to influence you.
4) And then be relentless, unleashed, and unstoppable, and let your purpose just come through you.

*Information Diet - The information that reaches your brain on a daily basis. Controlling and limiting what you intake from social media and the news media is especially important to maintaining a happy, healthy, wealthy, and fully alive life.*

You see, the magic comes when you become even more eccentric, not less. You see, those who made history never blended in.

So stop trying to conform to the middle of the bell curve, so as not to make too much of a wave. Just do you and be you in every moment. Become the fully expressed and authentic version of yourself.

In other words: Do you.

As the musician Kurt Cobain once said, "Wanting to be someone else is a waste of the person you are."

*"Weirdness is why we adore our friends. . . . Weirdness is what bonds us to our colleagues. Weirdness is what sets us apart, gets us hired. Be your unapologetically weird self. In fact, being weird may even find you the ultimate happiness."*
*- Chris Sacca, Lowercase Capital*

So many people lack the self-confidence to be themselves and to truly believe deep down they are worthy of their dreams. So if you take away nothing else from this book, know this:

> You are worthy of your dreams.

Yes, the world wants you to live with joy, passion, obsession, and purpose—not dread, drudgery, and a bad case of the Mondays.

The world wants you to wake up each morning thrilled about what you're doing and joyously excited to get to creating.

Of course, it can be annoying at times to see other people super happy when you haven't quite figured out your own roadmap to joyous living. You have to realize that for every vocal critic who tears you down, there are 1,000 fans quietly encouraging you.

As Robin Sharma wrote in The Everyday Hero Manifesto, "Yes, the media you consume might send you photos of people who appear to have thinner tummies and videos of actors driving spectacular sports cars. But that doesn't mean you're not startlingly worthy. Because you are. Absolutely one of a kind. And while I believe it's very important to keep making every aspect of your life better, every single day, please also know and trust that who you are right now is more than enough. So may I humbly suggest that you give yourself the words, praise, and encouragement you are waiting for forces outside of you to give. And become your own top cheerleader, your single finest supporter, and your number one fan."

## Thoughts Become Things

> "If you can conceive it, and you can believe it, you can achieve it."
> - Napoleon Hill in *Think and Grow Rich*

As you should know by now, thought is the catalyst for all human creation. Everything that becomes real first becomes real in our mind through our imagination and belief.

Then, thought repetition focuses our brain, naturally leading it to become crisply aware of what we want.

This leads to taking the actions that allow the desired dream to become real.

So curating your thoughts and creating a method to repeat the good ones is absolutely essential for an optimal life.

You should remember from earlier in this book that you can have ANYTHING you want in life, but you can't have EVERYTHING. Thus, focusing your mind on what is most important to you so you can make that real is key.

As my wife Morgan says, "Life is not about getting everything you want. Life is about having enough experience to know what you truly want."

Morgan has a very useful practice for focusing her thoughts on a daily basis. She writes herself letters, proclaiming exactly what she wants. One letter for each desired result. She even puts them inside envelopes.

She then reads these letters to herself every morning as part of her own miracle morning routine. She intentionally creates a sense of gratitude as she reads these letters to herself, imagining them already coming true and feeling the feelings she'd feel as if they'd already come true.

At any given time, I see her carrying around five or six of these little letters to herself for daily review.

Here's one of the letters she wrote to herself in January 2023 while in Bali just before we came back to Austin, TX for a few months before we moved to Nosara, Costa Rica.

### The Letter Morgan Wrote To Help Find The Perfect Home

Hello Beautiful Mamma,
I give you the perfect home in your ideal location with sidewalks, trees, beautiful sunsets, happy neighbors with families, and block parties. There will be people you adore and a totally amazing home experience that utterly delights you and you feel the coziness of family time everyday and all throughout your day. You feel grateful and overjoyed to be with your family. I give you an easy environment to create, parent, eat, play, dance, and sing with family. I give you easy support and joy for it all. I give you the perfect cozy creative loving environment to thrive.
Love, The Universe

Wow, I love this woman! I've learned so much from her about the way that she makes things real through vision, belief, action, and consistency.

So what are you giving to yourself? What letters do you wish you could open every morning? Well, you can. Write these affirmation letters to yourself and read them each morning as part of your miracle morning.

**Action Item #18: Write a Letter to Yourself**
Write a letter to yourself describing exactly what you truly want. Then read it to yourself every morning for the next week as part of your daily miracle morning routine.

Thoughts. Become. Things. One final time, I'll share this inspiring quote from my friend Salman, who I originally met in Bali. He's one of the few people in the world I know who has an Ivy League MBA degree and spends a lot of his time today between music festivals, DJing ecstatic dances, and visiting Bali and Costa Rica. Pura vida!

> "What if I told you that the secret to it all is simple? Our thoughts and our feelings create the blueprint for our reality. Every coherent thought and feeling is a lever to pull for generating change on a greater level, one that creates ripples far beyond that which our conscious minds are able to comprehend." - Salman Hatta

## Create Your Vision

"I am a big believer that if you have a very clear vision of where you want to go, then the rest of it is much easier." - Arnold Schwarzenegger

# MAGIC YEAR - 141

Remember, friends, the distance between a dream and reality is action. Here's my 2009 vision board that I created three full years before I got into Harvard. Take a look at what's at the very center. It's small—but squint. Yes, that's right—a diploma from Harvard University. Seemingly impossible for a college dropout like me—but seven years later, on May 17, 2016, I got the real thing.

Without even knowing it, I'd put **The Formula of Success** to work: Vision → Belief → Action → Consistency = Results.

My Actual Vision Board from 2009. A Harvard diploma was at the center, which I actually got 7 years later.

These days, I create an annual **vision board** using Google Slides. I then print it out and turn it into a single big poster board. You can make a copy to create your own at https://bit.ly/ryanvisionboard).

*Vision Board - A Google Slide Deck or physical cardboard that contains images of what you want to bring into your life over the next 3-5 years*

If you want to do the quicker version of the vision board, just go and get 5-10 images for each of these ten categories. Then, print them out and tape/glue them to your poster board. Here are the ten basic vision board categories:

| Basic Vision Board Categories |
|---|
| 1. Family     6. Career |
| 2. Health     7. Financial |
| 3. Education     8. Quotes |
| 4. Travel     9. Values |
| 5. Adventure     10. Goals |

I am obsessed with vision boards as they help me program my brain for the year ahead. I've come up with 38 categories and I often end up using four posters taped together to create my mega-vision board each year. There are 38 categories on my vision board.

### Ryan's Expanded Vision Board Categories

| | | | |
|---|---|---|---|
| 1. | Adventures | 20. | Inspiring Sayings |
| 2. | Agreements | 21. | Intentional Communities |
| 3. | Annual Theme | 22. | Nature |
| 4. | Art We Love | 23. | Purpose |
| 5. | Books | 24. | Relationships |
| 6. | Bucket List | 25. | Life Plan |
| 7. | Community | 26. | Love / Sensuality |
| 8. | Dreams | 27. | Office Design |
| 9. | Experiences | 28. | Rituals |
| 10. | Family | 29. | Service |
| 11. | Festivals | 30. | Shared Values |
| 12. | Finances | 31. | Spirituality |
| 13. | Goals | 32. | Strengths |
| 14. | Habits | 33. | Traditions |
| 15. | Health | 34. | Travel |
| 16. | Home | 35. | Visions |
| 17. | Hopes | 36. | Vows |
| 18. | Inspiring Words | 37. | Ways of Being |
| 19. | Inspiring People | 38. | Work |

I create a single slide for each category and then spend about 5-10 minutes on each category, adding photos from the internet that relate to what I want to bring into my life over the next 1-5 years. I update my digital vision board every year, but it takes many years for it to change entirely as some goals are long-term in nature.

I often end up with 300+ unique images on my vision board (5-10 per category times 38 categories). It takes me a couple of days to finish each year, and I always do this process the same week as I update my annual goals between Christmas and New Year's Day when few people are working.

Here's an example of one of the images on my vision board from 2019 that is getting closer and closer to becoming real every day.

*The Allis Family - 2027*

*3/4ths of this picture from my 2019 vision board has become real. Hopefully Aurora comes soon too!*

It's amazing what an image on a vision board can do to turn thought into massive action (finding Morgan at Burning Man, getting married, making Apollo, etc.)

Remember: **Vision → Belief → Action → Consistency = Results**. So go ahead and set aside a weekend and create your vision board.

### Ryan's Process for Creation a Vision Board

1. Use the digital template to find images in each category
2. Print out the images on a color printer
3. Get a friend (or assistant you pay if needed) to help you cut out the images.
4. Glue/tape them to an oversized white board from CVS/Office Depot
5. Display the vision board in your room

Don't skip the process of making it physical. That's the fun part. While that is what takes 3/4ths of the time -- it will be 10 hours very well spent as you program your mind toward what you actually want.

Make it digital. Make it physical. Make it real.

**VISION BOARD**

**Action Item #19: Create Your Vision Board**
Open up Google Slides and make a vision board, grabbing images from the internet representing what you want to embody, experience, and bring into your life within the above listed categories. For extra credit, print them all out and paste them on a physical vision board. Hang this vision board in your bedroom on a prominent wall.

## Create Your Bucket List

*"The big question is whether you are going to be able to say a hearty yes to your adventure."*
— Joseph Campbell, writer

Lastly, once you've written down your goals and made your vision board -- there's one more thing to do: create your **bucket list** of all the **epic adventures** you want to have over the next decade.

*Bucket List - A list of all the exciting and adventurous things you want to do for yourself and with your friends and family before you "kick the bucket."*

Here's my ten year bucket list from five years ago. Notice how many I've checked off already. YOLO, my friends. Well at least in this body and in this time.

1. Meet my wife at Burning Man (DONE)
2. Live in Bali for a year (DONE)
3. Climbing Mt. Batur Volcano in Bali at sunset (DONE)
4. Visit Gili Islands with my family (DONE)
5. Help start an intentional living community (DONE)
6. Sky dive (DONE)
7. Write a book on how to live a passionate, mindful, and healthy life (DONE)
8. Get married and create a family (DONE)
9. Go to the Envision Festival in Costa Rica (DONE)
10. Rented a beach house as our primary home in Nosara, Costa Rica (DONE)
11. Visit all 7 continents with my children and family
12. Attend at least two of these festivals: Ondalinda (Mexico), LoveBurn (Miami), AfrikaBurn (South Africa) and Labyrinto Festivals (Costa Rica)
13. Learn to scuba dive
14. Ride a motorcycle on the Carretera Austral in Chile
15. Visit the Alps with my family
16. Hang glide in Rio De Janeiro
17. Travel to space on Virgin Galactic
18. Learn karate or taekwondo
19. Experience a Berlin & London Sex Dungeon just to see what they are like
20. Go on a 100+ day around the world cruise. I've been eyeing Royal Caribbean's 274 day cruise to 60+ countries for Morgan, Apollo, and I. Now that would be an adventure of a lifetime!

Now create your own bucket list, just open a Google Doc or grab some post-it notes and write down all the amazing experiences you want to have in the next ten years of your life. Then print them out and put them somewhere visible in your room or office (bonus points for framing it).

Dream big--and trust that you can do absolutely anything you set your mind to. As Napoleon Hill once wrote, "Anything you can conceive and believe you can achieve."

See if you can write down at least 20 -- so that there's two bucket list items per year that you're checking off.

As Robin Sharma writes, "Do you really want to postpone what you most want to do until a time when it may be too late to do it?"

### Action Item #20: Create Your Bucket List
Open up a Google Doc and write down a list of at least 20 things you want to do before you die. Use the above list for inspiration. Think about what you want to do on your own, with a partner, and with your family. What epic adventures can you imagine?!

## Go on Epic Adventures

"Humans are happiest when we are progressing. And exploring. And venturing out into the vivid blue oceans of previously imagined places, potentials and pursuits that set our spirits aflight. You and I, at a primal level, are nomads. We are travelers. Voyagers. Pioneers, of sorts. We long to learn new skills, embrace novel experiences, enter foreign cultures, turn strangers into friends and advance through life with sparkling eyes and dancing hearts." - Robin Sharma

Have you let your life become a little bit *too predictable*? Have you lost a little of that inner soul spark?

Well ask yourself this question. When was the last time you had a truly **epic adventure**? When was the last time you struck up a conversation with someone from another culture or country?

*Epic adventures - Elements on your bucket list. Things that you'd absolutely love to do and would create lifelong memories.*

When was the last time you hiked up a volcano at sunset, taken on a new challenge like learning karate, or flown across the world to go to an art and music festival with your friends?

I like to ensure I have at least one "incredible adventure" every 3 months. Recent Epic adventures for me have included:

- Taking a speed boat through the Indian Ocean from Bali to Gili Air, an Indonesian island, where there are no cars and everyone gets around on horses and bikes for a Christmas Celebration with my family.

- A three-month Sabbatical in 1991 with my family where we traded our home in Florida for houses in Germany, France, and England. I was 6 years old and got to experience Europe. Even though we didn't earn much money my mom found a way for us to travel internationally every other year.

- Renting an ATV and driving 30 minutes to TierrAmor, my friend's 1200 acre ocean-view property in the hills of Nosara, Costa Rica. Then, getting on horseback to explore the land for two hours.

- A four hour sunset hike up the active Mt. Batur volcano in Bali with a good friend for some man-bonding time. There was nothing like seeing the steaming rocks at the top and feeling the accomplishment of making it.

*The top of Mt. Batur Volcano in Bali*

- Five days in Ibiza on a boat with a founder of a well-known circus performance company and 20 friends enjoying some of the best human performance art I've ever seen.

- Eight Burning Man festivals in the desert of Nevada, including four where I helped build my camp for a week before with a crew of 65 people (this was how I met my wife!)

- Going to a friend's Italian Castle one month into my relationship with my beloved Morgan for a four day gathering to align with other global leaders. This was during the first 30 days of our dating and was the cause of us truly falling for each other (though that lucky dose of MDMA from a friend might have helped a bit).

- Going on an unforgettable 10-day Mediterranean cruise with my girlfriend when we were 24 -- seeing Spain, Italy, Greece, and Turkey in a whole new way and deepening my love for Europe in the Summer. This was where I started my habit of striking up conversations with complete strangers everywhere we stopped to see what I could learn and contribute. As Jen Sincero says, "Talk to strangers, we're all family on this planet."

- Deciding at the very last minute (the day of) to fly from our home in Los Angeles to a festival in Thailand called Wonderfruit with our friends when my then fiancee Morgan spontaneously asked me, "if you could do anything, what do you really want to do tonight?" I replied "If I could do anything I'd go to Thailand tomorrow to dance with my friends at Wonderfruit." Three hours later, I hopped on a plane from LAX to Bangkok and made it just in time for the start.

- Taking sensual tantra lessons with a **tantrika** and my wife in Bali to make me last 3x longer in bed with about 16 hours of "hands-on" training over two months. This was quite the fun learning adventure, I must admit.

My wife and I have intentionally designed our lives to be a continual **epic adventure**—for the same cost or less than if we stayed in suburban America all year round. I work as a writer and CEO coach, which allows me to live anywhere. My wife works as an artist and creative producer, which also gives her the flexibility to live anywhere.

But even if you, due to family and/or work, choose to stay mostly in one place, there is absolutely nothing stopping you from planning an incredible adventure of your own every three months!

> **Action Item #21: Add Some Epic Adventures To Your Bucket List**
> Add to your bucket list at least 10 epic adventures you want to have in the next 5 years of your life.. Then schedule all 10 on your calendar, one every six months for the next 5 years. Just fucking do it!

It may be uncomfortable at times to actually do the things you've dreamed of doing. But it will definitely get you out of your uninspired and glazed-over boredom. You don't get a second chance at living life. Now is your moment. What will you do?

As Ayn Rand said, "Do not let your fire go out, spark by irreplaceable spark, in the hopeless swamps of the not-quite, the not-yet, and the not-at-all. Do not let the hero in your soul perish, in lonely frustration for the life you deserved but have never been able to reach. The world you desire can be won, it exists, it is real, it is possible, it's yours."

> **Action Item #22: Read a Book on Goal Setting**
> Take a look at the below list of books. Choose one and read it. If you haven't ever read *Think and Grow Rich*, I recommend starting there.

## Recommended Books on Goals

- *Think and Grow Rich* by Napoleon Hill
- *The Law of Success* by Napoleon Hill
- *Ask and It is Given: Learning to Manifest Your Desires* by Esther and Jerry Hicks
- *Be Your Future Self Now* by Dr. Benjamin Hardy
- *Excellent Advice for Living: Wisdom I Wish I'd Known Earlier* by Kevin Kelly

## Key Outcome from This Chapter

> **Write Down Your Goals & Frame Your One Page Life Plan** - Be sure you've written down your lifetime, five year, 1 year, and 90 gay goals. Also be sure you've created and framed and hung up your One Page Life Plan (OPLP).

## GOALS CHAPTER ACTION ITEMS

1. **Your Big Goal** - Reflect on and write down your Big Goal -- the #1 goal in your life over the next year.

2. **Big Goal Wristband** - Print yourself a wristband with your Big Goal on it. Start wearing this around your wrist.

3. **Frame Your Goals-** Using the template, print out and frame your goals sheet. Frame it and hang it up in your bedroom.

4. **Life KPIs** - Using the template, create your Life KPI Tracking Sheet and update it weekly at the same time.

5. **The Success Formula -** Study the Success Formula and apply it to your life. Vision + Belief + Action + Consistency = Results.

6. **Letter to Yourself** - Write a letter to yourself with everything you want to create and achieve and read it to yourself each morning.

7. **Vision Board -** Create a vision board with everything you want to bring into your life the next 5 years.

8. **Bucket List** - Create a bucket list of at least 20 experiences you want to have before you die.

9. **Epic Adventures -** Add to your bucket list at least 10 epic adventures you want to have in the next 5 years of your life.

10. **Goals Book** - Pick one book from the list of recommended books at the end of this chapter and read it.

# STEP 3

# HABITS MAGIC

**MAGIC YEAR**

MAGIC YEAR - 150

## KEY CONCEPTS FROM THE HABITS CHAPTER

**1. HABIT STACK**

The collection of all your current habits. Since your daily habits create your future, be very intentional about creating positive habits and removing any negative habits.

**2. TRIGGER ACTION PLAN**

Adding a new habit to your routine by tying it into something you already do. The existing habit becomes the trigger for the new habit.

**3. VISUALIZATIONS**

Running through in your mind how you want to feel or what you want to achieve. Many athletes and entrepreneurs use advance mind visualizations multiple times per day to achieve extraordinary athletic and business results.

**4. GAIN MOVIE**

A visualization of what you will gain when you install a new habit. For example: a six pack for summer if you do 100 sit-ups every single day.

**5. PAIN MOVIE**

A visualization of what you will lose if you don't install a new habit. For example: your girlfriend if you don't get yourself in shape.

**6. LIFE EXPERIMENTS**

Intentionally designed experiments trying something new in which you track the results and keep what works. These are what you do when you want to test out a new habit, role, relationship, or location before committing to it long term.

**7. WORKCATIONS**

Taking a long vacation (1+ months) where you take your laptop and work during Monday-Thursday and travel on the weekends. Common among remote workers.

**8. INNER INTEGRITY**

Following through and doing what you commit to yourself that you're going to do (i.e. exercise daily, lose 20 pounds, stop eating sugar, spend time with your family, etc.). By doing what you say you're going to do, you gain inner confidence.

**9. OVERCOMMITTERS**

People pleasers who say yes to everyone but then constantly don't do what they say they are going to do because they are overwhelmed and stretched too thin. It's better to only commit to your Fuck Yeses and then do what you say you'll do.

**10. VALUES STACK**

The current values that you actively work to embody in your life (i.e. kindness, helpfulness, presence, positive energy, playfulness, etc.).

**11. VALUES SYSTEMS**

Collections of values popularized in spiritual and cultural traditions. Examples include Tikkun Olam the Jewish concept of repairing the world and Ahimsa, the Sanskrit philosophy of do no harm.

**12. EMPATHY CIRCLE**

The collection of identity layers that you have empathy for. Those with the least empathy only value themselves. Those with the most empathy value all people and all life.

# STEP 3: HABITS MAGIC

*"We are what we repeatedly do. Excellence, then, is not an act, but a habit."*
*- Aristotle*

### YOUR MAGIC YEAR

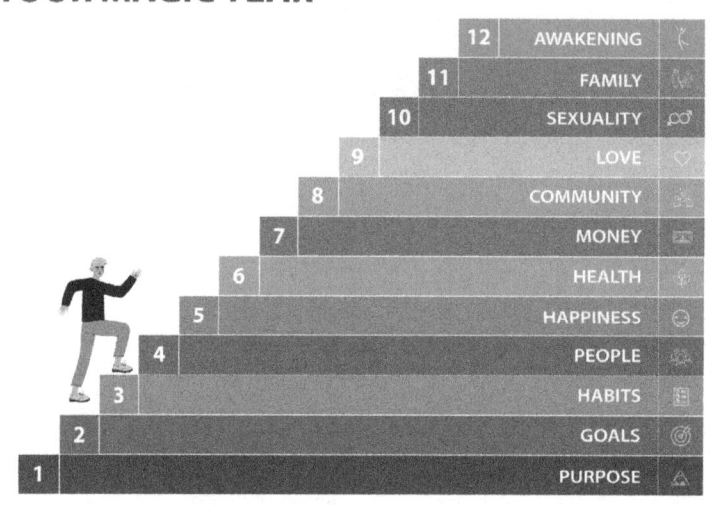

| Step | Area |
|------|------|
| 12 | AWAKENING |
| 11 | FAMILY |
| 10 | SEXUALITY |
| 9 | LOVE |
| 8 | COMMUNITY |
| 7 | MONEY |
| 6 | HEALTH |
| 5 | HAPPINESS |
| 4 | PEOPLE |
| 3 | HABITS |
| 2 | GOALS |
| 1 | PURPOSE |

## What's Your Habit Stack?

Habits and values form the basis of your life. If you install good habits and values, you'll live a great life. It's really as simple as that.

Good Habits + Strong Values = A Great Life

Show me a person's habits and I'll be able to tell a lot about them right away. Your **habit stack** is everything.

*Habit stack - The collection of all your current habits. If you can upgrade your habit stacks in each of the 12 areas of this book, you can completely transform your life.*

Of course, there are many good habits -- and there are many bad ones. Here's a short list.

| Good Habits | Bad Habits |
|---|---|
| Daily cardio workout | Smoking |
| Daily lifting | Vaping |

| | |
|---|---|
| Daily sauna | Eating processed foods |
| Daily cold plunge | Eating sugar |
| Daily journaling | Taking cocaine/heroin/meth |
| Daily reading | Watching lots of television |
| Morning 15 mins of Sunlight | Drinking alcohol |
| Keto/paleo diet | Complaining |

The key is to get addicted to the dopamine you get from the good habits and not the dopamine that you get from bad habits.

You can imagine the difference in life outcomes between a person who did ALL of the good habits and a person who did ALL of the bad habits.

As Samuel Johnson says, "True greatness consists in being great in little things."

You see, what you do repeatedly creates your life and your results. So, if you're not getting the results you want in life, adjust your habits.

"The Five Habits of Successful People" according to my friend Noeline Kirabo are:

1. **Positive Mindset** - Successful people believe in themselves and their abilities. They view setbacks as opportunities for growth and maintain a positive outlook even in the face of adversity. They also surround themselves with positive, supportive people who encourage them to succeed.

2. **Set Goals** - Successful people know what they want to achieve and set clear, specific goals to get there. They break down their goals into smaller, achievable steps, and regularly evaluate their progress.

3. **Continuous Learning** - Successful people never stop learning. They read, attend seminars, and seek out mentors to expand their knowledge and skills. They also embrace new experiences and challenges to push themselves out of their comfort zones.

4. **Time Management** - Successful people are masters of their time. They prioritize their tasks and use calendars and to-do lists to ensure they stay on track. They also know how to say "no" to distractions and delegate tasks to others when necessary.

5. **Persistence** - Successful people don't give up easily. They are willing to put in the hard work and effort required to achieve their goals, even when faced with obstacles or failures. They maintain a long-term focus and are willing to make sacrifices to achieve their vision.

So now you know some good habits to have. But how do you install new habits? Well, installing a new habit should always be seen as a 21-day experiment. If you do it for 21 days -- and it goes well -- integrate into your ongoing routine. Later in this chapter, I'll share an advanced technique for habit stacking called the Trigger Action Plan, which works for me every time.

As Jen Sincero says in *You Are a Badass*, "How do you form a habit? Decide to. Make it a part of your regular, everyday activities. Make it as non-negotiable and thoughtless as brushing your teeth or getting out of bed. Schedule it in."

Definitely follow that last point from Jen -- put new habits in your calendar on repeat.

**Action Item #23: Keep, Stop, Start Habits List**
Make a list of all the habits you'd like to start, stop, and keep. Then implement this list for at least 30 days, actually doing all the new habits and stopping the bad habits.

Here's what this would look like for me currently. Because I do this exercise often, I only have items in the middle "Keep" column.

| STOP | KEEP | START |
|---|---|---|
| None | Sleeping 8-9 hours per night | None |
| | Lifting weights every day (135 lbs x 30 reps) | |
| | Playing active games with my friends (Padel, Pickleball, Racquetball) | |
| | Getting at least 15 minutes of direct sunlight every morning | |
| | Writing at least 1000 words (1 hour) every single day of the week | |
| | Drinking green tea every morning instead of coffee | |
| | Daily Sudarshan Kriya breathing meditation (20 minutes) | |
| | Surrounding myself with joyous and easeful people | |
| | Limiting social media + television to 30 minutes per day max | |
| | Limiting "work" to 20 hours per week so I can spend lots of time with my family | |
| | Reading books on my Kindle daily | |
| | Weekly practice of another language on Duolingo (often I'll practice my Spanish or Indonesian since I spend so much time in Costa Rica and Bali). | |
| | Choosing to live an unconventional life with my family | |
| | Investing lots of time into my young son's education -- making it based on curiosity, nature, and adventure | |
| | Morning steam sauna and cold shower/plunge | |

Give hugs when I meet people instead of handshakes

Reviewing my goals the last week of every year and setting new ones

Quarterly 3-day solo writing/reading reflection sessions at different retreat centers

Every 3 years doing an Ayahuasca ceremony

Every 5 years doing a 10 day Vipassana silent meditation

These are my core habits -- and they have directly led to the quality of the life I lead and the quality of the output I produce as a creator, entrepreneur, and writer.

Here are some other "good habits" I've tried in the past (but don't currently always do if I'm being honest).

1. Drinking a full glass of water with lemon within 30 seconds of waking up
2. Doing 20 pushups every morning
3. Once per year Art of Living 3-day silent retreat
4. Intentionally reducing the number of commitments I make to give me more time to do the existing things I'm doing well and freeing up my mind for creative thinking.
5. Weekly walk in nature.

Here are some "bad habits" that I've ended over the past 20 years.

1. **Ending all alcohol consumption.** Alcohol dulled my brain and made me dumb and slow. It wasn't worth it so I stopped entirely.

2. **Stopping drinking coffee** - Coffee made me anxious due to the cortisol and adrenaline it releases. By age 30, I had stopped all forms of caffeine other than green tea and an occasional oolong tea. Cutting out caffeine quickly can be hard (I remember the withdrawal headaches), so it is advisable to slowly reduce intake over the course of a couple of weeks. Green tea has much less caffeine, as well as antioxidants, and can lead to a lower risk of heart disease, cancer, and diabetes.

3. **Checking my phone right when I wake up.** This can cause a lot of unnecessary anxiety. I keep my phone on airplane mode the first 30 minutes of each day. My morning routine has me wake up, drink green tea, take supplements, lift weights, shower, and eat scrambled eggs. Only then do I turn on my phone -- after my miracle morning is already secured.

4. **Endless phone scrolling.** On those scrolling social media apps (TikTok, Instagram, Facebook), I limit my "scrolling" time to about 60 seconds. I understand the value of my brain's attention, so I only pop on every so often to check my messages and the first few items on the news feed, and that's it.

5. **Spending time with uninspiring people.** I don't spend time with people unless I find them both inspiring and kind. I think everyone has the potential to be inspiring. It's just

that most people aren't exactly living inspiring lives. I find those who are -- and then I consciously spend a LOT of time with those people.

6. **Watching mindless television.** I limit my social media and television usage to a maximum of an average 30 minutes per day in total. Although sometimes I watch part of a playoff NFL or NBA game or a World Cup match, I avoid spending hours per day watching television. When I do watch, it's usually documentaries, sports, kids movies, and occasionally an episode of Amazing Race (I love travel). I also don't play video games, although I did enjoy playing FIFA on Playstation occasionally back in my 20s.

7. **Reading the news.** The news is usually negative and inflammatory (in order to drive more scared readers and sell more ads). Commercial news media has been one of the biggest sources of division in our world. My attention is my most important resource. If something is truly relevant and important, I will hear about it from friends in person, via my friend groups on WhatsApp, or during my limited use of social media. As Robin Sharma says, "Cognitive bandwidth deserves a bandwidth around it."

8. **Eating processed food.** My rule is: if it's in a package or if it has ANY ingredients I don't recognize -- I don't eat it. This one change can shift so much with your health and brain function.

Take a moment and add up how many hours per week you spend doing the above seven activities.

**Action Item #24: Add Up Your Wasted Weekly Time**
Add up all the hours you spend each week watching television, reading the news, scrolling on social media, hanging out with uninspiring people, and drinking alcohol. See if you can cut this amount of time by 50% next week and by 80% the following week. Put the extra time instead into reading, exercising, writing, creating, walking in nature, learning, building a cashflowing side project, and spending time with people you actually find inspiring.

Many people will average **20 hours per week on social media and television** and be in a continuous cycle of lots of caffeine to wake up in the morning and alcohol to slow them down in the evening.

I call this the **Caffeine Alcohol trap**. If you can simply reduce caffeine to a maximum of 50mg per day (one cup of green tea) and cut out alcohol entirely -- I bet you will feel a LOT better (after the first week of withdrawals ends). And just cut out alcohol entirely. Its downsides are much bigger than any upsides from sociability (which can be hacked easily without needing alcohol).

Further, if you can cut the cord on time wasting social media scrolling and television -- you will suddenly find a LOT more is possible in your life. Time for you to spend with your family, create the life of your dreams, travel, see the friends you already have, build meaningful friendships, read books that make your life better, and play active sports with your friends.

It's simply to live a healthy and optimal life. But will you actually do it?
Expanding on the earlier list, here's a little bit longer list of good habits and bad habits.

| Good Habits | Bad Habits |
|---|---|
| Green Tea | Coffee |
| Juices | Alcohol |
| Real Food | Processed Food |
| Time with Friends & Family | Mindless Scrolling |
| Reading Non-Fiction | Mindless Television |
| Active sports with friends | Excessively Reading the News |
| Morning sun exposure | Hiding from the sun |
| Living in the moment | Worrying about the past & future |
| Appreciating life and friends | Complaining about life and friends |
| Being kind and honest | Talking badly about people |
| Daily heart rate above 160 BPM | Smoking cigarettes/vaping |
| Spending less than your earn | Spending more than you earn |
| Investing in cash flowing assets | Buying things you don't need |
| Sleeping 8-9 hours per day | Not prioritizing your sleep |
| Daily Sauna and Cold Plunge | Staying in a job you don't like |
| Quarterly Digital Detox | Excessive working |
| Daily meditation | Daily highway commute |

This next sentence is one of the more important ones in this book: You can edit your future reality outcomes by changing your present thoughts, dreams, actions, and daily patterns.

> You can edit your future reality outcomes by changing your present thoughts, dreams, actions, and daily patterns.

As Stephen Covey says, "Our character is basically a composite of our habits. Because they are consistent, often unconscious patterns, they constantly express our character." So be very thoughtful about which habits you want to remove and add to yourself. Remember that you are in control, not your reptilian brain. Train yourself to be consistent and always do what you say you're going to do -- and your life will flourish.

Below I summarize the most important habits that will help you create a happy life.

### The 12 Most Important Habits for a Happy Life

1. Writing down your purpose statement and keeping it updated annually.
2. Writing down your goals and framing them and displaying them where you see them every day.
3. A willingness to try out new life experiments and keep what works.
4. A curated inner circle of men and women who support you in life.
5. An optimistic and positive mindset.
6. A personalized daily health routine.
7. Saving at least 20% of what you earn after taxes, every single month.
8. Thoughtfully choosing where you want to live and visit, and which communities to be in.
9. Choosing the right life partner.
10. Creating a weekly sensuality ritual with your romantic partner.

11. Going on epic adventures with your partner and kids
12. Being willing to try out new things that lead to greater presence and awakening (like Vipassana or Ayahuasca for example).

## How to Add a New Habit to Your Life

"Small, daily, seemingly insignificant improvements, when done consistently over time, lead to stunning results." - Robin Sharma

Once there's a new habit you want to add -- here's how to add it. The simple version is just do it every day for 21 days.

Here's the more sophisticated version of how to add a new habit... in case the "just do it for 21 days straight" thing isn't working...

A good way to add in a new habit to your routine is by creating a **Trigger Action Plan**, also known as a TAP.

*Trigger Action Plan - A way to add a new habit to your routine by tying it into something you already do. The existing habit becomes the trigger for the new habit.*

Trigger Action Planning is a technique created by Psychologist Peter Gollwitzer to create new habits.

An analysis of studies involving over 8,000 participants found that those who used trigger action plans performed measurably better creating the desired habit.[12]

So how do you actually do this?

Well, a trigger can be something you already do that can remind you to do the new habit. A good trigger occurs at a specific moment and is a memorable sensory experience that your brain will notice when you do it.

In other words, tie the new habit to something you are already consistently doing (like shower, brush your teeth, etc.).

Here are a few examples of potential "new habit" triggers, adapted from the Center for Applied Rationality Course Workbook.

1. When I get to the office, I will take the stairs and not the elevator every day.

2. I will meditate for 20 minutes every morning after I shower.

3. In order to heal my inner critic, whenever I notice I made a mistake, I will say "Yes!" and feel good about noticing the mistake.

---

[12] Gollwitzer, P. M., & Sheeran P. (2006). Implementation intentions and goal achievement: A meta-analysis of effects and processes. Advances in Experimental Social Psychology, 38, 69-119.

To really "install" the new habit, take 3 minutes to do a couple of quick **visualizations**. I use visualizations before I begin each day's work, and before any important meeting. I find that by visualizing and imagining in my mind's eye how something will do before it happens, I can usually be better prepared, happier going in, and create better results.

*Visualizations - Running through in your mind how you want to feel or what you want to achieve. Many athletes and entrepreneurs use advance mind visualizations multiple times per day to achieve extraordinary athletic and business results.*

Here's a visualization that can help you add a new habit more easily. Do this right now with a habit you want to add.

Now, close your eyes and imagine all the benefits of taking it on and successfully adding it to your daily habit stack. Watch yourself doing it every single day. Like an elite athlete who visualizes winning before every race, watch yourself "performing" the new habit in your mind's eye. This visualization is called a **Gain Movie**.

*Gain Movie - A visualization of what you will gain when you install a new habit. For example: a six pack for summer if you do 100 sit-ups every single day.*

And to make it even more real, take 3 minutes to visualize in detail the downsides of not taking on this new habit. This is called the **Pain Movie**.

*Pain Movie - A visualization of what you will lose if you don't install a new habit. For example: your girlfriend if you don't get yourself in shape.*

After following these steps you should have it baked in...

### The 7 Steps to Install a New Habit

1. Find something you already do (the trigger).
2. Tie your new habit mentally to the existing habit (the action)
3. Visualize yourself doing it after the trigger in your minds eye
4. Visualize the benefits of doing it
5. Visualize the benefits of not doing it
6. Draw a short visual of the new habit (example below)
7. Then, of course, actually do it when the trigger comes up

As I'm integrating the new habit into my life, I also like to add it to my calendar so I see it every day.

Here's a template for creating your own Trigger Action Plan, as well as a handy little diagram that "locks it in." Create your own on a sheet of paper or notepad.

> **Example: Adding in 50 Morning Pushups Habit**

- **Big Picture Goal:** Improve my cardio health
- **Specific Habit to Install In My Life:** Do 40 pushups every morning
- **Trigger From Pre-Existing Habit:** After I drink my morning glass of water, immediately do 40 pushups
- **Gain Movie Visualization:** I close my eyes and imagine being 80 years old and being able to mentor my little grandchild and hold him on my lap because I am alive due to my commitment to my daily pushup routine
- **Pain Movie:** I imagine not being alive to mentor and spend time with my future grandchildren

I also really like to draw the new habit as a simple flowchart in my notebook to really lock it in. Here's the drawing I made in 2015 when I decided to incorporate a 30-minute breathing meditation into my **habit stack**.

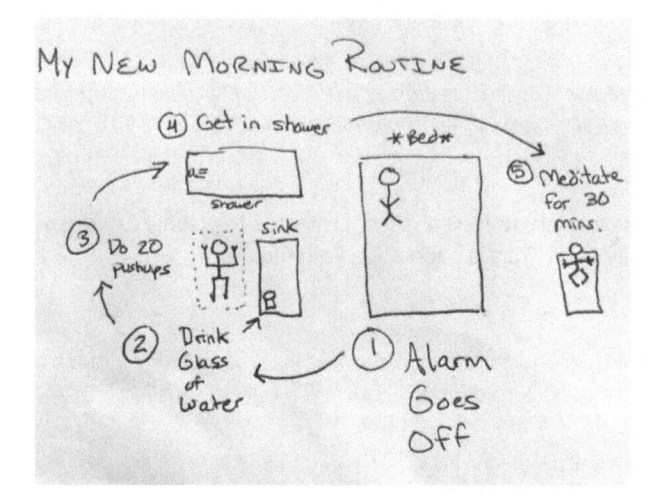

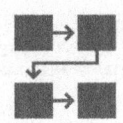

**Action Item #25: Draw a Habit Flowchart For Your Mornings**
Draw out a simple flowchart of how you want the first 120 minutes of your day. Begin to design your own Miracle Morning routine -- and actually start doing it for the next 30 days.

## How to Track Your Daily Habits

A great spreadsheet to track your habits is the "Ultimate Habit Tracker" from EmilyExcels.com. Here's what it looks like. You can get your own copy of it for $10 and use it to track how you do against your daily habits.

## MAGIC YEAR - 160

[Habit Tracker spreadsheet for August showing 72.1% completion rate, with habits tracked including: Exercise, breakfast, Practice mindfulness, Read news, Plan meals, Review budget for the day, Spend time with loved ones, Get 8 hours of sleep, Do my skin-care routine, Use social activities to connect, Write in the down cell for a new line. Weekly Done %: 74%, 64%, 67%, ✓, 39%]

I now use this habit tracking spreadsheet to track all of my daily habits, which are currently:

| Morning Routine | Nighttime Routine |
|---|---|
| 1. Wake up at 630am<br>2. Read my daily affirmation<br>3. Sex with wife (every other day)<br>4. Green Tea<br>5. Supplements<br>6. Swim<br>7. Bench Press<br>8. Pull Ups<br>9. Sit Ups<br>10. Cold Plunge<br>11. Dry Sauna<br>12. Wet Sauna<br>13. Visualizations<br>14. Meditation<br>15. Breakfast<br>16. Brush Teeth<br>17. Take Apollo to daycare | 1. Put Apollo to sleep<br>2. Celebrate the days wins with wife<br>3. Write in my gratitude journal<br>4. Write down a challenge or opportunity I want to reflect on while I'm asleep<br>5. Brush teeth<br>6. Phone off and in bed by 9pm |

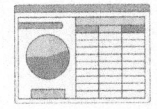

**Action Item #26: Daily Habit Tracking**
Start using a daily habit tracking tool like the one mentioned in this chapter. Every single day, take 5 minutes to fill it out as part of your before-bed night routine. Do this for at least 30 days to lock in the habit.

## Living Life As An Experiment

*"When we live life as an experiment, we are far more willing to take risks, to acknowledge failure, to learn and develop. That's what experiments are all about: discovery and growth." - Peter Bregman, Harvard Business Review*

So how do you test new habits before you implement them for good? Well, you conduct mini experiments. You keep what works. And you throw out what doesn't.

I live my life as a series of **life experiments**.
Cope

*Life Experiments - Intentionally designed experiments trying something new in which you track the results and keep what works. These are what you do when you want to test out a new habit, role, relationship, or location before committing to it long term.*

To create this book, it has been a two-decade process of living an intentional and extraordinary life, trying hundreds of experiments, and a decade-long process of note collecting. Then, there was a three-year process of organizing and writing to create this book.

As Abraham Lincoln once said, "Give me six hours to chop down a tree and I will spend the first four sharpening the ax."

That's essentially what I did to create this book -- except instead of sharpening an ax I was intentionally living life as a series of experiments and seeing what I could learn.

1. Could I build and sell a technology company for $100M+ in my 20s?
2. Could I get into Harvard's MBA program without a college degree?
3. Could I start a global community of purpose-driven leaders?
4. Could I create a workshop that teaches how to upgrade yourself?
5. Could I actually find my wife at Burning Man?
6. Could I help start an international living community in Bali?
7. Could I start a stuffed animal company with my wife?
8. Could I start a band with my friends and publish on Spotify?
9. Could I start an annual festival for my friends in Austin, TX?
10. Could I have a baby who learns through curiosity, play, & adventure?

In addition to living life as a series of joyous **life experiments**, I spent a significant amount of time reading books. I carefully curated my **information diet**, aiming to maintain a positive mindset while gathering the most valuable ideas from over 200+ books on health, wealth, purpose, goals, habits, and optimal living.

*"There is no real failure in an experiment because it's all data. If something doesn't work, that's simply data that leads to changing behavior to see if something else does work." - Peter Bregman, Harvard Business Review*

So, how do you find which habits you want to add? Well, you conduct experiments to see what works for you.

Living life as a series of continuous experiments is the best way to live. If an experiment goes well, integrate it into your life. If it doesn't, tweak the variables, learn from the experience, and try again. There is no failure if you're learning and growing.

If you live life like it is an experiment, conquering fears becomes so much easier. Peter Bregman said it best in an HBR article:

"When we're experimenting, we're willing to do all sorts of things we might be embarrassed to do otherwise. Like ask for something when we don't particularly "deserve" it. Or say something in a conversation that might create a breakthrough (or might appear dumb). If it's an experiment, then taking a risk is the win — whether it pans out or not." - Peter Bregman

## A Template for Creating Your Life Experiments

"My recommendation is to treat life as a series of little experiments."
- Derek Silvers, Entrepreneur

Back in January 2023 my wife and I were deciding on whether to stop by Sunshine Coast, Australia for a week or not on the way home from Bali to Austin. One of our good friends was from there and kept recommending it to us as a potential place for one of our homes. Plus my wife got an astral cartography reading and was told that we would thrive at the exact longitude and latitude that is Sunshine Coast.

The weather is great all year round, it is on the ocean, there is lots of nature, there is organic food, the streets have sidewalks, and the people are kind. Plus, there's very low gun violence and a much healthier population compared to the USA. So, we figured it might be worth a short trip while we were already in Bali.

This was before we moved to Nosara, Costa Rica as our home base. We were still looking for where our eventual primary family home would be.

It was certainly easier, faster, and cheaper to skip Australia—as traveling with a baby can be challenging. If you're a parent, you'll know what I mean. But after reflecting on it, we realized that easier, faster, and cheaper weren't what we were optimizing for in our lives. Instead, we were optimizing for *experience, memories,* and *finding potential long-term communities.*

So we designed the following experiment (you can use a similar template for your own life experiments).

### Experiment Example: Explore a New Potential Home for Our Family

**Time of Experiment:** February 4-11, 2023

**Location:** Sunshine Coast, Australia

**Participants:** Ryan, Morgan, and Apollo (and Nanny Prima)

**Goal of the Experiment:** Assess whether Sunshine Coast, Australia may be a good potential home base for our family. Spend 6 days in Cotton Tree in a two-bedroom unit within walking distance to the ocean and two days in Brisbane. Go every day to GoodLife Community Center for our miracle morning activities and Ryan's writing. Look for sidewalks, healthy cafes, kind people, and good weather. Explore the nearby nature. Visit the nearby city of Brisbane on the way out to see if we like it.

**Potential Upside of the Experiment:** If we like it, we may come back many times to this part of the world to live and work from and meet many interesting people. This could become where Apollo goes to school for a few semesters of his life and where we choose to buy our first home together.

**Potential Downside of the Experiment:** It will delay when Morgan can begin her brain training work with Dr. Dan by a week. It will add extra travel during February when we will already be traveling between Bali, the USA, and Costa Rica for the Envision Festival. I may not want to go to Envision with all the added travel.

**Added Cost of Experiment:** $4000 in added flight, car, and lodging expenses

**Decision:** As Richard Branson says, "Screw it, let's do it." We decided to go. The upsides far outweighed the downsides.

After visiting, we ended up loving our time on the Sunshine Coast so much that Australia has now become one of our homes that we visit and live in from time to time. Thank God we listened to our gut to go, even if it was a bit challenging with the extra travel with a seven-month-old baby.

Citizens of 34 countries, including the USA, can visit and live in Australia for up to 3 months at a time by filling out a ten-minute form on a mobile app called AustralianETA.

For people from outside the country, becoming a longer-term resident in Australia is much easier than in the USA. With some of the best beaches and weather in the world, modern healthcare and infrastructure, world-class cities, top schools, very low crime, and proximity to beautiful New Zealand and Bali, Australia is one of our favorite escapes.

One of the things we love most about Australia is that there is very low crime, thankfully very few guns (just 0.14 guns per person compared to 1.2 guns per person in the USA[13]), and minimal history of leading military interventions in other people's territory.

We absolutely love Brisbane, Sydney, Melbourne, Perth, and the Gold Coast, and have had many adventures in these very walkable, family-friendly, European-esque towns like Mooloolaba, Noosa Heads, Caloundra, and Byron Bay. We love the Brisbane/Sunshine Coast/Gold Coast area the most due to the direct flights to SF/LA and the perfect year-round weather, which is always between 70-90 degrees.

I was so sad at the end of my first week on the Sunshine Coast that I had to remind myself of Dr. Seuss' inspired life maxim...

*"Don't cry because it's over. Smile because it happened" - Dr. Seuss*

---

[13] Gun Ownership by Country - https://worldpopulationreview.com/country-rankings/gun-ownership-by-country

**Action Item #27: Write Down Your Life Experiments**
Read the list of my life experiments above. Write down at least three life experiments you'd like to test over the next year. Then add actually doing them to your calendar. If you'd like, follow the format from the template above.

# The Experiment We Designed to Get Over Fear

Back in February 2023, we were about to leave Bali after three beautiful months there. I didn't want to leave at all—I wanted to stay and finish my book. But Morgan needed to get back to Austin for three months of specialized medical treatments before we moved to Costa Rica, so we decided to go.

I wrote in my journal that I was feeling a bit scared to leave Bali and head back to Austin. I had been healing my nervous system for three months in Bali (lots of massages, cranial sacral, and a calm, happy populace without any of the overwork traumas of America). I was learning Tantra and had finally mastered my miracle mornings at the nearby community wellness center.

Even for me, travel and change can still be a disruptive force. I didn't want to lose all the habits that I had worked so hard to establish while in Bali. I was worried about becoming an "American Fuckface" again and turning into a workaholic in order to pay for all the added costs of living an upscale lifestyle in the USA. I wasn't certain I could actually be in America and not get addicted to work, news, and sports again—three addictions from my 20s.

Of course, we had to go back to Austin for Morgan's medical care for four months. We definitely had to go. I needed to change my mindset about it and not let the American Matrix affect me too much. So, here's the experiment we designed

### Experiment: Live in Austin

**Time of Experiment:** February 13-June 30, 2023

**Location:** Austin, TX

**Participants:** Ryan, Morgan, and Apollo

**Goal of the Experiment:** Depart Bali and return to living Austin for 4 months to work on improving Morgan's health. While there, get a furnished home with walkable sidewalks that is within 10 minutes of a community wellness center with a gym, pool, and sauna so we can continue our daily miracle morning routine.

**Potential Upside of the Experiment:** We can demonstrate that we can live in Austin and keep our nervous systems strong. We can strengthen our friendships in Austin. We may find that Austin becomes our USA hub for our family or learn that we actually want to live in Costa Rica.

**What Could Go Wrong:** When I don't do my miracle morning basics (lift, pool, cold plunge, sauna) I often feel overwhelmed and anxious. Without full-time nanny coverage I may have less time to write -- which may make it hard to finish this book.

**Protecting Against the Downside:** Go to the nearby Austin LifeTime wellness center, gym, and pool each morning 7 days per week. Keep writing this book from 11am to 1pm daily. Host sensuality nights in Austin so I can continue my learnings with tantra. Keep intentionally not reading the news and curating my information diet carefully on social media. Find a live-in nanny who is interested in working with us so that we can afford coverage for 40 hours per week so we can continue our creative pursuits of writing and art. Each night and weekend, spend lots of family time together with Apollo and visit the nearby trails, parks, and family activities.

**Added Cost of Experiment:** Around $5,000 per month in added costs over what we would spend living in Bali (where we were coming from).

**Result of Experiment:** We realized that for us, Austin was either too cold in the winter or too warm in the Summer. We ended up deciding to do Oct-May in Nosara, Costa Rica and May-Oct in Boulder, Colorado each year.

During the time I was in Austin, seven days per week at 9am I'd drive 3 miles to our local wellness center, LifeTime South Austin (I'm a creature of habit) and do my **miracle morning** of gym, pool, cold plunge, and sauna -- and then voila -- writing.

I'd write from around 10am to 1pm each day -- then do CEO coaching calls from 2pm to 5pm on Mon-Thu (which pay the bills while I'm building up my writing career) -- then have the rest of the time spending time with my family and friends.

Mornings for self-care and creativity. Afternoons for "work." And evenings for family and friends. A great life. Life is good as a new dad. I have so much to be grateful for.

## A Few Experiments From My Own Life

Here are fifteen of the life experiments I've conducted over the last twenty years. I share them to inspire a sense that anything is possible within you. What are the experiments you want to create in your own life for the next few years?

1. **Could I build a company to $1M in sales by 21?** - When I was 16, after reading the book *Think and Grow Rich*, I wrote down my first ever goal -- to build a company to $1M in sales by my 21st birthday. I missed the goal by 18 days. iContact reached $1M in sales when I was 21 years old and 18 days on September 1, 2005.

2. **Could I build and sell a tech company for $100M+ in my 20s?** - Once we got to $10M in sales in 2008. I decided to up the game. Starting that year, I wore a wrist band that said $100M in 2012. I saw this everyday, and it motivated me to stay focused for another four years. iContact reached $50M in annual sales in 2011 and we sold the firm for $169M in February 2012 when I was 27 years old. What a life experience -- only possible due to focus, obsession, recruiting a great team, building systems that made money while we slept, and sweating the details of creating value for others for a

decade.

3. **Could I get into Harvard's MBA program without a college degree?**
Hurdles are built to see who can get over them—and to keep out the masses. Don't be the masses. Be uniquely you. When I was 26, there was a case study done on iContact at HBS[14] by the head of the entrepreneurship department. I went up to Boston and presented the case study and met the professor. The next year, my mom passed away, and we sold the company. I was seeking a change in life. I wanted to go to HBS but not finish the year of undergraduate studies I had left. I reached out to Professor Sahlman, and he helped me get into the HBS MBA program—even though I didn't have the required college degree. I still had to take the GMAT and apply, of course. With the professor's advocacy, they let me in, reasoning that if I could build a successful company, I could successfully contribute to the class and my alumni group. Anything is possible when you have the right relationships.

4. **Could I start a global community of diverse leaders and build a recurring workshop that helped them find their purpose?** I was part of many leadership communities in my 20s that were usually 80% men and mostly people from the USA. I wanted a leadership community to exist that would actually be truly diverse, with at least 50% women, and with people from all over the planet. So in 2013, I co-founded Hive (www.hive.org), a diverse global community of purpose-driven leaders. We've had over 3,600 graduates from 135 countries complete our three day *Designing Your Life* workshop -- and we've hosted these workshops in nine countries so far including USA, Canada, Germany, Romania, India, Pakistan, Nigeria, Kenya, and Rwanda. Though we had to slow down a bit during Covid, in the last year we've had events in the USA and Africa and are still going strong.

5. **Could I try nearly every plant medicine in 36 months?** - From 2015 to 2018, I tried many different plant medicines as part of ceremonies in California, New England, Costa Rica, Mexico, and Bali. I became fascinated by these entheogens and experienced tremendous personal growth during this time. I tried ayahuasca, peyote, mescaline, san pedro, sassafras, White Lily, MDMA, iboga, LSD, psilocybin, and 5-MeO-DMT—all of which have either been used in indigenous spiritual ceremonies as sacraments for thousands of years or have been clinically shown to reduce depression and PTSD and have benefits for creative ideation. The only one I've never tried is the toad medicine Kambo, and I have a feeling that its turn will come soon enough. If I were to do it all over again, I would simply spread out the experiences a bit more and limit usage to once per quarter so that I had time to fully integrate each experience. More than that can cause a bit of instability in my own experience. These days, I limit my usage to just 2-3 ceremonies per year, as I truly value the consistency within myself that sometimes these medicines can disrupt.

6. **Experiment #6 - Could I actually find my wife at Burning Man?** - My good friend Bear Kittay met his wife, Katiyana, at Burning Man in 2012, and I was always enthralled by their love and story. Starting in 2016, when I was 32, I was ready to find my long-term partner. So, I created an experiment: could I find my wife at Burning Man within

---

[14] HBS Case Study - Providing Liquidity for Shareholders of Privately Held iContact
https://store.hbr.org/product/secondmarket-providing-liquidity-for-shareholders-of-privately-held-icontact/812072

three years of actively searching? My strategy was to get deeply involved with my camp, Camp Mystic, and see if there would be someone within the camp whom I would fall in love with. I began by showing up a week early to the festival to actively participate in building my camp. We worked on various tasks, such as scaffolding, planks, shade structures, domes, rugs, and decor, from 8am to 8pm each day, accompanied by Nahko Bear songs playing in the background. This process of spending a week each year in the desert, engaged in manual construction labor with 60 of my closest friends, proved to be incredibly rewarding. In September 2018, on the very last day of Burning Man, I met my future wife. She had joined our camp to create a mural for the Cosmic Heart Temple. Nine months later, we began dating after reuniting in California during our annual Camp Mystic campout. Two years later, on September 7, 2022, we were married. Thank you Camp Mystic. ☑

***Pro Tip on Finding an Extraordinary Romantic Partner:** I highly recommend this strategy to anyone looking for an incredible long term partner to start a family with. Get deeply involved in a single community (whether it's a church community, Burning Man community, sports community, arts community, dance community, whatever) and develop an earned reputation as a high-integrity leader of that community. Then you'll be first to meet all the incredible people who come through -- and more importantly everyone in the community will know you're looking for someone special and they can help connect you with extraordinary people with similar dreams. It's not an overnight solution if you're super picky like me -- but within 36 months of me getting deeply involved with Camp Mystic, my Burning Man camp, I met "the one."*

7. **Could I help start an international living community in Bali?** - In November 2020, my wife Morgan and I had just gotten married and had moved to Bali. It was our dream to someday raise our children in a diverse international community where our kids could run safely around without needing supervision. During a hot tub session at The Istana in Uluwatu (a major Bali hangout for biohackers) -- we met Raio, a DJ, who introduced us to Sergey -- one of the founders of a new living community in Bali that was about to get started called Nuanu. We got involved, started hosting cacao ceremonies at our house for the initial collaborators, and started putting together decks and dreams for what it would be like to someday build a community there, and went on a team retreat on a pirate ship near Lombok (ask me about that story if you ever see me). Nuanu is 108 acres so far and located on the west coast of Bali, just 20 minutes north of Canggu. Nuanu has the goal of getting 2,000+ residents to live there by 2026. As of publication, Nuanu is now open to its first few hundred residents and has plans to achieve its goal of 2,000 residents just in time for its goal. Nuanu is a home for leaders, creators, and makers. They are "re-thinking systems and developing a game-changing future destination, moving beyond sustainability to thriveability with a regenerative mindset for living and working." You can learn more and get involved at www.nuanu.com.

8. **Could I start a weekly newsletter on digital assets and pass 100k subscribers?** - In December 2020 the price of one Bitcoin passed $20,000. This caught my attention, as this was the highest price ever recorded during the prior bull market of 2017-2018. As I've been involved in building web 2.0 software companies since 2002 - I became really passionate about web3 and especially Ethereum, a blockchain that anyone can build applications on top of. I started writing a weekly newsletter sharing everything I

was learning about blockchains, digital assets, programmable money, and decentralized finance. Over the last few years, the newsletter has grown to over 100,000 subscribers and has become one of the largest weekly newsletters in the institutional crypto market. We summarize the news, reports, and funding deals each week. This is a good example of turning passion into a side project and later into a sustainable entrepreneurial business.

9. **Could we intentionally get pregnant on our one year wedding anniversary?**
We got married (the first time) in a small 14-person ceremony on Lake Tapps, Washington on September 7, 2020. A year later, on our one year anniversary, we created a very intentional six hour sex temple together where we wrote down our dreams and intentions for the next year of our marriage and then entered into our red lit room filled with massage oil and sexy music and proceeded to make love for hours. One of the intentions we wrote down that day was to get pregnant. Four weeks later, we found out that we were four weeks pregnant with our son, Apollo. Apollo was conceived, beautifully out of deep love, on our first wedding anniversary.

*Our wedding ceremony on Lake Tapps, WA in Sep 2020*

10. **Could I start a stuffed animal company with my wife?** - In Spring of 2021, Morgan and I were living in Bali. She started drawing for me a new mythical creature each day (she's an artist). She did this for 137 days in a row. I started taking photos of them and turning them into art NFTs on OpenSea. We called them LuvMonsters. Each has its own mythology. I turned one of Morgan's more famous creations, Llamacorn Angel, into a stuffed animal as a Christmas gift for her in 2021. We were walking around the SXSW festival in Austin, TX in March 2022 when person after person asked, "Where can I get one of those Llamacorns?" So we decided to turn it into a business. We incorporated LuvMonsters, Inc. and made our first three stuffed animals for Llamacorn Angel, Slinky Sloth, and Alpaca Cupcake. Check them out on Amazon. Now these characters are getting ready to be featured in an animated movie! Anything is possible if you keep going after your dreams!

*Our first three stuffed animals we made together for LuvMonsters*

11. **Could we start a band with my friends and publish on Spotify?** - We decided to make a song for each LuvMonster and put the songs inside each animal and also online. We gather our friends about once per month and make improvised music together. We have 14 published songs so far. Search for "LuvMonsters" on Spotify. I'm Mr. LuvBubble. I'm particularly fond of the songs: Llamacorn Fan Club and Alpaca Cupcake. I'm looking forward to these songs someday being in a Disney movie about the LuvMonsters. We sure love to make life fun!

12. **Could we start an annual festival for our friends?** - In May 2022 we attended a small festival with 80 friends called Mostly Woke and figured, we can do this! So for our big wedding celebration in 2022, we invited 175 friends and threw a two day festival on a 10 acre ranch in Drippings Springs, TX. We called it LuvBubble (after Morgan's artist name). Now, every October we host LuvBubble for about 150-200 of our closest friends. We have a blast with it--and it breaks even each year.

13. **Could we educate our baby through curiosity, play, & adventure?** - Apollo (the namesake for this book) was born in Austin, TX on June 14, 2022. We let his curiosity guide his learning (like Maria Montessori taught). When he wants to learn about vikings, we go to Scandinavia and take a ship through the Fjords of Norway. When he wants to learn about robots, we build one together. When he wants to learn about birds, we go bird watching in Costa Rica for a week. We know we're lucky to be able to give him this direct experience-based education. We count our blessings every day. The principle remains regardless of income -- let your children learn through their desire and curiosity -- with around half of their learning time happening outside exploring nature and the world rather than inside a classroom. We're designing his education to be based on the four principles of curiosity, play, adventure, and nature.

14. **Could I lose 30 pounds in three months?** - Nearly every night during Morgan's pregnancy, she would ask me to make her a roast beef wrap or a venison sandwich. Since she needed the calories to nourish Apollo inside her, I generously added butter and mayonnaise. And because these 10 pm snacks were so delicious, I always made one for myself too. The outcome was predictable: I went from 160 pounds at conception to 190 pounds at birth. The stress of pregnancy and childbirth affects both partners, and it certainly affected me. After Morgan gave birth, I had had enough of

being an overweight American Fuckface and decided it was time for a change. My doctor prescribed me an appetite suppressant called Semaglutide, which was originally used for diabetes but had recently gained popularity in Hollywood for helping actors slim down before movies. In just 90 days, through a combination of a good diet, daily exercise, and Semaglutide, I went from 190 pounds to 160 pounds. The experiment was successful. Since then, I have managed to further reduce my weight to 145 pounds and maintain it solely through a good diet and daily exercise. Currently, I am using Tirzepatide, which has proven to be even more effective than Semaglutide.

15. **Could I learn to make love for hours without needing to orgasm?** This one took a while for me to learn, twenty-three years to be precise. I first had sex in the year 2000 with my high school girlfriend. For many years in college and afterward, sex was usually a 15-20 minute activity where the male orgasm was prioritized over the female orgasm. I didn't even realize how selfish I was being. Fast forward to 2023, and I was in Bali, finally taking Tantra lessons and learning how to become a "Tantric Sex God" and give a woman the cathartic sensual experience of her lifetime. Through working directly with a Tantra teacher in early 2023 in Bali, I was able to practice "edging" -- getting very close to orgasm but not ejaculating, over and over. Each time I'd get close, I'd slow down, guide the energy up my spine (with her help), and be able to continue onwards. Now I can go for hours in our weekly temple sessions -- and I have a MUCH happier wife. I write about this more later in this book in the love and sexuality section.

16. **Could we live in 4 countries in one year, with a baby?**
In 2023, as I was editing this book--Morgan and I decided we would spend 3 months per country in four places. Apollo was between 6 and 18 months old during this year. We picked Austin (USA), Ubud (Bali), Tamarindo (Costa Rica), and Sunshine Coast (Australia). Apollo got his passport when he was five weeks old and we haven't looked back since. Suffice to say--this was one of the best years of our life. We met incredible people -- lived in 80-85 degree weather nearly the entire year -- and made extraordinary memories with our baby Apollo. Start living life now.

What are the experiments you want to run in your life? And <u>when are you going to do them?</u>

## Self-Discipline - The Key Habit of Winners

"The more you deliver on what you promised to yourself, the more your confidence will grow to realize even more challenging enterprises." - Robin Sharma

As Jocko Willink, Jiu-Jitsui Black belt & Navy SEAL trainer says, "Discipline equals freedom."

Discipline = Freedom

Self-discipline is simply the habit of actually doing what you tell yourself you're going to do. It's the habit of follow-through and of consistency.

In my own life, I've found that the most successful people are those who:

1. Clarify internally what they want and have crystal clear big goals
2. Write down the habits and actions needed to get there
3. Get others aligned toward the roadmap if needed
4. Consistently take the actions in alignment with the roadmap
5. Stay committed for years to the goal, while varying the actions as they learn more about what works.

As Robin Sharma says, "Consistency is the DNA of any great athlete." My goal, which I am consistently working towards, is writing a bestselling book. What am I committed to doing consistently?

I am committed to going to my gym and wellness center every single day at 9 am and completing my miracle morning, which includes strength training, swimming, and sauna.

In Austin, my center is Lifetime Austin. In Bali, my center is either Titi Batu Ubud or Amo Spa. In Nosara, I go to the Bodhi Tree Gym, followed by the sauna and plunge at Outpost and Plunge Nosara. In Sunshine Coast, Australia, my center is the Good Life Community Center. The key is to find a place that offers everything needed so you don't have to drive to multiple places.

After my morning workout, swim, sauna, and cold plunge, I usually have scrambled eggs or chicken salad before beginning to write for 2-3 hours. On weekday afternoons, I engage in CEO coaching calls to earn income for our family. In the evenings, starting from 5 pm onward, I am dedicated to family time.

By looking at my weekly schedule in visual form, you can see my own consistency. The schedule below allows me to allocate approximately 15 hours per week to writing, 15 hours per week to Magic Year Course Building, and 30 hours per week to family and friends.

| Day | Morning | Afternoon | Evening |
| --- | --- | --- | --- |
| **Monday** | Workout & Writing | Course Building | Family & Friend Time |
| **Tuesday** | Workout & Writing | Course Building | Family & Friend Time |
| **Wednesday** | Workout & Writing | Course Building | Family & Friend Time |
| **Thursday** | Workout & Writing | Course Building | Family & Friend Time |
| **Friday** | Workout & Writing | Family & Friend Time | Family & Friend Time |
| **Saturday** | Workout & Writing | Family & Friend Time | Family & Friend Time |
| **Sunday** | Workout & Writing | Family & Friend Time | Family & Friend Time |

My Weekly Schedule

It's the consistency and level of mastery in your work that matter more than the number of hours. I have designed my life for maximum happiness, not for maximum work hours. As Robin Sharma says, "Small, consistent, and regular always beats all fire and bravado at the beginning with a gigantic flameout at the end."

This consistent schedule, executed with joy, flow, and discipline, and with frequent travel adventures incorporated, has allowed me to thrive. When my family and I travel for **workcations**, we usually prefer flying on a Saturday, giving us Sunday to settle into our new location before starting the work week on Monday. We typically stay at least a week wherever we go to ensure maximum consistency during the work week.

*Workcations - Taking a long vacation (1+ months) where you take your laptop and work during the work week and travel on the weekends. Common among remote workers.*

It is crucial to design your life for maximum happiness, creativity, and health, rather than focusing on the maximum number of hours worked.

If you prioritize maximum happiness, creativity, and health in your life, you will soon discover that working 20-25 hours per week on something deeply meaningful in a sustainable and enjoyable way can lead to greater financial success and overall happiness, compared to grinding out 50+ hours per week on something soul-sucking.

As Albert Einstein once said, "Only those who devote themselves to a cause with their whole strength and soul can be true masters. For this reason, mastery demands all of a person."

Get your daily discipline on lock. Let your higher self dom your lower self into blissful submission. Learn to love it. And become a master.

**Action Item #28: Schedule a Workcation**
Schedule at least a 2 week workcation (on your own or with your partner/family) to somewhere you've never been before where you work during the workweek and travel and adventure on the weekends.

# The Secret to Self-Confidence

In my experience, there are two major types of people in the world...

1. People who do what they say they are going to do
2. People who don't

People Who Do What They Say They're Going to Do

People Who Don't Do What They Say They're Going to Do

Be in the first circle. Don't be someone who makes empty promises to themselves and others. Actually do what you commit to. Actually follow through. Actually do what you tell yourself you will do.

Be someone with **inner integrity**.

*Inner Integrity - Following through and doing what you commit to yourself that you're going to do (i.e. exercise daily, lose 20 pounds, stop eating sugar, spend time with your family, etc.). By doing what you say you're going to do, you gain inner confidence.*

Integrity with yourself will change everything. Yes, actually doing what you say you're going to do TO YOURSELF is the foundational principle for an excellent life. You see, actually doing what YOU commit TO YOURSELF is the foundation of self-confidence.

### The Foundation of Self-Confidence

Actually doing what you commit to yourself.

Robin Sharma has a great quote on the importance of getting commitments made to yourself on lock first... "Even more important than the consistent keeping of the promises you make to others are the self-promises you set and then keep for yourself. Practice delivering on these and you'll experience explosive gains in your willpower, confidence and talent to get giant things done. You'll also grow beautifully in the honor and self-respect that then turns into the self-love that causes you to stand steadfast against any obstacles that threaten to stop the making of your mesmerizing movement."

So actually run that fucking marathon, lose that 20 pounds, wake up early to finish a book, climb that volcano at sunrise, complete that course, get that black belt in karate, go do your bucket list, finish that New Year's resolution, make beautiful love to your partner, launch that side business, and reach your savings and investments targets.

The self-discipline of following-through on your commitments to yourself will change everything in your life for the better. Let's repeat this important principle for emphasis.

> The self-discipline of following-through on your commitments to yourself will change everything in your life for the better.

Of course, this will require making commitments thoughtfully. Many people go around people-pleasing and saying yes to anything they are asked to do -- then constantly running late on everything -- greatly decreasing their own happiness, effectiveness, and workability of their own lives. Don't be an **overcommiter**.

*Overcommitters - People pleasers who say yes to everyone but then constantly don't do what they say they are going to do because they are overwhelmed and stretched too thin. It's better to only commit to your Fuck Yeses and then do what you say you'll do.*

These over-committers are sabotaging their own lives by not thoughtfully making commitments -- wasting their own time and the time of others. Be like Tom below, not Ollie.

| Thoughtful Tom | Over-Committed Ollie |
| --- | --- |
| Makes commitments thoughtfully | People pleaser |
| Says "no" or "not right now" a lot | Says yes to everyone |
| Willing to disappoint people upfront by saying no | Disappoints people more in the end by leading people on then not delivering |
| Shows up on time/early | Shows up late to everything |
| Delivers quality work on time | Delivers shitty work late or not at all |
| Believes in himself | Lacks self-confidence |
| Knows what he says matters | Gives lip service, doesn't follow through |

And if it helps, hire a weekly **accountability coach** to get on a 30 minute Zoom call per week and check-up on:

1) What you want to achieve
2) What you committed to
3) What you actually did
4) What results you got, tangibly and emotionally

My wife, Morgan, is a good example of someone who is fanatical about consistency when she really gets committed to something.

- She recently completed a 43-day body cleanse that involved taking 18 different supplements and doing three different liver flushes (those aren't fun)!

- She's painted over 1,500 paintings in the last ten years (yes that's about 3 per week), becoming a master of her artistic craft.

- She's now obsessed daily about creating a storyboard for a LuvMonsters movie -- a movie she will be working on with a major animated film studio to turn into a feature-length film.

As Robin Sharma so beautifully writes in *The Everyday Hero Manifesto*, "Consistency is the Mother of Mastery and persistence breeds the longevity demanded to become legendary."

**Action Item #29: Write Down Your Commitments to Self**
Write down all of the commitments you've currently made to yourself. Then, grade yourself A-F on how you're actually doing against the commitment you made. Then, rewrite the commitments that you are choosing to renew and that you are committing 100% to completing successfully on time. Finally, communicate with the people whose choices impact.

## Honor Your Word To Others

"So simple. So *transformational*. So unusual, these days. Try very hard not to make even one promise that you cannot keep, to be the kind of creative leader, exceptional performer and outstanding human being who follows through on each promise you offer, whether it's to deliver spellbinding quality on a project (before a certain date), send the book you told a top client you'd send them at a lunch meeting, start the running group you told your friends you'd set up, or have a family dinner at least three nights a week as you vowed you would. Each promise you keep increases the trustworthiness you have in the mind and heart of the person on the other side of the promise. Do what you say you will do, without fail, and you'll soon become a hero in the eyes of all who know you. The esteem, loyalty and admiration they have for you will soar." - Robin Sharma

In an organization without integrity, nothing works. Meetings start and finish late, projects are delayed, budgets are exceeded, people make promises they can't keep, accountability is unclear, and teams fail to follow through on their commitments. Leaders also fail to uphold their word.

Similarly, with people without integrity nothing works. Their rent is late and they are often getting kicked out of their homes. Their credit is bad and they aren't able to buy a home. They are late for important appointments, upsetting both friends and colleagues. They rarely get promotions, as they are known for not following through on their commitments. For a person, integrity is a matter of keeping their word.

You can be a person of integrity, and enjoy the benefits of things working in your life, when you do what you say you're going to do. And when you can't do what you said you'd do- you communicate, clean it up, and make up for it right away. This practice allows you to **honor your word**, even if you can't *keep your word*.

*Honoring your word - Doing your very best to do what you say you're going to do every single time. And when you can't, communicate early and more than make up for it.*

Surprisingly, you will gain a great degree of trust (and admiration) when you do not keep your word but you do **honor your word** – by being sure to communicate early and more than make up for it.

You'll also be much happier if you always honor your word – and will start noticing that others in your life will also start honoring theirs more often.

It's like the babysitter who gives you 24 hours notice when she cannot come and 20% off next time (she honored her word) instead of the one who gives you two hours notice and then ghosts you (she didn't honor her word).

It's important to note, that unless you give your word to virtually nothing, you will not be able to always keep it. Leadership is all about giving your word to something that you may not fully know how to accomplish yet. You have to start the journey to discover the next step.

So yes, you do sometimes have to give your word and commitment to things you're not 100% sure you can do. But the key is to always honor your word.

Some people think it is okay to do a cost/benefit analysis of honoring their word—and only if the benefits outweigh the costs do they do what they say they will do.

While this may work in the short term, in the mid-term no one will trust you or like you or be willing to work with you. So always honor your word. When you do this, your word becomes powerful. And you start believing in yourself.

The time to do a cost/benefit analysis is when you are considering giving your word, not after. When you give your word, you are in effect saying "I will make this happen."

Consider, what would your life be like if…

1. You do what you said you would do and you do it on time

2. You do what you know to do, and you did it the way it was meant to be done, and you did it on time; and

3. Whenever you realized you were not going to do the above, you communicated that to the relevant parties and cleaned up any mess you made.

Back in 2014 I was part of Werner Erhard and Michael Jensen's *Being a Leader & The Effective Exercise of Leadership* course. The above section was inspired by their course. I give enormous credit to Werner for creating both this course as well as the original EST program and the Landmark trainings. I recommend everyone do the Landmark Forum and Landmark Advanced Course for a wonderful course on how to live an extraordinary life.

**Action Item #30: Write Down All Your Commitments to Others**
Write down all of the commitments you've currently made to others. Then, grade yourself A-F on how you're actually doing against the commitment you made. On page two, rewrite the commitments that you are choosing to renew and that you are committing 100% to completing successfully on time. Get in touch with anyone where you need to adjust your commitments.

# Preparation - Winning Before the Game Begins

*"My work isn't done tonight. My work was done three months ago, and I just have to show up."* - Whitney Cummings, Stand Up Comedian

High school cross country is a sport that involves running three miles as quickly as possible.. My best 3 mile time was 17 minutes (5:40 per mile). Where I went to school, the overall team time was calculated by adding up the times of the top six finishers from your team, which you want to be as low as possible.

I was able to make varsity at my high school with that time and ended up being the 3rd or 4th fastest in my school.

By my final year, I knew that it mattered very little what I did on Saturday (when I ran the race). No matter how much resolve or perfect pre-race diet I had, my time would only change by ~30 seconds based on what I did on race day.

What actually mattered more was the preparation I had put in in the 90 days prior to race day. That is what took many minutes off my 3 mile time.

In July, when we began running, my time would usually be around 22 minutes. It took running 50 miles per week for 12 straight weeks (plus sprints and leg lifts) to get my time down to 17 minutes by October, when the races counted.

It wasn't the 3 miles in Saturday's race that really mattered. It's the 50 on Monday-Friday that made my cardiovascular and muscular system ready.

Preparation was everything. Absolutely everything.

I am writing this sentence on January 29, 2023, while in Ubud, Bali. What's today's date that you're reading this? The preparation I was doing from 2002-2022 led me to write this chapter in 2023, which then finally came to you years in the future. Preparation in the past creates the results of the moment.

Well-known comics and politicians often experience the same thing when preparing their joke material or stump speeches. The real preparation is done a few months before the outcome is achieved. In the case of Barack Obama, it was his 2004 Democratic Presidential Convention speech, when he was a barely known junior Senator from Illinois, that propelled him to the presidency four years later.

I took this lesson into business when I started my company, iContact, the following year in college. Before every single big meeting, including new employee meetings, recruiting meetings, and venture capital pitches (roughly 1,000 meetings over 10 years), I religiously researched who I was meeting with -- reviewing their LinkedIn profiles and anything I could find about them before the meeting.

My Executive Assistant, Michelle, would often make me dossiers on key people I'd review before in-person meetings. Before I went into a meeting, I would make sure I knew what their goal was, what my goal was, and what a win/win outcome would look like.

I also memorized the names of all 300 employees using flash cards with photos so that when I walked around the office, I'd be able to say hi to every single person with their name. We then rolled out digital flash cards to all employees and encouraged everyone to learn everyone's name. This made a huge difference inside the company in terms of trust and the ability to collaborate across teams.

As young Abraham Lincoln once wrote, dreaming of someday being of service to his country: ""I will study and prepare myself, and someday my chance will come." The day came indeed.

So in the silent moments before the big game or the big meeting -- do your inner work. It's in that work that all the results will come.

It's the preparation that matters. Your big day is coming.

## Do This Before You Go To Sleep

Preparing for the next day starts with getting great sleep (at least 8-9 hours). Before I go to sleep, I have three habits that come after I brush my teeth...

1. I tell my loved ones (spouse/children, etc.) I love them
2. I write down 3 things I was grateful for that day
3. I write down a problem to reflect on while I'm asleep.

I then take some melatonin, put on my earplugs and eye mask, and head to sleep. This last action -- writing down a problem to reflect on while I'm asleep has proven especially useful. As Thomas Edison said, "Never go to sleep without a request to your subconscious." In these late night requests to myself, I've asked for:

- The solution to a sticky HR situation with an employee
- The solution to the title of this book (I went through 100+ title options).
- The solution to a growth challenge we were having with our son
- Guidance on how to talk to my wife about something that was challenging me
- Guidance on whether or not to accept a certain publisher
- Guidance on how I can be kinder
- Guidance on how I can better serve my CEO coaching clients

Reid Hoffman, at LinkedIn and Graylock fame, does the same thing. He writes down the biggest challenge he's currently facing right before he goes to bed and then lets his latent mind go to work. Then, when he wakes up (according to *Tools of Titans*), he journals in his notebook any potential solutions when his brain is best primed. He then writes down the gratitudes he has in his life. Talk about a great start to a Miracle Morning!

**Action Item #31: Pre-Sleep Ritual**
As a nightly pre-sleep ritual, write down 3 things you are grateful for and a particularly challenging problem you are facing in school, work, or life that you'd like to solve in your subconscious while you sleep tonight. Do this for 30 straight days.

# Writing Down Your Values

"If it's not right, do not do it. If it's not true, do not say it." - Marcus Aurelius

If you get only two things right in your life, get your habits and your values right. Now that you know how to get your **habits stack** locked -- let's create your **values stack**.

*Values Stack - The current values that you actively work to embody in your life (i.e. kindness, helpfulness, presence, positive energy, playfulness, etc.)*

Values create a system through which you interact with others. You might value showing up on time, being kind, and being honest, for example.
As you consider your own values, let's look at the values of other societies and then certain well known individuals throughout history.
Let's look at a few global **values systems** to begin with. Across many spiritual traditions, a key guideline is kindness and caring for others.

*Values Systems - Collections of values popularized in spiritual and cultural traditions. Examples include Tikkun Olam the Jewish concept of repairing the world and Ahimsa, the Sanskrit philosophy of do no harm.*

| Origin | Concept Name | Description |
| --- | --- | --- |
| Judaism | Tikkun Olam | The concept of repairing the world |
| Sanskrit | Ahimsa | A philosophy of do no harm |
| Confucian | Li | A set of norms that teaches brotherliness and community |
| Islamic | Ummah | A perspective on a supranational community |
| Christian | Golden Rule | A practice of treating others as you want to be treated |
| South Africa | Ubuntu | A spirit of cooperation between people of all colors and creeds |

Each of these concepts has led millions (and sometimes billions) of people toward living a more values-centered life. Most of these values systems are centered around treating all people with kindness and expanding your **empathy circle** as widely as possible.

*Empathy Circle - The collection of identity layers that you have empathy for. Those with the least empathy only value themselves. Those with the most empathy value all people and all life.*

**EXPAND YOUR EMPATHY CIRCLE AND CARE FOR ALL PEOPLE**

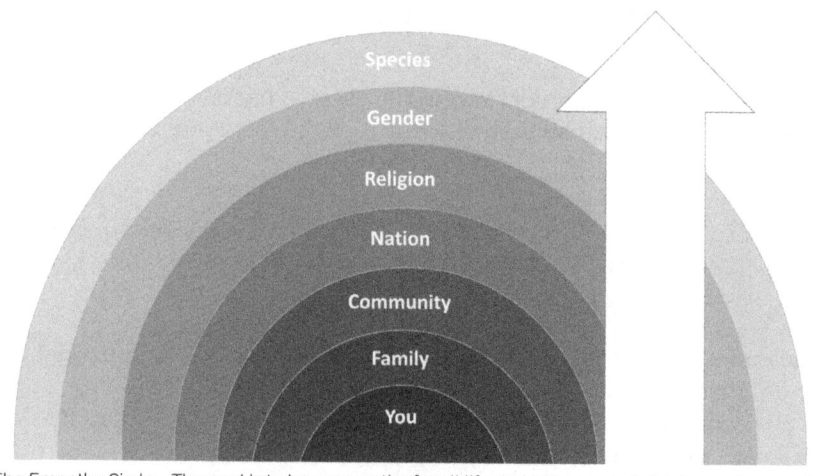

Species
Gender
Religion
Nation
Community
Family
You

The Empathy Circle - The goal is to have empathy for all life and to transcend division and separation

Yes, compassion for all sentient beings is definitely the way. As futurist Ray Kurzweil says, "To be human is to have the ability to transcend our egocentric preconditioning and care so deeply for our children, partners, friends, or even strangers that we would put their interests above our own no matter what it might cost us personally."

As you prepare to select your own set of values, we can also learn a lot from the values systems of some well-known people who did their best to publish and then live in adherence with their values. Let's study some of the greats throughout history as we build our own **values stack**. Here are Confucius' five values.

### Confucius' Values Stack

1. Benevolence
2. Wisdom
3. Integrity
4. Righteousness
5. Ritual

And here were Benjamin Franklin's 13 Values...

### Ben Franklin's Values Stack

1. **Temperance:** Eat not to dullness; drink not to elevation.
2. **Order:** Let all your things have their places; let each part of your business have its time.
3. **Resolution:** Resolve to perform what you ought; perform without fail what you resolve.
4. **Frugality:** Make no expense but to do good to others or yourself; i.e., waste nothing.
5. **Moderation:** Avoid extremes; forbear resenting injuries so much as you think they deserve.
6. **Industry:** Lose no time; be always employed in something useful; cut off all unnecessary actions.
7. **Cleanliness:** Tolerate no uncleanliness in body, clothes, or habitation.
8. **Tranquility:** Be not disturbed at trifles, or at accidents common or unavoidable.
9. **Silence:** Speak not but what may benefit others or yourself; avoid trifling conversation.
10. **Sincerity:** Use no hurtful deceit; think innocently and justly, and, if you speak, speak accordingly.
11. **Justice:** Wrong none by doing injuries, or omitting the benefits that are your duty.
12. **Chastity:** Rarely use venery but for health or offspring, never to dullness, weakness, or the injury of your own or another's peace or reputation.
13. **Humility:** Imitate Jesus and Socrates.

So, what are your own values? Once you write them down and commit to them, your life will be enriched, and you will sleep soundly at night knowing you are living with a conscious set of values. You can see my fifty personal values below. Take a look as you go through the exercise of writing down your own values. There 50 personal values are my **values stack**. These are the ones that I hold dearly and do my best to always live by. If you're reading this in a print edition, I encourage you to grab a pen and **circle the values below that really resonate with you**.

## My Values Stack

1. Acceptance - I shall accept what has already occurred
2. Action - Though deliberate & careful I shall have a bias toward action
3. Adaptation - I shall maintain in a state able to flow, learn & modify myself to fit new surroundings or occurrences
4. Analysis - I shall analyze what I do and do not do and attempt to derive inherent laws, axioms, tenants and guideposts
5. Best Effort - I shall put forth my full and best effort on what I strive to accomplish and create, within the boundaries of proper physical & mental health
6. Care - I shall intentionally wrong no one
7. Challenge - I shall often challenge myself & step outside my comfort zone so as to reach worthy goals
8. Collaboration - I shall work collaboratively with others who are better than I am at what they do
9. Commitment - I shall uphold my commitments and under-promise and over-deliver
10. Communication - I shall make it a priority to learn to communicate extremely well with others.
11. Confidence - I shall always be confident & optimistic and set my goals high
12. Contentment - I shall be only where I am and savor everything about that moment
13. Deferred Consumption - I shall save and invest today so as to gain for tomorrow.
14. Detail - I shall not dally needlessly in detail but examine to the full extent needed
15. Diversity - I shall recognize the uniqueness and humanity of those who differ from myself.
16. Environmental Consciousness - Though I shall promote the mastery and utilization of nature for the betterment of living conditions of humans, I shall never forget that the Earth should be treated as precious and that sustainability must be required if we are to survive as a species, and that there is inherent value in all species. I shall conserve and protect nature and ensure it remains for my grandchildren
17. Focus - I shall recognize that while I can do anything I can't do everything.
18. Forgiveness - I shall forgive those who have mended ways including myself
19. Generosity - I shall give to others however I am best and most able
20. Health - I shall maintain my health and eat, sleep, & exercise in such a manner as to maintain a high level of energy.
21. Honesty - I shall be honest and fully forthright in all representations of and deliberations with myself, and truthful about all that I have witnessed
22. Humility - I shall not be afraid to ask for help and not assume myself above another.
23. Industry - I shall lose no time and always be active or employed in creating or experiencing something useful. Reflection, relaxation, sleep, family time, and adventure shall definitely be included in the definition of useful.
24. Integrity - I shall act with integrity and in alignment with what I say I will do.
25. Joy - I shall always remember that "seriousity is poo" and strive to have lots of silly fun with my friends and family.
26. Kindness - I shall live a life of kindness & compassion. I shall wrong no one and be friendly toward all people.
27. Learning - I shall be a lifelong voracious learner.

28. Listening - I shall strive to listen & understand before I speak
29. Mentorship - I shall give the knowledge I have and will gain to others, as well as seek out mentors from whom I can learn.
30. Optimism - I shall always see the glass as half full
31. Organization - I shall keep my life & belongings in order while keeping space for exuberance & creativity
32. Passion - I shall always strive for that which I believe
33. Perseverance - I shall not give up nor give in too soon as long as I feel a goal is worthy of the effort. I will continue with tenacity on what I believe in.
34. Planning - I shall plan for my life and upcoming events and meetings. I shall turn my bucket list of desired experiences into real lived experiences.
35. Positivity - I shall be positive during all times and believe in the power of a positive mental attitude. I shall eliminate negative energy as my body is a temple that houses my spirit.
36. Preparation - I will be prepared for every meeting I have. I shall attempt to enter each situation with an intellectual framework primed & ready. I will also prepare my body for lifelong health.
37. Presence - I shall focus my complete attention on the single individual I am speaking with
38. Punctuality - I shall be on time
39. Reflection - I shall take moments to review what has been done and examine society as well as my goals, habits, and actions. I will live an examined life. I will value what I can learn from the mistakes I made. I shall strive to learn from my mistakes and to not make them twice
40. Sincerity - I shall be sincere and only talk about people in an empowering way.
41. Spirituality - I shall realize I am a very small part of the universe and have great gratitude for life. I shall realize that all of consciousness is one -- and that all beings are one. I shall work to end the false narrative of good vs. evil.
42. Solitude - I shall have a period of peace, meditation, and solitude at the beginning of each day in which I shall give thanks and envision the day ahead
43. Spontaneity - I shall perform weekly either an act of kindness or an activity which I have never done before
44. Superficiality - I shall not focus on the outer but on the inner
45. Teaching - I shall transfer both knowledge & energy in teaching. I shall work to capture and share the lessons I have learned.
46. Tranquility - I shall not be disturbed by trifles or by that which is not truly important.
47. Transparency - In order to make a positive impact on the lives of my readers, I shall live a public life and share the contents of my dreams & plans in my writings.
48. Travel - I shall make a priority to see and explore the world.
49. Truth - I shall always tell the truth.
50. Work Ethic - I shall work both hard and intelligently and not leave for tomorrow what can be done today.

**Action Item #32: Write Down Your Values**
Read my 50 values above. Circle or make note of any you want to commit to for yourself. Then come up with a list of at least 10 values you want to live by.

I'll end this section on habits and values with a quote from the great Mahatma Gandhi on how your habits and values become your destiny. "Your beliefs become your thoughts. Your thoughts become your words. Your words become your actions. Your actions become your habits, Your habits become your values. Your values become your destiny." Wise words from a wise man.

## Recommended Books on Habits

- *The Seven Habits of Highly Effective People* by Steven Covey
- *The Power of Habit* by Charles Duhigg
- *Atomic Habits* by James Clear
- *Tools of Titans* by Tim Ferriss
- *The Four Hour Workweek* by Tim Ferriss
- *The 5AM Club* by Robin Sharma

## Key Outcome from This Chapter

**List of Habits You're 100% Committed To** - Make a list of all the habits you're 100% committed to keeping on a daily, weekly, and monthly basis. Commit to them fully. Share them with a friend or partner. Hold yourself fully accountable to them. Reward yourself when you achieve them consistently.

# HABITS CHAPTER ACTION ITEMS

1. **Habits List** - Make a list of all the habits you'd like to start, stop, and keep. Then implement this list for at least 30 days, actually doing all the new habits and stopping the bad habits.

2. **Time Redirection** - Add up all the hours you spend each week wasting time. Put the extra time instead into reading, exercising, writing, creating, walking in nature, learning, and spending time with people you actually find inspiring.

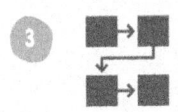

3. **Miracle Morning Flowchart** - Draw out a simple flowchart of how you want the first 120 minutes of your day. Begin to design your own Miracle Morning routine -- and actually start doing it.

4. **Habit Tracker** - Start using a daily habit tracking tool like the one mentioned in this chapter. Every single day, take 5 minutes to fill it out as part of your before-bed night routine. Do this for at least 30 days to lock in the habit.

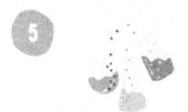

5. **Life Experiments** - Read the list of my life experiments. Write down at least three life experiments you'd like to test over the next year -- then add the dates you want to actually do them to your calendar.

6. **Workcation** - Schedule at least a 2 week workcation (on your own or with your partner/family) to somewhere you've never been before where you work during the workweek and travel and adventure on the weekends.

7. **Commitments to Self** - Write down all of the commitments you've currently made to yourself. Grade yourself A-F on how you're actually doing against the commitment you made. Then, rewrite the commitments that you are choosing to renew and that you are committing 100% to completing successfully on time. Finally, communicate with the people those choices impact.

8. **Commitments to Others** - Write down all of the commitments you've currently made to others. Grade yourself A-F on how you're actually doing against the commitment you made. On page two, rewrite the commitments that you are choosing to renew and that you are committing 100% to completing successfully on time. Get in touch with anyone where you need to adjust your commitments.

9. **Pre-Sleep Ritual** - As a nightly pre-sleep ritual, write down 3 things you are grateful for and a particularly challenging problem you are facing in school, work, or life that you'd like to solve in your subconscious while you sleep tonight. Do this for 30 straight days.

10. **Values List** - Read my 50 values. Circle or make note of any you want to commit to for yourself. Then come up with a list of at least 10 values you want to live by.

# STEP 4

# PEOPLE MAGIC

MAGIC YEAR - 186

# KEY CONCEPTS FROM THE PEOPLE CHAPTER

**1. MASTERWORK** 
The most important contribution you will make in your life to society. For some it's raising kids, for some it's a book or movie, for some it's a scientific advancement, for some it's a painting. Don't let yours die inside of you.

**2. INNER CIRCLE** 
The 10-15 people you spend the most time with. You have to choose your core very very wisely and intentionally (and not be afraid to remove people from your core when needed).

**3. CHOSEN FRIENDS** 
The people you invest in building meaningful long-term relationships with because they are truly extraordinary people who inspire you. While most people end up friends randomly, chosen friends are intentionally sought out, selected, curated, and invested into.

**4. SOUL FAMILY** 
People who are not blood family but you are as close with them as you are with your blood family, if not more. You commonly share a lot of values and dreams with these people.

**5. PADAWAN** 
Sanskrit for "learner." An apprentice or mentee, someone who learns from a Jedi Master.

**6. JEDI** 
A competent, super-connected, and deeply compassionate soul & systems thinker, whose passion has been fully unleashed toward achieving an identified deeply meaningful mission that awakens them with extraordinary focus and immense energy daily.

**7. JEDI MENTORS** 
A person who is operating at an extremely high level of consciousness, skill, and integrity who agrees to be your mentor.

**8. AUTHENTIC SELF** 
Who a person really is once they take off the facade of their work identity. Someone who is fully expressed and living in their purpose.

**9. MASTERMIND GROUP** 
A highly curated and formal group of your best connections who commit to helping each other achieve each of their big goals in life. These groups usually meet in-person monthly.

**10. POSITIVE ENERGY EDGE** 
The huge edge in life, business, and relationships that you gain from going up to people with authentic energy, optimism, and excitement.

**11. PRESENCE** 
Being fully focused on the people you're speaking with rather than in your own head or looking elsewhere. Choose to look people in the eye and actually listen to what they are saying, and magic will happen with your career and goals. Deep presence is the magic of True Kings.

**12. RADICAL TRUTH** 
Choosing the tell the complete truth 100% of the time in all circumstances. Follow this practice in order to greatly simplify your life.

# STEP 4: PEOPLE MAGIC

*"Hang out with people who are living on purpose, who meet their challenges with a "step aside suckers" attitude, who are dating super awesome people, making exactly the kind of money they want to be making (or working toward it) or taking the kind of vacations they, and you, want to be taking, and you'll not only see what's possible for you, too, but you'll have more incentive to follow suit." - Jen Sincero, Author of You Are a Badass*

**YOUR MAGIC YEAR**

| Step | Category |
|---|---|
| 12 | AWAKENING |
| 11 | FAMILY |
| 10 | SEXUALITY |
| 9 | LOVE |
| 8 | COMMUNITY |
| 7 | MONEY |
| 6 | HEALTH |
| 5 | HAPPINESS |
| 4 | PEOPLE |
| 3 | HABITS |
| 2 | GOALS |
| 1 | PURPOSE |

## My Journey With People

Finding your tribe of curiously weird, creative, and unique people like you can take some time. But it's easier if you look in the right place. I've spent 20 years building a personal network of unique creatives who think differently than most. When I look at my closest friends -- they are all either entrepreneurs, healers, artists -- or both.

I am friends with a disproportionate number of tantra coaches, reiki healers, massage therapists, clothing designers, conscious musicians, travel bloggers, personal growth authors, venture capitalists, and technology entrepreneurs. There's just something about creative people that I love. People who know how to get into flow and give their master gifts to the world are my type of people.

I've been fortunate to have been surrounded by loving parents, caring mentors, and extraordinary people my whole life, from 1984 to today.

I had two loving parents who worked hard, saved up as much as they could, and took me traveling to other countries every other year (giving me a huge advantage in life and in childhood brain development through exposure to cultural complexity).

Then, as an adult, I went to college at a top 30 global university (UNC-Chapel Hill) and then went to graduate school at the top university in the world (Harvard).

Through college and graduate school, I met many well-connected, ambitious, and successful people that I can reach out to when I need encouragement, support, or guidance.

And through my other adventures (Burning Man, Bali, Costa Rica, Envision) and other communities I've been part of (Summit Series, EO, YPO, Mindvalley, Hive), I've been so very lucky to know thousands of truly extraordinary people.

I've been mentored by Marc Benioff, helped Barack Obama execute his digital marketing campaigns, became friends with Tim Ferriss, and danced with billionaires in Ibiza and Black Rock City.

It's been quite a life so far. All due to seeking out and being around people who truly inspire me.

This result of being around people who truly inspire me and carefully building relationships over decades wasn't just an accident, however.

It all came from reading the book *How to Win Friends and Influence People* by Dale Carnegie when I was 17 years old.

Here are some of the lessons I've learned from that book and along the way.

## Surround Yourself With Extraordinary People

*"Surround yourself with relentless humans. People who plan in decades, but live in moments, train like savages, but create like artists, obsess in work, relax in life. People who know this is finite, and choose to play infinite games. Find people climbing up mountains and climb together."* - Zach Pogrom, @BehaviorHack on IG

There's an old saying from Jim Rohn that "you become the average of the five people you spend the most time with." This is exceptionally accurate. Who you surround yourself with is who you become over time.

Just imagine how different you'd become over 5 years if you were person A vs. person B and C vs. person C.

| Person A | Person B | Person C |
|---|---|---|
| Surrounded by childhood friends in his hometown, drinking and smoking and gossiping about others and working jobs he hates just to pay the bills | Surrounded by business mercenaries who sell their soul for the highest price, back out of agreements, think life is all about money and showing off, and deep down feel insecure and unhappy | Surrounded by happy, healthy, kind people who are working on what they love every day and are committed to life mastery |

It's clear that person C would have a much higher chance of becoming a happier person who is in touch with living his soul's purpose and is able to give his gifts and eventually his **masterwork** to the world.

*Masterwork - The most important contribution you will make in your life to society. For some it's raising kids, for some it's a book or movie, for some it's a scientific advancement, for some it's a painting.*

The key is to be sure to give your masterwork to the world before you die – especially critical considering we don't really know when we are going to die. If you died today, what would have been your masterwork?

The heights to which your masterwork can rise (as well as the quality of it) are a direct function of the people around you.

Let's look at the fabulous Robin Sharma quote: "Your inner circle absolutely drives your external mastery." A truer sentence has rarely been written.

Your **inner circle** are the 10-15 people you spend the most time with. You have to choose your inner circle very very wisely and intentionally (and not be afraid to remove people from your core when needed). I am very intentional with the people I go deep with. I like to surround myself with only positive, happy, kind, smart, and adventurous people.

> *Inner Circle - The 10-15 people you spend the most time with. You have to choose your core very very wisely and intentionally (and not be afraid to remove people from your core when needed).*

On the topic of the people you surround yourself with being a huge factor in who you become...

- Zach Pogrom likes to say, ""Surround yourself with people who make extreme goals feel normal. Surround yourself with humans who create their lives. People who change more than they complain. Who create more than they consume. Live actively instead of accepting life as is. Find people changing their potential and sprint together."

- Robin Sharma says, "if you're really serious about rolling at world-class, make sure you regularly hang with human beings who are behaving at such a level of amazingness that you'll never ever be able to catch up to them!"

- Robin also says... "We rise to the level of our conversations, associations and relationships. Your inner circle absolutely drives your external mastery. If you're the most successful person you know, maybe it really is time to get to know some new people."

- Bill George, the HBS Professor and author of *True North* says, "Having people around you who support you gives you the confidence to listen to your inner voice, even when the outsiders are attacking or criticizing you. Your closest confidants give you the resilience to get through hard times and enable you to recognize what is truly important in life."

- Jen Sincero, the author of You Are a Badass says "The people you surround yourself with are excellent mirrors for who you are and how much, or how little, you love yourself."

- Vienna Pharon, a marriage and family therapist says, "Look for the people who can take ownership and accountability. Look for the people who care about how you feel. Look for the people who align their words and their actions. Look for the people who care about what's going on in your inner world. Look for the people who prioritize seeing, hearing, and understanding you."

- Andrew Carnegie, the great Scottish American steel industrialist, has the following on this epitaph of his tombstone, "here lies one who knew how to get around him men who were cleverer than himself."

For me, I mainly look for people who inspire me. People who I think I can really learn from. Personally, I believe that we should only invest our time with people who truly inspire us to be around them. If your friends don't uplift and inspire you, it's time to find new friends!

While every human being is inherently valuable, not EVERY human being has truly "done the work" to master their life. It is these "masters," or at least those "on the path of mastery," that I seek out in my personal life.

This means I can sometimes go years with many acquaintances but only a couple truly close best friends. Here's what I look for in the people I surround myself with:

Positivity, Kindness, Joy, Purpose, Compassion, Passion, Intelligence, Adventurousness

I tend to avoid conspiracy theorists, people who live in a victim mindset, those who are too serious, those who can't see the bigger cosmic picture of why we are here (to learn, grow, be kind, and help), and those who complain a lot.

I look for friends living in the "Hero Mentality" who see the silver lining in every experience and choose to see through the lens that "life is happening FOR you" instead of "life happening TO you."

As Tony Robbins says, "Life is always happening for us, not to us. It's our job to find out where the benefit is. If we do, life is magnificent."

So don't let chance determine who is in your life. Instead, take a proactive approach to designing your community and friendships.

Intentionally seek out amazing people in your life. And instead of "random friends," find "**chosen friends**."

*Chosen Friends - The people you invest in building meaningful long-term relationships with intentionally because they are truly extraordinary people who inspire you. While most people end up friends randomly, chosen friends are intentionally sought out, selected, curated, and invested into.*

MAGIC YEAR - 191

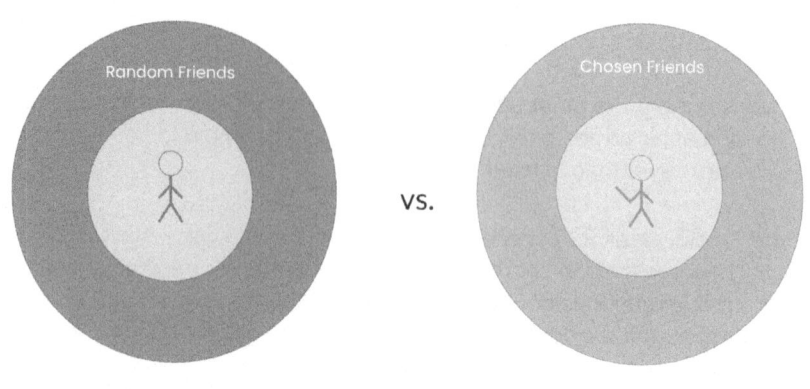

|  Random Friends  |  |  Chosen Friends  |
|:---:|:---:|:---:|
|  (figure)  | vs. | (figure) |
| An ordinary life | | An extraordinary life |

There are about 20 people in my life who keep consistently showing up -- regardless of whether I am in Bali, Austin, or Costa Rica. Some are lovers (my wife and I are in an open relationship, more on that in the love and sexuality sections). Some are colleagues. Some are deep brothers. And some are guides and mentors.

These are the people I consider my **soul family**.

*Soul Family - People who are not your blood family but with whom you are as close as you are with your blood family, if not more. You commonly share a lot of values and dreams with these people.*

I am so fortunate to have found these people along our journeys. Usually the common denominator across all the people I'm close to is that they are committed to continual personal growth and life mastery, and they've been to Burning Man, Landmark Forum, Mindvalley A*Fest, or a Vipassana retreat. They tend to hang out at the networks and conferences I mention later in this chapter.

Here's a quick exercise... In the left circle below, write down the names of the 10 people you spent the most time with today. Then, next to it, write down the names of the 10 people you want to be spending the most time with 3 months from now--if you were optimizing for joy, growth, learning, and happiness.

| Actual Inner Circle | Desired Inner Circle |

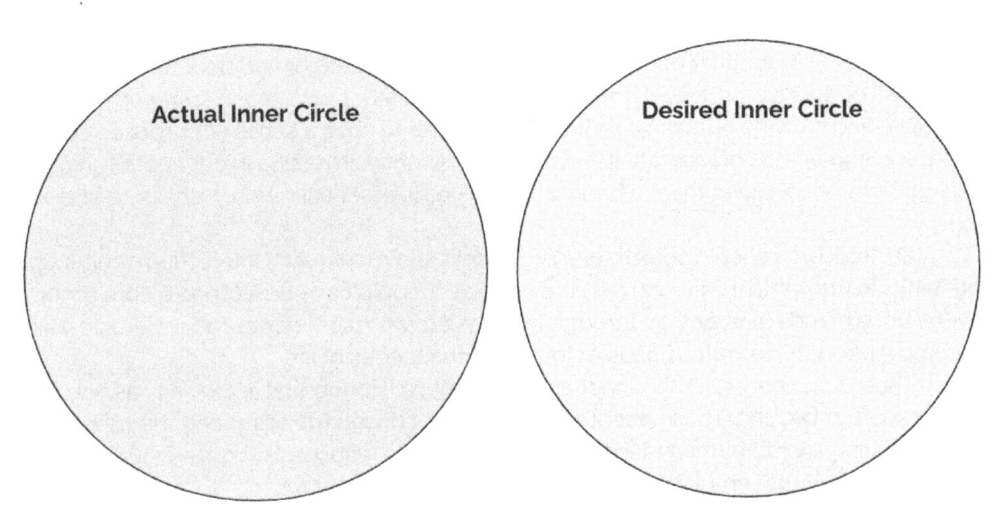

*The 10 People You Spend the Most Time With Today*  —  *The 10 People You Would Spend the Most Time With If Optimizing for Growth, Joy, Learning, and Happiness*

How many people in Circle 1 are in Circle 2? If there's not a big overlap, it's time to get to work. The goal is to make your Actual Inner Circle look like your Desired Inner Circle over the next three months.

Think deeply about the men you want to be in your Inner Circle of Brothers and the women you want to be in your Inner Circle of Sisters.

**Action Item #33: Your Inner Circle**
Write down the names of the 10-15 people you currently spend the most time with. This is your Current Inner Circle. Now, write down the names of the 10-15 inspiring people you want to spend the most time with in a month. This is your Desired Inner Circle. Spend the next month making your Desired Inner Circle your Actual Inner Circle.

## Relationships Lead to Happiness

The Existentialists, Stoics, Epicureans, and Confucians all believe that meaningful relationships are essential to a happy life. And now, so do the researchers at my alma mater, Harvard.

The Harvard Study of Adult Development is one of the longest-running longitudinal studies in history; it started in 1938 and continues to this day. The study has followed the lives of 724 men for over 80 years, tracking their physical and mental health, relationships, careers, and overall well-being.

One of the most significant findings of the study is that relationships are critical to our happiness and well-being. The study found that the quality of our relationships, not the quantity, is what matters most. Participants who reported having strong and supportive relationships with their family, friends, and partners tended to be happier, healthier, and live longer than those who did not.

The study found that people who were socially isolated or had poor relationships had higher levels of depression, anxiety, and other mental health problems. In contrast, those who had positive and fulfilling relationships were more likely to have a sense of purpose, feel fulfilled, and experience greater life satisfaction. Apparently, investing in our relationships, nurturing them, and making them a priority in our lives is essential for our happiness and well-being.

So, while you should seek to explore widely and meet many interesting people up to good things in the world, I've found that the happiest people have developed a core group of 3-5 very close friends that they go through many years with (sometimes many decades) and get to know through the various phases, joys, and challenges of life.

Those you choose for this inner circle are critically important, especially as you get into your 30s and beyond. These people become your **chosen friends** -- and they should be chosen intentionally rather than randomly. Choose people who inspire you, encourage you, have good habits worth emulating, and are kind.

According to a study from the UC Berkeley Greater Good Science Center, human connection is the best predictor of happiness in life. Humans are simply happier when they live near their friends and inspiring peers. Those with close bonds are happier, less lonely, and have higher self-esteem. So invest heavily in these close bonds with your chosen friends and soul fam.

These are the bonds that will change your life for good.

## Find Extraordinary Mentors

"Finding exceptional role models to mentor you will create a total right-angle turn in your life. This, I promise you." - Robin Sharma, Author

Very very few people actually have mentors. Yet mentorship is crucial to living the life you want.

Whoever mentors you directly impacts who you become -- and what you can learn how to accomplish and create. Whoever mentors you determines which networks you can access.

By mentors, I mean people who are about 10-20 years ahead of you in life. People that you'd like to model yourself after. People that you'd like to be like.

It always confounds me why people will spend 832 weeks going to school and 0 weeks reaching out to potential mentors that could change their entire life in one phone call or email.

With **chosen friends** and **Jedi mentors,** you can create for yourself an extraordinary life.

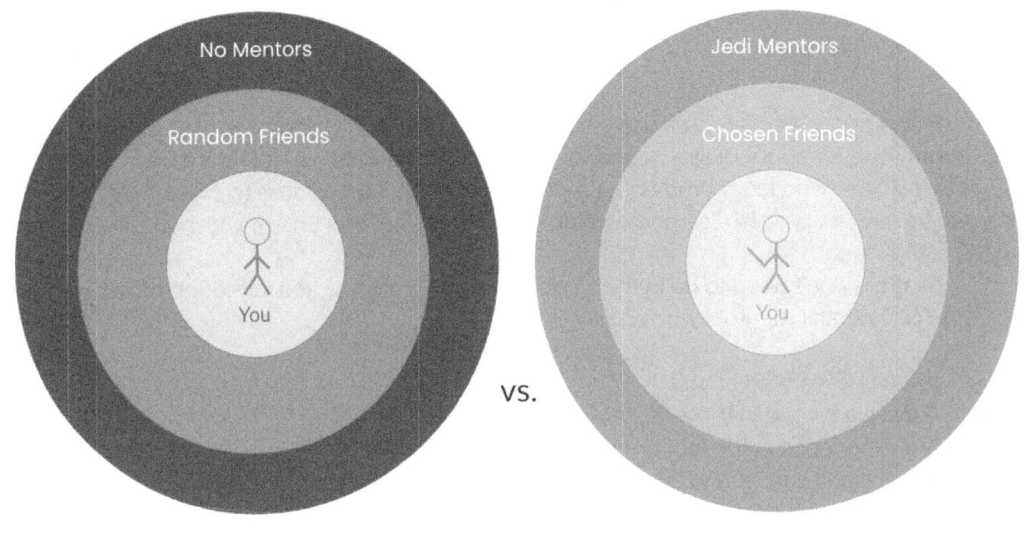

| No Mentors / Random Friends / You | vs. | Jedi Mentors / Chosen Friends / You |
|---|---|---|
| An ordinary life | | An extraordinary life |

So how do you find amazing, high-integrity mentors? And what's in it for them? Well-- every high-achieving person wants to be able to share what they've learned with someone else.

Most high-achieving people want a "padawan" to pass their knowledge down to -- whether within their company or outside of it.

*Padawan - Sanskrit for "learner." An apprentice or mentee, someone who learns from a Jedi Master.*

As a Padawan (learner), your goal is to find a **Jedi** to train from. Let's look a my definition of Jedi that I first published in my *Lessons from My 20s* slides online in 2014.

*Jedi - A highly competent, super-connected, and deeply compassionate soul and systems thinker, working at the highest levels of societal structuring, whose passion has been fully unleashed toward achieving an identified deeply meaningful mission that awakens them with extraordinary focus and immense energy daily.*

To find a **Jedi mentor,** just research potential mentors online and then reach out to them via email or by sending them something small, like a book in the mail via FedEx (more on that in a moment).

*Jedi Mentor - A person who is operating at an extremely high level of consciousness, creativity, and integrity and agrees to be your mentor.*

Some of my mentors over the years have included Tim Oakley, the CFO of iContact (who taught me a lot about business and venture capital fundraising), and Marc Benioff, the CEO of Salesforce (who taught me about meditation and doing business to make a positive impact in the world). I've also learned a lot from Tim Ferriss, Robin Sharma, Vishen Lakhiani, and Michael Singer.

Mentors don't need to be in the same geographic area as you (although they could be). Look for potential mentors who are:

- 10-20 years ahead of you
- Are experienced in the industry you want to grow in
- Are experience in the job function you want to learn
- Are brilliant, caring, and kind
- Share a similar passion
- Are looking to give back through sharing their knowledge and experience

**Mentor Recruiting Tip:** You can find nearly anyone's email address in seconds using Seamless.ai, Uplead, or LinkedIn Sales Navigator.

When you reach out to the potential mentor -- send them a very short email -- no more than 20 words.

Most people send very long, multi-paragraph emails to potential mentors. That's fine for email #10 once you've established a back-and-forth relationship -- but definitely not for email #1.

In your first email, keep it to two sentences.

Sentence 1: Why you emailed them
Sentence 2: A quick question for them

In my experience, it can take 6-7 short emails over the course of a few weeks before people actually reply -- so be persistent and don't give up.

Here are a few tips for your later emails to potential mentors (just remember, keep each message short to maximize your chances of getting a reply). People will either kindly ask you to stop or respect you for your chutzpah. In your messages:

- Explain why you're reaching out
- Explain any shared passions you both have
- Show that you've done your research on them and what they are interested in
- Explain the "why" behind what you do.
- Explain your eventual goals
- Explain how you may be able to help them

If you can get a 5% response rate -- that's really good. So be prepared to email 20 people to get 1 to reply.

Fortunately, it only takes a few hours of work to research, identify, and then get email addresses for 50 potential mentors.

Do what very few people do -- and spend a few weeks working on finding extraordinary mentors.

Then, once you have them engaged and replying, every month or so reach out to them for their quick advice.

The funny thing is -- you don't even have to "ask" them to be your mentor until later on, after you've established some back-and-forth connection. -- you just send them emails, and if they like you and see them as being able to contribute to the world or share their knowledge by helping you out, they will reply.

Don't send long messages. If you send a long message, a busy professional will think, "I don't even have time to read this. Delete.""

Instead, send 2-3 sentences to start. Something like this:

"Sally--I'm a [describe yourself in one sentence]. I'm also really passionate about [example: solar panel efficiency]. What do you [insert a short, to-the-point question]?

Here's what a busy professional who gets this thinks: "I'm glad they respect my time. Will only take 30 seconds to reply. Might as well do now.

Using this reach out process, see if you can find 3-5 experienced people who you can send questions to via email.

After you've established a back-and-forth for a couple months -- you can even let them know you "just happen to be in town" and schedule an in-person lunch or coffee to learn more from them.

Just say you're going to be in their city in about 2 weeks -- and if they say yes, book the flight!

One can see much further by standing on the shoulders of giants, so find mentors who are giants in their field and stand on their shoulders.

**Action Item: Jedi Mentors**
Write down the names of 5-10 people you'd love to be mentored by and reach out to them to ask them to be a resource for you as you progress. Use LinkedIn if needed to find people who are doing today what you want to be doing in 5-10 years.

# Finding Great Mentors Using FedEx

Another good way to reach out to mentors is by sending them books in the mail via FedEx. You can look up home addresses online or simply send a package addressed to them at their corporate office.

Back in 2015, my mentee, who I've worked with for eight years now, Mike Gavela, sent me a copy of the book "The Alchemist" in the mail.

Mike was 21 at the time and a junior at Seton Hall University. Mike realized something that few 21 year-olds know.

While successful CEOs usually have Executive Assistants (EAs) who screen their mail for them, most EAs will directly deliver FedEx packages to their bosses without opening them.

So, Mike bought *The Alchemist* by Paulo Coelho on Amazon and had it delivered to my house. And then he added a handwritten note that said that he was willing to intern for me for free for the summer, that he admired me, and that he wanted to learn.

While I had received dozens of mentorship requests via email, I had never received one via FedEx before.

I said yes -- and today Mike is my right hand person and #1 asset in growing my web2 and web3 investment advisory business, Coinstack Partners.

Here's an example of how many messages "busy and important" people receive each month by channel:

Emails: 1,000
WhatsApp Messages: 300
Texts: 300
LinkedIn Messages: 100
Instagram DMs: 50
FedEx Packages: 5

So if you want to reach someone busy and important, send them a FedEx package. And be persistent and consistent with your reachouts to these potential mentors. This is your life we're talking about!

If you join networks of other inspiring people, live a purpose-driven life where you are clear on why you're alive, practice beneficial habits with your relationships (like sending handwritten thank you notes and staying in touch every couple months over time), and surround yourself with amazingly smart and caring people, you will be on the path to becoming a Master of Life yourself.

## Finding Mentors Via Your Podcast

Another great hack for finding extraordinary mentors is to start your own podcast and then ask your targeted mentors for an interview.

You will likely get a much higher response rate (around 10% instead of 2%) if your initial reach out email says:

"I'd like to interview you on my podcast, *Podcast Name*, and talk with you about the topic of XYZ. Would next Wednesday at 2 p.m. ET for 30 minutes work for you?"

You'll get an even higher response rate if you stay consistent with high content quality and marketing efforts for a year or two and are able to get more than 50,000 weekly listeners/viewers. This is around the mark that a podcast is considered to have "made it" and can start signing large brands as sponsors and be enough to drive a full-time income for you -- while allowing you to live anywhere with a strong internet connection.

I recommend distributing your show on both YouTube (as a video recording of the Zoom call) and Anchor.FM, which distributes to all the major platforms.

While your initial guests may be doing you a favor by joining your show, by year two or three -- you may be doing *them* a favor by bringing them on. Then, suddenly, you can get nearly *anyone* on your show, and the world is your oyster.

Here are some suggested interview questions that were proposed by the experienced podcast host Alex Blumberg (of Reply All, StartUp, Mystery Show, and This American Life).

1. "Tell me about a time when . . ."
2. "Tell me about the day [or moment or time] when . . ."
3. "Tell me the story of . . . [how you came to major in X, how you met so-and-so, etc.]"
4. "Tell me about the day you realized ___ . . ."
5. "What were the steps that got you to ___ ?"
6. "Describe the conversation when . . ."
7. "How did that make you feel?"
8. "What did you make of that?"
9. "If the old you could see the new you, what would the new you say?"
10. "You seem very confident now. Was that always the case?"
11. "If you had to describe the debate in your head about [X decision or event], how would you describe it?"

Enjoy the process of building your own podcast!

## Use Your Educational Network

Your undergraduate & graduate schools are critically important networks, so prepare well and go to the best schools you can get into while avoiding getting into mountains of debt. These networks can be great sources of chosen friends and mentors.

In the USA, these schools are generally considered to have some of the best alumni networks: Harvard, Yale, Stanford, MIT, Princeton, UPenn, Colombia, Brown, Dartmouth, and UChicago.

Outside the USA, these schools are generally considered the best: Oxford, Cambridge, University of Tokyo, University of Hong Kong, Tsinghua University, Peking University, National University of Singapore, University of British Columbia, University of Toronto, University of Melbourne, Imperial College London, and University of Geneva.

So if you can attend for undergrad, grad school, or take an exec program at these above schools,

And if you can't afford it (or can't get in), you can still take many of the same courses online for free on EdX and Coursera. Do whatever it takes to get the knowledge needed to thrive in life.

I was in the class of 2014 at HBS (and graduated in the class of 2016 after taking two years off to launch the Hive community in San Francisco). I knew how important LinkedIn was becoming in the business world as both your online resume and support network.

So during my 2012-2013 school year, I sent LinkedIn requests to all 1800 members of the class of 2013 and 2014. And in my 2015-2016 final year, I sent LinkedIn requests to all 1800 members of the class of 2015 and 2016. The end result: I have over 3,000 HBS connections on LinkedIn, meaning I can find strong connections in nearly any business industry around the world in minutes.

## Use Professional Networks

For those who work at traditional companies (and aren't entrepreneurs like me), the alumni network from the companies you've worked at can be very useful and helpful in finding extraordinary people to be your chosen friends and mentors.

So choose the individuals you report to and the companies you work for carefully.

I always find it mind-blowing that people will spend 832 weeks in school (16+ years) and then only spend 4 weeks trying to find a job that will determine the direction of their life and career. They take the first job they get offered as if suddenly it's urgent after ~20 years of not being employed.

Only go to work for a company if:

- You think you will learn from the people there
- You think you will know more after a year of working there
- You think it would be beneficial to what you think you want to do in your career
- Your supervisor is kind and a good mentor
- They allow you to work remotely -- allowing you to travel as you desire as long as you're getting your job done
- You thinking working there will allow to gain skills that will make it even easier to work fully remotely in the future
- You believe in their bigger mission, the change they are trying to make in the world

The mission of the companies you work with really matters. Make sure you join a company with a mission that resonates and aligns with your personal purpose. Ultimately (besides the alumni network and money), this is what you're trading your life's energy for.

If you don't like your job, find a company whose mission you're passionate about and do whatever it takes to get in there.

And remember -- your LinkedIn is your public facing professional persona to the world -- so be sure to give and ask for recommendations, add your projects to your page, and add your work colleagues to your professional network.

## Show Up Early to Events

*"People who succeed at the highest level are not lucky; they're doing something differently than everyone else does." - Tony Robbins, motivational speaker*

Here's a strategy that can 5x the number of quality people you meet at events and relevant conferences.

Show up a couple hours before the registration desk is scheduled to open -- volunteer to help the people there get it set up (so you become friends with the organizers), and then introduce yourself to every single person as they arrive. This worked like a charm. I figured this out at one of the first Summit Series events in 2009.

By the end of day one, I'd met every single one of the 120 people who showed up to the Summit Series in Aspen, Colorado. Suddenly, I knew everyone, so I could use day two to deepen my relationships with the people that were most relevant and interesting to me.

What I found was that people are super open on the first day of an event, and become more and more guarded and closed off toward the end -- wanting to deepen their relationships with the people they've already met rather than meet more new people.

So be one of the first people they meet -- and then you can play the role of connecting people with similar interests and needs who can help each other out.

## Networks Filled With Great People

Here are some networks that are worth looking into for making additional friends who are achievers, creators, entrepreneurs, investors, and C-level leaders. Just Google them to learn more about each one. I've been involved with many of the professional communities and organizations on the below list.

- Aspen Institute
- Clinton Global Initiative (CGI)
- Daybreaker (pop up sunrise dance community)
- Dreamers and Doers (women-only)
- Eden World (community for couples)
- Entrepreneurs Organization (EO)
- Forbes 30 Under 30
- Habitas
- Hedoné
- Hive (the community I founded)
- Humans I Trust
- Ivy
- International School for the Temple Arts (ISTA)
- Nexus Global Summit
- Renaissance Weekend
- Sandbox
- Skoll World Forum
- SoCap (Social Capital Markets)
- SoHo House
- Singularity University
- StartingBloc
- Summit Series
- Tech Stars
- TED
- Unreasonable Institute
- White House Fellows
- World Economic Forum Young Global Leaders (YGL)
- Y-Combinator
- Young Presidents' Organization (YPO)

There are new great organizations popping up all over the world -- so find -- or create a group to be part of.

**Action Item #34: Communities & Networks**
Write down what communities and networks you're currently a member of and which communities you'd like to join over the next 5 years.

# Meeting Epic People at Festivals

You can meet truly extraordinary great communities like those mentioned above (Summit Series, TED, Unreasonable Institute, Renaissance Weekend), at personal growth events (you can meet really fantastic people at a Tony Robbins, Deepak Chopra, Joe Dispenza, or ISTA event), at community ecstatic dances and community service organizations, and also at art and music festivals. I especially love meeting new people at festivals.

I met my wife at Burning Man, sold my house to someone from my camp, and made over half of my good friends in life at either Burning Man, Bali Bloom, Wonderfruit, or the Envision festival.

These festivals are often the tip of the spear in human experimentation, learning, and culture creation. They are at the forefront of artistic and cultural evolution. Here are the seven themes of Envision, the seven day festival on the Costa Rican beaches. They focus on the themes of music, art, movement, education, health, sustainability, and spirituality.

These types of extraordinary events, counter-intuitively, are often also the most concentrated "business development" environments in the world -- because everyone is open and their **authentic selves** and you can actually go talk to everyone from Tim Ferriss to Sergey Brin to Vishen Lakhiani. If you want to hang out with Elon Musk riding a spaceship art car around a desert at 5 a.m., just go to Burning Man.

*Authentic Self - Who a person really is once they take off the facade of their work identity. Also someone who is fully expressed and living their purpose.*

Burning Man brings out the authentic self inside of you. Yes, at Burning Man, you can find an orgy dome or a psilocybin experience if that's what you're looking for -- but you can also find incredible workshops on every imaginable topic. Going to Burning Man for the learning adventure alone is worth it. Going to Burning Man is a great way to find out who your authentic self is once you drop the facade of your work identity. You have permission there to be whomever you truly are.

You can be a naked cowboy, an art aficionado, an experimental bi-sexual, a painter, or a caring and kind alpha male who protects and cares for others. Whatever you really are deep down, will come through.

Good festivals are also art-filled showcases of the sublime impermanence of life, memory-making extravaganzas, and a time to connect deeply with extraordinary people who have escaped the Matrix.

Here are what I consider to be festivals that are worth going to, regardless of how old you are. Do yourself a solid and pick one or two of these and go to them in the next year. You'll thank me.

MAGIC YEAR - 202

Here's an entire calendar of festivals that we love and those that have been recommended to us. Go -- and meet some incredibly adventurous, kind, and brilliant people.

1. KiwiBurn (January in New Zealand)
2. LoveBurn (February in Miami)
3. Envision (March in Uvita, Costa Rica)
4. Burning Seed (March in Australia)
5. Lucidity (April in Santa Barbara, California)
6. Afrika Burn (April in South Africa)
7. Bali Spirit Fest (May in Ubud, Bali)
8. Lightning in a Bottle (May in Buena Vista Lake, California)
9. Meadows in the Mountains (June in Bulgaria)
10. Terraforma (June in Italy)
11. Waking Life (June in Portugal)
12. Electric Forest (June in Michigan)
13. Fusion Festival (June in Germany)
14. Rainbow Gatherings (July in the USA, rotating locations)
15. Shambhala Music Festival (July in Canada)
16. Nowhere (July in Spain)
17. Xplore Berlin (July in Germany)
18. Burning Man (August in Black Rock City, Nevada)
19. Midburn (October in Israel)
20. Ondalinda (November in Careyes, Mexico)
21. Labyrinto (December near Nosara, Costa Rica)

**Action Item #35: Go to a Festival**
Take a look at the above list of transformational art and music festivals. Pick one (or two) and actually go this year, buy a ticket, and put it on your calendar. I promise it will change your life!

I haven't done this yet -- but I've often dreamed of going to 10 festivals in a year and seeing all the incredibly artistic people that I meet. Perhaps Morgan and I will do this with our son Apollo someday when we're in our 50s or 60s. That would be fun!

My favorite two festivals are Envision and Burning Man. Imagine being in a desert with 70,000 people when suddenly the following happens (this is from my journal from an actual Thursday night at Burning Man in 2018).

8:30pm - My friends and I take a dose of MDMA at Playa Alchemist
9:00pm - Fireworks go off
9:15pm - A drone show goes up in front of us
9:30pm - A fire dancing troupe spontaneously performs in front of us
10:00am - We jump on the Anastraca Pirate Ship Art Car for our friends anniversary
12:00am - My friends and I go to a friend's wedding celebration at Red Lightning
1:00am - We go dancing next door and then mutant vehicle hop for the next 5 hours
4:00am - We return to Camp Mystic to refill our CamelBaks with water
6:00am - We find ourselves dancing at sunrise while the wooden Lighthouse burns
7:00am - One final dance before we fall asleep at Camp Mystic
8:00am - Time for sleep

Yes, these were some very good times. You don't have to be in a camp to go to Burning Man, as they have an open camping section where anyone can set up their tent, yurt, or RV. That said, being part of a Burning Man camp really does add to the experience -- and having access to a food plan, electricity, and a camp shower can add a lot of comfort.

To find a good camp, go to BurnerMap.org and see if you know anyone that is going this year or went last year. Reach out and ask if you can join their camp. My favorite camps are Camp Mystic, Playa Alchemist, Disco Space Shuttle, IDEATE, and Opulent Temple. Many of these camps host Spring or Summer fundraising parties in the Bay Area of California that you can find on their Facebook group or website. Get involved and don't be afraid to volunteer for camp build week in order to get into a camp for the first time.

Have yourself an absolutely epic adventure!

## The Value of Mastermind Groups

*"Masterminding is the principle through which you can accomplish in one year more than you could accomplish without it in a lifetime if you depended entirely on your own efforts for success." - Napoleon Hill*

Once you've found some people you want to learn from -- form a mastermind group with them.

One of Napoleon Hill's greatest contributions was popularizing the concept of forming a **mastermind group** with 5-10 other high achieving people who commit to mutually supporting and guiding one another. There is tremendous value in forming or joining a mastermind group of these high achieving and well-connected people.

*Mastermind Group - A highly curated and formal group of your best connections who commit to helping each other achieve each of their big goals in life. These groups usually meet in-person monthly.*

A mastermind group is NOT a casual group of people who listen to each other complain and socialize. A mastermind group IS a highly curated and formal group of your best connections who commit to helping each other achieve each of their **Big Goals** in life. Sort of like your own Bones and Skulls club, but probably without all the weird fire and death rituals.

Mastermind groups help professionals and entrepreneurs get peer support, brainstorm ideas, and create accountability. They are typically goal-oriented and success-driven. Mastermind groups can also sometimes act as a personal board of directors or an advisory board.

For many years in North Carolina, I would host a group of my closest friends (the ones I wanted to mastermind with) every Wednesday night from 7 p.m. to 10 p.m. Sometimes we would play board games, sometimes we'd go out for a meal, but we always focused on helping each other with our biggest personal and professional challenges.

I was also a member of the Entrepreneurs' Organization (EO), a networking organization for CEOs of companies with $1M+ in annual revenues, in Raleigh and later in Los Angeles. Every month we would hold a "Forum" with 6-8 other members. You'd meet with the same people every month, allowing for the opportunity to go deep into getting to know each member. This Forum was essentially a mastermind group, with some added personal and emotional depth so that you could share your personal and business challenges with the group and get feedback.

The monthly forum location would rotate between the offices of each forum member. Over the years, I was able to get advice on all kinds of personal and professional challenges -- from getting a mortgage as an entrepreneur (it's not easy), to relationship struggles, to business scaling, to the death of my parents.

This monthly mastermind group -- mostly of people in their 40s -- was my secret to getting iContact to $50M in annual sales by 26. I highly recommend all entrepreneurs who have reached the $1M in sales mark join the EO chapter in their city. They have around 220 chapters in 60 countries so far.

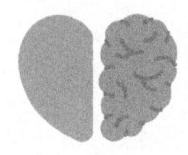

**Action Item #36: Form Your Mastermind**
Write down a list of 6 people you'd like to be in a monthly in-person mastermind group with you (people that live in the same city as you). Then, write down another list of 6 other people you'd like to be in a virtual mastermind group with (these people can live anywhere). Lastly, when you're ready, reach out to these people and pitch them on actually forming a monthly 2 hour mastermind group with you and the others on your list (or others they suggest).

## WhatsApp Groups Really Matter

Most of the events I hear about these days (and most of my friends' communications) happen on WhatsApp. The rest happens on Telegram and Signal -- two other messaging apps.

So, the opportunities you will have in your life these days will be a function of which WhatsApp groups you are in.

Here are some examples of the most important and relevant WhatsApp groups in my life. The only way to get added to a WhatsApp group is to be added by an admin, so these tend to spread just through word of mouth.

- Austin Boom Spiral
- Austin Magic Friends
- Bali Magic Friends
- Bali Tantra Tribe
- Boulder Magic Friends
- Davos Burners
- EO Los Angeles
- HBS Alum CEOs/Presidents
- HBS Alum VCs
- HBS Section F
- Humans I Trust Envision
- Humans I Trust Global
- Hive Global Community
- Nexus Global Community
- New Earth Land Projects
- Nosara Buy & Sell
- Nosara Magica Collective
- Nosara Magic Friends

- Nosara Long-Term Rentals
- Nosara Parents
- Nosara Tantra Tribe
- Summit Series Burners
- Summit Series LA
- Summit at Sea

In each city we live in -- we form a group of our favorite people there. We've created four groups so far:

- Boulder Magic Friends
- Austin Magic Friends
- Bali Magic Friends
- Nosara Magic Friends

You can imagine how helpful it is to our life to be in these groups for finding great events and getting help on whatever you need. So, if you're not on WhatsApp, get on it.

## Public Speak Every Chance You Get

> "I always advise young people to become good public speakers. Anyone can do it with practice." Scott Adams, creator of Dilbert

I used to have this eye opening routine when I'd come on stage to give a talk. I'd turn on Eminem's song, *Lose Yourself* over a speaker that was loud enough for the whole room to hear. You know that song that goes:

> "Look If you had One shot Or one opportunity To seize everything you ever wanted In one moment Would you capture it Or just let it slip?" - Eminem

I would do a cartwheel on the way in just to ensure I had everyone's attention as I came into the room. Forget boring intros.

I found out later that President Obama would listen to the same song before going into his debates with John McCain and later Mitt Romney. While Obama would use it to pump himself up -- I'd use it to ensure that the audience would never forget the main message of my speech, which was...

> ❗ To seize the opportunity for living and do something extraordinary, joyful, and meaningful with your time on this planet. In other words, to follow your bliss.

I gave a version of that same speech at over 50 colleges between 2006 and 2011 as part of the Extreme Entrepreneur Tour and the Collegiate Entrepreneur Organization conferences. And all told, I've probably spoken live in front of 25,000 people in my life so far (and I have a feeling more of this is ahead of me).

I have three tips for public speaking:

- One of the best tips I ever learned about public speaking is to always think about your audience, not yourself. What do they need/want to hear? Before your talk, fill this out: *As a result of my presentation, I want the audience to know [X], and do [Y].*

- Avoid saying the words um and uh when you're speaking in public. Instead, just pause in between ideas. Film yourself speaking to an audience and watch it afterwards to ensure there aren't any ums or uhs in your talk
Ideally use one big powerful picture and no more than 10 words (or sometimes no words at all)

- For presentations you plan to actually present, never have more than 15 words on a slide. Anything more and the text will be too small to read — and will distract the audience from you as a presenter. Use just enough to trigger your mind.

- On slides, follow the TED-style of presenting and use one big powerful picture and no more than a 2-5 word headline in the center of the slide (or ideally no words at all). It is better to be authentic and talk directly with your audience without using anything more than a picture on a slide to prime your memory. Kill the bullet points, my friend. Those are so 2004.

But why did I intentionally set up my schedule to publicly speak every couple weeks when I had a busy CEO schedule? Simple: because it helped me overcome the initial fear I had of public speaking -- an essential skill for leaders, CEOs, workshop presenters, and authors like me.

I didn't always get a huge dopamine rush when I spoke on stages. In high school, I ran for President of Key Club, a community service organization. Part of running was giving a five minute speech about our plans as future President. I was so nervous that my knees knocked together during the speech -- leaving a wobbly speaker above.

Needless to say, I lost that election -- but I gained a strong desire to overcome this fear of public speaking by doing exactly what Dale Carnegie taught me in *How to Win Friends and Influence People* -- to publicly speak hundreds of times until I was no longer afraid, and, in fact, I've come to love it.

That talent for public speaking propelled me to become a CEO with 300+ employees, speak in front of 1,500 people as a keynote speaker, and create a workshop called *Hive Designing Your Life Workshop* in which I was presenting for six hours each day -- and of course to have many stages with Eminem blaring as I cartwheeled onto them.

I'll leave you with a few 3,000 year old tips from Aristotle on public speaking:

1. Sooth people's fears
2. See the emotional side of an issue
3. Make it funny as attention spans are short
4. Use illustrations and examples to make your point come alive

**Action Item #37: Practice Public Speaking**
Join Toastmasters or reach out to your local TEDx event. Within the next 30 days, get on stage and give a talk in front of at least 100 people on a topic you're passionate about.

## Developing Deep & Authentic Relationships

*"If you're like most people, you probably seek first to be understood; you want to get your point across. And in doing so, you may ignore the other person completely, pretend that you're listening, selectively hear only certain parts of the conversation, or attentively focus on only the words being said, but miss the meaning entirely. So why does this happen? Because most people listen with the intent to reply, not to understand." - Stephen Covey*

Learning how to get unobsessed with yourself and instead become interested in other people is a key to happiness in life. Whether it's great listening, exceptional presence, recalling names, or asking meaningful questions -- there are a number of little things you can do that add up to a huge advantage in your personal and professional relationships, let people know you're actually interested in them, -- and directly translate into what you can get done in this world.

Here are a few tips I've learned along the way about people, getting them to authentically like you, and becoming great at communicating with them. Props to the school of hard knocks, lots of practice as a CEO, and Dale Carnegie for how I learned many of these.

1. **Live with Positive Energy** - Whenever you greet people, go up to them with authentic energy and excitement. People will remember how they feel when they're around you more than what you say. I call this the **Positive Energy Edge**. It gives you a huge advantage in friendships, relationships, and business. When you talk to people, smile, be joyous, and not stressed. Focus on sharing what you're excited about and what lights you up inside. Always let your passion shine through.

*Positive Energy Edge - The huge edge in life, business, and relationships that you gain from going up to people with authentic energy, optimism, and excitement.*

2. **Be Present or Nothing** - When you talk to people, look them in the eye. Bring all your presence and awareness to just them, as if nothing else exists. If you need to go do something else, simply excuse yourself. But either be 100% present with those who are with you or not present at all. As Robin Sharma says, "Being flawlessly present and genuinely engaged, instead of checking messages, thinking about what you'll eat for dinner, or rehearsing your answer, exponentially makes the other feel important, connected, and safe with you. All this accelerates trust massively. And trust is the bedrock of any great relationship, whether at work or within your private life."

*Presence - Being fully focused and attentive on the people you're speaking with rather than in your own head or looking elsewhere. Choose to look people in the eye and actually listen to what they are saying, and magic will happen with your career and goals. Deep presence is the magic of True Kings.*

3. **Ask About Their Family** - Whenever you are meeting someone who will become important in your life (new work colleague, close friend intro, etc.) ask them about their family. Note down the names of their spouse/partner, and kids in a digital notepad (like Evernote or a personal wiki). Then when you see them every so often ask about their family by name. They'll be both surprised and so appreciative that you took the time enough to recall the names of those close to them.

4. **Listen More Than You Speak** - If you're speaking to someone else, listen as much as you speak and ask good questions like, "what is really lighting you up right now?" As Tara Branch says, ""Be the silence that listens." Remember that the purpose of conversation is not to be heard, but rather to hear.

5. **Restate Their Points** - In important conversations restate the other person's point and then wait for them to confirm you got it before saying anything new. I like to use this formula in important conversations, especially in my romantic relationship with my spouse:

    a. Restate their point in your own words
    b. Ask them if you got it right.
    c. If you did, only then add your own point/perspective

6. **Ask a Lot of Questions** - If you want to be well liked and gain a lot of wisdom, ask a lot of questions of the people you meet. As the 19th century French politician, Pierre Marc-Gaston once said, "Judge a man by his questions rather than his answers." Care about what is going on in the other person's life.

7. **Have Crucial Conversations In Person** - Anytime you have something difficult to communicate (in business or personally) do it in person if possible (or at worst on a video call if you're not in the same city.

8. **Avoid Using But** - Whether at work or with your family, never start a sentence with BUT. The but is a signal that you disagree with them — which will turn off any remaining ounce of listening in the other person. Instead of the word *but*, use the word *and*. Instead of: I hear what you're saying, but I think XYZ. Say: I hear what you're saying, that's interesting. I am also thinking of XYZ.

9. **Study People's Names** - There's no more beautiful word to describe someone than their name. Whenever someone tells you their name, come up with a mnemonic device (memory cue). So if someone's name is Ryan, in your mind, call them "Ryan the Lion" and see a Lion's mane around them. If someone's name is Apollo, think of Apollo the Astronaut and see them on a spaceship. Then, when you see them next, you can happily call them by their name instead, which people love. I learned this from reading about former U.S. President Bill Clinton, who always remembered names, helping him

rise from an Arkansas lawyer to American President.

10. **Master Digital Communication** - When my dad was born in 1938, personal computers, tablets, and mobile phones were still a dream in science fiction novels. Today, the average American spends an incredible 7 hours per day on these devices.[15] So, becoming a master of digital communication is just as important as becoming a master of in-person communication. Here are some tips for mastering digital communication.

    a. Avoid sending emails with more than 5 sentences in them. That's a surefire way to get your email deleted and never responded to.
    b. Avoid sending emails with emotional content. Email is a terrible place for emotions.
    c. Use WhatsApp, Messenger, or SMS for personal communications or to alert someone you sent them an important email. Don't expect people to be continually on their email.
    d. For presentations you plan to actually present as a speech, use a full-screen picture and a short headline per slide. The only time you get to use bullet points in a presentation is if you're a McKinsey consultant or you're making an informational deck that isn't meant to be presented but simply read.

"Never forget that you're an evolved ape with consciousness, staring at a screen or book, trying to decide how to spend your time on Earth. We are all lost travelers. Love everyone. Love every moment." - Zach Pogram @BehaviorHack on IG

11. **Be Kind** - Go out of your way to be kind to everyone you encounter. As British action Ian MacLaren encouraged, "Be kind, for everyone you meet is fighting a hard battle." Everyone has a detailed and nuanced inner world -- and is doing their best to make it through this thing called life. Help them out by being nice to everyone -- whether they are your Instacart delivery person, your Uber driver, or your boss.
    a. I've found that karma is a real force in the universe. The energy you put out will come back, perhaps not during the same day, but eventually. By delighting others, they will delight you.
    b. Do random acts of kindness for people you don't know weekly. Give exceptional service if you can. Delight in making people happy. Make people feel great around you. As Maya Angelou said, "People may forget what you say and people may forget what you do. But no one will ever forget how you made them feel."

12. **Tell the Radical Truth** - No matter how hard it seems, tell the truth. Every single time. Each time you lie it reduces your connection to your own soul, dims your light, and makes your life infinitely more complicated (now you have to remember what you told to whom to keep it all straight!). Don't go down the path of lying. It's much better to simply tell the truth. Every. Single. Time. Choose the path of **radical truth**. It will set you free.

---

[15] Screen Time Stats - https://www.comparitech.com/tv-streaming/screen-time-statistics/

*Radical truth - Choosing to tell the complete truth 100% of the time in all circumstances.*

As Robin Sharma writes, "Any lies you make are being witnessed by the sovereign self that is your essential nature. Your best dimension sees any dishonesty that your weakest, egoic side feels the need to participate in. Every mistruth stains your character, and all breaches of integrity scar your soul. Each breach of your sterling power through the speaking of that which is not true not only dissolves the faith another person has invested in you, it harms your conscience and steadily remakes you into a human being who has zero intimacy with your own values, virtues, and ability to realize a meaningful mission that somehow uplifts society while owning more of your hidden potential."

**Action Item #38: Winning Friends and Influencing People**
Read the above list of 12 ways to develop authentic and meaningful relationships. Write down what you learned from it and what you plan to change in your own life based on it.

## Avoid Conspiracy Theorists

There are a number of relatively obscure conspiracies out there that are often peddled by rather poorly educated people that sometimes pop up in the "spiritual community" or the alternative right wing community ("alt-right").

I am very very grateful for my Harvard Business School MBA, where I read hundreds of cases on how the world works -- and learned how to sift through and evaluate claims with evidence and proper research. I personally, tend to avoid anyone who promotes these beliefs.

1. The Earth is flat (if it were flat, how the heck could airplanes fly all the way around the world?). Thankfully, this is being disproved further each year as more people go into space and see the beautiful sphere-like nature of Earth.

2. The moon landing in 1969 (and the six successful moon missions afterwards) were all faked and filmed in a Hollywood studio (no way you could keep thousands and thousands of insiders silent about this for 75+ years).

3. The world is controlled by a group of Alien Reptile Overlords (lol).

4. The world is controlled by a group of evil pedophiles who like to sexually abuse children (ah, the silly QAnon crap).

5. The 19th century European banking family, the Rothschild Family, secretly controls the world (this an insane anti-semitic conspiracy that is rather laughable).

6. 9/11 was an inside job (no way you can keep the hundreds of people who had to be involved to pull that off silent for 20+ years).

7. Bill Gates is an evil man who is trying to control the world through microchipping people (this is just silly).

8. The World Economic Forum is evil and attempting to remove the world of individual liberties (this is ridiculous).

9. The vaccine industry is evil. In reality, the large majority of people, scientists, and companies in the vaccine industry are working hard to create life saving, rigorously researched and tested interventions that have saved the lives of hundreds of millions of people over the last 200 years.

10. That coronavirus wasn't real (it was, it killed over 7 million people worldwide). That said, the world probably did overreact to it, especially after the first year when more was known about it and vaccines became available to those who wanted them. A similar global effort put into accelerating solutions for heart disease, cancer, and obesity would have probably saved more lives and many of the extended lockdowns caused more damage to society and people than they prevented.

For the record, here are a couple "conspiracies" that I do think have some merit after digging into them enough:

1. There have been many documented cases of human contact with advanced non-human aircraft (UFOs) that are unexplained and likely evidence of sentient life on other planets. Pretty cool to know we're most likely not alone in this universe.

2. Genetically Modified Organisms (GMOs) in our food supply may be introducing complex interactions that we may not fully understand, some of which may be dangerous.

Conspiracy theories can, at times, seem attractive because they offer explanations for complex and confusing events in the world. They spread widely during times of chaos and upheaval, offering a sense of control and stability in the face of complex and confusing events.

Conspiracy theories provide simplistic answers to overwhelming issues, giving the illusion that the problems can be solved by targeting a certain group. Especially during economic crises, social unrest, wars, political revolutions, and pandemics, these theories become more prevalent, providing a way to make sense of the chaos.

So yes, avoid people who promote unfounded conspiracy theorists, while at least keeping your mind open that, once in a while, one of them might end up being right.

## Keep Relationships Even in Failures

I have failed many times in my life. The only way that I get to write about successes with iContact and Hive is because I have many more failures that I learned from. While iContact reached $50M in sales and Hive Digital, our marketing agency, does $3.5M per year in sales -- I also founded a few other companies that didn't quite make it.

Back in 2012, two months after selling iContact for $169M I founded Connect.com. Our goal was to build a new social media application that showed you a map of where your friends had most recently posted. We did this to help increase the amount of time you spend in-person with your friends instead of being addicted to a newsfeed. We integrated with Facebook, Instagram, LinkedIn, and the phone address book. I put $6M of my own money into the company, and we raised $10M more from venture investors.

While we won the 2014 Launch Festival in San Francisco, we never were able to figure out our business model, and after Facebook's friend graph API got turned off in 2015 following the Cambridge Analytica scandal, our product didn't work very well. We tried to pivot into being an events application, but it didn't work. By 2017, we shut down, and five years of work and $16M were lost.

Was it a failure? Yes, it was definitely a business failure. But in terms of life, I learned a lot from this. Namely, don't raise venture capital until *after* you've figured out your business model. Venture capital is best meant to provide fuel to grow an already successful company -- not to fund development in a company that hasn't yet reached product-market fit.

Whenever things don't work out, it's important to communicate early and often and share bad news up front (some people say that CEO stands for Communicate Early and Often).

Investors will remember that you lost their money, yes. But they'll also remember how you communicated with them during the process. And if you do that well, many will back you again.

To become a success you have to be willing to fail. It comes with the territory. I recommend checking out the book *How to Fail at Almost Everything and Still Win Big: Kind of the Story of My Life* by Scott Adams, the founder of the Dilbert comic strip.

**Action Item #39: What You Learned from Failure**
Write down all the personal and professional failures you've had in your life and what you learned from them and how they made you who you are today.

# Recommended Books on People

- *How to Win Friends & Influence People* by Dale Carnegie
- *Conflict = Energy: The Transformative Practice of Authentic Relating* by Jason Digges

# Key Outcome from This Chapter

**Define Your Uplifting Inner Circle** - Make a list of the 10 people (friends, family, colleagues, and mentors) who you would want to be spending the most time with if you were optimizing for growth, joy, learning, and happiness. Then actually adjust your life so that those are the 10 people you spend the most time with.

## PEOPLE CHAPTER ACTION ITEMS

1. **Your Inner Circle** - Write down the names of the 10-15 people you currently spend the most time with. This is your Current Inner Circle. Now, write down the names of the 10-15 inspiring people you want to be spending the most time with in a month. This is your Desired Inner Circle. Spend the next month making your Desired Inner Circle your Actual Inner Circle.

2. **Jedi Mentors** - Write down the names of 5-10 people you'd love to be mentored by and reach out to them to ask them to be a resource for you as you progress. Use LinkedIn if needed to find people who are doing today what you want to be doing in 5-10 years.

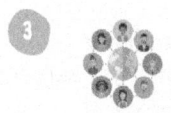

3. **Communities** - Write down what communities and networks you're currently a member of and which communities you'd like to join over the next 5 years.

4. **Go to a Festival** - Take a look at the above list of transformational art and music festivals. Pick one (or two) and actually go this year and buy a ticket and put it on your calendar. I promise it will change your life!

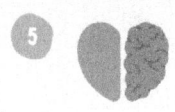

5. **Form Your Mastermind** - Write down a list of 6 people you'd like to be in a monthly in-person mastermind group with you (people that live in the same city as you). Then, write down another list of 6 other people you'd like to be in a virtual mastermind group with (these people can live anywhere). Lastly, when you're ready, reach out to these people and pitch them on actually forming a monthly two hour mastermind group with you and the others on your list.

6. **Public Speak** - Join Toastmasters or reach out to your local TEDx event. Within the next 30 days, get on stage and give a talk in front of at least 100 people on a topic you're passionate about.

7. **Build Meaningful Relationships** - Read the list of 12 ways to develop authentic and meaningful relationships. Write down what you learned from it and what you plan to change in your own life based on it.

8. **Lessons from Failure** - Write down all the personal and professional failures you've had in your life and what you learned from them and how they made you who you are today.

# STEP 5

# HAPPINESS MAGIC

**MAGIC YEAR**

# KEY CONCEPTS FROM THE HAPPINESS CHAPTER

**1. HAPPINESS**

When one's spiritual needs are met by an untroubled inner life with inner peace and deep fulfillment. Lasting happiness comes when your work and words are of benefit to yourself and others.

**2. SMILES PER DAY**

One of the most important life success KPIs. Those who have the most deep "I love this moment" smiles are generally the happiest in life. Aim for smiles over possessions and joy over stress.

**3. EGO DEATH**

The dissolution of the identity of who you are in order to prepare you for who you're becoming. This process can be very challenging.

**4. IDENTITY RISKS**

When people fear failure because of what it would mean for how they view their own identity. For example, an entrepreneur deathly fearing the failure of a business because of what it would mean for their identity as a successful businessperson changing.

**5. UNCONDITIONAL HAPPINESS**

The choice to be happy no matter what the external circumstances.

**6. PURPOSE OF LIFE**

To enjoy it, be kind, learn, and give your gifts to the world.

**7. PURPOSE OF SUFFERING**

To teach us, to guide us, to help us evolve and change.

**8. DHARMIC CHALLENGES**

Challenges that are given to you for the evolution of your soul, as part of your learning path here on Earth.

**9. CRITICISM CRAVER**

Someone who realizes that if they are not getting criticized that they are playing too small. These people desire criticism because it's a sign they are doing something of note. They use fair criticism to get better and ignore the noise from the haters.

**10. THE ARENA**

The playground of life where you can both do extraordinary things and potentially be criticized by others. Purpose-driven leaders get into the arena and aren't willing to get dust on their face in order to make a positive contribution.

**11. NEGATIVE VISUALIZATION**

Imagining ahead of time the worst case scenario so you can be mentally and emotionally prepared for it if it happens. Best if combined with positive visualization where you also visualize the outcome you want.

**12. EMOTIONAL RESILIENCE**

The greater the chaos and challenge around you the calmer your inner core becomes -- in order to help you get through difficult moments and periods in life.

MAGIC YEAR - 216

## MORE KEY CONCEPTS FROM THE HAPPINESS CHAPTER

**13 HEDONISM**

Says that pleasure is the highest good, and one should always strive to maximize their own pleasure and happiness.

**14 STOICISM**

The Stoics believed that by learning to control one's emotions and desires, and to accept whatever comes their way with equanimity, one could attain true happiness.

**15 EPICURIANISM**

A belief in making balanced choices that maximize long-term pleasure. Epicureanism posits that pleasure is the ultimate good, and pain the ultimate evil. Known as connoisseurs of the arts of life and the refinements of sensual pleasures. In between Hedonists and Stoics.

**16 EXISTENTIALISM**

Happiness comes from developing your authentic identity, developing meaningful relationships, laughing at the absurdity of life and finding a purpose in life. Encourages people to find joy in life, even in the midst of difficulty and adversity.

**17 DAOISM**

Places great value on being content with the present moment. Daoists embrace simplicity, minimize external distractions, and develop personal relationships with their inner selves and nature in order to increase their feelings of happiness

**18 HUMANISM**

A philosophy of those in love with life. Humanists believe that we owe it to ourselves to make life the best possible for us and everyone we share this planet with. Humanists believe in reason, science, and education and that all individuals should have equal rights and opportunities.

**19 GRATITUDE JOURNAL**

A notebook by your bed that you write nightly in. Write down everything you're grateful for from that day and Three Good Things that happened. Re-read this writing as the first thing you do when you wake up.

**20 IMPERMANENCE**

The reality that in the universe everything experiences entropy and nothing can last forever. This realization leads to appreciating each moment as it happens as well as realizing that any difficult moments will pass.

**21 HAPPINESS CHEMICALS**

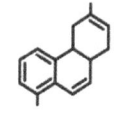

The four primary happiness chemicals are Dopamine, oxytocin, serotonin, and endorphins. They form a handy acronym: DOSE.

**22 FUCK YESES**

Things that light you up inside with joy, pleasure and happiness. Live a life where you are just committing to doing fuck yeses and say no to all the maybes.

**23 DAILY AFFIRMATIONS**

A short written encouragement letter to yourself that you read every morning when you wake up. You can also record it as audio and play it before you go to sleep.

**24 HIGH-FLYING DISC**

An upbeat and positive feeling. Make sure you're on a "high flying disc" before making any important decisions about your life.

# STEP 5: HAPPINESS MAGIC

*"Can't nothing bring me down. My level's too high to bring me down. Can't nothing bring me down. Clap along if you feel like happiness is the truth." - Pharrell Williams, Musician*

**YOUR MAGIC YEAR**

| Step | Area |
|---|---|
| 12 | AWAKENING |
| 11 | FAMILY |
| 10 | SEXUALITY |
| 9 | LOVE |
| 8 | COMMUNITY |
| 7 | MONEY |
| 6 | HEALTH |
| 5 | HAPPINESS |
| 4 | PEOPLE |
| 3 | HABITS |
| 2 | GOALS |
| 1 | PURPOSE |

I am writing this section as thunder clouds form over the hills of Nosara, Costa Rica -- a town my family lives in for most of the year that is on the Pacific Coast within the Blue Zone of the Nicoya Peninsula. It's one of the happiest places on Earth -- and a perfect place to write this chapter.

Let's begin with a definition of happiness.

> *Happiness - When one's spiritual needs are met by an untroubled inner life with inner peace and deep fulfillment. Lasting happiness comes when your work and words are of benefit to yourself and others.*

Pretty cool definition, huh? I found it on a Tibetan prayer flag inside my daily cold plunge place in Nosara, Costa Rica. Sometimes you find the coolest inspiration in the most unique places. Let us always remember that the goal in life is happiness, meaning, and fulfillment, NOT vanity, what others think, or even possessions.

## My Personal Metric of Life Success

Do you want to know what my #1 personal metric of success for my life right now is? A personal life success KPI that is more important than money in the bank. For me, it's simple. I count my **smiles per day**. Not just regular fake hello smiles. But real, deep down, "wow, I love this moment" smiles.

*Smiles per day - One of the most important life success KPIs. Those who have the most deep "I love this moment" smiles are generally the happiest in life. Aim for smiles over possessions and spend your time with people that make you smile and doing what you enjoy.*

Back in April 2023, I was on a trip to Nosara, Costa Rica, and I was at the Sunday morning ecstatic dance at Nosara Blue. At the end, they played the classic song, "Don't Worry, Be Happy" by Bobby McFerrin.

There I was, dancing my heart out with friends old and new. I realized just how serious I'd been as of late as I worked to grow my income from CEO coaching. I realized deep down that what I was truly seeking was community connection with people committed to personal growth -- and tropical paradise living.

I found myself in that perfect moment -- getting lots of community connection in a beautiful tropical paradise with Birds of Paradise flowers, little puppies playing, and forty happy people dancing around me -- people that came together twice per week and had formed a really strong community bond around them.

What I realized in that perfect Nosara moment was that:

1. Life is about making memories with the people you love.

2. Life is about smiling and enjoying yourself.

Even at 38 years old, even after being married to "Morgan the Joy Queen" for 2+ years, I was still way too serious most of the time. So I decided to change my primary two life KPIs from things like stability and money to "smiles per day" and "magical moments per week."

I knew that if I made this mental shift, I'd be much happier -- making choices that optimize for happiness and moments of family and friend connection over anything else.

Here's a question: Would you rather be around someone who's serious and grouchy all the time or someone who's constantly smiling?

Well, that answer is sort of obvious. So be that person for others. Be the person who's constantly smiling, and do the inner work (cold plunges, exercise, movement, good sleep, saunas, good nutrition, meditation, etc.) so that you can authentically be the cheerful person in the room. Be the rising tide that lifts all the boats around you -- and live your life with authentic, infectious enthusiasm.

And if something is in your way that is preventing you from truly being infectiously enthusiastic most of the time -- look at it very closely -- and see if you can shift, move, or heal whatever is in your way. Commit to being the alive, playful, and joyful person that you would want to be around -- and your entire world will change in an instant. The typical child smiles an average of 400 times per day, while the average adult smiles just 20 times per day. That means kids smile on average 20x more than adults!

Be the rare adult who smiles like a kid (all day long) and watch your life change and the type of extraordinary people who are attracted to your energy multiply!

Why is it important to smile? Smiling provides not only a boost to our mood, but also triggers the release of cortisol and endorphins in our bodies, leading to numerous health benefits such as reduced blood pressure, increased endurance, reduced pain and stress, and a strengthened immune system.

People who smile are perceived as more likable, courteous, and competent. Smilers have also been shown to be more productive at work and make more money.

It is easy to increase your daily smile average - simply start your day with a smile and intentionally smile more when in group settings. Smiling is contagious and activates neurons in the brain that fire synchronously. You may even find that your smile leads to additional smiles from those around you.

As Morgan and I like to often say to each other, "seriousity is poo."

**Action Item #40: Smiles Per Day**
What changes would you make in your life if your actual metric of success was the number of smiles per day that you either had or created in others? Write down the answer.

## My Journey With Happiness

I've been lucky to have had a relatively sunny disposition most of my life. As long as I get my **miracle morning** in, I thrive mentally. This means getting a daily 10-15 minutes of morning sunshine, my green tea, 20 minutes of strength-training, 10 minutes of swimming laps, 10 minutes of sauna time, and scrambled eggs with a banana smoothie. Tweak as needed for you. Then I start writing. If I do those things -- I feel good inside and am exceptionally happy.

While life has been pretty good, I've also had some major challenges, like when both of my parents passed away suddenly from cancer or when I got addicted to taking too many plant medicines. There were phases of years when I was exceptionally anxious, overweight, had chronic neck pain--and was dealing with very difficult moments like a business failure. It was through these times that I learned how to put the right **habit stack** in place to ensure both my health and my happiness. These challenges led to my strengths today.

When I was 27, I lost my mom, Pauline, to a glioblastoma brain tumor. I remember pounding the cement sidewalk outside the doctor's office after I was told she had less than six months to live and that the diagnosis was terminal. I was used to controlling everything in my life and winning -- and suddenly there was something I couldn't control. I had won at nearly everything up until I was 27 -- and here was something I couldn't win at -- no matter how fast I could learn or how much I could throw at it. There just wasn't yet an effective clinical trial anywhere in the world against this type of fast growing brain cancer.

Her passing woke me up to the brevity of life and the need to live now and follow my bliss. It also woke me up to the reality that I couldn't continue being fifty pounds overweight, eating processed foods, and suffering from chronic neck pain. It came to a boiling point.

I decided to make a big change after her death in 2012 -- and when my dad died of cancer in 2014, it only accelerated my commitment to health. By 2015, I was down from 212 pounds to 150 through healthy eating and daily exercise, had learned yoga positions that healed my neck (it was as simple as a daily sun salutation), and had started a daily breathing practice using alternate nostril breathing and bhastrika breath of fire (called the Sudarshan Kriya from Art of Living) that reduced my anxiety. I was on the path to full health by 2015.

## Conscious Drugs Messed Up My Consistency

"Live like a hero. That's what the classics teach us. Be a main character. Otherwise what is life for?" —J.M. Coetzee

But then I faced another challenge. For about two years (2016-2017), I got addicted to entheogenic plant medicines and microdosing on psychedelics for creativity. Thankfully, I wasn't addicted to the truly terrible drugs that can destroy you quickly (meth, heroine, fentanyl, etc.).

Instead, I got addicted to doing **medicine ceremonies** and "conscious parties" with some of my friends in California every month or so. These medicine ceremonies usually involved 10-40 people getting together for a Saturday afternoon where we would use "medicines" like psilocybin, ketamine, LSD, MDMA, Sassafras, White Lily, 2CB, or GHB and then hang out, have fun, make music, and talk late into the night.

Sometimes these events would be led by a facilitator -- and sometimes these would be free-for-all parties involving costumes, cuddle puddles, and sometimes invite-only orgy rooms (gasp!). There was nothing quite like living in San Francisco in the mid-2010s!

Microdosing had become "all the rage" in San Francisco among tech entrepreneurs -- with profiles in mainstream newspapers like the NY Times becoming quite common.

These medicines not only gave me enhanced creativity, empathy, and connection -- but also did something else for me -- they got rid of my anxiety completely for 4-6 hours. Wow, the feeling of having complete peace of mind with enhanced sociability was so desirable to me that I got hooked on them -- at times using these "medicines" more than once per week.

Because they masked my anxiety and made me a bit more creative, I started **microdosing** 10mg (about 1/10th of a common dose) of LSD or 0.1g of psilocybin (also about 1/10th of a common dose) a few times per week. At one point, I even tried microdosing Iboga powder. While the LSD, mushrooms, and Iboga microdoses helped me with my creativity and anxiety in the short-term -- it really messed with my linearity, work ethic, and consistency -- what made me so powerful in the first place.

The issue that I realized later was that **the drugs weren't solving the underlying anxiety that was still stored in my body from the unprocessed trauma of losing my parents**. They were simply covering it up for a few hours -- helping me forget about it and not feel it.

So there I was -- 32 years old -- after a 14 year career as a successful CEO -- using drugs a couple times per week to mask my anxiety. Along the way, the combination of all these different drugs messed up my brain chemistry and my stomach lining -- leading me to move to San Diego, leave my SF community, and switch to a gluten-free keto diet for three years to get my gut and brain back in working order.

While the infrequent use of some of these above medicines in controlled environments has been clinically shown to be able to reduce PTSD and anxiety -- the way I was using them (weekly and testing various combinations without any expert clinical oversight) led to me actually becoming *more anxious*, *more unstable*, and *more ungrounded*.

Instead of me being a consistent executor who could make anything happen through the combination of **Vision + Belief + Action + Consistency = Results**, I became convinced that God was giving me guidance through these medicines and that I should follow the signs they were showing me. Whether that was God or my own delusional mind, I will never know.

All I know is that I started changing my mind on key projects I was working on every few weeks, ended up unable to be calm without drugs, and the two businesses I was working on at the time deeply suffered. I had to turn things around.

# How Do You Know When Too Much is Too Much?

*"Silence, sunshine, and strength training will solve 99% of your problems."*
- Zach Pogrob

I was feeling exceptionally anxious in 2016 due to a combination of too many medicine ceremonies, unhealed trauma that came up following an ayahuasca ceremony, losing my girlfriend Nadia, and my tech startup Connect failing. I remember falling on the floor of my bedroom, pounding the floor uncontrollably, and screaming.

"WHY IS LIFE SO HARD"

This was only the second time in my life I'd pounded the floor (the first time was when my mom got her terminal diagnosis), crying and screaming, not knowing what to do as I saw my "identity" as a "successful entrepreneur" evaporate in front of my eyes. Apparently, **ego death** can be almost as challenging as actual death. It certainly was for me.

*Ego death - the dissolution of the identity of who you are in order to prepare you for who you're becoming. This process can be very challenging -- and often occurs somewhere around age 28-35 for people who are on a growth path.*

Who was I if I wasn't a "successful entrepreneur" who could make any business thrive instantly?

The hard part about ego death is that it's not an instant process. It can take 5-10 years!

While I laugh about it now, at the time, I was undergoing the beginning of my personal transformation process. I was undergoing the **dissolution of the identity of who I was as a successful and busy tech entrepreneur in order to prepare myself for who I was becoming as a loving and present family man**. You can think of this phase (which often happens between ages 28-35) as a metamorphosis process. In the middle of this process, it's common to not even know who you are anymore -- similar to how a caterpillar ceases to be a caterpillar before it turns into a butterfly. The caterpillar's body breaks down into a kind of soup inside the pupa. Over the course of two weeks, the caterpillar's body is completely reorganized into the structures of the butterfly. This has to be really uncomfortable for the caterpillar, and yet it's entirely necessary for it to become what it is destined to become.

For humans, some people in the spiritual community call this upgrade process a "Saturn Return," as it often happens around age 29, which is how many years it takes for Saturn to orbit the sun.

For me, my personal transformation process began in 2015 (when I was 30) and ended in 2021 (when I was 36). Damn, it was uncomfortable at times. I had to keep trusting the process.

When I was 31, I realized I had to make some changes in my life. After a decade of being a successful tech entrepreneur, I had gone too deeply into the Burning Man/plant medicine culture of California. I looked around and realized too many of my friends were either fake shamans or unemployed creatives. Too many of my friends abuse ketamine on a weekly basis--wanting to escape from reality. They were using it to disassociate and forget --

not to heal. Suddenly the "conscious" medicines were being used the same way as the unconscious medicines

My romantic relationships and my businesses were falling apart around 2016 due to my lack of solid habits and consistency. I had become very different from the consistent, goal oriented guy who had built a company to $50M in annual sales just five years before.

While I never contemplated suicide for more than a fleeting thought -- I had two brilliant entrepreneur friends (one male and one female) who had gone through similar challenges with drugs, anxiety, and business failure and ended up killing themselves in their early 30s.

It was all getting too close to home. I needed a new life. **I had to take full responsibility for my own life.** I needed to go back to what worked for me and run away as fast as I could from all the medicine ceremonies and culture of frequent drug use to cope. It was time to heal naturally.

While I'd had incredible, life changing, mind-opening, and spiritually enlightening experiences -- I'd gotten careless and combined too many things and did them too often. I had to come to terms with the reality that I'd gotten addicted to the feeling that came from doing these drugs.

As Arthur Brooks wrote in his famous Atlantic essay, *How to Want Less*, "Addiction is a by-product of homeostasis. As the brain becomes used to continual drug-induced production of dopamine--the neurotransmitter of pleasure, which plays a large role in nearly all addictive behaviors -- it steeply curtails ordinary production, making another hit necessary to simply feel normal."

I'd gotten stuck in the dopamine trap of conscious drug microdosing on LSD and psilocybin, which I was using to temporarily mask my anxiety.

So, how did I heal myself?

**Step one was to throw away all my "medicines"** like psilocybin and LSD and to get out of the entrepreneurial, creative tech community of San Francisco, where using them was a normal thing to do on a Saturday afternoon (and a Monday morning for that matter).

**Step two was to change my diet to paleo** (the drugs had led to an ulcer in my stomach that made me gluten-intolerant until it healed).

**Step three was to start working out every single day.** It worked.

### How I Healed My Anxiety Naturally

1. Threw away all my drugs
2. Change my diet to gluten-free paleo for a year
3. Start working out every single day

THAT last step was the fucking real solution to the underlying anxiety I felt. Working out every single day... Who knew?

I just had a lot of energy in my body that I needed to move through strength training and cardio. Once I added that in, everything in my brain got fixed very quickly.

I moved south to Encinitas, California, in the fall of 2017 and found a new romantic partner, Danielle, who helped change my diet and help me heal and re-establish positive habits. She and I dated for a year.

I got my gut lining healed within a year and began the three year journey to heal my brain chemistry. In 2019, I started dating Morgan, and she continued the path of helping me heal naturally through good habits.

I am exceptionally thankful to both Danielle and Morgan, who helped me get back to the fully alive and consistent version of myself and overcome my anxiety through working out rather than through drugs.

In 2020, Morgan and I got married, and the next year we got pregnant with our son Apollo. I write all of this in this book in the hope that our son Apollo and many other readers, including you, will be able to learn these lessons without having to go through the entire trial and error process.

The key lesson to all this -- if you have chronic anxiety -- before you try covering it up with drugs, alcohol, or pharmaceuticals -- try the natural solutions that I call **The 5S Formula For Healing Anxiety Naturally.**

### The 5S Formula for Healing Anxiety Naturally

1. Sunshine (15 mins every morning)
2. Silence (breathing exercises)
3. Strength-training (15-20 minutes per day does wonders)
4. Sustenance (limit sugar, alcohol, caffeine, and processed foods)
5. Supplements (try ashwagandha, magnesium, GABA, valerian, and L-theanine)

Only then, after I tried the natural solutions, would I try ketamine-assisted or psilocybin-assisted psychotherapy (with a trained and experienced clinician).

**Action Item #41: The Root of Anxiety**
Write down everything in your life that you believe may be causing you anxiety. Then, based on the above list and anything else you know to do, write down what you are going to do to naturally reduce your anxiety.

Today, I've healed my anxiety through daily strength training and my gut lining through a good diet. I still utilize some of the above mentioned medicines, but I limit their use to once every 3 months and very rarely combine them. **I no longer treat my brain like an experimental petri dish.** My businesses and personal relationships are now thriving again, and I have a fantastic wife and son. And I've never been happier.

In fact, one of the reasons I took on this extensive book project was to retrain my own brain on everything I learned in my 20s and 30s so that I could go into my 40s with an optimized mindset and systems for living.

It took me my entire 30s to learn these critical lessons about how to stay consistent and heal anxiety from the inside. I hope you can learn them much much faster. I am excited to see what I can create in my 40s now that I have my happiness back, my anxiety gone, my habits on lock, and my consistency going strong.

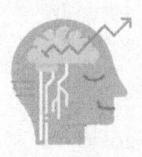

**Action Item #42: Habit Fortification**
Remove from your life anything that doesn't bring you joy, inspire you, or help you. Delete your news apps. Block the news sites. Unfollow downer social accounts. Delete any addictive apps that don't actually make your life better. Consider pausing or slowing down on any addictive stimulants or depressants.

Write down your new commitments to yourself and follow them for at least the next month.

# The Vow Of Unconditional Happiness

In Michael Singer's extraordinary book, *The Untethered Soul*, he shares one of the most important lessons about happiness ever written -- that happiness truly is a choice -- even when things aren't going well around you.

He encourages his readers to make a vow that they will choose to be **unconditionally happy** -- regardless of the circumstances or environment around them. This is the exact same technique that Victor Frankl described using to maintain his inner peace while being a Holocaust prisoner in the 1940s.

*Unconditional Happiness - The choice to be happy no matter what the external circumstances.*

Read this powerful excerpt for yourself -- and then consider making your own **vow of unconditional happiness**.

### The Vow of Unconditional Happiness By Michael Singer

To begin with, you have to realize that you really only have one choice in this life, and it's not about your career, whom you want to marry, or whether you want to seek God. People tend to burden themselves with so many choices. But, in the end, you can throw it all away and just make one basic, underlying decision: Do you want to be happy, or do you not want to be happy? It's really that simple. Once you make that choice, your path through life becomes totally clear.

Most people don't dare give themselves that choice because they think it's not under their control. Someone might say, "Well, of course I want to be happy, but my wife left me." In other words, they want to be happy, but not if their wife leaves them. But that wasn't the question. The question was, very simply, "Do you want to be happy or not?" If you keep it that simple, you will see that it really is under your control. It's just that you have a deep-seated set of preferences that gets in the way.

The question is simply "Do you want to be happy?" If the answer is really yes, then say it without qualifying it. After all, what the question really means is "Do you want to be happy from this point forward for the rest of your life, regardless of what happens?"

Now, if you say yes, it might happen that your wife leaves you, or your husband dies, or the stock market crashes, or your car breaks down on an open highway at night. Those things might happen between now and the end of your life. But if you want to walk the highest spiritual path, then when you answer yes to that simple question, you must really mean it.

There are no ifs, ands, or buts about it. It's not a question of whether your happiness is under your control. Of course it's under your control. It's just that you don't really mean it when you say you're willing to stay happy. You want to qualify it. You want to say that as long as this doesn't happen, or as long as that does happen, then you're willing to be happy. That's why it seems like it is out of your control. Any condition you create will limit your happiness. You simply aren't going to be able to control things and keep them the way you want them.

You have to give an unconditional answer. If you decide that you're going to be happy from now on for the rest of your life, you will not only be happy, you will become enlightened. Unconditional happiness is the highest technique there is. You don't have to learn Sanskrit or read any scriptures. You don't have to renounce the world. You just have to really mean it when you say that you choose to be happy. And you have to mean it regardless of what happens. This is truly a spiritual path, and it is as direct and sure a path to Awakening as could possibly exist.

Once you decide you want to be unconditionally happy, something inevitably will happen that challenges you. This test of your commitment is exactly what stimulates spiritual growth. In fact, it is the unconditional aspect of your commitment that makes this the highest path. It's so simple. You just have to decide whether or not you will break your vow. When everything is going well, it's easy to be happy. But the moment something difficult happens, it's not so easy. You tend to find yourself saying, "But I didn't know this was going to happen. I didn't think I'd miss my flight. I didn't think Sally would show up at the party wearing the same dress that I had on. I didn't think that somebody would dent my brand-new car one hour after I got it." Are you really willing to break your vow of happiness because these events took place?
Billions of things could happen that you haven't even thought of yet. The question is not whether they will happen. Things are going to happen. The real question is whether you want to be happy regardless of what happens.

The purpose of your life is to enjoy and learn from your experiences. You were not put on Earth to suffer. You're not helping anybody by being miserable. Regardless of your philosophical beliefs, the fact remains that you were born and you are going to die. During the time in between, you get to choose whether or not you want to enjoy the experience. Events don't determine whether or not you're going to be happy. They're just events. You determine whether or not you're going to be happy. You can be happy just to be alive. You can be happy having all these things happen to you, and then be happy to die. If you can live this way, your heart will be so open and your Spirit will be so free, that you will soar up to the heavens.

    So, what do you think? Are you ready to make your own vow of unconditional happiness? Are you ready to keep that vow through any challenge you face? Are you ready to see the positive in every difficult experience? Are you ready for your soul to know deep down that any challenges that arise are there for your own growth?
    Never forget that you are the co-creator of your own reality and that your life is a cosmic adventure to accelerate your soul's growth.

**Action Item #43: The Vow of Unconditional Happiness**
Write down the following (if you actually do commit to this). "I hereby commit to taking the vow of unconditional happiness from this moment forward. No matter how dire the circumstances, I will commit to seeing the bright side of any challenge and making the best of any situation I am in." Then print it out and sign it beneath the statement to make it official.

## Life is Happening For You, Not To You

*"Life is always happening for us, not to us. It's our job to find out where the benefit is. If we do, life is magnificent."* - Tony Robbins

**The purpose of your life is to enjoy it, be kind, learn, grow, and give your gifts to the world.** Your soul is here to learn, grow, and contribute to the evolution of consciousness in the universe toward higher complexity, order, and love.

The Purpose of Life - To enjoy it, be kind, learn, and give your gifts to the world.

The Purpose of Suffering - To teach us, to guide us, and to help us evolve and change.

Let's recap some answers to some basic universal and philosophical questions from my vantage point...

**What's the purpose of all life?** The purpose of all life is the evolution of consciousness.

**What's the purpose of your life?** To enjoy it, be kind, grow, and give your gifts to the world.

**Why did your soul come here?** To learn, grow, and contribute to others and the continual evolution of consciousness in the universe.

**What is the purpose of suffering?** To teach us, to guide us, and to help us evolve and change.

You see, there's a bigger force that we are all a part of that holds us. Whether you call that God, Allah, Yahweh, spirit, the universe, or something else -- it's there. There's a web that supports us. It is invisible to our eyes, yet omnipresent. Our higher selves are part of this energy. It's where we come from.

And so, when challenges in life inevitably arise, the opportunity is to see them as part of our journey within a field that we are part of but do not control and to appreciate the learnings that come from the challenges.

Suffering happens to every being. The key is to recognize that suffering gives us benefit. Properly utilized, suffering teaches us and guides us. Some suffering (difficulty/challenge) is inevitable. It's how you interpret and react to the suffering that matters. There's a lot of unnecessary suffering caused by resistance to inevitable change.

You see, it is often our challenges that give us our unique gifts. I recently met a young woman in Austin who told me her story. She had been abused by her father. This type of thing could set another person back a lifetime. She turned the difficulty into ingredients for finding her passion to serve. She has now found her purpose -- and is working on becoming a trauma therapist to help others who have been through similar situations heal. Her deepest challenge became her greatest gift to others.

My mom's passing from brain cancer when I was 27 was a challenge that changed my whole life. Within a few days, I decided to sell my software company, go to graduate school, and actually take my health and wellness seriously. Without the gift of her early passing -- I would be an entirely different person, less healthy, less happy, and not writing this very book for you right now. I would have stayed in North Carolina, met a different partner, and my son Apollo wouldn't even be here to inspire this book. My greatest struggle has become my greatest gift.

As author Robin Sharma writes, "When things get super-hard, I encourage you to default into being an opportunity seeker. Ask yourself how you can *profit from* the setback to reveal the peak of your powers, turn calamity into victory, and rework the apparent failure into an *even better* life than you previously enjoyed. This is how warriors operate. And how heavyweights roll."

The journey of our soul is to learn. And the way we learn is through challenges. So don't be surprised when challenges come up. Our role is to trust the process and accept the present moment while working to shift the future and make the next moment a better one.

The key is to recode from "my life sucks right now" to "wow, I'm learning a lot right now." The key is to see your life challenges as **dharmic challenges** that are there for your soul's growth.

*Dharmic Challenges - Challenges that are given to you for the evolution of your soul, as part of your learning path here on Earth.*

I look for friends who see the silver lining in every experience and choose to see through the lens that "life is happening FOR me" instead of "life is happening TO me."

I certainly looked for a life partner who understood this key principle. My wife, Morgan, has taught me a lot about reprogramming my mind to see the challenges as perfection -- and that everything that occurs is truly happening "for me" instead of "to me." Here is one of her top Principles for Living that she wrote in her notebook recently.

### Morgan's Principle for Living #1 - Everything Is Happening Perfectly For Me

The whole experience of life is perfect and in divine timing, always working out for me, my family, my friends, and my projects. Even the hiccups are perfect, benevolent manifestations always working toward my highest goals and desires, even when I cannot see the full path ahead. The Universe and all its parts are absolutely in love with me, helping me and supporting me in every way. Whether I like the experience or not doesn't really matter because it is all in service to me. Move your heart into immense gratitude for every aspect -- all conspiring for your goodness. It is all happening perfectly for you. The pristine perfectness of life is extraordinary to behold. It is all happening for a good reason. God's got you!

You must transcend spending all your time fighting what has already happened (the past) or worrying about what might happen (the future) and instead work to make the next moment better. Thrive on your challenges.

As Emperor Mulan said in the Disney movie Mulan, "The flower that blooms in adversity is that most rare and beautiful of all."

And give up obsessing about the challenges that are in the past. They are over. Each of us must realize that our past is nothing but a construct. A fading memory inside some synapses in our brain that is no longer real. Your past is a mental box, and it's a mental box you don't have to be within any longer. Do the work. Forgive. Heal. And focus on the now.

If we can re-code the difficult things that happened in life as gifts, we can move forward powerfully and "**surf the wave of now**."

## Accept Continual Change As the Way of Life

"Life is a series of natural and spontaneous changes. Don't resist them; that only creates sorrow. Let reality be reality. Let things flow naturally forward in whatever way they like." - Lao Tzu, founder of Daoism

Suffering happens when you resist what is.

Let's say that again -- as it's one of the most important lines in the book. **Suffering happens when you resist what is.** As such--it is very important to accept what has already happened -- and to look for the gift in every situation -- no matter how terrible or challenging. The key is to find the silver lining in every moment -- and to surf the wave of continual change that is life.

Learning to accept continual change and appreciate the **impermanence** of every moment is so important in life. Nothing ever stays the same. You won't be 25 forever. Your baby won't be 6 months old forever. Your parents won't always be alive. Things change continually. That is the natural way of the world.

As the spiritual writer Eckhart Tolle says, "Surrender to what is. Say "yes" to life and see how life suddenly starts working for you, rather than against you."

While there is a natural desire to "hold on to what was," the *Way of Life* is to surf the ever changing waves. Learn to "surf the wave of now."

Instead of holding on tightly to what was, the easier way is to fully enjoy and appreciate each good moment while knowing it won't last forever.

And when times are tough, similarly to be able to tell yourself the great Persian adage, "This too shall pass."

As Robin Sharma writes, "The great saints, sages and spiritual geniuses all understood that a main aim on the path to awakening was to stand in any mess that life sends and remain contented, courageous, serene and free. To stay tranquil while all appears to be falling apart. To construct an inner axis of power so strong, and yet so flexible, that nothing on the outside could shake its roots. Imagine this: making an interior life that stays graceful, quiet and grateful, regardless of what is happening outside of you. To have your strength depend not on worldly stability but upon your primal heroism. As you release resistance to change in your personal life or professional career or external environment, and embrace the new circumstances that destiny has sent, you will come to see any volatility that has unfolded as a grand blessing."

You see, nothing is forever, except perhaps our souls. While our inner soul, our **True Self**, may be forever (in my view, we have many many lifetimes, and the purpose of life is the continual learning and evolution of consciousness), this body and even this Earth is not forever. It is important to accept this in order to find true inner peace and happiness.

And since time never stands still and this life is short -- it is important that you live your best life and leave behind on this planet what you are meant to leave behind.

In other words, give your gifts to the world now, not in 20 years. Begin the **masterwork** of your Life now -- and don't delay in the joyous effort of doing what you have come here this time around to do.

I'll end this section with a great quote from my favorite writer ,Robin Sharma, "We live in a period of tremendous volatility, uncertainty, and high-velocity change. Disruption is tearing at the foundations of a lot of organizations. And hurting the spirits of many good people. Many of us have lost our confidence in a predictable future. The majority of people face constant worry. Most of the population has been overwhelmed with unhelpful negativity. Yet a spectacular minority of human beings are able to remain strikingly positive and profoundly bullish in the face of exponential upheaval. And amid challenging personal times. One of their primary strategies to stay centered on possibility rather than descend into toxicity is to fill their minds with such great dreams that there's simply no room for stressful concerns. I'll reinforce the idea again so we can process it together: Fill. Your. Mind. With. Great. Dreams. So. There. Is. No. Room. For. Petty. Concerns."

> Fill your mind with great dreams so there is no room for petty concerns.

So give yourself some dedicated time for yourself. Create your special temple workspace. Build your mental armor. Fill your mind with great dreams. And give your gifts to the world.

## Reframe Suffering as Learning

> "The last of human freedoms is the ability to choose one's attitude in a given set of circumstances." - Victor Frankl, Author, *Man's Search for Meaning*

In order to truly feel the heights of joy, one must have felt the depths of suffering. Often, the more difficulties you've faced, the stronger you become. The hotter the fire the iron is forged in, the stronger the steel becomes. The more difficult the circumstances you've faced, the stronger your character and resolve.

The key is to not let life break you -- but instead to bend to the challenges and grow from them -- knowing that everything will eventually pass.

Mihaly Csikszentmihalyi, the author and creator of the concept of "flow," once wrote, "The ability to persevere despite obstacles & setbacks is the most important trait for succeeding in life."

So don't be afraid of struggle.

Often, the greatest individuals who make the largest contribution to society are those who have been through the most.

- Think of Nelson Mandela, who after 27 years in prison became President of South Africa and led efforts to end apartheid in the country.
- Think of Gandhi who took down the British Empire in India after being jailed for two years for non-violent resistance.
- Think of Martin Luther King, Jr. who persisted through entrenched racism and death threats, to spread his message of unity, equality, and brotherhood.

While the obstacles may not make sense at the time, you'll eventually be able to understand why going through them was important. As Robin Sharma writes, "It's only when we look back on our lives that we can connect the dots and see how everything that happened was for our highest good. And finest growth. What we saw as a burden—in the heat of the difficulty—through the passage of time turns out to be a blessing that makes our lives vastly better."

Here were some of the hardest obstacles I faced in the first three decades of my life:

- Dealing with chronic neck pain from a 2001 car crash
- Helping my dad through prostate cancer in 2008
- My mom's death from brain cancer in 2012
- Panic attacks from stress at work while CEO of iContact
- My dad's death from Leukemia in 2014

We all go through really hard times. I'm sure you've been through tough times yourself. It is our response to the crucible moments that makes us great.

While I wish so much that my parents could have met their grandson Apollo, this book would never have been written had I not found the deep reservoir of resolve in the sea of struggle after my mom's passing in 2012 and my dad's passing in 2014.

It is the **inner resilience** and resolve that come from the faith that you will get through to the other side that are valuable time and again in life. It is often in our struggles that we learn the most about ourselves.

You have to, as Robin Sharma says, "reframe setbacks into setups, reperceive hardships into advantages, and reprogram troubles into triumphs."

It is often in our struggles that our soul learns what it has come here this time around to learn.

Yes, the very purpose of our lives -- to learn, be kind, and upgrade our consciousness -- can be achieved through what we gain from our suffering.

So, as counterintuitive as it may sound, learn to appreciate the challenges and suffering you experience. When something challenging occurs, learn to pause and breathe before you react. Take a moment or two so that you can respond thoughtfully from your brain (prefrontal cortex) rather than rashly from your limbic system.

"Between stimulus and response there is a space. In that space, is our power to choose our response. In our response lies our growth and our freedom." - Victor Frankl, Holocaust Survivor and Author, *Man's Search for Meaning*

Suffering can produce various benefits, such as compassion, creativity, relatability, and genuineness. Suffering can also be the gateway to profound self-discovery. Adversity eliminates the superficial, fearful, and egotistical aspects of our personalities. It redirects us towards our inherent brilliance and creativity, but only if we are brave enough to confront the wounds that afflict us.

So appreciate the suffering you've been through -- as it has made you who you are today.

**Action Item #44: Silver Linings**
Write down the 10 most difficult and challenging things that have ever happened to you. Then, in a second column, write down all the positive things that came from each of those experiences -- that you would not have learned or experienced without the first challenging event occurring. Recognize that you wouldn't be who you are today without the challenging experiences.

## Make a Comeback & Create a Magic Decade

*"I've grown the most when my life has looked its worst. It's been thanks to my troubles that I've been introduced to my virtues. Misery is the very fire that forged courage and persistence, patience and gentleness, the optimism to forgive and the devotion to work for the world. These priceless benefits were developed not in the days of ease, but in the seasons of my deepest suffering. They have been the rewards Fortune has sent me for remaining present to the difficulty and for converting hardship into healing, purification and spiritual ascension."*
- Robin Sharma

As Conan O'Brien once shared in a commencement speech, "Your path at 22 will not necessarily be your path at 32 or 42. One's dream is constantly evolving, rising and falling, changing course. I'm here to tell you that whatever you think your dream is now, it will probably change. And that's okay. But the point is this. It is our failure to become our perceived ideal that ultimately defines us and makes us unique. It's not easy, but if you accept your misfortune, and handle it right, your perceived failure can become a catalyst for profound reinvention."

Yes, your traumas and failures have given you your gifts and deep wisdom that you can share with others. So use the wisdom gained from them to your benefit. See your challenges and misfortune as what have forged your character and made you who you are.

It doesn't matter if you're a drug addict, drug dealer, ex-con, alcoholic, victim of sexual abuse, homeless, unemployed, high school dropout, or you lost your parents at an early age. Or if you were just a normal person who's had some tough times. No matter what has happened -- you can learn to use this fire of life experience to forge your character, develop resilience, change your life for the better, get on a good track, and become anyone you want to be in the next decade of your life.

As John Lennon said, Everything will be okay in the end. If it's not okay, it's not the end."

Yes, that's right. Anyone of any background can make a decision today to make the next ten years different from the last ten years and make a comeback.

No matter what has happened to you in the past, you can choose right now to keep fucking going, keep your head up, and start on a new path.

Give yourself a new shot at life and be honest about where you are. Fix your habits, create your vision, create your goals, and start working on having one good day after another. Magic mornings turn into magic weeks, which turn into magic years, which turn into magic decades, which turn into magic lives.

Get started today and re-build yourself cell by cell, neuron-by-neuron to be a consistent, caring, athletic, healthy, motivated, and alive person who recognizes what a gift it is to have this opportunity to be alive.

Look, you've got one shot, one opportunity, to seize everything you've ever wanted. Will you capture it? Or let it slip?

## Thrive on Criticism

> "Caring too much about what people think about your visionary venture —the one that is flooding you with energy—is an excellent way to ensure you do nothing that matters." - Robin Sharma, The Everyday Hero Manifesto

I'm a big fan of the 20th Century French-Algerian existentialist philosopher Albert Camus. He believed that life is worth living, but we have to create the meaning in life for ourselves, that we all should live with passion, and that all of our lives are absurd (we are just biological matter spinning senselessly on a tiny rock in the corner of an indifferent universe). He recognized that once you realize that life is absurd, you can live more intensely without worrying about criticism from others.

So are you worried about criticism? Does it stop you in your tracks, trigger you, or cause you to give up on your dreams? Well, perhaps you should realize that life is absurd, we are simply intelligent monkeys on a rotating rock in space, and there's nothing to really worry about.

Reprogram your mind to realize that **criticism is good** -- because it means people care enough about what you're doing to say something about it. If you are never criticized, you may not be doing much that is noticeable or makes a difference.
Criticism is good -- because it means you're making a dent in the universe that matters.

Yes, you want to be a **criticism craver** rather than a **criticism avoider**!

*Criticism Craver - Someone who realizes that if they are not getting criticized, they are playing too small and not doing anything meaningful. These people desire criticism because it's a sign they are doing something of note. They use fair criticism to get better and ignore the noise from the haters.*

Reprogram your mind to **love criticism,** as it means people give a damn about what you're doing. Crave it, seek it, learn from it, and appreciate it. And as long as you are living in alignment with your personal values and are kind to everyone, use the controversy as free publicity for your mission. Many great entrepreneurs and entertainment celebrities intentionally stir up controversy to get massive media coverage. So get over the need to avoid criticism.

Here's what a few leaders and authors have said over time about overcoming the fear of criticism.

- Do not waste your precious time giving one single crap about what anybody else thinks of you. - Jen Sincero, author
- "No one can make you feel inferior without your consent." - Eleanor Roosevelt
- "Struggle and criticism are prerequisites for greatness. That is the law of this universe." - Prince EA, motivational poet
- "You know you're releasing genius into the world when you're being laughed at. Trust you're not only on the right track but sending out genuine masterwork when the trolls mock, condemn and ridicule you. Nice job. You win." - Robin Sharma, author
- "Feeding the trolls is a waste of your time. Most critics are jealous because you did what they couldn't do. Ignore them. And allow mastery to be your response." - Robin Sharma, author
- "Have no fear. You've got one chance here to do amazing things, and being afraid of being wrong or making a mistake or fumbling is just not how you do something of impact. You just have to be fearless." - Dr. Adam Gazzaley
- "Is it so bad, then, to be misunderstood? Pythagoras was misunderstood, and Socrates, and Jesus, and Luther, and Copernicus, and Galileo, and Newton, and every pure and wise spirit that ever took flesh. To be great is to be misunderstood." - Ralph Waldo Emerson
- "It is a rough road that leads to the heights of greatness." - Seneca
- "When you are immune to the options and actions of others, you won't be the victim of needless suffering." - Don Miguel Ruiz, author

Self-belief, even to the point of being considered borderline delusional by some, is often necessary to make true breakthroughs in society. At various times, people thought Tesla, Einstein, Copernicus, and Musk were all to be bat-shit crazy. In some sense, they were. In other senses, they were brilliant.

You learn later in life that there is a fine line between exceptional brilliance and craziness. It's somewhat crazy to obsessively spend 20 years writing down all my life lessons in order to someday write a book about them all that I could give to my future children. And yet, that's exactly what I did. And someday some people will criticize this book. And the moment they do, that's when I will know I've arrived as a writer.

The desire for criticism and an exceptionally strong sense of self-belief go hand-in-hand. Here are some very helpful quotes to read to yourself out loud as you create your internal matrix of steel and get locked in on your dreams.

- "The most successful people I know believe in themselves almost to the point of delusion." - Sam Altman, *How To Be Successful*

- "Without a high grade of self-confidence, you'll never have the resolve to translate your silent fantasies into everyday reality." - Robin Sharma, author

- Because one believes in oneself, one doesn't try to convince others. Because one is content with oneself, one doesn't need others' approval. Because one accepts oneself, the whole world accepts him or her. - Lao Tzu

The key to being able to withstand criticism and maintain strong self-belief over the years is to ensure you have a strong internal value system built -- so that the criticism of others doesn't even phase you as your soul knows what you are pursuing is your truth. Ensure you follow your values and The Golden Rule as you go about your big missions and creative endeavors.

Hitler was maniacal with self-belief, but he violated The Golden Rule. He became a maniac hell-bent on genocide. He was quite immune from criticism, but didn't have the right values-system installed -- to disastrous effect.

So, a very important nuance here. **As long as you are operating within your values system and are kind to all people, fuck the critics**. As Teddy Roosevelt so famously said in 1910 at a speech in Paris:

"It is not the critic who counts: not the man who points out how the strong man stumbles or where the doer of deeds could have done better. The credit belongs to the man who is actually **in the arena**, whose face is marred by dust and sweat and blood, who strives valiantly, who errs and comes up short again and again, because there is no effort without error or shortcoming, but who knows the great enthusiasms, the great devotions, who spends himself in a worthy cause; who, at the best, knows, in the end, the triumph of high achievement, and who, at the worst, if he fails, at least he fails while **daring greatly**, so that his place shall never be with those cold and timid souls who knew neither victory nor defeat." - Teddy Roosevelt, U.S. President

So get in the fucking **arena**, my friends, and do something, create something, build something -- and stop hiding meekly from your very purpose on this planet -- to give your gifts to others. Dare greatly. Thrive on criticism. Crave criticism. And be worried if you're not getting criticized.

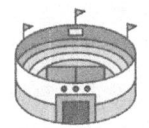

*The Arena - The playground of life where you can both do extraordinary things and potentially be criticized by others. Purpose-driven leaders get into the arena and aren't willing to get dust on their face in order to make a positive contribution.*

Yes, there is one way to avoid criticism. It is to do nothing and stand for nothing. The world will then leave you alone. If you're up to something that matters in the world, criticism is inevitable and comes with the territory.

Crave the criticism. It means you're making waves.

**Action Item #45: Reprogram Criticism**
Write down the answer to this question: What have you been not doing at all or not doing as boldly as you should be -- out of fear of being criticized by others? After writing down that answer, write down: "I commit to living my life boldly. I now know that when I'm criticized, it means I'm on the right track to doing something people are noticing. I will always be kind, do my best, follow my creative truth, live in the arena, and welcome the critics--seeing them as a

sign I'm on my way."

## Fuck Fitting In

"Be yourself. Everyone else is taken." - Oscar Wilde

We think we have to fit into the life that our parents expect us to live. We think we have to fit into the life that our society expects us to live. We think we have to fit into the life that our boss expects us to live. Well, you know what, fuck everyone's thoughts about who you should be. Just be yourself.

Do you. Follow your bliss. Follow your obsessions. Do what you love. Be kind. And keep your curiosity open as you discover who you truly are.

We think we have to live a busy and stressed out life like everyone else. The truth is You don't.

Be the fucking wind instead of letting life blow you around. Be a calm center in a storm of continual change.

But no, instead of being the wind -- you let the wind fuck you up. Why do you do that? And instead of living the life of our dreams, we get sucked into a great vortex of passionless mediocrity.

After just a few months of this passionless mediocrity, our eyes start to go dead, we glaze over, and we lose touch with what lights us up inside.

Most human beings become overwhelmed by "the demands of life" and the "judgments of others" and subconsciously, ever so slowly, like a frog in boiling water, without really noticing until it's too late, begin to give up on our dreams.

Soon, we no longer believe our dreams are "reasonable," and we give up on them.

Soon we start worrying a lot about what other people will think rather than dancing to our own beat like we did as children.

Eventually, some of us, beaten down, become cynical and resigned and think, "Is this all that life can offer?"

But the truth is simple. We get to choose how we live our lives. And even if you're "stuck" in a life you don't like -- you can make your life better, while staying in integrity with your existing commitments by making new choices over the next couple years.

**Fuck fitting in.** Be you. Do you. And walk to your own strange drum beat. Get out on the edge of your own creative niche. As Kurt Vonnegut said, "Out on the edge, you see all kinds of things you can't see from the center. Big, undreamed-of things—the people on the edge see them first."

Be your own unique self. We need your evolutionary mutations to push humanity forward.

As Steve Jobs said, "Your time is limited, so don't waste it living someone else's life. Don't be trapped by dogma—which is living with the results of other people's thinking. Don't let the noise of others' opinions drown out your own inner voice. And most importantly, have the courage to follow your heart and intuition.."

And as Zach Pogrob says, "Be a paradox. Build an empire. Have fun doing it. Train like a savage. Create like an artist. Dream in decades. Act in days. Lift, run, and sweat. Learn, build, and design. If you're easily defined, you're easily forgotten."

What would the existentialists say about all this? Well, Sartre would have encouraged you to be authentically true to your own personality, desires, and characters, despite external pressures.

And Camus would encourage you to realize just how absurd life is so that you can live more intensely and let your own freak flag fly. If he were still around today he might even hear this quote…

> "Life is r-i-d-i-c-u-l-o-u-s. It so seriously is—we have no freakin' idea what we're even doing here spinning around on this globe in the middle of this solar system with who-the-hell-knows-what out there beyond it. Making a big fat deal out of anything is absurd. It makes much more sense to go after life with a sense of, "Why not?" instead of a furrowed brow. One of the best things I ever did was make my motto "I just wanna see what I can get away with." It takes all the pressure off, puts the punk rock attitude in, and reminds me that life is but a game." - Jen Sincero, *You Are a Badass*

## Learn From Failure

Holy shit I've failed a lot. I lost $10M of venture capitalists money building a startup that didn't work out called Connect.com. I lost $6M of my own money investing in that same startup. I lost millions in a business lawsuit. I lost a $2M deposit on a San Francisco church I was turning into a community center when I couldn't get the zoning changed to allow for meditation, yoga, classes, and co-working. I got addicted to plant medicines and entheogens for two years.

But only through all those "failures" did I become who I am today and achieve my greatest successes with my businesses and family. Going through failures can be traumatizing if you fight them, - and easier if you let them pass right through you.

I remember pounding the floor in 2015 when my third startup, Connect, was failing. What I should have done was let it go out of business, wind it down, and communicate with investors. But I was "addicted" to the internal identity (ego) of being a "successful entrepreneur." If I let the company fail, I feared my identity would dissolve and I wouldn't know who I was. I remember pounding the floor of my bedroom in San Francisco, deeply afraid of what this business failure would mean.

This sounds ridiculous to write, but it actually felt like I was dying when I was facing the death of a company I'd founded. So instead of just letting the company wind down -- I put another $2M of my own money into the business to pivot and keep it alive for 24 more months. That pivot failed too -- and the inevitable shutdown happened in 2017.

I deeply respect Elon Musk for putting his last penny into SpaceX in 2009 after two rocket launch failures to prove that commercial rockets and spacecraft were feasible. The difference was that he was deeply passionate about his mission. By 2015, I was no longer passionate about the Connect mission. And so instead of investing my money passionately in the change I wanted to see happen in the world -- I was investing it to save face and reduce ego death pain. I was worried way too much about what others would think. A $2 million mistake.

There are actual physical risks, and then there are **identity risks**. Both can scare the crap out of you and cause your body to shut down or run.. It can feel like you're dying when your mental identity (ego) is challenged.

> *Identity Risks - When people fear failure because of what it would mean for how they view their own identity. For example, an entrepreneur deathly fearing the failure of a business because of what it would mean for their identity as a successful businessperson changing.*

It can feel like we're dying if we're not successful. And some entrepreneurs and creators can't handle the internal conflict and choose to stop going after their dreams and play small, or worse, end their own lives--unable to realize that their company and them are not the same thing.. I've had two friends kill themselves very sadly during business failures. Don't do that. Your value to others is much greater than one company.

Because of the way our nervous system is wired from millions of years of primate evolution to respond quickly to threats, many people live their lives deathly afraid of **identity risks,** as if there is grave danger ahead like a lion. Don't attach too much to your own identity or to how others perceive you, and life will be much easier.

> Don't attach too much to your own identity or to how others perceive you, and life will be much easier.

You see, just 20,000 years ago, our species was surviving primarily as nomadic species, having to be continually aware of physical threats in our environment. Evolution of our bodies' nervous systems hasn't yet caught up with cultural evolution, where these threats mostly don't exist any longer. DNA evolution has been slower than cultural evolution, at least in the pre-CRISPR world.

We get amygdala attacked and go into fight or flight responses with cortisol and adrenaline flooding whenever our own conception of ourselves (or egoic identity) feels like it is at risk.

We end up spending our lives constrained and worrying about what others will think. When you can transcend this limitation, so much more becomes possible.

Real creators fail so many times that they often will fail themselves right into a big success if they stay humble, kind, and keep listening for how they can help others in a big way. Tell yourself, over-and-over, failure is the path and to trust the path toward your long-term best-possible growth, even when it's shitty.

## How to Heal PTSD

If you are suffering from chronic pain, mental health challenges, post-traumatic stress disorder (PTSD), or something else that prevents your full happiness and from realizing just how beautiful and precious life is -- do all you can to work with professionals who are skilled at healing that.

Post-traumatic stress disorder (PTSD) is a mental health condition that can develop after a person has experienced or witnessed a traumatic event. Treatment for PTSD typically involves a combination of therapy and medication.

Many friends of mine have been able to heal from deeply traumatic experiences ranging from fighting in overseas wars to sexual abuse to the deaths of loved ones by working with trained professionals and various medicines that have been shown through initial clinical research to be effective at reducing PTSD, including **Psilocybin**, **Ketamine**, **MDMA**, and even **ayahuasca**.

The Multidisciplinary Association for Psychedelic Studies (MAPS) has dedicated more than three decades to conducting clinical research on the use of MDMA in combination with therapy for individuals with post-traumatic stress disorder (PTSD). The outcomes of their studies have been incredibly promising, leading to the FDA expediting the Phase III trials. This expedited process signifies the recognition of this therapeutic approach as a crucial treatment option for those experiencing major trauma.

Other more traditional treatments include cognitive behavioral therapy, exposure therapy, and eye movement desensitization and reprocessing (EMDR), or taking prescribed SSRI medications. My wife Morgan even did some transcranial direct current stimulation work (her doctor called it "brain training") to overcome anxiety and PTSD and increase the amount of oxytocin naturally in her body, and it helped her a lot.

Transcranial Direct Current Stimulation (tDCS) is a non-invasive brain stimulation technique that involves applying a low-level electrical current to the scalp to modulate brain activity. tDCS has been extensively studied in recent years and has been found to have potential therapeutic applications in several areas, including treating depression, enhancing cognitive performance, managing chronic pain, treating addiction, and managing neurological conditions like Parkinson's disease, MS, and strokes.

I encourage you to talk to a trained medical professional and take on the healing of your PTSD. It's time to put the past in the past and live in the present to experience the magic of the now.

## Become A Mental Black Belt

"We've become a culture of the too easily bruised, the too terribly delicate and the too readily weakened. We've become a society of snowflakes, complainers and hedonists who wish for only ease, pleasure and luxury, at every turn of each of our hours." - Robin Sharma, *The Everyday Hero Manifesto*

I want you to be tough. No, not a tough heart. I want you to keep your heart open and soft. I want you to be tough minded.

I want you to have a stoic mind that welcomes difficult circumstances -- almost craves challenge due to the learning that can come from it. For it is that challenge that makes us who we truly are.

Here's what my friend Lindsay Sukornyk recently shared on this topic:

"Life can be hard. In fact, it can be fu@&ing brutal. I have danced in the darkness and met more thresholds than I even knew existed, in the last many years. I have been in the fetal position, crying on the bathroom floor (many times), pushed so far past my limits of what I thought I could handle, I couldn't even see my comfort zone behind me. But then, somewhere in the depths of despair, I realized, I can handle this. I am equipped. In fact, I was born for this! Life does not give us any experiences we are not ready to navigate. And it makes us stronger. And braver. And more resilient and compassionate and kind. It brings us closer to our true nature - love. To be truly alive is to be available to feel it ALL. To accept it, to embrace it, to celebrate each moment on this wild, ecstatic journey called life. Because whatever it is, this too shall pass." - Lindsay Sukornyk

Yes, I want you to be tough minded and know that whatever you are going through, this too shall pass.

Here's what the Instagram account @insidehistory had to say about this topic of realizing that all challenging times eventually pass. Whatever you're going through now, this too shall pass.

### Putting Everything Into Perspective - From @InsideHistory

"For a small amount of perspective at this moment, imagine you were born in 1900. When you are 14, World War I starts, and ends on your 18th birthday with 22 million people killed. Later in the year, a Spanish Flu epidemic hits the planet and runs until you are 20. Fifty million people die from it in those two years. Yes, 50 million.

When you're 29, the Great Depression begins. Unemployment hits 25%, global GDP drops 27%. That runs until you are 33. The country nearly collapses along with the world economy. When you turn 39, World War II starts. You aren't even over the hill yet.

When you're 41, the United States is fully pulled into WWII. Between your 39th and 45th birthday, 75 million people perish in the war and the Holocaust kills twelve million. At 52, the Korean War starts and five million perish.

At 64 the Vietnam War begins, and it doesn't end for many years. Four million people die in that conflict. Approaching your 62nd birthday you have the Cuban Missile Crisis, a tipping point in the Cold War. Life on our planet, as we know it, could well have ended. Great leaders prevented that from happening.

As you turn 75, the Vietnam War finally ends. Think of everyone on the planet born in 1900. How do you survive all of that? A kid in 1985 didn't think their 85 year old grandparent understood how hard school was. Yet those grandparents (and now great grandparents) survived through everything listed above.

Perspective is an amazing art. As this year ends, let's try and keep things in perspective. Let's be smart, help each other out, and we will get through all of this. In the history of the world, there has never been a storm that lasted. This too, shall pass."

Yes, things are really good for humans now compared to 100 years ago. Across the world, life expectancy is much longer, infant mortality is lower, per capita income is much higher, and literacy is higher.

So don't complain when you have to wait in line for 30 minutes at the airport or when you have to get a tooth taken out. **Life is pretty damn good right now for humans compared to every other time in human history.**

And yet, from time to time, things can get cloudy and difficult. So like a karate master, I want you to be able to hold your mental form even while the waves are high and the sky is cloudy.

Train your mind to be a black belt in acceptance, appreciation, gratitude, and riding the wave of now while creating the future.

No matter the external circumstances, keep the inner realm calm, peaceful, and hopeful—just like the Holocaust survivor Victor Frankl trained his mind to do during the last few years of WWII when he was imprisoned and unsure if he would live.

Achieving victory in the midst of chaos can lead to incredible self-confidence. The true master learns to become, as Nassim Taleb calls it, "antifragile," where the greater the chaos around you, the calmer your inner core becomes.

People who have developed the skill set of being antifragile are naturally **emotionally resilient**.

*Emotional Resilience - The greater the chaos and challenge around you, the calmer your inner core becomes -- in order to help you get through difficult moments and periods in life.*

So yes, place yourself intentionally in harsh places from time-to-time, whether that's in the middle of a forest on a three-day solo hike, in the midst of a morning cold plunge, or in a spartan motel for a month-long retreat to work on the book that's been inside of you for years.

"To do towering work that stands the test of time and builds a life that you'll be ever so proud of demands that you place yourself in harsh places. And force yourself to do difficult things. So that the struggle introduces you to your hidden strength. And confidence. And brilliance." - Robin Sharma

It's interesting to observe that those who are the happiest, ironically, are those who don't require a lot to be happy. Air to breathe. Water to drink. Food to eat. Shelter over our heads. People who we love. What more is there to need? **Require little. Enjoy everything.**

Be a Stoic in your needs, and an Epicurean in your delights. Savor every little delight, every joy, and every friendship. For it will all be gone someday.

## Choose a Growth Mindset

"Lord, I thank you for sunshine. I thank you for rain. I thank you for joy. I thank you for pain. It's a beautiful day." - Jermaine Edwards, Musician

I realized early on in life that a clear vision, self-belief, consistent action, and having a **growth mindset** were essential to success.

*Growth Mindset - Someone who accepts responsibility for their life and believes that the challenges in their life are for them to grow. Has clear goals and purposes. Sees life as happening for them. The opposite of the victim's mindset.*

On the other hand, the **victim mindset** is the perspective that everything is difficult and unfair and that life is happening to you.

> *Victim Mindset - The perspective that everything is difficult and unfair and that life is happening to you The opposite of the growth mindset.*

What's an example of applying a Growth Mindset in my own life?

Back in 2017, I'd lost around $10M from real estate investments, bad angel investments, and a challenging business lawsuit. I had also lost both my parents by age 30 to cancer and gotten addicted to entheogenic ceremonial shamanic drugs, which caused me to lose my ability to be a consistent producer and maintain a clear mindset. It was a rough start to my 30s for me, to say the least, during this phase of massive personal growth.

Instead of becoming a victim and complaining about how life was unfair -- I took personal responsibility for all that had happened, chose the path of healing I was on, and did the work to get out of the hole I'd put myself in. I remember holding onto a wooden hexagon that said, "Trust the Process," during many moments in my recovery process. Thankfully, I knew that mentally becoming a victim would get me nowhere.

As Robin Sharma writes in *The Everyday Manifesto*, "It's about no longer acting like a victim (letting your circumstances control your life) and instead acting like a superhero (creating a life that has you waking up in giddy disbelief that you get to be you)."

So instead of living in the **victim mindset,** choose consciously and intentionally to live in the **growth mindset**.

*Victim Mindset = Everything is difficult, unfair, and terrible. Life is happening "to me."*

*Growth Mindset = I appreciate what I have, I accept what has already happened. The challenges in my life are for my soul to grow. Life is happening "for me."*

Here's what Robin Sharma says about these two very different mindsets...

| Victim Mindset | Growth Mindset |
| --- | --- |
| Has the mindset of can't | Has the mentality of can |
| Makes excuses | Delivers results |
| Lives in the past | Makes their future brighter |
| Is busy being busy | Is productive |
| Takes from the world | Gives to the world |

As Robin Sharma wrote: "I will show up as a leader, not as a victim. As an originator, not a copier. As a visionary, instead of a follower. Today, I choose to be extraordinary rather than average. And brave, instead of timid. A hero in my own distinct way, instead of giving away my potent powers by blame, complaint, and excuse".

People with a **growth mindset** follow the guidance of George Bernard Shaw, who encouraged us to follow on purpose and contribute to the world rather than complaining. He said, "This is the true joy in life, being used for a purpose recognized by yourself as a mighty one. Being a force of nature instead of a feverish, selfish little clod of ailments and grievances, complaining that the world will not devote itself to making you happy."

## Never Complain

"When you complain, nobody wants to help you. If you spend your time focusing on the things that are wrong, and that's what you express and project to people you know, you don't become a source of growth for people, you become a source of destruction for people.
- Stephen Hawking

**We are living in the most prosperous time in human history.** We have buses that fly through the air. We have penicillin and antibiotics that prevent life-taking infections and bacteria. We are nearing universal access to mobile phone service, something only the wealthiest could afford when I was born. Life expectancy and global income are higher than they've ever been.

We have electricity and engines that take away so much of the difficult labor of the past. We have free generative AI bots that can do research for us. We have festivals that celebrate the magic of life, from Burning Man to India's Kumbh Mela. Most of us have a cornucopia of grocery options within 15 minutes of our homes. And importantly, we also now have renewable energy sources that are now cheaper than fossil fuels. We're on track to be a highly prosperous and low carbon society.

We can fly to the literal other side of the world (LA to Sydney) in 16 hours. The same expedition would have taken two months by boat when my Grandma Eva was born in 1902.

Yes, life ends in death, and everyone we know will someday die. But if you are still alive and breathing -- celebrate this time you DO HAVE with yourself and your friends. Your candle is not yet out. What you will lose someday hasn't yet been lost. And that is worth celebrating. If you're reading this, you still have time.

Yes, challenges happen. But the key for winners is to never complain, appreciate the challenges, and put yourself in a state of gratitude every single day through your **miracle mornings**. As author Jen Sincero writes, "You cut yourself off from the supply of awesomeness when you are not in a state of gratitude."

Don't be a drama mama, a term that Robert Sharma coined in *The 5AM Club*. "Drama mamas. That's what I call men and women who've caught the virus of victimitis excusitis. All they do is complain about how bad things are for them instead of applying their primal power to make things better. They take instead of give, criticize instead of create, and worry instead of work."

So if you want to be happy -- limit your complaining and instead aim to maximize the amount of spontaneous hand-written mini-thank you cards you randomly give out to everyone in your life, including your waiters, drivers, delivery people, and even the cute girls at the bar.

**Action Item #46: The Incredible Now**
Write down the answer to this question: What are all the things that are possible in your life because of the inventions that have happened since 1900? Take a moment to research everything that has been discovered and created since then, and then write down what's possible in your life now because of these inventions.

## Choosing a Positive Outlook

*"Happiness is a way of interpreting the world, since while it may be difficult to change the world, it is always possible to change the way we look at it." - Matthieu Ricard, monk and French author*

It is your mindset that controls your happiness. Your mindset is:

1) How you interpret what happens in your life

2) How you prepare your mind to get through the inevitable challenges that come up

The exact same life challenges could lead two different people to either appreciation and happiness or resignation and sadness -- simply based on their mindset.

Those who have taken a **Vow of Unconditional Happiness**, those who have read this book, or those who have studied the stoic practice of **negative visualization** might do quite well during challenges.

*Negative Visualization - Imagining ahead of time the worst case scenario so you can be mentally and emotionally prepared for it if it happens. Best if combined with positive visualization, where you also visualize the outcome you want.*

Some may let a single challenge delay the pursuit of their purpose for years or forever. It's all about the mindset you choose to have and the mindset you build. Never let a challenge stop you from giving your gift to the world.

You can decide whether you want to live in an ordinary world full of stress & suffering or an extraordinary world full of joy, wonder, and possibility.

You can choose to live in the default ordinary world (what I call "The Matrix") -- or a world where anything is possible ("The Extraordinary World").

MAGIC YEAR - 244

## The Ordinary World

fear, insecurity, scarcity, disappointment, upset, danger, desperation, limitation, anger, victimization, cynicism, mistrust, manipulation, defensive, reason, inaction, greed, resignation

The extraordinary world happens through a mindset shift -- through a simple choice to be happy and look at things through a positive lens -- and to look at challenges as beneficial for growth.

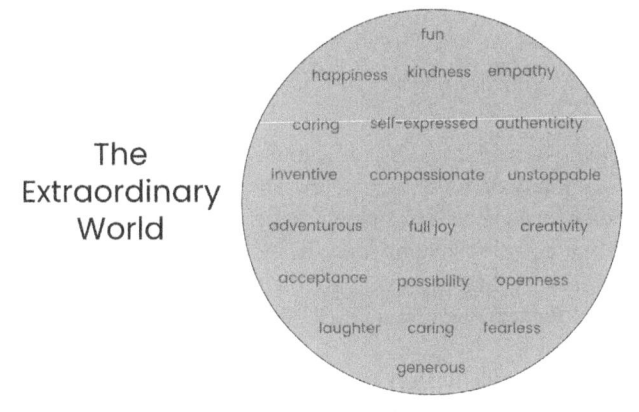

## The Extraordinary World

fun, happiness, kindness, empathy, caring, self-expressed, authenticity, inventive, compassionate, unstoppable, adventurous, full joy, creativity, acceptance, possibility, openness, laughter, caring, fearless, generous

Living with joyfulness and ease is a choice you can make. So where are you right now on the happiness scale? On a scale of 0-10 where would you rate your overall happiness?

**DEAD INSIDE** 0 — 10 **FULLY ALIVE**

| Dead Inside | Fully Alive |
|---|---|
| Sad and pessimistic | Happy and optimistic |
| Hating life and work | Loving life and work |
| Given up on your dreams | Pursuing your dreams |
| Not doing what you love | Doing what you love |
| Not contributing to others | Contributing to others |
| Cynical & resigned | Positive and engaged |
| A world of despair | A world of joy |
| Mental chaos & confusion | Mental calmness and clarity |
| Feeling anxious & depressed | Feeling relaxed and excited |
| Feeling angry | Feeling welcoming |
| Feeling blocked | Feeling creative |
| Feeling unexpressed | Feeling expressed |
| A lack of love | Receiving and giving love |
| A lack of confidence | Confident |
| Eating dead foods | Eating live foods |
| Unhealthy body | Healthy body |
| Low energy | High energy |
| Driven by fear and anger | Driven by love & compassion |
| Driven by material possessions | Driven by contribution |

**ON A 0-10 SCALE, WHERE WOULD YOU RATE YOUR OVERALL HAPPINESS?**

*Are you dead inside or fully alive?*

Once you know where you're at today, ask yourself, "What is your plan to increase your baseline happiness level over the next few months? What habits can you introduce that are likely to lead to greater life satisfaction?"

### Action Item #47: Your Happiness Number

On a scale of 1-10, rate your current happiness level as an average over the last few weeks, with 10 being the highest possible. Now that you have your baseline happiness number, write down the answers to these two questions: What is your plan to increase your baseline happiness level over the next few months. What habits can you introduce that are likely to lead to greater life satisfaction? Actually, do these for the next 30 days.

## Quit Your Job?

"You see, the secret to happiness is simple, find out what you truly love to do and then direct all of your energy towards doing it." - Robin Sharma, author

If you're working at a job that you don't love, aren't growing in, or that restricts you from doing what you actually do love to do -- you should quit. No amount of money is worth spending your life doing work you don't enjoy.

My belief is that you'll make way more money over time doing what you love to do and becoming so obsessed with it that you become world class at that specialized offering or skillset. If you love what you do, over time you'll become much better at it and make much more money.

So while it's fine to work at a job for a few years if you are learning skills and being surrounded by great mentors -- if you don't love the work -- then you should eventually make plans to leave and spend some time exploring so you know what you truly love to do.

Your happiness demands it.

### Be Sure You Do Work You Actually Love To Do

"We're born, and roughly around 20 we start to work. Then we work work work work work. We keep working all the way until we're 65 years old. If you die at 80, this is most of your life. So it is very important to spend this time doing something you love. Being a kid is nice. Retiring is nice. But what about the years in between? These should not just be a "write off" and just "waiting for Friday" and "just get through it." So, if you're working at a job that you hate just for a paycheck, then you need to make a change in your life."
- @SuccessOwner on IG

**Action Item #48: A Job Transition Plan**
Do you love what you do? If so, great. If not, write down a simple plan to transition out of doing work you don't love within the next 12 months into a new field where you truly love what you do while achieving your financial goals. How will you serve the world in the future? What will be your work contribution to society that lights you up?

# Forgiveness Is a Key to Happiness

"Holding on to resentment is like taking poison and then waiting for your enemies to die." - Jen Sincero, author

I once had a CEO I hired for one of my companies who didn't do the best of jobs. Under his management, the company lost around $1M in 24 months, and the staff came to me with lots of concerns about his style. I let him go.

About two years later, he sued the company for millions of dollars, claiming we'd promised him half of the firm when we had in writing that we offered him 25% over 4 years, which he never signed and thus never received.

50% of a firm losing $500,000 per year is probably worth nothing. But nonetheless, the guy persisted through a multi-year battle. It seemed we had very different perspectives on the matter. As a side note, it's best to assume in a misunderstanding that the other side simply had a different perspective rather than bad intent. Assuming positive intent in others whenever possible is a key to a happy life.

While we nearly went to court, I ended up settling as I wasn't sure whether a jury would hear the case based on the written evidence or simply side with the employee. The risk of losing the entire firm to bankruptcy was real. The total cost to me personally was in the millions when all was said and done, wiping out the majority of my net worth.

I am still to this day (eight years after I let him go) finishing paying off debts incurred from the suit and the business loans I took on to cover the settlement to keep the business and its mission alive. We couldn't declare bankruptcy because we had a profitable business -- we simply had to pay off the debts slowly over time.

Most people would be furious at this ex-employee. I was. But after a couple years, I realized that this hidden resentment was doing nothing for me.

I choose to reprogram the whole experience as a gift. I realized that without the lawsuit, I would have never slowed down enough to meet my future wife, which happened just three months after we settled in 2019. I would have never gone to a four day Burning Man camp out on a farm in California had I been the old, fast-moving entrepreneur version of myself.

You see, my wife Morgan is an artist who lived on a 650 acre intentional community and wouldn't have been interested in marrying a busy entrepreneur who didn't have time to make family a priority.

The suit slowed me down enough to actually be ready to meet my beloved. My wife and I now have our son Apollo, who inspired me to write this book in the year after he was born..

And so, without this challenge, I wouldn't have my wife, my son, or this book. You wouldn't be reading this word right now without that lawsuit that slowed me down. This great challenge led to my greatest gifts.

Now let's zoom in on January 2023. I was at a "Dark Masculine Tantra Workshop" in Ubud, Bali, Indonesia. The facilitator asked us to do an exercise around expressing our rage. They matched us up with a partner and asked us to imagine that partner as the person who had challenged us the most over the last decade. I imagined the former CEO who had led to years of headaches and millions of dollars in losses.

Then the facilitator asked us to scream and shout and let out all our rage on our partner. My workshop partner went first and screamed at me, imagining I was her sexual abuser. I went second.

I didn't scream, yell, pound pillows, or express my rage. Instead, I thanked my partner for challenging me and slowing me down enough so that I could actually get healthy, meet my wife, and give myself the greatest gift ever -- my family.

I said something like: "What you did was terrible. What you did, in my opinion, was unethical. And I want to thank you because without the challenges you created for me, I wouldn't be the person I am today."

So if you're reading this, the person I once hired who later sued me, know that I've forgiven you fully and hope you can find the same forgiveness in your heart for me and the misunderstandings we had. I no longer hold any resentment and have turned it into appreciation. Thank you for the deeply challenging lessons.

Afterwards, my partner in the tantra exercise said that what I had said to her was the most powerful example of forgiveness she had ever seen. She decided to forgive her abuser, which gave her mental freedom after years of feeling rage.

Following the exercise, a long discussion continued in the tantra class circle around whether "expressing our rage" more is what is really needed or if "expressing our forgiveness" is what is really needed.

The conclusion we reached in that tantra classroom in Bali: Expressing emotions fully is very important. Bottling them up doesn't do anyone any good. But after you do that, the way you actually move on for good and achieve lasting happiness in your life is through forgiveness and seeing the true gifts from what happened. Let's repeat that one more time for emphasis...

> Expressing emotions fully is very important. Bottling them up doesn't do anyone any good. But after you do that, the way you actually move on for good and achieve lasting happiness in your life is through forgiveness and seeing the true gifts from what happened.

Yes, whatever suffering you've experienced -- it's been a gift. What is this gift? Being thankful for the gifts that have come from challenges is one of the keys to internal freedom and happiness.

**Action Item #49: The Forgiveness List**
Write down the names of all the people you still need to fully forgive for past transgressions. Write down what you are forgiving each person for. When done, write at the bottom: "I thank you for the lessons you taught me and hereby forgive you completely and fully."

# Be Like a Kid

*"Play! Play more. I feel like people are so serious, and it doesn't take much for people to drop back into the wisdom of a childlike playfulness. If I had to prescribe two things to improve health and happiness in the world, it'd be movement and play." - Jason Nemer, founder of AcroYoga*

As kids, we were all joyful. As kids, we were all fully-self expressed. Of course, most four year olds are very, very good at "self-expression." But then, sometime usually between ages 10 and 30, traumas (big and small) pile up that cause us to disconnect from our inner soul and our vibrant expression.

As Robin Sharma writes, "When we were kids, we were emotionally naked. We held our vulnerability in our open palms for all the world to see. Yes, we were that strong. We spoke honestly of our fears, cried innocent tears, risked taking risks, stayed true to ourselves, and felt safe revealing our brilliance to anyone who cared to see it. Then, as we proceeded through life—and met with disappointments, difficulties, and discouragements—we gathered the emotional residue of our challenging encounters. To protect ourselves, we unconsciously began to construct a suit of armor over our tender, wise, and powerful hearts. To escape the hurt. To avoid the suffering. To forget the trauma. Yet in dismissing our pain, we also disassociated from our light."

Various events, from as small as scraping your knee to as large as sexual abuse or losing a parent, teach us to be "safe" and no longer fully express ourselves. Something teaches us to prioritize being "safe" and no longer prioritize being fully expressed and fully alive. Something teaches us to be "safe" and no longer take big chances.

### Examples of Events That Teach Us To Be "Safe"

You scraped your knee on the playground
You made a speech and were laughed at on stage
You ripped your pants at recess and your underwear showed
You got yelled at for playing at the wrong time
Your parents yelled at you for making a mistake
Your dad hit you for doing something wrong
Your boyfriend or girlfriend broke up with you
You gave the wrong answer in class
You were sexually abused
You blamed your parents' divorce on yourself
You broke your leg while doing something you love
You lost money on an investment and were yelled at
You were discouraged from starting your own company
Your business failed
You broke your leg after jumping off a waterfall
Your parents passed away early

Of course, when we lose our spark -- our magic dies with it. We have to become self-aware of our own internal repression in order to become the fullest version of ourselves again.

As youngsters, we possessed an innate sense of vitality and wonder, finding joy in simple pleasures like gazing at the stars, playing in the park, and chasing butterflies.

As we grew older, we became detached from our humanity, losing our sense of passion, enthusiasm, and love for life. Our once-boundless optimism dwindled, and we resigned ourselves to mediocrity.

We became preoccupied with conforming, acquiring wealth, and gaining popularity, allowing our wellsprings of creativity, positivity, and self-awareness to wither. But we need not submit to the disillusioned, uninspired world of adulthood, characterized by scarcity, indifference, and fitting in.

Do you think a four year old boy cares what others think? Of course he doesn't. He doesn't give a flying hootenanny about what people think. He's just himself--present and joyful most of the time -- and when he's upset, he cries for a few minutes, and it's all gone.

*Be like this kid -- well into your 30s, 40s, 50s, 60s, and beyond*

But we often lose our joy as we get older, and part of us dies inside. There's a fix. Want to know?

To regain our joy and childlike wonder, we must **reconnect with what makes us come alive**. To regain our joy and childlike wonder, we must live a life that lights us up inside. To regain our joy and childlike wonder, we must live a life that inspires us and others. To regain our joy and childlike wonder, we must be brave and actually pursue our dreams. And we must remember to play. Every single day.

Do you need a little reminder to help you remember your inner joy? Well, whenever my wife and I get a little crusty, we do two things.

1. We shout out loud, "Seriousity is poo."

2. We sing and dance to Hakuna Matata like animals in the midst of a wild rumpus

So if you need a little reminder for yourself each day, set an alarm for 6 p.m. each day to sing this song refrain. It will remind you to play like a kid every single day and have no worries for the rest of your days.

"Hakuna Matata! What a wonderful phrase.
Hakuna Matata! Ain't no passing craze.
It means no worries. For the rest of your days.
It's our problem-free philosophy, Hakuna Matata!"

Here's what's inside my wife's notebook right now here in Bali about play and love. I find it a great affirmation and reminder of what life is all about.

### Morgan's Principle for Living #2 - Devote to A Life of Play

I am devoted to play and loving my life every single day. I shall enjoy the whole ride, the ups and downs, and do it from a sense of utter gratitude, awe, love, joy, and fun. I shall celebrate what it means to be alive now with my family, on the incredible Mamma Gaia (Earth), and in my luscious body. I choose to live from this play and love every single day.

# Your Best Work Comes From Flow States

"JPF (joy, peace and freedom) are a million times more valuable than FFA (fame, fortune and applause)." - Robin Sharma

Over the millennia, many philosophers have asked the fundamental question -- what is the source of joy?

I believe that joy comes from living with flow, purpose, and connection.
Flow is the state of consciousness people achieve when they are so engaged in an activity that nothing else seems to matter.

What I've found is that true joy occurs when you can fully express yourself and bring your full passion into your EVERYDAY WORK.

True joy occurs when your daily work involves sharing the greatest contribution you can give to humanity with the gifts you have.

True joy occurs when you're making a difference in the lives of others -- whether your kids, your spouse, your blood relatives, your friends, your community, -- and even the lives of people you don't know.

True joy comes from service and from the habit of living with gratitude. True joy comes from living in flow and finding your flow state in what you create. As I wrote earlier: you know you've found your purpose when you find your **flow state**, when you're so engaged in what you're doing that time melts away, you can achieve superhuman performance, and your inhibitions about revealing your true self are extinct.

As Marc Benioff, CEO of Salesforce, says, "The real joy in life comes from finding your true purpose and aligning it with what you do every single day."

To find your own internal joy, do these six things.

1. Decide and declare your **purpose statement**
2. Choose to be **unconditionally happy**
3. Appreciate what you learn from your **dharmic challenges**
4. Do what brings you into **flow**.

5. End your **unhealthy addictions**.
6. Follow your **healthy obsessions**.

Do these six things, and life becomes so much easier. So. Much. Easier.

> Common people who find uncommon success don't find their passions -- they follow their obsessions. - Michael Moritz, investor

## The Eight Sources of Joy

So what leads to long lasting joy? I've been able to track eight causes and sources of deep joy inside of me.

1) **Presence:** Being actually present in every moment rather than worried about the past or the future and spending time with close friends and family.
2) **Achievement:** Achieving meaningful goals that matter to you.
3) **Alignment:** The satisfaction of doing what you say you're going to do
4) **Commitment:** And being committed to something bigger than yourself
5) **Flow:** Getting in deep flow on a creative project or adventure that you enjoy so much that time seems to melt away.
6) **Love:** Finding a deep love for nature, people, family, yourself, and creation
7) **Obsession:** Becoming truly committed and even obsessed with creating something bigger than yourself.
8) **Wonder -** Appreciating the beauty & impermanence of life

Yes, the world wants you to live a life of joy, play, connection, and contribution -- a life of meaning. But you must be bold, actually think through and then follow your dreams, and go after living the life of your dreams. For it is only through living the life of your dreams that a life of true meaning and authentic expression can emerge.

Yes, living the life of your dreams is the path to living a life worth living. But of course, that brings up the question, "What are your dreams? And what is your vision for your life?" Be sure you've written those down and have them framed in your bedroom or office!

## Live in the Moment

> "If you are depressed, you are living in the past. If you are anxious, you are living in the future. If you are at peace, you are living in the present."
> - Lao Tzu, founder of Taoism

Whatever happened to you in the past -- your obsessive thoughts about it are limiting you, holding you back, and keeping you small.

But what if you could put what happened in the past, in the past -- rather than letting it hang around your neck like a permanent albatross -- continually causing undesired anxiety and fear?

What would be possible for your life then? What if you could live again with full excitement in the present?

What if you could absolutely SAVOR the joy that comes from small things like smelling a flower, holding a baby, or going on a walk in nature?

You see, true joy comes from being completely present and in the flow of a moment.

Learning how to be in the present with something you absolutely love and out of the past and the future is a key to happiness in life. **The key is to enjoy each and every moment along the way... the challenging ones and the sublimely magnificent ones.**

Like this moment, where I'm sitting next to two palm trees and a pool in Canggu, Bali, writing these very words on this screen while a butterfly flutters by -- completely enmeshed in my flow-guided effort to offer a helpful guide to life and transformation for my son and for others.

The key to presence is to train your mind to stop thinking about the past or future. It's hard, but doable -- especially through meditation and a silent Vipassana retreat.

You see, people spend much of their mental energy worrying about either the past or the future.

True joy comes when you focus instead on enjoying the present moment and don't worry about whatever happened in the past or what might come in the future.

Of course, all of eternity has been lived in the now. There is nothing (at least to the human observer) other than the continuous present moment.

And so this is how people lose their whole lives, stuck in the past or the future rather than actually being "in the now," as Eckhart Tolle likes to say.

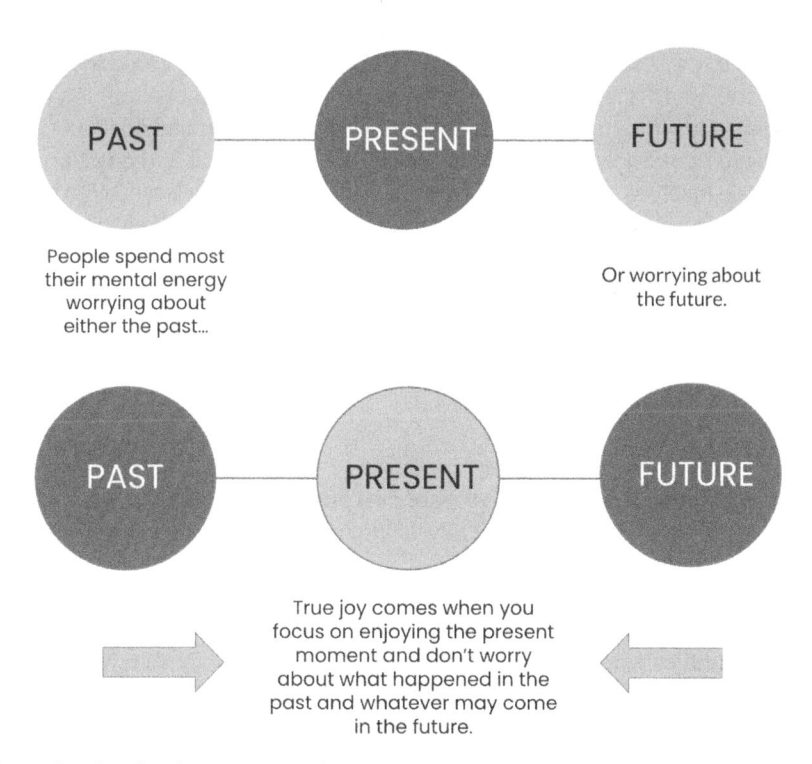

PAST — PRESENT — FUTURE

People spend most their mental energy worrying about either the past...

Or worrying about the future.

PAST — PRESENT — FUTURE

True joy comes when you focus on enjoying the present moment and don't worry about what happened in the past and whatever may come in the future.

Every leader that has ever made an inspiring speech or taken a heroic act -- all of those actions were taken in the then-present moment. Everything in life -- your whole life -- is a series of these precious moments. Don't waste them by mentally being checked out and doing something else.

You see, the key to both happiness AND communication, AND leadership is **presence**.

> *The key to happiness, communication, and leadership = Presence*

Great leaders have it. They are focused, clear, and when you speak to them, you feel like they are actually with you rather than somewhere else.

> *Presence - Being fully focused on the people you're speaking with rather than in your own head or looking elsewhere. Choose to look people in the eye and actually listen to what they are saying, and magic will happen with your career and goals. Deep presence is the magic of True Kings.*

As my friend Aliya Daniels says, "Presence is our *superpower* as humans, and we each have access to it *all the time*."

Bad leaders don't have a clear presence. They are scattered, anxious, and rarely present with their team, colleagues, or family members. You simply don't feel like they are "there with you" when they speak with you. It feels as if they are reading a script or just going through the motions without being connected to their inner humanity.

The key to presence is having a clear mind, a good morning breathing practice, slowing down enough to actually feel the people you are with, and overcoming looping anxious thoughts and worry through meditation and reducing sugar and caffeine in your diet.

There are two major types of presence: **physical presence** and **emotional presence**. Physical presence involves looking people in the eye and being physically with them. It involves commanding energy and attention at the right moments, and paying incredibly close attention to others at other moments. Emotional presence involves actually feeling what others are feeling -- and taking the time to inquire as to how they are truly doing inside. The best leaders are A+ at both physical and emotional presence.

If you find yourself often worried and anxious in moments and unable to be fully present, check out the great classic 1948 book, *How to Stop Worrying and Start Living* by Dale Carnegie.

**Action Item #50: The Presence Test**
Decide in this moment that going forward, you are going to be fully present in each moment with the people you are with. No more smartphone distractions or thinking about the past or the future. Just be present, moment-to-moment. If a conversation is boring or uninspiring, either work to make it interesting or excuse yourself so you can be fully present elsewhere. Write down the following: "I commit to being fully present whenever I am with another person."

# Give Your Master Gift Before You Die

"How long does a masterwork take?" the apprentice asked the master. "As long as it takes" was the master's simple reply. "And don't stop until it's magic. Otherwise you might as well not even start it." Handcrafting your tour de force is far from easy. It will call on you to develop extreme patience with the process, dig deep, pull out your greatness and come face to face with your dragons. Yet if you continue to completion, you'll become a totally new person. And the confidence, expertise and self-respect gained in making the project will last an entire lifetime. - Robin Sharma, The Everyday Hero Manifesto

    The only thing we owe the world is to be kind and leave behind something worthy of our lives. Your gift to the world could be a company, a book, a clothing line, an invention, a philosophy, music, art, or various other things.
    You see, as we get into our 20s, 30s, and 40s, we often become more afraid of being criticized (or being canceled) than of wasting our lives being mediocre and not "finding the time" to give our gifts.
    Your **masterwork** is worthy of your time. And you giving it in this lifetime, before you die in this body, is essential.
    It has been a twelve year process to create the book. Ten years of notetaking and two years of writing and editing. Yes, creating this book is me giving one of my master gifts. If you're reading this sentence, I've likely succeeded in getting it out before I passed on. Go Ryan.
    I mean, this book is sort of an insane project. To capture everything I've ever learned in one massive metabook? Right now, this book is at 125,000 words, and I'm not even done editing it yet. That's a long book -- but hopefully one you're getting a lot of inspiration and value from. What motivates me? The thought that sometime in 2038 my young son Apollo is going to be reading this line and pondering what his **masterwork** is going to be.
    You may not know what your masterwork is going to be yet. But once you do, it will grip you and give you an uncomfortable choice. Do you get out of your comfort zone and change around your life to ensure it becomes real -- or do you delay and take the chance that this magic will never flow from your hands.
    Of course, the truth about life is that you rarely know when it will end. My mom, Pauline, died at age 60 from a brain tumor. She went from being perfectly healthy to no longer breathing within 6 months. 180 days. Bam.
    She told me in those later months that she always had a premonition that she would die young like her mom, Jean, who passed at age 53.
    And so she, at age 43, decided to "retire" and move to Florida with our family so she could live her last years doing yoga, walking on the beach, watching her son grow up, and reading books. Her big gift to the world, she often told me, was making me.
    Her gift to me was the way she encouraged and guided my education, including lots of reading and travel adventures (while our family earned just $32,000 per year), and told me I could do absolutely anything I set my mind to.
    Your parents gave up a big chunk of their lives to create you. If you have a compelling interest, a grabbing passion, or a distracting healthy obsession -- follow it until the ends of the earth. Become a world class expert in something you love. And then sing your song, write your book, raise that incredible baby, paint your painting, or build that company.
    Dedicate yourself to the mastery of something you love. And share the gift. The world is counting on you.

**Action Item #51: Your Masterwork**
Write down what you think the most important gift will be that you will someday give the world, your community, or your family? Will it be a book, a movie, a company, an invention, a child, or an artwork? Something else. Speculate in your writing what might be the possible masterworks of your life.

## Study Happiness Philosophy

*"Everything in life happens for a reason. Disappointment comes with a lesson. It's for me to get wiser. Got to work harder. In the end it will get better."*
- Jermaine Edwards, Musician

The greatest leaders are happy and encouraging of themselves, their families, and their teams. People want to be around happy people and avoid grumpy complainers. So learning to become truly happy not only makes a huge difference for yourself, -- it also has cascading effects on your work and brings your masterwork and gifts to the world.

Making a Vow of Unconditional Happiness (see prior section) is a start -- but deeply understanding happiness philosophy will lock it all in and give you the edge you need to maintain happiness in all conditions and circumstances.

The various philosophical traditions have a lot to say about happiness. Here's a quick rundown.

### Philosophical Views on Happiness

**Hedonism -** Says that pleasure is the highest good, and one should always strive to maximize their own pleasure and happiness.

**Epicureanism -** A belief in making balanced choices that maximize long-term pleasure. Epicureanism posits that pleasure is the ultimate good, and pain is the ultimate evil. Known as connoisseurs of the arts of life and the refinements of sensual pleasures.

**Stoicism -** The Stoics believed that by learning to control one's emotions and desires, and to accept whatever comes their way with equanimity, one could attain true happiness.

**Existentialism -** Happiness comes from developing your authentic identity, developing meaningful relationships, laughing at the absurdity of life, and finding a purpose or mission in life. Encourages people to take risks, pursue their own goals and ambitions, and to find joy in life, even in the midst of difficulty and adversity.

**Confucianism -** Happiness is achieved through leading a virtuous life, developing meaningful relationships, and achieving success in one's chosen field. Happiness is found in the realization of one's true potential.

**Daoism -** Places great value on being content with the present moment. Daoists embrace simplicity, minimize external distractions, and develop personal relationships with their inner selves and nature in order to increase their feelings of happiness

**Humanism -** Believes that we owe it to ourselves to make life the best possible for ourselves and everyone we share this planet with. Humanists believe in reason, science, and education and that all individuals should have equal rights and opportunities.

The Stoics, especially, had a lot to say about suffering and happiness. According to the Stoics, much of our suffering is caused by attachment to external events, such as wealth, status, power, and health, which are beyond our control.

To overcome suffering, the Stoics recommend developing a sense of inner peace and calm by focusing on things that are within your full control, such as your thoughts, emotions, and behaviors.

By practicing rational thinking, mindfulness, and living in accordance with your values and priorities, the Stoics believed that you could reduce negative emotions and increase positive ones, ultimately leading to a more content and fulfilling life. Check out the great modern stoic book *The Obstacle Is the Way* by Ryan Holiday for even more stoic philosophy.

Personally, I'm a combination of a Stoic, an Epicurean, and an Existentialist. I like that Stoics can deal with difficult challenges and make the best of them. I like that Epicureans can enjoy the celebrations of life. And I like that Existentialists work hard to become their authentic selves and actually live their purpose.

If you re-read the definition of Existentialism it pretty much sums up this entire book.

*Existentialism - Believes that happiness comes from developing your authentic identity, developing meaningful relationships, laughing at the absurdity of life, and finding a purpose or mission in life. Encourages people to take risks, pursue their own goals and ambitions, and to find joy in life, even in the midst of difficulty and adversity.*

There is a nihilistic side to existentialism that I don't like (thanks, Nietzsche!) that posits that life is pointless. However, I think when you really read Camus, Heidegger, and Sartre enough, you realize that they suggested that there is immense meaning in life -- if you choose to create it for yourself. They believed, as I do, that you create the purpose in your life that pulls you forward into inspired action.

Give me the non-nihilist existentialists combined with the ethical hedonists, and I'm a happy man.

**Action Item #52: Define Your Happiness Philosophy**
Write down in your notebook: which of the above philosophies speak to you most? Why? If you had to describe your personal philosophy to someone else as a mix of 2-3 other philosophies, which ones would you choose?

## Buddha, Epicurus, & 3 Existentialists Walk Into a Bar

"Everything that I need I already have
Everything that I have is all that I need
Anything I desire I will receive
Because my reality is created by me
I am successful I am peaceful I am free I am wise
I am potential energy and like a Phoenix I shall rise
I am healthy I am wealthy I am power I am talent
I am mind I am body I am spirit I am balanced
I am enlightened I am fearless I am outside the realm of time
I am a part of the all and I am one with the divine."
- Michael Seven, The Energy Mantra

My favorite philosophers in terms of their views on happiness were: Buddha and Epicurus, and my favorite three existentialists: Martin Heidegger, Albert Camus, and Jean-Paul Sartre. Let's learn a little bit more about each of them.

### The Beliefs of Siddhartha Gautama "Buddha"

Buddha (roughly 563-483 BCE) believed that the source of all suffering and dissatisfaction in life is ignorance and craving, and that the key to achieving lasting happiness and peace is to overcome ignorance and craving through cultivating wisdom, compassion, and acceptance. Buddha's key beliefs included:

1. One should not live in luxury or abstain from food and comforts. Instead we should live in moderation ("The Middle Way") so we can best cultivate compassion for others and seek enlightenment.
2. There is suffering and constant dissatisfaction in the world.
3. This suffering is caused by our desires.
4. We can transcend suffering by removing or managing our desires.
5. To be happy we can change our outlook and be happy in any circumstance no matter how difficult.

### The Beliefs of Epicurus, The Father of Epicureanism

Epicurus (341-270 BCE) is one of my favorite philosophers, as he focused on what actually makes people happy. He argued that money and luxury did not align well with happiness. Epicurus formed communal living centers with his friends so he could see them more regularly. I do the same thing in Boulder and Nosara, Costa Rica.

Epicurus was a Greek philosopher who founded the Epicurean school of philosophy in ancient Greece. His philosophy, known as Epicureanism, was based on the idea that the highest good is pleasure, and that the key to living a happy and fulfilling life is to seek pleasure and avoid pain.

Epicurus argued that pleasure was the chief good in life. Hence, he advocated living in such a way as to derive the greatest amount of pleasure possible during one's lifetime, yet doing so moderately in order to avoid the suffering incurred by overindulgence in such pleasure. He observed that what makes most people happy is:

1. Seeing friends regularly in real life
2. Helping others and improving the world (making a difference)
3. Finding calm within your own mind

## The Beliefs of Existentialist Martin Heidegger

Martin Heidegger (1889–1966) is my favorite existentialist philosopher. He believed that true happiness is found in living a life that is meaningful and focused on self-fulfillment and being your authentic self. Do you, my friend. Heidegger thought:

1. We had lost touch with the beautiful mystery of existence – the uncanny strangeness that we are in fact here on this planet and alive.
2. We had forgotten that we were all connected and that there is a unity of being.
3. We had forgotten to be free and live for ourselves (being authentic by doing what we truly love rather than the inauthenticity that comes from trying to be like others by following "The Chatter" of the crowds). He encouraged people to **Escape the Matrix** of society and think for themselves from first principles.
4. That when we realize that we will be dead someday (and be in "The Nothing") we will give up trying to impress people and instead lead the lives we want. He believed we should spend time in graveyards to gain perspective on our life.
5. We should become more conscious of The Nothing (our future death) every day and that we should escape the clutches of The Chatter of society in order to become more authentic.
6. We should be appreciative of the time we have on this planet.
7. Happiness should stem from a deep personal understanding of oneself and the world around you, rather than from external sources like material objects or money.
8. We should try to live in harmony with nature, as nature can provide us with a sense of contentment.
9. Happiness is an individual journey and that it is up to each person to find the path that leads them to contentment.

> True happiness is found in living a life that is meaningful and focused on self-fulfillment and being your authentic self

## The Beliefs of Existentialism Jean-Paul Sartre

Jean-Paul Sartre ( 1905 – 1980) was a Frenchman who popularized Existentialism, including these ideas:

1) Life is weird. For example: We're actually living on a planet spinning around an exploding fusion reactor at 66,000 miles per hour.

2) We are free. Things in the future don't have to be the way they are today. Everything is possible. Humans are making it up as we go along. Things don't have to be the way they are. We should create new ideas and institutions.

3) We should not assume that we have to maintain the same professional identity throughout life. We humans are free creatures who can go do anything.

4) Authenticity is the degree to which one is true to one's own personality, spirit, or character, despite external pressures.

5) We shouldn't let concerns about money and work hold us back from living an authentic life and doing exactly what we want to do. We shouldn't let anything deny our freedom. We should consider living in other ways and experimenting with our freedoms to live how we wish.

6) We shouldn't feel oppressed by the weight of tradition and the status quo.

**The Beliefs of Existentialist Albert Camus**

Albert Camus (1913 – 1960) was a 20th Century French-Algerian existentialist. In his writing, Camus drew on the ideas of existential writers and philosophers such as Nietzsche to examine themes of disillusionment and alienation in a time of war and turmoil, when people felt forgotten (by God) and without purpose. He believed that:

1. All of our lives are absurd. We are just biological matter spinning senselessly on a tiny rock in the corner of an indifferent universe.
2. Life is worth living, but we have to create the meaning in life for ourselves.
3. Once you realize that life is absurd, you can live more intensely without worry of criticism from others. We should live with passion.
4. There is great beauty in the little things in life like sunshine, kissing, and dancing.
5. We should be pacifists and oppose the death penalty.

Together, these five wise philosophers (Buddha, Epicurus, Heidegger, Sartre, and Camus) have changed my life and helped me focus on being happy in any circumstance and realizing that I get to create the meaning inside of my own life. I thank Werner Erhard of Landmark fame for turning me onto the Existentialists.

These philosophers have allowed me to see the pattern in others of using diversion to escape from boredom and instead **create the meaning** in my own life by creating a clear purpose and goals revolving around making a positive contribution to society and transferring human knowledge around living a great life onward to the next generation.

# Express Your Emotions, Bro

"Unexpressed emotions will never die. They are buried alive and will come forth later in uglier ways." - Sigmund Freud

Most women are pretty good at expressing their emotions as they come up. Most men, not so much. Because of this, many men have lots of emotions that get bottled up. A good way to get over your traumas is to express/share your emotions about them.

Yes, crying can be deeply cathartic for all human beings. So can sharing with a close friend, hiring someone to listen, or doing a guided psilocybin, ketamine, or MDMA ceremony with a trained practitioner. To heal an emotional wound, it's important to fully feel the suppressed emotion underneath it.

As Robin Sharma says, "Feelings left unfelt form a subconscious field of hurt that degrades your genius, cheats your promise, and blocks your greatness."

The worst thing you can do is bottle up your emotions, become resentful, and turn to numbing yourself with alcohol or drugs. The moment you resign yourself to a resentful life is the moment you begin to die.

The future can be anything you want it to be. As my friend Robin Sharma says, "Just because your past was painful doesn't mean your future won't be miraculous."

The key is to share your emotions openly and actually be real and vulnerable with yourself, your loved ones, and your friends. Tell them what is really going on. Ask them for their support in helping you re-find your passion. As writer Neil Gaiman said, "The moment that you feel that, just possibly, you're walking down the street naked, exposing too much of your heart and your mind and what exists on the inside, showing too much of yourself. That's the moment you may be starting to get it right."

He's got it right.

Let's look at a technique that Robin Sharma recommends for releasing emotions in *The Everyday Hero Manifesto*. It's called The AFRA Tool. The A stands for *awareness*. The F stands for *feel*. The R stands for *release*. And the second A stands for *ascend*.

1. Awareness - Find the feeling in your body
2. Feel - Stay with the sensation
3. Release - Let the hurt go
4. Ascend - Move forward higher

So first find the feeling inside, fully feel it (even if it means crying), then choose to consciously release it and let it go. Then, decide to move on and let the past be in the past.

Take the time to let go of the traumas that have happened in the past, so that you can enjoy living in the magic of the present. Make sure you take the time to actually fully feel your emotions around your childhood, your parents, past relationships, your siblings, your children, your career, your spouse, your body, your money, your sexual desires, your habits, your death, and the deaths of others.

Here's a great quote from my friend Allan McGrath:

### You Are Good Enough by Allan McGrath

Every man has a list he hides in his heart of all the reasons why he isn't worthy to lead, to love, or to be loved. And it's the very things on that list that make him worthy of all those things and more. Every man has a list. He keeps it close to his chest, rarely - if ever - does he let anyone else in on its raw contents. Not his intimate partner. Not his family. Not his friends. It's a list that he believes isolates him & keeps him uniquely alone in his suffering. It's a list that contains all the events, imprints, and experiences that were too vulnerable, too unsafe, too downright f*cking scary to share with anyone else.

Scrawled on its crumpled pages is the truth about his past That he wishes was different. The things that he's done. The things that were done to him. And it's a list that implies all the reasons why he isn't enough. Why he isn't really a man. Why he isn't worthy of love. But the truth is: it's the very things on that list that make him who he is. It's those very things that, if healed, would allow him to reach the full potential of greatness he senses is his real destiny.

Most men pretend that list doesn't exist. And they bear a heavy burden because of it. They hide behind a facade of impenetrability, invulnerability, & perfection. And they end up burned out, alienated, and powerless because of it. I know because I've been there. I know the fracturing pain of pretending that list didn't exist. But I also know... There is another way. A way that says: Yes, it's true. This is me. All of me. See me, feel me, know me. This is who I really am.

So yeah, share what is really going on with you with the people in your life with your partner, your friends, and your family. Sometimes growth, connection, and deep healing come from sharing just how imperfect you've been -- and in so doing, you create unbreakable bonds of connection and trust with your mentors, family, beloveds, band of brothers, and band of sisters.
Don't keep it inside. Share.

## Start a Gratitude Journal

"Reflecting on your blessings instead of your burdens alters your neurochemistry, which in turn elevates your moods. Remember that brain cells that fire together wire together, so actively seeking out things you can appreciate in your life will create stronger neural pathways around gratefulness. And the more appreciative you become, the more there will be no space for discouragement to show up and distort reality toward the perception of negativity." - Robin Sharma

If you have two arms, two legs, ten toes, and ten fingers, and are young enough to be able to read this sentence and clearly understand it -- holy shit it's time to be thankful!
As Wallace Wattles wrote in *The Science of Getting Rich*, "You cannot exercise much power without gratitude; for it is gratitude that keeps you connected with Power."
Once you start appreciating what you have, it becomes so much easier to live with joy as you work toward your dreams.
Maintaining a **gratitude journal** by writing in it for at least 5-10 minutes each day can help you overcome the negative bias of the human brain and cultivate an attitude of gratitude.

*Gratitude Journal - A notebook by your bed that you write nightly in. Write down everything you're grateful for from that day and Three Good Things that happened. Re-read this writing as the first thing you do when you wake up.*

One of the most effective and proven ways to increase happiness and productivity is the daily practice of noting three positive or uplifting experiences in a "Three Good Things" exercise at the end of each day.

**Action Item #53: Create a Gratitude Journal**
Go buy a blank journal. Put it beside your bed. Every night, write for 5-10 minutes about everything good that happened and everything you're grateful for. List at least Three Good Things that happened each day. Re-read this the moment you wake up to prepare your mind for another day of gratitude. Good things happen to those who think positively.

You can also use Robin Sharma's practice of "**Gratitude Value Chains**" to really amp up the good vibes.

"Go deep by engaging in what I call "value chain gratitude," displaying thankfulness from the beginning to the end of any benefits that cause your life to be better. For example, at a grocery store checkout, say a prayer of silent thanks to the cashier who is assisting you, the stock clerk who put food on the shelf, the truck driver who carried the supply to the store, and the farmer who raised the crops that you and your family will eat. Run this strategy across all areas of your daily experiences, and soon your entire life will be one giant immersive experience in granular gratefulness. And, therefore, inescapable joy."

Is there any evidence that gratitude makes life better? Tons. Shawn Achor, author of the fantastic book, The Happiness Advantage, writes about the results of his well-known gratitude study, showing that those who write down their gratitudes for 21-days in a row train their brains to be positive and optimistic.

"We've found that there are ways that you can train your brain to be able to become more positive. In just a two-minute span of time, done for 21 days in a row, we can actually rewire your brain, allowing your brain to actually work more optimistically and more successfully. We've done these things in research now in every single company that I've worked with, getting them to write down three new things that they're grateful for for 21 days in a row, three new things each day. And at the end of that, their brain starts to retain a pattern of scanning the world, not for the negative, but for the positive first."

My wife, Morgan, wrote the following about gratitude recently in her notebook containing her lessons on living. It's worth sharing here.

> **Morgan's Principle for Living #3 - Live In Gratitude**

Every day, wake up and share gratitude with the people in your life. Thank your friends, your family, your partner, yourself, the Earth, the stars, the critters, the animals, the clouds, the sun, and your home for sweetly caring for you. Send thanks for all the ways they co-create and collaborate on creating a beautiful life for you and your family. At night, count your blessings for all the magic, miracles, love, and learnings -- and thank the day into completion as the last thing you do each night.

Yes, if you can **mix gratitude with faith**, you can achieve absolutely anything. As Jen Sincero writes, "Mixing faith with gratitude is the High Holy Moly of Manifesting. This takes some Jedi mastery, however, because basically what it entails is not only believing in the not yet manifested (having faith), but being grateful for it. In other words, you must be grateful for your imaginary friends and your imaginary life."

## Realize That Happiness Leads to Success

Many people think "success leads to happiness." Actually, it's the other way around. **Happiness leads to success.** Here's what Shawn Achor, author of *The Happiness Advantage*, has to say about this topic:

"What I found is that most people follow a formula for success, "if I work harder, I'll be more successful. And if I'm more successful, then I'll be happier." This undergirds most of our parenting styles, our managing styles, and the way that we motivate our behavior.

This is scientifically broken and backwards for two reasons. First, every time your brain has success, you just change the goalpost of what success looks like.

You got good grades, now you have to get better grades. You got a good job, now you have to get a better job. You hit your sales target, now we're going to change your sales target. If happiness is on the opposite side of success, your brain never gets there.

Your brain at positive performs significantly better than it does at negative, neutral or stressed. Your intelligence rises, your creativity rises, your energy levels rise. In fact, what we've found is that every single business outcome improves.

Your brain at positive is 31 percent more productive than your brain at negative, neutral or stressed. You're 37 percent better at sales. Doctors are 19 percent faster, more accurate at coming up with the correct diagnosis when positive instead of negative, neutral or stressed.

If we can find a way of becoming positive in the present, then our brains work even more successfully as we're able to work harder, faster and more intelligently."

# Realize That Everything is Impermanent

Living much of our year in Nosara, Costa Rica, a surfing hotspot, we are quite familiar with the surfer philosophy of enjoying the moment and not taking life all too seriously.

I encourage you to adopt The Surfer's Mentality. Surfing teaches us that life is a series of ups and downs, and we shouldn't get too attached to the highs or discouraged by the lows.

A surfer knows that every wave will inevitably crash and end, and yet, another will predictably come along soon. Embracing this perspective of impermanence allows us to fully embrace and enjoy the full range of experiences that life has to offer, both the challenging and the enjoyable ones, knowing nothing will last forever.

If you're on a great wave, enjoy that moment immensely, as in a few seconds it will be gone. And if you're on a terrible wave, be appreciative that it too shall pass and a new wave will soon come. If you can do this, you will have truly mastered the art of living. Enjoy every part of being alive—the ups and the downs, the wins and the failures.

I learned all about **impermanence** during my eight trips (so far) to the Nevada desert for the Burning Man Festival.

*Impermanence - The reality that in the universe everything experiences entropy and nothing can last forever. This realization leads to appreciating each moment as it happens as well as realizing that any difficult moments will pass.*

At Burning Man, they build a wooden temple every year on which attendees are encouraged to write messages to people who passed away that year. Then they burned the temple down on Sunday night in a silent ceremony. In 2014, the year my dad died, I wrote the following message to my mom and dad inside the temple.

> "I miss you both so much. Thank you for all you have given me and all your love. Thank you for teaching me the lesson that nothing lasts forever and that we must be grateful for every moment we have."

I'll end this section on impermanence with one of my favorite quotes of all time.

### You Will Lose Everything. But You Haven't Yet. So Celebrate.

"You will lose everything. Your money, your power, your fame, your success, perhaps even your memories. Your looks will go. Loved ones will die. Your body will fall apart. Everything that seems permanent is impermanent and will be smashed. Experience will gradually, or not so gradually, strip away everything that it can strip away. Waking up means facing this reality with open eyes and no longer turning away. But right now, we stand on sacred and holy ground, for that which will be lost has not yet been lost, and realizing this is the key to unspeakable joy. Whoever or whatever is in your life right now has not yet been taken away from you. This may sound trivial, obvious, like nothing, but really it is the key to everything, the why and how and wherefore of existence. Impermanence has already rendered everything and everyone around you so deeply holy and significant and worthy of your heartbreaking gratitude. Loss has already transfigured your life into an altar." - Jeff Foster, British Spiritual Teacher

Now that's one powerful quote, my friend! I recommend reading it twice.

## Understand Happiness Chemicals

"Dopamine, which floods into your system when you're positive, has two functions. Not only does it make you happier, it turns on all of the learning centers in your brain, allowing you to adapt to the world in a different way."
- Dr. Shawn Achor, The Happiness Advantage

Let's look at the science behind regulating your happiness levels in your brain. The primary "**happiness chemicals**" are Dopamine, Oxytocin, Serotonin, and Endorphins.

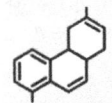

*Happiness Chemicals* - *The four primary happiness chemicals are Dopamine, oxytocin, serotonin, and endorphins. They form a handy acronym: DOSE. .*

| The Happiness Chemicals - DOSE ||
|---|---|
| **Dopamine** | **Oxytocin** |
| The "reward chemical" that controls the brain's reward centers, regulates emotional responses, stimulates happiness, and inhibits the stress chemical norepinephrine | Oxytocin is often referred to as the "love hormone" because it is released during intimate and social bonding experiences, such as childbirth, breastfeeding, sexual activity, and hugging. |
| **Serotonin** | **Endorphins** |
| The "soothing chemical" that helps maintain mood balance, regulate sleep and appetite, and reduce the likelihood of depression. | Endorphins are often referred to as "feel-good" chemicals because they are responsible for reducing pain and promoting feelings of pleasure and euphoria. |

| The Effects of Low Dopamine and Serotonin ||
|---|---|
| **Effects of Low Dopamine** | **Effects of Low Serotonin** |
| 1. Depression<br>2. Proneness to addiction<br>3. Craving for stimulants like caffeine | 1. Chronic fatigue<br>2. Sleep disturbance<br>3. A loss of appetite |

4. Chronic boredom
5. General apathy for life
6. Chronic fatigue and low physical energy
7. Parkinson's disease
8. Increased risk of Attention Deficit Hyperactivity Disorder (ADHD)

4. Craving for sweets and carbohydrates
5. Loss of sexual interest
6. Social withdrawal
7. Emotional sadness
8. Self-esteem and self-confidence are low.
9. Body sensations (hot flushes, temp changes, headaches, and stomach aches)

## How to Fix Low Dopamine & Serotonin

| How to Fix Low Dopamine | How to Fix Low Serotonin |
| --- | --- |
| 1. Eat foods rich in tyrosine like almonds, avocados, bananas, lima beans, sesame seeds, pumpkin seeds, and tofu. | 1. Get 15-20+ minutes of morning sunlight exposure |
| 2. Eat foods rich in antioxidants like spinach, asparagus, broccoli, beets, peppers, cauliflower, brussels sprouts, nuts, carrots, oranges, apples, blueberries, strawberries | 2. Exercising regularly (stimulates brain chemicals that reduce anxiety and depression) |
| 3. Some physicians recommend taking B6, vitamin C, and vitamin E | 3. Minimize carbs - Sweets and simple carbs, like white rice and white bread, quickly raise blood sugar, flood you with insulin, and then drop you in a hole. |
| 4. Exercise | 4. Cut out or substantially reduce caffeine, which suppresses serotonin (few people should be continually ingesting more than 100mg of caffeine per day) |
| 5. More laughter, cold plunges, get good sleep, sunshine, time in nature, new experiences, meditation, and breathwork | 5. Do meditations that empty the mind. Slow focused breathing can empty the mind. |
| 6. Avoid artificial light, binge watching, fast food, and endless scrolling | 6. Get a massage - massages have been shown to reduce cortisol and increase serotonin. |
| | 7. Try natural supplements like: B complex vitamins, St. john's wort, Folic acid, Omega 3, l-theanine, 5-HTP, and tryptophan |

As motivational Instagrammer Zach Porgrob says, "Chase real dopamine. Sun. Ice. Sauna. Weights. Runs. Walks. Hard work. Breathwork. Meditate. Visualize. Design. Service. Connect. Create. Spring towards your future self. Do real work. You'll never reach your potential if fake dopamine is always within reach."

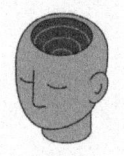

**Action Item #54: Fix Your Happiness Chemicals**
Review the above list of how to fix your happiness chemicals. Based on it, write down what you're committing to change or do to reset and optimize your dopamine, oxytocin, serotonin, and endorphins.

## Celebrate Your Wins

Creating anything of importance takes time. To stick with it all the way through, it's important to give yourself little dopamine hits along the way. You can do this by celebrating each little win as you go (both your wins and those around you).

I first learned the principle of celebrating wins while building my software company, iContact. We celebrated every major customer count milestone (1,000, 10,000, 25,000, 50,000, etc.) across the company with cakes and time off. In 2009, when we reached $1M in sales, I dressed up like Tina Turner in front of the company and sang. And in March 2010, I told people that if we reached $2M in sales that month, I'd shave my head. We reached the goal for the very first time, and my hair was gone. The more we celebrated each victory -- the more victories we had.

My wife also believes in the principle of celebrating even the tiniest of wins. Here is another one of Morgan's Principles for Living...

> **Morgan's Principle for Living #4 - Celebrate the Little Wins**

Life is comprised of many wins. Celebrating the little wins leads to bigger and bigger wins in yourself, in your partner, in your collaborators, in your children, in your life, and in the world. Start by taking notice of ten little recent wins you've had. Make life full of celebration. Celebrate your little wins every week.

## Know The Five Biggest Regrets of the Dying

> "The tragedy of life is not death but what we let die inside of us while we live."
> - Norman Cousins

Imagine if you could know the top five things that senior citizens regretted at the end of their lives.

Now imagine if you could find these out at 20, 30, 40 -- or however old you are today -- giving you hopefully many years of life to be able to make the needed changes so you don't end up with the same end of life wishes that things were different.

That would be helpful, right?

Well, Bronnie Ware, an Australian palliative care nurse, wrote a book called *The Top Five Regrets of the Dying,* sharing the top regrets that her patients would express to her in their final months of life. Here are the most commonly shared regrets that she wrote in her book.

1. I wish I'd had the courage to live a life true to myself, not the life others expected of me.

2. I wish I hadn't worked so hard.

3. I wish I'd had the courage to express my feelings

4. I wish I had stayed in touch with my friends

5. I wish that I had let myself be happier

Of course, this entire book is all about how to implement all five of these and live a life of your dreams. I encourage you to follow the great 19th century transcendentalist and nature-lover Thoreau and actually live the life you imagine instead of waiting until the end.

Thoreau wrote, "If one advances confidently in the direction of his dreams, and endeavors to live the life which he has imagined, he will meet with unexpected success in common hours."

I'll end this section with an excerpt from Matt Gray called "Things I'm Doing at 33 To Avoid Regret When I'm 85."

### Things I'm Doing at 33 To Avoid Regret When I'm 85 by Matt Gray

Things I'm doing at 33 to avoid regret when I'm 85...

1. Sip, don't gulp. Gently reminding myself that life is a marathon, not a sprint. Patience in my 30s will help me avoid rash decisions and ensure I am optimizing for the life I want.

2. Investing in personal relationships. Building relationships with incredible people gives me energy, ambition, and happiness.

3. Personal Health #1. I want to make sure I will have the energy and ability at 85 to keep pursuing my interests and passions.

4. Be aware that I'm breathing. Too often we never appreciate just living and what that truly means.

5. Read and write daily. They are the most nourishing forms of meditation and enable me to maintain a habit of continuous learning and curiosity.

6. Embrace the journey. I want to build a lifestyle that enables me to value each step I take and build memories that I can look back on.

7. Never conform to the norm. I want to make decisions built to optimize my family in the future (city selection, homeschooling kids, etc.)

8. Dispel hate. Hate is a pointless emotion that spreads rapidly.

9. Don't fall into the trap of constant aimlessness. I don't want to watch TV aimlessly. This doesn't mean to value TV less. Value it more by being selective when you watch it and why.

10. Be near nature. I want to build on a plot of land. I want to plant trees, be near trees and fall in love with nature.

11. Stop over worrying. I want to get rid of my habit of letting unrealistic scenarios dominate my brain.

12. Practice yoga and mindfulness. I want to have control over my mind and body in an era where technology's goal is to disrupt that.

13. Be transparent with myself. I want to let my thoughts flow and have a true conversation with my inner mind.

14. Build an understanding of philosophy. I want to understand fundamental human behavior and broaden my perspective.

15. Attain economic freedom. I want to build generational wealth and retire my parents. I want 3 generations of Grays to have the freedom of time together.

16. Be brave. I want to build a habit of believing in myself more.

**Action Item #55: Avoiding Regrets On Your Deathbed**
Write down what you are going to commit to starting to do now in order to avoid life passing you by and regretting not doing it later (examples: intentionally go see your friends twice per week, do 1 bucket list item per quarter, spend time daily with your kids, actually create your masterwork).

## What Robin Sharma Wishes He'd Known By 40

In one of the most powerful sections of the book *The Everyday Hero Manifesto* by Robin Sharma, he shares the forty lessons he wishes he'd known by age 40. It's an inspiring list that is worth sharing here. Read Robin's forty realizations below, and then see if there's anything else you want to commit to doing differently in your life going forward.

1. That family, flowers and walks in the woods would bring me more happiness than cars, watches and houses ever would.
2. That getting super-fit would multiply my creativity, productivity and prosperity considerably.
3. That your choice of relationship partner is one of the main sources of your success (or failure), joy (or misery) and tranquility (or worry).
4. That I'd do my finest work when I'd be working in hotel rooms and flying on airplanes rather than when chained to an office desk.
5. That good friendships are priceless treasures. And that old friends are the most precious ones.
6. That heaven helps those who help themselves. So do your best and let your higher power do the rest.
7. That people putting you down is a sign of your increasing success.
8. That the priorities I thought were most important in my youth are actually the pursuits I'm least interested in as I mature.
9. That silence, stillness and solitude form the sweet song that most attracts the Muse

10. That small daily victories, performed with disciplined consistency over extended periods of time, lead to revolutionary results.
11. That when I didn't get what I desired it was because the universe had something a whole lot better in mind.
12. That being scared just means you're about to grow. And that frequent discomfort is the price of accelerated progress.
13. That if you risk all for love and it doesn't work out, there is no failure because all love stories are, in truth, hero tales. And no growth of the heart is a waste. Ever.
14. That working diligently without concern for the rewards is the very behavior that brings the rewards.
15. That just because someone is aging doesn't mean they are growing.
16. That life has a fabulous feedback system showing you what you are doing right by where you are winning (and what you need to improve by where you're frustrated).
17. That it usually takes twenty years of working anonymously before you acquire the wisdom and expertise required to know what to leave out of a piece of work so it becomes extraordinary
18. That the humbler the person, the stronger the character.
19. That your income will never exceed your self-identity. And your impact will never be larger than your personal story.
20. That we get what we settle for. (So stop settling for what you don't want.)
21. That sometimes silence is the loudest reply you can give.
22. That the way people make you feel when you interact with them tells you everything you need to know about them.
23. That taking a lot of time off would make me twice as productive.
24. That feeding the trolls is a waste of your time. Most critics are jealous because you did what they couldn't do. Ignore them. And allow mastery to be your response.
25. That bullies become cowards once you stand up to them.
26. That journaling is praying on paper. And every prayer is heard.
27. That a genuinely rich life costs a lot less than you think.
28. That some people in business will tell you they'll do amazing things for you, but once the deal is signed, they'll end up doing nothing for you.
29. That the activities and places that fill you with joy are the activities and places where your wisdom wishes you to be.
30. That the best use of money is to create experiences and memories and not to secure objects and possessions.
31. That willpower is built by doing difficult things. So do more difficult things. (Daily.)
32. That it's better to read a few books deeply than consume many books lightly.
33. That hardship is the birthplace of heroism. Honor your scars as they have made you you.
34. That the majority of human beings have wonderful hearts and they'll show them to you if you make them feel safe.
35. That elderly people have the best stories. And deserve the highest respect.
36. That all life has huge value. Don't ever step on a spider.
37. That when you feel most alone, your higher power is closest to you.
38. That not every hour of the day and not every day of the week needs to be used "productively" and "grinding." Taking naps, staring at the stars and, sometimes, doing nothing are pursuits absolutely necessary for a life of unlimited beauty.
39. That respecting yourself is vastly more important than being liked by others.
40. That life's too short to play small with your highness.

## Don't Fear Death

*"I totally get that life's a fleeting voyage. And that it all ends too soon. And that even with its inevitable tragedies each day on Earth is a very precious and perfect gift. Yet I'm not concerned about leaving because I sincerely believe that after our bodies degrade to dust, all that we truly are continues. Our highest, wisest, strongest, undefeatable, noblest, eternal and all-loving selves—our souls—return to the source from which they came."*
- Robin Sharma, author

Those who have done the most work on themselves have imagined dying many times. They've already done the classic thought experiment of imagining they are dead and writing out their obituary. They've already done the exercise of writing their own eulogy at their own life celebration. That's all old hat to the truly developed.

You see, those who have done the most spiritual work rarely fear dying. They love their lives. Cherish it. Live it fully.

They know of its **impermanence**. They do all that they dream of -- and forge loving relationships. And they use the thought of death to motivate them. As Robin Sharma says, "Thinking about death refocuses our priorities, recalibrates our thinking, animates our emotions, and re-orders our routines."

And when the time comes for their body to pass on -- they go -- peacefully, easefully, knowingly knowing that they are part of something much bigger and more continual. They know their True Selves are immortal.

And yet, those who have done the least work have the most fear. Death of the body is natural. It is nothing to fear. In fact, death can be inspiring. The eye-opening oncoming reality of death is often a big motivating force for choosing to live your life now. Robin Sharma writes in his book *The 5AM Club*...

*"When many of us reach the half-time point of our lives, we make a right-angle turn. We begin to realize that we're not going to live forever and that our days are numbered. And so, we connect with our mortality. Big point here. We realize we are going to die. What's truly important comes into much sharper focus. We become more contemplative. We start to wonder if we've been true to our talents, loyal to our values and successful on the terms that feel right to us. And we think about what those we most love will say about us when we're gone. That's when many of us make a giant shift: from seeking legitimacy in society to constructing a meaningful legacy. The last fifty years then become less about me and more about we. Less about selfishness and more about service. We stop adding more things into our lives and begin to subtract—and simplify. We learn to savor simple beauty, experience gratitude for small miracles, appreciate the priceless value of peace of mind, spend more time cultivating human connections and come to understand that the one who gives the most is victorious."* - Robin Sharma

Getting past the fear of death is even easier when you know that your soul continues beyond the body.

As someone who, like my mother, aligns with many of the beliefs of the Buddhists -- I myself have come to believe in the continuation of the soul after death -- and the possibility of re-birth into other conscious forms.

I've found that those who are the most fearless are the ones who realize that their soul is immortal and that while this particular life on Earth at this time is unique, we have lived many times and will live many more lifetimes. This is a personal belief based on my own spiritual experiences with ayahuasca and 5-MeO and reading quite a few books providing the evidence of young kids who remember very specific and verifiable details of their past lives that kids that young could not have possibly learned elsewhere.

Read these two books if you're curious to learn more:

- *20 Cases Suggestive of Reincarnation* by Ian Stephenson
- *Children Who Remember Previous Lives* by Ian Stephenson

I'll end this section with a thought provoking quote from the spiritual teacher Sadhguru. "The Egyptian legend says that if one wants to enter heaven, at the point of entry, you're asked two questions. Only if you're one big yes to these questions is there an entry for you. The first question is, "Have you found joy in your life? The second question is, "Have you given joy to those around you? I must tell you that if you're one big yes to these two questions, you're already in heaven."

"Each day that I wake I will praise, I will praise. Each day that I wake I give thanks, I give thanks. And the day that I don't wake up and transcend the holy makeup.
I am capable. I am powerful. And the day that I don't wake up and transcend the holy makeup, I am on my way to a different place." - Nahko Bear, from Aloha Ke Akua

## Only Do The Fuck Yeses

"The thing that's so interesting about being alive is that you're all in; no matter what you do you're all in. This is going to kill you. So, I think you might as well play the most magnificent game you can while you're waiting because do you have anything better to do?" - Jordan Peterson

If you want to be happy, stop overcommitting yourself to stuff you don't want to do. Most people overcommit to a bunch of shit that they don't need to be doing because they want to **people-please**, look good, and don't want to disappoint their friends, family. and colleagues. Don't do that.

This overcommitment leads to ultimately disappointing everyone much worse when you show up late, turn in projects late, and then lose belief in the value of your word.

What's the solution to this? It's simple. Don't say yes to something unless it's a **fuck yes**.

*Fuck Yeses - Things that light you up inside with joy, pleasure, and happiness. Live a life where you are just committing to doing fuck yeses and say no to all the maybes.*

- Only accept jobs that are a fuck yes

- Only accept bosses that are a fuck yes (ask to get transferred or quite if you find someone who isn't)
- Only say yes to social engagements that are an absolute fuck yes
- Only say yes to dates that are a fuck yes
- Only move somewhere if its a fuck yes
- Take off any recurring commitments that are not fuck yeses
- Intentionally plan fuck yeses on your calendar every month

And don't say that your work makes you do a bunch of crap you don't love. You're a powerful force of nature, and instead of working a job you don't like, choose to follow your obsession. -- you'd create more value in the world, make more money eventually, and never again have to give into the tyranny of a boss.

I'd rather live as a pauper doing what I love than as a king doing what I hate.

I first heard the concept of "Fuck Yes" at the temple parties (adult sensuality play parties) we often go to in Bali, Costa Rica, and America. In nearly every opening speech on the importance of consent, the tantra-trained facilitators will often say: **"If it's not a fuck yes, it's a fuck no** -- meaning only do what you really want to do.

So let's apply that framework to our lives -- and start only committing to the things that we are big fuck yeses to. Let's create fuck yes jobs, fuck yes romantic partners, and fuck yes bodies. Let's go on fuck yes adventures with fuck yes friends.

A quick story: A few years ago, I was in a psychic reading in Denver with the psychic medium Rebecca Rosen. It appeared to me that she could actually talk to spirits and tell me things from them. Without knowing my name in advance, she told me a whole bunch of things that weren't findable online.

1. I had an alive spirit guide named Soraya (who happened to be the daughter of my former girlfriend that I helped raise for 7 months in a relationship). She actually told me the name.

2. That my grandfather Don was about to pass away in a couple months (she was right). His name was nowhere online.

3. That I should find the owner of a small white dog named Lily and follow her (which happened to be my friend Julia, which led me to moving to Bali a few months later).

Wow. These were quite incredible statements from someone that didn't know me! Rebecca ended by telling me that my mom had something special (from beyond) to tell me, "Don't measure your success in dollars. Measure it in joy. If you focus on doing what brings you joy, the money follows."

> "Don't measure your success in dollars. Measure it in joy. If you focus on doing what brings you joy, the money follows." - Rebecca Rosen, Psychic Medium

I just re-listened to the recording of the session today and found that beautiful quote in it. It's a perfect lesson -- follow your fuck yeses and you will thrive.

Follow your obsession, joy, and bliss, and you'll end up becoming so specialized in a particular field that you'll be able to name your price to your clients -- or you'll create a company that solves a problem that only people so obsessed would realize needed to be created.

As Zach Pogrob says, "Obsession turns average people into outliers. Obsession is the play where you lose yourself and find yourself at the same time. 5-9 years of obsession will save you five decades of working a 9-5. Greatness is the natural result of unnatural obsession."

So follow your obsessions and you fuck yeses to the very end. In relationships. In adventures. In work. As author Jen Sincero wrote in You Are a Badass, "There's nothing as unstoppable as a freight train full of fuck-yeah."

**Action Item #55: Only Do the Fuck Yeses**
Write down all the things you're currently committed to in your life that aren't actually big fuck yeses. Then write down your plan to either make those commitments fuck yeses or end those unaligned commitments. Who do you need to speak with to remove the energy drains from your life?

# Live the Four Agreements

*The Four Agreements*, a book written by Don Miguel Ruiz, has sold millions of copies worldwide and been translated into 48 languages. You may have heard of it. The book presents a code of conduct based on ancient Toltec wisdom. Ruiz comes from a family of healers and grew up in a family that practiced the Toltec tradition of indigenous Mexican spirituality. After studying to become a surgeon, he suffered a near-fatal car crash, which caused him to re-evaluate his life and follow his calling as a spiritual teacher.

Let's take a look at the four agreements...

| The Four Agreements by Don Miguel Ruiz |
| --- |

**1** Be impeccable with your words.
   a. Speak with integrity.
   b. Say only what you mean.
   c. Avoid using the word to speak against yourself or gossip to others.
   d. Use the power of your word in the direction of truth and love.

**2** Don't take anything personally.
   a. Nothing others do is because of you.
   b. What others say and do is a projection of their own reality, their own dream.
   c. When you are immune to the options and actions of others, you won't be the victim of needless suffering.

**3** Don't make assumptions.
   a. Find the courage to ask questions and to express what you really want.
   b. Communicate with others as clearly as you can to avoid misunderstandings, sadness, and drama.
   c. With just this one agreement, you can completely transform your life.

**4**  Always do your best.
   a. Your best is going to change from moment to moment; it will be different when you are healthy as opposed to sick.
   b. Under any circumstance, simply do your best, and you will avoid self-judgment, self-abuse, and regret.

It's rare that such a simple concept can have such a profound impact. If you actually live these four agreements, so much more becomes possible for your life. I encourage you to search online for an image of The Four Agreements, print it out, and paste it up on your fridge or in your bedroom.

## Create a Daily Affirmation

My wife Morgan, on New Year's Day 2023, hand wrote a declaration and affirmation in her notebook. It contained everything she wanted to program her mind to know and believe wholeheartedly. She reads it every morning in the first ten minutes of being awake. I'll share it here as an incredible example.

### Morgan's Daily Affirmation

Morgan is unconditionally happy. It's beautiful to watch and combined with how she is a total dominator in the best way, informing the world what she needs and how and the universe delights in giving it to her! It's a perfect pairing of surrender and will. She claims her space easily and joyfully, defends it if necessary without a problem and always boldly and joyously asks for what she wants! She is bold and has an easy time no matter what, taking right action from her heart!

She is the creator of our realm and absolutely believes in her magic and to fortify the frequency and grid of our space. Nothing can hurt us because we live in the LuvBubble frequency where magic, synchronicity, support, money and friends flow easily and joyously!

She loves and totally cares and shows up with delight and gratitude for every relationship in her life. She is an epically healthy person, who never gets sick. She is either deeply peaceful or utterly and joyously alive. She is cuddly, available, stable, healthy, playful, and happy. She cares about life in this effervescent way, where her attention is nutrition, and her being shines like a star. She is always in top physical shape with strong muscles and abs, and she sleeps like a rock.

She always gets eight hours of sleep. She is caring, kind, playful, super sexy and is one epic joyful mamma who is absolutely devoted to living a life of love and joy with her family. She is super dedicated to loving herself foremost to show up with the family in the most juicy love connected way, and absolutely adores her husband and baby. She and Apollo have so much fun together manifesting and creating the world around them!

She and Apollo are two peas in a pod. She dances between famliscious time, Apollo time and solo time seamlessly. She has an abundance of creative projects that joyously manifest.

Her nanny support is so delightful it feels light and easy

She is surrounded by a community of women and families that totally get us. Apollo always has someone to play with and learn with. He is totally raised in mamma's field of love.

She is a serial entrepreneur who easily takes ideas and finds aligned partnerships to bring them to life. She is the epic and successful lead of our family brand LuvMonsters and LuvBubble Studios animations and makes it profitable through her joy and play with people and the magic manifests in such profound ways. Her art is wildly successful and she loves bringing her ideas into the real world with joy aligned masterful partnerships across animation, music, real estate, plushies, media networks, education, clothing, lifestyle brand, and media.

She is a part of major company boards and is "an imagineer" that stewards their creative future. Sensually she is utterly alive in her most vital self and exudes light, grace, beauty and sexyness. She lives in the ever expanding pleasure of her being an open heart devoted to love.

She has created many nonlinear magic manifestations that fuel an unprecedented love story, money story, family story and life story.

You too should create your own **Daily Affirmation**.

*I am loved*

Daily Affirmation - A short written encouragement letter to yourself that you read every morning when you wake up. You can also record it as audio and play it before you go to sleep.

You can even record yourself speaking it and play it in your ears with headphones before you go to bed each night.

Combining an auditory daily empowering declaration with a visually read one in the morning can lead to extraordinary results.

There are two ways to read this book. To read it passively or actively do the exercises that are suggested. If you actually do these things you'll make so much more change in

So go ahead right now, and take some time to write your daily affirmation in your notebook.

Here's my daily affirmation. I read it every morning when I wake up, as it's printed out and in a frame on my bedside table.

## My Daily Affirmation

This day is a blessing. Each new day is a gift. Today I will do my Miracle Morning of green tea, strength training, swimming, sauna, and morning sunshine. Today I will write. Today I will love and support my family. Today I will make my beloved wife feel special. Today I will love and teach Apollo. Today I will help create a Magic Town full of connected Magic Friends. Today I will appreciate wherever I am. I will take chances and share my heart fully. I will be kind in all situations. I am a success magnet. I am a joy magnet.

Here's Robin Sharma's daily affirmation... it's a great one! He encourages others to read it and suggests that "reading this declaration aloud at dawn will—over time—reprogram both your conscious and subconscious minds.

### Robin Sharma's Daily Affirmation

This day is a blessing that I will honor, savor and make fullest use of. Tomorrow is an idea. Today is what's real. And so I choose to live it elegantly, patiently and immaculately. Over the moments coming, I will show up as a leader, not as a victim. As an originator, not a copier. As a visionary, instead of a follower. Today, I choose to be extraordinary rather than average. And brave, instead of timid. A hero in my own distinct way, instead of giving away my potent powers by blame, complaint and excuse.

Insecurity and meekness and the fear of rejection will not pollute my productivity, nor hinder my ability to uplift, respect and render value to other people. This day, I will make time for reflection and deep thinking, resist all time wasters, remain in the present moment and perform labor that reveals mastery while remaining true to my highest ideals.

Today, I will keep each promise I make to myself, defend my hopefulness, exercise my best habits and accomplish the things that make my heart sing. For I have much music in me. And I will no longer disrespect myself by keeping that song within. In the hours ahead, I will be supremely disciplined and incredibly focused, never confusing being busy with getting major feats done.

And should I need to rest, I will not measure this as a waste, understanding that first-class performance without honest recovery leads to the degradation of my native genius. Today, I will not leave the site of a great insight without taking some action to implement it. I know that ideation without execution is the sport of fools. And that making amazing dreams real is an enormous act of self-love.

This day, I will be more valiant than yesterday, more optimistic than I was last evening and kinder than I was last night. I understand that big people are the ones who make others feel bigger. And that on my deathbed, what will matter most will be the human beings I've inspired, the caring I've delivered and the generosity I've displayed.

So what are your daily affirmations and mental programming going to include? Make it good. And instead of reading the mind numbing news designed to hijack your amygdala and create unnecessary fear, read your uplifting affirmation when you wake up. Every. Single. Morning.

**Action Item #56: Create Your Daily Affirmation -** Write down a daily affirmation filled with encouragement for yourself. Include everything you want to bring into your life in the next year. Then print it out and read it every day when you wake up for the next 30 days.

How exactly do affirmations work? Let's see what Scott Adams, the creator of the Dilbert comic strip, says about their strange effectiveness at focusing the mind and the actions we take until we get what we dream of.

Scott says, "'You've got to try this thing called affirmations. All you do is you pick a goal and you write it down in some specific sentence form, like 'I will become an astronaut,' for example. And you do that every day. Then it will seem as if the universe just starts spitting up opportunities."

The key is to write them down, read them at least daily, and keep it primed in the front of your mind as you go through life. I do this same thing with a daily affirmation and with wristbands that I wear.

Here are some of the affirmations Scott has used throughout his incredibly successful career as a cartoonist and writer:

1. I, Scott Adams, will speak perfectly (he wrote this one down after losing his voice due to a medical issue)
2. I, Scott Adams will become a famous cartoonist (he wrote this one just before creating Dilbert, one of the most syndicated cartoons of all time).
3. I, Scott Adams, will become a number-one best-selling author. (He wrote this one down before his book *The Dilbert Principle* became the top selling book in the USA.)

This world is truly extraordinary. Butterflies on mountains at sunset overlooking the Indian Ocean. Eight billion plus people are all on a quest for soul learning and upgrades. Millions of species are all cohabitating. Earth is magnificent.

Yet sometimes we have our eyes closed to the magic all around us. This is where Morgan's next Principle for Living Comes in.

> **Morgan's Principle for Living #5 - Look for the Magic Everywhere**

My dominant intent is to look for what is going right, what I love, the beauty all around and in me, and how magic and miracles unfold everywhere for everyone. My dominant intent is to see and feel myself and that everyone is in their highest timeline and enjoying every moment of it. My dominant intent is to say yes to how good life is.

# Focus on What You Can Control

The happiest people focus on what they can control – and forget about what they can't control. So what can you control?

| Things You Can Control | Things You Can't Control |
|---|---|
| Your Affirmations | What Happened in the Past |
| Your Habits | What Other People Do |
| Your Experiments | What Other People Think |
| Your Goals | What People Say |
| Your Vision | What the Media Says |
| Your Purpose | What Happens in Politics |

| | |
|---|---|
| Your Information Diet | Social Media Algorithms |
| Who You Follow | Which Sports Teams Win |
| Your Self-Care | |
| Your Schedule | |
| Your Boundaries | |
| Your Attitude | |
| Your Gratitude | |
| Your Food | |
| Your Words | |
| Your Self-Talk | |
| Your Boundaries | |
| Your Energy | |
| Your Responses | |
| Those You Choose to Invest In | |

If you focus on what you can control and forget the rest – life will become a lot easier.

## Programs That Changed My Happiness & Health

When I moved to San Francisco in 2012, I was exposed to all kinds of new ways of living holistically.

Three programs especially changed me--the Landmark Forum, the Art of Living Happiness Program, and a silent meditation retreat called Vipassana.

I recommend taking all three of these programs, especially for those who work in stressful jobs.

In 2013 (and again in 2018), I took a 3-day course called the Landmark Forum. They offer the program in many cities across the USA and around the world.

What I got from Landmark was a better relationship with my dad in the year before he passed away, -- and also the motivation and encouragement to start a global community of impact leaders and entrepreneurs called Hive.org.

I also learned how to be fully present in deep conversations with friends and colleagues, how to become a really good listener in any situation, how to ensure I always honor my word, and how to make commitments thoughtfully.

I started to go from being "in my head all the time and moving 100 mph through the world" to being "embodied in my head and heart and moving 30 mph through the world."

In the spring of 2014, I took the Art of Living Happiness Program (offered in-person and online globally).

After learning some basic 20 minute breathing exercises from Art of Living (they call it the "Sudarshan Kriya"), my mind went from feeling anxious and racing to feeling calm, present, relaxed, and joyous--which has made me way happier and more productive.

Art of Living now runs programs in 150 countries and has taught 30 million people to meditate, slow down, and reduce stress.

And in the summer of 2015, I did my first ten day silent meditation retreat called a Vipassana in Montreal (I signed up on www.dhamma.org). I recommend doing this every five years, as a mental refresher, to every person I meet.

I left the retreat calmer, clearer, and happier than I'd ever been. Today, I weigh 150 pounds (down 62 pounds from the peak) and have calmed my racing mind through daily breathing exercises (specifically bhastrika and alternate nostril breathing).

And I have gotten rid of 90% of the chronic neck pain I had by learning two simple yoga moves (sun salutations + cat/cow poses).

I have learned to deepen the quality of my relationships and to play like a little kid again (through many adventures at Burning Man, and now as a father to a fantastic little boy named Apollo).

For anyone looking for a great in-person program to learn "how to be happy," I encourage you to look into these recommended programs and events, all of which are incredibly transformational.

1. Art of Living Happiness Program
2. Art of Living Silence Course
3. ISHA Foundation Inner Engineering Course
4. The Landmark Forum & Landmark Advanced Course
5. Dhamma.org 10-day Vipassana
6. International School for the Temple Arts (ISTA) - Level 1
7. Burning Man & Envision (two festivals, not a program, but both definitely taught me a lot about happiness)

**Action Item #57: Take a Happiness Course**
Take a look at the list above of recommended experiences, programs, and courses. Research each one. Pick one to attend in the next four months. Sign up now and put it on your calendar. Trust me on this one.

# Get on a 'High-Flying Disc' Before Key Decisions

*"When you first get on that high flying disc, you feel light-hearted and everything feels light and simple, just like the way you want to be forever. Get on the disc and then what's in your vortex [your true desires] will come." - Abraham Hicks*

If you haven't heard of Esther Hicks, it's time for you to know about her. She channels a wise deity named "Abraham Hicks." She's either actually really channeling wisdom from God -- or a damn good method actor who so fully gets into character when she is sharing wisdom.

She has fans all around the world and puts on epic cruises. The first time I went to an Abraham Hicks live event in Berkeley in 2016, I thought it was complete rubbish.

"People can't channel Gods,", I scoffed at myself. Now, I'm actually open to the concept that perhaps she really is channeling some divine intelligence. Regardless, her material is helpful.

One of her key concepts is to get yourself onto a **High-Flying Disc,** which basically means getting yourself to feel good.

*High Flying Disc* - *An upbeat and positive feeling. Make sure you're on a "high flying disc" before making any important decisions about your life.*

Abraham Hicks encourages everyone to get themselves onto a High Flying Disc before they make any important decisions.

If you're triggered, upset, tired, sad, or generally just feeling in the lower energies -- don't make any critical choices about your life.

Spend 30 minutes first to prime your state, get yourself on that high flying disc (joyous disposition), and then your path ahead will become immediately clear.

I learned this from my wife, Morgan, who listens to Esther often. Her principle is, "Only create when you're feeling good."

Whenever I'm upset or not feeling at my best, we have agreed not to make any decisions or plans. We wait until we're feeling good to make plans and make important decisions about our next steps.

For more on this topic, check out Esther's epic book she co-wrote with her husband Jerry, *Ask and It is Given: Learning to Manifest Your Desires.*

## Morgan's Ten Principles for Living

As we come to the end of this section, one big appreciation is due. This section on happiness has benefited from Morgan's Principles for Living, which she wrote in Bali in December 2022.

Thanks my love. Here are all of Morgan's Principles for Living in one place. Some wise words from Apollo's magical momma and the woman who deeply influenced so many of the ideas in this book!

**Morgan's Ten Principles for Living**

1. Everything is happening perfectly for me
2. Devote to a life of play
3. Live in gratitude
4. Celebrate little wins
5. Look for the magic everywhere
6. Devote to a life of love
7. Follow the joyous flow and enjoy the detours
8. Speak with intention
9. Only create when you're feeling good
10. Experience equanimity: nothing needs to change

## Recommended Books on Happiness

- *Happy* by Derren Brown
- *Flourish* by Martin Seligman
- *The Happiness Advantage* by Shawn Achor

- *Excellent Advice for Living: Wisdom I Wish I'd Known Earlier* by Kevin Kelly
- *The Good Life and How to Live it: Lessons from the World's Longest Study on Happiness* by Dr. Robert Waldinger and Marc Shulz, PhD

## Key Outcome from This Chapter

**Install the Growth Mindset** - Going forward, choose to see the challenges that happen to you as happening "for you" instead of happening "to you." See the platinum linings on all the hardships and difficulties you encounter. Take 100% responsibility for everything that happens in your life and choose to take the Vow of Unconditional Happiness.

## HAPPINESS CHAPTER ACTION ITEMS

1. **Smiles Per Day** - What changes would you make in your life if your actual metric of success was the number of smiles per day that you either have or create in others? Write down the answer.

2. **Anxiety Reduction** - Write down everything in your life that you believe may be causing you anxiety. Then, based on this section and anything else you know to do, write down what you are going to do to naturally reduce your anxiety.

3. **Bad Habit Remover** - Remove from your life anything that doesn't bring you joy or inspire you or help you. Delete your news apps. Block the news sites. Unfollow downer social accounts. Delete any addictive apps that don't actually make your life better. Consider pausing or slowing down on any addictive stimulants or depressants. Write down your new commitments to yourself and follow them for at least the next month.

4. **The Vow of Unconditional Happiness** - Write down the following (if you actually do commit to this). "I hereby commit to taking the vow of unconditional happiness from this moment forward. No matter how dire the circumstances, I will commit to seeing the bright side of any challenge and make the best of any situation I am in." Then print it out and sign it beneath the statement to make it official.

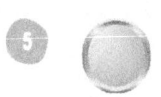

5. **The Silver Linings** - Write down the 10 most difficult and challenging things that have ever happened to you. Then, in a second column, write down all the positive things that came from each of those experiences -- that you would not have learned or experienced without the first challenging event occurring. Recognize that you wouldn't be who you are today without the challenging experiences.

6. **Overcome Fear of Criticism** - Write down the answer to this question: What have you been not doing at all or not doing as boldly as you should be -- out of fear of being criticized by others? After writing down that answer write down: "I commit to living my life boldly. I now know that when I'm criticized it means I'm on the right track to doing something people are noticing. I will always be kind, do my best, follow my creative truth, live in the arena, and welcome the critics--seeing them as a sign I'm on my way."

7. **The Incredible Now** - Write down the answer to this question: What are all the things that are possible in your life because of the inventions that have happened since 1900? Take few minutes to research everything big that has been discovered and created since then and then write down what's possible in your life now because of these inventions.

8. **Happiness Scale** - On a scale of 1-10, rate your current happiness level average over the last few weeks with 10 being the highest possible. Now that you have your baseline happiness number write down the answer to these two questions: What is your plan to increase your baseline happiness level over the next few months. What habits can you introduce that are likely to lead to greater life satisfaction? Actually do these for the next 30 days.

9. **Work You Love** - Do you love what you do? If so, great. If not, write down a simple plan to transition out of doing work you don't love within the next 12 months into a new field where you truly love what you do while achieving your financial goals. How will you serve the world in the future? What will be your work contribution to society that lights you up?

10. **The Forgiveness List** - Write down the names of all the people you still need to fully forgive for past transgressions. Write down what you are forgiving each person for. When done, write at the bottom: "I thank you for the lessons you taught me and hereby forgive you completely and fully."

# MORE HAPPINESS CHAPTER ACTION ITEMS

**11. The Presence Commitment** - Decide in this moment that going forward you are going to be fully present in each moment with the people you are with. No more smartphone distractions or thinking about the past or the future. Just be present, moment-to-moment. If a conversation is boring or uninspiring, either work to make it interesting or excuse yourself so you can be fully present elsewhere. Write down the following: "I commit to being fully present whenever I am with another person."

**12. Your Masterwork** - Write down what you think the most important gift will be that you will someday give the world, your community, or your family? Will it be a book, a movie, a company, an invention, a child, or an artwork? Something else. Speculate in your writing what might be the possible masterworks of your life.

**13. Happiness Philosophy** - Write down in your notebook: which of the above philosophies speak to you most? Why? If you had to describe your personal philosophy to someone else as a mix of 2-3 other philosophies, which ones would you choose?

**15. Gratitude Journal** - Go buy a blank journal. Put it beside your bed. Every night, write for 5-10 minutes about everything good that happened and everything you're grateful for. List at least Three Good Things that happened each day. Re-read this the moment you wake up to prepare your mind for another day of gratitude. Good things happen to those who think positively.

**16. Happiness Chemicals** - Review how to fix your happiness chemicals in this section. Based on it, write down what you're committing to change or do to reset and optimize your dopamine, oxytocin, serotonin, and endorphins.

**17. Avoiding Regrets** - Write down what you are going to commit to starting to do now in order to avoid life passing you by and regretting not doing it later (examples: intentionally go see your friends twice per week, do 1 bucket list item per quarter, spend time daily with your kids, create your masterwork.)

**18. The Fuck Yeses** - Write down all the things you're currently committed to in your life that aren't actually big fuck yeses. Then write down your plan to either make those commitments fuck yeses or end those unaligned commitments. Who do you need to speak with to remove the energy drains from your life?

**19. Daily Affirmation** - Write down a daily affirmation filled with encouragement for yourself. Include everything you want to bring into your life in the next year. Then print it out and read it every day when you wake up for the next 30 days.

**20. Happiness Course** - Take a look at the list of recommended happiness programs. Research each one. Pick one to attend in the next four months. Sign up now and put it on your calendar.

# STEP 6

# HEALTH MAGIC

# KEY CONCEPTS FROM THE HEALTH CHAPTER

### 1. BIOHACKING

Using a combination of quantified self devices, blood testing, functional medicine, and self-experimentation to create optimal physical and mental health.

### 2. REAL FOODS

Whole, minimally processed, and unadulterated food items that are as close to their natural state as possible. Real foods are often considered healthier choices compared to highly processed or heavily refined foods.

### 3. PROCESSED FOODS

Heavily modified food products that are usually bad for your health. They are often ready-to-eat or require minimal preparation. Examples include packaged snacks, breakfast cereals, frozen meals, sugary drinks, and fast food.

### 4. PALEO DIET

Eating the types of foods that early humans consumed during the Paleolithic era. The diet emphasizes whole, unprocessed foods such as meat, fish, vegetables, fruits, nuts, and seeds, while avoiding gluten, processed and refined foods, and most dairy products.

### 5. KETOSIS

A metabolic state in which the body primarily uses ketones, rather than glucose, for energy. Ketosis usually happens during periods of fasting, prolonged exercise, or when following a keto diet, which is low in carbs and high in fats.

### 6. TIRZEPATIDE

A prescription appetite suppressant that has been shown to be exceptionally effective at helping people lose weight.

### 7. MIRACLE MORNINGS

A routine for optimal mental and physical balance that you do in the first two hours of each day. Mine includes green tea, supplements, weight lifting, swimming, sauna, and a cold plunge.

### 8. STATE PRIMING

Exercises you can do quickly to get you mentally and physically ready for your day or your next meeting -- including push ups, sit ups, a cold plunge, a cold shower, sun exposure, kettlebell swings, or breath of fire.

### 9. KAROSHI

The Japanese term for working oneself to death.

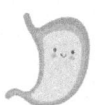

### 10. AUTOPHAGY

- A cellular process induced by fasting wherein cells recycle damaged components for energy and renewal. Derived from the Greek words "auto" meaning self and "phagy" meaning eating,

### 11. INTERMITTENT FASTING

Not eating for extended periods of time. For example, some people don't eat between 7pm and 11am each day so they can have 16 hours of daily intermittent fasting. Fasting can reduce the risk of cancer.

### 12. REM SLEEP

A stage of sleep with rapid eye movements, vivid dreaming, muscle paralysis, and heightened brain activity. This type of sleep plays a crucial role in mood, healthy, and memory.

MAGIC YEAR - 288

# MORE KEY CONCEPTS FROM THE HEALTH CHAPTER

**13 FUNCTIONAL MEDICINE** 
An approach to healthcare focusing on addressing the root causes of disease and promoting optimal health and wellness.

**14 STRESS CHEMICALS** 
The stress chemicals are cortisol, adrenaline, and norepinephrine. All three are released in the body in response to stress, preparing it for a fight-or-flight response.

**15 AMYGDALA ATTACKS** 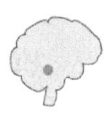
When the amygdala overrides rational thought and triggers a strong emotional response, often from of a perceived threat or intense stress. This can lead to impulsive or irrational behavior, as the emotional response takes precedence over logical decision-making.

**16 COLD PLUNGES** 
3 minutes per day in cold water around 40-60 degrees Fahrenheit can release endorphins which enhance mood, decrease stress, and increase mental clarity. I do this 7 days per week as part of my Miracle Morning.

**17 ACROYOGA** 
A physical practice combining elements of acrobatics, yoga, and Thai massage, emphasizing balance, trust, and connection between partners.

**18 CRANIAL SACRAL** 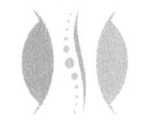
A holistic healing technique based on the idea that the skull, spine, and pelvis should be in proper alignment in order to allow the cerebrospinal fluid to flow freely. This therapy releases tension in the bones and tissues of the skull and spine.

**19 HOLOTROPIC BREATHING** 
Rapid, deep, breathing in and out for 30+ minutes designed to oxygenate your brain and naturally get into a psychedelic-like state. Do under guidance and with supervision until you're experienced.

**20 FLOAT TANKS** 
A sensory deprivation tank filled with water and Epsom salt where you can be weightless and relax the nervous system.

**21 CUPPING** 
A form of alternative medicine in which cups are placed on the skin to create suction. The suction helps increase blood flow to the area which can promote healing and alleviate pain.

**22 DIGITAL DETOXES** 
A break from using electronic devices, such as smartphones or computers, to reduce stress and improve well-being.

**23 DARKNESS RETREATS**
An extended period of time (usually a few days) spent in complete darkness or near-total darkness inside a specialized dark room for introspection, spiritual exploration, and heightened sensory experiences, often involving meditation and self-reflection.

**24 MEDITATION** 
A practice involving focused attention and breathing, aimed at achieving mental clarity, emotional stability, and enhanced self-awareness for overall well-being. I recommend learning from Art of Living or Transcendental Meditation.

# STEP 6: HEALTH MAGIC

"Splendid health is a key element of genuine fortune. Invest in it as the returns that will flow will be in an order of magnitude beyond anything you can fathom." - Robin Sharma

**YOUR MAGIC YEAR**

| Step | Area |
|------|------|
| 12 | AWAKENING |
| 11 | FAMILY |
| 10 | SEXUALITY |
| 9 | LOVE |
| 8 | COMMUNITY |
| 7 | MONEY |
| 6 | HEALTH |
| 5 | HAPPINESS |
| 4 | PEOPLE |
| 3 | HABITS |
| 2 | GOALS |
| 1 | PURPOSE |

## My Journey With Health

After 27 years of growing up on the East Coast of the USA and becoming a serious workaholic entrepreneur, I never thought I'd be one of those hippies living in Costa Rica, doing yoga, and writing books about living an extraordinary life -- but here I am.

In my 20s, I didn't think wellness had anything to do with being an entrepreneur. I was wrong. Big time.

As I wrote about earlier, at age 24, I was clinically obese at 212 pounds. I was often anxious and stressed out, had chronic neck pain from a car accident, and had a 'racing mind' that would keep me up past 2 a.m.

I ate a terrible diet of processed foods (lots of nachos, frozen dinners, bagel bites, and hot pockets) and had heartburn nearly every day. I drank a lot of coffee and was addicted to caffeine--fueling my anxiety.

At my most overwhelmed points in 2008 and 2011, I even had two panic attacks caused by stress.

During these panic attacks, my mind became deeply paranoid and hyperactive for ~5 hours. I know now that these panic attacks were caused by too much caffeine and too much stress, leading to too much cortisol, adrenaline, and norepinephrine.

My Sympathetic Nervous System (SNS), which manages the stress levels in my body, was completely overloaded.

At the time, the panic attacks made no sense to me, and I was scared.

I hadn't yet learned how to live with calm and ease while taking on big things in life. I hadn't yet learned how to take long, slow, deep breaths and meditate.

I worked all the time, but I wasn't exactly optimizing my productivity and effectiveness, and I was far from a shining example of vitality.

I thought being an entrepreneur required me to suffer and work hard.

I didn't get that for me to make a big impact externally, I had to be healthy and happy internally.

As I've written about, the passing of my mom, Pauline, from brain cancer in 2012 caused me to re-evaluate a lot in my life.

The unexpected passing of my dad in 2014 from leukemia and then my son's birth in 2022 both really inspired me to get my health in good order. These days, I look to optimize what Dr. Andrew Huberman calls **The Five Pillars of Health**:

1. Sleep - If you sleep better you function much better
2. Nutrients - 80% of nutrition should come from unprocessed or minimally processed sources
3. Movement - Cardio Exercises + Resistance Training
4. Light - Sunlight in the early part of the day, minimize artificial lighting at end of day
5. Social Connection - Relationships to others and self

This health section comes from my own experience living what is now a very healthy life and from interviews and reading the guides of people I trust the most in the health field – Dr. Daniel L. Stickler, Dr. Mark Hyman, and the father of **biohacking,** Dave Asprey.

Biohacking - Using a combination of quantified self devices, blood testing, functional medicine, and self-experimentation to create optimal physical and mental health.

After implementing my own biohacking learnings and creating the right morning routine and eating and exercise habits, I'm happy to be 150 pounds at 15% body fat at 40 years old, down from 212 and 25% body fat at age 24.

In this chapter, I am going to be writing about a lot of important health topics, including obesity, paleo diets, ketosis, miracle mornings, cardio, saunas, fasting, sleep, workaholism, functional medicine, blood labs, longevity, stress, cold plunges, holotropic breathing, acroyoga, reiki, cranial sacral, floats, cupping, gua sha, testosterone, digital detoxes, darkness retreats, state priming, and meditation.

Let's jump in!

### A Quick Medical Disclaimer for the Health Section

While the content below on health has been read by a couple friends who are doctors, it is not intended as medical advice. I am not a medical doctor, so please do your own research and it's usually helpful to speak with a physician (ideally a functional medicine doctor who works holistically across Western and Eastern modalities) before you implement any big change in your health care. Implement any of the below suggestions at your own risk.

## Don't Be An Average American

"It is no measure of health to be well-adjusted to a profoundly sick society."
- J. Krishnamurti

Okay, seriously, what the fuck is wrong with us Americans? Nearly 45% of us are now obese, up from 17% when I was born in 1984 – higher than any other country in the world. Terrible. Disappointing.

Look, I love America. But man, America is fat. The USA is the fattest country in the world – by far.

Let's take a look at the below graph of obesity rates by country. America is #1.

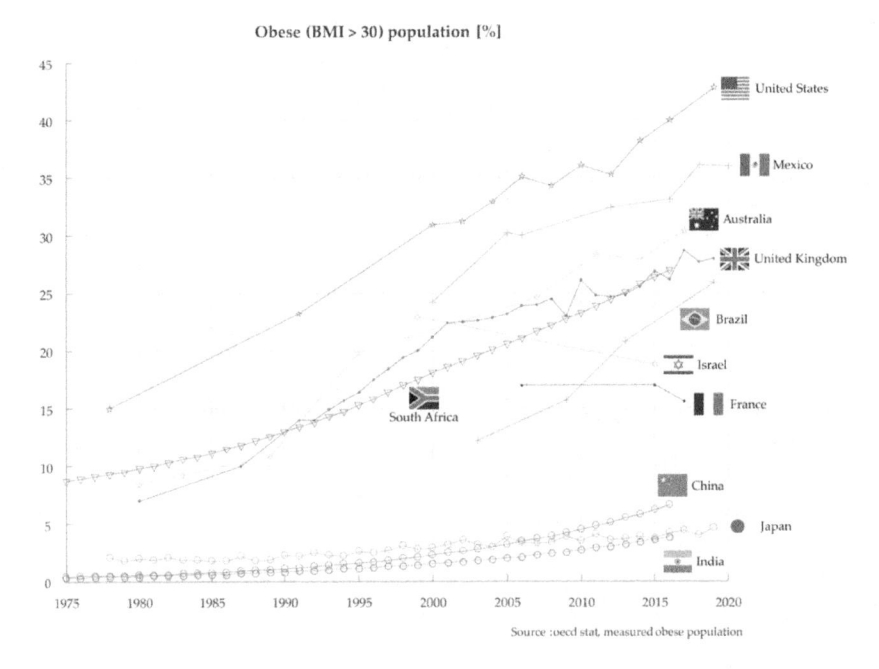

Obese (BMI > 30) population [%]

Source :oecd stat, measured obese population

Make America Healthy Again, that would have to be my slogan if I were running for President.

With the above chart, it's no surprise that American health care costs are higher per capita than any other nation in the world. In 2021, the United States spent an estimated $12,318 per person on healthcare — the highest healthcare costs per capita in the world.

Did these hundreds of millions of people just give up on living? Or was it something the American government failed to do to protect its own people from processed foods, sugar, and glyphosate. Or was it something the American food industry did to poison its own people and create an epidemic of diabetes and heart attacks.

Let's see what fellow author and friend Vishen Lakhiani has to say about the above graphic:

"The American diet is horrible. And it seems that the closer a country is to the USA in terms of culture (UK, Australia) or geography (Mexico, Canada) the worse their obesity rates get.

Canada is not on this graph but at 27% obesity would be between Australia and the UK. Today the average American dies two years earlier than the average European. And Americans are significantly more sickly. The #1 cause is the food in the USA. 80% to 85% of your body shape is what you eat (contrary to popular belief exercise is only responsible for around 15% of your weight loss/gain). This is why it's so important for governments to act to curb many of the practices of American food companies. We're killing our own people." - Vishen Lakhiani

This endemic of obesity (often in the suburbs and away from the coasts) is one of the reasons why we choose to live half our year in the much healthier regions of Bali and Costa Rica – and when we are in the USA, we live surrounded by our community of bio-hackers, life optimizers, and tantra practitioners in Austin.

I used to be clinically obese myself. I've gone from obese when I was 212 pounds in 2009 (at 5' 10") to 150 pounds today, which is right in the middle of the normal range for my height. Today I have a healthy BMI of 22, which is down from an obese BMI of 33 at my peak.

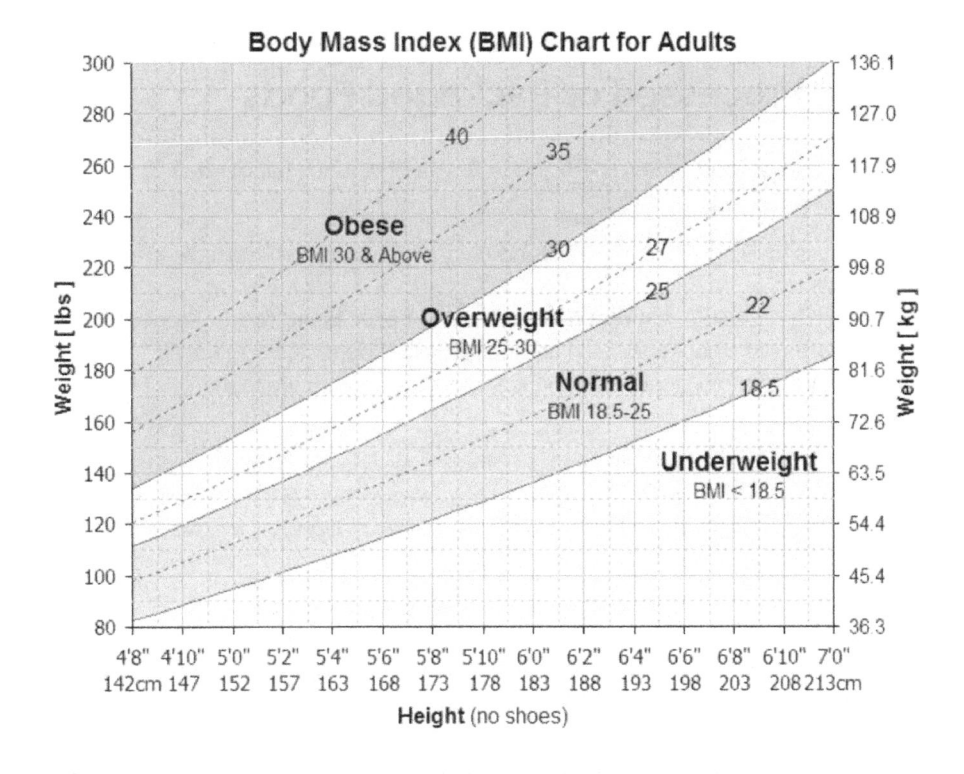

### Body Mass Index (BMI) Chart for Adults

**Action Item #58: Get a Smart Scale**
Get yourself a smart scale that measures weight, body fat %, and body mass index (BMI). I use the Renpho scale -- which connects to an app on my phone using Bluetooth. As of my weigh-in this morning I am at 14.7% body fat and 22.2 BMI. What are you at? Weigh yourself daily over the next 30 days.

```
          6.0%      13.0%      17.0%      25.0%
      ━━━━━━━━━━━━━━━━━━━━○━━━━━━━━━━━━━━━━━━━━
      Essential Fat  Athletes  Health  Acceptable  Obesity
```

Body composition fat tissue ratio

*My actual Body Fat % as of writing - 14.4%*

```
           18.5           25.0           30.0
      ━━━━━━━━━━━━━━○━━━━━━━━━━━━━━━━━━━━━━━━━
       Underweight      Normal     Overweight    Obesity
```

Body Mass Index

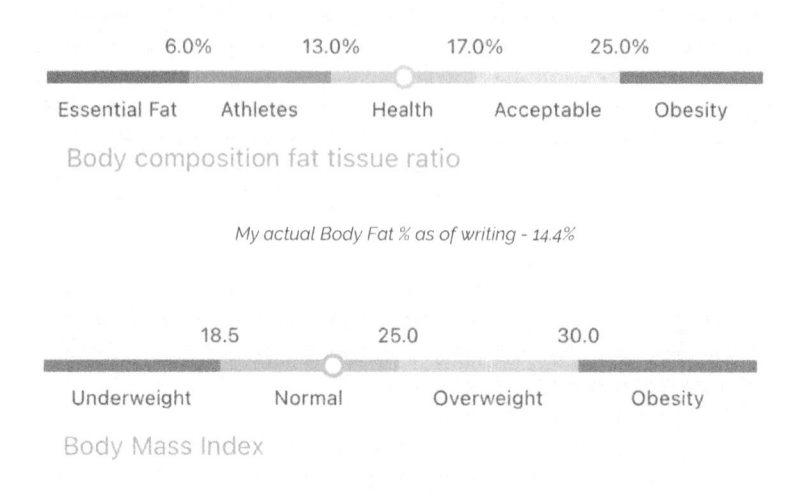

*My actual BMI as of writing - 22.0*

## Never Eat Processed or Packaged Foods

"Let food be thy medicine." - Greek physician Hippocrates

The key is to ensure you're exercising daily and eating well from the start. Let's talk about eating well.

As much as possible, eat **real foods** instead of **processed foods**. Processed foods (anything that comes in a package/box) are loaded with chemicals, sugars, and toxins that will reduce your mental and physical performance and shorten your lifespan.

*Real Foods* - Whole, minimally processed, and unadulterated food items that are as close to their natural state as possible. Real foods are often considered healthier choices compared to highly processed or heavily refined foods.

*Processed Foods* - Heavily modified food products that are usually bad for your health. They are often convenient and ready-to-eat or require minimal preparation. Examples include packaged snacks, breakfast cereals, frozen meals, sugary drinks, and fast food.

Real foods are items like meat, fish, fruits, nuts, and vegetables. Eat like a caveman would have, and you'll do well. Throw away from your pantry anything that goes through a process to make it. The epidemic of obesity in America is primarily caused by processed foods and sugar-filled sodas.

Here's what I would eat in 2008 when I was 212 pounds vs. what I eat today at a healthy 150 pounds.

| What I Ate in 2008 | What I Eat Today |
|---|---|
| Lots of carbs, sugar, and packaged foods<br>Bread<br>Hot pockets<br>Subs<br>Pasta<br>Pretzels<br>Fries<br>Chips<br>Desserts<br>Mayonnaise<br>Beer/wine/soda<br>Coffee | Keto and Paleo diet<br>Low carb, high protein, low sugar<br>Chicken, fish, steak, deer, pork<br>Almonds, nuts<br>Avocado, Broccoli, Corn, Cucumber, Green Beans,<br>Sweet Potatoes, Green Peppers, Carrots, Celery,<br>Spinach, Chia Seeds, Sprouts, Asparagus, Lima<br>Beans, Brussels Sprouts<br>Bananas, berries, kiwis, oranges, apples, dates,<br>grapes, peach, grapefruits, cantaloupe, Tangerines,<br>Watermelons<br>Almond milk<br>Green tea |

Not only do I feel a lot better and have kicked the heartburn— the meals I eat today actually taste better too. And my body looks 10x better, even though I'm a bit older now.

By making this change to my diet, I have likely gained about 20 years of quality life back -- years that I can joyously spend with my family, traveling, and writing.

The normal American diet is filled with sugar.

I've also substantially reduced sugar in my diet. Sugar is an inflammatory agent. It makes all the proteins in your bloodstream sticky. It slows down your metabolism and increases your hunger hormones, making you eat more.

Sugar makes you gain more weight, rots your teeth, gives you cavities, increases your risk of heart disease, and causes diabetes, mood swings, and skin issues.

Added sugars, which are added to processed foods and beverages, are particularly concerning because they provide empty calories with no nutritional value. Natural sugars, such as those found in fruits and vegetables, are generally considered healthier because they come packaged with fiber, vitamins, and minerals. These sugars are absorbed more slowly into the bloodstream, which helps regulate blood sugar levels. So just say no to added sugar.

## Eat a Paleo Diet

"I've found in my own life that there's a direct and profound relationship between the grade of my health and the quality of my craft. When I'm in superb condition, by training hard, eating well, fasting often, hydrating properly and resting intelligently, I produce my top work. My brain just works brighter, I feel happier (your moods dramatically affect your performance), I can sit at my writing table for many more hours, immersed in flow state, and I have access to a whole lot more willpower."
- Robin Sharma

With the support of close friends and partners, I changed my diet from chips, hot pockets, and bagel bites to healthier whole foods. Today I eat a mostly Paleo diet with intermittent keto diets once per month.

The **paleo diet**, sometimes known as the "caveman diet", is based on the idea of eating the types of foods that early humans consumed during the Paleolithic era, before the development of modern agriculture. The diet emphasizes whole, unprocessed foods such as meat, fish, vegetables, fruits, nuts, and seeds, while avoiding processed and refined foods and having minimal dairy products.

*Paleo Diet - Eating the types of foods that early humans consumed during the Paleolithic era. The diet emphasizes whole, unprocessed foods such as meat, fish, vegetables, fruits, nuts, and seeds, while avoiding gluten, processed and refined foods, and most dairy products.*

The theory behind the paleo diet is that early humans were better adapted to eat the foods that were available to them during the Paleolithic era, and that modern dietary habits and processed foods are contributing to the rise of chronic diseases such as obesity, diabetes, and heart disease. Proponents of the paleo diet believe that returning to a more natural way of eating can improve overall health and reduce the risk of chronic disease.

The main foods that are allowed on the Paleo Diet include:

- Meat and fish
- Eggs
- Nuts and seeds
- Fruits
- Vegetables
- Coconut oil, olive oil, avocado oil, lard, tallow, ghee/butter
- Minimally processed sweeteners, including raw honey, maple syrup, coconut sugar, and raw stevia

Paleo still allows carbs from groups of whole foods such as fruits, vegetables, and unrefined sweeteners. Conversely, the keto diet restricts all rich sources of carbohydrates, including starchy vegetables, most fruits, grains, sweeteners, and most legumes.

I'm not strict with my Paleo – it's just how I think about my base foods. Sometimes I'll add a little mayonnaise or ketchup. But I avoid processed foods like the plague.

In addition to eating mostly organic, non-processed foods, I recommend drinking a lot of water throughout the day. Hydration improves mitochondrial function, which is essential for maintaining high energy levels.

It's generally recommended to drink at least 8 cups of water per day – and more if you are physically active or live in a hot climate. Water can flush out toxins, aid in digestion, improve skin health, support cognitive function, lower the risk of heart attacks and strokes, and reduce your appetite. So drink a lot of water!

## Get Into Ketosis Monthly

The ketogenic diet, often referred to as "keto," is a high-fat, low carb diet plan that prompts the body to enter a metabolic state called ketosis, where it utilizes energy from stored fat instead of glucose or carbs.

**Ketosis** can be achieved through a variety of methods, including fasting, dietary changes, taking ketone supplements, or a combination of these approaches.

*Ketosis - A metabolic state in which the body primarily uses ketones, rather than glucose, for energy. Ketosis usually happens during periods of fasting, prolonged exercise, or when following a keto diet, which is low in carbs and high in fats.*

A keto diet optimized for ketosis typically involves consuming around 70-75% of calories from fat, 20-25% from protein, and 5-10% from carbohydrates.

I consume a paleo diet as my primary nutritional strategy, with occasional periods of intentionally inducing ketosis by following a keto diet for a few days each month.

Foods that are typically consumed on the keto diet include healthy fats such as avocado, nuts and seeds, olive oil, coconut oil, and butter, along with animal proteins such as meat, fish, and eggs. Low-carbohydrate / low glycemic vegetables like leafy greens, broccoli, and cauliflower are also included in the diet. It's essentially very similar to Paleo, but without the fruit and starchy vegetables like potatoes, squash, corn, and carrots.

The keto diet has been shown to have potential benefits for weight loss, blood sugar regulation, increased mental clarity, and reducing the risk of certain diseases, such as type 2 diabetes, neurological conditions, and some cancers.

**Action Item #59: Choose Your Diet**
After reviewing the above sections on diet, write down what foods you're committing to not eat (sugars, processed foods, etc.) and what type of diet you want to be on (paleo, vegan, keto, etc.). Write down any commitments you're ready to make about your diet.

## Appetite Suppressants That Actually Work

Thankfully, there is some hope for the obesity crisis in America. Prescription drugs like **Semaglutide** (often marketed as Ozempric or WeGovy) and **Tirzepatide** (sometimes marketed as Mounjaro) are becoming more commonplace for weight loss and are really the first generation of appetite suppressant drugs that actually have great results for both weight loss and insulin management.

Semaglutide has been shown to slow down digestion, stimulate insulin release, and lower the amount of glucose the liver releases.

After receiving a doctor's encouragement, I used semaglutide on myself for four months in 2022 and went from 190 to 160 pounds (and from a Body Fat % of 22 to 16%).

Here's what I wrote about my experience with semaglutide at the time. "About three months ago, a doctor friend recommended Semaglutide to me for weight loss. It's a prescription and a weekly home injection. It works. I've lost 30 pounds so far on Semaglutide (190 to 160 pounds). It reduces my appetite by 50-60%. I just eat much smaller portions as I'm not hungry, and only eat between 11 a.m. and 7 p.m. each day. I've been losing 2 lbs per week, predictably. I wanted to share it, as it's been incredibly helpful to me. I'm feeling a lot more energized and sharp."

The only negative side effect I noticed with Semaglutide was that I felt slightly depressed in the 24 hours after taking it. Talk to your doctor about these medicines, as they can have some side effects that you'll want to know about and consider.

After a few months of using Semaglutide, my doctor recommended I switch to a similar medicine that didn't have the depression side effect and has been shown to be even more effective at weight loss: Tirzepatide. I've now used Tirzepatide for a couple months, and it's even better than Semaglutide at appetite control, with no noticeable side effects for me. With Tirzepatide, I went from 160 to 145 pounds within two months and got down to 14.7% body fat.

Both Tirzepatide and Semaglutide are glucagon-like peptide 1 (GLP-1) receptor agonists, however, Tirzepatide is also a glucose-dependent insulinotropic polypeptide (GIP) receptor agonist, making it even more effective. It works by increasing insulin sensitivity, triglyceride clearance, lipolysis (fat utilization for fuel), and metabolic rate (metabolism), and decreasing appetite, fat storage, and the rate of digestion.

In a clinical trial of 3,731 patients, those who took Tirzepatide lost an average of 11.5% of their body weight, while those who took semaglutide lost an average of 9.2% of their body weight. Tirzepatide is also more effective in reducing abdominal fat and triglycerides.

So while Semaglutide and Tiirzepatide worked well for me, I combined them with healthy eating and daily exercise. As with any prescription or major health intervention, talk to your doctor about it before you begin.

Here's my daily scale tracking app results. As you can see, it worked for me – helping me lose 30 pounds in 3 months (followed by another 15 pounds after I took this screenshot)

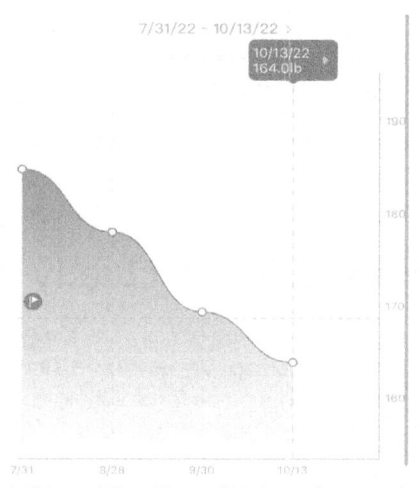

*I used Semaglutide and then Tiirzepetide to go from 190 to 145 pounds*

## Use Your Mornings for Self Care (Not Work)

"There is no way to well-being. Well-being is the way." - Thich Nhat Hanh

Most people wake up, have coffee, have breakfast, and go straight to work. You couldn't be making a bigger mistake.

Here's my daily schedule as of 2008, when I was at the height of my overwork (and weight), versus today:

| My Daily Schedule As of 2008 | My Daily Schedule Today |
|---|---|
| 8am - Wake up, shower, coffee, cereal | 7am - Wake up |
| 830am - Drive to work | 8am - Green Tea & Supplements |
| 9am - Start work | 830am - Walk/bike to wellness center |
| 12pm - Lunch | 9am - Gym, pool, sauna, breath, shower |
| 7pm - Drive home from work | 10am - Scrambled Eggs |
| 8pm - Dinner | 1030am - Writing |
| 9pm - More work | 1230pm - Lunch while writing |
| 12am - Sleep | 1pm - CEO Coaching Calls |
| | 4pm - Afternoon time with wife/family |
| | 6pm - Dinner |
| | 7pm - Family playtime |
| | 9pm - Work calls with USA (if in Bali) |
| | 10pm - Sleep |

Notice in the schedule to the left that there is:

- 13 hours per day of working
- 7.5 hours of sleeping
- 0 hours of personal care
- 0 hours with family

What an unhealthy workaholic I was! Notice in my schedule today there is:

- 5 hours per day of work (split between writing and CEO coaching)
- 5 hours per day of personal care
- 5 hour per day of family time
- 8 hours per day of sleeping

Now that's a balanced schedule designed for optimal results. In the **magic life**...

- Mornings are for self-care
- Afternoons are for work
- Evenings are for friends and family

> Mornings are for self-care, afternoons are for work, and evenings are for friends and family.

    Follow this daily work template, and your happiness, health, and joy will increase substantially.
    Of course – if you're working a full-time office job that requires you to be there from 9 a.m. to 5 p.m., it will be harder to achieve this type of integrated life – but you can still do it if you wake up at 5 a.m. and get your Miracle Morning in before 8 a.m.
    Then you just have to go to bed around 9 p.m., which is doable.

**Action Item #60: Design Your Optimal Daily Schedule**
Write down your optimal daily schedule. What time do you wake up, do each step of your miracle morning routine, go to work, go to sleep, etc.? Create your optimal weekday and weekend schedule and then actually live that schedule for at least 21 days to lock it in habitually -- making adjustments and improvements as needed.

## Prime Your State Before You Do Anything

Whenever you're about to do something important or make an important decision, it's very important to prime your body first so that you're in the right mindset.

Your entire **miracle morning** routine can be thought of as a priming process for your day ahead. But sometimes you are in the middle of your day and you need a quick little physiological and mental pick me up. That's where these rapid **state priming** exercises come in.

State Priming - Exercises you can do quickly to get you mentally and physically ready for your day or your next meeting -- including push ups, sit ups, a cold plunge, a cold shower, sun exposure, kettlebell swings, or breath of fire.

Here are some things you can quickly do in less than 10 minutes as a mid-day body and mind wake up so that you are ready to do your absolute best work, think positively and clearly, and nail that big speech, creative session, or crucial conversation.

1. 20 push ups
2. 20 sit ups
3. 20 pull ups
4. Quick cold shower (60 seconds)
5. 5 minutes of sun exposure (even cloudy daytime exposure helps)
6. 5 minutes of kettlebell swings
7. Bhastrika or Breath of Fire

Tony Robbins recommends the Breath of Fire breathing exercise as part of a morning routine. To do the Breath of Fire:

- Inhale deeply through the nostrils while simultaneously lifting the arms in a shoulder press motion, and then exhaling forcefully through the nostrils while bringing the arms back down to the body.
- This breathing should be done in quick succession, with three sets of 20 breaths and a short break in between each set.
- There should be equal time spent inhaling and exhaling, in rapid succession. Aim to breathe in and out every second.
- For extra impact, hold your breath for about 30-45 seconds in between each set of 20.

*An example of how to do the Bhastrika Pranayama (Breath of Fire)*

As I mentioned earlier in the book, I learned the Breath of Fire during the Art of Living Happiness Program (www.artofliving.com) in Palo Alto in 2014 and have done this exercise thousands of times since. It oxygenates my brain, helps me think more clearly, calms me down, and gets me ready for important conversations and presentations.

Another quick state priming exercise you can do is 5 minutes of sighing, as described below by my friend Dr. Andrew Huberman.

### Prime Your State with 5 Minutes of Sighing

"A brief, data supported protocol for reducing stress & improving mood *around the clock* is 5min/day of physiological sighing (= max inhale via the nose, then another short nasal inhale, then full exhale to lungs empty via the mouth (while saying Ahh); repeat for 5 mins). This outperformed 5 min/day meditation & other breathing protocols." - Dr. Andrew Huberman

**Action Item #61: Afternoon State Priming**
Schedule in a daily 10 minute state priming break each afternoon for the next 30 days at the same time each day. Choose a couple of the above exercises to do each day.

## Don't Overwork

"The most productive people on the planet do not "hustle and grind" 24/7/365. Instead, when they work, they work with supreme intensity. They do not snack on digital amusements or foolishly chit-chat about TV shows when they show up to advance their craft and pursue their trade. They are serious. They are professionals, not dabblers. Specialists instead of generalists. They go super-deep versus really wide when they work. When they sit down to produce, they bring the fullness of their human genius to the table and spend it all on their occupation." - Robin Sharma, author

Many people in the Western world work *way more than is optimal.* At the end of our lives, one of the most common five regrets among nursing home patients is, "I wish I hadn't worked so hard."

Why does it take us until we are 80 to realize that life is about so much more than work?

There's even a single term in Japan for working oneself to death: **karoshi**. I nearly karoshi'd myself in my 20s, and thank God I'm not doing that shit in my 40s.

Karoshi - The Japanese term for working oneself to death.

Now, I limit my computer work to 5 hours per day – about 3 hours every day of writing and 2 hours per day of CEO coaching. This amount is perfect for my productivity, flow, and desire to be present with my family (one of my biggest joys in life).

If I work less than four hours per day, I feel like I'm not giving my gift to the world. And if I work more than five hours per day, I feel like not giving my gift to my family. Four to five hours is the perfect sweet spot for me. Here's what Robin Sharma has to say about the optimal amount of work.

> "I recommend that my clients work only five hours a day (to me, five hours of undisturbed, fierce, steady and exquisite work is ideal) on those days reserved for work. Anything more is completely unnecessary and actually leads to diminishing returns because you're tired (so you won't produce anything substantial, so why waste the time?). Just five hours of glorious, majestic, monumental achievement on your workdays. Then recover. Regenerate. Refuel. And savor the rest of your day."

While I do take 3 day personal writing retreats every two months where I will write for more like 8 hours per day, my day-to-day habits are to limit computer time to five hours per day max.

I've found that consistently working ~20 hours per week in a high-focus, high-productivity environment is way more effective in terms of quality of output and results created.

What do I do with all that extra time?

- I sleep 8-9 hours per day
- I spend 4-5 hours per day with my family and friends (live life now!)
- I exercise and meditate an hour every day
- I read my Kindle about 30 minutes per day
- I actively think about how to help *Magic Year Course* clients succeed
- I plan travel adventures
- I plan adult sensual play parties with my friends in Austin and Bali (a really fun way to deepen with people in a community)

These other activities keep me fresh, alive, and able to continually and sustainably give my gift of information synthesis.

## Lift & Sweat Every Fucking Day

"Get physically strong to have greater concentration. To extend your stamina when you sit down to create. To toughen your body so you maximize your ability to generate the big ideas that solve enormous problems. Exercise regularly so you become a better artist. Work out harder so you become a better leader. And stay on that treadmill longer so you can roll like a movement-maker." - Robin Sharma

As I shared earlier, In 2016/2017 I got addicted to microdosing on too many "conscious drugs" like MDMA, psilocybin, and LSD in order to help me with my anxiety. In 2018, when I was living in San Diego -- I figured out something big that changed my life. If I simply bench pressed every morning, the anxiety would go away. Since then, I've bench pressed nearly every day. It's quite common for me to get 30, 60, or even 90 day streaks going -- only stopping if I travel somewhere that doesn't have access to a gym (which is rare).

I'm not trying to build muscle as much as I am simply trying to work out my natural masculine angst. I currently bench press 135 pounds between 30-40 times each morning. I also really enjoy doing daily sit ups, daily bicep curls, daily leg presses, and a daily short swim. I do this every morning between 9 a.m. and 11 a.m., then I write for 2-3 hours, then I do CEO coaching calls.

So, long story short -- if you're experiencing anxiety, try lifting every morning -- it may help a lot.

And don't just lift -- get some cardio in too. Sweat. Every. Single. Day.

"You should sweat like you're being chased by the police daily."
- Jocko Willink, Brazilian Jiu-Jitsui Blackbelt & Navy SEAL trainer

Exercising releases dopamine, which makes you feel more inspired during your day. It also reduces anxiety. As I wrote about in the section on overcoming drug addiction, I replaced microdosing on LSD or psilocybin with daily strength training (benching 130 lbs x 30 at the moment), and wow, I feel so much better and have a lot less anxiety.

As Zach Porgrob says: "Meditate to upgrade your software. Work out to upgrade your hardware."

You ideally want to get your heart rate to about 160 beats per minute (BPM) every day for at least five minutes. You can do this by jogging a kilometer or a half-mile around your neighborhood or on the treadmill each day.

"Stepping up your physical game will make you more money (because you're able to increase your productivity), help you remain more patient, peaceful and loving when you're in the presence of your family (thanks to the enhanced neurochemistry exercise turns on), and grow your sense of awe, wonder and aliveness. So my loving yet firm encouragement is to get super-fit so you push outright poetry into the universe."
- Robin Sharma

Exercising on a treadmill, skipping rope, or spinning on a bike immediately after waking up can cause you to sweat and trigger the release of BDNF (brain-derived neurotrophic factor). This protein aids in the development of new brain cells and the restoration of those that have been damaged by the stresses of the previous day. Additionally, BDNF enhances communication among your neural pathways, leading to a significant improvement in your brain's ability to process information.

You want to do both cardiovascular exercises and resistance training every single day of the week.

As Muhammad Ali said, "I hated every minute of training. But I said, 'Don't quit. Suffer now and live the rest of your life as a champion.'"

Engaging in physical activity in the morning can also result in the production of norepinephrine, a hormone that enhances concentration, which is particularly important in the age of constant digital distractions. Morning exercise can also boost the levels of serotonin, a neurotransmitter that helps to manage anxiety, improve memory, and promote relaxation. Additionally, working out increases your metabolic rate, providing you with more energy throughout the day. Establishing a routine of vigorous morning exercise can significantly improve the quality of your daily life.

As Robin Sharma says, "To play your greatest game, you want to be a PMM: a Perpetual Movement Machine."

One physical challenge you can work up to that will demonstrate you are truly in shape is to take on The Murph Challenge.

The Murph Challenge is a CrossFit workout where you run one mile, do 100 pull-ups, 200 push-ups, 300 bodyweight squats, and then run another mile while wearing a 20 pound vest. The challenge happens every Memorial Day in the United States, in honor of Lt. Michael Murphy, a SEAL team member who lost his life in Afghanistan in 2005.

The world record time is 22 minutes. My best time so far is 43:32. Can you beat me?

**Action Item #62: Design Your Daily Exercise Routine**
Write down your desired daily exercise routine. What are you committing to do seven days a week? At bare minimum, if you can lift weights for 5 minutes per day and also get your heart rate above 160 BPM for just 5 minutes per day, it can substantially reduce anxiety and also lead to a much longer and happier life. Follow the routine you design for the next 30 days.

## Sauna Your Way to the Top

Wow. The difference in my body and mind after ten minutes in a steam sauna and ten minutes in a dry sauna each day is night and day.

The sauna is a traditional Finnish practice that has been in use for thousands of years. It is believed to have been first used by the indigenous people of Finland. They used natural sauna-like structures, such as pits dug into the ground and covered with animal skins, to sweat and cleanse the body, and for ritual and medicinal purposes. Saunas are helpful in increasing endurance, mental clarity, and growth hormone levels.

The modern sauna, as we know it today, was developed in Finland in the 19th century. The first recorded sauna was built in 1837 in Turku, Finland, by a man named Juho Schreck.

Sauna-like structures have been used in many cultures around the world, from ancient Roman bath houses to Native American sweat lodges.

The most common types of saunas are Finnish saunas (dry with temperatures around 180°F), steam saunas (wet with temperatures around 120°F), and infrared saunas (around 140°F). Fifteen minutes inside these will do wonders.

Some of the benefits of a daily sauna practice include clearer thinking, toxins removed from pores, weight loss, relaxation, pain relief, improved skin, lower blood pressure, and muscle pain relief.

I often hear very interesting conversations in saunas – and they are where I'll often learn about community events or new biohacking techniques. I personally spend about 5-10 minutes per day in the dry sauna and 5-10 in the wet sauna.

I often also do my daily meditation practice, visualizations, and breathing practices while in the sauna.

Do like the Finns and sauna your way to the top.

And if you really like it hot, you can also do a sweat lodge every so often, which are indigenous saunas made with fire and stones.

Most sweat lodges last for about 60 minutes. Just be sure to drink lots of water, and if you find yourself getting dizzy, get out. Stones heated by a fire are placed inside the pit, and water is poured over them to create steam, which raises the temperature inside the lodge.

I did my first sweat lodge in Costa Rica before an Iboga ceremony in 2017 and my second in Tulum in 2020.

Participants sit inside the lodge in a circle and usually engage in prayer, song, or meditation as the temperature and humidity rise from the water poured on the hot rocks, inducing a state of intense sweating. Firekeepers continually bring new hot rocks every 10-15 minutes. There are sometimes short breaks where anyone who needs to leave can.

This traditional process is believed to promote physical and spiritual cleansing, the release of negative energy, and the healing of various physical and emotional ailments. The first time I did it, I felt great and clear. The second time, I stayed too long and ended up with an intense headache for the next 12 hours. So don't push yourself too much.

## Fast Often

"Fasting slows (and sometimes stops) rapidly dividing cells and triggers an 'energetic crisis' that makes cancer cells selectively vulnerable to chemo and radiation." - Dr. Dom D'Agostino

There are many health benefits to getting your body into **autophagy** through fasting – the biggest of which include reducing our risk of many cancers. During autophagy, our bodies clean out old, damaged cells and fix cells impacted by too much stress.

Autophagy - A cellular process induced by fasting wherein cells recycle damaged components for energy and renewal. Derived from the Greek words "auto" meaning self and "phagy" meaning eating,

In my 20s, when I was eating breakfast at 8 a.m. and dinner at 8 p.m., I'd only have about 11 hours per day of not eating.

Now, I eat breakfast after my workouts around 11 a.m. and my final meal of the day at 7 p.m. There's a full 16 hours between my last meal of the day and my next meal the following day. This is called **Intermittent Fasting**. This way, I have a mini-fast every night -- which is much healthier for my body.

Intermittent Fasting - Not eating for extended periods of time. For example, some people don't eat between 7pm and 11am each day so they can have 16 hours of daily intermittent fasting. Others do a 72 hour water fast once per quarter to get into ketosis and reset their body. Fasting can reduce the risk of cancer.

Let's look at my daily eating schedule and break it down.

| Normal Eating Schedule | Intermittent Fasting Schedule |
|---|---|
| Breakfast - 8am<br>Lunch - 1pm<br>Dinner - 8pm | Tea & Fish Oil: 9am<br>Breakfast - 11:30am<br>Small snack - 3pm<br>Dinner - 7pm |
| Total Eating Hours: 13 | Total Eating Hours: 8 |
| Total Fasting Hours: 11 | Total Fasting Hours: 16 |

A period of 16 hours without food (such as from 7 p.m. to 11 a.m.) is typically optimal for balancing autophagy, which is the process of consuming the body's own tissue for energy, and anabolism, which involves the building of muscle tissue.

Fasting has been found to increase the production of BDNF, a protein that aids in the development of new brain cells and has a beneficial effect on brain function. Additionally, fasting has been shown to reduce neurodegeneration and promote neuroplasticity, which can enhance learning capacity, improve memory, and lead to a decrease in blood sugar and insulin levels.

One fasting study[16] has revealed that reducing caloric intake can significantly increase human growth hormone levels by over 300%. Furthermore, limiting calorie consumption just a few times a week has been shown to activate certain genes, as seen in epigenetics, which signal cells to conserve resources and trigger a state called autophagy. In this state, the body works more intensely to eliminate old and damaged cellular material, and repair cells that have been impaired by stress.

Dr. Dom D'Agostino, a keto advocate and Professor at USF, has proclaimed the major benefits of fasting in reducing the risk of (and even killing) cancer. He writes, ""If you don't have cancer and you do a therapeutic fast 1 to 3 times per year, you could purge any precancerous cells that may be living in your body. Fasting slows (sometimes stops) rapidly dividing cells and triggers an 'energetic crisis' that makes cancer cells selectively vulnerable to chemo and radiation."

Research also indicates that fasts lasting three days or more can effectively regenerate the immune system through stem cell-based processes, essentially "rebooting" it.

So be sure to integrate both intermittent nightly fasts as well as 3-day quarterly fasts into your routines.

---

[16] Fasting Study - https://www.ncbi.nlm.nih.gov/pmc/articles/PMC329619/

For more on fasting, I recommend reading the fasting section inside the book *Tools of Titans* by Tim Ferriss. The book provides more details on how to quickly get into ketosis and what you can consume to help (MCT Oil, Coconut Oil, Lemon Juice, for example), as well as more on utilizing fasting as part of a cancer treatment protocol.

# Sleep... A Lot

"Legendary producers are professional resters." - Robin Sharma

Instead of asking friends, "How are you doing" -- I often ask them, "How are you sleeping." This question will usually reveal a LOT more about how they are actually doing, what they're worried about, and what is feeling a bit topsy-turvy in their life.

For good friends, this is what I really want to know, beyond the surface level "good" that usually comes back when you only ask how they are doing.

Sleeping is, of course, a core habit that leads to success. Almost all consistent high performers I know (save a few exceptions), are very good sleepers -- realizing that if they get 8 full hours of sleep per night, the quality of their brain and decision making while they are awake will be substantially higher.

Getting your REM (rapid eye movement) cycles in is essential to brain function. **REM sleep** plays a crucial role in emotional regulation, brain restoration, learning, cell repair, tissue repair, and transferring memories from short-term to long-term.

REM Sleep - A stage of sleep with rapid eye movements, vivid dreaming, muscle paralysis, and heightened brain activity. This type of sleep plays a crucial role in mood, healthy, and memory.

If a person's sleep is disrupted or shortened, they may miss out on some of the important later stages of REM sleep. You get about 25% of your total REM time in the first 4 hours of sleeping – and then the large majority of it (75%) in the second four hours of sleep. So if you're only getting 4 hours of consistent sleep, you're missing out on 3/4ths of your target nightly REM time.

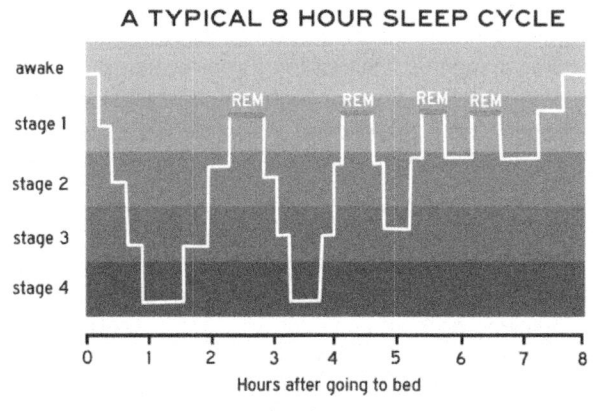

**A TYPICAL 8 HOUR SLEEP CYCLE**

This REM-backloading is why parents of young children, who have to wake up every 2-3 hours to take care of a newborn, have an especially difficult first couple of years, and it can sometimes feel like you're going crazy.

With enough REM sleep, you'll have difficulty concentrating, feel hazy, and be more likely to make poor decisions and emotionally overreact.

Dr. Matthew Walker, a professor of neuroscience and psychology and the founder and director of the Center for Human Sleep Science at the University of California, Berkeley, says that "REM is like a form of overnight therapy. We take those new pieces of information and start colliding them with our back catalog of stored information. It's almost a form of informational alchemy."

Insufficient amounts of REM sleep, regardless of age, can lead to a range of psychological drawbacks. These may include difficulties in learning, emotional processing, and problem-solving, among others.

Dr. Indira Gurubhagavatula, a sleep specialist at Penn Medicine, advises that "The way to get healthy REM sleep is to focus on getting healthy sleep overall and let your brain do the rest."

Robin Sharma agrees that good sleep is the secret for many top performers, "Rest is the elite producer's secret weapon… Championship athletes all have one practice in common: they sleep a lot."

Sleep is essential for maintaining physical and mental health. Not getting enough sleep can have a variety of negative effects on your health. It can lead to an increased risk of heart disease, diabetes, obesity, and other chronic health conditions. It can also impair your cognitive function and make it difficult to concentrate and perform well at work or school. Additionally, not getting enough sleep can lead to mood disorders like depression and anxiety.

Sleep can be highly disrupted by too much caffeine. So if sleep is important to you (and it should be!) you may want to limit your caffeine intake to one cup of green tea in the morning -- and never have any caffeine after 2 p.m. Caffeine not only keeps you awake when you should be sleeping – it also leads to anxiety.

There is about 100mg of caffeine in an 8-ounce cup of coffee and just 30 mg in a cup of green tea. So by switching from my former habit of drinking 2 cups of coffee to 1 cup of tea, I moved from 200mg down to 30 mg. I slowly reduced my intake over the course of two weeks (during a long meditation retreat at the Art of Living Center in Boone, North Carolina) in order to minimize the withdrawal headaches.

After making this change, my anxiety went down right along with it. According to Dr. Travis Bradberry, Ph.D., author of the book *Emotional Intelligence 2.0* explains the impact of being over-caffeinated…

> "Drinking caffeine triggers the release of adrenaline. Adrenaline is the source of the "fight or flight" response, a survival mechanism that forces you to stand up and fight or run for the hills when faced with a threat. The fight-or-flight mechanism sidesteps rational thinking in favor of a faster response. This is great when a bear is chasing you, but not so great when you're responding to a curt email. When caffeine puts your brain and body into this hyper-aroused state, your emotions overrun your behavior. Irritability and anxiety are the most commonly seen emotional effects of caffeine… Researchers at Carnegie Mellon University found that large doses of caffeine raise blood pressure, stimulate the heart, and produce rapid shallow breathing which deprives the brain of the oxygen needed to keep your thinking calm and rational." - Dr. Travis Bradberry

Top performers in business, sports, entertainment, and life have frequent periods of deep renewal. This is what enables them to perform at their highest level in bursts. Robin Sharma writes, "Recovery is not a luxury—it's a necessity and a priority that is beyond important for sustaining world-class productivity over not just years, but decades. Contrary to the dominant beliefs of our culture, hours spent renewing your depleted resources is time beautifully invested… Real renewal requires large blocks of time away from any influence that causes anxiety. This could include reading, having conversations with interesting people, enjoying a great film, going to the gym, traveling, and going out for dinner with someone you love."

He continues to say: "Real professionals trust their natural rhythms of productivity, alternating stunning intensity with deep recovery so that their prowess expands over a lifetime instead of experiencing a bright and quick flameout." So don't be a drop-in-the-bucket flameout. Let your star burn brightly for decades.

So take a weekly Sabbath away from digital distractions and social media. And take a quarterly digital detox retreat. And prioritize nightly sleep. As writer Maria Popova shares, "Ours is a culture where we wear our ability to get by on very little sleep as a kind of badge of honor that symbolizes work ethic, toughness, or some other virtue—but really, it's a total and profound failure of priorities and of self-respect."

**Action Item #63: Get Your Sleep Right**
Write down your optimal daily sleep routine. What are you committing to doing before you go to bed each night? What time will you start to wind down and turn off all devices. What time do you want to fall asleep and wake up each day? Make sure there's at least 9 hours between turning off all devices and your wake up time -- so that you get at least 8 to 8.5 hours of good sleep each night. Follow this sleep pattern for the next 30 days.

## Go See a Functional Medicine Doctor

The American (and global) medical system is thankfully in the process of a major generational overhaul that focuses on addressing root causes instead of symptoms and customizing medicines and interventions to the actual genetic profile and lab results of each patient. Even many prescription drugs will soon be produced

What may only be available today to people who can afford customized functional medicine treatments will thankfully become standard global practice in the 2030s as costs come down and technology advances.

The big advance in medical care over the past twenty years has come from the creation of the field of functional medicine.

Functional Medicine - an approach to healthcare that focuses on identifying and addressing the root causes of disease and promoting optimal health and wellness. It is a patient-centered, systems-oriented approach that views the body as an interconnected whole

**Functional medicine** was developed by a number of researchers, clinicians, and thought leaders in the field of integrative and complementary medicine. One of the early pioneers of functional medicine was Jeffrey Bland, PhD, who founded the Institute for Functional Medicine (IFM) in 1991. The IFM has since become a leading organization in the field of functional medicine, providing education, training, and certification for healthcare practitioners and conducting research into the underlying mechanisms of chronic diseases and health problems.

Other influential figures in the development and popularization of functional medicine include Mark Hyman, MD, a practicing physician and bestselling author who has written extensively on the topic of functional medicine, and David Perlmutter, MD, a neurologist and bestselling author who has incorporated functional medicine principles into his clinical practice.

Functional medicine is a patient-focused form of medicine that focuses on identifying and addressing the root cause of illness, rather than just treating symptoms. It is a personalized, patient-centered approach that takes into account an individual's unique genetic makeup, lifestyle, and environmental factors in order to develop a comprehensive treatment plan.

Functional medicine practitioners use a systems-based approach to evaluate the interactions among genetic, environmental, and lifestyle factors that can influence long-term health and chronic disease. They often use a combination of conventional and alternative therapies, such as nutrition, supplements, and lifestyle changes, to address the underlying causes of chronic diseases.

Functional medicine practitioners will spend more time with patients, listening to their health history, asking a lot of questions, and creating a detailed picture of the patient's health. They will also often order a wide range of lab tests, such as blood tests, genomic testing, and gut microbiome testing, to help understand the patient's health and identify any imbalances or deficiencies.

Functional medicine has gained popularity in recent years due to increasing interest in complementary and alternative medicine, as well as a growing awareness of the limitations of the conventional medical model for addressing complex and chronic health problems. As a result, more and more healthcare practitioners are incorporating functional medicine principles into their clinical practice, and the field continues to evolve and expand. Functional medicine is especially gaining popularity as a way to address chronic health conditions such as diabetes, heart disease, autoimmune disorders, and mental health conditions.

I personally work with the Apeiron Clinic in Austin, Texas, for all my functional medicine needs and lab tests.

Functional medicine doctors may run a wide range of blood tests, depending on the individual patient's health history, symptoms, and goals. These tests are used to identify underlying imbalances or deficiencies in the body's systems and processes, and to develop targeted treatment plans that address the root causes of health problems. Here are some common blood tests that may be run by functional medicine doctors:

1. Comprehensive metabolic panel
2. Complete blood count
3. Lipid panel
4. Thyroid panel
5. Vitamin and mineral levels
6. Inflammatory markers
7. Hormone panels

So, as a to-do item, go find a local functional medicine doctor and do their recommended panel of blood tests based on your body, your blood, and your genes so you can get truly customized medical care rather than the one-size-fits-all care of the mass produced insurance-driven traditional care system.

Some health insurance plans may cover certain aspects of functional medicine, particularly if they are deemed medically necessary and provided by a licensed healthcare practitioner. Some healthcare practitioners who practice functional medicine may be able to bill insurance for some of their services, such as laboratory tests and other diagnostic procedures.

**Action Item #64: Go See a Functional Medicine Doctor**
Set up an appointment to go see a functional medicine doctor in your area. See if you can find one your health insurance will cover, if applicable. Then go get your labs (blood tests and panels) run by the doctor so they can proactively assess your current health state. See what you can learn about your body and how to optimize your health.

# Run From Alcohol & Vaping

People think alcohol makes parties more fun and just gives you a hangover. The reality is, the impact of drinking alcohol is much worse, and it should be avoided. Here's what drinking alcohol does to you.

1. Depresses you
2. Increases anger
3. Doubles chances of liver cancer
4. Reduces the number of GABA receptors, an anti-anxiety neurotransmitter
5. Destroys your gut and disrupts your microbiome
6. Ages your skin
7. Compromises your intestinal barrier, leading to a leaky gut, allowing endotoxins to pass into your bloodstream
8. Depletes the liver's detox pathways with disrupt the ability to detoxify other harmful substances
9. Causes pufa peroxidation in the liver
10. Reduces gray matter in the brain
11. Lowers testosterone and increases estrogen levels
12. Depletes Vitamin A and NAD
13. Disrupts sleep cycle leading to cognitive impairment

Yeah, stay away from alcohol like the plague. Drinking is one of the worst things you can do for your health.

While I drank a bit during college at UNC-Chapel Hill (such was the culture there, and I didn't know better at the time), today I have less than 1 drink per quarter. And when I do drink, it's usually 0.5 to 1 drink, and it's usually either red wine, tequila, mezcal, or sake—three drinks that have some benefits when taken in moderation.

Thankfully, in the "conscious communities" that I tend to hang out with in Austin, Boulder, Los Angeles, San Francisco, Bali, and Costa Rica very very few people ever drink alcohol. We're much more likely to be seen drinking cacao or a non-alcoholic elixir.

Alcohol is not cool and will hurt your health and mental stability. What is cool is leading your friend group away from it.

Vaping has also been a trend for the last decade or so. Both smoking cigarettes and vaping are terrible for your health. Vaping has nicotine, which is highly addictive. Vaping causes breathing problems, heart problems, birth defects, and lung disease.

E-cigarettes contain 15 times the amount of formaldehyde found in traditional cigarettes. Formaldehyde is associated with an increased risk of lung, oral, and bladder cancer. Just say no to vaping, smoking, and alcohol – and you'll save your brain and body a lot of pain.

If you smoke or drink excessively, it's essential that you kick this habit during the next 30 days as part of completing the health chapter.

Remember the formula for success: Vision + Belief + Action + Consistency = Results. Anything that disrupts that consistency mentally or physically needs to be taken out of your environment.

## Reduce Your Stress Chemicals

*"When stress hormones build up, they cease to be a positive force, and begin to do damage: Overloads of cortisol will damage your memory, hurt your immune system, and increase the size of your gut." - Clive Thompson, writer*

Some stress can be helpful (to keep you moving), but too much stress for too long, and you are simply shortening (and worsening) your life.

If you stress yourself out for too long, you are putting yourself at risk of adrenal failure and a heart attack. Furthermore, stress makes you fat.

Let's take a look at the three major **stress chemicals** -- and how to reduce them.

1. Cortisol - Cortisol helps regulate metabolism, immune response, and blood pressure. In stressful situations, cortisol levels increase, preparing the body for the "fight-or-flight" response.
2. Norepinephrine - Works in conjunction with adrenaline to mobilize the body for action. Norepinephrine increases heart rate, constricts blood vessels, and enhances the release of glucose from energy stores to provide fuel for the body's response to stress.
3. Adrenaline - Released by the adrenal glands and the sympathetic nervous system in response to stress. It plays a crucial role in preparing the body for immediate action during times of stress or danger. It increases heart rate, blood pressure, and blood flow to muscles, while also providing a surge of energy.

Stress Chemicals - The stress chemicals are cortisol, adrenaline, and norepinephrine. All three are released in the body in response to stress, preparing it for a fight-or-flight response.

Cortisol is a major stress chemical, and prolonged elevated levels of it lead to fat storage. According to Dr. Ellen Weber, the effects of too much cortisol in the body include a weakened immune system, slower thinking, blood sugar imbalances, increased blood pressure, slowed wound healing, weakened muscle tissue, decreased bone density, and increased fat in the stomach area.[17]

---

[17] Dr. Ellen Weber, http://bit.Ly/effectsofcortisol

So how do you reduce the amount of cortisol in the body... well it's back to the basics we've been writing about in this book...

1. Substantially reduce caffeine from your diet (100 mg max per day)
2. Sleep deeper and longer. More deep sleep and more REM sleep.
3. Exercise regularly to build muscle mass and increase brain output of serotonin and dopamine, the brain chemicals that reduce anxiety and depression.
4. Avoid sugar in the diet (to avoid spiking insulin production)
5. Avoid refined carbohydrates (like white rice, white bread, most cereals)
6. Meditate or listen to relaxation tapes that promote the production of alpha (focused alertness) and theta (relaxed) brain waves.
7. Avoid jolting alarm clocks that take you from delta waves (deep sleep) to beta waves (agitated and anxious)
8. Some recommend taking DHEA, B vitamins, and herbal adaptogens

Now let's talk about norepinephrine. Norepinephrine is a neurotransmitter and hormone that plays a role in the body's stress response system. It is produced by the adrenal glands and certain neurons in the brain and is involved in a wide range of bodily processes.

It is also the chemical released during stress that ignites the fight or flight response and is a cousin chemical to adrenaline.

The effects of too much norepinephrine include elevated blood pressure, rapid heartbeat, skin paleness, nausea, dizziness, headaches, chest pains, and anxiety. Fun!

So here is how to reduce norepinephrine naturally:

1. Remove the root causes of your stress (stop doing the things that cause stress)
2. Take a few moments of silence each day
3. Meditate and use deep breathing techniques
4. Avoid or substantially reduce caffeine
5. Exercise regularly
6. Add a melatonin supplement 30 minutes before bedtime
7. Some recommend taking supplements l-theanine, omega 3 fatty acids, and the antioxidants nac and inositol
8. Avoid using artificial sweeteners, which contain l-phenylalanine

Finally, let's look at adrenaline. Adrenaline, also known as epinephrine, is a hormone and neurotransmitter that is produced by the adrenal glands and some neurons in the central nervous system.

Adrenaline is released into the bloodstream and the brain in response to stress or danger and helps to prepare the body for a "fight or flight" response. When adrenaline is released into the bloodstream, it causes several physiological changes in the body that help to prepare the body for action. These changes include an increase in heart rate, blood pressure, and respiration, as well as the dilation of the pupils and the release of glucose into the bloodstream.

Adrenaline can also act as a neurotransmitter in the brain, where it can affect mood, attention, and motivation. It has been linked to the development of stress-related disorders such as anxiety and post-traumatic stress disorder (PTSD). Adrenaline plays a crucial role in the body's stress response system, helping to prepare the body to respond to stress and danger. However, chronic or excessive stress can lead to dysregulation of the body's stress response system, leading to negative health outcomes.

Doctors recommend exercise, deep breathing, meditation, yoga, good sleep, and avoiding/reducing caffeine to reduce adrenaline in the body. It's amazing how important these things are for reducing stress. I've turned them into a handy acronym, **"GENTLY,"** so you can remember them quickly.

**G**ood Sleep
**E**xercise Daily
**N**o Caffeine After Noon
**T**ime for Meditation
**L**ie Down and Breathe
**Y**oga and Sun Salutations

I wasn't doing any of these things when I was having panic attacks in my 20s. Today I do each of these things as part of my miracle morning (which begins with 8 hours of sleep).

These basics will help you overcome stress and manage your stress chemicals so that you can become the best version of yourself, regulate your emotions, and create a happy and joy-filled life.

**Action Item #65: Your Stress Reduction Plan**
Review the above section on stress chemicals. Then write down in your notebook a plan to reduce the amount of cortisol, adrenaline, and norepinephrine in your body. Write down the new practices you commit to and which habits you will change to reduce stress on your body and help you be happier and healthier.

## How to Reduce Amygdala Attacks

"The amygdala regularly hijacks the conscious brain in the face of the mere threat of psychological, not physical pain. And the result can be highly counter-productive. We have all seen people "lose it" in reaction to some perceived insult or lack of respect. In the presence of an amygdala hijack there is almost no chance to have a productive set of interactions. It takes from 20 to 30 minutes of absence from the stimulus for the neurochemicals in the flooded brain to dissipate and thereby enable the possibility of a reasoned, rational interaction to occur." - Werner Erhard and Michael Jensen, Being a Leader Course

The amygdala is a small, almond-shaped organ deep in the brain that manages our primitive "fight or flight" response. This small organ, found in most mammals, controls the release of the stress chemicals (cortisol, adrenaline, and norepinephrine)

Let's look at the role of the amygdala in regulating our stress.

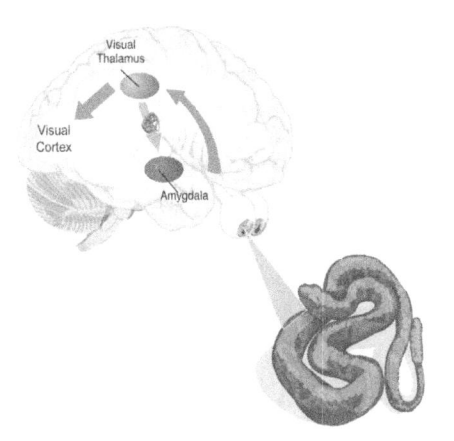

Sights and sounds enter the brain and go down two paths. One path leads to the amygdala, the other to the further away cerebral cortex, where we do our thinking and conscious reasoning.

If we see something that threatens us, like a snake, we often run away before we realize it and our amygdala queues our adrenal glands to release the stress hormone norepinephrine, which can temporarily increase our alertness.

The amygdala processes the danger signal first as an evolutionary advantage for increasing the likelihood of survival in a dangerous situation.

If the amygdala detects danger, it triggers the adrenals, which release stress chemicals norepinephrine and cortisol, quickening body reactions and heart rate and making us better at fighting or running.

Get this... this is big. The amygdala can be triggered not just by perceived physical threats, but also by psychological threats like when someone disagrees with you

So, when you get triggered during a conversation with a friend or loved one, this is what is happening... your body is getting flooded with stress chemicals. This is called an **amygdala attack**.

Amygdala Attack - When the amygdala overrides rational thought and triggers a strong emotional response, often in the face of a perceived threat or intense stress. This can lead to impulsive or irrational behavior, as the emotional response takes precedence over logical decision-making.

This is when your amygdala is hijacked and the body is flooded with stress chemicals for 20 minutes. Little progress can be made at this moment.

This is why it's better to take a short break when you get triggered instead of fighting and making things worse.

So how can you overcome these triggers that cause you to be defensive and fill up with cortisol?

Let's see what Being a Leader course founders Werner Erhard and Michael Jensen have to say about how to control the amygdala's responses.

"Individuals can learn to control the amygdala's response. To strengthen this neurological "muscle" one has to learn to move toward the source of the psychological or emotional pain. You do this by overcoming your resistance to negative feedback by willing yourself to

overcome the highly ingrained sense to "run" from or avoid situations in which you can discover your errors. Just like any rigorous physical conditioning campaign this is not easy but it can be done. It starts with recognizing the costs you impose on yourself from allowing yourself to be controlled by your own amygdala hijacks."
- Werner Erhard and Michael Jensen, Being a Leader Course"

When your amygdala is activated, your Sympathetic Nervous System (SNS) lights up, causing your heart rate to elevate, your digestion to shut down, and your breathing to quicken.

The human body's nervous system has two opposing sides, which you can think of as the accelerator and the brakes.

The accelerator is the sympathetic nervous system (SNS) and the brakes are the parasympathetic nervous system (PSNS). These are literally two parallel physical networks of nerves running throughout your body and affecting many metabolic systems (heart rate, blood pressure, perspiration, digestion, etc.).

|  | Sympathetic Nervous System (SNS) Activated | Parasympathetic Nervous System (PSNS) Activated |
| --- | --- | --- |
| Function | Governs stress and fight-or-flight response | Governs recovery |
| Heart Rate | Higher | Lower |
| Digestion | Shuts down | Available to function |
| Posture | Arms crossed | Open |
| Muscle Tension | Increased | Decreased |
| Speech | Faster and choppier | Slower and smoother |
| Breathing | Shallow and fast | Deep and low |
| Movement | Erratic and jittery | Measured and slow |
| Common Effects | Anger, irritation, impatience, amygdala attacks, fear, nervousness, unease | Peace, serenity, satisfaction, contentment |

Here are some keys to overcoming a heightened amygdala and SNS:

- Take deep long belly breaths for a few minutes and fill your brain with oxygen as you calm down your central nervous system again. You can also do alternate nostril breathing or bhastrika breathing.
- Get a full body massage and get your brain into a relaxed theta state
- Get a cranial sacral or reiki energy healing massage to get your brain back into a relaxed theta state
- Write down the things that trigger your defensiveness and then work with a trained therapist to uncover the original sources of these (using entheogens if desired).[18]

---

[18] Thank you to the Center for Applied Rationality Handbook from which some of the inspiration for this chapter was drawn.

# Do a Daily Cold Plunge

*"All the problems I have in the daily world subside when I do [cold exposure]. Exposing myself to the worthy cold . . . it is a great cleaning purifying force."* - Wim Hof

Back in 2017, Wim Hof, the Dutch motivational speaker known for popularizing holotropic breathing and ice baths, visited San Francisco and gave a talk at my house that we called The Light House.

We had brought in a kiddie pool, a tarp, and 100 pounds of ice for this special occasion -- where Wim himself demonstrated how to properly do the famed "Wim Hof" holotropic breathing while being submerged in ice -- and explained the benefits to our cells and nervous system of daily cold exposure.

Ever since then, I've always ended my showers with 30 seconds of cold -- and whenever I can (which is every day in Nosara) -- I do a **cold plunge** as part of my miracle morning routine.

Cold Plunge - A form of hydrotherapy where the body is immersed in water at a low temperature, typically ranging from 40 to 60 degrees Fahrenheit, to provide therapeutic benefits and promote overall health.

Just three minutes per day in cold water around 40-55 degrees Fahrenheit can release endorphins, which enhance mood, decrease stress, and increase mental clarity. I recommend starting at around 50-55° fahrenheit for first-timers, and then slowly working your way down to 40° F over six weeks of daily plunges.

Just 12-15 minutes per week of cold plunging will increase your natural dopamine release and make you happier.

A tip I picked up from Tim Ferris -- train yourself to say "It's so good!" when you're getting in to help reprogram your mind. Also, to make the cold more bearable -- pick a point in the distance to look at and keep staring at it while you submerge yourself.

It's not my favorite thing to do -- but I'm now myself on the daily cold plunge bandwagon. Thanks, Wim, I think.

Dr. Susanna Soberg, a metabolic scientist from Scandinavia, conducted groundbreaking research in which she determined the optimal thresholds for deliberate cold exposure to reap its benefits. Her paper reveals that subjecting individuals to 11 minutes of deliberate cold exposure per week, spread over multiple sessions and not just one, resulted in significant increases in healthy brown fat - which burns calories to maintain body temperature. Furthermore, participants became more tolerant of cold temperatures and **experienced a 2.5-fold increase in dopamine that lasted for hours**, along with substantial increases in norepinephrine and epinephrine.

A 2023 study in the BMJ Military Health journal found that regular cold exposure for soldiers led to higher life satisfaction and sexual satisfaction and lower abdominal fat and waist size.[19]

So, as part of your miracle morning routine, do about 3-5 minutes per day in a cold plunge and watch your life change dramatically. Spend some time right now finding your nearest cold plunge facility (or creating one at home).

---

[19] Impact of cold exposure on life satisfaction and physical composition of soldiers, Jan 2023

You can also get one for your home for around $5,000 at www.thecoldplunge.com or grab the much less expensive Yukon Cold Plunge for $800.

Cold showers are a good start -- but 2-3 minutes in a cold plunge daily will change your whole brain chemistry for the better and make you more resilient, happier, and better able to be a ninja of life.

**Action Item #66: Cold Plunging**
Search Google maps for your nearest cold plunge. Hopefully there's one less than 15 minutes from your house or office. Go there the next 30 days in a row and get in the cold plunge for at least 3 full minutes per day. If you can average 12-15 minutes per week in the cold plunge, you will start feeling immense benefits to your mood. Start around 50° F and then work your way down to 40° F over a few weeks.

## Do AcroYoga

"I'd always been repelled by yoga: too much mumbo-jumbo, too little excitement. AcroYoga is a different beast. You'll endure the occasional Sanskrit, but it's otherwise like a combination of body-weight strength training, dance, roughhousing, and hip rehab." - Tim Ferriss

**Acroyoga** is a form of yoga founded by two friends of mine, Jenny Sauer-Klein and Jason Nemer, that combines yoga, acrobatics, and Thai massage. I first saw it in the deserts of Burning Man in 2014 and then got interested in it as a great exercise and something fun to do with others.

Acroyoga - A physical practice combining elements of acrobatics, yoga, and Thai massage, emphasizing balance, trust, and connection between partners.

One person acts as the "base," who holds up the "flyer," who performs various postures and movements while being supported by the base. The practice can be done by people of all ages and fitness levels, and can be done solo or with partners.

Acroyoga classes typically involve a warm-up, skill-building exercises, and a "jam" session in which participants can practice and explore different postures and sequences with partners. The practice can be done for fun, fitness, or as a performance art.

Acroyoga helps train you on communication, trust building, and playfulness. The practice can help to improve strength, flexibility, balance, and body awareness, as well as creating a sense of community and connection with others

To find acroyoga classes, visit Acropedia.org, Acromaps.com, and Acropedia.org. And to learn more, check out Jason's book, *Move Connect Play*.

*One of the best books on AcroYoga*

## Book a Craniosacral & Reiki Session

If your central nervous system is feeling fried and you find yourself making rash decisions or not feeling grounded – book a **craniosacral** session.

Craniosacral - A holistic healing technique based on the idea that the skull, spine, and pelvis should be in proper alignment in order to allow the cerebrospinal fluid to flow freely. This therapy releases tension in the bones and tissues of the skull and spine.

Craniosacral therapy was developed in the United States in the 1970s by osteopath John Upledger.

During a craniosacral therapy session, the therapist uses gentle touch to manipulate the bones and tissues of the head, neck, and spine, with the goal of releasing tension and promoting relaxation. The therapist may also use techniques such as myofascial release, soft tissue manipulation, and stretching to help relieve pain and calm the nervous system.

Some of the benefits include pain relief, improved sleep, better immune system function, stress reduction, and emotional regulation.

In the craniosacral sessions I've done in Bali at the Yoga Barn, I've entered deep theta and delta brain wave states that have been incredibly healing and relaxing. Go see Adolf Brown there if you get a chance to go to Ubud. His hands are magic.

And if you like the craniosacral sessions, also try a reiki session.

Reiki is a Japanese form of alternative therapy that involves the transfer of energy from the practitioner's hands to the patient's body in order to promote healing and relaxation. The word "Reiki" is derived from two Japanese words: "rei," meaning universal, and "ki," meaning life energy.

Reiki was invented in Japan in the early 20th century by Mikao Usui. Usui was a spiritual seeker who was interested in understanding the healing practices of Buddha and Christ. He embarked on a spiritual journey that led him to study ancient texts and practice meditation and fasting. In 1922, Usui had a transformative experience on a mountain in Japan that led him to develop the Reiki system of healing.

MAGIC YEAR - 319

A 2018 meta-analysis of 24 studies found that reiki leads to reduced anxiety, stress, and fatigue.[20]

During a Reiki session, you lie down while the practitioner places their hands on or near the patient's body. The practitioner then channels energy into the patient's body with the goal of promoting healing and relaxation.

Reiki is based on the belief that the practitioner can channel universal life energy to the patient, promoting the body's natural healing process and restoring balance to the body's energy systems.

## Try Shirodhara (Ayurvedic Oil Dripping)

I had my first Ayurvedic oil drip treatment (called **Shirodhara**) at The Art of Living Retreat Center in Boone, North Carolina, in 2015, before a 4-day Art of Silence retreat held there, which was like a shorter and easier-to-do Vipassana.

ReLax — Shirodhara - An Ayurvedic therapy that involves pouring a continuous stream of warm oil or other liquids onto the forehead, specifically targeting the "third eye" area. It is designed to induce deep relaxation.

Shirodhara involves the continuous pouring of warm oil or other liquids onto the forehead or "third eye" area of the head. This therapy has been used in traditional Indian medicine for thousands of years to promote relaxation, reduce stress and anxiety, and enhance overall well-being.

The word "Shirodhara" comes from the Sanskrit words "shiro" which means head, and "dhara" which means flow. The therapy involves the use of special equipment from which the oil or other liquid is slowly and steadily poured onto the forehead in a rhythmic and repetitive pattern.

During the therapy, the person receiving the treatment lies down on a massage table with their eyes closed while the oil or liquid flows onto their forehead. The therapist may also massage the person's scalp, temples, and neck to enhance the overall relaxation experience.

Shirodhara is believed to help calm the nervous system, balance the body's energy, and promote a sense of deep relaxation and inner peace. It is often used to alleviate stress, anxiety, depression, and insomnia, and may also have other therapeutic benefits for the body and mind.

So next time you want to calm your nervous system down, book yourself either a Shirodhara, cranial sacral, or reiki session.

## Do Some Holotropic Breathing

"Breathe, motherfucker!" - Wim Hof

I was first exposed to **holotropic breathing** through the Art of Living breathing practices as well as through workshops at The Center in San Francisco. I then learned even

---

[20] Lee, M. S., Pittler, M. H., & Ernst, E. (2018). Effects of reiki in clinical practice: a systematic review of randomized clinical trials. Supportive Care in Cancer, 26(2), 371-377.

more when Wim Hof came to our house to demonstrate holotropic breathing while in an ice bath. Talk about combining two great modalities.

Holotropic breathing is a technique that involves using rapid, deep breathing combined with music and other forms of stimulation to induce an altered state of consciousness. It is based on the idea that accessing non-ordinary states of consciousness can facilitate healing and personal growth. is usually done lying down with your eyes closed in a comfortable and safe environment.

If you continue the deep and rapid breathing for long enough (30-60+ minutes), you can even begin to see a purple light in your third eye area (inside of your forehead) when you close your eyes and also start to have psychedelic-like visions.

Here are the basic steps for doing holotropic breathing:

1. Find a comfortable and safe place where you can lie down, and ensure that you will not be disturbed for the duration of the session.
2. Begin by taking a few deep breaths to relax your body and calm your mind.
3. Start breathing rapidly and deeply through your mouth or nose, inhaling and exhaling in a continuous cycle.
4. The recommended rate is about 2-3 breaths per second, or around 30-40 breaths per minute.
5. Focus on the breath and allow it to become increasingly rapid and deeper with each inhalation and exhalation.
6. You may start to feel lightheaded or experience tingling sensations in your body as you continue to breathe rapidly. This is normal and part of the process.
7. Allow any thoughts or emotions that arise to come and go without judgment, and simply focus on the breath.
8. Continue the breathing pattern for around 20-30 minutes, or until you feel a sense of completion.
9. When you're ready to stop, gradually slow your breathing down to a normal pace, and take a few deep breaths to fully ground yourself.
10. Take some time to rest and integrate the experience, and avoid any physical or mental exertion for an hour or two afterwards.

Some of the benefits that you can receive from this type of rapid deep breathing include higher oxygen levels, stress reduction, anxiety reduction, emotional healing, and new insights and inspiration.

## Get Daily Sun Exposure for 15 Minutes

"Imagine if there were a pill that could lower blood sugar, improve skin, decrease blood pressure, lower cholesterol, boost testosterone, improve mood, and give you dangerous sex appeal. It would make almost every medicine obsolete. This is why the sun is demonized." - @CarnivoreAurelius on IG

The four most important things you can do for your body are exercise, nutrition, sleep, and sunlight. Most people already know about the importance of the first three. Fewer people know just how important 15 minutes of morning sunlight are to our happiness.

Exposure to morning sunlight (even if the sun is behind a cloud) has a lot of benefits including mood improvement (more serotonin), reduction in depression, more vitamin D production (which helps with bone health), increased energy levels, improved sleep from better circadian rhythms, and lowered blood pressure, It's almost like God knew what she was doing when she put a fusion-ball eight light-minutes away.

It's best to get your sun exposure in the morning between 8 a.m. and 11 a.m. Excessive sun exposure can lead to sunburn, skin damage, and an increased risk of skin cancer, so it's important to protect your skin when spending time in the midday or afternoon sun – or when you're out for more than 15-20 minutes.

This is one of the reasons we love to live in some of the sunniest places on Earth, like the Sunshine Coast, Australia; Austin, Texas; Nosara, Costa Rica; and Bali, Indonesia.

The sun's significance to human beings is often undervalued. It serves as the primary source of all life on Earth and has the potential to enhance our moods, health, and physical attractiveness in powerful ways.

With just 15 minutes of full body sun exposure 2-3 times a week, you can rapidly transform your health and increase your vitamin D levels. Vitamin D is essential for immune, reproductive, and heart health, and the sun also produces antimicrobials that help fight disease, balance hormones, and boost mood.

Exposure to the sun's red and infrared light has been found to stimulate collagen synthesis, hair growth, muscle growth, fat loss, and even guard against UV rays. So if we wish to restore our health and humanity, we must also restore our connection with the sun.

Throughout history, people have recognized the sun as a natural marvel. Ancient Greek physicians prescribed "solar therapy," and named a God of the Sun (who happened to be called Apollo). And the ancient Egyptians even constructed the city of Heliopolis as a tribute to the sun.

Dr. Auguste Rollier operated a clinic in the Swiss Alps, where he discovered that the sun could aid in the treatment of numerous ailments, including tuberculosis, eczema, acne, and arthritis. Rather than remaining indoors beneath artificial light and staring at screens, it's time to venture outside and take advantage of the sun's natural light.

## Do A Monthly Float Session

*"I'm just about as excited about flotation therapy as I am about psychedelics, because not everybody is going to do a psychedelic. Maybe it's not in everybody's best interests to do it . . . but everybody can float. When prepped well and done consistently over time, it can still be an extraordinary 'psychedelic' arena. By this, I essentially mean coming back to a deeper connection with one's self." - Dr. Dan Engle, scientist*

To really relax the nervous system and bring on a greater sense of calm in your body, I recommend doing a weekly **float tank** session where you are completely weightless. These are sometimes called sensory deprivation tanks. You can probably find a few float tank centers in your city.

Float Tank - A sensory deprivation tank filled with water and Epsom salt where you can be weightless and relax the nervous system.

I did my first float in Encinitas, California, when I lived there in 2017/2018. It really helped me get through some of the stressful times I was going through as I transitioned out of tech entrepreneurship and into writing and hosting workshops.

The modern float tank, also known as a sensory deprivation tank or isolation tank, was invented in the 1950s by John C. Lilly, a neuroscientist and physician. Lilly was interested in studying the effects of sensory deprivation on the brain and developed the first float tank as a tool for his research.

Lilly's original float tank design was a dark, soundproof chamber filled with saltwater that allowed the user to float weightlessly on the surface. The tank was designed to eliminate all external sensory input, creating a state of sensory deprivation that Lilly believed could help induce altered states of consciousness and facilitate self-exploration and personal growth.

Lilly continued to refine the float tank design over the years, and his work helped popularize the use of float tanks for relaxation, stress reduction, and meditation. Today, float tanks are widely used in spas, wellness centers, and other settings as a tool for promoting relaxation, reducing stress, and enhancing mental and physical well-being.

Today, float tanks typically use water that is saturated with dissolved Epsom salt. The high concentration of salt in the water allows the user to float effortlessly on the surface, creating a feeling of weightlessness.

The water in a float tank is typically heated to skin temperature, around 93.5°F (34°C), to match the temperature of the human body, which can enhance the feeling of relaxation and reduce the sensation of being in water.

Float tanks create an environment of complete relaxation and reduced external stimulation. Some of the benefits can include stress reduction, pain relief, improved sleep, better focus and concentration, enhanced creativity, reduced muscle soreness, and improved athletic performance.

## Do A Cupping & Gua Sha Session

You can see below the results of my January 2023 experience working with Stephie, a gua sha and **cupping** masseuse in Canggu, Bali.

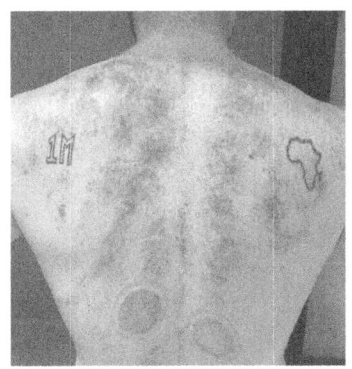

*My back after my first gua sha and cupping session in Canggu, Bali*

Cupping - A form of alternative medicine in which cups are placed on the skin to create suction. The suction helps increase blood flow to the area which can promote healing and alleviate pain.

Cupping works by creating a vacuum on the skin, which causes the skin and underlying tissue to be drawn into the cup. This suction can help increase blood flow to the area and promote healing. There are different types of cupping, including dry cupping, where no liquid is used, and wet cupping, where a small amount of liquid is used to create suction.

In traditional Chinese medicine, cupping is believed to help balance the flow of energy, or Qi, in the body. Some practitioners also use cupping to help release muscle tension, relieve pain, and improve overall wellness. Cupping can be done using various types of cups, including glass, bamboo, and silicone, and the cups can be left in place for several minutes or moved along the skin in a massage-like manner. The suction causes the skin to redden, which is considered a sign that the treatment is working. The redness usually fades in a day or two.

In the picture above, I got both a cupping session and a gua sha massage. Gua sha massage, also known as "scraping," is a traditional Chinese medicine technique that involves using a flat tool to scrape the skin in a downward motion. Gua sha can help reduce muscle tension, improve blood circulation, help with lymph drainage, and reduce skin inflammation.

## Take a Digital Detox Every Quarter

Many of our civilization's top imagineers spent considerable time in the wild. Long walks in the woods. Extended hours in a cottage by the sea. Quiet evenings staring up at the stars. In a documentary I watched about Greek shipping tycoon Aristotle Onassis, I discovered that after the stylish guests he entertained on his yacht would retire to bed, Onassis would remain on the deck, sipping cognac and simply staring up at the heavens to work through problems and download inspiration that would grow his business empire. Being near nature is a time-honored way to relax your mind. So your greatest ingenuity flows." - Robin Sharma

To optimize your mental health, be sure you're taking time to eat well, sleep well, and get into nature away from your laptop.

Every week, take your Sundays off of your phone and social media as much as possible – and spend the time with friends and family instead.

And at least every year, do a complete **digital detox** with no phones/laptops for at least four days.

Digital Detox - A break from using electronic devices, such as smartphones or computers, to reduce stress and improve well-being.

You could do an "Art of Living Silence Course" or a Vipassana, or simply go hiking with some friends in nature for a long weekend.

Whatever you do -- get off your phone for AT LEAST one day per week (I like Sundays) and four full days every year.

Here's what Robin Sharma has to say about the benefit of getting off devices and taking time to retreat from the world.

- "People who are constantly checking their devices, for example, soon suffer from digital dementia because each time they check for a message or look for a like, they leave a fraction of their valuable cognitive bandwidth on that activity. Do this daily (as many do), and you'll be installing Fragmented Attention Disorder as your general way of being. You'll never get anything sensational done."

- "One of the secrets of the immortal geniuses is seclusion. And the discipline of retreating from the world by placing themselves in a form of solitary confinement so they could produce their magic. All of history's great makers had this habit in common. They set up their workspaces to be completely diversion-free so they could get lost from society for extended periods of time, every day."

**KEEP CALM**

**Action Item #67: Slowing Down**
Review the sections on digital detoxing, holotropic breathing, reiki, cranial sacral, gua sha, oil dripping, float tanks, and morning sun exposure. Then, write down the new habits you want to experiment with and which ones you want to commit to doing regularly.

## Do a Darkness Retreat Like Aaron Rogers

In addition to doing a 10 day Vipassana every five years or so, it can be helpful to do a **silent retreat** or even a **darkness retreat** every couple years to refresh your own life plan and mind.

Darkness retreat - A few days spent in complete darkness or near-total darkness inside a specialized dark room for introspection, spiritual exploration, and heightened sensory experiences, often involving meditation and self-reflection.

Back in 2023, former Green Bay quarterback Aaron Rogers (who famously announced he sat with ayahuasca in 2022) did a four day darkness retreat at Sky Cave Retreats in Oregon to reflect on whether he was ready to retire from playing football in the NFL or play another season for the Packers. Rogers said at the time:

*"I've got a cool opportunity to do a little self-reflection in isolation. It's just sitting in isolation, meditating, dealing with your thoughts. It stimulates DMT, so there can be some hallucinations in there but it's just sitting in silence, which most of us never do. We rarely even turn our phone off or put the blinds down to sleep in darkness. I'm really looking forward to it. After, I feel like I'll be a lot closer to a final decision [about retiring]. It's going to be important to get through this week and to take my isolation retreat, contemplate my future, and then make a decision that is best for me and in the highest interest of my happiness."* - Aaron Rogers, NFL quarterback

Now this is an example of a conscious and aware person! You can sign up for a darkness meditation retreat in many places, ranging from your own bedroom (just hire someone to bring you two simple meals per day or ask a family member) to a silent retreat center in a beautiful location like Mexico, Costa Rica, Australia, Thailand, or Bali. Just Google "dark room silent retreat" in the location of your choice. The really cool things start to happen after you're about 48 hours in.

The result of his darkness retreat? He decided to move over to playing for the NY Jets after 18 years with the Packers, and continued his Hall of Fame career with a new team.

## Male Testosterone Supplements

Testosterone is a very important hormone, and if you don't have enough of it, you may end up with decreased sex drive, erectile dysfunction, fatigue, loss of muscle mass, changing moods, and more body fat.

Testosterone levels in men start to decline in their late 20s and early 30s. After doing a blood test as part of my functional medicine doctor's onboarding, at age 37, I was diagnosed as having about half as much testosterone as was ideal. It made sense, as my sexual drive at 37 had declined by 50% from age 35. I finally figured out why. Not enough testosterone.

I didn't need Viagra. I just needed to take daily supplements.

My doctor recommended I start taking the supplements Tongkat Ali and Fadogia Agrestis each day to help get my testosterone back on track. I found some on Amazon.

Within a week of starting to consistently take this daily supplementation, my sex drive returned, and suddenly I wanted to have sex every two days instead of every week.

A study published in the Journal of Sexual Medicine in 2017 found that testosterone levels in American men had declined by 1.2% per year over a 30-year period, for a total decline of 36%.[21]

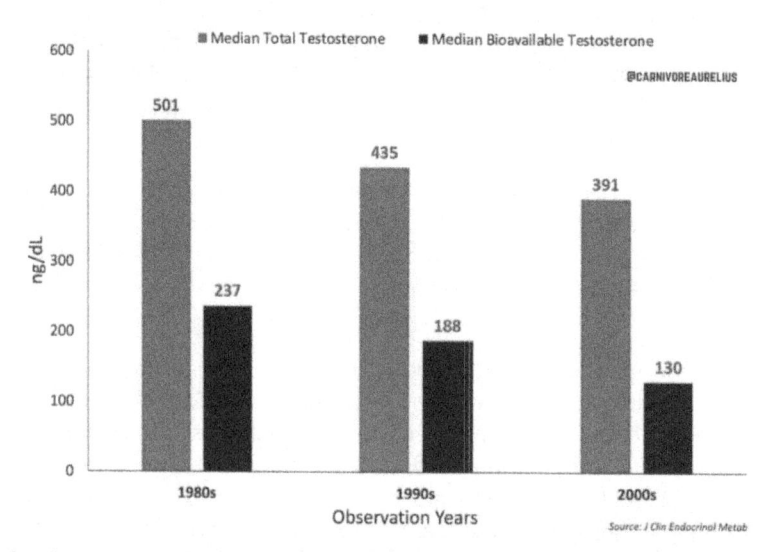

| Observation Years | Median Total Testosterone (ng/dL) | Median Bioavailable Testosterone (ng/dL) |
| --- | --- | --- |
| 1980s | 501 | 237 |
| 1990s | 435 | 188 |
| 2000s | 391 | 130 |

Source: J Clin Endocrinol Metab

So, for the men out there who are 35+, you may want to consider a testosterone supplement as part of your health care regimen. As always, check with your doctor first.

---

[21] Ramachandran, R., & Segraves, R. T. (2017). An observational study of serum testosterone levels and mortality in US men. The Journal of Sexual Medicine, 14(8), 1009-1018.

# Daily Meditation

> "More than 80% of the world-class performers I've interviewed have some form of daily meditation or mindfulness practice. Both can be thought of as cultivating a present-state awareness that helps you to be nonreactive." - Tim Ferriss

I used to think **meditation** was complete BS. I had no idea how to do it right. I thought meditation meant just sitting there and doing nothing.

Meditation - A practice involving focused attention and breathing, aimed at achieving mental clarity, emotional stability, and enhanced self-awareness for overall well-being. I recommend learning from Art of Living or Transcendental Meditation.

When I learned how to intentionally do breathing exercises (like alternate nostril breathing or bhastrika) during meditation, everything changed. In 2014, to learn how to meditate, I took a program on meditation I highly recommend called The Art of Living Happiness Program.

Art of Living is a non-profit organization founded in 1981 by Sri Sri Ravi Shankar and now has physical centers in over 180 countries. They teach their introductory meditation course online as well as in-person over the weekend.

There I learned some very helpful breathing techniques, including:

- Bhastrika - http://bit.ly/bhastrikademo
- Three stage pranayama - http://bit.ly/3stagebreathing
- Alternate nostril breathing - http://bit.ly/alternatenostrils
- Rapid nostril breathing - http://bit.ly/rapidnostril
- Holotropic breathing - https://bit.ly/holotropicbreathing

The Art of Living Sudarshan Kriya[22] meditation process combines these four breathing techniques into a single 30-40 minute practice.

After taking this course and learning how to breathe their special way, when I meditate with my eyes closed for more than 15 minutes I am able to see a deeply calming purple light (strange I know, but true).

**Action Item #67: Learn to Meditate**
Sign up for the Art of Living Happiness Program (online globally or in-person in 140+ countries) to learn their Sudarshan Kriya meditation technique. Then add in 30 minutes each morning to practice. Your life will change immensely!

I also did the more advanced course, The Art of Living Silence Course, a few times. I found that spending three days in silence was extremely beneficial to calming the mind and made me way more productive at work

---

[22] Learn more about the Sudarshan Kriya meditation practice at https://www.youtube.com/watch?v=O4HlTfVltjs.

There are other organizations as well that do a great job teaching meditation. I've also heard many friends say good things about Transcendental Meditation (TM), where you breathe in and out and say a given mantra over and over again.

If you need a full-system reset, here are some of the best retreat centers to visit in the USA and around the world

- Esalen - http://www.esalen.org/
- Art of Living Boone Retreat – http://artoflivingretreatcenter.org
- Harbin Hot Springs - http://www.Harbin.org/
- 10-day Vipassana (150+ centers around the world) - http://www.dhamma.org/
- Vedanta Society - http://sfvedanta.org/retreat/
- Tassajara Zen Mountain center - http://www.sfzc.org/tassajara/
- Earthrise - http://noetic.org/earthrise
- Hidden Valley Ashram - http://www.hvashram.org
- Green Gulch – http://www.sfzc.org/ggf/

You can find more programs and retreat centers at www.retreat.guru.

## The Science of Meditation

*"Meditation allows me to step back and gain a "witness perspective" (as with psychedelics), so that I'm observing my thoughts instead of being tumbled by them. I can step out of the washing machine and calmly look inside it." - Tim Ferriss*

Some of the earliest recorded practices of meditation come from ancient Indian traditions, particularly Hindu and Buddhist teachings. These traditions date back thousands of years and emphasize the importance of meditation as a way to achieve spiritual growth, enlightenment, and inner peace.

In Hinduism, meditation is known as "dhyana" and is one of the eight limbs of yoga, a practice that seeks to integrate the mind, body, and spirit. Buddhist meditation, known as "vipassana" or "mindfulness meditation," has been practiced for over 2,500 years and emphasizes the cultivation of awareness and compassion. Meditation is a practice that has been used for centuries in various cultures and religions to promote relaxation, calmness, and overall well being.

In recent years, scientists have begun to study the effects of meditation on the brain and body, and have found that meditation can have many positive effects on both.

Meditation changes the way the brain processes information. When we meditate, we are often instructed to focus on a particular object or thought and to let go of other distractions. This can help train the brain to become more focused and filter out unnecessary information. Over time, this can lead to improved cognitive abilities, such as increased attention, better memory, and enhanced problem-solving skills.

Meditation has also been shown to reduce stress, lower blood pressure, and improve immune function. It can also help alleviate symptoms of depression and anxiety.

When we meditate, we activate the parasympathetic nervous system, which is responsible for promoting relaxation and reducing stress. This can lead to a decrease in the levels of stress hormones in the body, such as cortisol, which can have many negative effects on our health over time. Overall, the science behind meditation suggests that it is a powerful tool for promoting both mental and physical health. By training the brain to become more focused and by reducing stress in the body, meditation can help us lead happier, healthier lives.

In a UCLA Laboratory of Neuro Imaging study, researchers looked at the link between meditation and the preservation of gray matter, the tissue where cognition occurs and memories are stored. They examined the brains of 100 participants, 50 people who had been meditating for an average of 20 years and 50 non-meditators. Both groups were made up of 28 men and 22 women between the ages of 24 and 77.

The participants' brains were scanned using fMRI technology. While both groups showed a decline in gray matter with older age, longtime meditators experienced smaller reductions in gray matter volume than those who did not meditate. It seemed that gray matter, in those who meditated, was better preserved.

Long story short, a daily meditation/breathing practice is essential to creating the best version of yourself. I do it every morning while in the sauna.

## Creating Your Miracle Morning Routine

"In a culture of cyber-zombies, addicted to distraction and afflicted with interruption, the wisest way to guarantee that you consistently produce mastery-level results in the most important areas of your professional and personal life is to install a world-class morning routine. Winning starts at your beginning. And your first hours are when heroes are made." - Robin Sharma

As W.H. Auden once wrote, "Routine, in an intelligent man, is a sign of ambition." You see, there is no more important part of your day than the first two hours. This is when heroes are made. As I shared in the introduction, here is my morning routine. It is the foundation of my physical, mental, and emotional health. It has 13 steps.

### My Miracle Morning Routine

1. Get 8+ hours of sleep (lights out and devices off by 10pm)
2. A cup of Green Tea
3. 10 Minutes of morning sun exposure
4. Take Supplements: Fish Oil, Tongkat Ali, Beef Liver, 5-HTP, & Magnesium
5. Bench 130 lbs x 30 (strength training) and do 30 pullups and 100 situps
6. 3 minutes in the hot tub
7. Swim 100 meters in the pool
8. 3-5 min in the Cold Plunge at 45-50° F
9. 5 mins in the Steam Sauna then 5 mins in the Dry Sauna (at around 176° F)
10. Alternate nostril breathing and breath of fire (Bhastrika Pranayama)
11. Visualization: imagining my day ahead and feeling grateful
12. Shower
13. Eat breakfast (usually scrambled eggs with avocado and sausage or chicken salad)

Only then do I begin my writing or other work. If I do these steps (they take me about 60 minutes plus a short commute to the wellness center/gym), I feel fantastic and am set up for a mentally healthy and productive day ahead of me with clear and calm thinking and extraordinary creativity. I tend to do the breathing exercises and mind visualizations during my 10 minutes in the saunas for some added time savings. A couple times per week, Morgan and I will also play racquetball or squash together.

> *Miracle Mornings* - *A routine for optimal mental and physical balance that you do in the first two hours of each day. Mine includes green tea, supplements, weight lifting, swimming, sauna, and a cold plunge.*

Own your morning, and you will 10x your life. Make your mornings your bitch and dom them into joyous submission to your intention and will.

Of course, every person's miracle morning routine is going to be a little different. Here is Morgan's for comparison.

### Morgan's Miracle Morning Routine

1. Wake up and play with Apollo
2. Read the Daily Affirmation she wrote for herself
3. Write out her gratitudes
4. Mouth scraping and oil pulling
5. Have a tea
6. Outdoor qi gong
7. Go for a walk
8. Do yoga and stretch at the gym
9. Paint and write at the gym cafe

The miracle morning is so essential for Morgan and I that when we moved to Austin in February 2023, instead of finding our home and then finding a nearby gym – we did it the other way around. Most gyms don't have pools, saunas, cafes, or places to write. So we found the ones that had everything.

We found the daily wellness center we go to in Austin (Life Time Fitness), and then we decided we would only consider houses within a 10 minute or less drive of it – knowing we'd be doing that drive twice per day. Lifetime even has a childcare center with free childcare if you book in advance. Now that's Gucci

Here are the other wellness centers we've become regulars at, depending on where we are living around the world.

- Ubud, Bali: Titi Batu Community Center
- Canggu, Bali: Amo Spa
- Sunshine Coast, Australia: Good Life Community Center
- Austin, Texas: Life Time Fitness
- Nosara, Bali: Bodhi Tree Gym + Plunge Nosara

So find a wellness center near you that has what you need to reliably do your miracle morning seven days per week. And if you can't find one, either move it or create one in your home. For around $15,000, you can get a sauna, pool, cold plunge, and gym installed at your place. Here's what the author of *Miracle Morning*, Hal Elrod, says should be the six components of every morning practice (they make the acronym SAVERS).

- Silence - Decreases stress & anxiety while increasing happiness & focus
- Affirmations - improve self-esteem and self-confidence
- Visualization - Rehearse in your mind performing at your best
- Exercise - Increase energy and physical well-being
- Reading - Learn how to change any area of your life
- Scribing - Reflect, track progress, and cultivate gratitude

*Silence*
Decreases stress & anxiety while increasing happiness & focus.

*Affirmations*
Improve self-esteem and self-confidence.

*Visualization*
Rehearse in your mind performing at your best.

*Exercise*
Increase energy and physical well-being.

*Reading*
Learn how to change any area of your life.

*Scribing*
Reflect, track progress, & cultivate gratitude.

The Six Parts of a Miracle Morning from Hal Erod

**Action Item #68: Create Your Miracle Morning**
Based on what you learned from this chapter, write down ALL the steps of your miracle morning from the moment you wake up until the moment you begin work. What is essential for you to do in the first 120 minutes of your day? What is so important to your wellness and presence and happiness that you will commit to doing it every day, seven days per week, rain or shine? Actually do this miracle morning everyday for the next 30 days and watch the change in you!

## Recommended Books on Health

- *The Myth of Normal* by Gabor Mate
- *Tools of Titans* by Tim Ferriss
- *Smarter Not Harder* by Dave Asprey
- *Young Forever* By Dr. Mark Hyman
- *Move Connect Play* by Jason Nemer
- *The Body Keeps the Score* by Dr. Bessel van der Kolk
- *The Myth of Normal: Trauma, Illness, and Healing in a Toxic Culture* by Gabor Maté

## Key Outcome from This Chapter

**Create a Personalized Magic Morning Routine -** Based on what you learned in this chapter, write down and 100% commit to a magic morning routine for yourself based on what is going to make you most ready to be present, happy, productive, creative, and ready to have rocking and positive days every day. Then do this routine every single day, seven days per week, for the next 30 days to install it -- and reap the benefits. At minimum, we recommend strongly considering including some form of daily cardio, daily strength training, daily cold plunge, and daily morning sun exposure.

# HEALTH CHAPTER ACTION ITEMS

1. **Get a Smart Scale** - Get yourself a smart scale that measures weight, body fat %, and body mass index (BMI). Weigh yourself daily over the next 30 days.

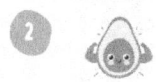

2. **Choose Your Diet** - After reviewing the above sections on diet, write down what foods you're committing to not eat (sugars, processed foods, etc.) and what type of diet you want to be on (paleo, vegan, keto, etc.). Write down any commitments you're ready to make about your diet.

3. **The Optimal Schedule** - Write down your optimal daily schedule. What time do you wake up, do each step of your miracle morning routine, go to work, go to sleep, etc.? Create your optimal weekday and weekend schedule and then actually live that schedule for at least 21 days to lock it in habitually -- making adjustments and improvements as needed.

4. **Afternoon State Priming** - Schedule in a daily 10 minute state priming break each afternoon for the next 30 days at the same time each day. Choose a couple of the above exercises to do each day.

5. **Daily Exercise Routine** - Write down your desired daily exercise routine. What are you committing to do seven days a week? At bare minimum, if you can lift weights for 5 minutes per day and also get your heart rate above 160 BPM for just 5 minutes per day, it can substantially reduce anxiety and also lead to a much longer and happier life. Follow the routine you design for the next 30 days.

6. **Get Your Sleep Right** - Write down your optimal daily sleep routine. What are you committing to doing before you go to bed each night? What time will you start to wind down and turn off all devices. What time do you want to fall asleep and wake up each day? Make sure there's at least 9 hours between turning off all devices and your wake up time -- so that you get at least 8 to 8.5 hours of good sleep each night. Follow this sleep pattern for the next 30 days.

7. **Functional Medicine -** Set up an appointment to go see a functional medicine doctor in your area. See if you can find one your health insurance will cover, if applicable. Then go get your labs (blood tests and panels) run by the doctor so they can proactively assess your current health state. See what you can learn about your body and how to optimize your health.

8. **Stress Reduction -** Review the section on stress chemicals. Then write down a plan to reduce the amount of cortisol, adrenaline, and norepinephrine in your body. Write down the new practices you commit to and which habits you will change to reduce stress on your body and help you be happier and healthier. Follow this plan the 30 days.

9. **Cold Plunging** - Search Google maps for your nearest cold plunge. Hopefully there's one less than 15 minutes from your house or office. Go there the next 30 days in a row and get in the cold plunge for at least 3 full minutes per day. If you can average 12-14 minutes per week in the cold plunge, you will start feeling immense benefits to your mood. Start around 50° F and then work your way down to 40° F.

10. **Slowing Down** - Review the sections on digital detoxing, holotropic breathing, reiki, cranial sacral, gua sha, oil dripping, float tanks, and morning sun exposure. Write down the new habits you want to experiment with and which ones you want to commit to doing regularly.

11. **Learn to Meditate -** Sign up for the Art of Living Happiness Program (online globally or in-person in 140+ countries) to learn their Sudarshan Kriya meditation technique. Then add in 30 minutes each morning to practice. Your life will change immensely!

12. **Miracle Morning -** Based on what you learned from this section, write down ALL the steps of your miracle morning from the moment you wake up until the moment you begin work. What is essential for you to do in the first 120 minutes of your day? What is so important to your wellness and presence and happiness that you will commit to doing it every day, seven days per week, rain or shine? Do this for 30 days straight.

# STEP 7

# MONEY MAGIC

**MAGIC YEAR**

# KEY CONCEPTS FROM THE MONEY CHAPTER

### 1. PASSIVE CASHFLOW
Money that is made from your assets not from your labor. Work once, earn multiple times. You can earn passive income from stocks, bonds, real estate, and royalties.

### 2. MONEY TRACKING
Using an app like Rocket Money to auto-categorize your personal expenses on a weekly or monthly basis and determine your total income, total expenses, and total savings for each month. An essential habit for achieving financial freedom.

### 3. PERSONAL FINANCIAL STATEMENT
A listing of your current assets, debts, and net worth along with your monthly income, expenses, and savings. You can create this in a spreadsheet or use a money tracking app.

### 4. PERSONAL FINANCIAL PLAN
A future target for how much money you want to be earning, spendings, and saving monthly, along with your future net worth. Sophisticated financial plans also create suggested investment plans with what to invest in for your risk-profile and goals.

### 5. TIME FREEDOM
When you can do whatever you want with your time, either because you have very low expenses or you have lots of money.

### 6. INCOME FREEDOM
When your monthly income is high enough to cover all your expenses, taxes, and still have 25% left over for savings and investments.

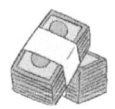

### 7. NET WORTH FREEDOM
When your passive cash flow from your businesses and investments is high enough to more than cover your total annual expenses, so that your net worth continues to grow over time.

### 8. SLEEP PROOF BUSINESSES
Businesses you own part or all of that make money even while you're sleeping or gone -- because they are built with systems that don't go home at night. Owning these is the key to creating large amounts of wealth.

### 9. STREAMS OF INCOME
Wealthy people almost always have a few sources of monthly cashflow including real estate, bonds, businesses, and dividend-producing stocks.

### 10. AUTOMATIC WEALTH
Wealth that is built up gradually over time through saving and investing each month over many decades. If for example you can save $3k per monht from age 25-65, you'll have $10M when you retire (see Automatic Decamillionaire).

### 11. AUTOMATIC MILLIONAIRE
Reaching $1M in net worth on autopilot by saving and investing $1000 per month, investing it at an average 8% annual return, and not taking any out for 25 years

### 12. AUTOMATIC DECAMILLIONAIRE
Reaching $10M in net worth by saving and investing $2,000 per month for 45 years, $3,000 per month for 40 years, or $4,000 per month for 35 years. Assumes an 8% average annual return.

# MORE KEY CONCEPTS FROM THE MONEY CHAPTER

**13. ENTREPRENEURIAL WEALTH** 
Wealth that is built up through building a growing business and then selling ownership of it to someone else.

**14. CONSUMPTION TRAP** 
Getting a job and then massively increasing your monthly expenses before you have a chance to explore and find what you truly love.

**15. HIGH INCOME TRAP** 
The trap that people with high income and high expenses fall into. They may make $500,000 per year but they spend $500,000 per year, leaving them with nothing to invest for the long term.

**16. CASHFLOWING ASSETS** 
Investment assets like stocks, bonds, real estate, and royalty streams that generate monthly, quarterly, or annual cash flow paid to the asset owners. These are what you want to accumulate to grow your passive income.

**17. PRIVATE STOCK** 
Shares of a company that is private and not listed on a public stock exchange. A share is partial ownership of a company. Private company stock is usually not liquid, although some private share marketplaces are available for fast growing firms.

**18. PUBLIC STOCK** 
Shares of a company that is publicly traded on a stock exchange like the NYSE or NASDAQ. Shares entitle holders to dividends and their respective percentage of proceeds in the case of a sale. Shares sometimes also offer voting rights.

**19. INITIAL PUBLIC OFFERING** 
When a company lists its stock to be sold on a public stock exchange for the first time. This process creates liquidity, meaning, that the shares of the company can be easily bought and sold.

**20. REAL ESTATE** 
Land, homes, apartments, and hotels. Real Estate is often a good way to create cash flow, either buy buying it and renting it out, or by investing in large real estate projects or REITS.

**21. BONDS** 
A loan that you give to a company (corporate bond), city (municipal bond), or a country (treasury bond) in exchange for interest and your principal paid back over time.

**22. DISCOUNTED CASH FLOW** 
A method of valuing a business by forecasting its profits out 20-30 years and then calculating the present value of those future cash flows. While you can also estimate a company's value using revenue or profit multiples, a DCF is the best way to value a company.

**23. FINANCIAL STATEMENTS** 
The most commonly used business financial statements are the Profit & Loss Statement which shows revenues, expenses, and profits and the Balance Sheet which shows assets, liabilities, and equity. Use these statements to value a company and assess performance.

**24. ANGEL INVESTING** 
Investing in early stage private companies (usually technology-enabled companies) in order to earn big returns if those companies later sell or IPO. Warning: It's easy to lose a lot of money if you don't do this right.

# STEP 7: MONEY MAGIC

"Don't chase the paper, chase the dream." - P. Diddy

**YOUR MAGIC YEAR**

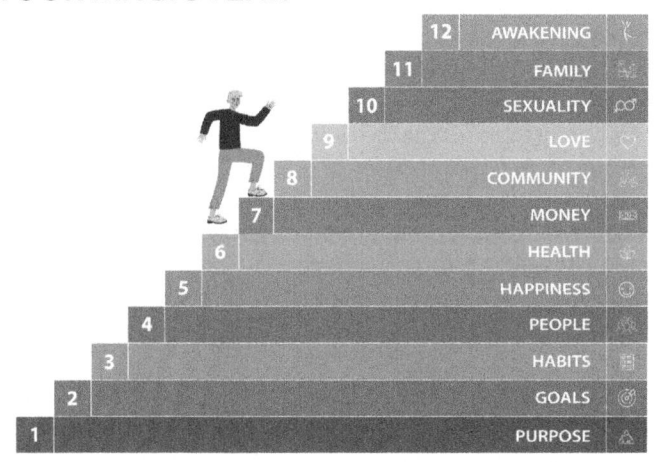

| Step | Area |
|---|---|
| 12 | AWAKENING |
| 11 | FAMILY |
| 10 | SEXUALITY |
| 9 | LOVE |
| 8 | COMMUNITY |
| 7 | MONEY |
| 6 | HEALTH |
| 5 | HAPPINESS |
| 4 | PEOPLE |
| 3 | HABITS |
| 2 | GOALS |
| 1 | PURPOSE |

Money is an important component of life and happiness. While money alone can't make you happy, having enough can certainly help. This chapter is designed to give you the skillsets needed to make, save, and invest more money so that you can become financially free and get out of the rat race.

Of course, the truth is, you don't need millions of dollars to be happy. You just need to cover your basic living expenses and spend your time doing things you actually enjoy with people you care about.

It is better to be a happy pauper than a rich, dead soul. That said, the ideal is to have both plenty of **passive cashflow** and a deeply fulfilling life. This life is possible -- and this step of the book will guide you there.

Passive Cashflow - Money that is made from your assets not from your labor. Work once, earn multiple times. You can earn passive income from stocks, bonds, real estate, and royalties.

This step of the book is also designed to show you the entrepreneurial path toward creating a business doing what you love that becomes a cash flow engine to fund everything you want to do.

I'll show you in the pages ahead how to be a financially prosperous creator with infinite **time** and **location freedom** by slowly building meaningful businesses over time that make money while you sleep.

While it may take 5-20 years to fully reach your financial dreams, by taking the right actions now, you can both do what you love and create automated cash flows that more than cover your expenses. With money, it's getting the basics right time and time again that matters most.

## My Journey With Money

My journey with money has been insane. It has felt like it's been guided by God at times. I've gone from the lower middle class growing up to earning $15M at age 27 from selling my company, then losing most of that, to then making much of it back. It hasn't been a straight path.

Some years, I've had a lot. Other years, not as much. Today, I'm focused on building sustainable wealth along with sustainable happiness.

I grew up in the middle class, with my family earning $32,000 per year on a single-income Priest/Chaplain income. We scraped and saved and cut coupons and did all we could to be able to go on a family trip to England every 2 years to see my mom's family there.

Then, at 16, my mom gave me *Think and Grow Rich* and *Rich Dad Poor Dad,* and the rest is history. I wrote down the goal of building a company to $1M in sales by age 21. Eighteen days after my 21st birthday, my company, iContact, reached that mark and would go on to grow into a company with $50M in sales per year.

By the time I was 27 years old, we'd sold the company for $169M and I'd earned around $15M after taxes (our other shareholders, including my co-founder, employees, and venture capitalists, got the rest).

Suffice it to say, I wasn't exactly smart about what to do with that $15M. What I should have done was put it in something relatively safe like stocks, bonds, or real estate and let it compound over time. Getting the basics of money right is everything.

I even had a meeting in NYC with UBS about managing my money for me. I should have just given it over to them and said, don't let me touch it for a decade.

I could have simply "retired" at 27, bought myself a $5M mansion in Raleigh, found myself a wife, had two kids, and lived a very traditional North Carolina lifestyle. But I was too fucking curious. I was an **achiever** and a **seeker**. I was deeply curious about the world. I couldn't stay in North Carolina.

The very day after my contract ended with the company that bought iContact, I was on a plane to San Francisco to attend the Singularity University Executive Program at the NASA Ames Campus in Menlo Park, California. After coming up with a business idea on day two of a four day program, I left and drove up to San Francisco to recruit a co-founder named Anima.

Two weeks later, we founded a new company called Connect together, with the mission of using mobile and social technology to bring people together more in the real world -- instead of getting stuck on Lord Algo's newsfeed.

Anima and I and a team of 15 people ended up spending much of the next five years (while also doing an MBA at HBS) attempting (and failing) to build Connect into a sustainable company. But we couldn't quite figure out the business model for a B2C Social App.

I learned as much from Connect's failure as I did from iContact's success. Sadly, I was overconfident and had put $6M of my own money into building Connect and $2M into building the Hive.org global community of purpose-driven leaders. I also invested $7M into angel investments in 34 other companies, mostly in Silicon Valley.

It was a comedy of unforced personal errors watching this $6M investment in my own company go to $0 and then watching the $9M of other investments I'd made turn into about $500k over the next decade.

At one point, a psychic told me I was meant to lose nearly all my money in my 30s so that I'd have the drive and work ethic again to create something extraordinary in my 40s. Whether he actually saw the future or it simply became a self-fulfilling prophecy, I will never know.

I like to think earning the $15M came from an extraordinary decade in my 20s, where I learned a lot about systems, scaling, and consistency. And then I like to think I traded the $15M during my 30s for some of the best friends, best experiences, and best family I could have ever imagined.

I could never have written this book had I purchased that $5M mansion in Raleigh and lived a boring "normal" life in the American suburbs. It would have been much easier, perhaps. But I'm a seeker. And I love experiences, and I love the eccentric weirdos, artists, nomads, and creators I meet in places like Bali, Costa Rica, and LA.

Today, I still own a digital marketing agency (Hive Digital) which does around $3.5M per year in sales. Hive Digital is really good at SEO and PPC. I also earn good money by coaching SaaS CEOs. Today, I prefer to guide other CEOs in creating the processes for growing from $1M to $100M in sales -- rather than be the CEO myself.

So we're very lucky and fortunate. But I'm definitely in a rebuilding phase in my 40s -- and this book is part of it. We actually have to keep a family budget, track our expenses, and be very intentional about our spending to get everything we desire. This has given me renewed understanding and empathy about what pretty much everyone goes through to manage their finances. We've learned to be happy with less.

Today we're spending $10k-15k per month and putting everything else we earn into long term investments and real estate.

**Action Item #69: Read This Essay**
Read the great essay in The Atlantic "How to Want Less: The Secret to Satisfaction Has Nothing To Do With Achievement, Money, or Stuff." by Arthur Brooks

Wow, the ups and the downs. The next time I make $15M I'm sending it straight to a trust managed by a professional financial advisor where I'm not allowed to touch the principal -- put it into muni bonds and REITS and only have access to half of the annual interest/cash flow. This way, the money keeps growing every year -- by design. Thankfully, I'm much wiser about money at 40 than I was at 30. Having a family requires that.

We have more than enough to fulfill all our dreams. But we still have to be thoughtful about what we buy, especially with the expenses of childcare and schooling coming up.

Today we have a more modest net worth of around $2M but are building it back up in our 40s -- and I have a feeling that this time around it will actually stick. Building (and keeping) wealth with a committed, long-term partner is easier for me. My monthly income has more than doubled since I started dating Morgan. The love she gives me enables me to be exceptionally consistent. A great romantic partner ends up being a great investment too!

Statistically speaking, I've probably earned (and lost) more money than 99.99% of humanity. In that process, I've learned a shit ton about what works and what doesn't. Below are some of the lessons that have come from that earned wisdom.

# The Eight Forms of Wealth

Interviewer: "Are you a rich man?"
Bob Marley: "When you mean rich, what do you mean?"
Interviewer: "Do you have a lot of possessions, a lot of money in the bank?"

Bob Marley: "Possessions make you rich? I don't have that type of riches. My riches is life forever"

Before I write too much more about how to make, save, and invest money, I need to say, money is only one form of wealth. There are eight different types of riches…

1. Time
2. Health
3. Purpose
4. Community
5. Family
6. Adventure
7. Sensuality
8. And last but not least -- money

You can be "rich" or "poor" in each of these areas. The key is finding the optimal balance for you. And the key is to realize that possessions that you don't truly enjoy or that don't generate cashflow are simply albatrosses around your neck that prevent mobility and adventure.

"The currencies of the New Rich are time and mobility" - Tim Ferris

There are many people who have lots of money, but don't have true happiness -- so be sure you know the value of "enough" and to always prioritize happiness over working to make more than you really need.

Robin Sharma writes on this topic. "Money is only one metric of success. It's only one form of wealth. There are many more, you know? Like being a good person and doing work that satisfies you, like having a fulfilling family life and being around friends who flood you with gratitude and hope. Many obsess over financial return on investment yet, tragically, ignore the value of character ROI, happiness ROI, and spiritual ROI. And I must tell you, from my experience as the adviser to a ton of industry captains, billionaires, and entertainment titans, that a lot of them have all the assets you could imagine, yet are troubled, unhappy, and fraught with worry. Too much money can become a formula for complexity, difficulty, and often outright misery. Personally, I place a vastly higher value on inner freedom than upon financial gain."

You don't want to wake up at age 60 with too much money but not enough love, friends, or experiences.

Always remember: **The goal isn't to be rich. It's to do something legendary and meaningful.** As P. Diddy says, "Don't chase the paper (the money), chase the dream."

The goal is to do something exceptionally worthwhile with your life that is in alignment with what brings you into flow. If you do that, you often become a world class expert in that field of specialty -- and usually make a lot of money, especially if you can build a business around it that makes money while you sleep.

To win at the game of entrepreneurship, we must always keep in mind that the true purpose of business is not to become a millionaire or make profits but rather to provide value to your customers, to create a positive impact, to innovate, to create great products, and to create jobs. Cash and profits should be seen as the lifeblood that allows you to strive for your company's true mission.

So while the goal of life is not to make a lot of money, having a good amount of money can help you do what you want to do in life and can certainly help you create jobs and pay it forward. Money is also a sign that you're creating value for others – which is a good thing. So let's learn how to make it, save it, and grow it.

**Action Item #70: The Different Forms of Wealth**
In your notebook, on a scale of 1-10 rate yourself on "how wealthy are you" for each of the eight different forms of wealth: time, health, purpose, community, family, adventure, sensuality, and money.

# Understand What Money Actually Is

"Money is simply the marketplace's return on benefit delivered." - Robin Sharma

What is money? Money is an agreed upon store of value that enables two parties to exchange even if they cannot barter. Over time, many different things have been used to represent money, ranging from seashells to cigarettes, to stones, to metals, to paper, to digital ledger entries.

In many ways, it's a digital entry in a database somewhere. It's certainly not something to fret about too much -- but definitely something you want to create good systems around saving and investing so that you earn money passively without having to work on anything that doesn't light you up inside.

As Jen Sincero says, "Money is an exchange of energy between people."

The amount of money you earn usually directly corresponds to how much economic value you are creating for others. If you're doing a job that is easily replaceable with low specialization, you won't earn much.

- If you're flipping hamburgers in a McDonalds and being paid $15 per hour, then you are creating about that much value in the labor market every hour, by providing the service of connecting hungry people with low cost food.

On the other hand, if you're doing a job that is highly specialized or building a business where you've **created a system that makes money while you sleep**, you can earn many millions of dollars. So learn to do high value things and become the best in a field that brings you joy. No matter what field you're in, if you love it and stick with it for 10 years, you can create a lot of value for others -- and thus for yourself.

- If you're the founder/CEO of a company that brings to market and then scales an industry-changing or world changing invention, you could earn millions or even billions of dollars

- If you're an investment banker helping companies raise hundreds of millions of dollars in venture capital and advising on large Merger and Acquisition deals, you could earn tens of millions of dollars. The value you're providing is getting capital into innovative projects that make a difference in the world.

- If you're a specialist surgeon who is one of the best in the world at performing a life saving treatment, you will likely earn a lot. High specialization = high income.

- If you're writing books that help millions of people become better and consulting with some of the top billionaires and leaders in the world to help them achieve optimal lives and companies -- you will likely earn a lot.

- If you're building a course on financial freedom for women that tens of thousands of people purchase and use to transform their lives -- you're going to do really well.

So to earn a good income, look to develop specialist skillsets that allow you to create a LOT of value for others in a short amount of time—or build businesses that make money while you're sleeping. Become world class in your niche -- and your income will grow.

Think about human society as groups ants working together to improve their villages, towns, cities, countries, and world. Every ant contributes to the communal effort. What's different about homo sapiens is that 7,000 years ago we invented currency to make it much easier to barter and trade. Thus, to obtain more currency, you create more value for others and tell more people about the value you provide.

Imagine if I created the *Magic Year Course* (magicyear.com) and then never ran any digital ads to share it with the world. I could perhaps sell $100,000 per year of the course just from my organic following on Facebook, Instagram, and email. Now, imagine that I took the value I already created (the course and the coaching program that comes with the course) and told 50 million people about it every month through Facebook, Instagram, and YouTube Ads.

That's called **value leverage** -- allowing a single online course to be distributed on a massive Archimedes Lever called social media advertising.

As long as the cost to acquire a customer plus the cost to deliver the product/service is less than the revenue earned from a customer, we will have a very profitable business that impacts a lot of people. So yes, don't obsess over money. Simply obsess with honing your craft and sharing your gifts with the world as widely as possible -- and the money will follow!

While some people obsess about their income, what I like to obsess about instead is:

1) How much I can save each month in order to stow away into long term cash flowing investments (like stocks, bonds, and real estate).

2) How much time freedom I have to spend with my family

3) How much value I can create for others in the fewest number of hours

## What I Obsess Over

- How much I can save
- How much time freedom I have
- How much value I can create for the world

I tend to work about 4-5 hours per day of intensely productive, high-value work. And that's been more than enough to fund our dreams. Too much money can really damage a person, especially if it's given to children who didn't go through the life lessons required to earn it.

So if you're a parent, instead of obsessing about making money, obsess about giving your children the best possible experience, education, and learning adventure in life.

That said, having financial freedom is key to being able to spend the time you want with your family. So that's what this section is all about --- how to achieve financial freedom.

Start where you are and build good habits (like spending only 50% of what you earn monthly, for example). Here's a quote from Arnold Schwarzenegger on how he got invested early in his 20s – not wanting to end up broke like many of the other young actors in LA.

"I saw over the years, the people that worked out in the gym and that I met in the acting classes, they were all very vulnerable because they didn't have any money, and they had to take anything that was offered to them because that was their living. I didn't want to get into that situation. I felt if I was smart with real estate and took my little money that I made in bodybuilding and in seminars and selling my courses through the mail, I could save up enough to put down money for an apartment building."

# My Four Rules for Money

*"One of the biggest mistakes people make in their financial lives (after accumulating too much debt and failing to practice the time-tested yet usually broken rule of living within their means) is to upgrade their lifestyle each time they increase their income. Huge error. If every time you make more money you increase your expenses, you'll never build any net worth. You'll always be on the hamster wheel." - Robin Sharma*

Twenty years from now, your financial situation will be a function of the plan you put in place and the actions you decide to take now. My rules about money are simple:

1. Spend less than you earn EVERY month.
2. Never ever go into debt for something you don't need
3. Save up money early in life as the law of compound interest makes a big difference over time.
4. Figure out how to make money while you sleep.

## Ryan's Four Rules for Money

- Spend less than you earn every month
- Don't go into debt for things you don't need
- Save up early in life
- Make money while you sleep

These four laws of money are exceptionally basic, yet the vast majority of people don't follow them

If you're committed to building financial wealth and having a nice nest egg for your family, follow these simple rules.

And when I say spend less than you earn: Target spending no more than 75% of your after-tax income each month. Yes, you read that right. **Spend no more than 75% of your after-tax income.**

This sentence is probably the most important line in this book about the initial phase of building up wealth. Short-term consumption deferment can lead to long-term riches.

It will require some short-term sacrifice in your 20s and 30s to defer unnecessary consumption, but it will start paying off big time in your 40s, 50s, and 60s.

Either learn to be a great saver OR a great builder -- and ideally both. Me? I'm an inconsistent saver, but an exceptionally consistent builder and creator. I've learned how to consistently scale businesses -- and that has made all the difference in my life.

**Action Item #71: Your Savings Plan**
Write down how much you earn per month after taxes. Then calculate what 25% of that amount is. That's the amount you should be saving and investing each month. Make the changes you need to make to your monthly spending so that next month you actually save 25% of your after tax income. See if you can actually accomplish this feat this month.

## Tracking Your Spending

The first step to getting a handle on your money is to track how much you're earning, spending, and saving each month. Being able to compare spending vs. your targeted budget each month for each category is also exceptionally useful. You're going to get really good at your weekly **money tracking** ritual. Pick a day of the week and stick to it. I do Fridays at 4 p.m. and stick to it every week.

*Money tracking - Using an app like Rocket Money to auto-categorize your personal expenses on a weekly or monthly basis and determine your total income, total expenses, and total savings for each month. An essential habit for achieving financial freedom.*

MAGIC YEAR - 344

I recommend using the free RockeyMoney personal financial expense tracker to get automated monthly personal financial reports that show how much you earned, how much you spent, and how much you saved. You can also keep track of your assets, liabilities, and net worth -- and the service can even cancel unneeded subscriptions for you.

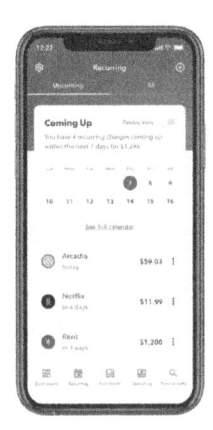

One of the coolest features is the auto-categorization of your expenses. So you can see how much you're spending in each category monthly without doing any work yourself.

While this is a lot of transparency, we're all about transparency in this guide to life. Right now, we have about $50k in our checking and savings accounts and a $2 million estimated net worth. Much of our financial net worth comes from the value of our stock in Hive Digital, Coinstack, Tatango, and a handful of other past angel investments. We're hoping to buy our first family home together at some point in the next 18 months, once we get a little bit of liquidity. We have an option to buy our little beach home in Costa Rica at the end of our 3 year lease, so we are saving up right now to buy it.

**Action Item #72: Track Your Money**
Use a free tool like RocketMoney to track your expenses and budget each month and cancel any unneeded expenses. Over the next 30 days, check in every Friday to review your progress and review the automatic expense categorizations. If you're engaged or married, meet with your partner monthly to review your progress.

## Creating Your Personal Financial Statement

One of the first steps to getting a handle on your own money is to create your **personal financial statement** in a spreadsheet.

*Personal Financial Statement - A listing of your current assets, debts, and net worth along with your monthly income, expenses, and savings.*

Use the below template to fill out your own **financial statement**, listing your assets, debts, and net worth in the first section and then your monthly income, expenses, and cashflow (savings) in the second section. Finally, list out what you want your monthly income, expenses, and cashflow to be in the final section to create a basic **financial plan**.

```
Financial Plan of _____
Assets           Debts              Net Worth




          Present Monthly Cash Flow
Income           Expenses           Cashflow




        36 Months From Now Monthly Goal
Income           Expenses           Cashflow





Signed X_____ this ___ day of _____ 20___
```

You can write a simple financial plan within 5-10 minutes on a sheet of paper or spreadsheet

*Personal Financial Plan - A future target for how much money you want to be earning, spendings, and saving monthly, along with your future net worth. More sophisticated financial plans also create suggested investment plans with what to invest in for your risk-profile and goals. You can create your own or get one made for you by a financial planner.*

It can be a good idea to consult a trained financial advisor when planning your future, as everyone's time frame, current state, and goals are different.

You can get a financial advisor to craft a customized plan for you from a place like Edward Jones, or you can use a digital robo-advisor service like SoFi, Wealthfront, or Betterment. As part of your financial plan, it's a good idea to purchase some life insurance - especially if you have kids. We have a $3M life insurance policy on me in the event that I die before age 65. This costs us just $2800 per year -- a good investment to ensure Apollo will always be financially taken care of if I happen to move on from this body early.

**Action Item #73: Your Personal Financial Plan**
Use the above template and create your personal financial plan. Be sure to list your monthly after-tax income, expenses, net cash flow, assets, liabilities, and net worth -- as well as what you want these numbers to be 3 years from

now!

## The 7 Steps for Building Wealth

Here are the seven steps for building wealth over time. Follow these to the letter, and you will do exceptionally well financially.

1. **Know How Much You're Earning.** Calculate how much you earn after taxes each month.

2. **Know How Much You're Spending**. Use a tool like Mint.com or Rocket Money to track how much you're spending automatically. Both tools connect to your bank account.

3. **Spend Less Than You Earn, Every Single Month.** This is the absolute most important skill to master for a long-term financial foundation. Track your spending closely and religiously, and once you have enough, hire a Personal Assistant to do this for you -- questioning anything they don't recognize. I suggest targeting spending no more than 75% of your after-tax income and saving and investing the other 25% so you can more quickly get out of the rat race.

| Monthly income after taxes | Monthly spending | |
|---|---|---|
| $3000 | $3200 | X |
| Monthly income after taxes | Monthly spending | |
| $4000 | $3000 | ✓ |

4. **Pay Yourself First:** If you get a paycheck or monthly income of some kind, set aside the needed amount for taxes and then pay yourself first by sending 25% into a long-term savings/investments account.

5. **Pay Off Debt:** Pay off all your debt, starting with the highest interest rates first. And never take on any credit card debt.

6. **Start Saving $1,000 Per Month, Every Month.** If you can get up to $2,083 per month and keep that going for 44 years (age 21-65 or age 31-75 for example) you'll end up with around $10 million (assuming an 8% average annual return on your investments). This is the automated way to wealth!

7. **Start Investing:** After building up 3 months of salary in your savings account (an emergency fund), start making long-term investments in stocks, bonds, and real estate/REITs. You can do this via an online robo-advisor app like Betterment, SoFi, or Wealthfront

### How to Become Wealthy The Automatic Way

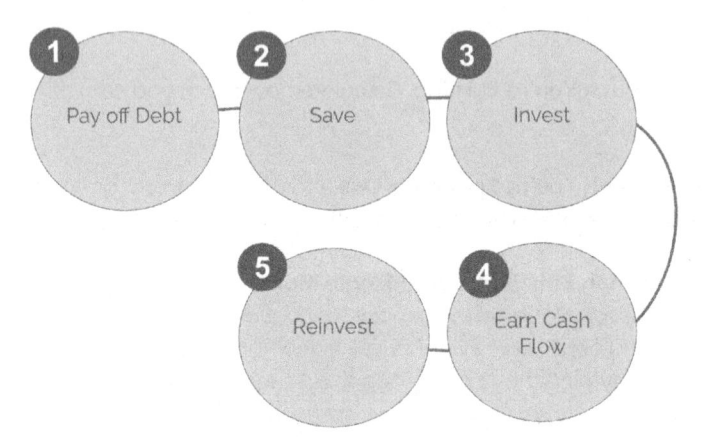

1. Pay off Debt
2. Save
3. Invest
4. Earn Cash Flow
5. Reinvest

If you want to earn more money each year than you currently do, you have to either increase the revenues or cash flows of the businesses you own.

If you work for someone else you have to either...

1) Acquire specialized knowledge and experience that is valuable to the firm you work with;

2) Or increase the sales and profits of the firm you work with, by either increasing sales, improving marketing, expanding distribution, or reducing costs – so that they can pay you more and offer you equity ownership.

People who consistently do these things tend to earn a lot more money than those who do not -- and thus can get a head start on the process of saving, investing, and compounding.

Specialization is critical to both monetary success and all types of success. Remember, you can do anything, but not everything. Focus on becoming the best in the world for 5-10 years at one thing you love doing that creates value for others -- then figure out how to make money doing that exact thing while you sleep by building a system that never goes home.

As entrepreneur Derek Silvers says, "I meet a lot of 30-year-olds who are trying to pursue many different directions at once, but not making progress in any, right? They get frustrated that the world wants them to pick one thing, because they want to do them all. The solution is to think long-term. To realize that you can do one of these things for a few years, and then do another one for a few years, and then another."

And as Scott Adams, the creator of the Dilbert Comic Strip, advises, "If you want an average, successful life, it doesn't take much planning. Just stay out of trouble, go to school, and apply for jobs you might like. But if you want something extraordinary, you have to either become the best at one specific thing or become very good (top 25%) at two or more things."

**Action Item #74: Your Debt-Free Plan**
If you have credit card debt, do the math and calculate how many more months it will take to pay it all off. Once you pay off all your high-interest debt, it's time to start saving, investing, and actually building wealth!

# The Four Types of Freedoms

In life there are four different types of freedoms. Let's take a look...

*Time Freedom* - When you earn more than your monthly living expenses in passive income from your businesses and investments or from very few work hours, so you have the freedom to invest your time as you choose.

*Location Freedom* - When you have the freedom to live and work from wherever you choose. You can work from anywhere with a strong internet connection.

*Income Freedom* - When your monthly income is high enough to cover all your expenses, taxes, and still have 25% left over for savings and investments.

*Net Worth Freedom* - When your passive cash flow from your businesses and investments is high enough to more than cover your total annual expenses, so that your net worth continues to grow over time.

## The Four Freedoms

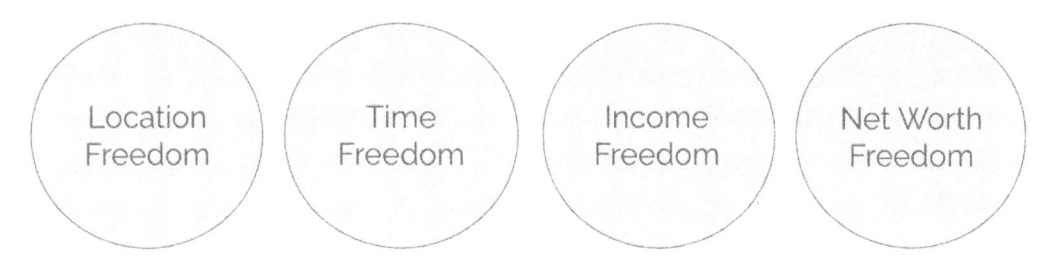

Location Freedom | Time Freedom | Income Freedom | Net Worth Freedom

Location freedom is something I've already written about earlier, so let's start with **Time Freedom** here. There are four ways to have time freedom as an adult...

1. Reduce your living expenses to as low as possible (say $1000 per month) by living in low cost places like Thailand, Cambodia, Bali, etc. so you can pay for all your costs by

working very little and only doing what you love.

2. Figure out how to turn what you love to do into a business that makes money while you sleep (a **sleep-proof business**) – so that you can own it without spending very much time on it after it's set up and has a good manager in place.

*Sleep Proof Business* - Businesses you own part or all of that make money even while you're sleeping or gone -- because they are built with systems that don't go home at night. Owning these is the key to creating large amounts of wealth.

3. Become a famous athlete, artist, actor, or writer (this is a hard path, beware)

4. Marry into a family that has a lot of money that pays for your expenses.

**Income freedom** comes when you have your financial life set up properly. Let's say you earn $150,000 per year before taxes, $100,000 per year after taxes, and have $75,000 per year of expenses. That means you can save 25% of your after tax income. Congratulations! You now have income freedom, and if you just keep going at that rate, you'll reach net worth freedom. The last freedom, **Net Worth Freedom** comes when your annual passive cash flow is at or above your annual expenses and taxes. When I say "get out of the **rat race**," this is what I mean.

*Rat Race* - The mindless race to do work you don't enjoy that barely keeps you afloat financially. Being stuck in a cycle of consumption, debt, and overwork and never choosing to do what you actually want to do with your life.

Let's look at the math here of what's needed to get out of the rat race once and for all and achieve **Net Worth Freedom** for someone with annual after-tax expenses of varying amounts.

| Cash Flowing Assets | Amount This Generates Per Year At 4% |
|---|---|
| $2.5M | $100,000 |
| $5M | $200,000 |
| $7.5M | $300,000 |
| $10M | $400,000 |
| $12.5M | $500,000 |
| $15M | $600,000 |

Active income is income you earn from your labor. Passive income is income you earn from your investments. As you can see, if you want to earn $400,000 per year in **passive cashflow**, you need to have about $10,00,000 invested in cash flowing assets like bonds and real estate.

To reach **net worth freedom,** you need to get your annual passive income to more than cover your annual expenses and taxes.

To generate the $400,000 in passive income in the example above, you'd essentially have your financial advisor take your $10M and buy municipal bonds, corporate bonds, dividend-producing stocks, real estate holdings, or REIT shares to generate this passive income.

I used 4% as the amount that can be generated relatively predictably and passively from safer, lower volatility investments like municipal bonds or real estate.

Since you are living off the income from the principal, you don't really want to risk loss of the principal base amount (the $10M you worked so hard to create), so we use 4% as the assumed annual return instead of 8% (what I used earlier when you weren't living off the capital and could accept more volatility of returns by incorporating equities into the mix).

# Time Freedom

"Many people forget that the goal isn't money.
The goal is to spend your time as you wish." - Luis Garcia

Today I am happy — very happy, in fact. And happiness is way more important than money to me -- though having both can be nice. Here's a comparison of me now vs. thirteen years ago, when I was working a lot more.

|  | Me at 26 | Me at 40 |
| --- | --- | --- |
| **Weekly Hours Worked** | 70 | 20 |
| **My Weight** | 212 Pounds | 150 Pounds |
| **Health Symptoms** | Heartburn, Anxiety Attacks, Neck Pain | None |
| **Happiness Level** | 5/10 | 9/10 |

It will be *very interesting* to update this table again when I'm 50. My intention is to maintain my health and happiness, spend a lot of time with my family, continue building our net worth, continue writing books and putting on seminars, and help popularize a new way of living.

At the time of writing, I'm in my late 30s and able to earn good money doing CEO Coaching (while living between Bali/Costa Rica/Austin) which only takes a few hours per week of my time. I feel like I'm richer than ever, regardless of what my portfolio is doing.

Today, I'm working about 25 hours per week on:

1. Writing this book

2. Coaching CEOs
3. Building Dow Janes, a firm that helps women achieve financial independence
4. Building Coinstack, a newsletter on digital assets and global finance.
5. Building an international community of extraordinary people in Costa Rica with both retreat centers and living communities for us to gather in.

We're definitely **Time Rich** — and are investing lots of time guiding our son Apollo as he grows up. My family is absolutely loving the life we've created for ourselves -- and we feel like we are wealthy in so many ways.

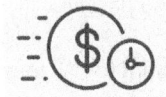

*Time Rich - People who have time available to do and create what they want because either their expenses are low and/or their income from their consulting work or passive income sources is high.*

We're still under 45, so we are still time billionaires (assuming we live past 65)...

"If you're under 45, you're a time billionaire. If you're 45 you have a billion seconds left to live. If you're 20, you have 2 billion. The world focuses on money and forgets about time. But dollars are replaceable and decades are not. A billion seconds feels like forever, yet in retrospect, will feel like a blink." - Zach Pogrob

We are very grateful to be time rich and have learned to prioritize living our lives now rather than waiting for retirement.

## Be Like Jack

There are two people. Which person is richer? Jim or Jack?

|  | Jim | Jack |
| --- | --- | --- |
| Age | 40 | 40 |
| Profession | Investment Banker | Entrepreneur |
| Lives in | NYC | Nosara, Costa Rica |
| After Tax Income | $800,000 | $400,000 |
| Annual Expenses | $700,000 | $200,000 |
| Money Saved Annually | $100,000 | $200,000 |
| Work Time | 70-80 hours per week | 15-20 hours per week |
| Family Time | Spends 1 hour per day with his family | Spends 5 hours per day with his family |
| Hobbies & Friends | Spends very little time on anything besides work | Surfing, gym, friend dinners, festivals, traveling, volunteering |

Jack is the richer person here, even though Jim earns twice as much. Jack not only works much less, he also saves more because he's chosen to live in a much lower cost environment and lifestyle.

$400,000 in Costa Rica goes a LOT further than $800,000 in NYC. Since the cost of living is about 4x higher in NYC.

What matters isn't how much you make. What really matters is:

1. How much you can save on an annual basis (for cash flowing investments and for family savings).
2. How much time you have free to do the things you truly love

The goal should first be to become **Time Rich** — so that you can spend your time however you like (whether with your family, friends, hobbies, or yes, even building a business you're passionate about).

Plus, someone who works consistently for 4 hours per day, 5 days per week, will often get much more done (and get the right things done) than someone who sits in front of a computer screen for 12 hours per day.

Tim Ferriss gave us three great examples of the Time Rich in *The Four Hour Workweek*

1. The employee who rearranges his schedule and negotiates a remote work agreement to achieve 90% of the results in one-tenth of the time, which frees him to practice cross-country skiing and take road trips with his family two weeks per month.
2. The business owner who eliminates the least profitable customers and projects, outsources all operations entirely, and travels the world collecting rare documents, all while working remotely on a website to showcase her own illustration work.
3. The student who elects to risk it all—which is nothing—to establish an online video rental service that delivers $5,000 per month in income from a two-hour-per-week side project that allows him to work full-time as an animal rights lobbyist.

# The Two Types of People: Workers & Investors

Broadly speaking, there are two types of people in the world...

1. Workers: People who work for companies and pay interest on loans. They earn "active income."
2. Investors: People who own parts of companies, receive dividends from stocks, and receive interest on loans. They earn "passive income."

Two Types of People In The World

**Workers**
People who work for companies and pay interest on loans. They earn "active income."

Over time, you want more of your income coming from investments not work

**Investors**
People who own parts of companies, receive dividends from stocks, and receive interest on loans. They earn "passive income."

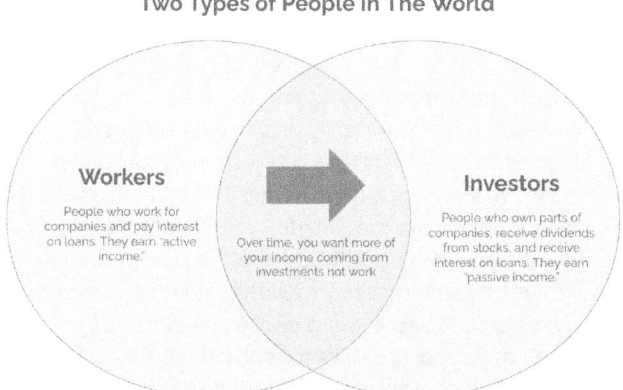

Over time, you want more and more of your income to be from investing and not from active work. The goal is to take your after-tax income from working and save 25% of it each month and invest it into cashflowing assets, so that after 15-20 years you don't have to work actively any longer.

While nearly everyone needs to start out in the worker category (unless you happen to have very wealthy parents), no one should STAY in the worker category for more than 20 years. There's just no reason to -- when all you have to do is:

1. Keep your costs low

2. Pay off any debts you have
3. Work to create multiple streams of income (a job, side hustles, products you sell online)

4. Save 25% of your after-tax income

5. Invest these savings into cash flow producing assets like stocks, bonds, and real estate.

6. Use the cash flow from these investments to buy more cash flowing investments

Only when the cash flow from your investments is covering 2x your monthly expenses should you start to splurge on unnecessary items that don't produce positive cash flow.

So, by the time you're 40 (or earlier if possible)--ensure that you end up primarily in the second category -- the investor. Make sure that the majority of your income by age 40 is coming from your investments and not your labor.

Life is way more fun as an investor than a worker.

## What Do the Rich Do Differently

The poor tend to live paycheck to paycheck, don't save much of their money, and are continually getting into debt. They are reliant on social security and family during retirement age to survive.

Too often, poor people work for others and not for themselves, spend more money than they earn and go into debt for unnecessary items, do not defer present consumption to invest, fail to take the initiative to improve their financial literacy and business education, and get married and have children before they secure a well-paying job, let alone a stream of passive and portfolio income. Don't let your life take this path-and if it already has, learn and apply these principles in everything you do, and you will overcome a challenging start to make it in the end. You can always change your habits and reinvent yourself.

The wealthy are able to achieve financial freedom by saving, investing, and building businesses, then having the passive income from their investments more than cover their living expenses -- allowing their wealth to grow even after retirement age.

The wealthy put off present consumption and the purchase of luxuries like vacations, boats, and big-screen televisions so they can invest in building an asset that will provide enough passive cash flow to buy 20 vacations, a cruise line, and a big-screen television company in the future. They never go into debt for something that is for pleasure and not investment. They buy things like businesses, securities, ties, options, bonds, and real estate.

They intelligently use their businesses to pay many of their expenses, thus receiving numerous tax advantages. They use their expenses to make them richer, and they have no fear of debt, as long as they are using debt to build an asset and not purchase unnecessary items.

While the poor often live frugally, they do not realize that time is more important than money.

The rich realize that time is more valuable than money because, with time, you can make money, but with money, you cannot make time. They understand the principle of opportunity cost and do not hesitate to spend $1,000 for someone to paint their house if, during that time, they can make $3,000 working at what they do best.

The rich have their money work for them. They do their due diligence and research, invest it in public and private companies, and then sit back while their money makes them more money.

The rich build companies that make them money while they are sleeping. Most mornings, they will wake up richer than when they went to bed. They realize the importance of developing **multiple streams of income** and creating **passive cash flow**, which brings in money whether or not they go to work. They stay out of the middle and lower classes by waiting, if possible, until they have consistent passive cash flow from their businesses and investments before they get married and have children.

*Multiple Streams of Income - Wealthy people almost always have a few sources of monthly cashflow including real estate, bonds, businesses, and dividend-producing stocks.*

So what do the rich do differently than people in the middle class?

| What The Rich Do Differently Than The Middle Class |
| --- |

1. They spend less than they earn monthly & build up savings to invest with. Even if this amount is initially small -- over time it grows and compounds.

2. They invest in profitable companies, both later stage private companies and publicly traded companies.

3. They start companies, earning founder stock in them.

4. They advise companies, earning early stage stock options in them.

5. They invest heavily in the financial, creative, and critical thinking education of their children to ensure the next generation can thrive.

Do these five things consistently, and you too can join the echelons of the financially wealthy over time.

## The Automatic Millionaire

*There is a big difference between walking around saying you want to make a million dollars a year, and having crystal clear intentions, fierce desire, and hell-bent action toward specific goals. - Jen Sincero*

So, how do you get out of the rat race and go from being the worker into the investor over time. There are two major paths to becoming financially wealthy.

1) Become a highly paid worker and then and then save & invest wisely for 30+ years

2) Build a profitable business and sell it

The first path is through consistency, and the second path is through creation. Let's start with path #1—the path of consistent savings and investments.

If you want to become a millionaire, it's really NOT THAT DIFFICULT from a mathematical perspective. It just takes consistency and dedication, which most people don't have.

Here's how to become an **Automatic Millionaire** in 25 years by saving and investing just $1,000 per month.

*Automatic Millionaire - Reaching $1M in net worth on autopilot by saving and investing $1000 per month, investing it in index funds or mutual funds at an average 8% annual return, and not taking any out for 25 years.*

It's really that simple. $1,000 per month in savings, invested at a 8% annual return, turns into $1 million after 25 years.

While you've only saved $300,000 ($1000x25x12), this principal turns into over $1M through the power of compounding.

If you can do it for 10 more years, you end up with $2.3M. And if you can do it for 20 more years, you end up with $5.3M. Pretty damn good—and enough to retire nicely on.

The slow-and-steady **automatic wealth** path can definitely work if you're consistent and get started in your 20s or 30s with saving and investing every single month.

*Automatic Wealth - Wealth that is built up gradually over time through saving and investing each month over many decades. If, for example, you can save and invest $3k per month from age 25-65 and can average 8% annual returns from your investments, you'll have $10M when you retire.*

You can even give your child a head start in becoming an automatic millionaire by starting a tax-deductible 529 college savings plan when they are born and putting $100 per month in it. If they don't end up going to college, they can always roll it into their IRA.

What do you invest in to achieve your slow-and-steady long-term investment goals? We'll cover that shortly. But the quick answer is a combination of stocks, bonds, and real estate.

You can also become a millionaire by building a business. If you build a business that has about $200,000 in annual net profits, you can usually sell it for around $1M on marketplaces like Acquire.com. This is the process of building **entrepreneurial wealth**.

*Entrepreneurial Wealth - Wealth that is built up through building a growing business and then selling ownership of it to someone else.*

## The Automatic DecaMillionaire

There are two major ways to earn $10M and achieve "**Net Worth Freedom.**" The first one requires consistency over 35-45 years. The second one requires consistency over about 10-15 years.

1. **The Automatic Decamillionaire Path:** Reach $10M in net worth by saving and investing $2,000 per month for 45 years, $3,000 per month for 40 years, or $4,000 per month for 35 years.

*Automatic DecaMillionaire - Reaching $10M in net worth on autopilot by saving and investing $2,000 per month for 45 years, $3,000 per month for 40 years, or $4,000 per month for 35 years. Assumes an 8% average annual return from index funds or mutual funds.*

2. **The Entrepreneurial Decamillionaire Path:** Build a business that has about $2M in annual profits and thus you could sell it for $10M. (Businesses are usually worth around 1-3x annual revenues or 5x annual net profits, and more if they are growing quickly).

You can also combine both methods by saving up consistently (at least until your business has a successful sale and you get a lump sum payout).

Let's take a look at what it would take to become a $10 millionaire in an automatic way.

| Monthly Savings | Time Required | Result |
| --- | --- | --- |
| $2,000 | 45 Years | $10M |
| $3,000 | 40 Years | $10M |
| $4,000 | 35 Years | $10M |

So, if you can save $2,000 per month for 45 years (at an 8% average annual return), you'll become an **automatic decamillionaire**. Pretty cool.

MAGIC YEAR - 357

Let's see some other possibilities in this chart that shows what you'd end up with if you save and invest a certain amount each month and let it compound...

### Compound Savings & Investing Chart

| Monthly Savings | 20 Yrs | 25 Yrs | 30 Yrs | 35 Yrs | 40 Yrs | 45 Yrs | 50 Yrs |
|---|---|---|---|---|---|---|---|
| $1,000 | $0.6M | $1.0M | $1.5M | $2.3M | $3.5M | $5.3M | $7.5M |
| $2,000 | $1.2M | $1.9M | $3.0M | $4.7M | $7.1M | $10.6M | $15.0M |
| $3,000 | $1.8M | $2.9M | $4.5M | $7.0M | $10.6M | $16.0M | $22.5M |
| $4,000 | $2.4M | $3.8M | $6.0M | $9.3M | $14.1M | $21.4M | $30.0M |
| $5,000 | $3.0M | $4.8M | $7.6M | $11.6M | $17.7M | $26.7M | $37.5M |

*Assumes 8% average annual return from investing*

Yes, that's right You can (through consistent saving and investing) build a net worth of $10.6M by saving and investing around $2k per month for 45 years. Take that statement in.

> Through consistent saving and investing, you can build a net worth of $10.6M by saving and investing around $2k per month for 45 years.

The key is to start saving and investing as early as you can – and ensuring your income is greater than your expenses.

**Action Item #74: Your Long-Term Savings Plan**
Take a look at the above Compound Savings chart. How much can you commit to saving and investing each month for the next 25-30 years? How much could that turn into if you stayed consistent with it?

What really matters isn't how much you earn – it's how much you save and invest. As Robin Sharma writes, "Avoid being hypnotized by "Top Line Seduction," the psychological attraction to being impressed by personal income rather than looking at the *profit*.
Your annual and monthly inflows matter a lot less than how much you have left over to save and invest, once expenses and taxes are paid. Don't confuse gross income with net profit. Ever. Please."
Let's see an example of the power of saving and investing over time... Below is a table that compares two different people "Rich Jack" and "Big Spender Bob."
Both Rich Jack and Big Spender Bob earn $100,000 per year after taxes. The difference between them is that Rich Jack saves and invests $25,000 per year of this, starting at age 21 and continuing to age 65 -- and Big Spender Bob spends all his money each year.

Both earn the exact same annual income, but made different choices and thus ended up in totally different places.

|  | Rich Jack | Big Spender Bob |
|---|---|---|
| Annual after tax Income | $100,000 | $100,000 |
| % Saved | 25% | 0% |
| Annual average savings | $25,000 | $0 |
| % of savings invested in cash flowing investments | 100% | 0% |
| Net worth at age 30 | $333,686 | $0 |
| Net worth at age 40 | $1,125,426 | $0 |
| Net worth at age 50 | $2,887,000 | $0 |
| Net worth at age 60 | $6,808,149 | $0 |
| Net worth at age 65 | $10,309,769 | $0 |

So all Rich Jack did differently than Poor Bob was invest $25,000 per year (around $2,083 per month) and then let the investments compound at an average rate of 8%.

The average annual returns of the S&P 500 the last 100 years have been 10.35%, so I'm picking a more conservative number, assuming you have some exposure to bonds and real estate as well as stocks.

What are the results of this consistent habit of saving $25k per year?

Rich Jack becomes a millionaire by age 40, but by "retirement age" (65) he's amassed over $10M through the power of consistent saving, investing, and compounding.

By the time Rich Jack stops saving at age 65, he's a decamillionaire! Assuming he then put his $10M into a municipal bond paying 4% per year, he'd be able to retire on $400,000 per year earned from the interest alone -- giving him the option to either spend or give away the $10M to his family and invest in companies and causes he really believes in.

Now, that's not the only way to become financially rich -- but it certainly one of the most predictable. It's a straight line path that anyone who can save and invest $25k per year consistently can have a good chance of achieving.

Of course, if you end up being able to save more than $25,000 per year, you can accelerate this path to $10M.

Or you can simply build a business and sell it for $10M. Frankly, I think that's the easier path than saving $2,000 per month for 45 years. But why not work on doing both?

## Avoid These Money Traps If You Can

There are a few major money traps in life to avoid if possible in order to create a clear path toward living the life of your dreams.

*The Consumption Trap* - Getting a job and then massively increasing your monthly expenses before you have a chance to explore and find what you truly love.

*The High Income Trap* - Earning a big salary but spending it all and having nothing left over for savings and investments at the end of each year.

*The Early Kids Trap* - Having kids before you've taken time to explore what brings you alive, what the world needs, and the major contribution you want to make in your life toward others.

If you can avoid falling into these three traps, life will be much easier. As you aim to become financially wealthy and create passive cashflow engines, it is very important to avoid the **Consumption Trap**, the **High Income Trap**, and the **Early Kids Trap**.

If you do fall into the **Early Kids Trap**, it's okay -- but work extra hard on savings. If you can save $750 per month for your child and put it into an index fund for them averaging 8%, they will have $1M by the time they are 30. Pretty cool, huh?

The **High Income Trap** is easy to fall into (I know, I've been there!). You think you're rich because you make $500k per year, but then at the end of the year, it's all gone because you've spent it all and didn't invest any .

In Texas, there's a saying for people who earn a lot of money but don't *have* a lot of money. It's "all hat, no cattle." This saying comes from ranchers and cowboys who'd talk a big game and wear a big cowboy hat in the saloons, but not actually own any land or have any cows.

If you had a choice between becoming actually wealthy over time (based on how much you saved per month) vs appearing wealthy in the short term (based on getting that expensive house that drains you), which would you choose?

A few years ago, while Morgan was pregnant with Apollo and in his first few months of life, I was living in Austin, Texas, and earning around $40,000 per month. Our family was, by most standards, quite wealthy. However, we were also spending $40,000 each month between housing, furniture rental, childcare, travel, food, and other expenses. We had a rich lifestyle, but we weren't actually becoming wealthy over time. We'd fallen into the High Income Trap ourselves.

We lived on a river in a big 4,500 square foot house for a beautiful part of time -- but we didn't own it. We were renters -- making our landlord wealthy.

While it appeared to our friends that we were living a wealthy lifestyle, it wasn't sustainable. I was working my butt off to bring in that $40k/month -- and my sex life with Morgan was really suffering. Four months into our son's life, we moved to Bali -- and then later to Costa Rica -- in order to create a much more modest lifestyle where we could actually save up, invest, and build actual wealth and passive income over time rather than being "fake wealthy" off a temporary high income from working.

You have to remember that the point of working is to save up and invest enough money so you don't have to work anymore (and can do whatever you want to create value in the world by following what lights you up inside). This only becomes possible if you consistently save up and invest 25% of your total income each year. This might require deferred consumption or some short-term sacrifices, but it is worth it!

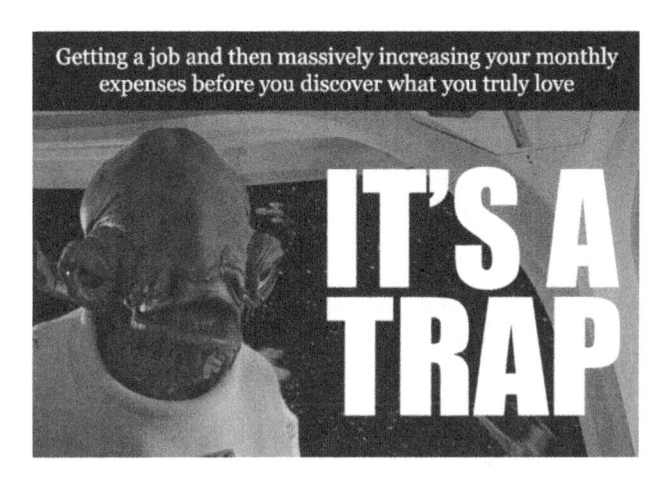

So don't get stuck in the hamster wheel of life by increasing your monthly expenses before you figure out what you truly love to do. First, explore widely to find what you're passionate about creating that serves others. Then make a lot of money creating it. Then buy cash flowing assets that create passive income. Only then should you increase your monthly expenses -- using your passive income to pay for them.

**Action Item #75: Avoid the Money Traps**
Write down in your notebook the definitions from above of the high income trap and the consumption trap. Do you fall into either of these traps? If so, what can you do to get out of these traps?

## Become the Authority in Your Field

One key to making lots of money is to provide a product or service people want and become the go-to authority online in that specific field by creating videos and content that demonstrate your expertise — so that whenever someone types in your niche keywords into YouTube, TikTok, Instagram, or Google — you show up.

Yes, you need to actually first become a world class expert within a specific field, which can take a few years — but once you are — the world truly opens up and you can consult in that field from anywhere.

You become the expert by producing content (video and written) about your niche, working in that field, and by becoming a consultant or creating information products or software products within your niche — allowing you to work from anywhere with an internet connection.

You can either provide a service (consulting/coaching) within your area of expertise, create digital products (courses/tools) that share your knowledge with others, or even create physical products (often sourced using Alibaba) that you sell online, with warehousing, fulfillment, and shipping handled by either Amazon or Shopify.

Here's a simple framework for nailing your niche by my friend Clay Hebert.

### How to Nail Your Niche by Clay Hebert

Nail your niche with this simple 3 step framework.

1. The Person: Who is the SPECIFIC person you help. Forget demographics and focus on psychographics. What are their problems, fears, hopes and dreams?

2. The Problem: What SPECIFIC problem do you help them solve? Acne? Weight? Clarity? Get specific.

3. The Promise: What is the SPECIFIC promise you're making? Not "lose weight." That's too generic. Are you promising 6-pack abs or "fit into your high-school clothes"? Those are two different things. Get specific.

When you nail your Person, Problem and Promise, everything from marketing, positioning, messaging and copy gets easier.

What are your 3 Ps?

While living here in Costa Rica, for example, I am earning money by coaching CEOs in the USA, writing a weekly newsletter on crypto that has sponsors, selling LuvMonsters stuffed animals on Amazon, and renting our property in Nosara on AirBnB. We currently have four sources of income — and all can be done from anywhere in the world.

Once you have built your sources of income and your monthly income after taxes is higher than your expenses, you can begin to make investments.

You can use the excess money you make by becoming the preeminent expert in your niche to invest in cash flow producing assets like businesses, franchises, real estate, stocks, and certain digital assets like Ethereum.

Always remember, the goal is to become **Time Rich** so that every month your savings account is going up while you're putting in no more than 3-4 hours per day maximum working on a computer.

Top Ivy League graduates will work 80 hours per week for a $250,000 per year job (and spend $5,000 per month to live in an urban box) when they could work just 15-20 hours per week and earn $500,000 by building their own business with multiple streams of income — and live in a luxury 4BR home in a place like Bali or Thailand for $2,000 per month.

## Learn The Basics of Investing

Once you become a consistent saver, it's time to learn about investing. There are three major types of investments:

*Stocks* - ownership in a company that entitles the holder to receive a percentage of the firm's profits and eventual sale value

*Bonds* - loans you make to a company or government that are paid back with interest.

*Real Estate* - Buying a home, apartment, hotel, apartment building, commercial space, land, or shares in a Real Estate Investment Trust (REIT)

You can think of a stock as a claim on a percentage of profits and sales value for a company. With stocks, your investment grows in value when the company you own a part of grows its net profits.

1. The value of a company grows when its profits go up, or are expected to go up.

2. The value of a company shrinks when its profits go down, or are expected to go down.

There are two major types of stocks, **publicly traded stocks** and **privately traded stocks**.

*Public Stock* - Shares of a company that is publicly traded on a stock exchange like the NYSE or NASDAQ. Shares entitle holders to dividends and their respective percentage of proceeds in the case of a sale. Shares sometimes also offer voting rights.

*Private Stock* - Shares of a company that is private and not listed on a public stock exchange. Private company stock is usually not liquid, although some private share marketplaces are available for fast growing firms.

When a company has an **initial public offering** (IPO), its stock goes from being private to being public -- making it easier to invest in -- and giving liquidity (the ability to sell shares) to early founders, team members, and investors. This is how entrepreneurs and venture capitalists get really rich.

*IPO* - When a company lists its stock to be sold on a public stock exchange for the first time. This process creates liquidity, meaning the shares of the company can be easily bought and sold.

One of the best books to read to learn the basics of investing is *Rich Dad Poor Dad* and *Rich Dad's Guide to Investing*.

In these books, author Robert Kiyosaki tells the story of his real dad (the poor dad), who was a teacher who could never save, invest, or build wealth – and his mentor (his rich dad), who was a business person who built businesses that provided products and services his community needed and thus became very wealthy.

Kiyosaki teaches in these books the importance of financial literacy and explains that most people acquire liabilities (that drain money from them) instead of acquiring assets (that put money in their pockets).

He shares the below graphic, which shows how money flows depending on whether you are poor, middle class, or rich.

- The Poor earn money from a job which all goes to pay expenses. They sell their time for money.

- The Middle Class earn money from a slightly better, usually salaried job, which goes to pay expenses. They own very few cash flow generating assets. They sell their time and expertise for money.

- The Rich do something different. They take their savings and invest it in **cashflowing assets** like real estate, stocks, bonds, and profitable private companies. Over time, their income from cash flows from investments becomes larger than their income from working.

*Cash Flowing Assets - Investment assets like stocks, bonds, real estate, and royalty streams that generate monthly, quarterly, or annual cash flow paid to the asset owners. These are what you want to accumulate to grow your passive income.*

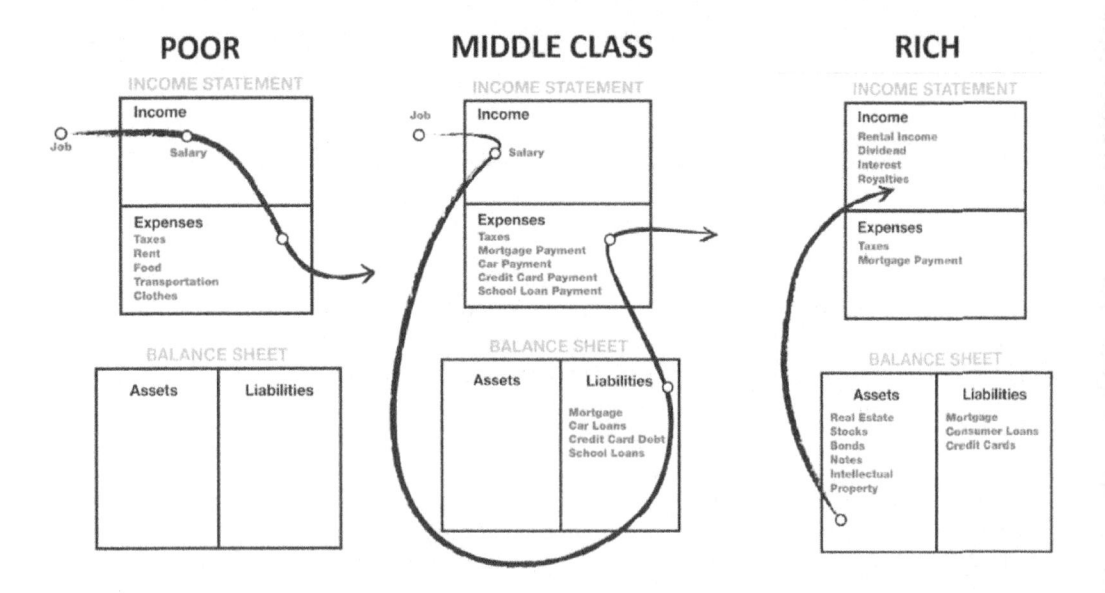

Robert Kiyosaki's classic diagram from Rich Dad Poor Dad showing how money flows differently for the poor, middle class, and rich

# Acquire Cash Flowing Assets

Let's assume that you now have some savings built up and your debts paid off. Now what?

Now that you have some savings, what should you invest in? If you're looking for more of the "sure thing over time" path, I would recommend sticking mostly to investments in:

1. Stock in profitable publicly-traded companies that pay dividends
2. Mutual funds (collections of stocks)
3. Highly rated corporate bonds that pay an annual/quarterly interest
4. Highly rated municipal bonds that pay an annual/quarterly interest
5. Real estate investment trusts (REITs). These are publicly traded companies that invest in real estate. (Easier than investing in real estate directly)
6. Real estate - You can buy a duplex or a multi-family house and then live in one of the units for free and use the rent from the other to cover the mortgage. This is called house hacking. You can also lease houses and then sublease them nightly on Airbnb (if your landlord allows it and you make a nice profit). Use AirDNA to find the best markets to buy in.

There's also a slightly riskier path of investing in angel investments in early stage private companies or buying real estate directly yourself for rental income -- though beware -- both of these paths require experience and a degree of sophistication. I suggest leaving making "riskier" investments separately from your "tried and true" consistent savings and investment plan.

If you're in the USA, also look into setting up a 401(k) or ROTH IRA to be able to make tax deductible contributions to your own retirement plan. This below table covers the four major forms of investment.

| Stocks | Bonds | Commodities | Real Estate |
|---|---|---|---|
| Public Stocks | Savings accounts | Oil | Residential |
| Mutual funds | CDs | Gas | Multi-Family |
| Index funds/ETFs | Treasury bonds | Gold | Commercial |
| Small/mid/large cap stocks | Municipal bonds | Silver | Retail |
| Value/growth stocks | Corporate bonds | Platinum | Office |
| SPACs | Foreign bonds | Copper | Hotel |
| Emerging market stocks | TIPs | Cryptocurrency | Industrial |
| Private stock | P2P lending | | REITs |
| Secondary stock | Microfinance | | |
| Stock options | Venture debt | | |
| Crowdfunding | | | |
| Venture Capital funds | | | |
| Private Equity funds | | | |
| Hedge funds | | | |
| Local Companies | | | |

The simplest thing to do is invest primarily in public stocks, index funds, and bonds. These assets will form the core of most financial advisor-structured investment portfolios.

As you get more sophisticated (and wealthy), you may begin investing in larger opportunities in asset classes like venture capital or private equity, investing in large multi-family or multi-zoned real estate units, or buying and then selling entire businesses.

Building wealth is just like playing Monopoly in the real world. Start with a few thousand dollars, invest in a cash flowing asset, continue saving and investing, and then eventually buy a house, multiple houses, then hotels. Soon enough, you'll be buying a few $100M businesses, combining them, and taking them public for $1B.

Robert Kiyosaki created a great board game called "Cash Flow" that I highly recommend playing to learn more about how the game of money works and how to get your passive income higher than your expenses as quickly as possible. In real life, I've seen people do this in as little as 3 or 4 years when they focus on it.

**Action Item #76: Your Investment Plan**
Go see a financial advisor at a place like Edward Jones. Get a free consultation and have them create a long-term investment plan for you or your family. Create a specific plan to achieve your net worth goals that tells you how much you need to save and invest monthly to hit it.

## Make Money While You Sleep

*There is only one way to make a great deal of money; and that is in a business of your own. - J. Paul Getty, once the richest man in America*

The key to making lots of money is making money while you sleep and building a **sleep-proof business**.

*Sleep proof business - A company that continues to make sales while you sleep. Figure out how to create one of these to unlock true riches and time freedom.*

If you aren't making money while you sleep, either from product sales, investment appreciation, or rental income -- your earning potential will be capped at whatever you can charge for your time or whatever you can sell personally.

It's very difficult to earn more than $500,000 per year by selling your time. There's a cap on what your time is worth when you sell it by the hour. However, it's much easier to earn much more by building a business that can operate even when you're not actively working. This requires building systems and teams.

Investors invest in systems that work 24/7 and don't go home at night. So build a system that can generate revenues and profits even while you're not working.

I first learned this lesson when I was 17. I was hired as VP of Marketing for a company in Florida called Synflex, which sold an arthritis supplement. Using digital marketing, we grew the company from $2000 per month in sales when I started to $200,000 in sales a year later when I went off to college. This was the very first multi-million dollar company I was involved with.

The owner agreed to give me $15 per hour plus $0.25 for every bottle sold. By the time I went off to college, I was earning a nice royalty stream of $2,000 per month. I was making money continually without needing to continue to work.

I became obsessed with finding ways to earn money while I slept and realized that the best way to do that was to build a business that would make money regardless of whether I was awake or not.

The next year, I co-founded iContact, and we grew that business to $4M per month in sales, or about $5,500 per hour every hour of the month. That means every time I slept, we'd make about $44,000 in sales. Now that was a good business. See if you can build an automated system that makes money while you sleep.

The secret to becoming extraordinarily wealthy is to build and invest in businesses and then use the excess cash flow from your businesses and the capital gains from any liquidity events to invest in future ventures, early-stage private companies, emerging markets, public securities, and other cash-producing assets such as real estate.

Today at Magic Year, we automate many of our webinars and follow-up systems and have figured out how to make sales even when we take a few days off.

**Action Item #77: Make Money While You Sleep**
Brainstorm a list of all the businesses you could start or invest in that would make you money while you're sleeping? Should you start an ecommerce business? An agency? An AirBnB rental business? A dropshipping firm? A chain of hotels? How can you turn your passion into passive income?

# How to Make $10M+ By Building Companies

*"Entrepreneurs are simply those who understand that there is little difference between obstacle and opportunity and are able to turn both to their advantage."* -Niccolo Machiavelli, 16th Century Italian Statesmen

The primary way people become financially rich is to build companies. That's what I like to do as an entrepreneur. I personally prefer this type of investing -- investing in my own businesses. I like businesses that make money while I sleep.

When you start a business -- you, as the founder and incorporated get issued the shares of the business. As the company grows in value, the value of the company's stock increases.

You can even create new shares of the company to raise money for the firm, or once the firm is big enough, sell your personal shares to diversify and make some money for yourself (this is called a secondary sale).

If you're good at sales, marketing, creating products or services people want, and building teams of people -- this form of wealth creation is the best. The wealthiest people in the world aren't politicians or athletes. They are business owners.

*It's the people who own these who make the wealth.*

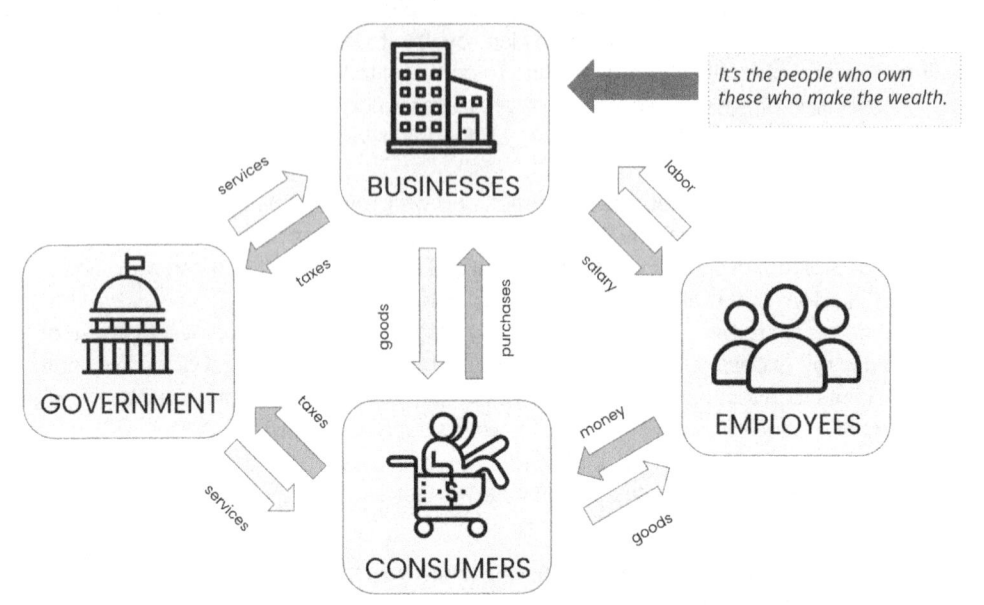

*It is business owners who make the most wealth. So become a business owner if you can -- and build a business that creates something people need, is a great place to work, and contributes to its community.*

While most people are concerned primarily with job security, it's way safer to focus on developing financial security by building a company you own.

And the best way to have long-term financial security is by creating (or buying) businesses that produce consistent cash flow.

> The best way of having long-term financial security is by creating (or buying) businesses that produce consistent cash flow

Read that last sentence again. It's one of the most important ones in this book.

You can think of the process of financial freedom as starting, growing, scaling, and investing in businesses that can generate positive profits and cashflow so you can live off of passive income from your businesses and investments.

If you're interested in learning more about this topic, read the book *Rich Dad's Guide to Investing* by Robert Kiyosaki.

You can incorporate a business in just a few hours online (I often use LegalZoom for my U.S. incorporations).

Once incorporated, all you need to do is find or create a product or service you can sell and build a business around -- and start selling.

The best type of business to start is a business in a field you are an expert or specialist in. By creating a business within your area of expertise, you will understand the particular problems and needs of the customers in that niche better than others.

You can also acquire an existing business (via a process known as a merger or acquisition) or start a franchise.

## Sell a Product, Not a Service

> "If you want better [business] ideas, fill your mind, read books, listen to podcasts, inhale inspiration. Then, empty your mind. Meditate, write, walk in silence. Ideas will storm your brain like fireworks. You won't have too few ideas. You'll have too many."
> - Zach Pogrob, @BehviorHack

     Often, I encourage entrepreneurs who don't yet have a product to start a service-based business using a skill set they already have (digital marketing, coding, graphic design, management consulting, real estate management, fundraising, etc.) and then, once they deeply understand a specific niche--then start a product-based business to solve a big problem in that niche.

     That's what I did with iContact. I started as a web site designer in 1998, when I was 14. For four years, I built dozens of websites. I noticed these websites needed ways to collect email addresses from their visitors. So in 2002, I worked with my co-founder to bring to market one of the very first email marketing software platforms.

     We found a problem in the market and solved it -- then built a company of experienced leaders to scale up the company.

     Businesses that sell products (whether digital products or tangible products) are the biggest companies in the world. Companies like Apple, Microsoft, Saudi Aramco, Alphabet, and Amazon.

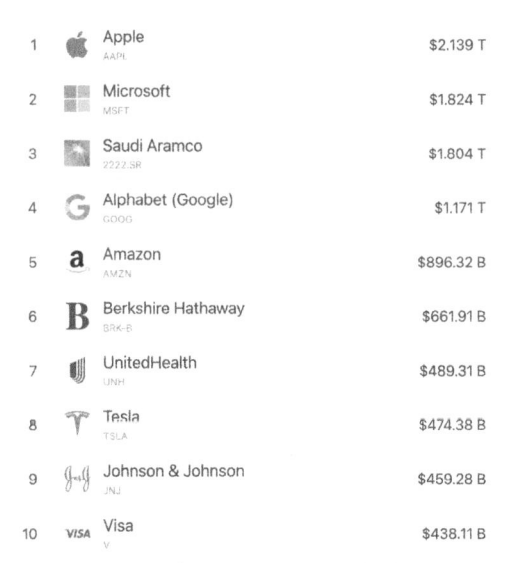

| # | Company | Ticker | Market Cap |
|---|---|---|---|
| 1 | Apple | AAPL | $2.139 T |
| 2 | Microsoft | MSFT | $1.824 T |
| 3 | Saudi Aramco | 2222.SR | $1.804 T |
| 4 | Alphabet (Google) | GOOG | $1.171 T |
| 5 | Amazon | AMZN | $896.32 B |
| 6 | Berkshire Hathaway | BRK-B | $661.91 B |
| 7 | UnitedHealth | UNH | $489.31 B |
| 8 | Tesla | TSLA | $474.38 B |
| 9 | Johnson & Johnson | JNJ | $459.28 B |
| 10 | Visa | V | $438.11 B |

*Every single one of the top 10 companies in the world by market capitalization primarily sells products (not services).*

## How to Value a Company

     I went to business school at Harvard for two years, and one of the most important things that got drilled into us was how to estimate the valuation of a company based on its cash flows.

Companies are generally valued based on their cash flows (profits), which can be estimated by taking their current cash flows and projecting them into the future. The faster a company grows its revenues and profits, the more valuable owning a piece of it becomes (as owning stock becomes a claim on both dividends as well as any future sale of the business).

So if you want to find a good stock, invest in a company that is likely to be in a fast growing market sector and thus is likely to increase its cash flows over the next decade. This is why investing in Google, Facebook, or Apple in 2008 was such a no-brainer.

Over the last 105 years, the average company in the S&P 500 index of five hundred American companies has been valued at 15.99x its annual earnings[23]. If a company is growing quickly (faster than 15% per year), it will usually trade above the average earnings multiple. And if it's growing less quickly or shrinking, it will trade below the average earnings multiple.

This means that for an average stock investment, it would take roughly 15.99 years to get your upfront investment back (assuming earnings were fixed and assuming all profits were distributed to shareholders).

So a company growing at 40% per year might trade at 20x annual earnings, while a company growing at 10% per year might trade at 5x annual earnings.

In the short term, a stock price is driven by supply and demand for the company's shares and speculation about its future products and the strength of its management team, but in the long-term a stock price is always equal to what the company could be sold for to a buyer.

While early-stage companies will sometimes be purchased based on revenue or profit multiples, the most accurate way to value later-stage companies that already have profits is to create a **Discounted Cash Flow (DCF) valuation**, which you can learn how to do on YouTube or at any business school.

*Discounted Cash Flow Valuation - An estimate of the current value of a company based on a projection of its future cash flows.*

To create a DCF, you simply project the revenues, expenses, and net profits of the firm going out in the future for 10-20 years, and then discount the value of that expected profit stream back to the present.

Start with the **financial statements** of a company (which are publicly available) and then project out what you expect the future revenues, expenses, and net profits to be.

*Financial Statements - The most commonly used business financial statements are the Profit & Loss statement, which shows revenues, expenses, and profits, and the Balance sheet, which shows assets, liabilities, and equity. Use these statements to value a company and assess its performance.*

Famous value-oriented investor Warren Buffet of Berkshire Hathaway always has his team create a DCF valuation estimate for each company he invests in or acquires. Buffett's investing method involves:

1. Understanding a firm well

---

[23] Historical Average PE Ratio - https://www.multpl.com/s-p-500-pe-ratio

2. Looking for firms with enduring products/services that the market needs continually
3. Calculating what he believes the firm is actually worth using a DCF
4. Purchasing shares when there is enough of a "margin of safety" between what his model says the company should be worth and what the company is actually trading at.

So for example, if his DCF model says the company he is looking at should be worth $10B but it's actually trading at $6B, then there will be a good $4B "margin of safety." Thus, he may buy a portion (and sometimes all) of the shares of the firm.

Buffett's team creates valuation models on each company they invest in and ensures there's a big margin of safety between what he thinks the firm
is worth and what the market thinks it is worth. While he's not always right, he's right more often than not.

Here are my tips for becoming a value-oriented investor:

1. Avoid stocks with Price to Earnings (PE) ratios over 25, unless they have extremely high revenue growth (over 50% year) and thus are deserving of such a high PE ratio.
2. Learn how to create a DCF valuation by taking current cash flows, estimating them out to the future, and then discounting their cash flows to the present.
3. Have the discipline to create a DCF valuation for every public company or late-stage private investment you make
4. Don't buy shares that are overvalued. Wait until the shares are undervalued compared to your DCF model, and then invest.
5. Invest only when you have a 30% margin of safety between what your DCF model says the company is worth and what the market says.

# How to Angel Invest The Right Way

For most people, I recommend avoiding angel investing (buying stock in early stage private technology companies before they reach product-market fit).

I find that **angel investing** is a good way to lose money quickly. For most people, the best thing to do is to make your money through work or building businesses and then keep your money by investing in safer vehicles like liquid public value stocks, index funds, real estate, and muni bonds. Angel investing is too risky (too much chance of complete loss of the invested amount) for most people.

*Angel Investing - The practice of investing in early stage private companies (usually technology-enabled companies) in order to earn big returns if those companies later sell or IPO. Warning: It's easy to lose a lot of money if you don't do this right.*

What I've found is that in order to make angel investing really work for you, you need to have at least $2.5M dedicated to it and make a LOT of similarly sized investments -- and you need to focus on investing in companies that have been de-risked and have already begun the process of starting to produce growing revenues.

Most angel investments are $25k to $50k. So $2.5M of capital allocated for angel investing would allow you to make 50 investments of $50k. Be sure to keep the amount per company either exactly the same or similar to avoid what happened to me (the large investments failing and the small investments winning).

In my angel investing career, I picked some good winners (SpaceX, LendingClub, Robinhood, Matterport, Kuli Kuli, and Catalant), but the amount I invested in the winners was small (about $25k per investment), while the amount I invested in the losers was big (about $250k to $1M per investment). Had I simply put an equal amount into each investment, I would have done pretty well. This was a lesson learned for future angel investing.

In your diligence process, look at their last two years of financial statements -- and if revenues haven't gone up in every quarter in the last four quarters (or if there are no revenues) -- seriously consider declining the investment opportunity.

To optimize the chance of finding eventual winners, look for companies that already have $1M+ in revenues and are close to cash flow positive.

You can find companies that you can invest in on AngelList, Fundable, and Republic.

Know that in angel investing, it's common 80-90% of the companies you invest in won't make it to an exit, and you'll lose your entire invested amount. So it often takes building a large portfolio to find enough winners to pay for the losers. You can make money in angel investing either when:

1. A company you invested in gets acquired at a price higher than your investment

2. A company you invested in goes public (has an "IPO"), creating a tradeable market for the shares of the firm. Companies go public on a stock exchange like the NYSE or NASDAQ in order to raise additional capital for growth and to enable founders and employees to gain liquidity for their shares and options.

3. A company you invested in reaches a large enough size that it can list its shares on secondary markets like ForgeGlobal

In my life, I've invested $5M into 34 private companies, and while I found some winners (SpaceX, Catalant, Kuli Kuli, Off Grid Electric, LendingClub, Matterport, and RobinHood), those seven winners weren't enough to make up for the 27 losers.

For a higher chance of success with private company investing, I recommend either:

- Investing in later stage private companies that already have substantial revenues (this reduces the risk of complete failure by a lot). You can use the site ForgeGlobal.com to find shares of later stage pre-IPO companies, some of which are already profitable.

- Invest in a Venture Capital fund that has full-time professional managers who focus on sourcing quality deals and helping their portfolio companies grow.

Here are Tim Ferriss' rules for angel investing from his book *Tools for Titans*.

1. If it has a single founder, the founder must be technical. Two technical co-founders are ideal.
2. I must be eager to use the product myself. This rules out many great companies, but I want a verified market I understand.
3. Consumer-facing product/service (e.g., Uber, Twitter, Facebook, etc.) or small-business focused product/service (e.g., Shopify), not big enterprise software.

4. More than 100K active users OR serial founder(s) with past exits OR more than 10K paying customers. Whenever possible, I want to pour gasoline on the fire, not start the fire.
5. More than 10% month-on-month activity growth.
6. Clean "cap table," minimal previous financing (or none), no bridge rounds.
7. U.S.-based companies or companies willing to create U.S.-based investable entities. Shopify started in Canada, for instance.

I'd agree with him on all of them except that I think it's good for one founder to be technical and one to be focused on business growth -- and I am open to B2B SaaS software companies since that's where my background and experience lie.

## The Traits of Billionaires

"Among the billionaires I've been mentoring for over a quarter of a century… they viscerally understand that all the money they want is already in existence. It's out there, waiting for their warm embrace. They believe that they simply need to unlock the hidden value within their marketplaces that will allow them to *access* all the riches they seek. These possibilitarians are deep believers in the boundlessness of *everything* in life. If they lose a business deal, they remain tranquil as they trust an even better one will appear when the time is right. They know that nature always unfolds for one's favor. And they abide by the spiritual law that *once you reach a place of inner freedom and everyday heroism, where you're unafraid to lose everything, you will not be scared of anything.*" - Robin Sharma

According to my favorite author Robin Sharma, here are the 13 traits of the billionaires he has known and worked with (reworded slightly from the original list for ease of understanding)

1. A Foolhardy Degree of Self-Faith
2. A Blinding Vision of a Brighter Future
3. A Terrific Thirst for Doing Things Their Own Way
4. A Childlike Level of Curiosity
5. An Acute Carelessness about the Opinions of Critics
6. A Gargantuan Commitment to Consistency and Persistency
7. A High Love of Winning and Being Best in World
8. A Deeply Trained Ability to Resist Instant Pleasure
9. A Learned Skill of Multiplying Wealth By Avoiding Consumerism and Focusing on Passive Income and Company Building
10. A Refusal to Be around Negative People
11. A Near-Infinite Sense of Self-Responsibility & Agency to Influence Their Own Accomplishments
12. An Ability to Identify Asymmetric Risk-Reward Opportunities
13. Investing Into Where the Puck is Going

Having gotten to know billionaire tech entrepreneur Marc Benioff of Salesforce.com fame when he was considering buying iContact in 2009/2010 – I have to completely agree with this list.

## Recommended Books on Money

- *Rich Dad Poor Dad* by Robert Kiyosaki
- *Rich Dad's Guide to Investing* by Robert Kiyosaki
- *Multiple Streams of Income* by Robert Allen
- *The Science of Getting Rich* by Wallace Wattles

## Key Outcome from This Chapter

**Create a Personal Financial Plan -** Use the templates in this chapter to create a personal financial plan that shows your current monthly income and expenses by major category, your current assets and liabilities, and your target monthly income, expenses, assets, and liabilities 36 months from now. Also start tracking your spending monthly using a free tool like Rocket Money.

# MONEY CHAPTER ACTION ITEMS

1. **A Great Essay** - Read the great essay in The Atlantic "How to Want Less: The Secret to Satisfaction Has Nothing To Do With Achievement, Money, or Stuff." by Arthur Brooks

2. **The Forms of Wealth** - On a scale of 1-10 rate yourself on "how wealthy are you" for each of the eight different forms of wealth: time, health, purpose, community, family, adventure, sensuality, and money.

3. **Savings Plan** - Write down how much you earn per month after taxes. Then calculate what 25% of that amount is. That's the amount you should be saving and investing each month. Make the changes you need to make to your monthly spending so that next month you actually save 25% of your after tax income. See if you can actually accomplish this feat this month. Short-term deferment will lead to long-term riches.

4. **Track Your Money** - Use a free tool like RocketMoney to track your expenses and budget each month and cancel any unneeded expenses. Over the next 30 days, check in every Friday to review your progress and review the automatic expense categorizations. If you're engaged or married, meet with your partner monthly to review your progress.

5. **Personal Financial Plan** - Use the above template and create your personal financial plan. Be sure to list your monthly after-tax income, expenses, net cash flow, assets, liabilities, and net worth -- as well as what you want these numbers to be 3 years from now!

6. **Debt-Free Plan** - If you have credit card debt, do the math and calculate how many more months it will take to pay it all off. Once you pay off all your high-interest debt, it's time to start saving, investing, and actually building wealth!

7. **Long-Term Savings Plan** - Take a look at the compound savings and investing chart. How much can you commit to saving and investing each month for the next 25-30 years? How much could that turn into if you stayed consistent with it?

8. **Avoid The Money Traps** - Write down the definitions from above of the high income trap and the consumption trap. Do you fall into either of these traps? If so, what can you do to get out of these traps?

9. **See a Financial Advisor** - Go see a financial advisor at a place like Edward Jones. Get a free consultation and have them create a long-term investment plan for you or your family. Create a specific plan to achieve your net worth goals that tells you how much you need to save and invest monthly to hit it.

10. **Sleep Proof Income** - Brainstorm a list of all the businesses you could start or invest in that would make you money while you're sleeping? Should you start an ecommerce business? An agency? An AirBnB rental business? A dropshipping firm? A chain of hotels? How can you turn your passion into passive income?

# STEP 8

## COMMUNITY MAGIC

# KEY CONCEPTS FROM THE COMMUNITY CHAPTER

### 1. LOCATION FREEDOM
The ability to live anywhere you want because your income can be sustained from working online (or you happen to be independently wealthy and living off of passive income).

### 2. FREEDOM SEEKER
Someone obsessed with living on their own terms, choosing where they want to live, going on adventures, and following their passions.

### 3. DEFAULT LOCATION
Where you randomly ended up living because of your family, your school, or your work. Don't end up in a place by default. Choose to explore the world and then decide on where to live.

### 4. DIGITAL NOMAD VISA
Visas to go live in other country for 1-3 years that are given out to people who can work remotely on their laptops and can show proof of earnings from a remote job.

### 5. SLOW TRAVEL
Traveling for 3-24 months at a time while working during the weeks on your laptop and traveling to new locations on the weekends. You usually will change countries every 30-90 days so you don't overstay your visa.

### 6. CONSCIOUS COMMUNITIES
Towns that have a lot of expats living in them and have a special focus on wellness, community, and personal growth. Global examples include Ubud, Bali; Chiang Mai, Thailand, and Nosara, Costa Rica. U.S. examples include Encinitas, Boulder, & Mill Valley.

### 7. INTENTIONAL COMMUNITY
A small village/town of 25-500 people where the residents have shared values, a system of new resident on-boarding, and a regular opportunity for community gatherings and festivals.

### 8. CO-LIVING
Sharing the same building or neighborhood with others who share your values and interests. Could include urban co-living in apartments or family co-living in the suburbs or in nature.

### 9. NEW URBANISM
A city planning movement creating more livable, walkable, and sustainable communities through the development of mixed-use, pedestrian-friendly neighborhoods with a variety of housing types near walkable parks, shops, entertainment venues, wellness centers, and community spaces.

### 10. 15-MINUTE CITIES
Towns (or parts of cities) in which everything you need is within a 15-minute walk or cycle from your home, from health care and education to grocery stores and green spaces

### 11. SMART CITIES
Cities that use advanced technology and data analytics to improve the quality of life of its citizens, enhance sustainability, and optimize urban services such as transportation, energy, and public safety.

### 12. GEOARBITRAGE
Earning your income from one place and then working remotely in another country where costs are much lower. (Example: earning American pay rates but rotating between Bali, Thailand, & Costa Rica).

# STEP 8: COMMUNITY MAGIC

## YOUR MAGIC YEAR

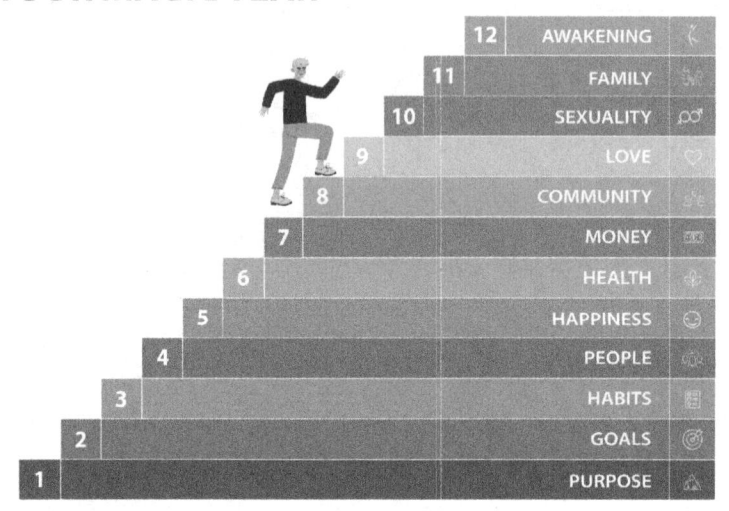

| | |
|---|---|
| 12 | AWAKENING |
| 11 | FAMILY |
| 10 | SEXUALITY |
| 9 | LOVE |
| 8 | COMMUNITY |
| 7 | MONEY |
| 6 | HEALTH |
| 5 | HAPPINESS |
| 4 | PEOPLE |
| 3 | HABITS |
| 2 | GOALS |
| 1 | PURPOSE |

## You Can Go Live Anywhere, Right Now

I don't know about you, but for me, **location freedom** is everything!

*Location Freedom - The ability to live anywhere you want because your income can be sustained from working online (or you happen to be independently wealthy and living off of passive income).*

While only 5% of people worked remotely before COVID-19, now around 25% of the American workforce works remotely.

The ability to work remotely is a huge benefit -- and a huge hiring differentiator for the companies that encourage it.

Here are a few helpful stats supporting the trend toward work flexibility, based on surveys of American professional workers:

- 94% of employees report feeling like their work productivity is the same or higher than before they worked remotely.
- 86% of professional employers now offer some work-from-home or remote-work option for their teams
- 75% of remote workers believe their work-life balance has improved.
- 68% of surveyed workers say they would want to work remotely if their employer allowed it.
- 62% of remote workers say that remote work positively affects their work engagement.

You see, where you live makes a huge difference in your life. It is literally your environment, which affects everything in your day-to-day life. So make the choice of where to live as thoughtfully as the choice of who to marry and whether to have children.

Spend some time exploring lots of different places and really reflecting on where you should live, rather than simply ending up somewhere out of chance. Don't just stay in your **default location** because it's where you were born, where you went to school, or where your company is headquartered.

*Default Location - where you randomly ended up living because of your family, your school, or your work.*

Far too many people stay in the town they grew up in. If you can believe it, 68% of Americans aged 25 and older still live in their hometowns! While that's fine, don't just stay somewhere because that's where you were raised. Go and explore the world. There's a lot of magic out there. Design your life to put your location first -- and then let everything else fit into that requirement.

If you want to be in the United States, here are the places in the USA I like the best for their combination of **conscious communities** with ambitious and kind people and lots of nature.

1. Encinitas, CA
2. Venice/Santa Monica/Topanga, CA;
3. Ojai/Santa Barbara, CA;
4. Shasta, CA
5. Nevada City, CA
6. Mill Valley, CA
7. Maui, HI
8. Kauai, HI
9. Boulder, CO
10. Ashland, OR
11. Asheville, NC
12. Sedona, AZ
13. Austin, TX

*Conscious Communities - Towns that have a lot of expats living in them and focus on wellness, community, and personal growth. Global examples include Ubud, Bali; Chiang Mai, Thailand, and Nosara, Costa Rica. American examples include Encinitas, Boulder, Mill Valley, Austin, and Nevada City.*

In every one of these cities and towns, you can find biohacking optimizers, yoga galore, grass-fed steak, organic food, paleo/keto diet options, supplements, wellness centers, ecstatic dances, massage, cold plunges, coworking spaces, and so much more. To plug in, just get on the local Facebook community groups and look at the flyers on the walls at every grocery store and yoga studio.

# Slow Travel Around the World

*"Try a few months of living the life you think you want, but leave yourself an exit plan, being open to the big chance that you might not like it after actually trying it.."*
- Derek Silvers, Entrepreneur

Where can you find both amazing people and all the things needed for an optimal and healthy life? Here are the places I recommend visiting or living in because of their strong communities of smart and conscious people.

- Bali - Ubud, Canggu, and Uluwatu
- Thailand - Koh Phangan and Chiang Mai
- India - Goa and Rishikesh
- Costa Rica - Nosara, Santa Teresa, and Dominical/Uvita
- Guatemala - Lake Atitlan
- Peru - Sacred Valley
- Mexico - Tulum
- USA - Austin, Boulder, Mill Valley, Kauai, Encinitas, Venice, Sedona, Asheville
- Spain - Ibiza
- Greece - Mykonos
- Portugal - Lisbon & The Azores
- Australia - Byron Bay & Sunshine Coast

In all of these places, you can find organic food, healing modalities like massage, float tanks, cupping, reiki, cranial sacral, saunas, and tantra -- and community activities like ecstatic dances, cacao ceremonies, festivals, play parties, and medicine ceremonies.

I have dozens of friends who actively **slow travel** the world, going on global adventures for months or years at a time while working during the week on their laptops.

> **SLOW** — *Slow Travel - Traveling for 3-24 months at a time while working during the week on your laptop and traveling to new locations on the weekends. You usually will change countries every 30-90 days so you don't overstay your visa.*

If you have a good passport, it is very easy to visit and even move all over the world today, with few roadblocks. Here are the most powerful passports to hold based on how many countries you can visit without needing a pre-arranged visa.

1. Japan (193 countries)
2. Singapore, South Korea (192 countries)
3. Germany (190 countries)
4. Spain (190 countries)
5. Finland, Italy, Luxembourg (189 countries)
6. Austria, Denmark, Netherlands, Sweden (188 countries)

7. France, Ireland, Portugal, United Kingdom (187 countries)
8. USA, Belgium, Czech Republic, New Zealand, Norway, Switzerland, (186 countries)
9. Australia, Canada, Greece, Malta (185 countries)
10. Hungary, Poland (184 countries)

So, if you're an American, you can visit 186 countries without needing a pre-arranged visa. Just bring your passport, book a ticket, and show up.

If you're ready for a change, you can also move to a lot of different countries very easily.

**Action Item #78: Where Will You Live?**
Review the list of towns and cities above in the USA and around the world. Spend a few minutes researching each one that calls to you. Then write down the names of all the cities in the world that you'd currently consider living in next. Set a specific date to visit any that are near the top of your list that you've never been to before.

# Move Globally With a Digital Nomad Visa

*"People can't get up in the morning and they can't get out of bed. I'm going to tell you why: because they can predict the feeling of everything that's gonna happen. And their bodies resign to the familiar. They say, "oh another mundane day." But remember when you were a kid and you were going on a field trip? What happened then. You were up and dressed before your parents. Why? Because you knew something unexpected was going to happen. So live your life so that unexpected things happen." - Dr. Joe Dispenza*

In many places (listed below), you can even apply for and get a 1-3 year remote work **digital nomad visa** by simply demonstrating that you earn around $3k per month and that you can support yourself.

*Digital Nomad Visa - Visas to go live in another country for 1-3 years that are given out to people who can work remotely on their laptops and can show proof of earnings from a remote job.*

These countries are smart -- as they are attracting a globally educated workforce that will help invest in and expand their local economies. Every year, more and more countries are launching their own digital nomad and second home visas in order to attract the global talent pool of remote workers who can log in from anywhere on their laptops.

These days, for many different types of passport holders, it's relatively easy to get a residency permit and move for a year or two to beautiful places like Portugal, Costa Rica, or Indonesia -- and then convert into a longer term resident if desired.

Here is a partial list of places where it's relatively easy to get a **digital nomad visa**...

## Countries You Can Live in With a Digital Nomad Visa

Albania, Anguilla, Antigua & Barbuda, The Bahamas, Barbados, Belize, Bermuda, Brazil, Cayman Islands, Colombia, Costa Rica, Croatia, Curacao, Cyprus, Czech Republic, Dominica, Dubai, Ecuador, Estonia, Georgia, Germany, Greece, Grenada, Hungary, Iceland, Indonesia, Italy, Latvia, Malaysia, Malta, Mauritius, Mexico, Montserrat, Namibia, North Macedonia, Norway, Panama, Portugal, Romania, Seychelles, Serbia, South Africa, Spain, Sri Lanka, St. Lucia, Taiwan, Thailand

Yes, that's right, depending on which passport you have, **you may be able to literally move to Costa Rica, Bali, Portugal, or Thailand next week**. You show proof of income (usually), pay a small amount (usually $500 to $2000) to get your long-term visa approved, and you're an official resident of another country. Generally speaking, as long as you can show proof of earning between $24,000 and $100,000 per year (depending on the country), you'll be granted your visa.

Here are a few resources for the adventure minded:

- Check out the Baseflow website (www.baseflow.io) for an ever-expanding list of countries that offer residency and even second passports.

- Check out the HiveGeist website (www.hivegeist.io) for their latest list of locations for their digital nomad homes that you can live in. They currently have homes that you can stay at in Bali, Mallorca, Barcelona, Lisbon, and the Grand Canaries.

- Check out Selina (www.selina.com), a network of community-friendly hotels that are designed with the digital nomad in mind -- offering daily, weekly, and monthly rates, co-working spaces, and community activities.

Selina has around 100 locations so far in 21 countries all over North America, Central America, South America, Europe, Africa, Australia, and Asia. Month-to-month prices range from $360/mo to $2500/mo depending on location and type of accommodations. These prices allow you to switch locations up to 3 times per month without adding lodging costs.

As the always inspiring Carnivore Aurelius says on IG, " I don't feel bad for people complaining about their job. You can move to a Latin American beach town and survive for like $500/month. People teach yoga, teach surfing, and literally sell cheese on the beach, and they make do. You can find a way to quit if you want it enough."

So say goodbye to long-term leases that keep you locked down and cooped up. Go on adventures and travel the world -- and in many cases, you'll pay less than you're currently paying to live in one place.

Be a relentless **freedom seeker** and get out there and see the world while you still have lots of energy and health.

*Freedom seeker - Someone obsessed with living on their own terms, choosing where they want to live, going on adventures, and following their passions.*

And if you don't yet have kids -- I would encourage you to take six months of your life and live entirely in Selinas--switching to a new location every 1-2 weeks. Having spent plenty of time at their Tulum and Nosara locations -- I know how life changing it can be to slow travel while you remote work globally. If you switched locations every week, it would take you 2 years to visit every Selinas location across the world. Now that would be a grand adventure!

I've even seen a few families live this nomadic, adventuring life. Check out The Bucket List Family (@thebucketlistfamily) on Instagram for a great example.

Some friends of ours took a year when their daughter was 7 years old and decided to spend one month living in twelve different cities. They got to live for a month in places like Paris, New York, Miami, Amsterdam -- and many other places that many people only dream of living in. And they did it all for the same cost as just staying in one place through a combination of advance travel planning and home exchanges. Both Mom and Dad worked from home on their laptops and owned their own businesses -- making this family adventure living possible.

The top 20 cities in the world based on livability (according to Monocle) are listed below. Important criteria in this ranking are safety/crime, international connectivity, climate/sunshine, quality of architecture, public transport, tolerance, environmental issues, access to nature, urban design, business conditions, proactive policy developments, and medical care. 12 of the top 20 are in Europe, 4 are in Asia, 3 are in Oceania, and 1 is in North America. None are in the USA.

1. Copenhagen, Denmark
2. Zürich, Switzerland
3. Lisbon, Portugal
4. Helsinki, Finland
5. Stockholm, Sweden
6. Tokyo, Japan
7. Vienna, Austria
8. Sydney, Australia
9. Vancouver, Canada
10. Taipei, Taiwan
11. Munich, Germany
12. Seoul, South Korea
13. Berlin, Germany
14. Amsterdam, Netherlands
15. Madrid, Spain
16. Auckland, New Zealand
17. Paris, France
18. Barcelona, Spain
19. Melbourne, Australia
20. Kyoto, Japan

**Action Item #79: Consider Living Internationally**
Review the list of countries above that many people can immediately move to easily and some of the top global cities for livability. Write down in your notebook any cities or countries that you'd consider moving to. Research any that call to you.

## Use Geoarbitrage To Keep Costs Low

"I've chartered private planes over the Andes, enjoyed many of the best wines in the world in between world-class ski runs, and lived like a king, lounging in the infinity pool of a private villa. Here's the little secret I rarely tell: It all costs less than rent in the U.S. If you can free your time and location, your money is automatically worth 3-10 times as much." - Tim Ferriss, *The Four Hour Workweek*

The great thing about living in a place like Costa Rica, Bali, or Thailand is that you can live like a King or Queen on $30,000 per year (as an individual) or around $60,000 per year as a family.

There's no need to earn $250,000 just to be able to afford nice things and live an upper middle class lifestyle (like it requires in Austin, San Francisco, Miami, or many other major American cities).

This means you can use more of your time to actually live and enjoy your life — while supporting the growth of a local economy in the place you live.

I call this, **geoarbitrage**.

Geoarbitrage - Earning your income from one place and then working remotely in another country where costs are much lower. (Example: earning American pay rates but rotating between Bali, Thailand, and Costa Rica.)

To illustrate what's possible with geoarbitrage, let's take a look at an example budget for a single person or family living in Bali or Thailand - who would be living really well.

| Monthly Expenses | Cost for Single Person in Bali | Cost for Family of Four In Bali or Thailand |
| --- | --- | --- |
| Housing | $1,000 | $2,000 |
| Meals | $300 | $750 |
| Transportation | $200 | $250 |
| Misc | $500 | $500 |
| Childcare/School | $0 | $500 |
| **Total Per Month** | **$2,000** | **$4,000** |

Yes, that's right - you can live like a King or Queen in Bali or Thailand for $24,000 per year - and for about $48,000 per year as a family of four. The costs of living that well in most U.S. cities are about four times that.

Use **geoarbitrage** to live in lower cost areas (where you can contribute in a big way to the local economy and you can much more easily save up at least 25% of your after tax income (or more!) for investing in cash flow producing assets). You'll get out of the rat race much more quickly this way.

I was in the sauna in Austin recently when I overheard a mid-40s guy tell his friends, "I spent the last 10 weeks in Koh Samui, Thailand. It's incredible. I can live the quality of life that it takes $240,000 per year to live in Austin for just $60,000. I can live like a king there. I can still come back to the USA a couple months per year to see family and friends -- and if I'm in the USA less than 90 days per year, the first $120,000 of my income is tax free. You've got to check this out."

Koh Samui is next to Koh Phangan, which is also known as Tantra Island. Go spend a couple months (by yourself, with your partner, or with your family) on Koh Phangan learning tantra. That would be a fun life upgrade!

As you adventure through the world, don't be a tourist. Be a traveler. What's the difference? A tourist wants to escape their life. A traveler wants to experience it.

## Using Remote Work To Achieve Location Freedom

I've been working remotely full time long before COVID made it common. I don't have an office. My "office" is usually the cafe I'm writing at. I thank God for background noise suppression on Zoom. My laptop is my world. I wrote this entire book on Google Docs while in Bali, Austin, and Costa Rica.

You too can make the switch to a full remote. If you have a job – just tell them you are going to start working remotely. If they don't let you, resign and get a similar role at a company that will. Your **location freedom** is too important.

Here are just a few examples of certain professions that either myself or my friends are able to do entirely remotely, working from places like Tulum, Mexico; Bali, Indonesia; Ibiza, Spain; and Nosara, Costa Rica.

| Good Jobs for Remote Work |
|---|

1. Business Owner (after putting a manager in place)
2. Ecommerce entrepreneur (using outsourced fulfillment or drop shipping)
3. Video Content Producer
4. Business Consultant/Coach
5. Digital Marketing Consultant
6. Writer
7. Upwork Gig Worker
8. Investment Banking (helping connect companies with venture capital)
9. Management consulting (taking gigs on Catalant)
10. Business Broker (helping companies sell themselves)
11. Business Scaling Coach
12. Personal Coach (Life Coach, Relationship Coach, Tantra Coach, etc.)
13. Software Engineer
14. Graphic Designer
15. Travel Blogger
16. Tech Entrepreneur
17. English teacher
18. Professional worker whose company allows them to work remotely

Entrepreneurial roles are especially aligned with remote work – but now more than ever, even many professional roles are allowing flexibility with where you work from as long as you are good, get your work done, hit your KPIs, and stay in communication.

While you work remotely, you can hire a low-cost high-quality remote Executive Assistant (often called a virtual assistant) to greatly increase your productivity. You can find a shared VA starting at $279/month from a firm like Wing, Belay, or Zirtual. Full-time 40-hour per week VAs with 3 minute response times start at $899/month. Leverage your time and do more of what you love to do by getting one.

Most passport holders can easily get a 2-3 month same-day visa to visit anywhere in Europe, Australia, Central America, South America, and much of Asia. And when you finish one country, you just go to the next one. I have many friends who simply rotate between Europe, Bali, Thailand, the USA, and Australia -- and don't actually "live" anywhere. Give it a try!

**Action Item #80: Planning for a Remote Work Life**
Write down the answer to this question: How would your life be different if you worked remotely and could live anywhere you chose? Where would you go? Where would you live? If this dream sounds appealing, what do you need to do to make it real?

## Finding My Home as a Dual-Culture Kid

I'm half British (on my mom's side) and half-American. Growing up, I lived in the USA, but we would save up our money and go to Europe every 2-3 years during the summers, often exchanging homes with other families to make it more affordable.

My dad earned around $32,000 per year as an Episcopalian Priest. My mom stopped working as a social worker when I was 4 years old to spend more time with me. So even though we didn't earn that much as a family, my mom was incredibly good at saving and reducing spending -- and we were still able to go on international adventures and see my family in England every few years.

I got to spend 3 months in Europe when I was 6 years old, in the summer of 1990. This cultural exposure to England, Germany, France, and Italy at a young age got me really interested in geography, travel, and culture. The exposure to other cultures was incredibly beneficial to my brain's development.

While I've lived in the USA for 95% of my life, I am currently living in Costa Rica with my family and many of our friends. I've lived in 14 places so far in my life.

1. Pittsburgh, Pennsylvania (Age 0-2)
2. Woonsocket, Rhode Island (2-10)
3. Anna Maria Island, Florida (10-13)
4. Bradenton, Florida (13-18)
5. Chapel Hill, North Carolina (18-27)
6. Cambridge, Massachusetts (28-29)
7. San Francisco, California (30-33)
8. Encinitas, California (33)
9. Los Angeles, California (35)
10. Ubud, Bali, Indonesia (35)
11. Canggu, Bali, Indonesia (35)

12. Boulder, Colorado (36)
13. Austin, Texas (37-38)
14. Nosara, Costa Rica (39)

The places I've loved living the most so far have been Anna Maria, Encinitas, Canggu, and Nosara. These all happen to be beach towns. There's just something about seeing the sunset over the ocean that calms my soul. So far, I've spent 38 years living in the USA and 2 years living in other countries. At this moment in my life, I'm really enjoying living in a community in Nosara, Costa Rica, with many friends and family.

## Learn From the Blue Zones

The concept of Blue Zones was created by Dan Buettner, a National Geographic Fellow and New York Times bestselling author. In 2004, Buettner teamed up with National Geographic and the National Institute on Aging to identify places in the world where people live the longest, healthiest lives. He called these regions "Blue Zones" based on the blue circles he drew around them on a map.

The original **Blue Zones** were located in Sardinia, Italy; Okinawa, Japan; Nicoya, Costa Rica; Icaria, Greece; and Loma Linda, California. Buettner and his team studied the lifestyles and habits of the people in these regions, and identified common factors that they believed contributed to their longevity and good health.

Blue Zone - Regions where people have longer lifespans due to factors like diet, lifestyle, and community. Examples include Okinawa (Japan), Sardinia (Italy), Nicoya (Costa Rica), Ikaria (Greece), and Loma Linda (California, USA).

Dan Buettner has since written several books on the subject, including *The Blue Zones: Lessons for Living Longer From the People Who've Lived the Longest* and has continued to study and promote the Blue Zones concept.

The Blue Zones approach to health and wellness emphasizes lifestyle factors such as diet, physical activity, social connections, and stress management, and has been adopted by communities and organizations around the world.

So what is it specifically that countries in the Blue Zones (where people regularly live to 100+) like Costa Rica and Japan actually do differently?

Disproportionately high numbers of people in the Blue Zones...

1. Eat diets rich in fruits and vegetables with minimal processed foods and eat smaller portion sizes
2. Drink lots of water.
3. Maintain a healthy Body Mass Index (between 18.5 and 24.9).
4. Are more physically active, engaging in daily activities like gardening and walking.
5. Have also formed strong social connections and a sense of community. They have a strong sense of belonging and purpose, often through family, friends, and spiritual communities.

6. Have lower levels of stress, stemming from mindfulness practices and meditation.
7. Don't smoke, which is a major contributor to longevity and health.

So take a page out of the book of the centenarians and follow their ways. This is one of the big reasons we now live most of the year in Nosara, Costa Rica -- right within the Blue Zone of the Nicoya Peninsula.

**Action Item #81: Learn from the Blue Zones**
Write down what you can learn from the people who live in the Blue Zones. Which of their habits do you want to apply to your life?

## Move to Nosara?

Nosara is a beautiful Blue Zone beach town with about 10,000 residents. It is where I live with my family most of the year.

It was founded in the 1970s and has some of the best surfing and yoga in the world. The main beach, Playa Guiones, has one of the most consistent surf waves in the world with over 330 days per year of surfable conditions. There are already two world class schools for kids here (Casa De Las Estrellas Waldorf and Del Mar Academy), and there are lots of land lots in the area that can be purchased for as low as $100k.

People get around on ATVs and golf carts. There are lots of people from all over the world who could live anywhere and choose to live here. It's definitely a paradise. In terms of the magic that happens daily here, There's a thriving ecstatic dance and tantra community and an active local farmers market. Nosara reminds me of Burning Man more than any other town in the world. Hopefully we can bring a few more epic people (like you) to live here too!

### How Nosara, Costa Rica Was Founded by Behnaz Love

"In 1967, An American businessman, Alan David Hutchinson, searching for a site to develop a residential community, flew along the coast of Costa Rica in a small rented airplane with a local pilot. He spotted the beaches of Guiones and Pelada and asked his pilot to land somewhere close by. They landed on a dirt strip near Nosara (which is still the city airport).

Hutchinson rode horseback out to the beaches and knew immediately he had found his dream spot. He bought the Nosara ranch and adjoining lands. Working with local technical experts in San Jose and his associates in the U.S., he developed a Master Development Plan and started advertising in American newspapers and publications. An ad in the New York Times in 1971 drew much attention and he began selling lots.

He paid great care to how his planned community would interact with its natural surroundings... In 1979, ten miles of dirt road were built, connecting Nosara with the beaches (that is still the road today). Great care was made NOT to develop modern mass tourism. He highlighted Playa Guiones as "one of the finest beaches in the whole world" - flat, smooth white sand and safe rolling surf"; Playa Pelada to the north with picturesque coves and tidal pools; and the all buttressing of the green jungle hills. All this remains today.

Hutchinson wrote in the mid-1970's, "The technological North is becoming less and less a place for an individual or family. To return to Costa Rica with its green mountains and wide open spaces – to our own beaches, what a joy it is. In Nosara there are cowboys and horses and wide beaches and I stop and shake hands with everyone. That is the local custom, and these gentle peace-loving people are genuine and smilingly friendly. This can become your custom too."

Here are some great communities in the Nosara-area in case you're interested in living here too.

- Shift Esperanza
- Tierra Amor
- El Bosque
- Eterna San Juanillo
- Pachamama Ecovillage

My friend Gunnar Lovelace, the founder of Thrive Market, is also working on building a community called Luna Sol in Nosara, though it doesn't yet have a website.

If community focused ecovillages aren't your thing, you can always live in existing Nosara neighborhoods like Guiones, Pelada, Esperanza, Delicias, or Huacas.

This is the short letter I wrote to Morgan when we decided to move to Nosara in April 2023 and finally experience our dream of living on land in Paradise and putting on festivals for our friends.

### The Letter I Wrote Morgan About Moving to Costa Rica
April 28, 2023

Wifie,
We gonna live in Garza, get a few hectares walkable to the beach, and build a few homes on our land for our core soul fam. We gonna have ATVs, eat organic food, make love a lot, and play with Apollo. He will go to Casa De Las Estrellas Waldorf school. I will work at Outpost. We will build a Titi Batu community center and a LuvBubble festival.
Yours, Ryan

Two weeks later, I'd convinced Morgan (and Apollo) to come with me back to Nosara to see if we could make it our home.

And less than 30 days after writing this above letter, we had secured a 3 year lease-to-own on some beachfront land with an existing home on it in the magical town of Garza, about 12 minutes south of Nosara. Today, we're working on building a local daycare, an animation studio (for Morgan's LuvMonster children's movies), and a wellness community center. Life is magical!

Always remember the **Formula of Success**: Vision + Belief + Action + Consistency = Results

# Why I Love Intentional Communities

I had the time of my life at Burning Man in 2016—my first year at Camp Mystic. We got to live next to 200 of our friends for 8 days in RVs and tents. I had a blast. After this experience,

I became obsessed with a search for communities where we could live near our friends all year around.

I began studying **intentional communities**—communities where people with shared values and interests would live together. I visited Damanhur in Italy (a community of 500 people that was founded in the 1970s), La Ecovilla and Alegria in Costa Rica, and studied Auroville in India, Findhorn in Scotland, and Tamera in Portugal.

> *Intentional Community - A small village/town of 25-500 people where the residents have shared values, a system of new resident on-boarding, and a regular opportunity for community gatherings and festivals. Some communities also create their own school, grow some of their own food, and share in profits from community-owned businesses.*

By 2019, when I started dating Morgan, I was certain that someday I wanted to live in an intentional community of passionate, brilliant, and diverse people from around the world. I wanted our future kids to be able to walk around unwatched and be free-range kids. I wanted them to be able to be mentored by others in the community.

Since then, we've gotten involved with a few different intentional communities, including the ones above near Nosara as well as Alegria, Holos, and Rise in Costa Rica and Nuanu and Parq in Bali.

Today, many of these projects are under development and getting close to being ready for move-in. You can learn more at these websites:

- Parq Ubud - They have built around 200 apartments and 30 townhomes so far, as well as restaurants, a gym, a sauna, a boxing center, a float center, retail shops, and coworking, and are now beginning work on 90 homes for families at Parq Family. This is one of the most impressive Bali-based communities so far. - www.parqubud.com.

- Nuanu Canggu - A home for leaders, creators, makers, and visionaries. They are planning for around 2,000 residents by 2026. We led some community building activities for the founding team in 2020/2021. www.nuanu.com

- Alegria Village, Costa Rica - A new ecological neighborhood in the foothills of San Mateo, Costa Rica with around 100 homes and 250 residents including many of my friends. Next door to La Ecovilla which has another 300 or so residents. Co-founded by a friend of ours Stephen Brooks. - www.alegriavillage.com

- Holos - A future-forward regenerative community with access to pioneering wellbeing programming and amenities located in the Diamante Valley of Costa Rica. They are planning for 43 homes. Lot prices range from $120k to $400k currently. Run by a friend of ours Ian-Michael Hebert. - www.holos.global

- Rise - A family-focused residential community in Costa Rica, with 800 acres, 53 home sites, and a Waldorf school, run by a friend of ours David Comfort, who is also the founder of the Kombucha Culture drink. The Kinkara retreat center is inside the property. www.risecostarica.com

- TierrAmor - A 500 acre ocean-view property in the hills of Nosara, Costa Rica. With large rolling hills, it's one of the most beautiful communities in the world. The plan to have 300+ residents there by 2027. I'm writing this chapter right now from this land. www.tierramor.cr.

- Shift Esperanza - A 140 acre community near Nosara, Costa Rica with around 70 homes and about 200 residents. The first homes are being finished in 2024. www.shiftliving.com

You can find a directory of intentional communities that you can live in at: https://www.ic.org/directory/. Many of these intentional communities are smaller (around 20-75 residents). Personally, if I'm going to live on land in a somewhat remote tropical paradise, I prefer to have around 200-400 residents living on the land so there are enough people to form schools, restaurants, and a co-working and wellness space.

**Action Item #82: Consider Living in Community in Paradise**
Review the list above of communities in Costa Rica and Bali. Go to the website for each one. Write down the names of any communities you'd consider living in. If any call to you, make a plan to visit them!

# Coliving and New Urbanism

**Co-living** is living near other people with whom you have shared values or interests. Coliving communities are usually structured—in principle and often in architecture—to encourage frequent interactions and the formation of close relationships between their members. Neighbors are encouraged to cooperate within the community, mentor each other's children, and care for their neighbors. There is a lot of emphasis placed on neighbors actually knowing each other and building sustainable and regenerative communities.

*Co-living - Sharing the same building or neighborhood with others who share your values and interests. Urban co-living involves sharing an apartment building with other people. Suburban or family co-living involves living in the same community as your friends in nearby homes.*

While there have been many companies that have built co-living in urban apartments for 20-somethings -- very few companies have yet taken on applying the principles of **New Urbanism** and community and "reimagining the suburb." There are only a few residential family-focused communities out there where residents are selected based on values-alignment and an intentional onboarding process rather than the randomness of Zillow and who happens to move there.

*New Urbanism - A city planning movement that seeks to create more livable, walkable, and sustainable communities through the development of mixed-use, pedestrian-friendly neighborhoods with a variety of housing types, public transportation options, and environmental sustainability features.*

Here are some of the design elements of **New Urbanism** and Family-Focused Residential Communities like those we mentioned above.

### Design Elements of Family Focused Residential Communities

Co-existing with nature. No more than 33% of the land built upon. The rest saved for parks and nature.

Car-free, pedestrian centric, and focused on walkability. Motorized vehicles parked in an external lot. Only golf carts, pedal bikes, e-bikes allowed internally to maximize safety for free ranging kids.

Globally diverse and often well-educated and accomplished residents and families from all over the planet who are masters of their fields and crafts and can work remotely or own businesses remotely -- and stay connected via fiber optic.

Definable town center and community edges

Variety of housing types available (apartments, townhomes, and homes) so people of varying compensation levels can join.

Attracts creator families including business owners, entrepreneurs, content creators, writers, teachers, healers, artists, community builders, and anyone who can work remotely

Both rentable and purchasable units available.

I've found that humans aren't happy when we live in disconnected ways. We've lost our tribal ways of being connected to those we live near. Further, we've created a global economic system that often centralizes wealth in the hands of a few and prioritizes individualism over connected celebration, expression, and interdependence.

I am so excited to see alternatives now being created to the 75-year failed experiment of the nuclear family (where you live on your own isolated from your friends, family, and soul fam) that has often led to misery, depression, and overwhelm. We aren't meant for tribal living -- not to be isolated worker cogs in a production machine churning out babies and GDP efficiency.

While Auroville in India and Damanhur in Italy were interesting alternative models from the 1970s--we need new options for values-aligned families that want to raise their family in community -- yet still being connected to the global economy via fiber optic internet.

Here are some of the incredible amenities that are being built in many of these new models for family living. But of course -- it's not about the amenities as much as it is about the exceptional people you get to interact with and co-raise your children with.

### Amenities for a New Way of Living

Organic food
Organic farmers market
Organic and paleo restaurants
Communal dining options
Steiner/Waldorf/Montessori Preschool s
K-12 Montessori-style school
Conversation pits
Yoga & pilates center

Community & wellness center
Spa and healing massages
Pool and hot tubs
Cold plunge
Steam & dry sauna
Sound healing room
Treehouses
Art & sculpting studios

|  |  |
|---|---|
| Indoor & Outdoor movie lounge | Retail shops |
| Volleyball, squash, padel courts | Town squares |
| Soccer/baseball/open play fields | Walkable promenades |
| Board games, air hockey & foosball | Food forests |
| Adult and kids sports leagues | Solar power grid with backup |
| Hotel for short-term stays | Fiber Optic Wifi |
| Underground music hall with classes | Large art sculptures |
| Innovation lab | Biking & running paths |
| Robotics, 3D Printing, & Computing Lab | Carless area for free-range kid safety |
| Music & Video recording studios | Teen mentoring center |
| Juice bars | Playgrounds |
| Quarterly community celebrations | Car and scooter sharing service |
| On-site doctor visits | Festival grounds |
| Functional medicine for all residents | Events pyramid |
| Community counselors | New resident onboarding workshops |
| Community elder counsel | Personal growth workshop space |
| Community concerts, plays, & field trips | Grandparent integration |

Each mini-town (especially the larger ones with over 200 residents) often has people who focus on community recruitment, architecture, permitting, government relations, town relations, food production, schooling, sports leagues, child mentoring, wellness, safety, and functional medical care.

It's time to change the way we live and raise our children. It's time to live in a community based on shared values and shared prosperity. It's time to create a harmonious and loving ecosystem to live in joyously. As you can probably tell, I'm quite passionate about this topic -- and my wife and I are dedicated to living in this type of structure ourselves and bringing as many of you along with us as we can.

So come join us!

**Action Item #83 A Different Life**
Write down the answer to this question: How would your life be different if you lived in a multi-generational community of 250-500 inspiring people who all supported and mentored each other? Would you consider living in a community like that?

## Try Living in a Peaceful Place Like Bali

Every time we go to Bali, it's pure peace for me. I've always wondered why I love it so much there. Here are my best theories. It is likely a combination of these factors:

1. We don't speak good Indonesian yet so we are saved from the daily news cycles that report on the daily drama of the political and economic machine. We get out of the "American Matrix" much more easily there.

2. People there tend to be highly satisfied with the joys of simpler daily living (taking care of their children, serving others, and living a balanced life).

3. Everything in Bali costs about 1/4th the prices of Austin -- reducing our stress as our income from consulting, art, and writing suddenly exceeds our expenses. This dynamic allows us to afford high-quality full time childcare here for around $1000 per month -- while still contributing in a big way to the family of our nanny here.

4. There are many community wellness centers that have pools, gyms, restaurants, wifi, and saunas (like Titi Batu in Ubud, where I am writing this section now, or Amo Spa in Canggu).

5. Every local person in Bali lives within and participates in a Banjar. You can think of a Banjar as a neighborhood, with required participation from at least one member of each family.

Regardless of why, all I know is that when I am in Bali, my whole system relaxes. My central nervous system, overstimulated by 20 years of being an "American Fuckface" overweight workaholic -- can finally relax -- allowing me time to build up brand new habits that help me lock in this lower and calmer level of cortisol and adrenaline in my body.

Many of my daily health habits were learned in Bali, including:

1. Going every single morning to a wellness center with a pool, gym, sauna, restaurant, and wifi. There aren't too many of these yet in America, but these could become the new "second place" in American lifestyle -- replacing Starbucks as the "go-to-place" at 8am for coffee and remote work. I sense there could be 1000s of these "Titi Batu" like places in the USA that act as the 21st century community center that combine a gym, cafe, pool, and co-working space.

2. Lifting weights, running 1 km (0.6 miles), swimming, using the wet sauna, cold plunge, and dry sauna, and having a Green Tea, and Scrambled Eggs, BEFORE I start my work.

3. Deleting the news apps from my phone and blocking the news websites from my computer (bye bye NY Times and CNN) that so often waste brain space reporting about scary things that have zero relevance to my life. Instead of these sites, I now read The Good News Hub, Positive.News, The Good News Network, and SingularityHub. This single change has made a huge positive impact in my life and happiness.

We've learned to only consider neighborhoods that have close proximity (10 mins or less, without needing a highway drive) to a community wellness center with an adult pool, kid-friendly pool, gym, sauna, cold plunge, restaurant, and wifi.

Yes, we could build this at our house, but it's way more fun to be around human beings while we workout and then do our creative work on our computers -- and way more fun for our son Apollo to come with us.

Long story short – if you find that you're too stressed out – take 2-3 months off and go live in a low-cost and relaxing place like Bali, Thailand, or Costa Rica to mentally and physically recover and change all your habits.

# Living in Walkable Cities

If you don't want to live in a family-centered **intentional community** yet, at least look into living in cities that are highly walkable. I find people are happier when they can walk or bike everywhere and don't have to drive as much.

There's a new trend in urban development and city planning called **15 Minute Cities**. These are towns (or parts of cities) in which everything you need is within a 15-minute walk or cycle from your home, from health care and education to grocery stores and green spaces.

*15 Minute Cities - Towns (or parts of cities) in which everything you need is within a 15-minute walk or cycle from your home, from health care and education to grocery stores and green spaces*

The aim of this movement is to make cities more livable and connected, with less private car use -- meaning cleaner air, greener streets, and lower levels of planet-heating pollution.

Examples of cities that have embraced this concept include Paris, Melbourne, Barcelona, Tokyo, Oslo, and Portland. We also really like Boulder, Colorado, Miami Beach, Florida, and Santa Monica, California.

Paris Mayor Anne Hidalgo has made the development of 15-minute cities a priority for her administration. The city has been working to create more pedestrianized areas, bike lanes, and green spaces and to promote public transport to reduce reliance on cars. Paris has also introduced a series of initiatives to encourage small businesses, such as local food markets, to flourish in each neighborhood.

Melbourne has launched a "20-minute neighborhood" initiative, which aims to create neighborhoods where residents can access all essential services and amenities within a 20-minute walk, bike ride, or public transport trip. The city has been investing in bike lanes and public transport and is promoting small businesses and community facilities in each neighborhood.

Barcelona has been working to create a network of "superblocks," which are groups of blocks that are closed to through traffic and are designed to prioritize pedestrians, cyclists, and public transport. The city is also investing in green spaces and promoting local businesses in each neighborhood.

Who came up with the idea for 15-minute cities?

Well, Clarence Perry is credited with developing the concept of neighborhood unit planning, which is often seen as a precursor to New Urbanism and the 15-minute city concept. In 1929, Perry published an influential report titled "The Neighborhood Unit: A Scheme of Arrangement for the Family Life Community," which proposed the idea of organizing cities into smaller, self-contained neighborhoods that would have all the necessary amenities within walking distance.

Perry's neighborhood unit concept was based on the idea that neighborhoods should be designed to support and enhance community life by providing access to essential services and amenities, including schools, parks, shops, and healthcare facilities. His vision was to create small-scale, walkable communities that were designed for people rather than cars.

# What Is a 15-Minute City?

A 15-minute city aims to provide everything you need within a short 15-minute walk or bike: jobs, schools, food, parks, community, medical, and more.

Building on the principles of New Urbanism and popularized by Parisian Mayor Anne Hidalgo, this urban design concept may be a solution to create more sustainable, equitable, and healthier cities.

A good example of a 15-minute walkable town is Serembe, which is about 40 minutes outside of Atlanta.

A great example of a 15-minute walkable town within Austin, Texas, is called Mueller. Mueller is a 700 acre idyllic walkable town within Austin, TX, complete with restaurants, a lake, an amphitheater, a children's science museum, a movie theater, and an Irish pub. Check it out!

## Smart Cities

There's also a trend of very wealthy entrepreneurs and even nation-states funding the development of new **smart cities** that may be intriguing and worth checking out for your family once they are developed.

> Smart Cities - Cities that use advanced technology and data analytics to improve the quality of life of its citizens, enhance sustainability, and optimize urban services such as transportation, energy, and public safety.

These cities use Internet of Things (IoT) devices, sensors, and data analytics to gather and analyze real-time data, which is then used to make informed decisions and improve city services. The ultimate goal of a smart city is to create a more efficient, livable, and sustainable urban environment for its residents. These could be existing cities like Singapore, Dubai, or Barcelona, or emerging cities like the ones below. Here are a few that we are tracking. We shall see which, if any, become real.

- Telosa, USA - Telosa, aims to establish a new American city that leads the way in urban living standards, broadens human potential, and serves as a prototype for forthcoming generations. The city will give priority to pedestrians and cyclists, with a limited number of "slow-moving autonomous vehicles." Designed by Bjarke Ingels Group to be an environmentally friendly city, it will be powered by renewable resources, with green spaces safeguarded and given priority while water is stored, cleaned, and reused on-site. In addition to environmental measures, the city will be founded on the concept of "equitism", an economic system in which citizens hold a stake in the city's land. The objective is to reach a population of 5 million by 2050. The team is now settling on the exact U.S. location.

- The Line, Saudi Arabia - Saudi Arabia's 100-mile long city, The Line, is set to receive an investment of $100-200 billion. The city's mirrored exterior will house a high-speed autonomous transit system, enabling it to eliminate cars and carbon emissions. The city will contain everything needed to live, work, and play. Construction on the city has already started, and it is slated for completion by 2030. I'm a bit skeptical of this project as who wants to be stuck indoors all the time and live in a desert – but we shall see.

- Snailbrook, Texas - A utopian city being built by Elon Musk for employees of Tesla and Boring Co. about 35 miles east of Austin, TX near Bastrop. Musk has acquired 3,500 acres so far. We'll see what happens!

## Recommended Books on Community

- *Belong: Find Your People, Create Community, and Live a More Connected Life* by Radha Agarwal
- *Creating a Life Together: Practical Tools to Grow Ecovillages and Intentional Communities* by Diana Leafe Christian
- *Finding Community* by Diana Leafe Christian
- *Designing Creative Communities* by Spud Marshall
- *The Four-Hour Work Week* by Tim Ferriss
- *Happy City* by Jeff Speck
- *Walkable City* by Charles Montgomery
- *The More Beautiful World Our Hearts Know is Possible* by Charles Eisenstein

## Key Outcome from This Chapter

**Living Where You Love, With People You Love -** Do a location assessment for your life. Are you living in a town/city you love to live in? Do you have a core tribe of epic inspiring friends who are encouraging? Is this where your partner/spouse wants to be living? If not, consider visiting and then potentially moving to a place filled with inspiring, health conscious, and caring people (some recommendations are in this chapter).

# COMMUNITY CHAPTER ACTION ITEMS

1. **A New Home Town** - Review the list of towns and cities above in the USA and around the world. Spend a few minutes researching each one that calls to you. Then write down the names of all the cities in the world that you'd currently consider living in next. Set a specific date to visit any that are near the top of your list that you've never been to before.

2. **International Living** - Review the list of countries that many people can immediately move to easily and some of the top global cities for livability. Write down in your notebook any cities or countries that you'd consider moving to. Research any that call to you.

3. **Remote Work** - Write down the answer to this question: How would your life be different if you worked remotely and could live anywhere you chose? Where would you go? Where would you live? If this dream sounds appealing, what do you need to do to make it real?

4. **Blue Zones** - Write down what you can learn from the people who live in the Blue Zones. Which of their habits do you want to apply to your life?

5. **Living in Paradise** - Review the list of communities in Costa Rica and Bali. Go to the website for each one. Write down the names of any communities you'd consider living in. If any call to you, make a plan to visit them!

6. **A New Way of Living** - Write down the answer to this question: How would your life be different if you lived in a multi-generational community of 250-500 inspiring people who all supported and mentored each other? Would you consider living in a community like that?

# STEP 9

## LOVE MAGIC

# KEY CONCEPTS FROM THE LOVE CHAPTER

**1. PRIMARY PARTNER**

Your primary romantic partner. Usually the one you live with, spend the most time with, and have a family with. If you have an open relationship each of you may have other secondary partners.

**2. OPEN MARRIAGE**

A marriage in which both people can have other emotionally and physically intimate connections.

**3. MDMA THERAPY**

Guided use of MDMA with a trained practitioner as an aid in couples relationship counseling. MDMA can increase feelings of empathy and connection with others. It is known as the love drug and often can help couples listen, open up, and connect more deeply.

**4. RELATIONSHIP ADVENTURE BOOK**

A blank notebook where you draw and write your key memories together as a couple. We make one for each year.

**5. COMPERSION**

Experiencing joy when your partner experiences pleasure, even if it's not you giving them that pleasure. Opposite of jealousy.

**6. POLARITY**

The push and pull of masculine and feminine energy that creates passion, excitement, and a sense of aliveness. In almost all romantic partnerships, there is one person who is more alpha and one person who is more omega. These opposite energies attract.

**7. MASCULINE ENERGY**

Builder, hunter, and protector energy that can create structure, think linearly, manage time, and be consistent. Also known as Alpha Energy.

**8. FEMININE ENERGY**

Goddess and nurturer energy. Beautifier of spaces. Feeler. Emotional connection. Flowing. Bringer of the softness. Also known as Omega Energy.

**9. ISTA**

The International School of the Temple Arts (ISTA), one of the world's best programs for learning tantra and connection with others. I recommend doing Level 1 and Level 2 on your own or with your romantic partner.

**10. RELATIONSHIP NORTH STAR**

The shared purpose that you have for your romantic relationship. Ours is "to live and then popularize a new way of living, loving, learning, working, and playing based on community, presence, slowness, connection, depth, sensuality, and joy."

**11. CONSTRUCTIVE CONFLICT**

Conflict that is honest yet still kind, where the result is people feel heard and the relationship gets stronger.

**12. DESTRUCTIVE CONFLICT**

Conflict that is so energetically off that it causes the relationship between those in conflict to get weaker over time.

# STEP 9: LOVE MAGIC

"What do you want from your partner? Bliss? No, no, you don't. You want periods of peace punctuated by a good fight. Because that means you respect them. It means you have something to offer each other. And it means that you're both growing. A real relationship is a wrestling match. It's a grappling phenomena that you both emerge transformed from."
- Jordan Peterson

**YOUR MAGIC YEAR**

| Step | Theme |
|---|---|
| 12 | AWAKENING |
| 11 | FAMILY |
| 10 | SEXUALITY |
| 9 | LOVE |
| 8 | COMMUNITY |
| 7 | MONEY |
| 6 | HEALTH |
| 5 | HAPPINESS |
| 4 | PEOPLE |
| 3 | HABITS |
| 2 | GOALS |
| 1 | PURPOSE |

## My Journey Finding Magical Love

Finding the right long term partner to build a life and family with is one of the most important correlates of long-term happiness and living a truly extraordinary life.

As I start writing this chapter, I'm sitting at the cafe at Life Time Fitness in Austin, Texas. I'm staring at a really beautiful woman across the cafe. She's wearing a white coat and orange bell bottom pants. I just caught her eye and smiled – and she smiled back. It looks like she is working on a pitch deck for an animated movie called LuvMonsters that she's working on selling to Disney.

This woman is, of course, my wife, and beautiful baby momma, Morgan Carson Allis. I feel incredibly lucky to have found her six years ago at Burning Man, when I was 34. Today, we are in a beautiful marriage, have a wonderful son, Apollo, and encourage each other's full expression of desire and love. **Complete freedom**. And **complete devotion**.

It wasn't always this way.

Starting in 2012, when I went to grad school, I began what became a seven year search to find *her*.

I had three major romantic relationships during this search – all of which I thought I would marry at some point (Nadia, Rebecca, and Danielle). These three women taught me a lot about personal health, wellness, and spirituality.

All three of these (fabulous) women left me either because I wasn't quite the right fit for them – or because I wanted an open marriage (where we both could have sensual intimacy with others) while they wanted a more traditional closed marriage.

I grew up the son of a rather monogamous Episcopal priest and a social worker from England. About once per year for ten years, my mom would often say to me, "I love your dad so much – but I'm just not sure if people are supposed to be with only one person for their whole lives."

While my mom only ever had one husband (my dad) until she passed away at 60, she seeded in me the question of whether I really wanted someday to commit to never kissing or making love to anyone besides my wife.

By 2016, when I joined Camp Mystic at Burning Man – I was sure that I personally identified as an open relater. I was looking for a solid, committed marriage to one woman—someone I would marry, have kids with, be my best friend, and live together with for life. But I was also looking for it to be okay, and even encouraged, for each of us to have sensuality, touch, and emotional connection with others that we were attracted to -- without it threatening or causing a rupture in the **primary partnership**.

*Primary Partner - Your primary romantic partner. Usually the one you live with, spend the most time with, and have a family with. If you have an open relationship each of you may have other secondary partners.*

While me finding someone who actually wanted an **open marriage** proved challenging in the default world, at Burning Man, it seemed many of the people there were open to having non-traditional relationships.

*Open Marriage - A marriage in which both people can have other emotionally and physically intimate connections.*

While open marriages aren't for everyone -- they tend to be pretty common in the ISTA / tantra / Burning Man community that we have found ourselves in. They definitely take a lot of work and good communication to maintain.

Our camp at Burning Man was a mixture of internet marketers (me), coaches (me), and open relaters (also me) – so I was right at home.

For four years, I invested as much time and energy as I could, becoming a core part of the Camp Mystic community. I helped build the camp in the desert every year with a crew of 60 volunteers a week before the festival began – and I got to know everyone.

Finally, in 2018, I saw Morgan across the desert. We both had other partners then, so we waited nine months until we re-found each other at another Camp Mystic event in California.

We've been together ever since. Yes, from time to time we are sensual and sexual with others – but that only increases our love for each other.

Our family is incredibly special to us – and we've made a lifetime commitment to each other and to our family. We think that being open *increases* our chances that we'll make it through the next 50+ years together!

# Meeting My Wife At Burning Man

In 2016, my former girlfriend Nadia left me because she was looking for something different. After I'd had a challenging Ayahuasca trip, it was a bit too much for her to take care of me, and this was the final step in her realization that we weren't quite right for each other. I was also still a workaholic at the time -- and perhaps not as present as I could have been.

I was devastated. God had other plans for me – and the path ahead, while challenging, would eventually become bright again.

Sometimes you don't end up marrying the first, or even second or third person you think you'll marry. You just have to trust the process along the way. Trust the process, as they say.

By 2017, I was so exhausted from the burnout culture of the tech entrepreneur game in San Francisco that I moved to Encinitas, California — a spiritual yoga hippie beach town just north of San Diego.

I was enthralled by the sun, the sand, and the beautiful women who seemed to all be into yoga and plant medicines.

There I met a new girlfriend, Danielle, who helped teach me about the power of gluten-free and keto eating. She helped me heal my stomach lining, which had gotten weak from too many medicine ceremonies (I went a little overboard in 2017-2018 and needed some time to slow down and "heal" from all the "healing work").

At the time, I had a sense I was getting close to meeting the person I'd ultimately marry, writing in my journal at the time, "I'm ready to build a life together with someone extraordinary."

It ended up not being Danielle – but the next person I would date after her.

Roughly two-thirds of the way through my healing journey (in 2018), I met my wife, Morgan, at Burning Man -- and whatever I hadn't learned by then on my own -- she helped me learn.

I first saw Morgan across the desert at Burning Man, the annual music and arts festival in Nevada that I had been to six times already. Yes, we met at the quirky, unexpected, outlandish, and magical event that teaches self-reliance, self-expression, playfulness, and impermanence. It had already taught me many life lessons and changed my life -- and it was about to shift my world one more time.

She and I ended up camping at the same camp, Camp Mystic, positioned in the top right of the map, near the open playa and the major sound camps. It was Monday afternoon, September 3, 2018 -- a holiday in the United States called Labor Day. We are all packing up the camp in an annual ritual called the Exodus.
She was about 30 meters away from me, wearing a black bra top, silky high-waisted leopard-print shorts, and a cowgirl hat.

At Camp Mystic (my camp), she was helping pack up The Cosmic Heart Temple into a trailer with her new boyfriend, a regenerative power designer.

I first saw her about 30 meters away across the desert while we were breaking down the camp. I found her drop-dead beautiful. A 5 foot 3 inch petite brunette, just like my mom Pauline (Oedipus Complex, anyone?). Who was this cosmic woman entering into my gaze? It would take me many more months to find out.

For some reason that day, perhaps because we both had another partner at the time, I never mustered the courage to say hello. I simply admired her from afar as I went about my work of dismantling the shade structures.

## Our First Meeting

Two weeks later, I found myself at a 500-acre **intentional community** called Hummingbird Ranch, a butterfly and bee sanctuary in northern New Mexico, at a first-time event called Collective Legacy that brought together indigenous elders with tech entrepreneurs with Burners.

My friend and fellow Camp Mystic member, David Weber, was hosting a four day event on the property for about one hundred of his friends -- focusing on aligning us all on how to create a better world. At the time, David was a 28 year old poet with long blonde hair and a penchant for all things spirituality and humanistic. He had invited many of us to come after meeting us at Burning Man.

My girlfriend, Danielle, really wanted me to stay in San Diego with her. But I had a deep intuition that I just had to go -- and I almost always follow my intuitive hits. At the time Danielle and I were having some trouble, as I was quite clear that I wanted an open marriage -- and Danielle wasn't open to that idea.

After flying into Albuquerque, picking up my good friend Gavriella Ravid in Santa Fe, and driving four more hours, we arrived on the beautiful green ranch. Gavriella was a mixture between a left-brained robotics engineer and a beautiful 23 year old Goddess, who pranced around the ranch in my bumble bee onesie.

The setup crew was days delayed -- so we got to work helping them with the final build efforts. On the third day of the event, I heard the good news... The Cosmic Heart Temple had finally arrived from Burning Man.

The Cosmic Heart Temple at Burning Man 2018:
Where I First Met My Wife Morgan

The Cosmic Heart Temple was created by our friends Brigitte Huff and Hannah Natali for Camp Mystic at Burning Man in August 2018. The temple was built as a "prayer for divine union" between the Masculine and the Feminine.

The "temple" was made from a large bell tent with plush rugs and beautiful lighting added. It had been transported from Burning Man to Hummingbird Ranch by none other than Morgan, the beautiful woman I saw across the desert, and her new boyfriend.

They were three days delayed in their arrival due to an axle breakdown and a tire blowout on their dusty old hauler. I walked into the temple as it was being set up at Hummingbird Ranch.

And there she was again. The beautiful woman. I still didn't know her name. This time, I thankfully said hello. I introduced myself and offered to help her build the Cosmic Heart Temple. She said thanks and asked me to come back later on. Our interaction may have lasted 20 seconds.

She later told me that she remembers telling her boyfriend that some nervous guy (me) had offered to help her with the building of the Temple.

But later that night, I had to leave the event early as my girlfriend Danielle needed me back in San Diego. I wouldn't see this magical woman again for seven more months.

In the Fall of 2018, Danielle broke up with me. She wanted a monogamous man -- and I was more into open relating. So I became single for a few months.

I had a really strong sense that the next woman I dated, I would marry. I was anything but patient. I was looking everywhere for "her."

I was trying to apply the **Formula of Success** to dating. Vision + Belief + Action + Consistency = Results!

But who was she? Where would I find her? I was 34 years old, and I truly wanted to find my Queen, my beloved, and my future wife. I was ready.

I tried introductions from friends and even Bumble and Hinge. I would go on dates and essentially interview each woman to be my wife. How many kids did she want to have? Was she interested in community coliving? Would she live with me in places like Bali and Costa Rica and build communities for our friends to live in?

# Camp Mystic MidBurn

Fast forward six months, and I would finally meet the one I had been waiting for all along. It was May 17, 2019, and my friends had convinced me to come to my Burning Man camp's annual camp out over a long weekend. Gavriella had asked me to be her roommate and share a teepee, and I was excited and said, "Yes."

The camp out was to be held at The Mushroom Farm, a 650-acre property in Pescadero, California, stewarded by about 30 renegade regenerative social good activists, hippies, and designers who loved to live in RVs, party, host festivals, and tend to their farm.

At the center of The Mushroom Farm was a renovated old Campbell Soup processing plant that had been turned into a dance floor, offices, a kitchen, and places to hang out. A large white geodesic dome had been added recently and was used for talks and panels.

The space was owned by the family of our friend Nadeem Kassam, a tech entrepreneur I had known through the Summit Series community who previously founded the Basis digital watch company and more recently had begun wearing balloon MC Hammer pants, studied the science of living in flow, and lived out of a "Gratitude Bus" for a year, just because.

There were about sixty Mystics in attendance, all friends of mine from Burning Man. It was the first time we had gathered as a camp in between burns. We would all sleep in various teepees recently set up on the property or in our own RVs.

*The view from the exact spot where we had a first ever conversation at The Mushroom Farm in Pescadero, California. The sun set over the Pacific Ocean as we had our first conversation.*

## The First Conversation

As I got ready for the first meal, I went to my teepee and put on my Green Dinosaur onesie to get warm. This turned out to be a smart move.

It was mid-May in Northern California, and the breezes from the Pacific Coast were creating a chill. Onesies were quite common at Burning Man, and well, this *was* a Burning Man camp gathering.

Just before dinner, Gavriella, in her bee onside, grabbed me and said, "Ryan, come get in this photo. It's for all the people wearing yellow."

Morgan (my future wife) was organizing the photo, and once she saw me, she said, "Get outta here; you're a green dinosaur, you're not wearing yellow!"

Fortunately, my yellow shoes saved me. I popped up my legs to show my shoes, and she let me stay in the photo. That was my first ever photo with my future wife.

*The first ever photo I was in with my future wife, Morgan. We are the people on the right side. Yes, I'm in a dinosaur onesie!*

# MAGIC YEAR - 406

After the photo, we talked for four hours on the nearby bales of hay as the sun went down over the Pacific Ocean and a beautiful full moon rose over the hills.

It was one of those picture perfect, movie-like moments we had both been waiting for our entire lives. My friend Brad snapped this photo without me knowing. It was a picture perfect moment!

In the first conversation I ever had with my future wife Morgan,
Still in that dinosaur onesie. A friend captured this moment for us.

Morgan was wondering, she later told me, "Who is this Harvard grad in a dinosaur onesie and San Diego Padres baseball hat?"

I learned in our four hour conversation that Morgan had been appointed the Chief Dream Officer of The Mushroom Farm a few months earlier and now lives and works there full-time.

We sat down on a bale of hay by the firepit -- and I did what I always did to attractive, smart women who would talk to me. I interviewed her to see if she was the one for me.

"Do you plan on getting married"
"How many kids do you want to have"
"Do you want to live in a community"
"What do you think of living in Bali and Costa Rica"

Morgan said, "Wow, you're a curious one, aren't you?"

The next day, we somewhat avoided each other, neither of us trying to seem too anxious to see each other. But there was some magic in store for the evening.

Each of us had separately decided to take **MDMA** that night, a drug commonly known as 'Molly' that is often used for healing trauma among veterans with PTSD as well as by festival-goers to experience feelings of compassion, connection with others, and wonder.

MDMA - A drug that can increase feelings of empathy and connection with others. It is known as the love drug and is sometimes used in relationship counseling sessions to help the couple listen and connect more deeply.

While MDMA used too frequently can drain serotonin and have negative effects on brain development, when used infrequently by people 25 and older (with fully developed brains), it has been shown to have many healing effects and be particularly helpful for couples to have deep and caring conversations. It's best used a few times per year and not more than quarterly — in our experience.

By the time we found each other in the hangout lounge after dinner, we were both on the "come up" on our molly journey. So there we were – on our second night ever in the same place – on MDMA together.

Over the following six hours (8 p.m. to 2 a.m.), we platonically cuddled, talked for hours more, danced, and skipped around the property. Morgan thought I was nerdy, smart, cute, and a lot of fun.

Around midnight, Morgan took me over to the magical tree by the geodesic dome and told me, "Ryan, I am so happy we are getting to know each other. It feels so good to feel such a close connection with someone else platonically."

Platonically? I sure hoped not! I responded calmly, "Sure. Yes, it's wonderful," hoping in the back of my mind that this connection wouldn't be platonic for too much longer.

Of course, Morgan still had a boyfriend who was away in Chicago for the week. And so, for the weekend at The Mushroom Farm, it was to be a platonic, yet fun experience of deep connection.

After getting home, I wrote Morgan a six page letter detailing the vision I had for our lives (a lot of the things later became true, like living in international intentional communities together). This letter became the vision for our future relationship.

## The Vision For Our Relationship

Here's the text of the first letter I ever wrote to Morgan on May 21, 2019, just a few days after meeting her for the first time.

I wrote the vision for our future relationship, which has now come true as we live together in a community in Costa Rica.

As you read this letter, think to yourself, What is the vision for your current or future romantic relationship? Where do you want to live? Who do you want to live near? What shared purpose will you have?

> **The First Letter I Ever Wrote My Wife Morgan**
> **Sharing the Vision for Our Relationship**
> May 21, 2019
>
> Dear Morgan,
>
> I write tonight to tell you of my soul's deepest dream. It is why I chose to come back this time around to Earth. Unlike you, you see, I sense I haven't always been "human." I go from sentient planet to sentient planet. Each time, that planet is on the brink of a transformation in culture, a transfiguration in the evolution of the consciousness of the beings on that planet.
>
> We are at one of those key moments in human culture. We are moving in our lifetimes from an "us vs. them" culture of division across racial, national, and religious lines to a culture of massive adoption of the notion that "I am you." The Great Non-Dual Awakening is occurring now and it precedes The Golden Age that is nearing. The teal/coral tipping point (from

Spiral Dynamics) of 5% of the human population is nearing. This is exciting!

My dream, my vision, that I co-hold in joint aspiration with you and so many of our brothers and sisters is a human society based on love, in harmony with nature.

What does a global movement based on love look like? And why I am so clear that this is what is worth my devotion to?

Well, what I see ahead of humanity is a world filled with love, joy, playfulness, creativity, art, and safety... a world in which the feminine inside all of us is protected and valued and uplifted... a world in which we recognize that we are living in the most peaceful time in human history, that we are living in the most educated and literate times ever, that we are healthier than we have ever been, and that from a human development standpoint we have so much to be thankful to our grandparents and parents for. See the book *Factfulness* by Hans Rosling for more on this.

And yet, with all our external, technological, medical, and educational achievements we still face a crisis in the internal world. So many still feel loneliness, disconnection, and anxiety -- due to the cultural norms of the way we have chosen to live in nuclear family based fiefdoms. Each group of 3-6 with their own property, cars, and traditions.

The fundamental societal structure of community so important to blue zones, happiness, elder care, and a thriving life is in breakdown in much of the world as the churches, synagogues, mosques, temples, and gathering halls of our elders are replaced by lonely enclaves and an all encompassing obsession with work. We must bring our temples and gathering halls back -- and reinvent what values-centered communities based on mutual support, shared traditions, authentic relating, presence, kindness, new narratives of story.

We must re-integrate our elders with our children for the generational knowledge transfer. We must and get to re-inspire childlike wonder and play in 30, 40, 50, 60, 70, and 80 years olds! We get to create a world around us in which no ones has to feel alone anymore, in which all are welcome, in an environment based on joy, services, contribution, play, and love.

Further we face an environmental crisis. While humanity has temporarily flourished, this species' position on this planet is precarious. Our planet will thrive the next 3 billion years with our without us. But in the short term due to our impacts, we're nearing systemic collapse in both biodiversity and greenhouse gasses.

The solution is both the external technological innovations (carbon capture, electric vehicles, geoengineering, drone tree planting, renewable energy at scale), the public policy innovations (like a carbon price to capture its true externalities and costs) and a cultural solution (conscious media, intentional communities, activism) that integrate the internal spiritual and healing processes that are needed more than ever in a society moving faster than ever.

Reimagining community together in a place with others devoted to creating a beautiful life and a beautiful world is why I am here. I am here to innovate and create a new model for living in community: To reimagine how humans live, work, learn, play, and love. I'd love to do that with you.

I have a sense that you and I will soon be working on this together -- with many others -- perhaps even sooner than we can fathom -- perhaps in as soon as 4-8 weeks from now.

In this new community you will have your gardens, full of hundreds of different veggies, fruits, and herbs. We will rejoice in their presence and make them feel loved.

In this community you will have your art, we will have <u>so much art</u>. This beautiful, plentiful, and uplifting art will inspire us, anchoring truth, beauty, wisdom, joy, peace, expression, trust, laughter, connection, and freedom.

You <u>won't even need benefactors</u> because the way we will structure our community -- the businesses that we all run together will ensure everyone in the community can thrive, give their gifts, and do what they are meant to do on this planet.

I dream all of this with a pure heart. I have been preparing for what is coming now my whole life -- as have you. It shall be thrilling and joyful to see what emerges ahead.

Together we are more powerful than apart and together we can all hold the vibration for each other. There is no battle to fight any more. Only a song to be sung.

Yours in service to you and our joint aspiration,
Ryan P. M. Allis

P.S. - Your builders are almost ready. Welcome Queen Bee. It's time to rise in love.

      Two weeks after she received this letter, Morgan and her boyfriend had separated, and Morgan was staying at my apartment in San Diego for a wedding.
      We connected intimately — changing both of our lives forever. And within 24 hours, we were in a relationship with each other.

### Action Item #84: Your Relationship Vision

Read the example in this chapter and then write a letter in your notebook to your actual or future long-term romantic partner sharing the vision for your life with them in as much detail as you possibly can. What do you want to create together?

      We spent the first year of our relationship living between Los Angeles and Bali -- and traveling all over the world for events in Italy, Thailand, Maui, NYC, Puerto Rico, and Seattle.
      I was so sure about her that after only 40 days of dating, I asked her to marry me. She said yes, and we got officially   September 7, 2020 (fifteen months after starting to date). We'd planned to get married at Burning Man -- but it was canceled that year due to COVID, so we had a small 14 person wedding on Lake Tapps in Washington with close family and friends.

*Our Engagement Photo in Ubud, Bali in January 2020*

After a year of traveling the world together and visiting 40 cities, we moved together to Bali– and lived there for 18 months before establishing our American home in Boulder, Colorado, and our global home in Nosara, Costa Rica.

## Creating an Relationship Adventure Book

Morgan and I both had other partners when we met each other. But we recognized the intense, undeniable emotional, spiritual, and physical connection and sought each other out. I wrote her a seven page vision letter for our relationship before we got together – and she had sung a song to the trees describing the man she wanted just two weeks before I showed up.

She lived on a 650 acre farm in Pescadero, California, called The Mushroom Farm. I lived in San Diego. Thankfully, her cousin Jimmy was getting married in San Diego, and she needed a place to stay. She stayed with me, and the rest was history. The next day, we drove to LA together.

I then went to Morgan's former husband's house where she was staying, picked her and her dog Smash up, and we moved into the Fairmont Hotel in Santa Monica for a couple days where we figured out exactly where we wanted to live together.

What a scene – a fifteen pound Brussels Griffon Shih Tzu barking inside our room at the Fairmont Santa Monica so much that the front desk had to take care of her at the reception and call us to come back.

After getting relocated to another part of the hotel where the barking wouldn't disturb neighbors, Morgan went off on a very special mission on her own, leaving me with Smash.

She went to find our very first **Relationship Adventure Book**. We've had many relationship adventure books over the years. We fill the pages with illustrations and details of all the magical and wonderful experiences we've had -- so we can look back on them later.

*Relationship Adventure Book - A blank notebook where you draw and write your key memories together as a couple. We make one for each year.*

Below is an example of one of our relationship adventure books from 2021.

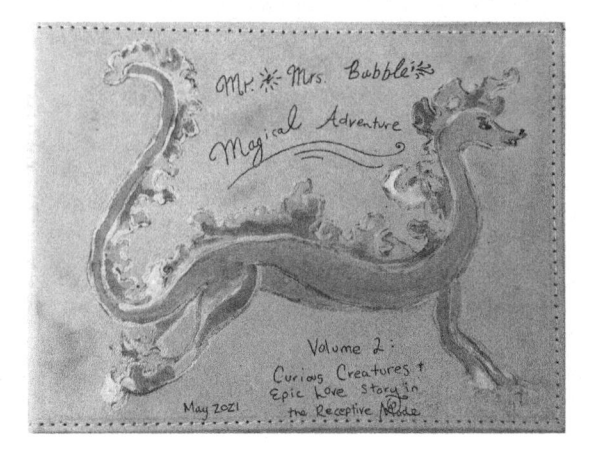

*Each year we start a new book. Here's a couple pages from the book so you can see how we capture the memories of our relationship.*

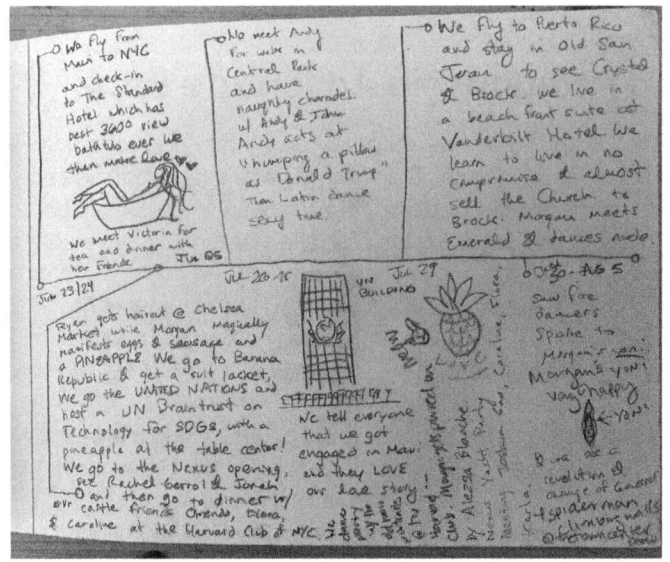

*A1 page from our relationship adventure book from our first summer together in 2019*

**Action Item #85: Create A Relationship Adventure Book**
Buy a leather bound notebook and make it your relationship adventure book. Every 30 days, get together with your partner for 30 minutes and have fun filling out the memories you've had together over the last month.

    Over the next year, we would visit Italy, Indonesia, Thailand, and over forty other cities together, going to festivals and hosting Hive events together.
    After 40 days of being together, I met her family in Seattle – and the very next day I asked her to marry me.
    We were in the Seattle airport about to go to San Francisco to present Hive to investors at the San Francisco Blockchain Society. We thought about it and decided we really

didn't want to go to San Francisco. We wanted to go somewhere new. We agreed we could go anywhere that was on the airport destination board. We looked up and saw that a plane was heading to Maui in 30 minutes. I asked her if she wanted to go to Maui. And she said yes. She then walked up to the customer service counter, and enrolled the lovely agent to switch our flights to go to Maui at no extra cost. It worked.

I was so inspired that I took out a $5 conch shell ring I'd been hiding in my backpack from when I bought it the week before, got down on one knee in the middle of the airport, and asked her to marry me.

She said yes.

I would ask Morgan to marry me three more times over the next eight months, each time with a slightly better ring. First in Maui with a humping pineapple gold ring, then at Hive with a bumble bee ring, then in Ubud, Bali, during our engagement photo shoot, and then in L.A. with a morganite ring.

She said yes every time I asked. Finally, we set a date to get married in September 2020 while at Burning Man.

And in February 2020, we had an engagement ceremony with our friends at our home in Los Angeles, where we lived at the time.

*Our Engagement Ceremony in Los Angeles, February 2020*

One of our good friends, the musician Gentle Sparrow, wrote this Engagement Song for us, capturing our love story, and performed it at our Engagement Ceremony in Los Angeles in February 2020.

### Our Engagement Song - Written by Gentle Sparrow

**Ryan Sings This Part:**
I saw your face in the swirling sand
A goddess in a desert land
I loved you long before I knew your name
Your hair was wild, your eyes were bright
And when the moon came out that night
I felt the spark ignite my heart in flames
And as it burns ever brighter
My eyes grow softer and my soul grows lighter
My hands grow stronger and my shoulders grow wider

**Morgan Sings This Part**
We build a home for everyone
In the beauty of the golden sun
And dance are dreams of heaven through the night And our circle grows forever into the light
You stumbled into my photograph
Dressed all wrong, you made me laugh
But I knew your heart was golden as your shoes
I took you home to my family
I've never seen them laugh so free
And the flower in my heart began to bloom

Cause I was born, I was born to be your man
And all around the world, roses line our way
Birds are singing, bells are ringing
At the dawn of every day

And as it opens to receive you
Brilliant colors blossom and deepen
Fragrance wafts out ever sweeter
Cause I was born, I was born to be with you

Sadly, Burning Man got canceled that year due to COVID, but we still got married in a beautiful small 14 person ceremony on September 7, 2020, at Lake Tapps, Washington. The vows we shared with each other that day are below.

## Steal These Marital Vows (And Customize Them)

I share our marital vows below in order to inspire you about what you want your marital vows to be. If you're already married, perhaps you'll find some vows you want to add. We wanted our vows to be a bit more customized than the standard: "I take you to be my wife/husband, to have and to hold from this day forward, for better, for worse, for richer, for poorer, in sickness or in health, to love and to cherish, until parted by death."

So, on the morning of our wedding day that September in Seattle, we each wrote our marital vows. It felt like I was channeling them for the 20 minutes I was writing. Here's what I came up with.

### Ryan's Marital Vows to Morgan

I promise to...

1. Love you unconditionally and into forever.
2. Create and hold a peaceful and joyous love bubble around us and our children
3. Be a great husband to you and a great father to our children
4. Be "The Loving Patriarch" of our family, into infinity.
5. Provide a stable and solid foundation for everything we create.
6. Build a beautiful world with you
7. Live with play, love, kindness, and joy
8. Dance with you everywhere we go
9. Take good care of myself
10. Reimagine how humans live, work, learn, and play with you
11. See you as magical and extraordinary
12. Share my vulnerability and my strength with you
13. Know my God-like nature and treat you as the Divine Goddess and Divine Mother that you are
14. Continually learn with you and from you as we expand into our divine nature
15. Encourage your sensuality and pleasure (with me and with others)
16. Build community with you everywhere we go.
17. Build joyous festivals that are celebrations of life with you.
18. Live with you globally and explore our world together as a family.
19. Create with you an Allis Family with values, traditions, and celebrations that last centuries.
20. Lovingly be with you and our family through any and all challenges and transform challenges into magic and play.

21. Joyously welcome you as the Matriarch of the Allis Family

Vow #15, to always encourage Morgan's sensuality and pleasure (whether with me or not), was an important one for Morgan.

Here are Morgan's vows that she wrote the same morning of our wedding.

## Morgan's Marital Vows to Ryan

I promise to...

1. Love you wholly.
2. Enjoy our beautiful world and life together.
3. Be soft with our hearts and be encouraging.
4. Be a beautiful, magical, divine mamma.
5. Be a wonderful loving wife, beloved, and Matriarch of the Allis Family.
6. Be a wild, loving, playful, stable mamma.
7. Create a wonderful life with us together into infinity.
8. Live in my magic and celebrate yours.
9. Always see our divine essence.
10. Honor our needs and vulnerabilities.
11. Keep creating a beautiful, playful, joyous, love story for us.
12. Nurture our love and love bubble every day for ourselves and our family.
13. Joyously care for myself and wholly be me and love me.
14. Embrace each challenge as an opportunity for more love and make what's important to you important to me.
15. Share what's important to me.
16. Joyously appreciate me and you each day.
17. Play with and love our community together and invite them into our beautiful world.
18. Lovingly honor our boundaries while keeping love in our hearts for all we care about.
19. Care for all that we create together.
20. Share our life with wonderful friends and family,
21. Be prosperous and share my dream and gifts with the world.
22. Be my Morgasmic self with your Roargasmic self.
23. Take care of our bodies.

Below are photos of the original handwritten vows – which are now framed in our home and hanging above our **love altar**.

Love Altar - a table or ledge that has your most important items related to your relationship or marriage.

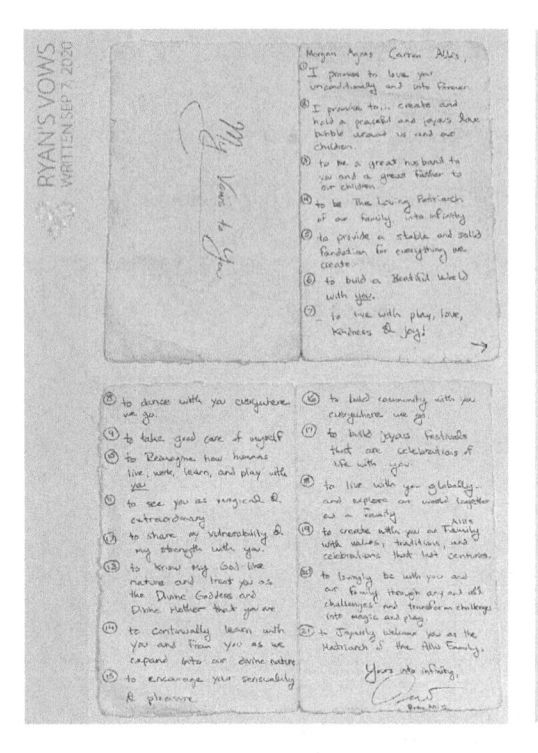

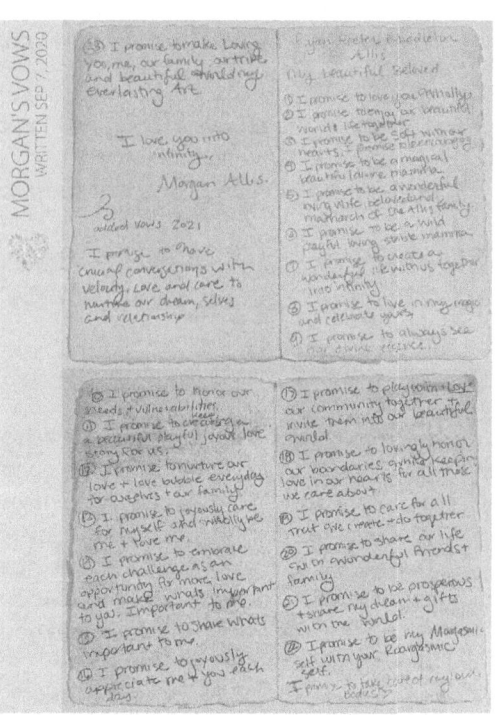

## Action Item #86: (Re)Write Your Marriage Vows

After reading this section, write down what you want your marriage vows to be -- for your current spouse if you're married or for your future spouse if you're not yet married. Put some real thought into them, and feel free to draw on the examples above.

# Reimagining Marriage, Family, & Divorce

*"Many years ago—as I endured a painful divorce—a respected mentor offered me this wisdom, for comfort during my crisis. 'This too shall pass.' It wouldn't seem like these four words could make a difference. Yet they totally did (and I remain most grateful to him for his generous advice). They were to me as balm on a tender lesion, serving to remind me about my brighter future. And of the reality that hard experiences never endure, but patient, steadfast people always will."* - Robin Sharma

Around 44% of marriages in the United States end in divorce. What Morgan and I have agreed to is to be together and live as husband and wife no matter what. Since our shared dream is to create a beautiful family – why would we ever want to separate and live in different houses. For us, we're committed to being committed for life.

Coming with this commitment, however, is openness and the encouragement of each other's pleasure, sensuality, and sexuality. If one of us is attracted to someone else – that's a good thing – not a bad thing. It's not a threat to our devotion to each other. And with total devotion comes total freedom.

If the sexual energy fades or you have an attraction to others, don't get divorced. The marital commitment is to living together and raising kids together – not to have sex only with each other. You can have other sexual partners – just keep your commitment to living under the same room so you can guide the kids together. The only good reason I can imagine for divorce is if you just cannot get along, no matter how much you try.

Morgan and I have reimagined marriage. One of my vows to her is to encourage her sensuality and pleasure – with me and with others. I have **compersion** – which means I want her to experience joy, pleasure, connection, play, and sensuality with me – and with other lovers. I get joy from knowing she's experiencing pleasure – regardless of who is giving it to her.

*Compersion - Experiencing joy when your partner experiences pleasure, even if it's not you giving them that pleasure. Opposite of jealousy.*

If something really threatens me, I can call a time out so we can talk and feel through it. But I rarely do that – as usually I'm really enjoying her experiencing pleasure, whether from a man, a woman, or a group.

Since we have a deep devotion and commitment to **always come back to each other,** and that's been proven time and again – I have no worry that she'll fall in love with someone else and leave me. We can add new lovers – but we've committed to always keeping our relationship primary and at the core. I will write more about this in the upcoming sexuality chapter.

This commitment is very important for the health of our family and the well-being of our children. It's very important for our children to know that their parents will always love each other, encourage each other, and continue to create the LuvBubble around them.

### What Most People Think Marriage Is

Living together, raising kids together, supporting each other, and committing to not having sensual or sexual relationships with other people.

### What We Think Marriage Is

Living together, raising kids together, encouraging each other's sensuality, supporting each other, helping each other grow, and committing to staying together no matter what

**Action Item #87: What Does Marriage Mean to You?**
After reading the above section, In your notebook, write down the answer to this question: What do you think marriage is?

## Divorce the Conscious Way

Morgan and I get along very well, and we love building a magic town in Costa Rica and creating and raising babies together -- so we do plan to stick together as primary partners far into the future. We don't anticipate ever getting divorced -- as there's no reason to. We love each other, our baby, our life, and what we're creating together.

That said, sometimes in relationships, it doesn't work out to last forever. Our friends Miki Agarwal and Andrew Horn recently had a conscious divorce. They have a son and plan to stay a family for life -- even though they are no longer married. Here's what they shared on Instagram after they announced their separation.

### Miki's intention for her new relationship with Andrew

Being the best parents to Hiro Being true homies for life who love and support one another Celebrating each other's wins and being there during the tough stuff Knowing that family is about a constant game of rupture and repair and love and rupture and repair and love. It's an ongoing dance. Being a phone call / short drive away if he ever needs me. Basically family for lyfe. Lezz go!

### Andrew's intention for her new relationship with Miki

I want us to... Build a coparenting dynamic that is loving, supportive and infinitely fun. Celebrate each other in becoming the most authentic, highest version of ourselves. Help each other to be the best parents we can be. Hold deep gratitude for the experiences that we have shared and all the ones that will come next. Anchor into the belief that our friendship and family will just keep getting better and better, forever and ever.

Now that's the way to go through a conscious divorce. There's no need for any animosity -- that just hurts the kids. If you do ever choose to shift out of a marriage, keep it loving and appreciate all that person has done to catalyze growth in you!

## What Love Means to Me

To me, the word LOVE is an acronym. Love stands for:

**L**AUGHTER
**O**PTIMISM
**V**IBRANT
**E**NERGY

This is certainly what I have always looked for in my romantic partners -- and what I've found in Morgan. To me, there are key elements to building a great relationship.

Tell the truth
Build trust
Be vulnerable

Give time
Follow through
Show care with your actions

Morgan and I definitely follow all six of these steps with each other.

You see, a great woman can make a huge difference to her partner. And a great man can make a huge difference to his partner.

The partner you choose to build a life with makes a huge impact on your ability to reach your potential, live with joy and positivity, and truly create a beautiful world around you and your family.

So look for an extraordinary partner -- an extraordinary best friend -- and an extraordinarily wonderful adventure mate.

But before you really start looking for *the one*, develop yourself first.

# Develop Yourself First

If you are ready for a long-term partner, put a lot of emphasis and intentionality into developing yourself first so that you are ready to attract the partner of your dreams. To find an extraordinary partner, it helps a lot to be extraordinary yourself first.

This doesn't mean you need to be perfect. But it does mean you need to be following your dreams, doing what you love, enjoying life, and being healthy.

To find a partner who is living their dreams, it helps to first follow your own dreams -- and live a **purpose-driven life** that you love.

Women look for men who are living their purpose and know who they are. Princes wander. But kings know. Kings know who they are and why they are here. And kings are working on what brings them alive every day.

Great women are looking for kings. And kings have created 'meaning' in their lives already. Great women aren't going to marry someone who doesn't know who they are or has resigned themselves to being stuck doing something they don't enjoy.

So re-read the earlier purpose chapter if you need to!

Similarly, most men are looking for women who are joyous, happy, and doing what they actually love.

I can't emphasize this enough -- the path of actually living your purpose will lead you to your long-term partner.

To find a partner who is living passionately, it really helps to first live passionately yourself. Make sure your life force is running inside of you. Spiritually alive people tend to attract other spiritually alive people.

Developing "self-love" is also critical to attracting your mate. Before you find someone else to love you, you must fall in love with yourself first. Self-love is critical to a successful relationship -- and it just can't be outsourced.

I like to say: to find a partner who is on the path to becoming a Jedi, you yourself must be on the path to becoming a Jedi. All kinds of crazy good shit happens in the universe when two Jedis marry.

Before I met her, Morgan had traveled Europe and Asia, become a black belt in Tae Kwon Do, studied tea service in Taiwan and meditation in Bali, sat with Ayahuasca, painted over 1,000 paintings, and attended two Burning Mans. She had "done her work."

She is truly extraordinary -- and the only way I attracted her was by being extraordinary myself -- and having a very clear vision for our relationship that she resonated with (having a family while traveling the world and living in communities with friends).

That six page letter I'd channeled describing the vision for our future relationship three days after we had our first conversation—before we were even dating was some bold, confident magic. And it worked.

At 34, because of the self-work and exploration I had done myself, I had a vision for our lives and our family that she was attracted to. She liked my **alpha clarity,** and so she decided to align her life with my life and create a family together with me—a big decision.

On my side, I was attracted to her **feminine omega**—her beauty, kindness, and softness—something that I was deeply missing in my life and hadn't yet been able to lock-in within myself.

## Develop Your Masculine & Feminine Skills

Regardless of your gender, it's exceptionally helpful to have fully developed both your **Alpha/Masculine** and **Omega/Feminine** energies inside of yourself prior to selecting your long term partner.

***Masculine (Alpha) Energy*** - *Builder, hunter, and protector energy that can create structure, think linearly, manage time, and be consistent.*

***Feminine (Omega) Energy*** - *Goddess and nurturer energy. Beautifier of spaces. Feeler. Emotional connection. Flowing. Bringer of the softness.*

If you can have a healthy internal masculine and a healthy internal feminine -- prior to meeting your partner -- so much more is possible.

For most people, it usually takes until at least around age 35 to fully develop these skills. They are incredibly helpful in both business and personal relationships.

| Alpha "Masculine" Skills | Omega "Feminine" Skills |
| --- | --- |
| Rational Logic | Emotional Mastery |
| Thinking with the Mind | Feeling With the Heart |
| Taking Action | Knowing The Right Action To Take |
| Building Structure | Creating a Vibe Inside the Structure |
| Business and Law | Art, Dance, and Music |
| Hustle | Flow |

| | |
|---|---|
| Hunting for Short Term Results | Farming For Long Term Results |
| Finding What is Needed | Caring For What You Have |
| Left Brain / Analytics | Right Brain / Creative |
| Earning Money | Nurturing a Community & Family |
| Protection | Play & Joy |

The alpha skills are focused on protection, building, and providing, while the omega skills are focused on caring, nurturing, and feeling.

The alpha mentality is strong, confident, assertive, and in control of the environment. An alpha energy has the ability to lead, motivate and inspire those around them. An alpha often takes charge in difficult situations, providing guidance and stability to those around him.

It is very important to say that the "alpha" skills aren't only for men and the "omega" skills aren't only for women.

**The fully developed human being works to master both alpha and omega skillsets.** Regardless of your gender, you want to be able to be a master of both skillsets to be able to move easefully through the various challenges and moments of life.

While men more traditionally are in charge of the "masculine" skills and women the "feminine skills," as an individual, you want to develop both energies fully. You want to be able to be a 10/10 on alpha skills and a 10/10 on omega skills – and you want to know when and where to put each skillset to work.

You can learn more about developing your alpha skills in David Deida's book, *The Way of the Superior Man*. You can learn more about developing your omega skills in the ISTA Level 1 course.

**Action Item #88: How Developed is Your Masculine & Feminine?**
Based on the above description, rate yourself on a scale of 1-10 on your masculine/alpha skill sets (10 = most developed) and your feminine/omega skill sets. Which skill sets do you want to develop?

# Creating Polarity in Your Romantic Relationship

Now, let's talk about polarity -- which is the principle that sexual connection is strongest when one person has more alpha energy and the other has more omega energy.

In romantic and sexual relationships, you want the **polarity** to be strong. Polarity is the push and pull of masculine and feminine energy that creates passion, excitement, and a sense of aliveness. For attraction to last, you want one partner to have more alpha/masculine energy and one partner to have more omega/feminine energy. Just like a magnet, for there to be lasting attraction, you need opposite energies.

*Polarity* - The push and pull of masculine and feminine energy that creates passion, excitement, and a sense of aliveness. In almost all romantic partnerships, there is one person who is more alpha and one person who is more omega. These opposite energies attract.

In nearly all romantic connections, one person is the dominant, more masculine energy, and one person is the more dominant feminine energy. People who have similar polarities (two alpha males, two omega males, two alpha females, or two omega females) rarely have sustained sexual chemistry with each other.

When the polarity is strong, there is a deep sense of connection and attraction between partners. However, when the polarity is weak or non-existent, the relationship can become stagnant, and the sexual chemistry can fade quickly.

Even in homosexual relationships, there is almost always one partner who is more masculine and one who is more feminine. Which are you usually attracted to?

If there's low polarity in your current relationship -- then it means there's an opportunity for one or both of the partners to learn to embody either more masculine or more feminine energies -- and to learn how to switch energies when needed.

In my own relationship with Morgan, I am the dominant energy about 90% of the time, and she is the dominant energy around 10% of the time. We switch, depending on how we are feeling and the needs of the moment. It's exceptionally helpful to our relationship that we can alternate who is dominant and who is receptive.

When I'm feeling tender and soft and want to express my emotions, I let her know, and she quickly switches into the alpha energy so that she can hold what I'm sharing rather than be swirled by it. But generally, as we walk through life, I am the dominant alpha who leads moment-to-moment. And she is my partner and counsel and helps us determine the longer term direction that we together lead our family in.

**Action Item #89: How is Your Polarity?**
How is the polarity in your current (or most recent) romantic relationship? What is working? What needs to shift? Who is the more dominant/masculine/alpha energy and who is the more submissive/feminine/omega energy most of the time?

## How to Find Your Romantic Partner

As I began to write this section about finding your romantic partner, the song "I Found You" by Calvin Harris and Benny Blanco just came on at my local Austin cafe. Here are the very appropriate lyrics:

| I Found You By Calvin Harris and Benny Blanco |
|---|
| I traveled many roads<br>And I know what road to choose<br>Now my world is never changing<br>There's anything I can do<br>'Cause I found you, I found you |

'Cause I found you, I found you
'Cause I found you, 'Cause I found you

Yes, the right life partner can make your life better, easier, and more enjoyable. It's worth it to invest years into developing yourself and years into the search for the right person.

The Greek Philosopher Plato encouraged people to find a life partner from whom they could learn and become a better version of themselves. .

Plato said that true love is when you admire someone. This means you should find someone who has good qualities that you don't have. If you spend time with that person, you can learn from them and become better too. The best person for you is someone who helps you become the best version of yourself.

Plato thought that a couple shouldn't just like each other the way they are now. They should work together to learn new things and be there for each other during tough times. Each person should want to make the other person better.

I had two strategies to find my person – and one of them worked. First, I started a "global community of purpose-driven leaders" called Hive.org. As the co-leader of Hive, I got to know everyone in the community who came through. I ended up meeting my last girlfriend before I got married through Hive (Danielle). But it was at Camp Mystic where I met Morgan.

As I wrote about earlier, I highly recommend getting deeply involved in a single community (whether it's a church community, a Burning Man community, a sports community, an arts community, a dance community, or whatever) and develop an earned reputation as a high-integrity leader of that community.

## How to Find Your Future Spouse

To find your long-term partner, get deeply involved in a community you're passionate about. That way, you'll meet all the other people in the community.

If you become a leader in a community you're passionate about, then you'll be the first to meet all the incredible people who come through -- and more importantly, everyone in the community will know you're looking for someone special, and they can help connect you with extraordinary people with similar dreams.

It's not an overnight solution if you're super picky like me -- but within 36 months of me getting deeply involved with Camp Mystic, my Burning Man camp, I met "the one."

So think about it – which community of people do you want to get really involved with—so involved that you're volunteering your time for free?

Is it your church, synagogue, mosque, or temple? Is it a co-ed sports league? Is it a festival? Is it a triathlon organization? Is it plant medicine, ecstatic dance, or tantra community? Is it a single parents community? Is it a YMCA or wellness center? Find your passion – find the organization that promotes the field you love – and then find others who also love what you love. Then ask the cute ones out on dates.

As Robin Sharma writes, "Your choice of relationship partner is one of the main sources of your success (or failure), joy (or misery), and tranquility (or worry)."

So invest that extra effort during the years you're actively looking for your partner. It will be one of the most important decisions you make in your life – so don't leave it purely up to chance–and don't wait for them to come to you. Write down exactly what you are looking for in a long term partner. And then go get them.

## 25 Tips to Win A Heart

Once you find your potential partner and start actively dating, turning them from a boyfriend/girlfriend into a husband/wife takes some intentionality and skill. Here are some tips I have on how to win the heart of your beloved for good.

1. Don't lead your partner on. Be open and transparent about your intentions with the relationship.
2. Follow the Golden Rule in all relationships.
3. Be playful and let the little kid inside of you out.
4. Have a shared purpose / relationship north star that you work on together. Ours is below.
5. See your partner as the future perfect version of themselves and hold space for and encourage their evolution and growth as they become the best version of themselves.
6. Give them lots of neck massages.
7. Never ever take them for granted
8. Never stop telling them you love them
9. Create shared goals together
10. Hold hands... a lot.
11. Never yell at each other (unless the house is on fire)
12. If someone has to win an argument, let it be your partner.
13. Never criticize. If you have to share feedback, do it very rarely and lovingly.
14. Never bring up mistakes from the past.
15. Never go to sleep mad.
16. At least once per day compliment your spouse.
17. Grab their butts... a lot. Turn this into a way of flirting with them where you are telling them indirectly that you want to have sex with them later on that day. Let them anticipate the upcoming sex all day.
18. When you've done wrong or said something with bad energy, admit it
19. Kiss.. a lot.
20. Go on walks... a lot.
21. Be your partner's biggest fan and encourager
22. Turn your home together into a temple for your relationship and later on for your family. Put up framed photos of all your key moments together. Create a sacred altar space in your bedroom that has special letters or objects that represent your love for each other.
23. Schedule weekly 2-3 hour sex temples to practice massage, tantra, and sex with each other. Put them on the calendar for every Sunday 5-8pm.
24. Take baths together (in big bath tubs) nightly and have deep conversations. Install an oversized bathtub in your house if you don't have one -- just for this purpose. It's worth it!

And this is the **one tip** that may change your whole life and romantic relationship for the better...

25. Learn how to deeply love your partners' bodies and souls by taking the Level 1 and 2 training with the **International School of Temple Arts (ISTA)**.

ISTA - The International School of the Temple Arts (ISTA), one of the world's best programs for learning tantra and connection with others. I recommend doing Level 1 and Level 2 on your own or with your romantic partner.

ISTA offers courses every year in beautiful places like Iceland, Turkey, Bali, Guatemala, Australia, Greece, Mexico, Costa Rica, Hungary, California, Brazil, Italy, Norway, and Ecuador. Level one is called the "ISTA Spiritual Sexual Shamanic Experience." Sign up today and get ready to take your lovemaking and sensuality to a new realm.

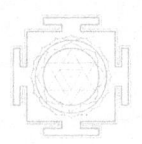

**Action Item #90: Sign Up for ISTA Level 1**
To develop your tantra skills and become more present with your partner(s), take the Level 1 course from the International School of Temple Arts (ISTA), held all over the world. If you like Level 1, you may want to take Level 2 afterwards.

## Create a Relationship North Star

Below is something Morgan just wrote and sent me recently--our **Relationship North Star**. I found it was worth sharing as an example of the types of exercises conscious couples go through. Fill one out for your relationship!

*Relationship North Star (n). - The shared purpose that you have for your romantic relationship.*

### Ryan & Morgan's Relationship North Star

To live and then popularize a new way of living, loving, learning, working, and playing based on community, presence, slowness, connection, depth, sensuality, and joy.

- To bring the LuvBubble realm of love, play, magic, and encouragement to life and share it with others.
- To be an epic sexy family living in their joy, creativity and soulful connection to life, love, community and each other.
- To reimagine how humans live, work, learn, love, and play and build a beautiful realm around us.

**Action Item #91: Create Your Relationship North Star**
Using the above example as a guide, write down your relationship's north star in your notebook -- for either your current relationship or a future desired relationship.

Morgan also shared the following with me recently, her thoughts on what our relationship needs to thrive. You can write the same type of document for your relationships and family.

> **What Our Relationship Needs to Thrive**
>
> At the center point of our relationship, what keeps our romance thriving and chemistry on fire is Tantra and health. We workout together, see nature, and challenge our bodies physically while we also hold our weekly sensual temple, up leveling our intimacy regularly while getting big doses of the chemicals that make us go boom boom. We also go to monthly sensual temple nights with our friends to deepen connections and keep things spiced up.
>
> To us, family looks like miracle mornings where the babies are running around and getting microdoses of our morning routines to learn from us, shared breakfast space, solo flow mojo! It includes working out, sauna, and yoga and meditation, and daily self care with good food, good hygiene, and daily movement.
>
> It looks like a daytime flow where we share new skills with Apollo, have nanny support, and go into our solo creative work! It looks like dinner time with the 'lil babe and play time, making memories and videos of the things we are learning, talent shows, and blessing food together.
>
> Dinner is always together with the whole family, except on date nights when we go out 1:1. Weekends are famliscious adventure and community bbq, waterfall hikes, and sports games. Saturday is banana pancake friend day, and Sunday is temple day.
>
> We go on family trips and vacations together, and we do learning expeditions and quests. We occasionally travel for fun projects, and at the core, weekends, mornings, and evenings are famliscious experiences for rituals and learning, connection, and love.
>
> For our inner selves to thrive, we need time to ourselves, time to build big projects (books and movies), and lots of family time to just be and love together. We always desire a very easy walkable safe environment and to be celebrated for the bigness we dream.
>
> We desire access to super clean organic food and water, a large, diverse community to play with, a few great deep friends, and snuggles and giggles daily. We take quarterly solo adventures on our own to keep ourselves renewed. Our lives are a joychevious sweet musical of fam love and epic romance with a big dream.

## Tips on Creating With Your Spouse (Holy Hell)

Holy shit, this is a hard one to get right. There are few things MORE TRIGGERING and GROWTH INDUCING than attempting to build a company with your romantic partner.
There's a constant ying/yang domination issue. Both parties want their ideas to be heard and to win. You can't really say no to your romantic partner's ideas; otherwise, your

sexual life together suffers. But if you don't say no, then you end up in a business that you don't actually want to build. Holy shit it's a fucking trap filled with spikes and spiders.

I failed miserably the first time I tried to collaborate with Morgan on building Hive in 2019. She wanted the brand color to be yellow. The brand color had always been red. I wanted it to be red. I wasn't going to change the fucking brand color. She told me it made her feel unsettled -- like blood or aggression. I told her it was red because Harvard and Stanford were red. She said that it needed to be yellow.

We kept trying. I had her come on stage to sing a beautiful song at our big annual event, and we attempted to host a 25 person entrepreneur retreat together, which was a bit of a hilarious mis-adventure in collaboration.

Imagine an uptight perfectionist (me) trying to work with a magical goddess who wanted an Australian actress to ride on a white horse around a candle lit flower labyrinth at dusk in the closing ceremony.

She won. She got the actress on the fucking horse and around the labyrinth. The shit actually worked. The horse actually made it around the labyrinth somehow, in one of the most spectacular displays of magic I'd ever seen. But I lost my goddamn mind trying to operationalize the un-operationalizable.

**How the fuck do you scale magic?**

Imagine a scalable systems focused Harvard MBA (me) trying to comprehend that my wife had hired a family circus performer troupe and a fire breathing melancholy clown comic to kick off the event. What the actual fuck. But it worked. It actually fucking worked.

She won. She got the fucking horse, the labyrinth, the circus troupe, and the melancholy fire breathing comic. The shit actually worked. But I lost my goddamn mind.

Then we moved to Bali (thankfully) just before COVID. We ended up in Ubud, Bali, living with 25 friends in a complex of ten homes during the craziness of the Spring of 2020. We called that time Poly in Paradise Season 1 for the amount of crazy love quadrangles that emerged in that unique time of lockdown. Someday that will have to be done as a Netflix special.

It nearly broke us up -- but our love shone through. We were meant (and I mean meant) to build something together. A family, a life, a fucking way of life. We were meant to bring this book, the community we're building in Costa Rica, and so much more to the world.

A few months later, we got married in America. We kept re-committing to creating together, no matter how much it would trigger us. We knew it was our destiny and held the vision to eventually create something truly special together.

We honeymooned in Croatia, then moved back to Bali for a year to get through the rest of the crazy COVID times when everyone seemed to have lost their minds.

We started collaborating together on Nuanu (www.nuanu.com), an incredibly innovative and unique coliving and arts community on the west coast of Bali that was just getting started at the time, in 2021. We played the informal role of bringing together all the initial collaborators for community connection and ideation (lots of cacao ceremonies!).

But after "perfectionist me" freaked out about -- get this -- the grammar of the worksheet she'd created -- I think she swore off working with me for a while. Her soul disconnected, and while she felt sad inside -- she decided that I was her "person" and that I was still right for her even if we couldn't play nice together professionally and creatively quite yet.

I went into an 18 month solopreneur hole -- working on SaaS CEO coaching and building Coinstack (a crypto newsletter) all by myself. We moved back to America, got pregnant with Apollo, and I became the workaholic American Fuckface working to build a crypto hedge fund with a friend for a while.

It wasn't until we decided to get married again with a big wedding that we actually had our FIRST TRULY SUCCESSFUL COLLABORATION.

This was our wedding, not a business -- so somehow it was easier to work together on it.

We'd had a 14 person small "Covid wedding" in 2020, but now it was time for the big wedding with all of our friends and family from around the world.

The theme for the wedding was "An Intergalactic Wedding." The marriage ceremony was performed as a one hour live opera -- complete with custom music, festival artist performances, violins by our bestie Claraty, beatboxing from Johnny Buffalo, and Amber Lily flying in from Boulder.

The wedding had a budget of $40,000. We ended up having 175 guests there. See the wedding website at www.intergalacticwedding.com to get a sense of what an incredible production it became. We charged our friends $111 to attend, so we could cover about half the costs.

Finally, we'd pulled something off that was truly exceptional and had come in on time and on budget. We'd somehow learned to work together.

In my heart, I was always hopeful that I'd figure out how to work with Morgan. She's a creative prolific artist, and epic producer. I just needed time to stabilize myself, heal, get over my own shit, kill my ego a bit more, and get ready to work with her.

So what's the key to the whole shabang? What's the magic to working together with your spouse?

Well, it's simple. Follow these three rules.

1. Don't try to professionally collaborate with your spouse unless you're ready for the most epic growth phase of your life.

2. Make sure before you start collaborating on a business that your relationship is already on very solid ground and you've created the ability to communicate exceptionally well about difficult topics. Read the book *Crucial Conversations*. It will help. Also make sure your sex life is really good before you start working together -- and work to keep it that way.

3. Establish very clear guidelines for WHO'S THE ALPHA OF WHAT AREA. Make sure you know in advance who the ALPHA is for each part of the business. Once we figured out who was the alpha/dom and who was the beta/sub for each area -- things started flowing. This was the thing we didn't know how to do initially. We both tried to be the dom 100% of the time initially -- which obviously didn't work because two doms can never play nicely unless they know when to sub.

Read rule #3 again, as that was the magic. Now read it one more time and let it seep into your brain.

So that was the key. For everything we've created since -- we now know to establish in advance who gets to make the final decisions.

For LuvMonsters, Inc. -- the animation, music, and stuffed animal business -- she's the alpha. I'm the advisor. She gets the final call. I help. I live with it if she makes a decision I don't immediately love.

For personal growth books like this one and our live courses -- I'm the alpha. She advises. I make the final calls. She lives with it if I make a decision she doesn't immediately love.

We still have conflict, but it's **constructive conflict** instead of **destructive conflict**.

*Constructive Conflict - Conflict that is honest yet still kind, where the result is people feel heard and the relationship gets stronger.*

*Destructive Conflict - Conflict that is so energetically off that it causes the relationship between those in conflict to get weaker over time.*

We're not yet perfect, but we're getting damn good at flowing and creating together.

So there you fucking go. How to create with your spouse Good fucking luck. You'll need it. But if you can crack the nut, and keep at it, then true, extraordinary magic is possible. The type of masculine and feminine magic that created the Universe, Earth, humanity, and all that is great in the world.

So yes, let's scale some fucking magic, babe. Let's not just make an epic family. Let's build a Magic Town, and let's get all of our gifts out into the world.

## Relationship MDMA Ceremonies

Overusing MDMA (known informally as Molly) can wreck your serotonin levels and lead to memory, attention, and decision making challenges. Research suggests that using MDMA more than a few times a year can increase the risk of developing negative consequences such as depression, anxiety, cognitive impairment, and addiction.

With that proper warning out of the way, using it about every 3 months as part of an intentional ceremony with your romantic partner can be extremely helpful. Doing it on the Solstices and Equinoxes is a very special way to bring in the new season into your lives and heal anything from the past 90 days.

For a couple years before we got pregnant with Apollo, Morgan and I would do an Relationship MDMA Ceremony every quarter or so (we stopped due to pregnancy, and now she's on a sober kick at the moment as she focuses on creating the script for her animated film LuvMonsters, which I deeply respect).

There are many trained relationship counselors and therapists who now use MDMA with their couples. So you can do it with just the two of you or have the session facilitated by a therapist. Just google "MDMA-assisted relationship coaching" or "MDMA Therapy" for your city, and you'll probably find some interesting options. Or ask around with your festival friends.

*MDMA Therapy - Guided therapeutic use of MDMA with a trained practitioner as an aid in couples relationship counseling. MDMA can increase feelings of empathy and connection with others. It is known as the love drug and can sometimes help couples listen, open up, and connect more deeply.*

The MDMA ceremonies Morgan and I did together led to beautiful connections between us, 4-6 hours of deep healing conversation each time, a deepening of our relationship and love, the ability to work through any challenges and heal the recent past, and the ability to make plans for the next quarter of our relationship.

After approximately an hour from the initial administration of MDMA, serotonin levels in the brain experience a significant increase. This surge in serotonin plays a key role in uplifting mood and enhancing perception. The release of oxytocin follows, which contributes to a reduction in fear and stress levels while promoting feelings of trust and fostering a sense of connection with others.

We were also able to have some very life changing conversations about the deeper nature of the universe, the soul, and our higher selves.

There has been growing interest in the use of MDMA-assisted psychotherapy for treating PTSD in veterans and other trauma survivors. Preliminary research suggests that MDMA can enhance the therapeutic process by reducing fear and anxiety and increasing empathy and trust between the patient and therapist.

One of the most notable studies in this area was conducted by the Multidisciplinary Association for Psychedelic Studies (MAPS), a non-profit research organization that aims to develop MDMA and other psychedelic substances into legal prescription medicines. In this study, veterans with chronic, treatment-resistant PTSD received three sessions of MDMA-assisted psychotherapy over the course of 12 weeks.

The results showed that 68% of participants no longer met the criteria for PTSD after treatment, and the effects were sustained at a 12-month follow-up. Additionally, participants reported significant improvements in depression, anxiety, and quality of life.

The research is demonstrating that it is beyond time that MDMA be reclassified from a Schedule I drug into a controlled and regulated prescription medication. Schedule I drugs are those with no known medical benefit -- and that is no longer true with MDMA.

It's absolutely ridiculous that adults have to go to drug dealers to obtain such helpful medicine that, when used properly, can do so much good. Requiring people to technically commit a crime to repair and strengthen the relationship bonds is fucked up. At least decriminalize it and make it available at certified therapy centers for infrequent use!

## Our Guide to Open Relating

Morgan and I together wrote this below guide to open relating to share our lessons learned for anyone who is simply curious – and for couples who may want to consider an open relationship or open marriage for themselves.

As we shared above, our shared purpose/dharma as a couple is to help reimagine how human beings live, love, learn, and play -- and to share the lessons we learn as we live an "alternative lifestyle" of semi-nomadic and sensual living.

We are in an open relationship -- meaning that we can have emotional or physical intimacy with others. Some people call this Ethical Non-Monogamy (ENM) -- others call it polyamory (aka "poly"). The key is to have clear communication about the open relating, and not hide it.

A lot of our friends have asked us for tips on making an ENM relationship work well, so we decided to write this guide to open relating together. Our hope is that this can be used as a guide to make it easier for you to either decide you want to actually be monogamous with your partner or to make it easier to make open relating work for you.

Some people use the term open relating when they are dating and having sex with multiple people. If you're not in a committed relationship with anyone, however, we just see that as casual open dating, but not open relating. People in their early 20s, for example, are often masters at casual dating with few strings attached – but rarely masters at long-lasting open relating.

True open relating comes in (in our view) when there's at least one solid main committed relationship – and others are added on top of that solid foundation.

## The Most Common Types of Open Relating

About 20% of the US population has practiced some form of consensual non-monogamy at some point in their lives, such as polyamory or open relationships – and 4-5% of American adults are in a polyamorous relationship currently.[24] The most common types of polyamory include:

1. Stable dyad with shared lovers - 2 people in a committed relationship with alternating shared thirds (common when one or more of the partners is bi-curious or bi-sexual)

2. Stable dyad with individual lovers - 2 people in a committed relationship, who separately date others

3. Stable triad - 3 people all in a committed relationship with each other, who all share sensual energy and raise children together

4. Stable quad - 4 people (often two couples) who all share sensual energy and sometimes live together and raise children together

There are all kinds of variations in the realm of polyamory – but there is, by definition, not a lot of plain vanilla going on – it's more like Rocky Road Ice Cream mixed with strawberry ice cream inside of a banana split.

## Our Form of Marital Relationship

In our case, we are currently a stable dyad (a married male and female couple) who have both individual lovers and shared lovers from time-to-time.

We are each other's primary partner, or main partner. We have other lovers in different parts of the world that we see from time to time as we travel and adventure. We date others both together (when we are both interested in them) or separately (if just one of us is feeling it).

We have a devoted partnership with each other, an active sex life with each other, and are also free to have sensuality and sexuality with other people.

---

[24] Prevalence of Experiences With Consensual Nonmonogamous Relationships: Findings From Two National Samples of Single Americans, Journal of Sex & Marital Therapy Volume 43, 2017 - Issue 5

From our perspective, the desire to have sex with other people in addition to your primary partner seems very human, very natural, and very normal.

How to actually do it well, however, ethically and lovingly, while keeping a thriving marriage — now that takes some practice, nuance, trust, and good communication and often leads to growth.

Open relating may not be the easiest path -- but we've found it to be the most fun, fulfilling, and one that keeps bringing us back to each other.

Yes, We're still learning. The moment you pretend to be an expert in this dynamic, ever changing field is the moment your whole world shifts.

That said, we have learned some good tips that we will share below that will hopefully be helpful to people who are curious about open relating. Here are some of those tips and lessons.

We believe that no person (even one you're married to) possesses, owns, or should control your sexuality. We find it a bit silly that many married people try to control access to the genitals of their partners – often to disastrous effects.

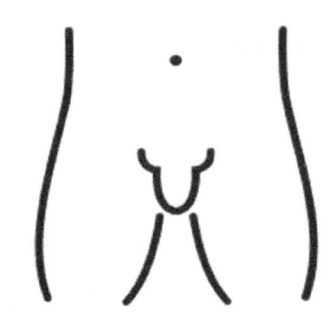

*Now, that we're married we control access to each other's genitals, right?*

**Key Lesson:** *If you repress a person's sexuality permanently, a part of their soul, a part of their vigor, a part of their spark often dies.*

When a person's choice is to either cheat and lie, repress their innermost desires to express themselves, or to lose their family – it's a lose/lose/lose scenario that has led many men and women to internal despair and separation.

It's one thing to ask your partner to slow down external connecting while you make your primary relationship thrive (that's fine in our view)

It's another thing to ban them from ever sensually touching another person and act like you control access to their body (that's not okay, in our view, unless both of you agree to it fully).

We believe that the only person who should control who touches your body is you. We believe in genital freedom, not genital control. We believe that more touch (a lot more touch, actually) would be a great thing for human beings and society in general.

While not everyone wants to be in a stable, open, loving relationship (many people are actually totally happy being with one person sensually for decades) – we do believe that everyone who does want to explore ethical non-monogamy should have that opportunity without shame, without it being a crime, and without risking losing their family or home.

What's important is that the family unit stays intact, especially when kids are involved.

Just because someone else touched your partner's vagina or penis doesn't mean that a family unit needs to separate. Celebrate your partner's explorations – while demanding that they please you as well and requesting that they use any needed precautions to keep sexually healthy (condoms, STI tests, vasectomies, etc.).

While some do actually prefer monogamy, getting married should not mean, by definition, that you're committing to only touching the genitals of one person for 50 years. Instead, it should mean that you're committing to being each other's primary sexual partner, living together, and building a family together (if you choose). Primary sexual partner, not an exclusive sexual partner.

## Full Devotion & Full Freedom

We believe in having full devotion and full freedom within our marriage. We've found that there is a correlation between the amount we are devotedly in love with each other, the health of our own sex lives with each other, and how safe we feel when our partner is intimate with others.

If your partner isn't feeling good about you connecting intimately with others, one of the reasons may be because they feel like you aren't intimately connecting with them as much as they desire.

**Key Lesson:** *For open relating to work — you have to first ensure that your core primary partnership is healthy.*

If things aren't feeling good / right in our relationship with each other — we stop exploring externally — and first come back to the center to make our primary partnership right before continuing to explore with others.

We've found that the more devoted we are to our long-term union and family -- the easier it is for us to feel at ease with our partner's full sensual expression with others.

## Make the Primary Relationship Solid First

So if you already have established a frequent and deep sexual and sensual relationship with your primary partner, THEN it becomes possible to bring in external players into the dynamic — for both additional learning and additional fun.

Things tend to go off the rails and end up in misery when a strong sexual and emotional foundation with your partner is not built first. People (especially women, but all genders) need to know that their partner is not going to leave them if they have sex with another person. This is the deepest fear — the fear of being replaced.

So, long story short — if your core relationship isn't solid — you may want to work on making that relationship fantastic first before you open it up to other energies. Maybe work with a relationship coach on the emotional connection or bring in a tantrika into your relationship bedroom to work on helping the two of you connect sensually at a 10/10 level.

Many look for external connections when their primary partnership is not working. We *only* look for new external connections when our primary marriage is *thriving*, which thankfully is most of the time.

The greater the devotion to our long-term bond, the easier it is to feel comfortable both exploring and encouraging each other to explore -- and then to bring back the juicy learnings to each other.

Here are six prerequisites to consider opening up to others' energies:

1. Good frequent (2x/week or more) sex with primary partner (presuming both of you still want to have sex with each other)
2. Deep emotional bond and trust with primary partner
3. Open communication and trust with each other
4. Desire to see your partner have all their desires & growth edges met
5. Desire to bring back what you learn into your primary sex life
6. Willingness to go slow and pause open relating when necessary

If any of these elements are not in place, it's a recipe for a blown up relationship rather than something fun and sexy.

The Camp at Burning Man we met through -- Camp Mystic -- is known for being a camp of quite a few non-traditional couples -- and so it isn't a surprise we are open.

I joined this camp in 2016, and this camp was where I first found models of married couples who were open about being open, including Camp Co-Leader Jennifer Russell and her husband Bryan Franklin, who were the inspiration behind the well known Android Jones "Union" artwork, made of their marriage and popularized within festival culture.

An Android Jones painting of our friends Bryan Franklin and Jennifer Russell

Morgan ended up in this same Burning Man Camp in 2018, and that's how we originally found each other — seeing each other from across the playa desert on the last day during Exodus, when everyone was breaking down the camp.

We started our relationship open, then we closed it while Morgan was pregnant (to make it feel safer for her during that tender time), and now we have opened it up again.

So in the five years we've been together, we've been "open" for about four of those years—at various stages of openness.

We've both had other lovers. Morgan's had one other male lover so far, a couple female lovers, and I've had one other female lover. We've also had quite a few "threesomes" and sexualities in the same rooms as others.

We recognize that we don't have to be absolutely everything for each other, emotionally or physically. Yet we have a strong desire to only have children with each other. So we do take some precautions to maximize that likelihood (like using condoms in the case of having vaginal sex with others to minimize the chance of both pregnancy and STIs).

We are both open to having other lovers -- some that last for just a night -- and some that may continue for decades. It's the long term lovers that can be the most emotionally meaningful – while the short term lovers can add the most spark and opportunity to explore a new fantasy.

## Well Known Open Relaters

From Warren Buffet to Will Smith to Angelina Jolie – there are many well known people past and present who have been open about being open (and many more who tried to hide it). Here's a few quotes on open relating that are worth reflecting on as you think through which type of relationship structure you want to have.

- "I doubt that fidelity is absolutely essential for a relationship. Neither Brad nor I have ever claimed that living together means to be chained together. We make sure that we never restrict each other." - Angelina Jolie

- "The experiences that the freedoms that we've given one another and the unconditional support, to me, is the highest definition of love." - Will Smith

- "I don't think it's natural to be a monogamous person. It's something I have a lot of respect for and have participated in, but I think it definitely goes against some instinct to look beyond." - Scarlett Johansson

- "I don't know if anyone is really naturally monogamous. We all have the same instincts as animals. But we live in a society where it's been ingrained in us to do these things." - Cameron Diaz

- "Do I think human beings are meant to be in 40-year-long monogamous, faithful, relationships? No, No, No. Whoever said they were? Only the Bible or something." - Hugh Grant

- "We became polyamorous without ever really trying, and we let each other go so often; I guess we finally realized it's the reason we are impenetrable." - Nico Tortorella

- " I think we're in a day and age where there should be no rules except for the ones designed by two people in a partnership — or three people, whatever floats your boat! But there has to be a level of responsibility in any relationship dynamic, and that responsibility is simply honesty and communication and trust. Apart from that, it's really none of our business what people choose to do with their lives." - Shailene Woodley

- "Sometimes in a relationship, people can't always get what they need, and if you have reputable people you can turn to in order to get what you need, I say go for it. It is a whole lot better than being frustrated and angry at the person you love." - Whoopi Goldberg

Other well known people who have been open relaters include former U.S. Presidents John F. Kennedy, Bill Clinton, and Franklin Roosevelt, billionaire Warren Buffet (who openly had two partners until one passed in 1977), psychologist Carl Jung; as well as Alfred Kinsey, the father of modern sex research. Philosopher Bertrand Russell, who wrote the 1929 classic *Marriage & Morals, and existentialist* Jean-Paul Sartre both had multiple long-term partners.

## Some Potential Benefits of Open Relating

While it's not for everyone, some of the benefits of open relating in our experience include:

1. **More Fun** - Both the fun of actually connecting with others as well as the fun of the pursuit of meaningful connections.
2. **More Close Friends** - It's just more interesting to make friends when you never know where it may lead and there's a possibility of both emotional and physical intimacy
3. **More Aliveness** - For people who enjoy variety (creative/entrepreneur/artist types), it's often this pursuit or experience of something new that keeps up the most alive.
4. **More Invigorated Spouse** - When sexual energy is running freely and not restricted or shamed magic can happen within someone's soul)
5. **More Sex** - Both with your primary partner AND with your other partners.
6. **Better Health** - You and your partner are extra incentivized to keep your bodies healthy and looking good for themselves, you, and their other potential partners.
7. **More Sexy Vacations** - There's nothing more fun than a week in a beautiful place like Cabo, Costa Rica, or Canggu with a few couples you love!
8. **More Personal Growth** - You might just be surprised how much personal growth is possible when you experience your first Berlin leather sex dungeon or Los Angeles GHB orgy. It's not for everyone, but maybe it's for you?

The biggest downsides of open relating are that you're continually on a path of growth — and that can be uncomfortable at times.

Open relating is NOT the easy path — but it can be the most fun and growth inducing path. Just remember to be willing to slow things down when necessary to get your core relationship thriving again.

We're not looking to have multiple husbands/wives -- we just want **one intact family unit of husband/wife/children**.

While originally we thought about us potentially having other husbands/wives — that got complicated too quickly, especially in a relationship where we move around a lot between Bali, Costa Rica, Australia, Europe, and America.

We wanted our core family unit to be clear and consistent — with other lovers being something we sometimes experience when we happen to be in the same place.

So family trips usually just involve me, Morgan, and Apollo (and sometimes a nanny). And we'll often meet up with friends or lovers wherever we go – but only rarely bring them with us.

## How Monogamy Led Me to Lose My Sex Drive

When Morgan (my wife) got pregnant in September 2021, she asked me not to have intimate relations with other women while she was carrying her child — as there were too many changes going on in her body and she wanted me, understandably, to be focused on her. It was something she'd never been through before.

However, there were some major repercussions on my soul from asking me to not connect sensually with anyone else for about a year. I went from a happy, joyous, playful, and sexually expressed Ryan to a serious, robotic, and repressed Ryan.

You see, when we moved back from Bali to America in 2021, I took a consulting role at a crypto hedge fund. This role ended up being very stressful.

By the end of the pregnancy, I was spending a lot of time on Zoom calls having conversations with potential investors. Over the course of a few months, I gained 30 pounds, started wearing collared shirts, and had turned into the "American Fuckface" that I wrote about earlier in the book (who was getting to be an obese workaholic America who had lost connection to his primal energy).

Because she was in the later stages of pregnancy, we weren't having sex. Things got so bad that we ended up moving back to Bali so we could reduce stress and living costs and learn from some very talented tantrikas. We also opened up our relationship again. Immediately, I was excited to lose the weight, and my primal energies came back online. I went from 190 to 150 in four months, and I was engaged and excited by life again – no longer sacrificing my body and spirit and repressing my sex drive in order to "be a good husband and "create financial stability for my family."

Monogamy caused me to lose my sex drive, overwork, and to even lose some of my passion for life itself. For the next pregnancy, we will likely stay open in some form so that this level of inner self-repression doesn't happen again.

## The Key Lessons We've Learned About Open Relating

While open relating isn't for everyone -- knowing the right lessons to do it well can help. We've learned a lot along the way--and it hasn't all been rainbows and unicorns. There have been some difficult moments—such as when we broke off our engagement for three months in the Summer of 2020 (more on that in lesson #3 below). Here are some of the most important lessons along the way, most of which we've learned through trial and error...

1. **Start Slow** - We're on a 50+ year journey together, there's no need to hurry anything. As long as the destination was clear (full freedom to explore sexually and sensually within complete devotion to each other), it was totally fine if it took us 2-3 years to get there (which it did). Maybe start with a threesome or making love in the same room as another couple you know. Consider building up to having sex with other people over the course of a year or two after creating a very strong foundation with each other.

2. **Talk About It Up Front** - If you're interested in open relating as a possibility, it's probably a good idea to talk about it up front. We talked about it in our very first conversation actually. Open relating tends to work best when both people in the relationship are willing to give it a try, when neither are in a huge hurry for something to happen, and when both partners realize that it only works in the long term if the core relationship is thriving first. If you're already in a marriage/relationship where open relating hasn't yet been part of the conversation - you can ease in by doing things like going to a conscious festival like Burning Man or Envision, reading the book *The Ethical Slut* together and then talking about it openly, or perhaps by taking some MDMA together as a couple either in a clinical setting or at your home and sharing your desires and fantasies (2-3 MDMA sessions per year in an intentional 6-8 hour container of love can do wonders for a marital relationship!).

3. **Pause Whenever Necessary** - When we were engaged in 2020 and living in Bali, we both had sex with other lovers. At the time, me having sex with another person (the first such person in our relationship) caused Morgan enough challenges that she asked me to pause and slow down. When I chose to keep going with my lover (thinking to myself "we're in an open relationship, why should I stop being with other people"), Morgan chose to end the engagement and relationship. It took an ayahuasca ceremony, a mushroom ceremony, and 90 days for us to re-find each other. The lesson: when your partner asks you to pause or slow down, you do it. Sometimes these pause may be days, sometimes they may be months — but *you have to get your primary relationship thriving again before resuming*.

4. **Consider Pausing During Pregnancy** - When we got pregnant we took 12 months off from sexually interacting with others (the pregnancy plus 3 months post birth). Why? Well we learned that being pregnant and bringing a new baby in is a tender time and it was good to have attention focused on taking care of Morgan and our newborn during that unpredictable phase. That doesn't need to be the case for everyone — but that's what we chose to do.

5. **Be Clear With Other Partners That You Are Taken in the Primary Department** - One of the biggest challenges in open relating is other sexual partners attempting to separate the primary partnership — so that they can establish themselves as the alpha mate. Other sexual partners need to know in advance that you are "fully taken" and aren't open to that — otherwise, things can get disastrous very quickly and hearts can get hurt. Make sure anyone connecting with you knows you have a long term primary partner you are deeply in love with (if that is in fact the case).

6. **Create a Policy of "Family Together Always"** - With your primary partner/spouse, make it clear (if it is in fact true), that you are wanting to build a long-term stable partnership with them and that no matter what happens, you will always come back to them and bring back your learnings. Create the feeling in your partner that the family is always together and that there will always be an environment of care, affection, love, and encouragement between the two of you. This is even more important if you have children together. You want the children to grow up, whenever possible, in a loving, caring, encouraging, and stable home. No matter what other lovers get added or subtracted — the core family unit always sticks together.

7. **Start With Sensual Massages Or Being in the Same Room With Friends -** We started our open relating journey in 2019 with receiving Yoni/Lingam massages from tantric friends of ours. You could do that with a friend or find an experienced provider from the tantra section of Eros. That felt like a safe way to start. Other good ways to start include having a couple friends that you have sex in the same room with — and perhaps make out with. Over time, you can ramp up to more if you all feel comfortable.

8. **Bring Sexual Learnings Back to the Core -** One of the benefits of interacting with others is that it can teach you skills that may be helpful to bring back into your primary sexual relationship (such as sub/dom energy play, shibari, tantra, Kama sutra, role playing, massage, and much more). Bring whatever you learn back to your primary partnership.

9. **Create a Weekly Temple Night -** We have set aside 4-7pm on Sundays, every week, for sacred temple time for just each other. We even get a babysitter for this time. This allows us to have slow, connected, sexy time with each other every single week — and ensures that at the very very minimum our bodies are connecting in deep intimacy weekly. Sometimes one or both of us may take a micro dose of GHB at the beginning of these sessions for extra juiciness and connection.

10. **Don't Try to Be Everything For Each Other -** It's not really possible for one human being to be absolutely everything for another human being. If you're already their best friend, sexual partner, spouse, roommate, and co-parent — do you really need to also be their Shibari teacher, Tantra teacher, or BDSM daddy? You could be — but someone else might enjoy some of those roles more than you. Don't feel like you need your primary partner to be everything. They might prefer slower, energetically nuanced sex while you might enjoy rough domination from time-to-time. All that is perfectly okay within the realm of open relating.

11. **Encourage Each Other To Flirt With Others -** Once you feel safe that your partner is not going to leave you if they have sex with someone else (the most common fear) and are ready to open up — encourage your partner to go have intimacy with others if they wish. Cheer each other on when you have a sexy experience. And tell each other about the best parts and the parts you want to bring back into the main relationship!

12. **Be Fully Honest With Each Other At All Times -** This one is self-explanatory. It's a recipe for disaster if you have to hide things from each other.

13. **Practice Compersion -** To the extent possible, practice compersion, which is the opposite of jealousy. Compersion is when you experience joy and authentic happiness from your partner getting loved up by another human being. We love when our partners feel pleasure and get loved up on especially well by someone else — especially if there's something we can bring back into our main relationship. An advanced practice (not for month one!) is actively watching your partner have intercourse with another person, and working to turn any feelings of jealousy or insecurity into feelings of joy that they are experiencing joy and pleasure.

14. **Talk Openly About Crushes -** Eventually, you'll get to the point when you can both talk openly about crushes on other people. It's fun for me to hear about the people Morgan likes, and vice versa.

15. **Play Together & Separately** - Some open couples prefer to only play together. We are open to both playing together (in the same room) or playing separately. It's often when we play separately that we learn the most about ourselves and have the most juiciness to bring back to our primary sexual relationship.

16. **Go to Play Parties Together -** We've found that all cities (at least in those in America and Europe) have "play party" communities of adults who like to have sex in front of each other — and sometimes share partners. We've been part of these types of sexual conscious communities in places like San Francisco, Los Angeles, Boulder, Austin, and Bali. If you join the local Burning Man community wherever you are, they are pretty easy to find. We much prefer "Burner conscious sensuality parties" which commonly are alcohol-free experiences and have clear guidelines on consent. Going to festivals like Burning Man and/or the regional burns is also an easy way to start getting invited to these sexy gatherings.

17. **Use Apps Like Feeld to Explore -** If you can't find your local sensuality parties immediately, you can always start your own by getting on an open dating app like Feeld and connecting with other open couples and singles. Maybe start a WhatsApp group for all the open couples in your area that you like — and then throw a couples play party to get them all together. That's a fun and easy way to meet 10-20 open sexy people in a week or two. In any town, there are underground communities serving this need for sensual expression without judgment, you just have to find them—or create them.

18. **Don't Use Polyamory to Fix Something Missing Within Yourself** - My mom passed away from brain cancer in 2012, when I was 27. So from age 27-34 I was on a journey to find a romantic partner who could "replace" the love I got from my mom. After living in the SF Bay Area and being exposed to Burning Man culture, I thought that open relating was the key to never again "quickly losing" the feminine in my life. If I had two or three partners/lovers, I'd never be without the feminine, he thought. I later realized I had to self-source that feminine love and self-care within myself. Only once I learned how to do that in 2020 (through a 2nd ayahuasca journey) was I ready to marry the love of my life, Morgan, and actually have a healthy, non-clingy relationship to open relating. It's sexy when you're not needy and can let sensuality and connection evolve naturally over time rather than forcing them to happen quickly to fill a gap inside of you.

19. **Delight Your Partner -** Sometimes when you meet someone new and exciting you can focus too much energy on them — leaving your main partner wishing you were spending more time romancing and delighting them. So even when you are dating others, be sure you are putting the majority of your romantic time and energy on your primary partner. Ensuring that you have a weekly romantic date on the calendar with your primary partner is a helpful step.

20. **When You Get Married, Make Your Marriage Vows Very Intentional -** We wrote out the day before we got married our vows to each other. I had 21 and Morgan had 23 vows. Consider including in your wedding vows that you read aloud at your wedding ceremony something like, "I promise to always encourage your sensuality and pleasure" instead of the more traditional implied vow of "I promise to never have sex with other people.

While open relating isn't for everyone and certainly isn't always easy -- or linear -- for us, we've found it fun, growth inducing, meaningful, and additive to our lives -- and it has certainly added to our health and vibrancy as creative beings.

**Action Item #92: Desired Relationship Structure**
Based on what you've read above and your own experiences, what type of relationship structure are you most interested in and why? Write this down.

Lastly, in this chapter, I'll leave you with one of Morgan's Principles of Living - devoting fully to living a life filled with love.

> **Morgan's Principle for Living #6 - Devote to A Life of Love**

I am devoted to love. I am devoted to loving my family, my partner, and myself. In this love lives my wealth, my well being, my satisfaction, my pleasure, and my happiness. Calling upon my devotion will immediately bring me into the frequency and my heart will pour forth with the overflowing love and truth for my husband, myself, God, and all of life. This is where I choose to live. This is what matters.

## Recommended Books on Love

- *The Ethical Slut* by Dossie Easton and Janet Hardy
- *Mating in Captivity* by Esther Perel
- *The Way of the Superior Man* by David Deida
- *Crucial Conversations* by Joseph Grenny, Kerry Patterson, Al Switzler, and Ron McMillan
- *Conflict = Energy: The Transformative Practice of Authentic Relating* by Jason Digges

## Key Outcome from This Chapter

**Creating Your Relationship Vision -** Create a written 1+ page description of the vision you have for your current or future romantic relationship. Where do you want to live? Do you want children? What is the purpose of your relationship? What do you want to create together? What are your shared values? See the example letter I wrote to Morgan in 2019 in this chapter for an example.

## LOVE CHAPTER ACTION ITEMS

1. **Relationship Vision** - Read the example in this chapter and then write a letter in your notebook to your actual or future long-term romantic partner sharing the vision for your life with them in as much detail as you possibly can. What do you want to create together?

2. **Relationship Adventure Book** - Buy a leather bound notebook and make it your relationship adventure book. Every 30 days, get together with your partner for 30 minutes and have fun filling out the memories you've had together over the last month.

3. **Marriage Vows** - Write down what you want your marriage vows to be -- for your current spouse if you're married or for your future spouse if you're not yet married. Put some real thought into them, and feel free to draw on the examples in this chapter.

4. **Meaning of Marriage** - Write down the answer to this question: What do you think the meaning of marriage is for you? See the examples in this chapter.

5. **Masculine & Feminine** - Rate yourself on a scale of 1-10 on your masculine/alpha skill sets (10 = most developed) and your feminine/omega skill sets. Which skill sets do you want to develop? Reference the description in this chapter.

6. **Polarity** - How is the polarity in your current (or most recent) romantic relationship? What is working? What needs to shift? Who is the more dominant/masculine/alpha energy and who is the more submissive/feminine/omega energy most of the time?

7. **ISTA** - To develop your tantra skills and become more present with your partner(s), take the Level 1 course from the International School of Temple Arts (ISTA), held all over the world. If you like Level 1, you may want to take Level 2 afterwards.

8. **Relationship North Star** - Using the example in this chapter as a guide, write down your relationship's north star in your notebook -- for either your current relationship or a future desired relationship.

9. **Relationship Structure** - Based on what you've read in this chapter and your own experiences, what type of relationship structure are you most interested in and why? Write this down on your notebook.

# STEP 10

# SEX MAGIC

# KEY CONCEPTS FROM THE SEXUALITY CHAPTER

**1. MONOGAMOUS RELATIONSHIP** 
A committed relationship in which the partners agree to reserve sensuality for only each other.

**2. OPEN RELATIONSHIP** 
A committed relationship in which the partners agree to also be open to some form of intimacy and sensuality with other people.

**3. FAST SEX** 
Having sex in 10-15 minutes quickly, generally to satisfy the desires of the male but not the female. While these quickies can be fun, women usually desire longer interactions.

**4. SLOW SEX** 
Sexual sessions that last 2+ hours with the goal of connection, pleasure for both parties, and deepening the relationship. Usually better when planned in advance and in the right setting.

**5. WEEKLY SENSUALITY TEMPLE** 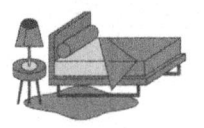
Your once per week sacred time scheduled with your partner for a sensual or sexual experience and heartfelt connection. We do ours every Sunday from 1-4pm.

**6. GHB** 
A drug that can be used to increase sensuality and help you get in touch with your emotions and feelings. Can be helpful to use a small amount before your weekly temple as part of connecting more closely with your partner. Just be careful on dosage and don't mix with it with alcohol or anything else.

**7. YONI MASSAGE** 
A massage of the female vagina, which is referred to as a Yoni in Sanskrit. Some yoni massages focus on the lips and clitoris, while others also may include penetration with the finger.

**8. LINGAM MASSAGE** 
A tantric sensual massage of the penis and surrounding areas. "Lingam" is a Sanskrit word that translates to "shaft of light." The purpose of a lingam massage is to provide a holistic and therapeutic experience that encompasses emotional, spiritual, and physical well-being.

**9. TANTRA** 
The use of sexual energy as a tool for spiritual transformation and connection. The primary goal of tantra is to harness and transmute sexual energy as a means of attaining spiritual enlightenment, self-realization, and a deeper connection with self, one's partner and the divine.

**10. TANTRIKA** 
A woman who practices Tantra as a path to spiritual growth through sacred sexual practices.

**11. DAKINIS** 
Sacred sex workers who share their life force energy and presence with others in sensual and sexual experiences in order to enable the other person to connect more fully with their divine essence.

**12. EDGING** 
Getting close to male orgasm but not finishing in order to extend your ability to make love longer. The more males practice edging the longer they'll last in bed.

# MORE KEY CONCEPTS FROM THE SEXUALITY CHAPTER

**13. SEX COACH**
An individual or couple who comes into the bedroom with you and your partner in order to help guide you both on re-establishing polarity and frequent good sex

**14. DEEP DICK MEDICINE**
The cathartic and emotionally healing release that can occur in a woman when she is penetrated all the way to her cervix.

**15. G SPOT**
The Anterior Fornix Erogenous Zone; a zone on the back of the vaginal wall near the cervix.

**16. C SPOT**
The Cervical Spot, a zone on the very back of the vaginal wall at the entrance of the cervix

**17. COUPLES EROTIC MASSAGE**
An erotic (yoni/lingam) massage for a couple designed to deepen the connection between the pair. You can often find these available in Thailand, or Bali, via Eros.com, or by Googling "couples erotic massage."

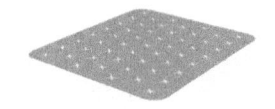

**18. PLAY PARTY**
A invite-only gathering of people who are open and curious to experience intimacy and sensuality with others in a safe, consent based environment.

**19. TEMPLE NIGHT**
What people who come from tantric backgrounds call a play party.

**20. DOM**
The dominant alpha energy in the room during a sexual experience. Can be a male or a female.

**21. SUB**
The submissive omega energy in the room during a sexual experience. Can be a male or a female.

**22. BDSM**
Sexual activity involving the use of physical restraints, the granting and relinquishing of control, roleplaying, and the infliction of pain. Stands for Bondage, Discipline, Sadism, and Masochism.

**23. SHIBARI**
The Japanese art of tying and binding a person using intricate and specific techniques. Shibari is often associated with the practice of Kinbaku, which is a more specific form of Japanese rope bondage that emphasizes aesthetic and erotic aspects.

**24. SEX TRANSMUTATION**
Using the heightened energy of a sexual experience with a partner to together work on putting a shared goal out into the universe. Also known as sex magic.

# STEP 10: SEX MAGIC

*"Don't ignore what Daoists, transcendental meditators, ayurveda, and yoga have been teaching for centuries. Your libido is your life force." - Dave Asprey*

**YOUR MAGIC YEAR**

| 12 | AWAKENING |
| 11 | FAMILY |
| 10 | SEXUALITY |
| 9 | LOVE |
| 8 | COMMUNITY |
| 7 | MONEY |
| 6 | HEALTH |
| 5 | HAPPINESS |
| 4 | PEOPLE |
| 3 | HABITS |
| 2 | GOALS |
| 1 | PURPOSE |

## My Journey with Sex

This section is a guide to sex and sensuality. It is a topic that isn't talked about nearly enough. I am going to do my best to be very transparent in this section.

Sensual energy is the creation force of the universe. It is what drives our species forward. And yes, we repress it and shame it. There is no need to repress or shame sensual energy. There is, however, a need to own it, claim it, be proud of it, and be honest about it.

Own the reality that you're a turned on being. Own the fact that you like to be sensual with multiple people (if, in fact, you do). Or own the fact that you feel better in **monogamous relationships**.

*Monogamous Relationship - A committed relationship in which the partners agree to reserve sensuality for only each other.*

An **open relationship** is a relationship where there's a primary long-term partnership between two individuals and they can both have sensual adventures and experiences outside that 'main' relationship. This is what Morgan and I have today—something that was very important to both of us when we met.

*Open Relationship - A committed relationship in which both people can have other emotionally and physically intimate connections.*

Whatever type of relationship you prefer, own your truth. And find people who not only accept you but people who encourage you to be who you are. When men and women aren't properly sexed, they die inside. While they may hold on and suffer through, they aren't thriving. And if you aren't thriving sexually, it's much more challenging to thrive emotionally.

So if you're a turned on being that isn't being properly fucked, start communicating about it, get in the best physical shape of your life, start finding and going to play parties and tantra temple nights in your area, and start putting the word out that you're looking for something more. There's nothing sexier than a fit person who puts his/her desires honestly out into the world.

After 18 years of being semi-repressed in monogamous relationships (2000-2018), I finally claimed my identity as an open relationship person. Since then, I've been open about being open.

Our marital relationship is based on the principles of **complete freedom** and **complete devotion**. We are completely free to do anything sexually or sensually with anyone we want. And we know we are totally and utterly devoted to always coming back to each other.

Another fun way of explaining it is: "We can sleep with whomever we want as long as they are high vibe and don't mess up our LuvBubble frequency." At this point, we trust each other's selection process. We know not to have continued sexual relations with people who are going to attempt to create separation or who aren't able to have care and love for both of us and for the family unit.

## Getting Outside of the Box

I would describe my sexuality as a hetero-open joysexual sapiosexual. What that means to me is that I'm attracted to people (mostly women) who are smart and very playful.

I'm also bi-flexible -- meaning that while I'm mostly hetero, I'm open to being in sexual situations with men and having male/female/male experiences. I just don't personally want to penetrate or be penetrated by men.

I've only had a few male/female/male sexual situations in my life -- but I've found all of them enjoyable. There's something about two men pleasing a woman at the same time that really turns me on.

I resisted those types of sexual situations prior to age 38, as I had a lot of conditioning from childhood growing up in conservative Florida in the 1990s around "gay" being "wrong."

I actually had some fear of being near another penis in a sexual situation that I had to get over through time. Thankfully, there's much greater acceptance of bi-sexuality and homosexuality around the world today.

While at a play party in Ubud in 2023, I had my first sensual situation with two men and a woman (in which we were both pleasing her), and I was able to heal a lot from that experience.

I've also had a few female/male/female sexual situations in my life. Those are definitely my favorites.

Regardless, the message here is to explore your sexuality and get outside the narrow confines of labels. Lean into your edges and see what you can learn about yourself. So, presuming you are of age… go to that play party. Go to that tantra night. Go try out one of those London, San Francisco, or Berlin sex dungeons. Exploring your sexuality is one of the biggest drivers of personal growth.

> **!** Exploring your sexuality is one of the biggest drivers of personal growth.

If you're wondering where you can find people to explore, learn, or play with consensually, you can check out your local play parties, the ISTA community, Xplor Berlin, the Feeld or Fetlife app, and of course the infamous annual Orgy Dome at Burning Man. Have fun and be safe!

## Fast Sex vs. Slow Sex

If you're in a romantic relationship, the next few pages might just save it. So read closely — especially if you're a guy wanting to learn how to become a tantric sex god and bring extraordinary pleasure to your partners.

There are, generally speaking, two very different types of sex: fast sex and slow sex. Fast sex is the sex that is most commonly practiced, at least in the West. It's the rough type of sex that is most often depicted in adult videos.

> *Fast Sex - Having sex in 10-15 minutes quickly, generally to satisfy the desires of the male but not the female.*

However, many women (and some men) truly desire the connection, intimacy, and pleasure that come from slow sex. With slow sex, the point is not to climax — the point is to deepen the relationship.

Yes, climax can and often does happen — but that's the side show. The main act is the feeling of connection and the sharing of pleasure.

In this slower form of sex, the purpose is mindful awareness and presence with each other. The purpose is to be centered and aware in the body.

> **SLOW** *Slow Sex - Sexual sessions that last 2+ hours with the goal of connection, pleasure for both parties, and deepening the relationship.*

Slow sex is usually best when planned in advance and in the right setting. It can be helped along with taking just the right amount of GHB about 20 minutes before beginning your sensual activity.

The goal of slow sex, as author Diana Richardson says, is to stay in the valleys of the experience longer, rather than always searching for the peak. She recommends, "having mind-filled sex when you want a rush or quick high—and having mindful sex when you want to nurture the connection between you."

Both fast sex and slow sex have their place. Sometimes fast sex is fun. The issue occurs when ALL you do is have fast sex — as if the goal is to get it over with.

Note that in slow sex, you can still be rough and thrust with vigor -- it's simply that you're not fast to orgasm and then quickly leave the room. Instead you have connected 60+ minute sex with many energetic waves of varying intensity versus 6 minute quickie sex.

Here's a comparison of the two types of sex:

|  | Fast Sex | Slow Sex |
| --- | --- | --- |
| Objective | Male orgasm | Deepening the relationship and shared pleasure |
| View of Sex | Satisfying biological needs | An art form, a gateway to transcendent transpersonal experiences, a path toward deep connection |
| Time | 10-15 minutes | 2-3 hours undisturbed time |
| Scheduled | Usually not | Specific date & day selected |
| Type of Sex | Mind-filled sex | Mindful Sex |
| Eyes | Closed, thinking of thoughts or fantasy | Open, looking at your partner |
| Modeled After | Porn | Ancient Indian Practice of Tantra |
| Male Orgasm | Quick | Lasting Much Longer |
| Female Orgasm | Rare | Multiple orgasms |
| Characteristics | Performance Pressure<br>Disconnection and Sadness<br>Seeing sex as duty<br>Loss of interest in sex | Relaxing and taking it easy<br>Bonding and connection<br>Feeling valued and appreciated<br>Longing returning |
| Intention | For the dominant partner/ male to have an orgasm and release | To be as aware and present as possible and take it moment by moment |
| Preparation | None | Setting a time and date<br>Flirting throughout the day<br>Scan your body<br>Breath deep and slow into the belly and the genitals together |
| Entering | Fast | Very slow, step-by-step, using lubrication |
| Movements | Back and forth friction | Each movement done with awareness, creating slowness and increasing sensitivity |

There's a very different pattern of energy with fast sex vs. slow sex. The pattern of fast sex is:

*Excitement—Excitement—Ejaculation—Exhaustion*

By the six minute mark, it's often over. Sad. With slow sex, however, the pattern looks more like this:

*Excitement—Relax—Excitement—Relax—Excitement—Relax—Excitement—Female Orgasm—Relax—Excitement—Male Orgasm*

To learn more about slow sex, watch the TedX talk by Diana Richardson, "The Power of Mindful Sex," and read the book *Slow Sex* by Nicole Daedone.

**Action Item #93: What Type of Sex Do You Have?**
In your relationship(s), what type of sex do you most commonly have? Fast sex or slow sex? What type of sex do you want to be having most of the time? If there's a discrepancy, you may want to pass this chapter along to your partner.

## Create Your Weekly Sensuality Temple

Let's say that you're in a long-term partnership and you're wanting to make the sex well, a little juicier, frequent, and hot.

A great way to rekindle and reignite a sensual relationship is to schedule a **weekly sensuality temple** with your partner.

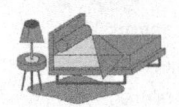

*Weekly Sensuality Temple - Your once per week sacred time scheduled with your partner for a sensual or sexual experience and heartfelt connection. We do ours every Sunday from 1-4pm.*

Morgan and I have been doing this nearly every Sunday since 2021. We originally did it from 4-7 p.m. but more recently moved up the time to 1-4 p.m. so we could more easily have childcare coverage during that window.

So every Sunday at 1 p.m., we know where we will be. In bed. With each other. And I got to tell you, it's better than any NFL football game.

In the first 90 minutes, we're usually holding each other and sharing what's on our hearts and sharing any feelings about the past week, and then we use the last 90 minutes for mutual massage and lovemaking.

The first 90 minutes can be thought of as our weekly love meeting to share our emotions and feelings and open up with each other in a present, relaxed way, and the last 90 minutes as our weekly dedicated love making session. We often will make love more than this one time -- but this temple ensures it is always at least one time.

The benefits of a weekly temple with your partner are many. Now, if you both happen to have a busy week, you'll know when you're coming back together. In my experience, women are a lot happier when they get well sexed. This type of weekly ritual can ensure your marriage stays hot for many decades to come.

I usually take a little bit of **GHB** to help me get into my heart and become more present with Morgan. This medicine helps me get into my heart and get out of my fast paced world within about 15 minutes. It allows me to be connected, a good listener, and much more in my body.

> *GHB - A drug that can. be used to increase sensuality and help you get in touch with your emotions and feelings. Can be helpful to use a small amount before your weekly temple as part of connecting more closely with your partner. Follow all local laws and only use with experienced guidance.*

GHB can be rather dangerous if you use too much or mix it with other things, as it can cause you to pass out or even go into a coma at high doses. So be very aware and careful about proper dosage, and don't mix it with alcohol, depressants, stimulants, opioids, benzos, sedatives, or really anything else at all.

GHB can have significant health risks and is a controlled substance in many countries. As with all drugs, it should only be used under the right supervision and in accordance with the law in your area.

While there is a lot of negative and scary stuff online about GHB, I have benefited a lot from using small amounts of it before sensuality. It both gets me into my heart and makes me much more sensually aware and tantric.

While I wouldn't necessarily recommend it for two people who are just getting to know each other, for a stable long-term partnership, the right dosage done in a romantic setting every so often with your beloved can create extraordinary and life changing magic. For safety, go slow, get the dosage right, and don't mix it with anything.

**Action Item #94: Schedule Your Weekly Sex Temple**
If you have a regular sexual partner, schedule a 2-3 hour weekly sensual temple with them. I recommend Sunday afternoons or evenings. Be sure to get a babysitter lined up if you have younger kids.

# Learn Tantra

"Tantra is about truly loving and embracing all of life and through this love remembering our essence. Tantra is a life path. How we make love is how we create the life we lead." - Osho

There are two major types of tantra -- white tantra (tantric practices done alone) and red tantra (tantric practices done with a partner).

White tantra is the solo practice which incorporates yoga, visualization, energy work, and meditation. Red tantra is a sexual practice. While both use sexual energy, the goals of the two practices are different. The goal of red tantra is to create a deeper bond with a partner through touch and sex, while white tantra is to create a deeper bond with yourself and the divine.

Red Tantra practitioners believe that sexual energy is a powerful force that can be harnessed for spiritual growth and that by learning to control and channel this energy, one can achieve a higher state of consciousness.

Treating yourself to a tantric sensual massage, sometimes known as lingam massages (for men) or yoni massages (for women), is a wonderful way to relax and improve your body's energy flow and your sexual abilities.

Yoni - Sanskrit for sacred gateway to the universe. Also refers to the female vagina.

Lingam - Sanskrit for "distinguishing symbol of generative power." Also the term used for the male penis in tantra.

Together, the lingam and the yoni symbolize the divine on-going process of creation and regeneration, and the union of the feminine and the masculine that continually recreates all of existence.

Of course, there is often a difference, however, between an "erotic massage" and a "tantric massage."

While the purpose of an erotic massage may be stress relief or sexual pleasure — the purpose of a tantric massage is more often to bring you into your body, help you reconnect to your own sensual energies (which can often get blocked after years and years of stress and being on a computer all the time), lengthen the time you can last in bed by moving your sexual energy throughout your body, and even deepen your sexual connection with your partner.

Sometimes during a tantric massage, there is an orgasm/ejaculation — and sometimes there isn't.

I received my first ever Tantric lingam massage in 2022 while in Bali from a friend of mine who was a tantric teacher and practitioner (a "tantrika"). It was done at my house.

She first prepared the bed with a cloth and essential oils, offered me a sarong to put on, checked in with me to see what boundaries I had, if any, and then started with 20 minutes of breathing exercises for me before offering a full body massage — with particular attention paid to my perineum (the spot between the penis and the anus) and my tailbone.

After about 20 minutes of deep breathing and 20 minutes of massage on my perineum and tail bone, my body began rhythmically pulsing on the bed. We ended by growling and play-wrestling with each other. Afterwards, I was exhausted for the next four hours — integrating the healing that had occurred as my energetic channels began to unlock after being partially closed for years.

One of the great things about Bali (and Thailand) is that there is a very large tantra community — and so finding this type of bodywork is relatively easy, especially in the expat hotspots of Ubud and Canggu. You should be able to find a tantra practitioner in any major global hub or through the International School of Temple Arts (ISTA) community.

## Become a Tantric Sex God

"Sex is the highest Temple. It's where we experience our deepest pleasure. It's where we experience our highest love. It's where we come fully alive through the electric merging of masculine + feminine polarity. It's how we create new life + grand visions. It's magic - if you know how to tap into it's potential. Tantra teaches us how to experience embodied sex + empowered love to live a life that's devoted to divine desire."
- Holly Turiya, Tantric Sex Coach in Costa Rica

Let me tell you what my wife did for me. If you recall, we met at Burning Man in 2018, so we have some unorthodox practices, to say the least.

In 2022, my wife noticed that after our first child, I had become a bit overweight. I gained 30 pounds during her pregnancy, perhaps due to increased levels of prolactin in my system. She also noticed that I had practically lost my sex drive, as she had asked me not to have any sensuality with others to help make her feel safer during pregnancy.

So when we went to Bali in October 2022 (four months after our son was born), she challenged me to learn **tantra.**

> *Tantra - The use of sexual energy as a tool for spiritual transformation and connection. The primary goal of tantra is to harness and transmute sexual energy as a means of attaining spiritual enlightenment, self-realization, and a deeper connection with one's partner and the divine.*

She wanted me to become, in her words, a "Tantric Sex God."

This was very smart of her. During our three months in Bali, this involved me working with four different **tantrikas** -- two of whom were friends and two of whom I found through word of mouth.

> *Tantrika - A woman who practices Tantra as a path to spiritual growth through sacred sexual practices. These practices may involve harnessing sexual energy to deepen the connection between partners, enhance intimacy, and promote spiritual awakening.*

Here's what I learned while working with these tantrikas.

- I learned how to give a yoni massage
- I learned how to really touch women sensually the way they want to be touched (I thought I knew, but wow, I didn't know)
- I learned the practice of "**edging**" -- getting close to orgasm but not finishing in order to extend my ability to make love longer
- I went to play parties and tantra workshops

> *Edging - Getting close to male orgasm but not finishing in order to extend your ability to make love longer. The more males practice edging the longer they'll last in bed.*

The freedom (and even encouragement) to learn with these women felt exhilarating -- and my sex drive and vigor for living naturally returned stronger than ever.

At the end of the three months "working" with these women, I could last 3 hours in bed (instead of 20 minutes -- yes 6x longer), I knew how to properly foreplay (something most goal oriented men sadly don't put nearly enough focus on), and I knew how to bring a woman to orgasm with my tongue, finger, and cock.

And of course, for whom did I bring all these lessons back? Well, none other than my VERY HAPPY WIFE.

Talk about a good use of time. Talk about a good challenge. Talk about a smart spouse.

But how do you overcome jealousy? Here's one way. Tell your partner their mission is to go learn with others and then bring all the learnings back into your bedroom for use on you. Your partner gets to have some enjoyable experiences -- and you get to benefit for many years to come.

Work with others who are trained in the art of tantra (which is an entire philosophy for living) and who know that everything they do must be in support of the primary relationship.

After a few weeks of experiencing the MUCH BETTER AND FREQUENT SEX with your partner, you'll be sending glowing voice notes to the people your partner is working with, saying, "Thank you so much for making my man/woman a fucking king/queen again and showing him/her how to properly please his beloved."

**Key Lesson**: If you find your partner wasting away, getting fat, and lacking motivation, it may be, in part, because you took their sexual freedom away when you got together. Did you? Set them truly free, and see the more motivated and healthier version of them emerge within a few months. They'll probably get happier, start getting in shape, and become much better in bed for you. It's at least worth a conversation with each other.

So if you haven't already done it, sign up for an upcoming ISTA Level 1 tantra program today and begin the process of becoming a Tantric Sex God yourself.

## Bring a Tantrika Into Your Bedroom

During our time living in Bali in 2022 and 2023, Morgan and I worked with a female Tantric Sex Coach over eight different weekly sessions. Each session cost around $250 and lasted 2-3 hours. We usually did them on Sundays around 4-7pm.

Here's how the sessions progressed – so you can get a sense of what we did and what we learned:

- **Tantra Session 1-3** - Lingam Massages, just the tantra teacher and I working on edging (me getting close to orgasm without actually ejaculating) so that I could last hours during sex without "finishing."
    - While it's okay if you do ejaculate during these types of sessions, the goal is to go as long as you can without, and practice getting very close and then moving the energy up the spine to spread it throughout the body.
    - These sessions were very helpful as they taught my body how to be in complete control of when I ejaculate. With premature ejaculation being a sexual challenge for many men, this edging training was invaluable.

- **Tantra Session 4** - Me practicing the five different types of tantric touch on the teacher, named after the elements:
    - Air - Tips of fingers, making light contact
    - Water - Long, slow, circular, and flowing movements
    - Earth - Harder, pressing and pushing with the hands, holding for a while, then releasing

- Fire - Fast, intense, and sharp touches like slapping, spanking, and scratching
- Ether - Touching the air above and around the body to move the energetic field

After we got through the first four sessions, we were ready to work together with my wife, Morgan, for session 5 and bring her into the sessions with the tantrika and myself.

- **Tantra Session 5** - Morgan and I together, working on developing a pleasure map of her body (what locations on her body and types of touch feel best), guided by the teacher. We used lots of coconut oil and the teacher showed me how to apply the five types of touch to each area of Morgan's body and also how to give a yoni massage to Morgan. Morgan and I then finished by making love. We also were able to heal some childhood wounds around "giving feedback during sex" that were very helpful to become aware of. Yes, every man should take the time to develop a pleasure map of their partner.

- **Tantra Session 6** - The Tantra teacher and I together, learning through the touching of her body and then learning how to give a yoni massage, including the Orgasmic Meditation (OM) technique developed by Nicole Daedone. Before this session, the teacher suggested I write down four affirmations of what I wanted to embody. I wrote down:
  - I am a tantric sex God
  - I am a confident love maker
  - I am a pleasure making machine
  - I am great at integrating feedback and pleasing my partners

- **Tantra Session 7** - Morgan and I together with the tantra teacher, with Morgan working on developing a pleasure map of my body (learning how I loved to be touched).

- **Tantra Session 8** - Graduation session: Morgan and I together, with the Tantra teacher observing us make love and giving up tips and encouragement.

In total, we spent about $2500 for these 8 sessions, and they completely upgraded our lovemaking and sensuality. It was a great investment. During this time, we also went to two play parties (aka temples) that allowed us to practice loving each other in front of others as well as easing back into the experience of kissing and sharing sensual energy with others in front of each other.

For individuals, these types of tantra sessions can make anyone a better, more present, lover. And for couples, I highly recommend hiring your own Tantric Sex Coach, who actually comes "into the bedroom" and guides you in your sensuality with your partner.

You can find them on Eros.com under tantra, on SacredEros.com, or by googling these terms for your city. So if you were in Austin, TX, for example, you could search for:

- Tantra teacher Austin
- Tantra relationship coach Austin
- Tantric sex coach Austin
- Tantric massage Austin
- Tantra couples sex coach Austin

- Dakini sex coach Austin

If you want to improve your sex life, you can also hire a **sex coach**. A sex coach is an individual (or a couple) who comes into your bedroom to help guide you and your partner on re-establishing polarity and having frequent hot sex again. My wife and I sometimes act as informal sex coaches for our friends in relationships who are looking to reignite their sexual spark.

*Sex Coach - An individual or couple who comes into the bedroom with you and your partner in order to help guide you both on re-establishing polarity and frequent good sex*

So yes, hire a tantrika or a sex coach. It will be one of the best investments you'll ever make in your partnership. And it's a lot of fun!

**Action Item #95: Hire a Sex Coach**
If you're in a relationship, search online and in tantra groups and ISTA groups for an experienced couples sex coach. Discuss with your partner whether you'd want to hire one for a couple sessions in order to get immediate feedback on your polarity and how to make your sex even better.

## Destigmatizing Dakinis & Sex Workers

Sex is an expression of the divine. Sex is a deeply healing way of connecting with the divinity and consciousness in ourselves and others.

So why in American culture do we sometimes shame women who have sex with people for pay? No really. Why? This is some of the most sacred and healing work there is. This type of work is seen for what it is in other cultures, such as in Central and South America, Europe, and much of Asia -- essentially for the orderly functioning of human society.

This type of work shouldn't be underground -- but instead there should be revered Tantric temples of sensual massage in every community -- designed to heal souls and reconnect us back to who we are.

Can someone please start a religion with sacred healing temples for men and women? Sign me up! I'll bring 100,000 people with me.

And why do we shame men who have sex with people for pay?

Why do we shame male businessmen and politicians who use these services for healing and relaxation? We are literally evolved apes, and there is absolutely nothing wrong with sex.

Sex between consenting adults, even for monetary compensation, should NEVER be illegal -- but instead should be celebrated as a form of true healing of the body and soul.

Sex is a very important thing for the human body and for personal growth.
**It's time to bring sex out of the shadows and into the light.**

There is nothing wrong with working with sex workers, tantrikas, or dakinis to learn to be better in bed for your partner or to regain confidence after a difficult relationship. In fact, this is, in my view, a very good thing.

*Dakini (n) - Sacred sex workers who share their life force energy and presence with others in sensual and sexual experiences in order to enable the other person to connect more fully with their divine essence and inner presence.*

The millions of women around the world who are working as sex workers should be celebrated and honored, rather than shunned.

If we took 1/10th of what we invest into prisons and incarcerating millions of people around the world for minor drug offenses and put that into funding an army of divine Goddesses trained to heal our warriors and most hardened men through tantric temple rituals (aka sensual massages), we would help heal the lost souls in our world. There is a lot of healing that can happen through sensuality. And destigmatizing sensuality is an important first step.

It's quite interesting how bombing people using drones in another country is still seen as societally acceptable (perhaps one of the worst things that could possibly be done), but creating sensual healing temples to heal our warriors isn't.

Let's change that.

**Key Tip:** Use a condom whenever you're having sex with someone who isn't your long term partner and practice safe sexual habits. The logistics of family life are generally WAY easier when you have all your kids with one person.

## Sexuality: Resurrect Your Fucking King

Morgan said to me during sex once: "Kill your victim. Kill your villain. And resurrect your fucking king."

What a truly powerful encouragement. The context was that she was giving me feedback on how to please her.

For some reason, instead of appreciating the feedback on how to please her more – my inner victim came out and was upset that she would give me feedback in the middle of sex.

As it turns out, I developed a sexual confidence issue between 2009-2014 due to a couple challenging experiences with partners.

Since then, I've done a lot of work with tantra and have become a powerful, skillful, and loving sexual partner. However I still had one Achilles heel…

When women give me feedback during sex about what would feel better, I sometimes collapse into a former version of my non-confident self.

| Stimulus | What Used to Happen | What Happens Now |
|---|---|---|
| Woman gives me feedback during sexual intimacy on how to improve | I'd lose my confidence and become submissive, killing the polarity and often ending the experience | I say thank you for showing me how to love you better, take a breath, change what I'm doing based on the input, and continue confidently |

I was able to finally get over this "fear of feedback during sex" by working with a **tantrika** in Bali in 2023.

During a specialized three-hour session designed to heal this issue (requested by Morgan), the Tantrika had me touch her and give her a **yoni massage** while giving me detailed feedback every step of the way so that I could work through the trigger.

> *Yoni Massage - A massage of the female vagina, which is referred to as a Yoni in Sanskrit. Some yoni massages focus on the lips and clitoris, while others also may include penetration with the finger.*

She gave me a lot of feedback while I was giving the tantrika a yoni massage. The process worked, and now whenever I get feedback in bed, I say thank you and calmly make the adjustment – while being able to maintain my confidence and my dominant energy.

## Orgasms Can Cure Hysteria

According to historian Rachel Maines, the practice of providing pelvic massages to female patients has a long history, dating back thousands of years. These massages were not considered erotic, but were seen as a medical treatment.

During the late 1800s and early 1900s, doctors administered pelvic massages involving clitoral stimulation by early electric vibrators as treatments for what was called "female hysteria."

After the Industrial Revolution, physicians began using medical vibrators as a tool to alleviate symptoms of "hysteria" and to bring women to orgasm more efficiently.

As technology progressed and batteries became smaller, portable vibrators started to appear in advertisements in ladies' magazines, newspapers, and catalogs, marketed as household appliances that could be used for self-pleasure. By the 1950s, the use of home vibrators had become mainstream, and was depicted in Hollywood films.

Long story short, if a woman is not having frequent orgasms (at least a couple per week, if not more), it can often seriously affect her mood, emotions, and stability.

Orgasms in women lead to better sleep from the release of endorphins, a natural pain reliever, improved blood flow and cardiovascular health, and better emotional well-being including increased feelings of happiness, contentment, and self-esteem.

So if you are with a woman, it is advisable to ensure you're doing your part to bring her to orgasm a few times a week. Please, for the love of God, and the continuation of the human race.

### The Huge Positive Impacts of Female Orgasms

Better sleep, release of endorphins, natural pain relief, improved cardiovascular health, better emotional well being, and greater happiness and self-esteem.

So, long story short, if you're not participating in ensuring your woman has multiple cathartic orgasms each week, you might not be around for too long!

# Deep Dick Medicine (DDM)

Sex can be a deeply healing, bonding, and cathartic experience, especially for women. Morgan has a rather funny and memorable term for what she receives from me 2-3x per week when we make love. She called it "**Deep Dick Medicine**."

*Deep Dick Medicine - The cathartic and emotionally healing release that can occur in a woman when she is penetrated all the way to her cervix.*

We haven't yet looked up the science, but her theory is supported by her experience. Whenever she gets that deep dick (the type that touches her cervix), she goes wild.

She tells me it is addicting and that it helps her stabilize her emotions and let things go. She tells me (in my very official WhatsApp interview I just conducted with her while sitting in Canggu, Bali) that:

- The G-spot touched by the fingers tend to release all the pent up emotions

- Cervical orgasms tend to create euphoria and overall peace

- And foreplay (touching her whole body with coconut oil) makes her feel super alive and connected to her body.

So there you have it, men (and women). If you want a happy partner, make sure you're giving your lady Deep Dick Medicine (DDM) every few days. As they say, happy wife, happy life. Here's an excerpt of a post from my friend Jordan Bowditch speaking to this exact topic.

### Your Woman Is Begging You To Fuck Her Stupid by Jordan Bowditch

Your woman is BEGGING you to fuck her stupid to set her straight.
She wants you to step the fuck UP.
She's requiring you to expand your capacity.
Seducing you into realizing your abilities.
Infinitely inviting you IN.
Inside of her & deeper into yourself as a means of reminding you both what's possible, and what's necessary.
This & much more are parts of her sacred role in testing your commitment - to her…to unwavering integrity…to extreme ownership…to a purpose-driven life.
She wants MORE from you.
It's not a matter of 'not enoughness'.
(and she's not 'too much')
This is a call UP for the BOYZ.
It's time to recognize the gift of your women's perceived 'irrationality'.
It's time to take ownership of EVERYTHING - not just what seems reasonable & fair.
It's time to prioritize $EX as integral to your personal growth - the port(hole) for eternally & exponentially revolutionizing your relationship.
It's time to acknowledge the power of your partner's Pussy.
She's not your best friend.
She's not your therapist.

She's not your mom.
She's your LOVER.
She's an unparalleled gateway to GOD.
She's the activating agent for actualizing your unique greatness.
Guys, you are capable of SO much more when your relationship is on FIRE.
Prioritize it accordingly. Raise the stakes.
Do something RIGHT now to show her (and GOD) that you mean it. Make a declaration. Take a BOLD stance for your romance.
Whatever it is, unabashedly OWN it. Not just once - FOREVER. And then...
Fuck her brains out. (as she fucks yours IN)
Behind every well-fucked woman is an unstoppably confident man (or woman, or both).

## The Secrets to the Pussy

Women love it when you light up some candles, grab your coconut oil or body butter, and give them a 20 minute yoni massage. The secret to the pussy is to go a LOT slower than you think. The key is to set aside some time when you both agree there will be no penetration with the penis -- and simply focus on her.

Start by rubbing around the thighs and outer lips. Make her really want it. Then spend a few minutes on the inner lips, a few minutes very very very lightly stroking her clitoris with your oiled up finger (you could spend an hour here), and only then ask her if it's okay for your fingers to enter her.

Then slowly use one (or two) fingers to reach her G spot (the ribbed spot directly above with fingers curled toward you), the A spot (further back behind the G spot), the C spot back in the cervix area (fingers fully extended back), and the K spot (with fingers curled down). With each spot, you can try a circle motion, a left-to-right motion, and an up and down motion.

While most adult films demonstrate more aggressive moves, most women really enjoy a much, much slower approach. You can win the heart of your woman for a very long time and be considered a sensual master with this knowledge. In review, the four inner vagina spots for making your woman go wild are:

| The Four Erogenous Zones Inside a Vagina |
| --- |

**The G Spot** - The Gränfenberg Spot - an inch or two inside the vagina, toward the upper front wall

**The A Spot** - the Anterior Fornix Erogenous Zone; a zone on the back of the vaginal wall near the cervix.

**The C Spot** - The Cervical Spot, a zone on the very back of the vaginal wall at the entrance of the cervix

**The K Spot** - The Kundalini Spot - the spot reached with curled down fingers, activates the sensual energy flow of your partner

**Action Item #96: The Secrets to the Pussy**
Study the above list of erogenous female spots. See if you can identify them in yourself or in a female partner (if desired).

# Get A Couples Erotic Massage

I had my first erotic massage (from someone that wasn't my girlfriend or wife, that is) in 2020 in Bali. I will never know why I waited until age 35 for this; they are pretty fantastic and helpful for both individuals and couples.

Morgan and I went to the Flame Spa in Seminyak, Bali, and we got the "Couples Inferno" which was their "Unique service for couples: a sensual massage for two in our spa room with two specially trained female therapists."

We added on the Nuru Gel, a Japanese body gel, for added delight. After selecting the two women from a lineup of twenty, we were escorted to our spa room by the front desk manager. There was a large five person jacuzzi inside, a shower, and a large massage area.

The two women helped us take our clothes off, and then asked us to lay face down on the large cushiony massage area to begin the massage.

We followed their instructions, now both entirely naked, and the two women proceeded to give us both a fantastic full body massage for the next hour.

Halfway through, they asked us to turn over — and began touching all over our bodies. This was a highly erotic experience, to say the least. All very turned on, the therapists asked if we wanted to have sex with each other (sex with the therapists was prohibited at this particular establishment, of course) — and so we did.

While it wasn't the first time we'd made love to each other in front of others — it was definitely one of the most memorable — with the ladies cheering us on and smacking our butts every so often.

These types of massages are commonly available in Europe and Asia (especially South East Asia). In the United States, you can go to the massage or tantra section of Eros.com to find this type of massage or ask for what you desire on Seeking.com or Feeld. You can also Google "erotic massage," "tantra massage," "lingam massage," or "yoni massage" for your area.

*Couples Erotic Massage - An erotic (yoni/lingam) massage for a couple designed to deepen the connection between the pair.*

You can often find couples massages easily available in Thailand, Bali, or any major city via Eros.com, or by Googling "couples erotic massage."

You can also find other couples to share erotic massages with on Feeld, at your local swingers hangout, through the ISTA community, or through the Hedoné community. Hedoné is a community based in Berlin that is all about ethical hedonism. It is a "movement to liberate and share pleasure."

They describe what they do as "We aim to deconstruct the misconceptions surrounding hedonism by shining a light on its ethical aspects. We empower those who want to be free from the conventions and prejudices that keep them and others from experiencing joy and pleasure and from being the happiest versions of themselves. Our vision is to create a global network of conscious individuals and intentional spaces liberated to experience and enjoy pleasure consciously." They host events annually in Paris, Berlin, and Austin. Check them out!

## Go To a Play Party

We have friends who host play parties in different parts of the world – Austin, Bali, San Francisco – and many other places...

A play party is a gathering of adults where people connect physically and sensually, and sometimes have sex in front of each other.

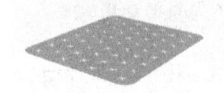

*Play Party - An invite-only gathering of people who are open and curious to experience intimacy and sensuality with others in a safe, consent based environment.*

It may sound a bit edgy, but it's one of the most natural things in the world to have sex in front of other humans. It's been going on for hundreds of thousands of years :).

As a husband and wife who are working on getting pregnant with our second child, we appreciate these types of events to spice things up a bit. Anything that is consensual goes.

There are often guides (aka angels) to make sure everything goes well in the space – and that there aren't any creepers.

Generally, the only people invited to the play party are those the hosts know quite well – to maximize the chance of a great experience for all.

Morgan and I went to one of these play parties in Bali recently. It was called a **Temple Party,** as it was held by people who were long-term practitioners and teachers of the tantric traditions -- and graduates of the International School of Temple Arts (ISTA).

*Temple Party - What people who come from tantric backgrounds call a play party, an adult-only invite-only gathering where people can consensually have sensuality with each other.*

The organizers do it for two reasons – first, because it's really hot and sexy to experience a play party with your friends – and second, because they really believe that through greater communication and intimacy, they can make a positive difference in the world and build community.

We put on our sexy attire, took our motorbike over, and showed up at the designated arrival time. The event was scheduled for about five hours, from 7 p.m. to 12 a.m.

*Morgan and I at a Temple Party in Bali in January 2023*

As we arrived at the Bali Temple Night, we were (of course) saged by a shirtless, long haired man – to welcome us to the space.

There was some fruit available upon arrival—think pineapple, papaya, and mango. And the space was covered by lots of red squish and mats on the floor, making it very comfortable.

We circled up around 730 p.m., were led through some connection games by the two lead organizers, and were taken through a process of agreeing to ask for consent for anything we wanted to do with others. Yes, consent is very sexy! And getting a "no" is perfectly okay.

Couples were asked to identify themselves and share their current relationship agreement in front of the group.

Morgan (my wife) and I raised our hands, and we shared with everyone that we were married and in an open relationship. Morgan added that we were committed to "**complete devotion and complete freedom,**" which lit up my heart.

At this particular Bali play party, there were about 15 women and 18 men. Usually, you want the gender ratio to be pretty close to even.

After circling up, the organizers had each person say their name and two words that described the energy they were bringing that night.

I said: Ryan and Lion Energy – which got a nice rouse from the group.

We were then put in groups of 3. We were told to request from the other two people what we wanted to receive from them, which was pretty cool. The ability to ask for whatever type of touch you wanted to receive was nice. We all took turns being the giver or the receiver – for 3 minutes each. Of course, for something to happen, everyone had to agree to it.

Every minute or so, the organizers encouraged us to ask ourselves: "What would make this even better?"

I ended up getting a nice body massage, giving a soft touch to a new female friend, and then spanking some guy I didn't know (with pants on) 15 times (per his request, of course!).

I was inspired by the triad on the bed next to us, who were really getting into it with some sexy flogging and licking.

After a number of warm up activities, we moved into **open play** at Bali Temple Night. Now the fun really began.

Open play meant minimal facilitation—just do whatever you want to do in a consensual way. Condoms and lube were provided by the organizers for safety and enjoyment.

There were various marked different areas in the home for:

1) Cuddling
2) Dancing
3) Being blindfolded
4) Kink and flogging
5) Shibari
6) Sex
7) Being alone

When we left a bit early due to having to get home to our baby boy, one of our friend couples were tying each other up with rope while a threeway on the bed was getting sexy. There was also a couple making love while dripping hot red candle wax on their naked bodies.

The closing circle was held at 1130 p.m. for each person to share their greatest moments of joy from the evening, and then everyone went home by midnight.

Overall, it was a truly beautiful night and a highlight of the human experience for us. We ended up becoming good friends with a couple of the people there for later connection and deepening.

One of the things you learn at temple parties is to have a short conversation before you engage in sexual activity with a new partner. There is a simple framework you can use for this quick check-in that's easy to remember and goes by the acronym BDSM.

B = Boundaries - any current boundaries you have
D = Desires - what would you love to experience
S = Status - relationship status and STD status
M = Meaning - if you two connect sensually, will it mean you're in a relationship?

Here's an example of a short check-in conversation that I used with a first time play partner at a recent play party in Austin:

Boundaries = nothing in my butt, no pain
Desires = To give massage, to receive massage, oral sex, penetrative sex
Status = In an open relationship, STD clear
Meaning = Seeking short-term or long-term play partners, not girlfriend/wife

So how do you find these play parties? You can find play parties (or "temple nights," as they are sometimes called) in any city across the world. They tend to spread more via word of mouth and private WhatsApp groups than online.

You can often find these play parties via the Burning Man community, the open relating community, the ISTA community, and via the app Feeld, which is for non-traditional relationships and threeways.

I've found that open relating and sensuality are not only some of the most fun experiences but also one of the most growth inducing!

Enjoy!

### Action Item #97: Go to a Play Party (For Adults-Only)

Find a play party or temple party in your area through searching the web and Facebook. Join any local Burning Man or ISTA communities, or find them through word of mouth from people on the Feeld app. Just attending will likely become a major personal growth and sexual growth experience!

### An Example Play Party Schedule

6:30pm - Arrivals
- Welcome people
- Collect people's phones upon entry

7:00pm - Circling up

7:15pm - Introductions
- Introducing the facilitators
- Each person sharing their desires for the evening
- Couples identifying themselves and their relationship boundaries if any
- Basic overview of consent
- Sharing what the various zones of the room are
- Explaining where condoms/lube are
- Identifying who the "angels" are in the room who can be available for help if needed

7:45pm - Getting to know each other exercises
- Moving around the space
- Slowly dancing with various partners
- Giving hugs
- Groups of 3 for requested touch
- Prey and Predator (see below)

8:30pm - Open Play
- No facilitation
- People connect with others as desired
- Full sexuality allowed -- whatever is consensual

10:45pm - Closing Circle

11:00pm - End of Evening

### A Fun Play Party Warm Up Game: Predator Vs. Prey

Here's a really fun and sexy warm up game that you can put on at your local play party. It's called Predator vs. Prey. I learned it from my friend Aaron Kleinerman in his "Dark Masculine" tantra workshop in Bali in January 2023. Note that this exercise was done only after an introduction about the importance of consent and boundaries. This exercise is best done as a warm up when people still have clothes on.

**Instructions:**

1. First, separate the group into half on one side of the room and half on the other. You can separate people by gender -- or just randomly.

2. Designate half of the group as Predators and half as Prey.

3. Explain the exercise to the group and let anyone knows if they want to opt-out of the exercise they can by simply sitting against the wall.

4. Create a memorable safe word that the prey can use if they at any point feel uncomfortable or don't like what's happening. We used "yellow" at our workshop to mean slow down and "avocado" to mean "stop and leave me alone."

5. Encourage the prey to get into their feminine receptive mode and to embody this mode with some movement and dancing.

6. Encourage the predators to get into the masculine penetrative mode and to embody this mode with some growling.

7. Next, tell the predators their job is to go find someone they'd like to play with.

8. Then put on a 5 minute song and tell the predators to go after their prey. If someone is already taken by another predator -- the predators can go find someone else they are attracted to.

9. The Predators start with simple touch in places like shoulders, arms, backs, and knees -- but then can proceed as they wish to "devour" their "prey" as long as it is consensual and desired and no safe word has been used.

10. Finally, after 5 minutes, switch who is predator and prey and allow the new predators to select a new person to go after.

11. Afterwards, you can take a few shares from the group if desired about what it was like for them to be Predator or Prey and which they preferred.

## Set the Scene for Your Sex

When you're getting ready to make love (or host a play party), setting is everything. Here are some things you'll probably want to make sure of as you create your love temple. There is a huge correlation between the right setting, the calmness of the female nervous system, and the ease of the female orgasm.

Here's what you should be sure to have in your sensuality room at all times to make it ever ready for the fun romp.

**Sex Room Checklist:**
- King bed
- Silk sheets
- Extra squish / padding on the floor
- Lots of Coconut Oil or Olive Oil for massage
- Lots of lube
- Towels to protect against oil on the bed

- Body butter
- Music playlist (Search for "The Balanced Butterfly" or the "Shamanic Tantra" playlist on Spotify)
- Portable speaker
- Red lighting (pretty essential)

**Optional But Helpful**
- Sexy outfits
- Hot Tub
- Sauna
- Blindfolds
- Collars
- Whips, floggers, and paddles
- Handcuffs or wrist cuffs
- Vibrators
- Condoms (if needed)

**Action Item #98: Set Up Your Sex Room**
Take a look at the above checklist. See what you need to create a truly memorable and orgasmic experience for your lovers. If you are able to, go buy what you need to create the ultimate sex palace.

# Find a Dom

Recently, Morgan went on a date with a bisexual professional dominatrix female named Jane (name changed) that I helped set up for her using the Feeld app – the app for threeways and fourways and alternative dating. They met at Meteor, a bar in the South Congress district of Austin, near where we live.

A dom is the person who takes the lead energetically in the bedroom--the alpha of the moment who gives the directions.

Morgan asked Jane what she should wear to their first get-to-know each other date and got a very specific and clear reply. Jane replied, "Wear a tight pair of jeans, off the shoulder shirt, booties with a small heel, hair half way up, make up minimal with a bright lipstick and bright cheeks, a chain choker or long pendulum necklace, no other rings other than your wedding band. If you can meet these outfit specifications, it would bring me great joy to know that you're obedient and want to be a good girl." Now that's an experienced dom!

After spending the afternoon excitedly getting this outfit together, Morgan arrived at the date, got herself a tea, and sat down with Jane.

At the date, Jane explained she was a professional **dom** from New York who was now a bisexual, polyamorous ecologist living in Austin. She loved "domming" people (telling them what to do in the bedroom).

*Dom - The person who takes on a dominant role in a sexual experience. The dom is responsible for exercising control and authority over their submissive partner ("sub"), who consents in advance to relinquish power to the dom.*

In a dom/sub play session, a **dom** may create rules, boundaries, and expectations for their sub and engage in various activities that involve dominance and submission, bondage, discipline, or sensation play.

Jane explained to Morgan that there were four types of **subs**.

- Good girls - Who do what they're told
- Brats - Who don't do what they're told in order to get punished
- Pets - Who do what they're told
- Fuckdolls - A sex toy to be used by her lover as desired

*Sub - The submissive omega energy in the room during a sexual experience. Can be a male or a female.*

The first coffee date went well – and Jane the Dom agreed to take Morgan on as her sub for a more in-depth date. After a two week pause due to Jane's visit to New Zealand, the dom fling continued. Morgan booked an Airbnb in east Austin for a night (as having a dom at your house at the same time as a night nanny and a baby isn't easy).

Morgan asked the dom how she should prepare for their second date. In true dom fashion, Jane replied to Morgan with one of the most incredible and specific text messages I've ever read...

"As for your preparation, before I arrive I want you to take a long hot bath, rub your favorite oils and lotions all over your skin, and wear your favorite perfume. Adorn yourself with the softest material, wear minimal to no makeup, pin your hair up with a pencil or chopsticks, and wear no jewelry. When I arrive I want you to answer the door in a pair of heels and your softest robe or wrap dress with nothing underneath.

The more sheer the material, the better. I want to see the outline of your body through what you wear. I want to watch the material shift over your curves as you move.
If you have free reign of the house, I want you to have your toys and tools laid out on the kitchen counter, organized first by size and then by color. If you are more confined to a room, have them laid out on the bed or another applicable surface.

Our first meeting will be soft and firm. It will be to establish limits and enthusiastic yes's. Your body will belong to me during this time where I will treat it with all the respect, desire, and love that it deserves.

I will watch for how your body responds to my direction. Keeping an eye out for untold flinches or hesitation. Silent no's are still no's and are to be adhered to.

As your breathing grows deeper from my touch and your body begins to quiver and pulsate I will dive in deeper. I will press harder. The goal is for my control to bring you to your ultimate climax. Your orgasm is my orgasm.

Just as my hands and fingers are tools and toys, so are my lips. I look forward to exploring your hills and valleys, pulling and spreading you apart, and putting you back together again. After you transform from a strong beautiful woman into a puddle of pure pleasure, I shall envelope you. Your journey will be a beautiful thing to watch."

Now that's a person who knows what she wants!

Morgan was excitedly looking forward to their time together. She followed Jane's instructions explicitly. Morgan arrived early for the date, got the environment ready, set up candles, and used the hot tub, cold plunge, and shower to get relaxed.

While I won't go into complete details here of every activity that commenced, suffice it to say that Morgan healed a lot that night and both women had a great time. As it turns out, being dommed by a woman she trusted in a safe environment helped Morgan heal some sexual trauma from the past. So if you're working on healing some sexual trauma yourself or want to let the feminine inside of you learn to feel safe again, consider working with a dom that you deeply trust to take you into uncharted territory and explore the growth-inducing world of **BDSM**.

*BDSM - Sexual activity involving the use of physical restraints, the granting and relinquishing of control, roleplaying, and the infliction of pain. Stands for Bondage, Discipline, Sadism, and Masochism..*

## Try Some Shibari

I first experienced **Shibari** in February 2020 in Bali. My friends Phillippe and Yani came over and hosted a Shibari workshop at The Joy Villa in Ubud, Bali,, where we lived next door to 15 of our friends. My wife was out with a dance teacher that night, so I partnered up with a friend of mine named Daria. Daria tied me up, with Phillippe and Yani's guidance.

*Shibari - The Japanese art of tying and binding a person using intricate and specific techniques. Shibari is often associated with the practice of Kinbaku, which is a more specific form of Japanese rope bondage that emphasizes the aesthetic and erotic aspects.*

I absolutely loved my Shibari experience. For once, I couldn't be the dominant person. I was completely restrained, and I had to trust others to care for me and respect any boundaries and desires. It was incredibly liberating for someone who is almost always the "alpha male" in the room to be able to simply surrender to a 5'2 brunette.

If you've never been tied up, I highly encourage you to Google "Shibari + Your City Name" where you live and find someone who can show you how to tie up others and how good it can feel to get tied up yourself!

I'm currently learning the basics of Shibari from a male dom that I met in Nosara at a tantra temple party. "Would you like to be tied up?" works exceptionally well as a pick up line at tantra parties.

## Name Your Masculine & Feminine

During a special recent MDMA ceremony with friends (we limit those to every 3 months at maximum to give our brains time to recover), we learned from our friends that they had named their inner man and inner woman – as a way of connecting with the energies opposite of their gender. Suddenly, our male friend became Jacqueline, and our female friend became Johnny.

Morgan and I loved seeing our friends in these new energies. So much so that we decided to name our own alter-egos.

Morgan decided to name her inner masculine Damian. And I decided to name my inner feminine Amy. So if you ever see me and call me Amy, I'll get a good laugh out of it.

Suddenly, I had a "character" that I could give voice to whenever I felt tender or soft. When I was "Amy," it transformed how I related to Morgan. I felt safer being vulnerable, open, or soft. I didn't have to have a veneer of masculinity all the time any longer. I could just be myself. Of course, 95% of the time my masculine is dominant, and I am definitely "Ryan," but in the 5% of the time that my feminine is dominant, it is so helpful to be able to be "Amy" and express my tenderness.

While most of the time I like to be the dominant energy during sex, there are some times when I like to be the submissive person. So in those rare situations, I just ask Damian (Morgan's masculine name) to listen to me and then fuck me, and life is good. I can move through emotions much more quickly that way.

So what is the name for your alternative gender? Naming him or her may just help unlock a new form of expression.

## Wait for Sex on the First Date

So here's the issue with some men as it relates to sexuality. They go for sex way too fast. Probably because we crave it so damn much.

So men -- stop trying to have sex with people on the first date. If your date is going well and things seem to be going well, let your date know that while you welcome sensuality, you will wait on having sex until after you know them a bit better. That boundary is likely to turn on your new potential partner. There's nothing that makes people want something more than knowing they can't yet have it!

Women will appreciate this clear and direct guidance, respect you even more, and feel much more at ease knowing that they aren't going to be pressured into doing something they may feel completely comfortable with so soon.

I remember back in my twenties doing just that -- implying that I was actually interested in something longer term when all I wanted was to have sex once or twice. At the time, I lacked the necessary empathy and compassion to see how much this hurt the people I was connecting with.

Women often need time to mentally and emotionally prepare to onboard a new ongoing sexual partner into their lives. So let them see if they really like you first and demonstrate that you could be a solid, trustworthy, and consistently interested person. This doesn't mean you can't sensually connect in the first two weeks. Do that all you want. I'm just specifically referring to waiting on penetrative sex -- the type of sex that can lead to some very big life changes (like pregnancy).

So if you want to actually develop an ongoing meaningful relationship with someone -- then, as a rule, wait at least two weeks after meeting someone to have sex with them. Let them at least meet a few of your friends first and spend a few hours getting to know them -- at least.

If you want to have a "no strings attached" one night stand, great -- but be honest about this upfront. Some people are just fine with that as long as it's clearly communicated. Just don't use the carrot of a potential relationship to get women to sleep with you. This is done way too often -- and it causes a lot of heartache.

The rule of thumb with sex is never ask someone to have sex with you under any false pretenses. Make sure any new sexual partner knows before you have sex.

a)   Your relationship status
b)   Your relationship agreements
c)   What you are looking for (a one night stand, a casual relationship, friends with benefits, a potential long-term partner, a primary partner, a secondary partner, a BDSM play partner, someone to learn from, etc.)

Before I onboard any new sexual partner into my life, I make sure they know I am happily married, that I am in an open relationship with full freedom and full devotion, and that I'm open to additional lovers every so often. I also insist that every new sexual partner that might become an ongoing lover meet Morgan before we have sex.

I only bring people into our relationship that can benefit the entire relationship ecosystem. And Morgan only brings people into our relationship that can benefit the entire relationship ecosystem. Morgan has a pause button and can put a stop to me seeing anyone if needed, and vice versa. By going slow, communicating openly, and intentionally integrating new partners into the marital ecosystem and inner community, sensuality becomes sustainable and longer lasting rather than short-lived like a firecracker.

I've learned to not crave, to slow down and pause when necessary, and to give women time to actually get to know each other (which can take weeks) before I go forth with my own sensual desires.

This practice has saved us lots of heartache on all sides and has made ethical non-monogamy easeful and fun and not require hours and hours of emotional processing every week.

## Listen to Napoleon Hill About Sex Transmutation

*"When harnessed, this motivating force of sex... may be used as a powerful creative force in literature, art, or in any other profession or calling, including, of course, the accumulation of riches." – Napoleon Hill*

A hundred years ahead of his time, the great successful researcher and writer Napoleon Hill, wrote about the concept of **sex transmutation** in Think and Grow Rich. Sex transmutation is channeling sexual energy into other areas of one's life, such as creativity, productivity, and business. It involves focusing the mind together on a shared goal during sex and using the exceptional heightened states achieved during sexuality to create clarity in the mind about the intended goals.

*Sex Transmutation - Using the heightened energy of a sexual experience with a partner to together work on putting a shared goal out into the universe. Also known as sex magic.*

Hill believes that sexual energy is a powerful creative force that, when harnessed and channeled properly, can be used to achieve great things in all areas of life. He suggests that individuals who are able to transmute their sexual energy into creative and productive outlets can experience increased motivation, focus, and vitality.

Hill wrote, *"When driven by this desire [for sex], men develop keenness of imagination, courage, will-power, persistence, and creative ability unknown to them at other times."*

Morgan and I often dedicate our sexual sessions to achieving a specific goal. Yesterday we dedicated our "sex magic" to her getting Disney to say yes to turning the LuvMonsters animated movie into a globally released featured kids film.

In the section on sex transmutation, Hill also talks about how people who are oversexed and undersexed. Hill wrote that individuals who engage in excessive sexual activity or allow their sexual desires to control their behavior are wasting their creative energy and hindering their potential for success. He also noticed that many undersexed people are unable to make their goals real in the world. The key is to find the right balance of sexual expression for you.

Hill saw sexual transmutation as an important tool for achieving success and personal growth, and suggests that individuals who are able to master their sexual energy can unlock their full potential and achieve their goals more easily.

**Action Item #99: Read the Sex Transmutation Chapter of TAGR**
Read the Sexual Transmutation section (Chapter 11) of the classic book *Think and Grow Rich* by Napoleon Hill. Then write down in your notebook what you learned from it.

## Recommended Books on Sexuality

- *The Ethical Slut* by Dossie Easton and Janet Hardy
- *The State of Affairs* by Esther Perel
- *Mating in Captivity* by Esther Perel
- *Slow Sex* by Nicole Daedone
- *Erotic Hustle* by Lana Shay

## Key Outcome from This Chapter

**Creating Your Weekly Sensuality Temple -** If you have a regular sexual partner, schedule a 2-3 hour weekly sensual temple with them. I recommend Sunday afternoons or evenings. Be sure to get a babysitter lined up if you have younger kids. Set up your bedroom for optimal delight (red lighting, comfortable sheets, good massage oils, and desired play devices). Get rid of all expectations and just massage and touch each other to start and see what emerges.

# SEX CHAPTER ACTION ITEMS

1. **Sex Type** - In your relationship(s), what type of sex do you most commonly have? Fast sex or slow sex? What type of sex do you want to be having most of the time? If there's a discrepancy, you may want to pass this chapter along to your partner.

2. **Weekly Sex Temple** - If you have a regular sexual partner, schedule a 2-3 hour weekly sensual temple with them. I recommend Sunday afternoons or evenings.

3. **Hire a Sex Coach** - If you're in a relationship, search online and in tantra groups and ISTA groups for an experienced couples sex coach. Discuss with your partner whether you'd want to hire one for a couple sessions in order to get immediate feedback on your polarity and how to make your sex even better.

4. **The Secrets to the Pussy** - Study the list of erogenous female spots. See if you can identify them in yourself or in a female partner (if desired).

5. **Go to a Play Party** - Find a play party or temple party in your area through searching the web and Facebook. Join any local Burning Man or ISTA communities, or find them through word of mouth from people on the Feeld app. Just attending will likely become a major personal growth and sexual growth experience!

6. **Your Sex Room** - Take a look at the sex room checklist. See what you need to create a truly memorable and orgasmic experience for your lovers. If you are able to, go buy what you need to create the ultimate sex palace.

7. **Sex Transmutation** - Read the Sexual Transmutation section (Chapter 11) of the classic book *Think and Grow Rich* by Napoleon Hill. Then write down in your notebook what you learned from it.

# STEP 11

## FAMILY MAGIC

# KEY CONCEPTS FROM THE FAMILY CHAPTER

**1. FAMILY PURPOSE STATEMENT**

A 10-30 word statement that describes your purpose as a family. Why does your family exist? What are you all about? What do you want to create together as a family in the years ahead?

**2. PREGNANT DAD BELLY**

The extra 20-30 pounds that new dads often gain during their wife's pregnancy due to the added stress and change in hormones like prolactin and cortisol.

**3. NEW DAD UPGRADE**

The motivation you feel as a first time dad in your baby's first year of life to get your act together and become the best possible version of yourself. It's no longer just about you!

**4. LUVBUBBLE**

An environment of love, play, magic, tenderness, presence, and encouragement that we are raising our children in and that we are creating around our family, beloveds, and closest friends.

**5. FAMILISCIOUS**

An environment that is full of welcoming loving family vibes.

**6. JOYDICULOUS**

Being joyfully ridiculous and playful. This is a term we use within our family.

**7. HEAVEN ON EARTH**

A state of living in bliss while here on Earth. We do our best to work toward creating Heaven on Earth around us by living immersed in nature, and eating organic food from our community farm, in a free-range environment.

**8. FREE-RANGE KIDS**

Kids who can safely run around their community for many hours at a time, stopping by neighbors' homes and being guided and mentored by the other inspiring families who live nearby.

**9. 10 YEAR FAMILY VISION**

Your written vision statement of what you have created and accomplished as a family ten years from now.

**10. FAMILY VALUES**

The set of 5-15 values that your family strives to embody. Create it together with your partner and kids and frame it and hang it in your house.

**11. CHILDHOOD ADVANTAGES**

The advantages you can give your kids to give them a leg up in life and maximize the chances they will turn into happy and thriving adults.

**12. CONFLICT REPAIR**

The process of softening, apologizing, taking time to actually hear each other and making up. If you ever have an argument in front of your kids, be sure that you close the loop and show them that mommy and daddy have reconnected.

# STEP 11: FAMILY MAGIC

"You know what success is? Success is when your children want to be with you when they're adults. That's success. I've been called many things in my life. The coolest thing I've ever been called is Dad." - Paul Orfalea, American Billionaire and Kinkos Founder

**YOUR MAGIC YEAR**

| Step | Theme |
|---|---|
| 12 | AWAKENING |
| 11 | FAMILY |
| 10 | SEXUALITY |
| 9 | LOVE |
| 8 | COMMUNITY |
| 7 | MONEY |
| 6 | HEALTH |
| 5 | HAPPINESS |
| 4 | PEOPLE |
| 3 | HABITS |
| 2 | GOALS |
| 1 | PURPOSE |

Even if you don't yet have a family of your own creation, reading this section may help you prepare to create one someday and visualize your vision, values, and dreams for your family. Kids are one of the biggest catalysts and accelerants of personal growth.

If you do have kids or want kids -- be sure to read this chapter. If you aren't so interested in having kids -- you can skip this section and move right on to the Awakening chapter.

## Our Family Purpose Statement

My wife Morgan and I are very intentional about creating a family that will stay intact as a caring and active family for the next seven generations. We are here to create our legacy through the traditions of our family, more than anything else.

We've chosen to make a lifelong commitment to living together, being each other's best friends, raising families together, and working on our shared purpose of creating an environment of love, care, encouragement, play, and joy for our family and close friends. Thankfully, we get along very well.

If you read our marital vows earlier in the Love chapter -- you know how intentional we are about our relationship, encouraging each other, and building a stable, loving family for our children and hopeful future grandchildren.

For us, divorce isn't really an option we'd consider, as that would undermine the very purpose of our lives -- to create a loving multi-generational family as an example of a new way of living, loving, playing, and learning.

A few weeks after we gave birth to Apollo, we created a **family purpose statement** that described our broader purpose as a family that has such strong traditions and cultural expressions that we will impact the next seven generations of our future downline.

*Family Purpose Statement - A 10-30 word statement that describes your purpose as a family. Why does your family exist? What are you all about? What do you want to create together as a family in the years ahead?*

A family purpose statement is similar to the **Relationship North Star** from the Love chapter, but includes the broader intention of why we are building our family. Here is our family purpose statement.

### Our Family Purpose Statement

Create a loving multi-generational family that serves as an example to others of a new way of living, loving, playing, and learning -- and creates a LuvBubble realm around our family and close friends.

**Action Item #100: Create Your Family Purpose Statement**
Working together with your partner (and kids if old enough) create a 10-30 word statement that describes your purpose as a family. Why does your family exist? What are you all about? What do you want to create together as a family in the years ahead? How do you want people to feel around your family?

## Having Our First Baby

Morgan and I got married on September 7, 2020, in Lake Tapps, Washington, and exactly one year later, on the day of our one year wedding anniversary, we conceived our son Apollo in Boulder, Colorado. On June 14, 2022, he was born in Austin, TX. Now our LuvBubble family is three people --- and someday it may turn into four (or five!). Here's a photo of Apollo just a week after he was born.

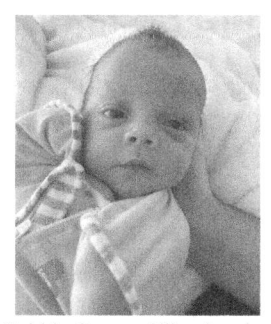

*Our son Apollo LuvBubble Carson Allis when he was a few days old*

The experience of giving birth to Apollo really brought us together as a family. We love the challenge of designing a life and educational experience for our son based on adventure, curiosity, play, travel, and nature.

We plan for Apollo to have many schools – and build networks of friends in each place we visit. He has already lived in four countries, and as of the time of publication, he's just two years old!

Kids aren't easy. They are definitely a commitment. But they are also the biggest joy in the world. I like to think of having kids as giving you DNA immortality and passing along 250,000 years of homo sapiens ancestry onward, especially when they later have kids themselves.

So yes, they are worth it. The coolest part is you become their leader. They look up to you. They see you as their #1 role model -- giving you an incredible incentive to get your shit together and be an extraordinary person in every way.

In Apollo's first year of life, I was so motivated that I lost 45 pounds, found our future home in Costa Rica, and wrote the entire first draft of this book. I went from 165 → 190 → 145 pounds over 2 years. I turned my **pregnant dad belly** into a six pack in twelve months through a combination of motivation and a little help from the tirzepatide appetite suppressant.

*Pregnant Dad Belly - The extra 20-30 pounds that new dads often gain during their wife's pregnancy due to the added stress and change in hormones like prolactin and cortisol.*

My **Magic Year** was Apollo's first year of life, when I was inspired to become the best version of myself and write this book, sharing what I've learned over the last 20 years with you. I call this the **New Dad Upgrade**.

*New Dad Upgrade - The motivation you feel as a first time dad in your baby's first year of life to get your act together and become the best possible version of yourself.*

## Creating a LuvBubble Around Our Friends & Family

Apollo's full name is Apollo LuvBubble Carson Allis. We gave him the middle name LuvBubble because it is a very special concept that Morgan and I created together a few years ago.

*LuvBubble - An environment of love, play, magic, tenderness, presence, and encouragement that we are raising our children in and that we are creating around our family, beloveds, and closest friends.*

We realized a few years ago that it was too big of a task to create a beautiful world for all people in one human lifetime – but that we could create a beautiful realm around us, in our home, and among our family and closest friends in our lifetime -- and then use that as a living example of a new way of living that others can model.

Rather than attempt to change the entire world at once, we've found it's better to build a beautiful world around us -- and hopefully inspire many thousands of other towns that are regenerative and focused on family, community, and connection.

So, we've devoted ourselves to building the LuvBubble all around us – which of course starts by getting into a really happy, positive, and joyous state of mind ourselves – and having a beautiful, creative, and loving relationship with each other, and attracting into our realm joyous, kind, and uplifting people.

We now have our own language inside the LuvBubble – like **famlicious** (which means full of loving family vibes) and **joydiculous** (joyfully ridiculous). We also say the phrase seriosity is poo whenever someone is getting too high strung. We love building culture within small groups of people!

*Famlicious - An environment that is full of welcoming loving family vibes.*

*Joydiculous - Being joyfully ridiculous and playful.*

Yes, one of our greatest **sevas** (spiritual acts of service to others) is creating an ecosystem of love around our children, family, and soul family.

While we may not be able to create Heaven on Earth for everyone – we can at least create **Heaven on Earth** for our family and friends – and create a model that others can copy to do the same for their community.

*Heaven on Earth - A state of living in bliss while here on Earth. We do our best to work toward creating Heaven on Earth around us by living immersed in nature near our closest friends, eating organic food from our community farm, and raising our kids in a free-range environment where they can roam free without worry.*

The annual festival that we put on for our close friends is now called LuvBubble – as a two day experiential peak into what LuvBubble is like. I encourage you to create an energetic LuvBubble in and around your family and closest friends – or come experience what ours is like. Here's how we think about extending our LuvBubble first with us, then our family and closest friends, then our broader community, and eventually the world.

We're starting small with our LuvBubble and intentional community -- and hoping to develop a model for a new way of living that grows and is eventually copied.

What we found was that when Morgan and I were on our own before we knew each other, it was hard to maintain our good vibration all the time. Then we found each other, and it became much easier. Then we made Apollo, and it got easier. Then we found other good friends like Clara, Joe, Kelly, Lotus, Nicole, and Aladdin, and it became easier. Now, it's easy to maintain the LuvBubble vibe among the nine of us -- and the crew keeps growing as the vibe gets stronger. Together in Costa Rica, we're building a community filled with love -- built one person at a time. Perhaps someday you'll come visit!

## Our Dream for a New Way of Living

When we got engaged, we wrote down the following dream for our lives and our family so that we'd never forget it.

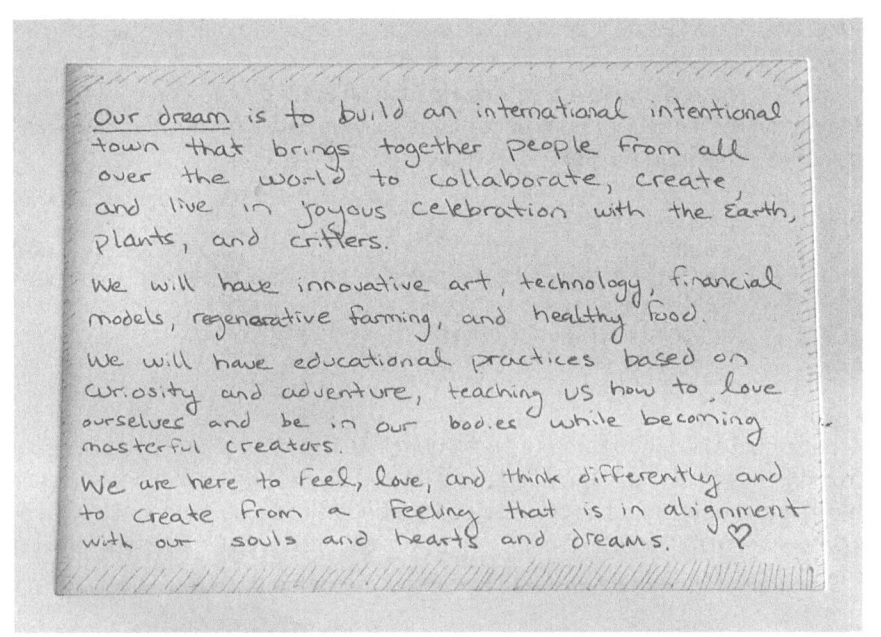

> Our dream is to build an international intentional town that brings together people from all over the world to collaborate, create, and live in joyous celebration with the Earth, plants, and critters.
>
> We will have innovative art, technology, financial models, regenerative farming, and healthy food.
>
> We will have educational practices based on curiosity and adventure, teaching us how to love ourselves and be in our bodies while becoming masterful creators.
>
> We are here to feel, love, and think differently and to create from a feeling that is in alignment with our souls and hearts and dreams. ♡

*The Original Framed Dream For Ryan & Morgan from 2021*

What is your dream for your current or future family? I encourage you to write it down.

**Action Item #101: Create Your Family Dream**
Write down, in as much specificity as you can the dream you have for your family. Where do you want to live? How many kids do you want to have? What do you want to create? What type of life do you want to offer your children? What will your family be about? Do this exercise with your partner if you have already found them -- or on your own if you are still looking for the right person.

Having little things like the above family dream framed around your house makes a HUGE difference as kids grow up. They start to get super curious about everything that hangs around the house around age 3-7. We like to have lots of inspiring things all around the house that give Apollo a sense of who his family is.

We want our kids to be **free-range kids** who can safely run around their community for many hours at a time, stopping by neighbors' homes and being guided and mentored by the other inspiring families who live nearby.

*Free-range kids - Kids who can safely run around their community for many hours at a time, stopping by neighbors' homes and being guided and mentored by the other inspiring families who live nearby.*

If you think it may be too dangerous for your 4-12 year old kids to run around the neighborhood for hours at a time without you worrying -- then it may be time to find a new neighborhood that allows you to rest easy. We chose where we live in Nosara, Costa Rica, based on safety, community, and the incredibly inspiring and global families that live nearby.

Here is Morgan's "Seven Divine Dreams" for the way she wants our kids to feel around our soul family. Reading her writing almost feels like reading a deeply divine prayer. This dream is now informing the way we go about building our community and home in Nosara.

### Morgan's Seven Divine Dreams For Our Soul Family

Yes, my heart yearns for a space for our soul family where we all can be ourselves, free of worry and shadow, free of anything hiding our lights, so that we may shine bright and love and care for one another.

1. I dream of our soul family holding my son Apollo and playing with his heart and giggles, knowing exactly how to connect to a child.
2. I dream of a home where our children roam free, and are safe to play, adventure, and take risks as they learn the secrets of the cosmos and being in physical form.
3. I dream of a world where we laugh and giggle, cry and care, tell the truth and know we are utterly safe and loved.
4. I dream of a world of great friends and collective upliftment, that our love story is beyond our own, it is all of us rising in love together as a soul family in full devotion and full freedom.
5. I dream of a world we play in and feel utterly safe within nature, that the plants and animals and critters have us and we have them, equals in the great harmony of it all.
6. I dream of a world where we light up the cosmos with our art and self expression, where we love our physical forms and know them as the divine and end separation from ourselves.

7. I dream of a world where magic is real, our wings sprout from our hearts and back, our forms can go through sacred changes and our hearts are pure and full of love.

I know this dream is big and getting us there is my epic adventure to make real.

It is my grandest adventure yet, to be family, making this real, creating this world in joy and of joy all around us, through us, with us, as us, in each breath, in the body, with each friend, in each moment, each child, each critter, the living earth and air, water and fire swirling in its alive form for us to dance inside of, on top of, and feel how deeply held in devotion and freedom we are–that we are all come from stardust and are infinite starlight bursting from our hearts and souls, collectively holding the new.

It is my greatest devotion to give this to my child, and future generations so they wander the skies and meet our friends out there. So they may be in the infinite galaxies of love and meet their epic life. That we become once again a part of the great tapestry in our remembering of who and what we are, what we are capable of and give the biggest yes to a life of love.

Deeply moving words from my beloved Queen who has touched my heart and soul and brought me to tears of ecstatic joy over and over again!

## Create a Ten Year Family Vision

In the first week of 2023, Morgan and I did a ten year family visioning exercise together for our new life intentions now that we have a family together.

*Ten Year Family Vision - Your written statement of what you have created and accomplished as a family ten years from now.*

Here's what we came up with, thinking ahead ten years. While dreams evolve over time, it's always helpful to write them out at least once per year.

| Our Ten Year Family Vision |
|---|

It's 2033 (ten years from when we did this exercise)...

- Morgan is 46
- Ryan is 48
- Apollo is 10 (born 2022)
- Aurora is 7 (born 2025) → our future child, not yet conceived

We own a fully paid off home with a pool, yard, garden, and an oversized bathtub near Nosara, Costa Rica. We have 4BR inside and then 3BR outside in converted shipping containers and tiny homes that our friends live in.

When we're not there, this home generates cash flow for us as well as home exchange opportunities. We use this cash flow for further investments and family expenses.

Together, Ryan, Morgan, Apollo, and (our future daughter) Aurora have pioneered and lived a reimagined way of family living — living in many different safe walkable intentional communities and allowing our kids to be free-range, mentored by many inspiring people who are our neighbors.

By exchanging our home in Nosara, we've experienced living as a family in: California, Bali, Spain, France, Italy, Australia — and many other wonderful places.

Apollo and Aurora have gone to incredible schools like Green School, Del Mar Academy, Casa De Las Estrellas Garza, and Austin Montessori.

Over the last decade, Ryan has:

1. Published this book and turned it into an online course and eventually a NY Times Bestselling Book.
2. Created an in-person course on creating the life of your dreams
3. Help build community in Nosara, Costa Rica
4. Helped raise money for many local Nosara-community development projects
5. Built a CEO Coaching business
6. Built Hive Digital, our digital marketing agency
7. Sold the Coinstack digital assets newsletter business
8. Enjoyed being a great dad to Apollo and Aurora, giving them an incredible education based on adventure, curiosity, play, and nature
9. Written multiple books on living an extraordinary life
10. Raised Apollo and Aurora, and mentored many other community kids

Over the last decade, Morgan has:

1. Painted beautiful works of art
2. Created a LuvMonster animated movie
3. Been an incredible mama to Apollo and Aurora
4. Lived slowly and enjoyed every moment of family time
5. Help build community in Nosara, Costa Rica
6. Co-hosted Temple Nights with Ryan
7. Been a sensuality coach to many friends

Over the last decade, Apollo has:

1. Grown from age 0 to age 10
2. Lived in five different countries
3. Learned to follow his joy, bliss, and obsessions
4. Had had an education based on curiosity, adventure, play, and nature
5. Become a big brother to Aurora

This is what we are now working on manifesting as a family. What is your ten year family plan?

**Action Item #102: Create Your Family Vision**
Working together with your partner (and kids if old enough), do a visioning exercise where you each write down what you want to achieve over the next ten years. Then print it up and frame it in the house. Do a new one every two years -- keeping the original ones behind the new one in the frame so you can see how your family's dreams evolve over time.

## Our Family Values

As a family, we've created our own set of values that we live by. We have these values framed on our love altar in our home. I encourage you to create your own family values that you, your partner, and your children can live by.

1. **Family** - Always put the health and stability of the family and children first.

2. **Community** - Live in a tribe, next door to or near our closest friends, in community, near nature, that is consistently full of love and support.

3. **Growth** - Always working on becoming the best version of ourselves (healthy, active, present, holistically well).

4. **Joy** - We have lots of fun and play!

5. **Presence** - Always time to be in presence with each other and our children

6. **Honesty** - Life's just more interesting when we share our deepest truths with each other--plus we grow more.

7. **Love** - We work to keep our hearts open to each other, and to others in our lives, as we work to set an example for creating a community based on love

8. **Openness** - Being open-minded to presence and intimacy with other people we both trust, as long as it feels safe to both of us, leads to our growth, and our values of family and stability stay true

9. **Education -** We'd like to worldschool our children as we adventure around the world together. We'd like to bring our kids to programs focused on learning through curiosity, play, joy, and adventure.

10. **Adventure** - We'd like to travel often and immerse ourselves in nature. We enjoy going to gatherings of heart-centered people working on inspirational projects. We travel the world in order to learn about new topics and cultures.

11. **Intentionality** - We communicate with and interact with presence, care, and love -- and integrate slowness into our lives.

12. **Relationship Stability** - We want to have one spouse and make a commitment to build a loving and harmonic home together as we raise our kids. We'd like to do all we can to minimize trauma on our children and provide a healthy, consistent family environment. Within this context of stability, we commit to continual growth and openness.

13. **Financial Stability** - We wish to ensure we have financial stability and strong passive income sources so that life is very comfortable and we can travel and we never have to concern ourselves with money.

Of course, it's the moment you set these values that you begin to get deeply tested by them in the cauldron of reality.

**Action Item #103: Family Values Statement**
Working together with your partner (and kids if they are old enough), create your family values statement with between 5 and 15 values. Once done, print it out, and frame it in your home. Read it together with your family at least once per year.

As a bonus exercise, you can create a short family song. Our Allis Family Song that we sing together with Apollo many times per week is…

Joyful like a Bubble<br>
Calm Like a Buddha<br>
Strong Like a Lion<br>
Playful like a Monkey<br>
Allis Family<br>
Kai Ya, Kai Ya, Kai Ya

# How to Give Your Kids a Big Leg Up in Life

*"What could possibly be more important than your kid? Please don't play the busy card. If you spend 2 hours a day without an electronic device, looking your kid in the eye, talking to them and solving interesting problems, you will raise a different kid than someone who doesn't do that. - Seth Godin, author*

My parents were masters of giving me as much of a head start in life as possible. On one hand I'm from a middle-class family that earned only $32,000 per year. On the other hand, I was extremely lucky and privileged.

I had…

- Two caring parents in a secure marriage
- A loving, calm, and stable home environment
- Well educated parents (both had masters degrees)
- A safe neighborhood to grow up in
- Thoughtful parents who gave me books like *Think and Grow Rich*, *Rich Dad Poor Dad*, and *How to Win Friends and Influence People*
- Role models to look up to

- The opportunity to play team sports like baseball, soccer, and track
- The opportunity to travel internationally every couple years (through house exchanges) which gave me an interest in other cultures
- Been taught from a young age to care about learning and to have good habits
- A sense that the world is a generally safe place in which the large majority of people are caring
- Day care from age 3 onward that gave me a head start with counting and words and socialization

If you can give your kids even some of the above, there is a much greater chance they will thrive in life.

My parents also gave me spiritual advantages -- the deeply ingrained and felt sense that I was part of a bigger divine and benevolent consciousness -- and that that I was able to be taken care of and rely upon my family and the greater universe as a source of care -- enabling me to feel safe that I was living in a world based on love.

I am also lucky to be American, to natively speak English (which gives you a big leg up in the world), and to have developed really high confidence levels. These were my **Childhood Advantages** and they contributed enormously to my life.

*Childhood Advantages - The advantages you can give your kids to give them a leg up in life and maximize the chances they will turn into happy and thriving adults.*

From this foundation that my parents gave me, I was able to get into a good college at the University of North Carolina, start a successful tech business, find mentors to help me grow it, sell it, and then get into Harvard for graduate school. I made the most of the advantages I had -- but nonetheless, I had huge advantages.

Regardless of where you live, what ethnicity you are, or how much money you make – if you can give your kids the above strong foundation for life, there is a very good chance that they will leave the nest feeling confident, grounded, secure, and able to make good decisions for their lives.

**Action Item #104: What Do You Want to Give Your Kids?**
Write down: What environmental advantages are you absolutely committed to giving your kids in life? A stable marriage, loving parents, calm home environment, safe neighborhood, travel, reading, role models, team sports, pre-school?

## Repairing Conflict In Front of the Children

If Morgan and I ever do argue, we come back to each other to "repair" very quickly. Earlier this week, Morgan came in at 11:15pm when I was about to fall asleep, which I really needed due to parenting challenges.

She decided to "play wrestle" with me and jump on top of me. I was rather upset as this woke me up, and I ended up saying in an upset tone that "she'd ruined my next day by waking me."

I realized right away that I'd erred. I apologized and told her I loved playing with her but needed to get some sleep. The next morning, I apologized again -- and so did she.

It's inevitable that conflict will happen. The key is to get to the repair part quickly, realize that seriousity is poo, and be sure that your kids know that their parents have done the **conflict repair** and are deeply in love.

*Conflict Repair - The process of softening, apologizing, taking time to actually hear each other and making up. If you ever have an argument in front of your kids, be sure that you close the loop and show them that mommy and daddy have reconnected.*

Too many parents get into arguments in front of their kids and then repair them behind closed doors -- leaving the kids to think that mommy and daddy are still mad.

As a parent, you are the primary role model for nearly everything your child is learning about relationships -- so be sure to fight rarely, when you do fight make up in front of the kids, and model a loving family environment that your kids can feel safe in.

# Raising Curious & Adventurous Kids

"Kids don't do what you say. They do what they see. How you live your life is their example."
- Paul Levesque, WWE Wrestler

While we are relatively new parents, here's what we've learned so far about raising children. We play with our son – a lot. We travel with him – a lot. We took him to the USA, Bali, Costa Rica, and Australia in his first year of life.

We encourage his education to be based on the principles of curiosity, play, adventure, and nature. And we live purpose-driven lives so that he can see us as inspired, passionate, healthy, and fully alive people.

We want to set an example for him of happy, loving, and creative people who love their work. Think about the example you're setting for your children with your work. Are you teaching them that work should be mundane and just used as a way to make money. Or are you teaching them that they should pursue their bliss, become a master at their craft, give their gift to the world, get into a daily flow, and earn money doing what they love?

Here's a quote from my friend Trey Stinnett. I first met Trey and his wife Grace through Camp Mystic at Burning Man. Trey wrote in a recent Facebook share:

"For the first 3 years after my daughter was born, I was afraid to take risks. I played small because she was depending on me. But, by the time my second daughter was on the way, I was overweight, out of money, with no inspiring purpose beyond putting food on the table. Everything changed at a marriage retreat when I heard the speaker ask, 'What example are you setting for your children with your work?' For better or worse, we are the example our children are modeling. If they see you "sacrificing" for them, then their model for being a parent will be sacrifice. If they see you pursue your dream AND make it happen they'll be unstoppable forces for good." - Trey Stinnett

Becoming a dad or a mom will change your entire world. Here's another great quote on parenting from a father named Jon (@frontiersman.living on IG):

*"When I became a father it changed my entire world. I think every father can say that. With my son he made me think about who I was as a man because I was his model for becoming one. But having a daughter exploded my brain. With a son you're modeling how to act. Every son wants to compete with his father and become better than his father. That's the ultimate goal of being a father: to strain your potential until it cries for mercy and then have your kids do even better than you. But when you have a daughter, the stakes change. She isn't looking to compete with you. You are the blueprint of her entire definition of what a man should be. And that's a heavy weight and huge responsibility for anyone to carry: to act like the man you would want your daughter to marry. Are you showing up like the man you would want your baby girl to choose as a partner?"*

## Parenting Is Really Hard

*"Children are like violins. They play the stress of their parents. If you want to raise a mentally strong child, you have to work on being mentally strong yourself."*
- Dr. Daniel Amen

Holy shit. Having a child is hard. No mistake about it. The mentoring/teaching/playing part is the fun part. It's the labor + delivery + recovery + sleep-challenged nights for 3 years that are the hardest parts.

Imagine making love to your beloved, having a baby with them, and then having so much love for that little bundle of joy who came out that you are actively willing to trade away your time, energy, and money to raise them into epic humans. That's parenting.

The more difficult part is waking up as a parent 3-4 times per night to feed them. And suddenly, 6 a.m. is wake up time every day, regardless of when you fell asleep. You can kiss many of your full REM cycles goodbye. Sleep. Wake up. Sleep. Wake up. All night long.

Welcome to the first year of being a parent.

Many parents will tell you when you're about to have kids, "Enjoy your sleep now when you can." What they don't seem to mention is that for the first year, one of you (or a night nanny if you can afford one) is waking up every 2-3 hours to bottle feed them and put them back to bed, making deep sleep very challenging. You become either an indentured servant to your baby or end up having to work extra hard to earn the money to pay for childcare.

Choose two: Sleep, savings, or a baby.

You can have a baby and some savings, but you'll get no sleep as you're up taking care of them. You can, of course, have sleep and savings, but no baby. Or you can have sleep and a baby, but spend all your savings on child care. Choose wisely.

The only way out of the trap is to have your income on autopilot before you have kids – so that you make enough passive income from your investments to cover your expenses – before you bring another human into the world. Otherwise, you're on a 20 year journey with kids where you're inside the **rat race** just trying to get the mortgage paid off and save up for college.

In some ways, having a kid is like a reverse pyramid scheme. In a normal pyramid scheme, the people at the bottom (the new people who just got in) pay for the people at the top who have been there awhile. Bernie Madoff used new recruits to pay off exiting investors in his investment scheme. With parenting, it's the opposite. It's the people at the top who pay for the people at the bottom (the babies).

With kids, you invest money into an ever growing hole that theoretically is going to pay you back when you're retired, maybe. Maybe.

But when it actually comes time to pay you back, the grown up kids grow their own downline, and all their extra money goes there for 20 years. And you become a grandparent and are suddenly expected to be a free babysitter.

So instead of the new people paying off the early investors in a classic pyramid scheme, it's you, the early investor, continually paying until you die.

The limitless joy, play, and laughter are your payoff. Along with the DNA immortality that you achieve when your kids eventually have kids themselves.

For many, having kids is part of their purpose in life. For me, it certainly was. I knew I wanted to have kids and a family since I was very young. When I was interviewing Morgan to be my wife that magical night at the Camp Mystic Burning Man campout, I asked her lots of questions to be sure she and I shared the same dream. We did. And now we are parents to Apollo, with potentially more to come.

We had to figure out a good system that worked for us for daytime work and nighttime sleep. In Bali, it was easy to have 24-hour nanny care for Apollo. This only costs $2,000 per month there. But in the USA, 24-hour nanny care costs around $14,000 per month.

So you either have to ensure you have read the chapter on money and building up investments and cash flow so that you can generate an extra $14,000 per month easefully by the time you have kids, or you have to spend some of your time being an unpaid babysitter (aka parent). Of course, you're paid in other ways, just not in money. Pretty much every parent ends up being an unpaid babysitter, at least some of the time – including at night.

So what did we do when we went back to Austin, where the going rate for childcare is $20 per hour instead of $3 per hour in Bali. We hired someone to cover 8 a.m. to 4 p.m. so we could do our miracle mornings and work out, and then had someone else available to do overnight nannying. Long story short, just to have our normal days and nights back, we were paying around $10,000 per month in child care costs. They are worth it, though. For some strange evolutionary reason, we want more.

Yes, it can be challenging to have babies and to raise them. But there is no greater joy that this life offers from my perspective. It is so meaningful to be there for many of the magic moments. Yes, it can be hard to be a **deeply dharmic man** and a **deeply present dad**. This is the balance we all must achieve. And if you take yourself on now, and make your magic year happen, and create a life you're truly proud of -- it will change the entire way your current or future kids or grandkids look at you.

Spend meaningful quality time with them. And become someone kids look up to. That is one of the greatest true measures of real success.

## Recommended Books on Family

- *Playful Parenting* by Lawrence Cohen
- *Hunt, Gather, Parent: What Ancient Cultures Can Tell Us About The Lost Art of Raising Happy, Helpful Little Humans*

## Key Outcome from This Chapter

**Write Your Family Vision & Values Statement** - Working together with your partner (and kids if old enough), do a visioning exercise where you each write down what you want to achieve over the next ten years. Then print it up and frame it in the house. Do a new one every two years -- keeping the original ones behind the new one in the frame so you can see how your family's dreams evolve over time. Do that same with your family values -- creating 5-15 values you share as a family. As a bonus exercise, create a short family song.

# FAMILY CHAPTER ACTION ITEMS

1. **Family Purpose Statement** - Working together with your partner (and kids if old enough) create a 10-30 word statement that describes your purpose as a family. Why does your family exist? What are you all about? What do you want to create together as a family in the years ahead? How do you want people to feel around your family?

2. **Family Dream** - Write down, in as much specificity as you can the dream you have for your family. Where do you want to live? How many kids do you want to have? What do you want to create? What type of life do you want to offer your children? What will your family be about? Do this exercise with your partner if you have already found them -- or on your own if you are still looking for the right person.

3. **Family Vision** - Working together with your partner (and kids if old enough), do a visioning exercise where you each write down what you want to achieve over the next ten years. Then print it up and frame it in the house. Do a new one every two years -- keeping the original ones behind the new one in the frame so you can see how your family's dreams evolve over time.

4. **Family Values** - Working together with your partner (and kids if they are old enough), create your family values statement with between 5 and 15 values. Once done, print it out, and frame it in your home. Read it together with your family at least once per year.

5. **Childhood Advantages** - Write down: What environmental advantages are you absolutely committed to giving your kids in life? A stable marriage, loving parents, calm home environment, safe neighborhood, travel, reading, role models, team sports, pre-school?

# STEP 12

## AWAKENING MAGIC

**MAGIC YEAR**

MAGIC YEAR - 492

# KEY CONCEPTS FROM THE AWAKENING CHAPTER

**1. AWAKENING** 
The process of re-remembering who you truly are and bringing your spirit back into full aliveness and connection to the oneness of all that is.

**2. STATES OF CONSCIOUSNESS** 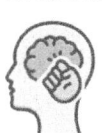
There are many different states of consciousness that are possible. The one to work toward is called pure presence where you are present, compassionate, and connected to all those around you. This is the state of Enlightenment.

**3. PURE PRESENCE** 
The holding of an enlightened awake state continually where you can be completely aware, connected, and present with the people in front of you and around you. You are able to feel their feelings and empathize with their experience.

**4. NON-DUALITY** 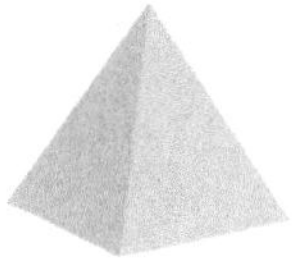
The concept that we are all part of something much bigger than ourselves and are all one with all human beings and in fact with all consciousness in the universe. The belief that I am you. Also known as oneness.

**5. CHALLENGE OF ENLIGHTENMENT** 
Enlightenment often comes in during brief moments and holding onto your awake state continually usually takes many years of practice.

**6. ENERGY DIET** 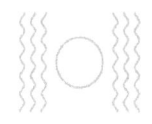
Only exposing yourself to positive uplifting "good vibe" people. Essential to learning to hold pure presence and begin to achieve a continual awakened state.

**7. ENTHEOGENS** 
Psychoactive substances that induce alterations in perception, mood, consciousness, cognition, or behavior for the purposes of engendering spiritual development or otherwise in sacred contexts

**8. VIPASSANA** 
A ten day silent meditation retreat designed to help you let go of the past and become the new version of yourself. Sign up for one at www.dhamma.org.

**9. INNER ROOMMATE** 
The anxious hyperactive voice inside your head. It can be quieted through meditation. Learn to observe your thoughts rather than be your thoughts.

**10. LSD** 
A synthetic hallucinogenic crystalline or liquid compound that can lead to creative thinking, visions, and visuals. It was first produced in 1938 in a lab by Albert Hoffman.

**11. IBOGA** 
A rainforest shrub and psychedelic native to Gabon in western Africa. The bark of the root is chewed for various pharmacological or ritualistic purposes. Ibogaine, the active alkaloid, is also used to treat substance abuse disorders and depression.

**12. SHAMAN** 
A trained traditional healer and medicine carrier, often offering ceremonies with healing medicines such as ayahuasca, peyote, sassafras, iboga, or psilocybin.

# MORE KEY CONCEPTS FROM THE AWAKENING CHAPTER

### 13. PEYOTE
A Native American medicine used ceremonially that contains mescaline. The peyote trip is characterized by visual effects, philosophical and introspective insights, and feelings of euphoria.

### 14. SAN PEDRO
A cactus, native to the Andes region of South America, that contains mescaline, one of the longest-studied psychedelics in the world—and the first to be labeled with the term "psychedelic."

### 15. MESCALINE
The active ingredient in San Pedro and Peyote. Mescaline induces a psychedelic state similar to those produced by LSD and psilocybin, but with unique characteristics.

### 16. AYAHUASCA
A plant brew grown in Central and South America. Drinking ayahuasca often leads to an 8-14 hour intense spiritual experience that leads people into greater connection to their heart and nature and compassion for all beings. Do with care and a good guide.

### 17. PSYCHEDELIC VISIONS
Intricate geometric patterns and vivid intense colors that can often be seen during an LSD, psilocybin, ayahuasca, DMT, 2CB, or mescaline experience.

### 18. 5-MEO-DMT
A inhaled vapor from the secretion of a Sonoran desert toad (Bufo Alvarius) that provides a 15-30 minute psychedelic experience of being connected to God and oneness, providing a parallel experience to the Near-Death Experience of seeing a white light.

### 19. HAPÉ
A sacred shamanic snuff made from powdered tobacco and various medicinal plants. It has been used for centuries by indigenous tribes in South America, particularly in Brazil and Peru, for healing, spiritual, and ceremonial purposes.

### 20. KAMBO
Poison from the a frog applied to a burnt spot on the skin by a trained shaman. Indigenous tribes used this to heal and cleanse the body, increase stamina, and improve hunting skills. Kambo often leads to vomiting for 5-30 minutes and a puffy face for a couple hours.

### 21. SASSAFRAS
A hallucinogen that's also known as methylenedioxyamphetamine (MDA). It's derived from the oil of the sassafras plant. It is an empathogen, and thus promotes feelings of closeness, compassion, affection, and empathy.

### 22. PSILOCYBIN
Psilocybin is a naturally occurring psychoactive compound found in certain species of mushrooms, commonly known as "magic mushrooms". When ingested, psilocybin produces psychedelic and spiritual effects.

### 23. WHITE LILY
An herbal aquatic flower plant that increases feelings of euphoria and sexual arousal. This is one of the milder entheogens.

### 24. KETAMINE
A synthetic dissociative discovered in 1962 as a surgical anesthetic that relaxes the mind and body. Ketamine is being researched for its potential in treating depression and PTSD.

# STEP 12: AWAKENING MAGIC

**Important Note:** This section discusses entheogens and psychedelics that can help in the process of awakening, presence, personal growth, and trauma healing. But overused or used incorrectly they can mess with your consistency and ability to actually make things happen in the world. So… seek experienced guidance with all mind-altering substances and always follow the law in your area.

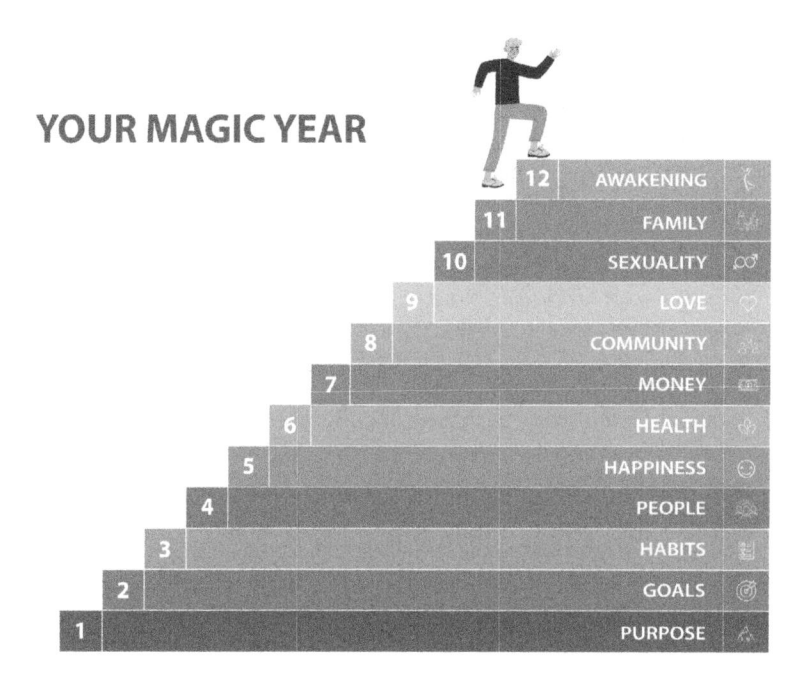

**YOUR MAGIC YEAR**

- 12 AWAKENING
- 11 FAMILY
- 10 SEXUALITY
- 9 LOVE
- 8 COMMUNITY
- 7 MONEY
- 6 HEALTH
- 5 HAPPINESS
- 4 PEOPLE
- 3 HABITS
- 2 GOALS
- 1 PURPOSE

## What I Mean by "Awakening"

In this section, I'll cover the process of **awakening** to your true nature as an infinite being and how to appropriately use **meditation** and **entheogens** that have been used for millennia to help homo sapiens transcend the illusion of ego-based separation and realize some of the deeper truths about the universe, like **non-duality**, the concept that we are all part of something much bigger and are all one.

First, a definition:

*Awakening - The process of re-remembering who you truly are and bringing your soul back into full aliveness and connection to the oneness of all that is.*

**Action Item #105: How Alive & Awake Are You?**
On a scale of 0-10, how fully alive is your soul? Is your soul dead inside or completely thriving? What changes do you need to make to get yourself to a 10/10? Write the answers.

The awakening I'm referring to in this section is the transformative shift from:

1. Overly serious to continual bliss (**ananda**)
2. Overly heady to integrated between body, mind, and spirit
3. An inability to feel to an ability to reconnect to your heart
4. Self-centered to we-centered
5. Following your obligation to following your obsession
6. Following others expectations to following your joy
7. Mediocre to extraordinary
8. Lonely to community-driven

*Ananda - A Sanskrit word meaning a feeling of intense pleasure or eternal bliss. The concept of Ananda inspired Joseph Campbell's famous encouragement to "Follow your bliss."*

While you could learn many of these concepts yourself on a single magic mushroom or ayahuasca journey or by doing a Vipassana, having a guide to these esoteric realms *might be helpful* and save you some time and brain cells.

Awakening is the process of re-remembering who you truly are and bringing your spirit back into full aliveness and connection to the oneness of all that is. It happens slowly, usually in one's late-20s or early 30s. Sometimes you meet people who are incredibly awake at 13 and others who stay fast asleep until they die.

Another way of explaining awakening, is that it is a realization (sometimes sudden, often gradual) that you are not separate but in fact part of all that is and a part of God, leading toward a **state of consciousness** characterized by greater compassion, kindness, presence, and humility.

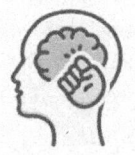

*States of Consciousness - There are many different states of consciousness that are possible. The one to work toward is called pure presence where you are present, compassionate, and connected to all those around you. This is the state of Enlightenment.*

Jesus, Buddha, and Lao Tzu are three examples of people in history who were said to have achieved extraordinary levels of compassion, kindness, and presence during their lifetimes -- influencing the creation of Christianity, Buddhism, and Daoism.

Other examples often mentioned are Ramana Maharshi, the 20th century Indian Sage, Rumi, the 13th century Persian poet, St. Teresa of Ávila, the 16th century Spanish Mystic, and Meister Eckhart, the 13th century German theologian.

All of these people across many different lands and times shared a unified message focused on the tenets of: love, compassion, kindness, forgiveness, simplicity, humility, inner peace, and the union between the individual soul and the divine. They were all also described as having an extraordinary **pure presence** in the moment with the people they were in front of.

> *Pure Presence - The holding of an enlightened awake state continually where you can be completely aware, connected, and present with the people in front of you and around you. You are able to feel their feelings and empathize with their experience.*

It is almost as if these extraordinary beings were tapping into a universal law -- that presence, enlightenment, awakening, compassion, and **non-duality** all go hand-in-hand based on a deeper truth that, when we remove the illusion of separation, I am you and we are all brothers and sisters on this planet (and in this universe, for that matter).

> *Non-duality - The concept that we are all part of something much bigger than ourselves and are all one with all human beings and in fact with all consciousness in the universe. The belief that I am you.*

Non-duality, also known as oneness, is a philosophical and spiritual concept that describes the fundamental unity of all existence.

Originating from the Sanskrit word "advaita," which means "not-two," non-dualists believe that there is no ultimate separation between the individual self (the observer) and the rest of reality (the observed). Instead, everything is interconnected and part of the same singular, undivided reality once we turn off the illusion of ego.

Non-duality is a core tenet in various philosophical and religious traditions, such as Hinduism, Buddhism, Taoism, and certain branches of Christianity, Islam, and Judaism. These traditions emphasize the idea that the distinctions we perceive in the world are ultimately illusory or superficial, and that realizing the underlying oneness can lead to spiritual awakening, liberation, or enlightenment.

It can certainly be challenging to be awake in a world where there is still so much unnecessary suffering. The **challenge of enlightenment** is that it comes in waves, and it can take a long time to become awake enough to hold onto your awake state all the time, even when in denser and less conscious environments.

> *The Challenge of Enlightenment - The challenge of enlightenment is that enlightening often comes in during brief moments. Holding onto your awake state continually after sleeping and being exposed to other lower vibrational influences usually takes many years of practice.*

You realize certain things in a ten day Vipassana, then you have the same "Eureka" at Burning Man at 3 a.m. on psilocybin, then you realize the same thing years later during an Ayahuasca ceremony. It's hard to hold your knowing that you are one with all that is -- and are an immortal part of God.

While in theory it should be easy to realize the truth of unity and to be able to maintain **pure presence** during your everyday life, when we read about warfare, school shootings, and people numbing themselves all day long -- and experience so many people who are "stuck inside" and have forgotten their true nature -- it can take time to hold this vibration of continual compassion, presence, and kindness. It sometimes requires moving to a very nature-oriented, calm, and peaceful place in order to lock in your connection to your Higher Self and the divine continually.

This temporary self-isolation in order to complete a personal upgrade process is what 28 year old Henry Thoreau did when he moved to Lake Walden for two years from 1845-1847 during his Saturn Return process.

His path was the same path many spiritual seekers choose to go through to be able to hear their inner voice. From monasteries to ashrams to temples, many **seekers** choose to have a period of societal isolation in order to remember their divine nature and get into a pure energetic state.

This is why **Escaping the Matrix** and getting outside of your regular environment, even if for only a few months, is critically important to being able to know thyself.

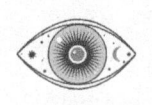

### Action Item #106: Mystical Experiences
Have you ever had a deeply spiritual or mystical experience, either sober or after meditation, holotropic breathing, or on psychedelics? Write about this experience and what you learned from it.

I would not have even understood this section, let alone been able to write it fifteen years ago. It took me three Ayahuasca journeys, two 5-MEO journeys, eight Burning Mans, a ten day Vipassana, thirty GHB sessions, twenty MDMA sessions, one hero's dose of magic mushrooms, eleven years of watching my dad preach in Church every Sunday, and forty years of life to realize the above as truths -- that I am part of the whole and that my greatest challenge is to maintain **pure presence** and bring an awake and compassionate perspective to every human interaction.

I still have some gunk in front of me. I'm still not 100% clear 100% of the time. But I may be 80% clear 80% of the time, which is good progress. The more I live on land in nature with friends and the more I can get out of the **American Matrix** that so often perpetuates the lies of separation and "us vs. them", the more present, aware, and awake I become.

I find that the more I maintain a really good **information diet** and **energy diet** (being around only positive, uplifting people) and the more I do my full **miracle morning routine,** the more I am able to maintain my own level of **pure presence**.

I've had to temporarily leave America, surround myself with inspiring and positive people, and block all news websites and apps from my phone and computer in order to not only hear my inner voice -- but also remember who I truly am.

Many people say that once you achieve full enlightenment, you can hold pure presence continually, even in energetically disruptive environments where there is conflict or suffering occurring. This, apparently, is what Jesus was able to achieve. I'm not there yet, but I'm working on it!

*Energy Diet - Only exposing yourself with positive uplifting people and sources of information. Essential to learning to hold pure presence and begin to achieve a continual awakened state.*

**Action Item #107: Your Energy Diet**
Are there any negative people, non-conscious news sources, or draining things you do that should no longer be part of your life? Journal the answer.

Thankfully, culture is slowly evolving as well, away from the tired "us vs. them" narratives that pit good against evil, into more nuanced narratives that recognize that we are all one and that there are both enlightened and unenlightened energies within each of us. The Ying and the Yang.

Certain movies have been said to have been written in a very awake manner in the last 30 years. Perhaps the most heralded awake movies are the original *Avatar* by James Cameron, the original Star Wars movies by George Lucas, and the original *Matrix* by the Wachowski Brothers. There was even a deleted scene in *Avatar* where protagonist Jake Sully takes a psychedelic worm that producer James Cameron said was influenced by the world of **ayahuasca**.

Many people are sleepwalking through life, having numbed their feelings and deadened their souls. They are resigned and cynical -- and certainly not joyous.

The truly enlightened, they say, can be joyous in any circumstance or situation. This is what we're working toward for the life you're designing for yourself -- a life of **Ananda** (continual bliss in Sanskrit) or **Shifuku** (supreme bliss in Japanese).

# My Personal Awakening Process

"Everyone holds his fortune in his own hands, like a sculptor the raw material he will fashion into a figure. . . . The skill to mold the material into what we want must be learned and attentively cultivated." —Johann Wolfgang von Goethe

I've found that most people's personal transformation and awakening processes start getting accelerated when they experience what I call "**The Triad of Transformation**." These are three types of experiences -- that once had -- change you forever, and accelerate the speed of your personal growth process -- and your understanding of many of the nuances of the universe. To recap from earlier, this triad of transformations is:

1. Plant Medicine -- especially Ayahuasca
2. Conscious Festivals -- especially Burning Man
3. Meditation -- especially a Vipassana

I can tell you this from personal experience, and from watching hundreds of friends go through the same process, If you do these three things, your life is guaran-fucking-teed to change forever, and your personal growth process will start to really kick into high gear.

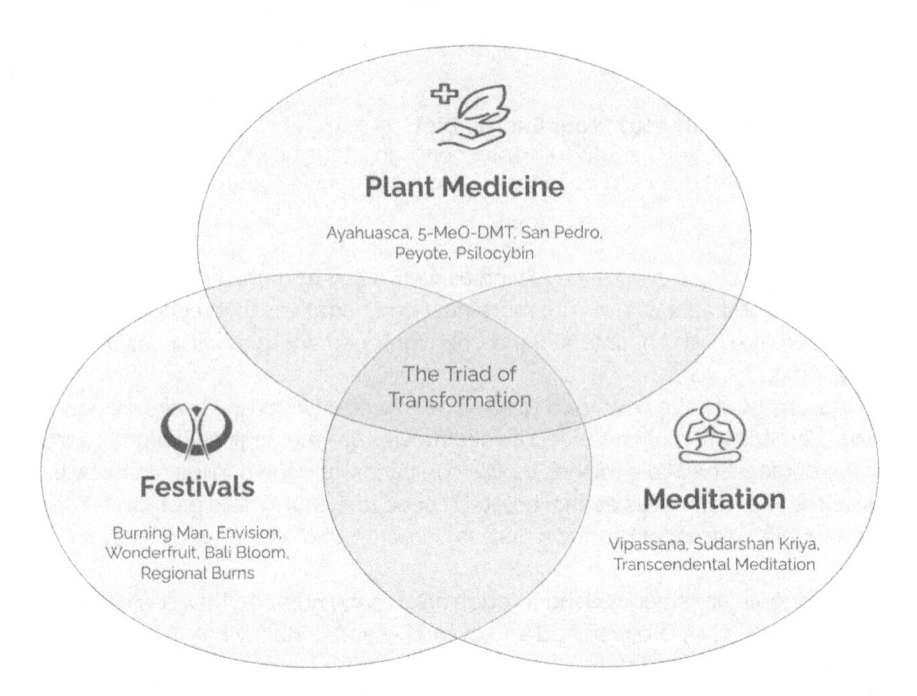

## The Triad of Transformation

**Plant Medicine**
Ayahuasca, 5-MeO-DMT, San Pedro, Peyote, Psilocybin

**Festivals**
Burning Man, Envision, Wonderfruit, Bali Bloom, Regional Burns

**Meditation**
Vipassana, Sudarshan Kriya, Transcendental Meditation

Here are a few more key parts of my ten year personal growth and transformation process between 2012 and 2023 that I now recommend to everyone I know. If you are ready for a wild ride of growth and adventure, look into some of these for yourself as well.

1. Conscious Festivals -

    - Burning Man - An annual art and music festival in the Nevada desert in late August. I've been going since 2012 and am part of Camp Mystic (one of about 2,000 different camps — or you can go without a camp too)

    - Envision Festival - An annual art and music festival on the Costa Rican beach in late February. We usually join the Humans I Trust Envision Camp.

    - Other great festivals like Wonderfruit (Pattaya, Thailand), Ondalinda (Careyes, Mexico), Lucidity (Santa Barbara), Lightning in a Bottle (California), Labyrinto (Costa Rica), LoveBurn (Miami), AfricaBurn (South Africa), Beloved (Oregon), and Bali Spirit (Bali)

2. Meditation -

    - Sudarshan Kriya - a short daily breathing practice I do that I learned at the Art of Living Happiness Program (held online and around the world, see www.artofliving.org)

    - Vipassana - A 10 day silent meditation that operates by donations. Sign up at www.dhamma.org.

- Transcendental Meditation - A form of silent mantra meditation developed by Maharishi Mahesh Yogi in the mid-1950s. The technique involves the use of a given mantra, which is repeated silently in the mind to help you achieve a state of relaxation and calm.

3. Facilitated medicine ceremonies with:

- Ayahuasca - a Peruvian plant medicine. You can find Ayahuasca ceremonies commonly in Peru, Costa Rica, and Mexico. I especially recommend the 1Heart Retreats in Costa Rica. I first experienced ayahuasca in 2016 and then again in 2019 and 2020. I recommend it to anyone who wants to live from their heart instead of their head — and to anyone who wants to understand the deeper nature of reality. Just be prepared to take a week or two off of working afterwards to integrate your experience. 1Heart is my recommended Costa Rica-based program for aya.

- Other transformative natural medicines like: 5-MeO-DMT, White Lily, Sassafras, San Pedro, Peyote, and Psilocybin (see the section later in this chapter on entheogens for a more in-depth review and set of cautions).

Other major transformation accelerants that I've experienced include:

1. Health transformation - Paleo diet plus daily lifting, cardio, cold plunge, & sauna

2. Sensual transformation - Tantra classes, yoni/lingam massages, ISTA 1 & 2

3. Mindset transformation - Landmark Forum, Tony Robbins' UPW, Hoffman Process

4. Nervous System Transformation - Reiki, cranial sacral, float tanks, breath of fire

Here is what I was like before and after experiencing these personal transformational processes over the last decade.

| Before My Transformation | After My Transformation |
| --- | --- |
| Stuck in my head | Feeling my feelings and heart |
| Hard to understand women | Much easier to understand women |
| Clinically obese (212 pounds) | Fit and healthy (160 pounds) |
| Anxious | Calm and clear |
| Workaholic | Balanced worker |
| Sensitive to Criticism | More Self-Assured |
| Overly Serious | Very Playful |
| Masculine Dominant | Masculine & Feminine Integrated |
| Achievement Focused | Achievement + Happiness Balanced |

In case you're wondering, my transformation process to a happy and healthy person wasn't an instant process. It was a full ten year journey from age 28 to 38. It's not like you can simply go to Burning Man, do some meditation, sit with Ayahuasca, and a month later be transformed. It takes time.

So take your time and let everything integrate as you go. Even for a dedicated person on "The Path," it can take 5+ years to get your body and CNS back into homeostasis after severe burnout. It took me from 2012 until 2022, I would say, until I considered myself "95%+ Healed" from the craziness of 2002-2012's entrepreneurial journey building iContact. Yes, it took me ten years of recovery to heal from ten years of burnout.

The Ten Year Transformation Process

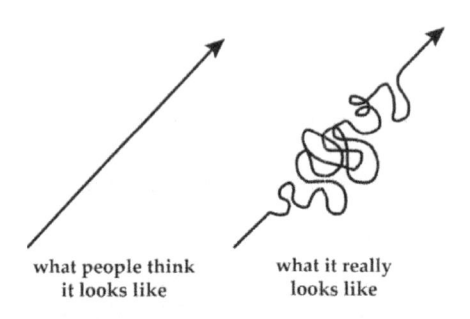

what people think it looks like        what it really looks like

These "breakthrough experiences" and the process of "waking up" to your true self can be accelerated by certain catalysts like long-term travel, festivals like Burning Man or Envision, silent retreats like Vipassana, and certain plant medicine ceremonies involving **entheogens** like Ayahuasca, 5-MeO-DMT, San Pedro, Kambo, and psilocybin that have been used as religious sacraments by indigenous tribes in spiritual ceremonies for many centuries to lead to major breakthroughs in consciousness and self-awareness. Just go slow and don't overdo it.

> *Entheogens* - Psychoactive substances which are used for religious, shamanic, or spiritual purposes. Entheogens can alter perception, mood, and cognitive processes, often leading to profound insights or experiences of unity and transcendence.

Take it from someone experienced: just don't mix too many variables in the same month. Know that breaking through to your higher self is usually a 5-10 year process -- involving many striking single experiences that unveil the next clue in the journey.

The key to personal transformation accelerants is to be sure to keep your achiever integrated as you go. You want to integrate both the masculine and feminine energies inside of you, not have too much of one or another and be unbalanced!!

If you do too much "personal transformation work" and don't properly integrate it, you can get unbalanced, lose your ambition and consistency, and become a spiritual hedonist drifter. Always remember the formula for success as you go, which is: **Vision + Belief + Action + Consistency = Results**.

> **Action Item #108: Look Into the Triad of Transformation**
> Look into Burning Man, a 10-day Vipassana silent retreat, and Ayahuasca. Take some time to research each of them and study all the potential benefits and downsides. Then choose one to do this year as part of your Magic Year and your transformation process. Schedule it now.

# How Ten Days in Silence Helped Me

Eleven months after my dad's death in 2014 – and after a failed Series B venture capital round for Connect, where I pitched in-person 62 VC firms and got 62 no's, I decided to take a 10 day re-calibration break.

I signed up for a ten day silent meditation program called **Vipassana** at www.dhamma.org. I found one near Montreal, Quebec, that was starting a couple weeks later and registered. Vipassana is a meditation technique discovered 2500 years ago by Buddha that focuses on observing the sensations in your body.

*Vipassana - A ten day silent meditation retreat designed to help you let go of the past and become the new version of yourself. Sign up for one at www.dhamma.org.*

I showed up in this rural Eden a few hours early—just enough time to get to know a few people before we'd be silent. Soon, all the men and women would be separated for ten days to avoid any distraction.

Everyone who attends a Vipassana course agrees to the following conditions for the duration of the course :

1. to not kill any being (including insects or animals for food);
2. to not steal
3. to not have any sexual activity;
4. to not lie:
5. to not have any intoxicants (including caffeine).

This seemed like a reasonable enough list of commitments for 10 days. I was in for the adventure.

The hardest part for me was getting off caffeine cold-turkey. I had already reduced my intake substantially, but I was still addicted to my two cups of green tea per day. After a couple days, my caffeine headaches finally went away.

The first night we went into the meditation room, and the **noble silence** was called to order by our teacher. The only sounds we'd hear for the next 10 days would either be the sounds of nature, the guidance of our teacher, or the video guidance of the Burmese man S. N. Goenka (1929-2013), the most recent advocate and modern popularizer of the ancient Vipassana tradition.

We were to wake up at 430 a.m. and go to bed at 9 a.m. each day. The Vipassana daily schedule was:

| The Vipassana Daily Schedule | |
|---|---|
| 4:00am | Morning wake-up bell |
| 4:30am | Meditate in the hall or in your room |
| 6:30am | Breakfast break |
| 8:00am | Morning meditation in the hall |

| | |
|---|---|
| 11:00am | Lunch break |
| 12:00pm | Rest, walk in the woods, or get guidance from the teacher |
| 1:00pm | Afternoon meditation in the hall |
| 3:30pm | Meditate in the hall or in your own room |
| 5:00pm | Dinner break |
| 6:00pm | Evening meditation in the hall |
| 7:00pm | Teacher's discourse in the hall |
| 8:15pm | Group meditation in the hall |
| 9:15 pm | Retire to your own room--Lights out |

If you add it up – we did five hours of meditation before lunch, four hours before dinner, and two hours after dinner – for a total of 11 hours of meditation per day. Can you imagine meditating for eleven hours per day for ten straight days?

We slept in a very basic bed, had only short showers and vegetarian meals, and mostly meditated in the meditation hall, which was about 50 meters away.

The daily lunchtime walks in the adjacent woods became my escape. I made 10 slash marks on a nearby rock – one for each day I had made it through. I was thankful that this particular facility allowed for forest hikes. Many did not.

Days 1 and 2 weren't too hard. I knew I could do nearly anything for a couple days. Day 3-4 got a bit difficult as there was a temptation to leave – and a couple people had already left – not able to get through the inner boredom – and the very slow pace of instruction that had spent 72 hours teaching us to breathe through our noses and sit in a proper position.

You see, in the first four days of Vipassana, all you do is sit there, and they show you how to sit properly and properly breathe through your nose. During the first 3 days, you simply observe your breath from your nostrils as your mind settles down. After a few days, the mental chatter inside begins to stop. And your mind becomes quiet and calm.

During days 4-10 you learn the vipassana technique of Calmly observing your own body sensations. After a few days, you can observe these sensations without reacting and can break the constant internal cycle of craving and aversion.

They take these three days to essentially prepare you for the "real Vipassana," which happens on days 4-10. It is during these days that "The Chatter" of the world and inner critic finally fades away, and some people are able to achieve true inner peace. By day 7, some students reported (they told me after it ended) being able to feel the vibration of the atoms in their body.

Vipassana is ultimately about getting still enough to clear the mind – and then once the mind is cleared – to be able to feel, at an atomic level, the vibration of the atoms in your body – in order to learn that everything, including you, is impermanent.

Humans, of course, are made of cells, which are made of atoms, which are made of particles, and those so-called particles are actually just vibrating energy. According to the tradition of Vipassana, if you get still enough, you can actually feel this vibrating energy.

The other goal of Vipassana is to be able to witness your cravings and aversions in your own mind – and to be able to watch them and consciously choose your actions based on what is actually good for you rather than what you are addicted to.

After a few days of sitting there and watching your breath, you learn to "observe your thoughts" as a witness rather than "be your thoughts." The goal is to be able to watch your thoughts (sometimes called your "inner roommate") and discern at a higher level which thoughts are helpful and which are unhelpful and should be thrown out/edited.

When you end up just observing your Sensations for 10-11 hours per day you experience pain, itching, fatigue, cramping, and you end up sensing the reality that all sensations and everything in fact will soon pass

By day 7, I could feel a deep sense of inner peace, could feel the vibrations in my arms and upper lips, and could notice the cravings constantly coming up (for meat, for sex, for caffeine, etc.).

I have to confess—I did cheat on one thing to make it through the Vipassana. Around day 5 I started reading the one book I brought under my covers at night before I went to bed. I even had to hide it from my roommate in the top bunk. The book was *The Untethered Soul* by Michael Singer, a spiritual classic.

While I probably would have had an even deeper experience had I not spent an hour per day sneaking reading – I will say that this book has become one of the most impactful books of my life – and I recommend it to everyone.

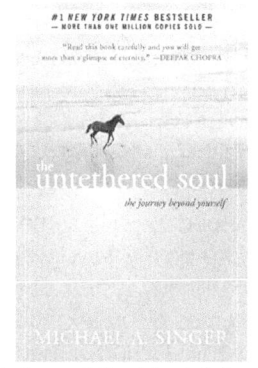

The Untethered Soul by Michael Singer
The book I secretly read during my Vipassana

**Action Item #109: Read *The Untethered Soul***
Get yourself a copy of the book *The Untethered Soul* by Michael Singer and read it over the next two weeks. Write down what you learn from it in your notebook.

# What I Learned from Vipassana

At the end of the 10th day I recall going outside near sunset and appreciating the intense beauty of the sunset and the flowers. Here's what I took away from the 10 day Vipassana (from my journal at the time).

1. I learned that I am the **Objective Observer** (the being watching) not the **Inner Roommate** (the voice in my head)

> *Inner Roommate - The anxious hyperactive voice inside your head. It can be quieted through meditation. Learn to observe your thoughts rather than be your thoughts.*

*Objective Observer - The witness to your thoughts. The real you. Learn to distinguish anxious thoughts from your "inner roommate" from your true intuition, which comes from your Higher Self.*

2. I will celebrate the small and big victories in life and take time to enjoy life with the ones I love
3. I will watch for my anger in my breath and cut it off before it begins through deep calm breathing
4. I will do my best to not let anything anger me or get me off my balance
5. I have learned that nothing is forever and that regardless of whether what you are going through is pleasurable or not it too will pass
6. I have learned to keep a balanced mind without extremely quick reactions to irritations or pleasure
7. I have learned to no longer immediately react to the cravings in my body and stay centered during times whether I otherwise would have been emotional and triggered
8. I learned that it is ultimately my choice to have inner peace
9. I learned that I can choose to be happy
10. I will take the "Vow of Unconditional Happiness" from the book The Untethered Soul

The Vipassana course also helped me with some mild anger issues that I had. Between ages 16-31 – when things didn't go my way, I'd get triggered, defensive, and upset. There was certainly a lot of testosterone in my system at that age – and there was quite an immense rage that I would feel a few times per week whenever something wasn't going my way. I learned to suppress the rage – afraid I'd hurt someone.

Fortunately, I never hurt with my inner rage – but I do remember punching two holes in the wall in my 20s when upset things weren't going my way. At that age, I didn't know how to calm or channel my masculine anger toward constructive means.

The Vipassana allowed me to notice the beginning of becoming angry (the sign was a quickening of my breath), allowing me to catch myself and calm myself through taking deeper, slower breaths.

Ultimately, Vipassana helped me get past losing my dad, overcome my anger, learn to be the witness of my own thoughts, appreciate nature even more, and notice my habit of continual overwork.

You should schedule a vipassana for sometime this year. While not exactly easy or blissful the whole way, the process will completely change your perspective on life and give you a major life upgrade. The courses are by donation only, so you can give whatever you can afford.

## How Plant Medicines Helped Me End Overwork

After selling iContact, I started another tech startup in 2012 called Connect.com. That company ended up failing miserably -- and taking $6M of my own money along with it. We had a meaningful mission of using technology to bring people together in the real world – but we couldn't quite nail the business model.

So after 10 years of building iContact, I had another harrowing experience building Connect, and my nervous system got even more fried. I should have just done nothing other than my MBA program and life exploration for a couple years after building and selling iContact – but I was still addicted to building companies.

So even while I was starting the healing and awakening process through festivals, meditation, yoga, and plant medicine work -- I was STILL ADDICTED TO WORK. I was still addicted to "success." I was still addicted to "doing." Can you relate?

Something else was needed to knock me out of my over-hyper entrepreneurialism. Thankfully, I discovered the world of plant medicine and entheogens. This discovery was the next stage in my personal transformation.

Thankfully, a friend introduced me to the world of plant medicines, which was still rather underground at the time.

### A Longer Safety Note on Plant Medicines and Psychedelics

Below I describe what I learned from plant medicines and psychedelics. These gave me incredible insights into myself, the nature of reality, and spirituality and helped me slow down. Many of these medicines have since been shown in studies to have major therapeutic benefits with reducing depression and PTSD. That said, it is very important to be careful using these types of "medicines" and follow the guidance of experience practitioners. Traditional entheogenic medicines are designed to create a deeper connection to spirit and self. However, they can turn from helpful medicines into harmful drugs very quickly if overused, misused, or mixed.

I encourage supervised use of them from people who really know what they are doing and are wise about the right dosages and settings and who understand how to comply with local laws. Without careful and thoughtful use, these substances used too frequently or combined in the wrong way can lead to lasting brain changes--some of which aren't positive.

Further, since the brain is still developing, I do not recommend using any of these plant medicines or psychedelics be used by people under 25. Lastly, while laws for these types of potentially beneficial medicines are thankfully trending toward decriminalization, there are various laws in each country and locality that you should be aware of. I recommend only using these medicines in supervised circumstances where they have been legalized.

## My Experience With Plant Medicines

I grew up the son of an Episcopal priest from Pennsylvania and a Buddhist social worker from England. While I had heard of meditation and yoga growing up – I had never heard of the world of plant medicines.

During my 10 years building iContact from 2002-2012 I also never heard of plant medicines. As far as I'd been taught by my 7th grade DARE class, "drugs were bad," and while I had the occasional puff of marijuana a few times in my 20s – I generally stayed away. I was Mr. Consistency and Mr. High Achiever.

Something about moving to San Francisco and going to Burning Man began opening me up to other perspectives and allowed me to start to differentiate between harmful drugs and those that could be helpful **entheogens** that could teach me lessons about spirituality and actually improve my life.

While it wasn't a straight line—and I made some naive mistakes that I'll share — I am very happy I discovered plant medicine work. Overall, my quality of life and level of happiness benefited immensely.

Please note that these ritualistic entheogens are not yet legal in all locations, so I recommend going to a place where they have been legalized (such as in some Native American lands, as sacraments for a registered church, or in other parts of the world where they are often used, such as Costa Rica, Mexico, and Peru).

You can find a recommended directory of experienced professional guides for the various entheogens that I'll be writing about at TheThirdWave.co.

Here's a timeline of my first experiences with each major psychedelic, entheogen, plant medicines, or "conscious medicine."

2014 - LSD & MDMA
2015 - Iboga and San Pedro
2016 - Sassafras, White Lily, Ayahuasca, and Psilocybin
2017 - Mescaline, 5-MeO-DMT, 2CB
2021 - GHB

I tried **LSD** at Burning Man 2014 for the first time -- and it definitely opened my eyes quite a bit.

*LSD - A synthetic hallucinogenic crystalline or liquid compound that can lead to creative thinking, visions, and visuals. It was first produced in 1938 in a lab by Albert Hoffman.*

Here's what Apple founder Steve Jobs has to say about how LSD impacted his life. "Taking LSD was a profound experience, one of the most important things in my life. LSD shows you that there's another side to the coin, and you can't remember it when it wears off, but you know it. It reinforced my sense of what was important—creating great things instead of making money, putting things back into the stream of history and human consciousness as much as I could."

I discovered I'm rather sensitive to LSD, so if I ever do use it, I tend to use very small amounts between 10 micrograms (a microdose) and 50 micrograms (a half-dose).

Today, I stayed away from it, as I found that when I was using it, I ended up becoming a different person after each use. Each time I used it, I'd come back the next day with an entirely new plan for what I wanted to do with my time and company.

I really value consistency, so LSD wasn't my medicine of choice. It can really mess you up as an achiever, so I stay away from it these days. The initial benefits from the mental perspective shifts from the first couple experiences were helpful to me -- but I don't find LSD useful for continual usage.

## My Time With Iboga

In 2015, during my second year at Harvard Business School, a friend of mine invited me to go to an Iboga Plant Medicine ceremony in a farmhouse in Connecticut. Iboga is a plant medicine used in Gabon, West Africa.

I had never heard of Iboga, but I was intrigued and decided to go with her. I had many friends in San Francisco who were talking non-stop about plant medicine and ayahuasca and all their revelations, and I wanted in on what it was all about.

After a couple hours' drive from Boston, we arrived at the Connecticut farmhouse. A group of four eccentric French shamans who had been initiated into the Gabonese practice of offering Iboga came to the door to welcome us. They had spent the last decade of their life being initiated into becoming medicine carriers in West Africa -- and were on a mission to bring the psychoactive medicine that was sacred in the Gabon culture to different parts of the planet.

That night, we worked with the medicine in a group of about 20 others. The night included traditional drums, face paint, fortune telling, talk of soul guides, and a bitter tasting green powder called **Iboga** from a rainforest shrub from Gabon that made me enter into a transcendental meditative state for 6 hours. It was all new to me.

*Iboga - A rainforest shrub and psychedelic native to Gabon in western Africa. The bark of the root is chewed for various pharmacological or ritualistic purposes. Ibogaine, the active alkaloid, is also used to treat substance abuse disorders and depression.*

I left with a positive enough experience to be open to other types of plant medicine ceremonies. While this first plant medicine experience was a bit strange and a far cry from the more familiar halls of Harvard Business School for me, it was eye opening -- and left me wanting to explore more. I felt like I was on the leading edge of a cultural surge of traditional indigenous medicines, bringing their benefits into America's heady culture of overwork and financial success at all costs.

Iboga has been used for centuries in traditional medicine and spiritual practices. The primary psychoactive component of iboga is ibogaine, which is known to help treat addictions to heroin, meth, and alcohol.

Due to its psychoactive effects, ibogaine can cause hallucinations and disorientation, which can be dangerous if you're not in a safe and controlled environment – so only take it with experienced guides.

Dr. Dan Engle, a friend of mine, stated that "Iboga is four to five orders of magnitude [superior to] anything in the general psychiatric rehab arena [for treating opiate addicts]. You have the same level of success using MDMA-assisted therapy to treat chronic post-traumatic stress disorder (PTSD). That's why MDMA is going into Phase III trials. Psilocybin is similarly going into Phase III trials because you have such a high success rate with people going through [cancer-related] end-of-life transitions being relieved of anxiety, and really being able to walk through death with dignity and strength."

**Side Note:** I don't recommend starting with Iboga as your very first plant medicine. It can be quite harsh. It just happened to be first for me. Iboga can be one of the harsher and more challenging plant medicines. If I could choose, I would look into an experience with San Pedro, Mescaline, Peyote, Sassafras, or even Ayahuasca as a better entry into the world of plant medicine work. As always, work with trained and experienced practitioners and research extensively beforehand so you know what you're getting yourself into. And follow the laws of your local area.

## The Softer San Pedro & Peyote

My next plant medicine journey was just a few months later, on New Year's Eve 2016, at a friend's home in Southern California. That magical night, we took **San Pedro**, a cactus native to the Andes Mountains that has been used in traditional medicine and spiritual practices for centuries. The cactus has a long history of use in indigenous medicine and shamanic rituals.

The primary psychoactive component of **San Pedro** and **Peyote** is **mescaline**, which is a psychedelic compound known to alter perceptions of reality. Some people report feeling euphoria, increased empathy, and a sense of connection to the natural world when taking San Pedro.

*San Pedro - A cactus, native to the Andes region of South America, that contains mescaline, one of the longest-studied psychedelics in the world—and the first to be labeled with the term "psychedelic."*

*Peyote - A Native American medicine used ceremonially that contains mescaline. The peyote trip is characterized by visual effects, philosophical and introspective insights, and feelings of euphoria.*

*Mescaline - The active ingredient in San Pedro and Peyote. Mescaline induces a psychedelic state similar to those produced by LSD and psilocybin, but with unique characteristics.*

Mescaline can have a positive effect on emotional well-being and has been shown to help people overcome trauma, anxiety, and depression. Some people describe the experience of taking San Pedro as a "spiritual journey" that helps them gain a deeper understanding of themselves and the world around them.

As with any entheogen, be sure you're working with trained professionals and be aware of any local laws that may be relevant to their use in your area.

For me, the San Pedro ceremony was much softer and easier to experience than iboga. All I remember is that we had a very heart opening night, formed many deep friendships that I still have to this day, and that the fireworks going off at midnight over the ocean were particularly spectacular.

I posted on my personal Facebook l the following week: "I am learning to feel deeply with my heart rather than being stuck in my mind. Building the head-heart connection, one week at a time. Like a toddler again, I am. But learning. Thank you for your help on this journey to so many amazing friends."

## My First Heart Opening Ceremony

Four months later, I was back in San Francisco, and a group of friends I trusted invited me to what they called a "Heart Opening Ceremony." I had no idea what that meant, but apparently they were working with a great **shaman,** and the goal was to bring us all into further alignment so that we could make a bigger positive impact in the world.

*Shaman* - A trained traditional healer and medicine carrier, often offering ceremonies with healing medicines such as ayahuasca, peyote, san pedro, 5-MEO-DMT, sassafras, iboga, or psilocybin.

We met up on a Saturday afternoon at a good friend's house in Marin, California, just north of San Francisco. Marin was not only home to some of the best hiking and biking trails in California -- but also had an active plant medicine community.

I attended, and many of my closest friends from Burning Man were there. That night we were given a choice between taking White Lily or Sassafras (MDA) -- both mild (compared to ayahuasca or iboga) heart opening natural entheogens. We sat in a circle, shared our intentions, selected our desired medicine, and swallowed it down around 4 p.m.

Within an hour, the whole room was abuzz in empathic, present, and meaningful conversations. Many people were cuddling and massaging each other in large cuddle puddles.

For an East Coast tech entrepreneur from Florida and North Carolina who grew up the son of a Minister, I was taken aback by how "free" the love was flowing that night.

People were cuddling and massaging people who weren't their romantic partners. And somehow it was all okay. Everything was clear, consensual, and talked about.

I realized that my first Bay Area Plant Medicine Ceremony had turned into my first Bay Area Polyamory experience. Everyone seemed to be having a REALLY GREAT TIME.

As I was single and had crushes on at least three of the women in the room, I had a blast having meaningful conversations with them as the night continued. My mind was blown at the level of care, presence, communication, and sensuality in the room.

I often joke that this night was the night I turned polyamorous -- the night I realized I would always love many people. In the love chapter, I have a section on open relating in case you're interested in how to "open relate" in an ethical way.

Around midnight at the ceremony, we gathered everyone together again to share their experiences. I remember sharing that I had never before felt so connected to others, so connected to my body, and so inspired by a field of love within a group of smart, talented, and sexy friends.

I was hooked. If this is what people did on Saturday evenings in California -- I was happy to live in California. It sure beats drinking alcohol at a bar (by a lot)!

Since 2016, I've now done this type of plant medicine ceremony in groups of friends about 25 times (about 4 times per year, though I've slowed down to 1-2 per year now) and absolutely have loved these types of experiences that I knew nothing about growing up becoming a common occurrence in my life.

## How Ayahuasca Changed Everything

*"Ayahuasca is very successful in helping people transition from chronic depression into what would be called euthymia , or normal mood. Many people don't even know what having a normal mood feels like; but optimism, faith, courage, strength, [and] personal empowerment are some of its qualities." - Dan Engle, scientist*

Since I first got exposed to plant medicines in 2015, mainstream interest has exploded, with many well known personalities like Joe Rogan, Aubrey Marcus, Aaron Rogers, and even Prince Harry actively talking and writing about the topic and the massive transformations they went through.

Google search interest for the term **ayahuasca** has increased by 3x over the last fifteen years, peaking when Green Bay Packers quarterback Aaron Rodgers talked about it on the Joe Rogan podcast in August 2022.

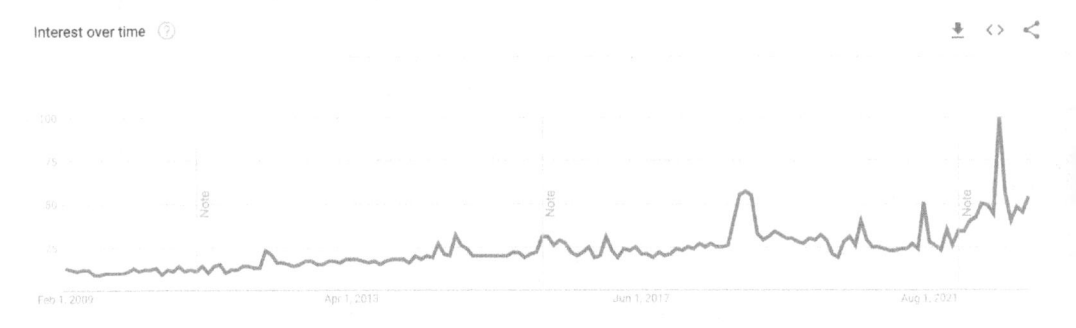

A study published in 2020 by researchers in Spain found that bereaved adults who took part in **ayahuasca** ceremonies at a retreat center in Peru reported a decrease in the severity of their grief, and those benefits lasted for at least a year.[25]

*Ayahuasca - A plant brew grown in Central and South America. Drinking ayahuasca often leads to an 8-14 hour intense spiritual experience that leads people into greater connection to their heart and nature and compassion for all beings. Do with care and a good guide.*

In May 2016, about a week before I graduated from Harvard Business School, I was invited by a friend in California to join my first Ayahuasca Ceremony. It was held at a friend's house in Northern California and facilitated by two **shamans**.

Ayahuasca is called "Grandmother medicine" because of the particularly wise teachings you learn from her consciousness. Yes, I do believe that plant are exceptionally conscious.

I was told to follow a strict diet, avoiding meat, alcohol, sugar, and sex for 4 days before the ceremony. I didn't listen. I had already experienced three plant medicine ceremonies by that point, and I thought I knew what I was doing. How challenging could aya be?

On the way to our Ayahuasca ceremony, I even had an ice cream cone, enjoying one last delight before two nights of sitting with the medicine. The medicine got me back for that transgression later on.

We arrived at the venue in Northern California around 3 p.m. on Friday afternoon. There were 12 total participants. The Shamans were relatively young, in their early 30s, and each had about 3 years of experience serving Ayahuasca. I later learned that it's much better to

---

[25] Ayahuasca Peru Study - https://www.ncbi.nlm.nih.gov/pmc/articles/PMC7113212/

look for very experienced Shamans who have been working with the medicine for at least a decade.

At 5 p.m., the ceremony began with the Shaman blowing tobacco smoke on our bodies, saging us (the process of using burning sage to remove unwanted energies from the body), and then blessing each of the directions of north, south, east, and west – as is done in many native or indigenous ceremonies.

After an hour of preparation, we were each offered a cup of the Ayahuasca medicine -- and one by one we drank it while Icaros (songs) were sung by the two Shaman. When it got to my turn, I drank the cup fully, expecting a mild experience.

Nothing happened for the first 30 minutes, and then around the 40 minute mark I started wiggling my body and "feeling it come on." Three hours later, I was having the most intense experience of my life. I was seeing **psychedelic visions** so intense that they'd be in full color whether I had my eyes open or closed.

*Psychedelic Visions - Intricate geometric patterns and vivid intense colors that can often be seen during an LSD, psilocybin, ayahuasca, DMT, 2CB, or mescaline experience.*

After drinking the aya for the first time, in what appeared to be straight from an Android Jones dome experience at Burning Man, I saw psychedelic kundalini-like golden snakes dancing—for roughly a half hour.

I then, for what seemed like hours, lived through an experience that seemed to be designed to deepen empathy inside me. I lived through five extraordinarily vivid experiences:

1) Being my mother while she was taking her last breaths while dying from brain cancer

2) Being U.S. President George W. Bush during the Iraq War and feeling what it was like to receive criticism coming from many sides

3) Being Saddam Hussein (the former dictator of Iraq) in his last moments hiding in a fox hole before being captured by American troops

4) Being Jesus on the cross, being nailed to the cross and crucified

5) Being a cow just before being slaughtered to become meat (I ended up a vegan for the next two months after that experience!).

Each experience had me actually believing *I was them*. I was seeing through their eyes, feeling their emotions, and feeling their pain. I became them for 5-10 minutes per experience.

I no longer had a sense of "Ryan," and instead I was, for a time, fully immersed in a hyperrealistic 3D world, as if I were in a VR headset so realistic that it seemed entirely real and connected to my own brain.

My first night of ayahuasca gave me greater empathy for all beings, a greater understanding of the nature of reality, and smacked my ego in the face.

The second night, after resting and eating a small vegan meal during the day, we again took a full cup of the medicine in the circle.

My entire view of "what was reality" was shifting. Ayahuasca showed me that I, as a soul, was immortal, everlasting, and that I certainly was not my body. It was a LOT to take in.

I remember the day after the second ceremony sitting outside of a coffee shop in San Francisco, on the floor, wearing "Free Hugs" pajamas, playing with an avocado shell on my head and completely still out of it while my friends got breakfast inside.

I spent the next week in bed in my San Francisco home, shaking trauma out of my body 6-8 hours per day.

Ayahuasca had shaken me up a lot inside.

## Starting the Healing Process

*"It's so critical to have preparation before the [ayahuasca] experience and then a period of integration afterward, because you are in this opened-up and receptive state and more suggestible." - Dr. Martin Polanco*

Ages 31-33 were really difficult for me due to my experience with ayahuasca messing up my internal navigating systems for a couple years -- and me learning how to integrate my head and my heart and truly heal my body while being a continual top level creator and builder.

Here's what I learned about how to set yourself up for success with taking ayahuasca.

If I could do it all again, I would have taken a half cup for just one night instead of a full cup two nights in a row. That lower dosage would have been much more conducive to my overstimulated nervous system.

For me, Ayahuasca brought out the underdeveloped feminine inside of me. This was incredibly helpful in expanding my compassion and kindness -- but it made me a pushover in business for a couple years afterwards, which made it easy for others to take advantage of me. Sometimes in business, you need 'get shit done' energy and alpha energy to win. That energy dissipated in me for a couple years.

| Me Before Aya | 1 Week After Aya | 3 Years After Aya |
|---|---|---|
| In my head a lot | In my heart only | Head & Heart Integrated |
| Very Masculine | Very feminine | Balanced Between Masculine & Feminine |
| Very serious | Unable to fully take care of myself for a few weeks | Balanced between playfulness and focused work |
| Overly driven, always working | A loss of interest in the "real world" | Balancing work & health |
| Firm | Flimsy | Firm Yet Compassionate |

Overall, I'm very glad I came across ayahuasca. I've now experienced the medicine three times (2016, 2020, and 2021). Now when I do it, I take a half dose of what everyone else is taking, and that works out okay for me.

While dosage amounts can be different depending on preparation, I recommend asking your shaman for a smaller dose the first time you do it.

I took a full cup for two nights in a row during my first ceremony in 2016, and it overstimulated my nervous system so much that I had to take a full MONTH off of email and working. I became a collapsed version of myself and lost much of my business acumen and ability to make tough decisions for a couple years–ultimately costing me a few million dollars.

So even though my business affairs took a beating for a couple years after taking ayahuasca in 2016 (due to soft boundaries and too much kindness on my side), throughout the process afterwards I learned how to integrate a strong masculine and strong feminine energy inside of my body at the same time -- which has proven invaluable.

What I recommend is that if you're a hard charging CEO or entrepreneur, take 2-4 weeks off of work after sitting with ayahuasca and make sure you fully integrate the experience before going back into the world of meetings, emails, and spreadsheets.

So in advance, block off at least 2-4 weeks after your first session for integration and vacation. You can always come back earlier if you feel ready. Aya has the potential to change your life and "way of being" that much. In traditional indigenous communities, taking ayahuasca was, for most people, a once in a lifetime experience that was treated with great respect, appreciation, and preparation.

Yes, there are huge benefits, like becoming kinder, more compassionate, and more aware of all beings. But go slowly initially to ensure you don't lose your business edge and analytical acuity. So if you are a business entrepreneur and want to experience ayahuasca, just start with a small amount, and then in future sessions, you can try larger amounts if the first session goes well.

My wife, Morgan, also had a very difficult first experience with Aya her first time. Long story short – it's worth it – but tread lightly initially until you know the full power of what you're working with (actual consciousness that can open you up). Also, fully read the health screening pages of those you're working with so you can ensure you're not taking any prescriptions that may contraindicate the medicine.

There's a common saying in the world of psychedelics: "If you get the answer, you should hang up the phone."

So after you get the lessons you came for, you shouldn't keep having more experiences, at least until you've integrated the lessons and used the clarity gained to make meaningful changes in your life. Use these tools with intention, not addiction.

If you decide to experience the magic of Ayahuasca, I recommend going with 1Heart Journeys (www.1heart.com) or you can find a provider on The Third Wave Directory.

## My Experience With 5MeO-DMT

"What we like about 5MeO-DMT, and what is particularly useful for drug addiction, is that it reliably occasions mystical experiences. In our patients, about 75% report experiencing an intense and profound sense of awe, divine presence, peace, joy, and bliss that transcends time and space. People often describe their 5-MeO experience as one of the peak transformational and spiritual moments of their entire lives. - Dr. Martin Polanco

There was one more major life changing medicine experience that made a big difference for me. In the summer of 2017, I went to a **5-MeO-DMT** ceremony in the San Francisco Bay Area of California with a group of about 10 friends. We paid our $200 donations and went off, and a few days later we went for a short drive.

> *5-MeO-DMT - A inhaled vapor from the secretion of a Sonoran desert toad (Bufo Alvarius) that provides a 15-30 minute psychedelic experience of being connected to God and oneness, providing a parallel experience to the Near-Death Experience of seeing a white light.*

After about an hour's drive south of Oakland, we arrived at Native American land in the Bay Area Hills – and found ourselves with a Shaman. He explained the medicine to us and told us it came from the Sonoran Desert toad in Arizona and Northern Mexico. If it is collected, dried, and smoked, the medicine produces a powerful, 15-25 minute psychedelic experience.

One-by-one, he would have us sit on a blue cushion and inhale the smoke from a pipe. Each person would take about twenty minutes and end up flat on their back within seconds of inhaling the vapor. Each person came back with wide open eyes, and some even shouted things toward the beginning of their journey, like "Oh my God."

Soon it was my turn. After inhaling the vapor, within about 15 seconds I fell back on the cushion, with my limbs temporarily feeling slightly paralyzed. I then proceeded to have **the most spiritually beautiful (and intense) next twenty minutes of my life**.

Immediately, I was rushing through a white cloud portal toward a bright white light. It was just like the stories you hear of people who have near-death experiences and then come back alive to share them (white light, feeling of calm). Once I reached the white light – everything was incredibly peaceful. I was no longer inside my body. I didn't even have a body at all. I was simply an aware consciousness, filled with love, care, and compassion.

The same university group had the following to say about 5MeO-DMT in 2022, "Although limited, the studies offer converging evidence of the potential ability of 5-MeO-DMT to provide fast-acting, and potentially immediate, therapeutic relief for depression, anxiety, and stress-related disorders (such as PTSD) in particular."

5-MeO seems optimal as a quickly acting tool for ego-dissolution. In 2019, researchers at Maastricht University studied the effects of 5-MeO-DMT and found that a single inhalation in a natural setting led to an improvement in overall life satisfaction and a reduction in symptoms of depression, anxiety, and stress, which persisted for up to a month after the experience.

Inhaling the medicine, according to user reports, often leads to transpersonal experiences, where the individual's sense of self extends beyond the personal level to encompass humankind, nature, and even the cosmos, which contributes to the mystical nature of the experience. 5-MeO-DMT also reliably induces ego dissolution, which can help create a non-dual awareness that we are all part of a greater whole instead of separate beings.

The presence of multiple ancient ceramic frog designs discovered in the Santarem region of the Amazon suggests a potential indigenous association with the medicine. However, the medicine was mostly unknown in modern times until 1983, when the book *Bufo Alvarius: the psychedelic toad of the Sonoran Desert* was published by Albert Most (a pseudonym for Ken Nelson), giving detailed instructions on how to milk the toads to acquire their sprayed substance, which is inhaled. Thankfully, a synthetic version of the medicine has been created in labs, which is chemically identical but spares the stress on the toads.

In 2019, former boxer Mike Tyson openly talked about his spiritual awakening that resulted from his use of 5-MeO-DMT, greatly increasing mainstream awareness. Former Navy SEAL Marcus Capone has created a campaign to help other Special Operations veterans access 5-MeO-DMT for its PTSD benefits. He told the NY Times that he "experienced a full nervous system reset" and referred to DMT as the God Molecule.

One 5MeO user online described the experience as: "If LSD is a rollercoaster, 5-MeO-DMT is an intergalactic faster-than-light rocket that takes you to a wholly unrecognizable state of being. Landing back from a high-dose experience, you are left with more questions than you came in with, but what an amazing ride it is."

What is nice about the 5MeO experience is that it usually lasts less than 30 minutes, and then you're back to normal very quickly, but with a whole new perspective on life. I've even seen people take a flight just 4 hours after the ceremony and be perfectly stable and back to normal – but now they're looking at the magic of life wholly anew.

I am convinced that if part of their training, every political and business leader in the world were required to experience the ancient traditional medicines of Ayahuasca and 5-MeO-DMT, we would immediately have a much more peaceful and beautiful world, filled with greater trust.

5-MeO DMT was also offered to heroin and cocaine addicts at Crossroads in Rosarito, Mexico, with substantial success. The founder, Dr. Martin Polanco, shared, ""[Addicts] realize that they are divine beings, and when you have this realization that you're indestructible and infinite and divine, it's very hard to put a needle in your arm and continue using."

While Crossroads Treatment Center has since closed down, Dr. Martin Polanco now recommends heroin and cocaine addicts go see the folks at the Beond Ibogaine Clinic (www.beond.us) in the Yucatan Peninsula of Mexico, or if you're a veteran, work with MissionWithin.org, which offers a six-week clinical psychedelic program for veterans experiencing PTSD that works with ibogaine, 5MeO, and psilocybin.

You can also find retreat centers that offer 5-MeO on **The Third Wave Directory** and you can also find it through word of mouth in the Burning Man community or through The Universal Shamans of the New Tomorrow Church in Huntsville, TX.

Once your brain is fully developed at 25, experiencing ayahuasca, 5-MeO, psilocybin, and MDMA (spread them out at least a few months apart) may lead to a number of beautiful insights about your true nature, spirituality, consciousness, and life.

As Dr. Dan Engle says, "[5MeO-DMT] is extraordinarily strong in its flavor and acts as a rocket ship back to God. . . . It does take you back to source consciousness."

# A Guide to Entheogens

As we shared earlier in this section, entheogens are drugs or "medicines" that often offer spiritual and emotional healing when used properly, and a deeper connection to self. These "medicines" are used traditionally by indigenous cultures as part of their rituals and communities.

The word itself, entheogen, means "meeting the divine within." Entheogens are used for religious, magical, shamanic, or spiritual purposes in many parts of the world. Entheogens have traditionally been used for practices geared towards achieving transcendence, including divination, meditation, yoga, sensory deprivation, healings, asceticism, prayer, trance, rituals, chanting, imitation of sounds, hymns like peyote songs, drumming, and ecstatic dance.

The term "psychedelic" comes from the Greek word meaning "mind-revealing" and refers to substances that can induce a state of altered consciousness, often leading to experiences of transcendence or mysticism. These substances are known for their ability to detach one from their sense of self and ego.

The psychedelic experience is often compared to non-ordinary forms of consciousness such as those experienced in meditation, near-death experiences, and mystical experiences. Ego dissolution (the ability to see yourself as part of a bigger whole and not separate) is often described as a key feature of the psychedelic experience."

Yes, the Psychedelic Renaissance is here, as many universities now study their benefits and many States and Nations decriminalize their usage. To end this section, below is a handy guide to some of the most commonly used Entheogens, Empathogens, and Psychedelics.

## ENTHEOGENS, EMPATHOGENS, & PSYCHEDELICS OFTEN USED IN SPIRITUAL PRACTICES OR FOR PERSONAL GROWTH

As always, follow local laws and ensure you have the right guidance before utilizing any of the below entheogens, psychedelics, and drugs.

### ~ NATURALLY OCCURING ~

5MeO-DMT - A inhaled vapor from the secretion of a Sonoran desert toad (Bufo Alvarius) that provides a 15-30 minute psychedelic experience of being connected to God and oneness, providing a parallel experience to the Near-Death Experience of seeing a white light.

Ayahuasca - A blend of the vine Banisteriopsis Caapi and the DMT-laden leafy plant Psychotria viridis. Often grown and made in Central and South America. Often served by experienced shamans. Drinking ayahuasca often leads to an 8-14 hour intense spiritual experience that leads people into greater connection to their heart and nature and compassion for all beings. A 2021 study found that Ayahuasca reduced anxiety in 94% of users who had anxiety and reduced depression in 90% of users who were depressed. I recommend the 1Heart Medicine ceremonies in Costa Rica for those looking to experience the medicine.

GHB (gamma hydroxybutyrate) - A depressant often used for increasing erotic connection. It produces feelings of euphoria, relaxation and sociability, and an increased sensuality and desire for sex. Research the right dosage for your body size as too high of a dose can lead to falling asleep into a few hour coma. Repeated overdoses can lead to negative brain changes. Don't mix with alcohol or other medicines/drugs.

Hapé - A sacred shamanic snuff made from powdered tobacco with (nicotiana rustica and various medicinal plants. It has been used for centuries by indigenous tribes in South America, particularly in Brazil and Peru, for healing, spiritual, and ceremonial purposes.

Iboga - A rainforest shrub and psychedelic native to Gabon in western Africa. The bark of the root is chewed for various pharmacological or ritualistic purposes. Ibogaine, the active alkaloid, is also used to treat substance abuse disorders and depression.

Kambo - Poison from the Phyllomedusa bicolor giant monkey frog applied to a burnt spot on the skin by a trained shaman. Indigenous tribes used this to heal and cleanse the body, increase stamina, and improve hunting skills. Kambo often leads to vomiting for 5-30 minutes and a puffy face for a couple hours.

Mescaline - Mescaline induces a psychedelic state similar to those produced by LSD and psilocybin, but with unique characteristics. Subjective effects may include altered thinking processes, an altered sense of time and self-awareness. Color appears brilliant and intense. Recurring visual patterns observed during the experience often include stripes, checkerboards, multicolor dots, and fractals. Found in San Pedro and Peyote.

San Pedro (huachuma) - A cactus, native to the Andes region of South America, that contains mescaline, one of the longest-studied psychedelics in the world—and the first to be labeled with the term "psychedelic." According to The Third Wave, "San Pedro has been an important element to the spiritual ceremonies of various indigenous cultures for thousands of years. In the context of these ceremonies, the San Pedro experience is known for being empathogenic (similar to MDMA) and potentially life-changing, promoting radical introspection, healing, and a sense of wonder and awe."

Sassafras - An empathogen that's also known as methylenedioxyamphetamine (MDA). You might also hear it called sass. It's derived from the oil of the sassafras plant. It often can promote feelings of closeness, compassion, affection, and empathy.

Peyote - A Native American medicine used ceremonially that contains mescaline. Found in cactus Native to Mexico and the Southwestern US. According to The Third Wave, "In ceremonial use, peyote is typically either chewed to release the active alkaloids or brewed as a tea. The peyote trip is characterized by visual effects (such as enhanced colors and breathing environments), philosophical and introspective insights, and feelings of euphoria."

Psilocybin - Research from Johns Hopkins has shown that a 3 gram dose has helped people with anxiety and smoking cessation. Early testing of psilocybin includes the 1962 Marsh Chapel Experiment, conducted by physician Walter Pahnke under the supervision of psychologist Timothy Leary and the Harvard Psilocybin Project. In this double-blind experiment, volunteer graduate school divinity students from the Boston area almost all claimed to have had profound religious experiences subsequent to the ingestion of pure psilocybin. Generally speaking a micro dose is considered 0.25g, a small dose 0.5g, a normal dose 1-2g, and a big dose 3g. It's a good idea to start with a smaller dose to see the impact before exploring larger doses.

White Lily (Nymphaea Alba) - An herbal aquatic flower plant that increases feelings of euphoria and sexual arousal.

## ~ SYNTHETICALLY PRODUCED ~

2CB - An aphrodisiac synthetic psychedelic. It is a stimulant, empathogen, and hallucinogen. In his book PiHKAL (Phenethylamines I Have Known And Loved), the legendary psychopharmacologist and author Alexander Shulgin named 2C-B one of the six most important phenethylamines for healing trauma.

Ketamine - A synthetic dissociative discovered in 1962 as a surgical anesthetic that relaxes the mind and body. Ketamine is being researched for its potential in treating depression and anxiety. While it isn't an empathogen, psychedelic, or entheogen per se, it can slow your mind down and has some data-driven benefits in controlled delivery situations.

LSD (Lysergic Acid Diethylamide) - A synthetic hallucinogenic crystalline or liquid compound that can lead to creative thinking, visions, and visuals. It was first produced in 1938 in a lab by Albert Hoffman. Generally speaking, 10mg is considered a microdose, 50mg is considered a half-dose, and 100mcg is considered a full-dose. It's a good idea to start with a smaller dose to see the impact before exploring larger doses. This one can really mess you up if you use too much or too often. It's bad for you if you want to be consistent in life.

MDMA - MDMA is an empathogen that primarily acts by increasing the activity of the neurotransmitters serotonin, dopamine, and norepinephrine in the brain. Research has shown that MDMA can reduce PTSD and depression. It can also be used for couples therapy and marriage counseling. First synthesized in 1912 by Merck.

**Action Item #108: Research The Benefits & Risks of Entheogens**
Spend some time researching some of the benefits and risks of the above entheogens and drugs. Write down in your notebook if any appeal to you and why--and those that don't. While many of these remain not yet legal in some places, many of these medicines have been legalized or decriminalized in other countries like Peru or Costa Rica or where they are used traditionally. Do your own research on safety, dosage, and legality. And as always, treat them with reverence and give time between them to integrate the lessons.

## Caution About Entheogens & Psychedelics

As I mentioned above, it's important to be very cautious while using any psychedelic or entheogen. Earlier in the Happiness chapter, I wrote about how I got addicted to using these medicines, and how it took me three years to recover my brain chemistry and consistency. Definitely read that section too. For now, here are some notes of caution about entheogens and psychedelics.

- **Do Your Own Research First:** With any mind-altering substance, it is very important to do your own research on the benefits and risks and ensure you are receiving the medicine from a trusted and experienced source. I am not a medical doctor and have only limited experience. I have seen some friends overuse the above substances with negative impacts on them. Also do research on the proper dosage amounts. The websites www.thethirdwave.co, www.erowid.org, and www.healthline.org are good resources. If you have a history of mental illness, you may wish to entirely avoid these types of medicines, or only use them under supervision from a trained clinician or experienced shaman, starting with smaller doses.

- **Don't Combine With Alcohol:** It is especially important to never combine alcohol with entheogens or psychedelics — as that can lead to danger, unconsciousness, and death. I once had a friend at Burning Man combine Ayahuasca, Ketamine, and Alcohol. He literally forgot who he was for four days and did enough crazy things to get kicked out of camp and moved to the Burning Man Ranger Camp where guards watch you and don't let you leave your RV. Don't be that guy.

- **Limit Usage to Every Few Months:** For me, a good rule of thumb is that I am open to sitting with medicine about once per quarter — and only within an intentionally held ceremony. If you find yourself using the above medicines more frequently than every few months, you should do additional research into the potential negative effects of frequent use, especially on mood and brain health. While some indigenous populations have at times offered some of the above medicines to youth as young as 14 years old, we suggest waiting until the brain is more fully developed (around age 25) before using the above medicines. Many people use the Equinoxes (start of Spring and Fall) and Solstices (start of winter and summer) as good times to explore quarterly ceremonial medicine use in the community.

- **Avoid the Bad Stuff:** The above mentioned entheogens which have been shown to have some benefits contrast with the following drugs that are known to cause a lot of harm and are definitely not recommended like cocaine, heroin, methamphetamine, and fentanyl.

- **Be Smart About the Law:** While my personal belief is that all the above entheogenic medicines are much less harmful than alcohol, have many proven benefits, and should be decriminalized and legal to use — there are still many countries where use of some or all of the above medicines is against the law, even in ceremonial or spiritual contexts. Do your own research and be careful. You can find a list of retreat centers where you can legally use the above medicines at The Third Wave Directory and Retreat Guru. Be especially careful not to travel with any of these medicines into countries with very strict drug laws in places like South East Asia and the Middle East where even small amounts can lead to huge fines or jail time. Hopefully soon enough the groundbreaking research being conducted by Johns Hopkins University, UCLA, Imperial College London, and Emory University on the beneficial and therapeutic use of entheogenic and psychedelic drugs will lead to the law being updated around the world and recognizing that these medicines, when used properly, are very important for healing.

I'll end this section with a great Twitter Thread from Jeremiah Dupin on his advice for using psychedelics properly.

## How to Use Psychedelics Properly by Jeremiah Dupin

In the last 11 years, I've had 100+ experiences w/ various psychedelics, including mushrooms, ayahuasca, ibogaine, LSD, 5MeODMT, & ketamine IV. I've also facilitated experiences for around 100 others & have learned several lessons along the way. Here is some of what I learned:

1. Psychedelics are a tool, not a solution. They can show you where the fish are, but they won't teach you how to catch them, filet them, or cook them.

2. It's crucial to understand how to regulate your nervous system before taking psychedelics. This means learning how to shift from the sympathetic state (fight or flight) to the parasympathetic state (rest and digest), as all deep healing occurs in

the parasympathetic state.

3. There is no such thing as a "bad trip". Instead, "bad trips" are when someone resists or fights against part of the experience, which can be painful but still holds purpose and can lead to valuable discoveries.

4. Real change comes from integrating what you learned from the psychedelic experience into your everyday life. Simply having insights during the experience isn't enough, you must also make changes to your environment to support your growth.

5. The combination of your mindset (set) and physical and social environment (setting) is crucial for a successful and safe experience. Safety should always be the top priority in a proper setting.

6. Surrendering and letting go of expectations can greatly enhance your experience. Your power and healing come from accepting whatever arises and discovering its purpose.

7. Your breath is a powerful anchor during the experience. Using it to ground yourself and shift focus from thoughts to physical sensations can lead to deep healing.

8. If you go into an experience w/ a mindset that you need to fix yourself, it creates an addictive relationship w/ psychedelics & distracts from addressing the root cause of discomfort, which is often nervous system dysregulation. Better to address healing your nervous system first.

9. It's highly effective to journal about your experience.

**Maintaining consistency in your life while taking too many entheogens or psychedelics is challenging.** Because of this factor, I encourage you to be sparse in your use of them -- and to treat each experience you do have as a sacred one. Take the time needed (many months usually) in between experiences to fully integrate the lessons from the journey. And always remember throughout that the Formula of Success is:

*Vision + Belief + Action + Consistency = Results*

While entheogens, psychedelics, dissociatives, and psychedelics may help you better understand yourself and God and offer a portal into the divine and deeper presence with others -- they can also destabilize you and make you inconsistent if you do too much (I know, this is what happened to me).

So -- if you are the adventurous type -- do go exploring with the right guides and see what you can learn -- but always come back to the knowing that there's nothing you truly need other than your breath, sunshine, good food, good water, and good people around you to live a deeply happy life.

Drugs are like salt. Just the right sparse amount of the right kind makes everything better. But use too much and you'll ruin yourself. Remember that the real goal here is awakening and presence, not addiction.

## Recommended Books on Awakening

- *The Untethered Soul* by Michael Singer
- *Recapture the Rapture* by Jamie Wheal
- *Seeding Consciousness* by Tricia Eastman
- *The Psychedelic Explorer's Guide* by James Fadiman PhD & Ross Douglas
- *How to Change Your Mind* by Michael Pollan
- *The Promise of Psychedelics* by Dr. Peter Silverstone and Rory Barnett
- (And not a book -- but check out The Psychedelic Mom podcast!)

## Key Outcome from This Chapter

**Experience Ayahuasca or Vipassana -** Do your research, then choose one of these life changing adventures (or both). Sign up for the next available Ayahuasca journey at 1Heart.com and the next available 10-day silent Vipassana meditation at www.dhamma.org.

## AWAKENING CHAPTER ACTION ITEMS

1. **Alive & Awake** - On a scale of 0-10, how fully alive is your soul? Is your soul dead inside or completely thriving? What changes do you need to make to get yourself to a 10/10? Write the answers.

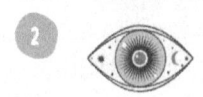

2. **Mystical Experiences** - Have you ever had a deeply spiritual or mystical experience, either sober or after meditation, holotropic breathing, or on psychedelics? Write about this experience and what you learned from it.

3. **Energy Diet** - Are there any negative people, non-conscious news sources, or draining things you do that should no longer be part of your life? Journal the answer.

4. **Triad of Transformation** - Look into Burning Man, a 10-day Vipassana silent retreat, and Ayahuasca. Take some time to research each of them and study all the potential benefits and downsides. Then choose one to do this year as part of your Magic Year and your transformation process. Schedule it now.

5. **Read The Untethered Soul** - Get yourself a copy of the book *The Untethered Soul* by Michael Singer and read it over the next two weeks. Write down what you learn from it in your notebook.

6. **Research Entheogens** - Spend some time researching some of the benefits and risks of the above entheogens. Write down in your notebook if any appeal to you and why. While many of these remain not yet legal in some places, many of these medicines have been legalized or decriminalized in other countries like Peru or Costa Rica or where they are used traditionally. Do your own research on safety, dosage, and legality. And as always, treat them with reverence and give time between them to integrate the lessons.

MAGIC YEAR - 524

# BONUS STEP

# OPTIMISM MAGIC

**MAGIC YEAR**

MAGIC YEAR - 525

# KEY CONCEPTS FROM THE OPTIMISM CHAPTER

**1. INFECTIOUS ENTHUSIASM**

Enthusiasm for living that is so beautifully intense and obvious that it rubs off on the people around you, and suddenly many other people are now having better days.

**2. LIFE OPTIMISM**

Optimism for your own life and your family

**3. WORLDVIEW OPTIMISM**

Optimism for the world and our species

**4. HUMAN DEVELOPMENT INDEX**

The Human Development Index (HDI) measures a country's overall well-being based on life expectancy, education, and income.

**5. SUSTAINABLE DEVELOPMENT GOALS**

THE GLOBAL GOALS

A set of global targets aiming to address various social, economic, and environmental challenges by 2030.

**6. INFANT MORTALITY**

The death of infants under one year of age per 1,000 live births. This percentage has declined from 10% to under 4% in my lifetime.

**7. LIFE EXPECTANCY**

The estimated number of years a person is expected to live. Average life expectancy globally has increased from 63 to 73 years during my lifetime and continues to improve.

**8. EXTREME POVERTY**

The percentage of people globally living on under $2.15 per day in today's dollars. This % has declined dramatically in my lifetime from 42% of humanity to 8% of humanity and continues to go in the right direction.

**9. RENEWABLE ENERGY**

The percentage of total energy supply that comes from renewable sources like solar, wind, geothermal, hydroelectric, and biomass. This has increased from <3% to over 30% in my lifetime so far.

**10. ANNUAL PER PERSON INCOME**

The average annual income a person globally earns in today's dollars. This has increased substantially in my lifetime from $3,574 to $18,603.

**11. MALTHUSIAN ERROR**

The flawed 18th century prediction by Thomas Malthus that unchecked population growth would lead to resource and food scarcity, disregarding technological advancements and human ingenuity. He believed we'd never pass 1 billion people.

**12. EXISTENTIAL RISK**

Threats that could lead to the extinction or irreversible decline of human civilization, such as global pandemics, nuclear war, catastrophic climate change, or advanced artificial intelligence gone wrong.

# A BONUS STEP: OPTIMISM MAGIC

> "Optimism is different than blind positivity. We can be in a dark tunnel but we can still stay focused on the light at the end of the tunnel. Optimism is the belief that the future is bright."
> - Simon Sinek

Okay, if you've gotten through the first 12 steps -- it's time for a bonus step on optimism. While happiness is your state of mind in the moment, **optimism is your outlook for the future**. I'm very optimistic about life and the world in general -- and this chapter will share why -- sharing the real data about how we're doing as a species.

## My Journey With Optimism

I've always been a joyful and optimistic person. It's part of what draws people to me. It's also part of my magic. By seeing a positive present and a positive future, I can bend reality toward that outcome more often than not.

While optimism is always beneficial -- overconfidence is not. I've had to properly calibrate my confidence levels over time. After having really big success selling my company at 27, I thought I had the Midas touch. I thought everything I touched would turn to gold. Of course, I was wrong. I was too confident.

I had to re-learn in my 30s that it takes a clear vision, self-belief, and consistent action to achieve magnificent results. You have to be both good and consistent to become great.

> It. takes a clear vision, self-belief, and consistent action to achieve magnificent results. You have to be both good and consistent to become great.

You can't just wish for good results. You have to make them happen one day at a time. You have to show up consistently to make your dreams come true in tangible reality.

Once I calibrated my levels of self-confidence and re-learned the lesson that Vision + Belief + Action + Consistency = Results, then I became a superhero, able to accomplish anything again and set big goals.

## Optimism As Your Secret Advantage

Optimists have the tendency to expect favorable outcomes, to believe that good things will happen in the future, and to see the world as it is (an incredible miracle and getting better with each generation) as opposed to what the media matrix frames it as.

I'm also naturally much happier because I know a data-driven truth that few people recognize -- that life on Earth keeps getting better. More on this in a moment.

Optimistic people tend to focus on the bright side of things, even in challenging situations, and have a strong belief in their ability to overcome obstacles and achieve their goals.

Optimism has numerous benefits, including better physical health, greater resilience, increased motivation, lower blood pressure, and improved relationships. Optimistic people also tend to have lower levels of stress and anxiety, better immune function, a reduced risk of heart disease and diabetes, and are more likely to experience positive emotions like joy, gratitude, and contentment.

I work hard to have an optimist's mindset and fortify my mind against the standard pessimism of society.

While some people are naturally more optimistic than others, optimism can also be learned and cultivated through various practices, such as positive self-talk, gratitude exercises, and reframing negative thoughts. Developing a more optimistic mindset can lead to a happier and more fulfilling life and can be your secret weapon in life, relationships, and business.

I have a good friend named Barry Stamos who is always happy and joyous. Every time I talk to him on Zoom or in person, he's glowing, smiling, and deeply content. He's always doing something fun and meaningful. Being around him is infectious. Be like Barry and live a life filled with **infectious enthusiasm**.

*Infectious Enthusiasm - Enthusiasm for living that is so beautifully intense and obvious that it rubs off on the people around you, and suddenly many other people are now having better days.*

## Why I'm Optimistic For the World

I like to say there are two types of optimism, **life optimism** and **worldview optimism**. Life optimism is about my own life and what is local to my family. Worldview optimism is a positive-forward looking perspective on humanity and our world. In this chapter, I write about both types of optimism.

*Life Optimism - Optimism for your own life and your family*

*Worldview Optimism - Optimism for the world and our species*

Let's talk about **worldview optimism**. Since the year 2000, when I first read the books *Lexus and the Olive Tree* and *The Commanding Heights*, I've been obsessed with understanding the reality of how our world and species are doing -- beyond the short-term hyperbole of the clickbait media.

After spending a couple decades learning, reading, and tracking many of the data sources, I'm incredibly optimistic for our world.

It's quite refreshing to have a view of the world based on actual data and not on media-driven fear designed to addict us to keep coming back and generating ad and subscription revenue for them. One uber important mental task is zooming out to see the big picture --outside of the day-to-day media headlines that are designed to grab readers' attention.

So, it's time to share a big secret with you. A secret your soul may be quite happy to hear. When you look at the data -- **the world is actually getting better – much, much better.**

We're literally living in the most incredible, healthy, educated, and wealthy time in human history -- yet many people don't realize just how well our species is doing compared to the past. Below is the data to back up this statement.

When I zoom out, I realize just how much extraordinary progress the human species has made just in the last forty years alone -- across many different categories like health, money, literacy, electricity, the internet, and renewable energy.

Nearly everything is better off than when I was born forty years ago in 1984, including life expectancy[26], infant mortality[27], per capita income[28], the number of people living in poverty[29], education[30], deaths from war[31], violent crime[32], and renewable energy generation.[33] And not even a little bit better. A lot better.

Let's look at just what has happened in my lifetime.

## The World Has Improved In The Last 40 Years In Many Areas

| Global Stat | 1984 | 2023 |
| --- | --- | --- |
| Average Human Life Expectancy | 63.5 yrs | 72.9 yrs |
| % of Population in Extreme Poverty (<$2.15 per day) | 42.3% | 8.2% |
| % of Adults Who Can Read | 69% | 88% |
| Average Annual Income Per Person | $3,574 | $18,603 |
| Infant Mortality Rate, Under 5 | 10.1% | 3.7% |
| Electricity Access | 58% | 92% |
| Internet Access | 0% | 65% |
| Renewable Energy as % of Total Supply | 3% | 31% |

Source: World Bank Open Data

Yes, **life expectancy**, literacy, **annual per person income**, **renewable energy**, electricity access, and internet access are up, while **infant mortality** and **extreme poverty** is way down. Nearly everything is going in the right direction when you zoom out and get our minds out of the gutter of the fear-based media matrix.

---

[26] Life Expectancy - https://ourworldindata.org/life-expectancy
[27] Infant Mortality - https://ourworldindata.org/child-mortality
[28] Income - https://ourworldindata.org/grapher/maddison-data-gdp-per-capita-in-2011us-single-benchmark
[29] Poverty - https://ourworldindata.org/explorers/poverty-explorer-2011-vs-2017-ppp
[30] Education - https://ourworldindata.org/grapher/average-harmonized-learning-outcome-scores
[31] War - https://ourworldindata.org/grapher/deaths-in-state-based-conflicts-per-100000
[32] Violent Crime - https://www.statista.com/statistics/191219/reported-violent-crime-rate-in-the-usa-since-1990/
[33] Renewable Energy - https://ourworldindata.org/grapher/modern-renewable-energy-consumption

*Life Expectancy* - The estimated number of years a person is expected to live. Average life expectancy globally has increased from 63 to 73 years during my lifetime and continues to improve.

*Infant Mortality* - The death of infants under one year of age per 1,000 live births. This percentage has declined from 10% to under 4% in my lifetime.

*Extreme Poverty* - The percentage of people globally living on under $2.15 per day in today's dollars. This % has declined dramatically in my lifetime from 42% of humanity to 8% of humanity and continues to go in the right direction.

*Renewable Energy %* - The percentage of total energy supply that comes from renewable sources like solar, wind, geothermal, hydroelectric, and biomass. This has increased from <3% to over 30% in my lifetime so far.

*Annual Per Person Income* - The average annual income a person globally earns in today's dollars. This has increased substantially in my lifetime, from $3,574 to $18,603.

Pretty cool data, right? Humans are healthier, wealthier, and living longer than ever. To learn a bit more about the many reasons to be optimistic and to protect your mind from the negativity of the media, read these books:

- *Factfulness: Ten Reasons We're Wrong About the World – and Why Things Are Better Than You Think* by Hans Rosling
- *The Rational Optimist* by Matt Ridley
- *Abundance* by Peter Diamandis
- *Getting Better* by Charles Kenny

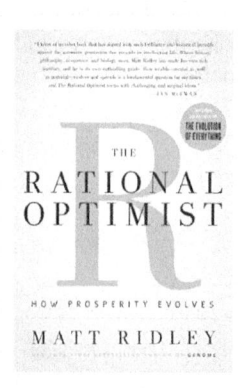

### Action Item #110: Read One of the Above Books
Pick one of the four books above on worldview optimism that look most interesting to you. Buy it, read it, then write down your reflections. How did it change your perspective? If you like the first book, consider reading another.

Yes, read these books. They will change your life. They will make you feel a lot better about the world, from a rigorous, data-driven perspective. Reading these will give you a force field so that the negativity and pessimism of the news media and other people doesn't impact you as much.

So build your mental defenses through the right **information diet**. Don't let the media matrix that is designed to sell ads and subscriptions by hooking your attention hold you back from being a hopeful, optimistic, and positive thinker. See the real data, and let it give a little smile on your face.

The entire story that there's some evil, coordinated reptilian entity making the world terrible for average people is a laughable fake conspiracy theory that is popular among people with a **victim mindset**.

The truth is that the world has more opportunity than it ever has -- and anyone who consistently focuses on delivering value to others will thrive over time.

There's a lot of nonsense out there about the World Economic Forum, Klaus Schwab, and Bill Gates that is worth addressing.

The truth is that the World Economic Forum (WEF) is an exceptional organization run by German professor Klaus Schwab, who's dedicated his life to bringing people together to create a more prosperous, sustainable, and peaceful world. The guy is exceptionally caring and certainly isn't trying to empower Nation-States to stamp out individual liberties or whatever hogwash is out there.

Bill Gates is an extraordinary entrepreneur and great philanthropist who has saved hundreds of millions of lives through his tens of billions of dollars of donations to life saving causes.

And there is no liberal conspiracy to abduct and molest children. QAnon was complete bullshit that was likely a Russian tool of information warfare. Thankfully, its followers have dissipated after its predictions stopped coming true.

So if you're susceptible to the non-sense of QAnon or "the world is ending" bullshit out there -- get your mind out of the gutter and learn to differentiate good sources from fantasy. The ability to critically think and continually learn from good sources is everything.

Fearing a Malthusian crisis that has never actually materialized, I've even heard some people say that they are choosing not to have children out of concern that it isn't right to have children in a world in which so much carbon dioxide is being emitted. This is also crazy.

The thing that is going to make carbon emissions sustainable is going to be innovators in business, science, and government who create the companies, technologies, and policies that address this challenge. So have that baby, if you choose, and teach them well. Train them to be critical thinkers, purpose-driven innovators and to follow their bliss. That is what the world needs.

I don't know who needs to hear this. But we're going to make it as a species. Barring an asteroid hitting the planet in the next few decades before we can properly backup our species in space, homo sapiens is going to make it.

Thankfully, NASA has recently published that there is a 0.00151% chance of a major asteroid passing within the orbit of the moon in the next 1000 years. Long story short -- we're going to be okay.[34]

In fact, the kids that are being born now are the very ones who are going to have the realistic opportunity to go live in space and on other planets and be part of bringing humanity to other parts of the galaxy. By 2050, when our son Apollo is 28 years old, it will be quite common for humans to go to Mars. So, people of child making age, go make some incredible babies.

And teach them to be optimistic -- especially if the data continues to demonstrate that we're continuing to make immense progress as a species.

I'll end this section with this quote. Harvard educated Professor of Economics at UC Berkeley Brad DeLong shares why he has a strong preference to live in the present time in his book *Slouching Toward Utopia, The Economic History of the 20th Century*.

### Excerpt from Slouching Toward Utopia by Brad DeLong

"Suppose that you stuffed me and my family into a time machine, sent us back a century to 1890... I would want, first, health insurance: the ability to go to the doctor and be treated with late-twentieth-century medicines. Franklin Delano Roosevelt was crippled by polio. Without antibiotic and adrenaline shots I would now be dead of childhood pneumonia.

The second thing I would want would be utility hookups–electricity and gas, central heating, and consumer appliances. The third thing I want to buy is access to information–audio and video broadcasts, recorded music, computing power, and access to databases.

None of these were available at any price back in 1890. I could not buy a washing machine... I could not buy airplane tickets... I could do nothing for medical care. And I could do nothing for access to information, communications, and entertainment technology save to leave the children home with the servants and go to the opera and the theater every other week.

How much are the central heating, electric lights, fluoridated toothpaste, electric toaster ovens, clothes-washing machines, dishwashers, synthetic fiber-blend clothes, radios, intercontinental telephones, xerox machines, notebook computers, automobiles, and steel-framed skyscrapers that I have used so far today worth–and it is only 10am?"

**So what's true?** Are we living in the best time ever (with all the comforts of modern living, improved life expectancy, improved education attainment, rapidly declining global poverty, and low infant mortality)? Or are we living in a challenging time with an obesity and anxiety epidemic in the Western world while we risk our planet's sustainability and biodiversity with modern progress?

Well, the truth is that for the first time in human history, we now have the ability to provide basic necessities (education, food, water, shelter, electricity, and internet) for every human being in the world -- and soon (within another decade or two), we'll be able to do it in a sustainable and even regenerative way. Things are getting better. Way better.

The real crisis is a **crisis of meaning**. In a world in which nearly all our basic needs are taken care of for us -- we have to actually use our time to do things that bring us alive and are meaningful. We have to use our time to invest in meaningful relationships. We have to learn to be **homo creatis** instead of **homo workaholis**.

---

[34] MIT Technology Review - Earth is probably safe from a killer asteroid for 1,000 years

It's time to solve the real crisis of meaning and human connection -- through purpose-driven living and community living.

In the next section, let's look at some more of the data that gives us reason to be optimistic. If we can solve the current crises of meaning, community connection, obesity, and climate change in the next couple decades, we can be on a very good trajectory for expanding into a multi-planet species in the 2nd half of the 21st century.

> "Science and technology promise the means for raising per-capita food production while decreasing materials and energy consumption, both of which are preconditions for successful long-term conservation and a sustainable economy."
> - E.O. Wilson, biologist

## Grandma Would Be Proud of Humanity

Forget the media matrix that has been designed to hook us and capture our attention. They so rarely present the real big picture.

In so many ways, things are better than ever. That is cause for celebration. But first, let's look at the data. It might just make you quite a bit happier if you realized that across many important metrics, the world is doing quite well and generally going in the right direction.

> Across many important metrics, the world is doing quite well and generally going in the right direction.

My grandmother, Eva Allis, was born in 1902 in Pennsylvania. She was 36 when she had my dad in 1938. And my dad was 46 when he helped bring me into the world in 1984.

When Eva was born at the beginning of the 20th century, global life expectancy was 32, 19.5% of infants died before they reached their first birthday, and the average person globally made $2,000 per year (in today's dollars, adjusted for inflation).

Now let's fast forward a little over a century to today. As we saw above, today's global life expectancy is 73, infant mortality is 3.7%, and the average person globally makes $18,603 per year (in today's dollars).

|  | When My Grandma Eva Was Born in 1902 | Today |
| --- | --- | --- |
| Life Expectancy | 32 | 73 |
| Infant Mortality | 19.5% | 3.7% |
| Annual Per Person Income (inflation adjusted) | $2,000 | $18,603 |

Since the beginning of the 20th century, global **life expectancy** has increased by 128%, **infant mortality** has declined by 81%, and **annual per person income** has improved by

730% (in real dollars). This is all while the human population has increased by more than 4x from 1.7 billion to 8.2 billion. Now that is a lot of progress for three generations!

My grandma Eva would be exceptionally proud of the world that her great-grandson Apollo lives in today. It's way better than the world of 1902!

As a species, we've made immense progress over the last century. We've made this progress during a period in which we saw the Green Revolution in agricultural productivity, the invention of personal computing, and the creation of the internet.

We've made immense improvements in measures of health, economics, and education.

For the first time in human history, a world in which every person has access to food, water, shelter, healthcare, and education is within reach. This goal of sustainable prosperity is not only within reach, it is amazingly within reach during our lifetime. Jim Yong Kim, Former President of the World Bank said back in 2013 "For the first time ever, we have a real opportunity to end extreme poverty within a generation."

The rapid advances in markets, technology, and public awareness that are currently taking place will allow us to move to a carbon neutral world by 2050 in which we have both environmental sustainability and shared human prosperity in which every person has access to opportunity and basic human needs like food, water, shelter, healthcare, and education.

## The Most Peaceful and Advanced Era Ever

In his book, *The Better Angels of Our Nature*, Harvard professor Steven Pinker makes the case that we are living in the most peaceful time in human history. After a tumultuous 20th century that saw events like WWI, WWII, the Holocaust, the Sino-Japanese War, the Korean War, Mao's Great Leap Forward, the Vietnam War, the Cambodian Genocide, the Gulf War, the Bosnian War, and the Rwandan genocide, it seems that over the last quarter century since the fall of the Soviet Union and the beginning of the widespread use of the Internet, we've entered a time of substantially less deadly conflict between and within nations, even including events from terrorism.

By the mid-1990s global trade was greatly expanding, creating interconnections that increased human understanding and reduced the likelihood of armed conflict as the calculus changed and populations realized they were usually better off pursuing peace than warfare. The 1990s also brought us the internet, which provided a way to share information with people anywhere in the world. The Internet has just begun to create an interconnected web of humanity that no "Berlin Wall" could stop.

Today, in 2024, over 65% of humanity will have access to the internet. Across cultures, we're now connected on WeChat, WhatsApp, Telegram, Twitter, TikTok, Instagram, and Messenger like never before. As these tools combined with internet-enabled smartphones have reached mass global distribution, humanity has finally found a tool through which it can spread information and understanding across cultures, greatly reducing the likelihood of popular support for armed conflict except in the most egregious situations. Wisdom is now distributed – and trust is being built across language and cultural boundaries.

Today we have access to Wikipedia, Udemy, Khan Academy, EdX, Coursera, SkillShare, and iTunes University. Twenty five years ago, none of these resources for self-directed learning existed. The power of knowledge and truth – distributed across eight billion people – is compounding. There is more light than ever in the world – even if everyone hasn't realized it yet.

Modern humans (Homo sapiens) have been around for about 200,000 years. It took us

190,000 years, from 200,000 BC until 10,000 BC, to reach 15 million people. With the advent of agriculture and the growth of cities and civilization, starting in Mesopotamia and then expanding outward, the human population reached its first major tipping point, growing from 15 million in 10,000 BC to 1 billion by the year 1800.

In the 19th century, the human population grew by 60% from 1.0 billion to 1.6 billion. Then, in the 20th century, the population skyrocketed nearly 300% from 1.6 billion to 6.1 billion. Today, the population has surpassed 8 billion and is expected to peak at 10 billion by 2050 (at least on this planet).

Only through the progress of medical science, the development of advanced agriculture, and the industrial revolution, which brought together both energy and engines, has this immense growth been possible over the last two hundred years. And with a greater population comes the ability for scientists to finally have the economic incentive to solve rare diseases and the ability for economies of scale to enable complex supply chains that bring every good to your local markets, greatly expanding choice.

> "The cornucopia that greets you as you enter the supermarket dwarfs anything that Louis XIV ever experienced." - Matt Ridley, *The Rational Optimist*

## Why Do Some Think the World is Getting Worse?

In 1798, Thomas Malthus made a famous prediction in *An Essay on the Principle of Population* that the world population would level off due to famine. At the time, the population was just under 1 billion people. Unfortunately for Malthus, he didn't properly take into account the impact of the industrial revolution and the agricultural revolution in expanding the food production capabilities of the 19th and 20th centuries and advancements in medical science (like penicillin) in greatly expanding our life expectancy. This was **The Malthusian Error**, which still affects the thinking of many academics who don't understand exponential technological improvements.

*The Malthusian Error - The mistaken belief that improvements in technology and science happen linearly rather than exponentially, causing even well-educated researchers to be overly pessimistic about the world. The name comes from Thomas Malthus who famously incorrectly predicted in 1798 that the world population would never be able to surpass 1 billion people.*

Today, I find the same principle often holds–those predicting doom are either doing it for the sake of selling news or are doing it because they aren't factoring into their models how rapidly the combination of the market system, specialization, and investments in technology are creating solutions to the major challenges facing humanity.

News publishers know that the human brain is instinctually structured to pay more attention to bad news and danger. Our brain's amygdala developed on the grasslands of Eastern Africa 50,000 years ago to ensure that information connected to possible danger was processed and remembered with much higher priority than information connected to opportunity and safety.

The early homo sapiens who paid attention to and remembered danger were those who were prosperous and reproduced, creating an evolutionary selection for those with amygdalas that easily recalled danger. Peter Diamandis writes about this principle extensively in his book *Abundance*.

Thus, people tend to pay attention to negative and scary news, even if it's actually completely irrelevant, far away, and statistically rare.

In a 2021 study, it was found that instances of negative news have reached all-time highs[35], even though, factually speaking, our species is better off than it has ever been.

So perhaps the problem is our sources of information and the hyperbole of the media -- and not reality.

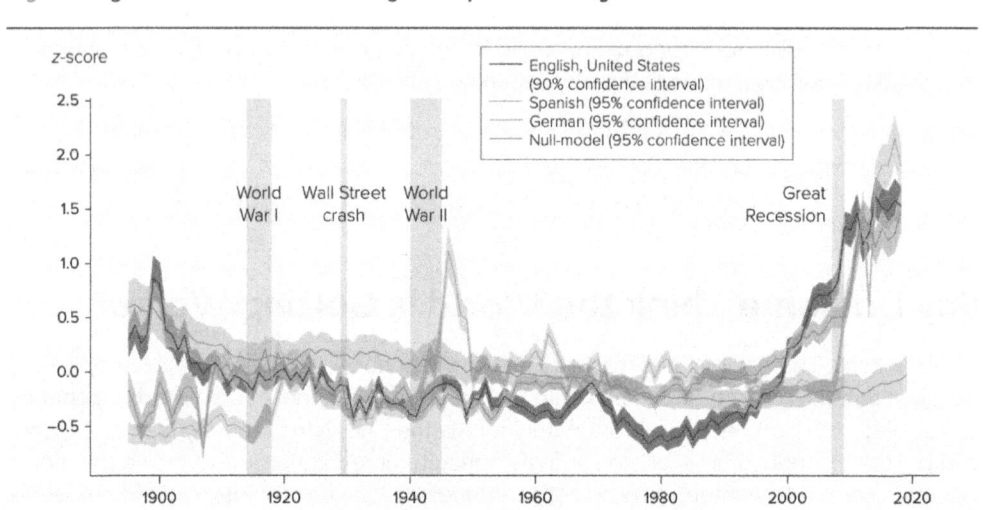

Figure 5 **Negative news about the world surges to unprecedented highs**

## The Progress With Renewable Energy

It's no secret that unless we make pretty rapid changes to a clean energy economy and away from fossil fuels over the next 20 years, we risk losing much of the progress we've made since 1900.

The earth's environment is not an issue delinked from human progress. The Earth is the place on which nearly all human progress has taken place. As the noted biologist E.O. Wilson says, "…the planet… is a little sphere with a razor-thin coat of life too fragile to bear careless tampering."

Yet even E.O. Wilson himself sees technology, science, and human progress as part of the solution to a sustainable future, not as part of the problem.

He wrote in The Future of Life, "Science and technology also promise the means for raising per-capita food production while decreasing materials and energy consumption, both of which are preconditions for successful long-term conservation and a sustainable economy.

Perhaps, then, it was the discovery of petroleum in 1859 in Edward Drake's steam engine well in Pennsylvania that has led to humanity having such high-standards of living today, standards of living that for once allow us to afford to invest in creating a carbon neutral

---

[35] UN Human Development Report 2022 - https://hdr.undp.org/system/files/documents/global-report-document/hdr2021-22overviewenpdf.pdf

world by 2050 that is prosperous for all of us, unlike the low carbon and low living-standard world of 1850 that was brutish, difficult, and short, with low literacy rates, a lack of sanitation, no electricity or sewage removal, and high infant mortality.

Historically, fossil fuels have been a great thing for humanity. Now that we know that the continued use of fossil fuels will threaten the progress they have so far enabled, we must use our wealth and scientific energy to move toward clean energy as quickly as possible.

As we create a prosperous world without poverty, we also must develop cleanly and sustainably to stop the destruction of habitats. This is not only the right thing to do, it's in our own best interest, as many species of plant and animal life may prove essential to medical advancements, and the full, complex ecosystem of millions of species provides essential services in keeping our planet in balance.

We need to move away from fossil fuels as quickly as possible, invest in companies and institutions researching synthetic algae, biofuels, wind, solar, and fusion power, tax carbon dioxide emissions, and invest in new carbon capture technologies like Bioenergy Carbon Capture & Storage.

Yes, my friends, a whole new and sustainable world is coming in which everyone has their basic human needs covered. This is cause for celebration—and more hard work and purpose-driven work as we get there. Thank you to all the scientists, entrepreneurs, investors, health professionals, and public servants who are helping us get there.

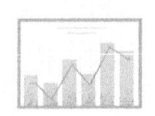

**Action Item #110: The World is Getting Better**
What was surprising in this chapter so far? What have you learned? Do you feel better knowing the world is getting better in so many measurable areas? Write a short reflection on what you learned from this chapter. Are you generally optimistic for humanity? Why or why not?

# The Human Development Report

There are still many challenges in the world today, and not everywhere is as rosy as the places I like to visit. Places like Syria, South Sudan, Afghanistan, and Ukraine have been sadly destroyed by major conflicts in the last decade -- and need time to rebuild new peaceful and thriving societies.

I encourage you to read the latest United Nations Human Development Report[36] to see where the best countries and biggest challenges are currently from a standard of living perspective. The top ten countries in the world in terms of human development are:

1. Switzerland
2. Norway
3. Iceland
4. Hong Kong (China)
5. Australia
6. Denmark
7. Sweden
8. Ireland
9. Germany

---

[36] UN Human Development Report https://hdr.undp.org/content/human-development-report-2021-22

MAGIC YEAR - 537

10. Netherlands

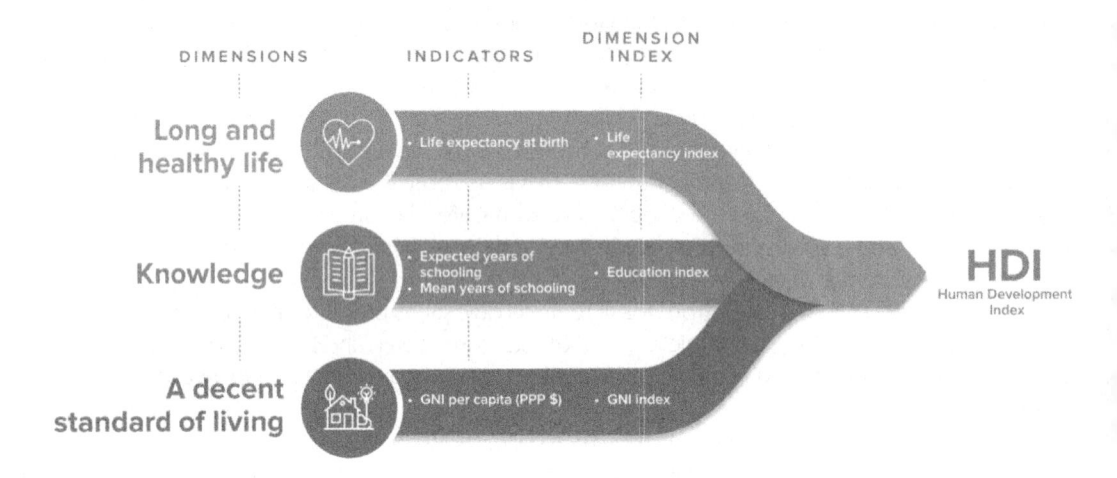

DIMENSIONS — INDICATORS — DIMENSION INDEX

**Long and healthy life**
- Life expectancy at birth
- Life expectancy index

**Knowledge**
- Expected years of schooling
- Mean years of schooling
- Education index

**A decent standard of living**
- GNI per capita (PPP $)
- GNI index

**HDI** Human Development Index

The UN Human Development Index (HDI) ranks countries based on life expectancy, education, and per capita income.

*Human Development Index - Measures a country's overall well-being based on life expectancy, education, and income.*

The United States is #21 on the list, declining from #1 in 1900.[37] The USA, while still doing better than ever, is falling behind its peers due to not making as much progress as others in education, per capita income, or life expectancy. It seems we have a lot to learn from Europe and Australia.

That said, the USA is still far above the world average -- and is getting better. We have a lot to be grateful for.

|  | World (2021) | United States (2021) |
| --- | --- | --- |
| Life Expectancy (yrs) | 71.4 | 77.2 |
| Avg. Years of Schooling | 12.8 | 13.7 |
| Per Capita Income | $16,752 | $64,765 |

The average American lives 5.8 years longer, gets an extra year of schooling, and earns 3.8x as much as the average human. And both the world and the USA have gotten a lot better since 1984. Life is good. And it's time to take a moment and appreciate just how good it is.

So, while there are some huge challenges in our world for us to address -- overall, as

---

[37] Interactive HDI Rankings - https://hdr.undp.org/data-center/human-development-index#/indicies/HDI

a species, when you look at the data, we are doing much better than we were at any prior point in human history.

At a global level, the United Nations is tracking how we're progressing from 2015-2030 using the **Sustainable Development Goals**. You can learn more about the SDGs and how we're progressing as a species at www.globalgoals.org.

*Sustainable Development Goals (SDGs) - A set of global targets aiming to address various social, economic, and environmental challenges by 2030.*

## The New Renaissance

Not only are we in the most prosperous time in human history, but we are also in the most creative time in human history.

We have generative AI that can research anything in milliseconds and design beauty in moments. We have 3D printers that can print homes for $25,000. We have robots that are thankfully removing grueling manual labor from humanity. We have decentralized currencies (like Ethereum) that are providing new competition for nation-state issued currencies. We have beautiful world class cities blooming (like Sydney, Singapore, and Hong Kong) and billions of people coming into the middle class across India, China, Africa, and beyond.

And we also have a Rising Gen Z and Gen Alpha that is getting wise to the war-ravaged Baby Boomers. As soon as the genocidal war-monger Putin departs, it will be a time for celebration in Russia and the world around as we move into a world no longer controlled by militarist septuagenarians and octogenarians born in the mental "us vs. them" context of the Cold War. Change is here. And more change is coming. Thank God.

The first Renaissance took place in Europe between the 14th and 17th centuries. It was characterized by a renewed interest in classical learning, humanism, and artistic expression. There are many similarities between today and the Renaissance in terms of the focus on creativity, innovation, and human potential. In the Renaissance, there was a belief in the power of human intellect and a renewed interest in classical texts, which led to the development of new ideas and technologies. Similarly, today, we are seeing a renewed focus on innovation and creativity in areas like technology, medicine, and the arts, which are driving rapid advancements and pushing the boundaries of what was previously thought possible.

The Internet is the Printing Press 2.0. Let us, as artists, entrepreneurs, and builders, create the art and writing that inspire a better humanity. Let the advances of science and the advances of spirituality and humanism bring forth a golden era of awakening and cultural flourishing.

Let the DJs, shamans, tantrikas, healers, street dancers, storytellers, athletes, teachers, and scientists among us from all nations all realize that we are all working together on the same global project—**working toward the evolution of human consciousness as we move closer and closer to building many little Heavens on Earth**.

Every single one of you, whether you realize it or not, has the potential to do good in the world around you, and join a community of people working in unison toward lifting the veil of worry and stress and creating a realm of joy, play, and celebration of life.

Let us use this global Renaissance happening today to create a beautiful world in which all people can live where they choose, do work they enjoy, and become the best versions of themselves.

Yes, there will be challenges ahead. There always are. The question, of course, is: how will we respond to them?

Things will never be perfect. But they are getting pretty damn good for being on a spinning rock orbiting around a fireball.

## We Are Consciousness First, Human Second

Here's an advanced optimism technique I discovered on one of my 5-MeO journeys in 2018.

During that 20 minute journey, I left my body, I saw my body down on the ground, and then entered a blissful white light that felt like heaven. It seemed like the same experience many people report when they are transitioning from life to death. But I wasn't dying. I was simply on a temporary 20 minute bufo alvarius toad medicine journey.

What did I learn from this experience? Well, we are souls that happen to temporarily be inside bodies. We existed before we were born, and we will exist after we die. I left that experience, as well as my ayahuasca experiences, knowing deep down that we are immortal as energy, even if we are mortal as humans.

So what does that make us? Well, what we actually are is part of consciousness. We are temporarily human but permanently part of consciousness.

So from a human perspective, I'm very optimistic because nearly everything is getting better in the large majority of places in the world every decade -- and because statistically, we are highly likely going to backup our species to other planets and to continual spaceships themselves before there's an actual existential issue here on Earth.

The universe has been around for 13.9 billion years, and the Earth has been around for about 4.6 billion years. Since the first Eukaryotes and Prokaryotes came about 3.5 billion years ago, there's been consciousness on Earth. And there are likely many millions of other planets where consciousness resides throughout this universe. There are also likely other universes that have unimaginable forms of consciousness.

Even in the unlikely event humans were to cease to exist due to an asteroid hit, supervolcano, AI takeover, or any other **existential risk** -- consciousness itself would make it. It survived the dinosaur's extinction and will survive all future challenges.

*Existential Risk - Threats that could lead to the extinction or irreversible decline of human civilization, such as global pandemics, nuclear war, catastrophic climate change, or advanced artificial intelligence gone wrong.*

From a consciousness perspective, even in the <1% chance that there's an existential crisis on Earth in the next 15 years before we permanently back up our species off the planet, we'll still survive as consciousness in other life forms. This makes me very happy - to know that we're going to make it no matter what.

Consciousness has been around for billions of years and has survived every challenge so far. It's not likely to ever go extinct. Consciousness is what we really are. And consciousness continues no matter what, even if a particular species doesn't make it.

So, IF you can wrap your head around this and believe that you are consciousness temporarily inside a human body -- and you trust that there is a greater universal web that holds you -- there's nothing to actually worry about. There's no need for anxiety. In the remote chance humans die out -- we'll still be fine, and we'll come back time and again. We might look completely different and come back on a different planet, but we'll come back. Since consciousness always makes it, there's nothing to be anxious about. This spiritual realization has made me very optimistic.

**Action Item #111: Share This Book**
If you liked this book, would you buy a copy of it as a gift for a friend and write a good review of it online? Thanks for helping spread the word!

## Recommended Books on Optimism

- *Learned Optimism* by Martin Seligman
- *Factfulness: Ten Reasons We're Wrong About the World – and Why Things Are Better Than You Think* by Hans Rosling
- *The Rational Optimist* by Matt Ridley
- *Abundance* by Peter Diamandis
- *Smaller, Faster, Lighter, Denser, Cheaper* By Robert Bryce
- *Getting Better* by Charles Kenny

## OPTIMISM CHAPTER ACTION ITEMS

1. **Worldview Optimism -** Pick one of the books mentioned above on worldview optimism that look most interesting to you. Buy it, read it, then write down your reflections. How did it change your perspective? If you like the first book, consider reading another.

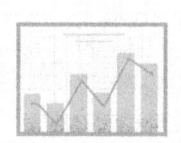

2. **The World Is Getting Better -** What was surprising in this chapter so far? What have you learned? Do you feel better knowing the world is getting better in so many measurable areas? Write a short reflection on what you learned from this chapter. Are you generally optimistic for humanity? Why or why not?

3. **Share This Book** - If you liked this book, would you buy a copy of it as a gift for a friend and write a good review of it online? Thanks for helping spread the word!

# CONCLUSION

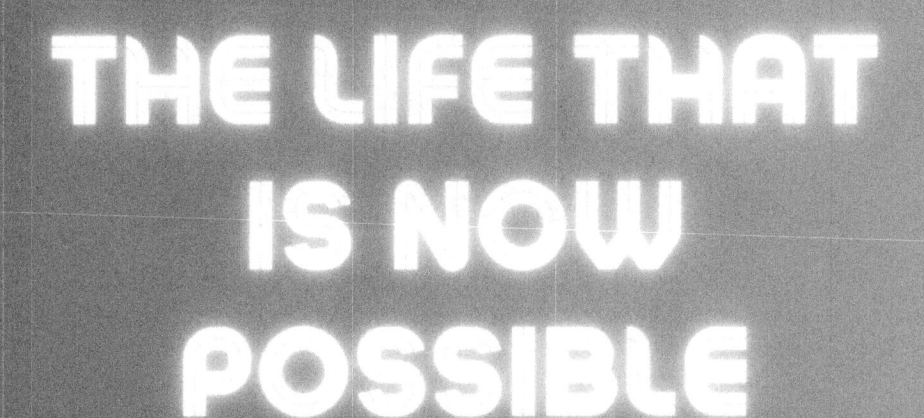

# THE LIFE THAT IS NOW POSSIBLE

**MAGIC YEAR**

# THE LIFE THAT IS NOW POSSIBLE

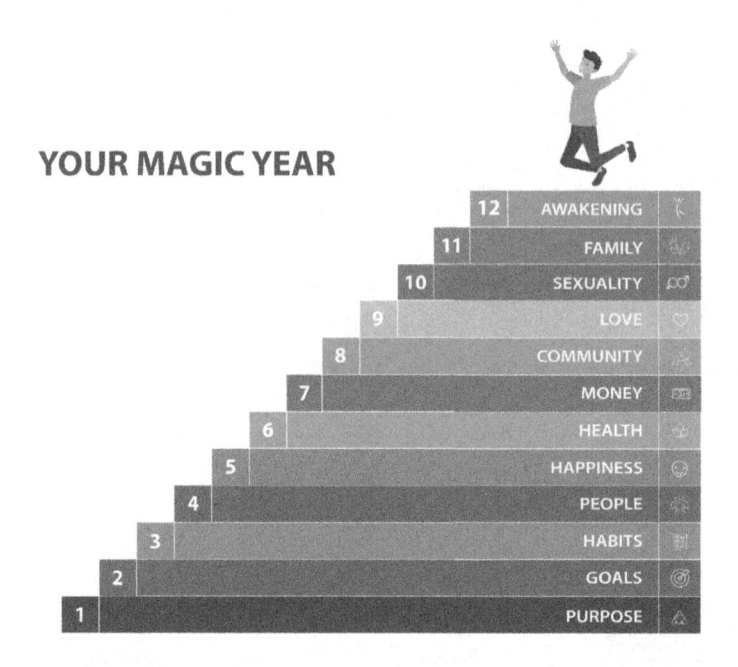

**YOUR MAGIC YEAR**

| 12 | AWAKENING |
| 11 | FAMILY |
| 10 | SEXUALITY |
| 9 | LOVE |
| 8 | COMMUNITY |
| 7 | MONEY |
| 6 | HEALTH |
| 5 | HAPPINESS |
| 4 | PEOPLE |
| 3 | HABITS |
| 2 | GOALS |
| 1 | PURPOSE |

The goal of this book was to provide a guide that you can use to rediscover the magic inside of you and become truly happy, healthy, wealthy, and fully alive. It is hopefully a guide that you can refer back to over time as you come across specific challenges.

Hopefully, more so than when you began the book, you have clear goals, good habits, and are committed to having an optimal mindset and uplifting people around you. If you can check these off, you'll be on the path toward being the happiest version of yourself.

If you can put the right healthy fuel in, get your miracle mornings in, build a strong body, meditate daily for a calm mind, and create a great sex life you'll get an A+ in the health department.

In the realm of money, if you can create and execute your plan to achieve **time freedom, income freedom**, and **net worth freedom** – you'll be on the path toward living the life of your dreams.

And if you can ensure you have an inspiring purpose statement, a caring family, and chosen friends and mentors, you too can feel like you're on top of the world with your spirit unleashed. This, my friends, is the big life upgrade that is possible when you work on all 12 major areas of your life – methodically and one-by-one – and install the right habit stacks.

If you still have some work to do, go back through the book one more time, and this time, actually do each suggested exercise as it comes up. Don't just read this book. Implement all the action items and **DO THIS BOOK**. This is when the magic happens. You can also take this book as an online course at www.magicyear.com with videos, community calls, optional coaching, and exercises. Join us!

No matter what, be sure you're not living, as Tim Ferris says, "a tolerable and comfortable existence doing something unfulfilling." Instead — do what you love to do. And do it now.

Here's a little recap of the major habit changes from this book that if you can make them -- anything is possible for your life.

## THE 12 STEPS TO A MAGIC YEAR

**1 PURPOSE** — An Inspiring Purpose That You Love

**2 GOALS** — Written & Framed Goals

**3 HABITS** — Doing What's Good For You, Over & Over

**6 HEALTH** — A Personalized Health Routine

**5 HAPPINESS** — A Growth Mindset

**4 PEOPLE** — An Uplifting Inner Circle

**7 MONEY** — Creating a Cash Flow Engine

**8 COMMUNITY** — Living Where You Love With People You Love

**9 LOVE** — Choosing an Extraordinary Partner

**12 AWAKENING** — Remembering Who You Truly Are

**11 FAMILY** — Raising Curious & Happy Kids

**10 SEXUALITY** — Creating a Weekly Sensuality Ritual

## The New You

So you're reaching the end of this book. I hope you've enjoyed it. You've now completed all 12 steps to creating the life of your dreams.

Just as I began in the introduction, imagine for a moment the upgraded version of yourself. The version of yourself that is possible after putting the knowledge in this book to work. A **magic life** is possible.

Imagine a fully integrated, healthy, healed, fit, confident, wealthy, and relaxed you. Yes, imagine...

1. The version of you who spent 10 days doing a Vipassana silent meditation retreat (see dhamma.org to schedule yours) and came out the other side with a clearer and happier mind.

2. The version of you who decided to finally lose that 25 extra pounds that's been hanging around -- either through diet and daily exercise or a combination of diet, daily exercise, and appetite suppressants like Tirzepatide or Semaglutide.

3. The version of you who decided to finally heal your central nervous system by committing to taking frequent digital detoxes -- getting yourself completely off your phone and into nature for *at least 3 days every quarter* and scheduled weekly full body massages and cranial sacral sessions.

4. The version of you that decided to limit television to 2 hours per week and put all that extra time into exercising, reading, and spending time with your family and friends.

5. The version of you who took a couple weeks out of your life to sit with the plant medicine Ayahuasca in Costa Rica or Peru and was able to heal childhood trauma as well as your fear of death.

6. The version of you who decided to buy a home inside of a community of inspiring and families living in paradise in a place like Bali or Costa Rica (read the Community chapter for more on that!).

7. The version of you who was able to overcome PTSD and anxiety through daily breathing practices and by working with a practitioner who utilized cutting edge entheogenic therapeutics like ketamine, psilocybin, or MDMA during guided sessions -- the same therapeutics that have been shown to heal PTSD in military veterans.

8. The version of you who realized life was short and proactively planned incredible adventures with your family and friends.

9. The version of you who left the job you hated and decided to actually make money doing something you truly enjoyed.

10. The version of you who decided to write down your goals, create a written purpose, and then take consistent action toward generating massive results in your life.

11. The version of you who (gasp!) decided to hire a sex coach and invite them into the bedroom to help you uplevel your sex life with your partner(s) and bring both of you to new heights of pleasure.

12. The version of you who realized that being happy is a relatively simple by-product of daily exercise, not eating processed foods, minimizing sugar and alcohol, installing the miracle morning routine, learning to not worry by letting go of obsessing about control, spending lots of time with people you care about, and then simply choosing to be unconditionally happy internally regardless of the external conditions.

This version of you is possible. It truly is. Yes, we're looking to create a version of you that is happy, healthy, wealthy, and fully alive.

But, friends, know that there is a whole other world out there. A world of connection, wellness, art, music, authentic people, adventure, purpose, and play. A world of wellness, festivals, magic, desert pyramids, art, music, and full expression. You just have to know where to go to find it. I hope you've found this book a good guide to living, upgrading your life, and creating the new version of you.

Now, if you've read the book through but haven't yet done the 111 action items, go back and do them on a second read through. It's those action items that actually create the changes in your life that are needed to create a **magic life**. Keep me updated on how it goes! Congratulations! You have finished this book! I'll end with this poem...

> "You were born with potential.
> You were born with goodness and trust.
> You were born with ideals and dreams.
> You were born with greatness.
> You were born with wings.
> You are not meant for crawling, so don't.
> You have wings.
> Learn to use them and fly."
> - Rumi

**One Bonus Action Item: Reflecting on This Book**
Write in your notebook the answers to these questions. What are the most important things you learned from this book? What new experiments are you committing to trying? What new habits are you committed to? What is the purpose for the next phase of your life?

*The Last word: Creating your magic life will require consistent action, self-belief, major habit shifts, and the right community and coaches. We've got your back every step of the way at www.magicyear.com. Come join our 12 month course and ongoing community of Magic Friends. See you there!*

Made in the USA
Coppell, TX
04 March 2024